# (ISC)²®

# SSCP® Systems Security Certified Practitioner Official

## Study Guide

### Second Edition

# (ISC)²®

# SSCP® Systems Security Certified Practitioner Official

## Study Guide

### Second Edition

Mike Wills

SYBEX®
A Wiley Brand

Development Editor: Kim Wimpsett
Technical Editor: Scott Pike
Production Editor: Lauren Freestone
Copy Editor: Elizabeth Welch
Editorial Manager: Pete Gaughan
Production Manager: Kathleen Wisor
Associate Publisher: Jim Minatel
Proofreader: Tiffany Taylor
Indexer: Johnna VanHoose Dinse
Project Coordinator, Cover: Brent Savage
Cover Designer: Wiley
Cover Image: © Getty Images Inc./Jeremy Woodhouse

ISBN: 978-1-119-54294-0
ISBN: 978-1-119-54295-7 (ebk.)
ISBN: 978-1-119-54292-6 (ebk.)

Manufactured in the United States of America

**Library of Congress Control Number:** 2019936132

# Acknowledgments

This book owes a great deal to the many teachers, coworkers, teammates, and friends who've worked so hard for so long to teach me what I know about information security and insecurity, and about risk management and mismanagement. Where this book works well in conveying that body of knowledge, skills, and attitudes to you is a testament to their generosity in sharing their insights with me. I would also like to acknowledge my faculty teammates here at Embry-Riddle Aeronautical University for sharing their frank and candid views throughout many conversations on making this body of knowledge accessible and engaging in the classroom. The ideas and experiences of Dr. Aaron Glassman, Dr. Wesley Phillips, Dr. Robert "Trez" Jones, and Mr. Hamid Ait Kaci Azzou have profoundly affected my approach to what you see before you here in this book.

The combined team at Wiley/Sybex and at (ISC)² worked tirelessly to focus, strengthen, and clarify what I wanted to say and how I said it, all while keeping my voice and my teaching ideas authentic and on point. My thanks go out to the editorial team at Wiley/Sybex: Jim Minatel, Kim Wimpsett, Pete Gaughan, Lauren Freestone, Elizabeth Welch, Tiffany Taylor, and their technical reviewers Jacob Penovich, Scott Pike, and Raven Sims, as well as to Tara Zeiler and Charles Gaughf, our reviewers at (ISC)². Johnna VanHoose Dinse, Wiley's indexer, has also made the art of finding what you want in this book when you need it more of a science (and I've always had a soft spot for a great index!). Where this book works well for you, it works because of the efforts of all of those people to make this book the best it can be. What errors, omissions, misspeaks, and confusions that remain are mine, not theirs.

Finally, I wish to thank my wife Nancy. She saved my life and brought me peace. Her strength inspired me to say "yes" when Jim first called me about doing this book and has kept both of us healthy and happy throughout.

# About the Author

**Mike Wills**, SSCP, CISSP has spent more than 40 years as a computer systems architect, programmer, security specialist, database designer, consultant, and teacher (among other duties). Starting out as a bit of a phone phreak in his college days, he sharpened his skills on the 1960s generation of mainframes and minicomputers, just in time for the first 8080 and Z80 microprocessors to fuel the home computer revolution. Learning about the ARPANET just added spice to that mix. Since then, he's had ones, zeros, and now qubits under his fingernails too many times to count, whether as part of his jobs, his teaching, or his hobbies.

Mike earned his BS and MS degrees in computer science, both with minors in electrical engineering, from Illinois Institute of Technology, and his MA in Defence Studies from King's College, London. He is a graduate of the Federal Chief Information Officer program at National Defense University and the Program Manager's Course at Defense Systems Management College.

As an Air Force officer, Mike served in the National Reconnaissance Office, building and flying some of the most complex, cutting-edge space-based missions, large and small. As a "ground control" guy, he specialized in the design, operation, and support of highly secure, globe-spanning command, control, communications, and intelligence systems that support US and Coalition missions around the world. These duties often required Mike to "optimize" his way around the official configuration management and security safeguards—all on official business, of course.

No good deed going unpunished, he then spent two years on the Joint Staff as a policy and budget broker for all command, control, and communications systems, and then taught in the School of Information Warfare and Strategy at National Defense University. He's taught at senior leader colleges in both the United States and United Kingdom, and has been a continuing guest lecturer at the UK's Defence Academy. He served as adviser to the UK's Joint Intelligence Committee, Ministry of Justice, and Defence Science and Technology Laboratories on the national and personal security implications of science and technology policy; this led to him sometimes being known as the UK's nonresident expert on outer space law.

Currently he is an assistant professor of Applied Information Technologies in the College of Business at Embry-Riddle Aeronautical University – Worldwide, where he is the change leader and academic visionary behind bringing the Microsoft Software and Systems Academy program into ERAU's classrooms at 13 locations around the United States. Prior to this, Mike helped create two new MS degrees—Information Security and Assurance, and Management of Information Systems—and was program chair of both during their launch and first year of teaching. He also taught in Worldwide's Security and Intelligence Studies program during its 2005 launch in ERAU's European Division.

Mike and his wife Nancy currently call Montevideo, Uruguay, their home. Living abroad since the end of the last century, they find new perspectives, shared values, and wonderful people wherever they go. As true digital nomads, it's getting time to move again. Where to? They'll find out when they get there.

# Contents at a Glance

*Foreword*                                                                                        *xxi*

*Introduction*                                                                                   *xxiii*

*Self-Assessment*                                                                                 *xlv*

**Part I**      **Getting Started as an SSCP**                                                      **1**

**Chapter 1**   The Business Case for Decision Assurance and
                Information Security                                                                  3

**Chapter 2**   Information Security Fundamentals                                                    25

**Part II**     **Integrated Risk Management and Mitigation**                                      **51**

**Chapter 3**   Integrated Information Risk Management                                               53

**Chapter 4**   Operationalizing Risk Mitigation                                                    111

**Part III**    **The Technologies of Information Security**                                      **173**

**Chapter 5**   Communications and Network Security                                                 175

**Chapter 6**   Identity and Access Control                                                         249

**Chapter 7**   Cryptography                                                                        297

**Chapter 8**   Hardware and Systems Security                                                       371

**Chapter 9**   Applications, Data, and Cloud Security                                              413

**Part IV**     **People Power: What Makes or Breaks
                Information Security**                                                            **477**

**Chapter 10**  Incident Response and Recovery                                                      479

**Chapter 11**  Business Continuity via Information Security and
                People Power                                                                        525

**Chapter 12**  Risks, Issues, and Opportunities, Starting Tomorrow                                 553

**Appendix**    Answers to Review Questions                                                         569

*Index*                                                                                           *605*

# Contents

*Foreword*                                                                    *xxi*

*Introduction*                                                                *xxiii*

*Self-Assessment*                                                             *xlv*

**Part  I**        **Getting Started as an SSCP**                              **1**

**Chapter   1**    **The Business Case for Decision Assurance and
                   Information Security**                                      **3**

Information: The Lifeblood of Business                                         4
   Data, Information, Knowledge, Wisdom...                       5
   Information Is *Not* Information Technology                   8
Policy, Procedure, and Process: How Business Gets
  Business Done                                                       10
   Who Is the Business?                                          11
   "What's Your Business Plan?"                                  12
   Purpose, Intent, Goals, Objectives                           13
   Business Logic and Business Processes: Transforming
    Assets into Opportunity, Wealth, and Success            14
   The Value Chain                                              15
   Being Accountable                                            17
Who Runs the Business?                                                         19
   Owners and Investors                                         19
   Boards of Directors                                          20
   Managing or Executive Directors and the "C-Suite"            20
   Layers of Function, Structure, Management, and
    Responsibility                                         21
   Plans and Budgets, Policies, and Directives                  22
Summary                                                                       23

**Chapter   2**    **Information Security Fundamentals**                       **25**

The Common Needs for Privacy, Confidentiality, Integrity,
  and Availability                                                   26
   Privacy                                                      26
   Confidentiality                                              29
   Integrity                                                    30
   Availability                                                 31
   Privacy vs. Security, or Privacy and Security?               32
   CIA Needs of Individuals                                     34

Private Business's Need for CIA ......... 35
Government's Need for CIA ......... 36
The Modern Military's Need for CIA ......... 36
Do Societies Need CIA? ......... 36
Training and Educating Everybody ......... 38
SSCPs and Professional Ethics ......... 38
Summary ......... 40
Exam Essentials ......... 40
Review Questions ......... 44

**Part II**    **Integrated Risk Management and Mitigation**   **51**

**Chapter 3**    **Integrated Information Risk Management**   **53**

It's a Dangerous World ......... 54
What Is Risk? ......... 55
Risk: When Surprise Becomes Disruption ......... 59
Information Security: Delivering Decision Assurance ......... 60
"Common Sense" and Risk Management ......... 63
The Four Faces of Risk ......... 65
Outcomes-Based Risk ......... 67
Process-Based Risk ......... 67
Asset-Based Risk ......... 68
Threat-Based (or Vulnerability-Based) Risk ......... 69
Getting Integrated and Proactive with Information Defense ......... 72
Trust, but Verify ......... 76
Due Care and Due Diligence: Whose Jobs Are These? ......... 76
Be Prepared: First, Set Priorities ......... 77
Risk Management: Concepts and Frameworks ......... 78
The SSCP and Risk Management ......... 81
Plan, Do, Check, Act ......... 82
Risk Assessment ......... 84
Establish Consensus about Information Risk ......... 84
Information Risk Impact Assessment ......... 85
The Business Impact Analysis ......... 92
From Assessments to Information Security Requirements ......... 92
Four Choices for Limiting or Containing Damage ......... 94
Deter ......... 96
Detect ......... 96
Prevent ......... 97
Avoid ......... 97
Summary ......... 100
Exam Essentials ......... 101
Review Questions ......... 105

**Chapter  4**    **Operationalizing Risk Mitigation**                    **111**

From Tactical Planning to Information Security Operations        112
    Operationally Outthinking Your Adversaries                  114
    Getting Inside the Other Side's OODA Loop                   116
    Defeating the Kill Chain                                    117
Operationalizing Risk Mitigation: Step by Step                  118
    Step 1: Assess the Existing Architectures                   119
    Step 2: Assess Vulnerabilities and Threats                  126
    Step 3: Select Risk Treatment and Controls                  135
    Step 4: Implement Controls                                  141
    Step 5: Authorize: Senior Leader Acceptance and
        Ownership                                               146
The Ongoing Job of Keeping Your Baseline Secure                 146
    Build and Maintain User Engagement with Risk Controls       147
    Participate in Security Assessments                         148
    Manage the Architectures: Asset Management and
        Configuration Control                                   151
Ongoing, Continuous Monitoring                                  152
    Exploiting What Monitoring and Event Data Is
        Telling You                                             155
    Incident Investigation, Analysis, and Reporting             159
Reporting to and Engaging with Management                       160
Summary                                                         161
Exam Essentials                                                 161
Review Questions                                                166

**Part  III**    **The Technologies of Information Security**    **173**

**Chapter  5**    **Communications and Network Security**         **175**

Trusting Our Communications in a Converged World                176
    Introducing CIANA                                           179
    Threat Modeling for Communications Systems                  180
Internet Systems Concepts                                       181
    Datagrams and Protocol Data Units                           182
    Handshakes                                                  184
    Packets and Encapsulation                                   185
    Addressing, Routing, and Switching                          187
    Network Segmentation                                        188
    URLs and the Web                                            188
    Topologies                                                  189
    "Best Effort" and Trusting Designs                          193

Two Protocol Stacks, One Internet                              194
    Complementary, Not Competing, Frameworks                  194
    Layer 1: The Physical Layer                               198
    Layer 2: The Data Link Layer                              199
    Layer 3: The Network Layer                                201
    Layer 4: The Transport Layer                              202
    Layer 5: The Session Layer                                206
    Layer 6: The Presentation Layer                           207
    Layer 7: The Application Layer                            208
    Cross-Layer Protocols and Services                        209
    IP and Security                                           210
    Layers or Planes?                                         211
    Software-Defined Networks                                 212
    Virtual Private Networks                                  213
    A Few Words about Wireless                                214
IP Addresses, DHCP, and Subnets                               217
    IPv4 Address Classes                                      217
    Subnetting in IPv4                                        219
IPv4 vs. IPv6: Key Differences and Options                    221
CIANA Layer by Layer                                          223
    CIANA at Layer 1: Physical                                223
    CIANA at Layer 2: Data Link                               226
    CIANA at Layer 3: Network                                 228
    CIANA at Layer 4: Transport                               229
    CIANA at Layer 5: Session                                 230
    CIANA at Layer 6: Presentation                            231
    CIANA at Layer 7: Application                             232
Securing Networks as Systems                                  233
    A SOC Is Not a NOC                                        234
    Tools for the SOC and the NOC                             235
    Integrating Network and Security Management               236
Summary                                                       238
Exam Essentials                                               238
Review Questions                                              243

Chapter    6    Identity and Access Control                   249

Identity and Access: Two Sides of the Same CIANA Coin         250
Identity Management Concepts                                  251
    Identity Provisioning and Management                      252
    Identity and AAA                                          254
Access Control Concepts                                       255
    Subjects and Objects—Everywhere!                          257
    Data Classification and Access Control                    258

Bell-LaPadula and Biba Models 260
Role-Based 263
Attribute-Based 263
Subject-Based 264
Object-Based 264
Mandatory vs. Discretionary Access Control 264
Network Access Control 265
IEEE 802.1X Concepts 267
RADIUS Authentication 268
TACACS and TACACS+ 269
Implementing and Scaling IAM 270
Choices for Access Control Implementations 271
"Built-in" Solutions? 273
Multifactor Authentication 274
Server-Based IAM 276
Integrated IAM systems 277
Zero Trust Architectures 281
Summary 282
Exam Essentials 283
Review Questions 290

Chapter 7    **Cryptography**    **297**

Cryptography: What and Why 298
Codes and Ciphers: Defining Our Terms 300
Cryptography, Cryptology, or…? 305
Building Blocks of Digital Cryptographic Systems 306
Cryptographic Algorithms 307
Cryptographic Keys 308
Hashing as One-Way Cryptography 310
A Race Against Time 313
"The Enemy Knows Your System" 314
Keys and Key Management 314
Key Storage and Protection 315
Key Revocation and Zeroization 315
Modern Cryptography: Beyond the "Secret Decoder Ring" 317
Symmetric Key Cryptography 317
Asymmetric Key (or Public Key) Cryptography 318
Hybrid Cryptosystems 318
Design and Use of Cryptosystems 319
Cryptanalysis (White Hat and Black Hat) 319
Cryptographic Primitives 320
Cryptographic Engineering 320
"Why Isn't All of This Stuff Secret?" 320

Cryptography and CIANA                                      322
    Confidentiality                                        322
    Authentication                                         323
    Integrity                                              323
    Nonrepudiation                                         324
    "But I Didn't Get That Email…"                         324
    Availability                                           325
Public Key Infrastructures                                 327
    Diffie-Hellman-Merkle Public Key Exchange              328
    RSA Encryption and Key Exchange                        331
    ElGamal Encryption                                     331
    Digital Signatures                                     332
    Digital Certificates and Certificate Authorities       332
    Hierarchies (or Webs) of Trust                         333
    Pretty Good Privacy                                    337
    TLS                                                    338
    HTTPS                                                  340
    Symmetric Key Algorithms and PKI                       341
    PKI and Trust: A Recap                                 342
Other Protocols: Applying Cryptography to Meet
  Different Needs                                          344
    IPSec                                                  344
    S/MIME                                                 345
    DKIM                                                   345
    Blockchain                                             346
    Access Control Protocols                               348
Measures of Merit for Cryptographic Solutions              348
Attacks and Countermeasures                                349
    Brute Force and Dictionary Attacks                     350
    Side Channel Attacks                                   350
    Numeric (Algorithm or Key) Attacks                     351
    Traffic Analysis, "Op Intel," and Social Engineering
        Attacks                                            352
    Massively Parallel Systems Attacks                     353
    Supply Chain Vulnerabilities                           354
    The "Sprinkle a Little Crypto Dust on It" Fallacy      354
    Countermeasures                                        355
On the Near Horizon                                        357
    Pervasive and Homomorphic Encryption                   358
    Quantum Cryptography and Post–Quantum Cryptography     358
    AI, Machine Learning, and Cryptography                 360
Summary                                                    361
Exam Essentials                                            361
Review Questions                                           366

| Chapter | 8 | **Hardware and Systems Security** | **371** |

Infrastructure Security Is Baseline Management 372
It's About Access Control... 373
It's Also About Supply Chain Security 374
Do Clouds Have Boundaries? 375
Infrastructures 101 and Threat Modeling 376
Hardware Vulnerabilities 379
Firmware Vulnerabilities 380
Operating Systems Vulnerabilities 382
Virtual Machines and Vulnerabilities 385
Network Operating Systems 386
MDM, COPE, and BYOD 388
BYOI? BYOC? 389
Malware: Exploiting the Infrastructure's Vulnerabilities 391
Countering the Malware Threat 394
Privacy and Secure Browsing 395
"The Sin of Aggregation" 397
Updating the Threat Model 398
Managing Your Systems' Security 399
Summary 399
Exam Essentials 400
Review Questions 407

| Chapter | 9 | **Applications, Data, and Cloud Security** | **413** |

It's a Data-Driven World...At the Endpoint 414
Software as Appliances 417
Applications Lifecycles and Security 420
The Software Development Lifecycle (SDLC) 421
Why Is (Most) Software So Insecure? 424
Hard to Design It Right, Easy to Fix It? 427
CIANA and Applications Software Requirements 428
Positive and Negative Models for Software Security 431
Is Blacklisting Dead? Or Dying? 432
Application Vulnerabilities 434
Vulnerabilities Across the Lifecycle 434
Human Failures and Frailties 436
"Shadow IT:" The Dilemma of the User as Builder 436
Data and Metadata as Procedural Knowledge 438
Information Quality and Information Assurance 440
Information Quality Lifecycle 441
Preventing (or Limiting) the "Garbage In" Problem 442

Protecting Data in Motion, in Use, and at Rest                443
    Data Exfiltration I: The Traditional Threat            445
    Detecting Unauthorized Data Acquisition               446
    Preventing Data Loss                                  447
Into the Clouds: Endpoint App and Data Security
  Considerations                                             448
    Cloud Deployment Models and Information Security      449
    Cloud Service Models and Information Security         450
    Clouds, Continuity, and Resiliency                    452
    Clouds and Threat Modeling                            453
    Cloud Security Methods                                455
    SLAs, TORs, and Penetration Testing                   456
    Data Exfiltration II: Hiding in the Clouds            456
Legal and Regulatory Issues                                   456
Countermeasures: Keeping Your Apps and Data Safe
  and Secure                                                 458
Summary                                                       459
Exam Essentials                                               460
Review Questions                                              470

Part IV    **People Power: What Makes or Breaks
           Information Security**                              **477**

Chapter 10    **Incident Response and Recovery**              **479**
Defeating the Kill Chain One Skirmish at a Time               480
    Kill Chains: Reviewing the Basics                     482
    Events vs. Incidents                                  484
Incident Response Framework                                   485
    Incident Response Team: Roles and Structures          487
    Incident Response Priorities                          490
Preparation                                                   491
    Preparation Planning                                  491
    Put the Preparation Plan in Motion                    493
    Are You Prepared?                                     494
Detection and Analysis                                        497
    Warning Signs                                         497
    Initial Detection                                     499
    Timeline Analysis                                     500
    Notification                                          500
    Prioritization                                        501
Containment and Eradication                                   502
    Evidence Gathering, Preservation, and Use             504
    Constant Monitoring                                   505

Recovery: Getting Back to Business                                    505
   Data Recovery                                       506
   Post-Recovery: Notification and Monitoring          508
Post-Incident Activities                                             508
   Learning the Lessons                                509
   Support Ongoing Forensics Investigations            510
   Information and Evidence Retention                   511
   Information Sharing with the Larger IT Security
   Community                                            511
Summary                                                              512
Exam Essentials                                                      512
Review Questions                                                     518

**Chapter 11    Business Continuity via Information Security
and People Power                                                     525**

A Spectrum of Disruption                                             526
Surviving to Operate: Plan for It!                                   529
Cloud-Based "Do-Over" Buttons for Continuity, Security,
   and Resilience                                      531
CIANA at Layer 8 and Above                                          537
   It *Is* a Dangerous World Out There                 539
   People Power for Secure Communications              541
   POTS and VoIP Security                              542
Summary                                                              543
Exam Essentials                                                      544
Review Questions                                                     547

**Chapter 12    Risks, Issues, and Opportunities, Starting
Tomorrow                                                             553**

On Our Way to the Future                                             554
   Access Control and Zero Trust                       555
   AI, ML, BI, and Trustworthiness                     556
   Quantum Communications, Computing,
   and Cryptography                                    557
   Paradigm Shifts in Information Security?             558
   Perception Management and Information Security       559
   Widespread Lack of Useful Understanding of
   Core Technologies                                   560
   IT Supply Chain Vulnerabilities                     561
   Government Overreactions                             561
CIA, CIANA, or CIANAPS?                                             562

|  |  |
|---|---|
| Enduring Lessons | 563 |
| You Cannot Legislate Security | 563 |
| It's About Managing Our Security and Our Systems | 563 |
| People Put It Together | 564 |
| Maintain Flexibility of Vision | 565 |
| Accountability—It's Personal. Make It So. | 565 |
| Stay Sharp | 566 |
| Your Next Steps | 567 |
| At the Close | 568 |

| **Appendix** | **Answers to Review Questions** | **569** |
|---|---|---|
| | Self-Assessment | 570 |
| | Chapter 2: Information Security Fundamentals | 576 |
| | Chapter 3: Integrated Information Risk Management | 579 |
| | Chapter 4: Operationalizing Risk Mitigation | 581 |
| | Chapter 5: Communications and Network Security | 583 |
| | Chapter 6: Identity and Access Control | 586 |
| | Chapter 7: Cryptography | 589 |
| | Chapter 8: Hardware and Systems Security | 592 |
| | Chapter 9: Applications, Data, and Cloud Security | 594 |
| | Chapter 10: Incident Response and Recovery | 597 |
| | Chapter 11: Business Continuity via Information Security and People Power | 601 |

| *Index* | *605* |
|---|---|

# Foreword

Welcome to the *(ISC)² SSCP Systems Security Certified Practitioner Official Study Guide, Second Edition*! The global cybersecurity talent gap represents a huge opportunity for you to leverage your information technology skills to help protect your organization's infrastructure, information, systems, and processes and to improve and grow in your professional journey.

The Systems Security Certified Practitioner is a foundational certification that demonstrates you have the advanced technical skills and knowledge to implement, monitor, and administer IT infrastructure using security best practices, policies, and procedures established by the cybersecurity experts at (ISC)² for protecting critical assets. This book will guide you through the seven subject area domains on which the SSCP exam will test your knowledge. Step by step, it will cover the fundamentals involved in each topic and will gradually build toward more focused areas of learning in order to prepare you.

The SSCP is a mark of distinction that hiring managers look for when recruiting for roles that include cybersecurity responsibilities. Your pursuit and maintenance of this credential demonstrates that you have the knowledge and the drive to meet a recognized standard of excellence.

Whether you are brand new to the field or just want a refresher on the core tenets of cybersecurity, this guide will help you build a solid understanding of the technical, physical, administrative and legal aspects of the information security and assurance profession, as well as the ethical fidelity required of the SSCP.

I hope that you will find the *(ISC)² SSCP Systems Security Certified Practitioner Official Study Guide, Second Edition* to be an informative and helpful tool and wish you great success in your preparation and your professional growth.

Sincerely,

David P. Shearer, CISSP
CEO, (ISC)²

# Introduction

Congratulations on choosing to become a Systems Security Certified Practitioner (SSCP)! In making this choice, you're signing up to join the "white hats," the professionals who strive to keep our information-based modern world safe, secure, and reliable. SSCPs and other information security professionals help businesses and organizations keep private data *private* and help to ensure that published and public-facing information stays unchanged and unhacked.

Whether you are new to the fields of information security, information assurance, or cybersecurity, or you've been working with these concepts, tools, and ideas for some time now, this book is here to help you grow your knowledge, skills, and abilities as a systems security professional.

Let's see how!

# About This Book

You're here because you want to learn what it takes to be an SSCP. You know this will demand that you build a solid understanding of many different concepts, not only as theories but also as practical tasks you can *do* to help make information systems more secure. You know you'll need to master a number of key definitions and be able to apply those definitions to real-world situations—you'll need to operationalize those definitions and concepts by turning them into the step-by-step operations that *make* security become real.

This book is your study guide. It guides you along your personal journey as you learn and master these ideas and technologies. It takes you on that journey concept by concept, starting with simple, fundamental ideas and growing them to the level of power and complexity *you* will need, on the job, as an SSCP. That is this book's focus, its purpose, and design.

In doing so, it's also a valuable reference to have with you on the job, or as you continue to learn more about information security, information risk management, or any of a number of other related subject areas. You'll find it more than covers the topic domains that (ISC)² requires you to demonstrate competency in, should you wish to earn their Systems Security Certified Practitioner credential.

---

### What Makes This the "Official" Study Guide for the SSCP?

Good question! This book exists because (ISC)² wanted a book that would teach as well as guide, explain as well as capture the common knowledge about keeping information systems secure, protecting information assets, and information assurance that all SSCPs should have at their mental fingertips. As creators of the SSCP program, (ISC)² defines that common body of knowledge, in continuous consultation with system security experts and practitioners from business, industry, government, and academia from around the world.

Using this official study guide, individuals can prepare for the SSCP exam with confidence. Businesses and other organizations can build their own in-house staff development and training programs around this book and have the same confidence that what they'll be training their people on aligns with (ISC)²'s structure and definition of the SSCP as a body of knowledge.

---

# What Is an SSCP?

The SSCP is actually three things in one: a standard of excellence, a credential that attests to demonstrated excellence, and a *person* who has earned that credential. Perhaps instead of asking "what" is an SSCP, we should also ask *why, who,* and *how*:

- *SSCP as standard of excellence.* The International Information System Security Certification Consortium, or (ISC)$^2$, created this standard to reflect the continually evolving needs for people who can help all sorts of organizations around the world keep their information systems safe, secure, confidential, private, reliable, and trustworthy. Working with businesses, nonprofits, academic researchers, and the thought leaders of the cybersecurity and information assurance communities of practice, they developed the list of subject areas, or *domains*, that are the SSCP as a standard. That standard is set as the starting point for your professional journey as an information security specialist. Its focus is on hands-on technical knowledge combined with procedural and administrative awareness. The knowledge, skills, and abilities that make up the SSCP domains become the foundation for other, more advanced certifications (and hence standards).

- *SSCP as a credential.* Earning an SSCP certification attests to the fact that you have solid working knowledge of the topic domains that are the SSCP. As a published standard of excellence, this certification or credential is portable—people in the information system business, or who know the needs of their own organizations for information security, recognize and respect this credential. People can easily consult (ISC)$^2$'s published standards for the SSCP and understand what it means. It is a portable, stackable credential, meaning that it can clearly pave the way for you to take on job responsibilities that need the knowledge and skills it attests to, and demonstrates you have the foundational knowledge to earn other credentials that can build on it.

- *SSCP as a goal or objective.* The SSCP as a standard answers the needs of hiring managers when they seek the right kind of people to help protect their organization's information, their information systems and processes, their IT infrastructure, and their ability to make informed decisions in reliable, timely ways. Training managers or functional department leaders in various organizations can design their own internal training and skills development programs around the SSCP, knowing that it is a reliable standard for information system security knowledge and experience. They can look at job descriptions or task designs, and use the SSCP as a standard to identify whether the job and the SSCP are a good fit with each other, or if other significant knowledge and skills will be needed by people filling that position.

- *SSCP as a person.* By choosing to earn an SSCP credential, you're declaring to yourself and to others that you're willing to hold yourself to a respected and recognized standard of excellence. You're willing to master what that standard asks of you, not only on the technical, physical, and administrative aspects of information security and assurance, but also on its legal and ethical requirements.

The *Systems Security Certified Practitioner* is thus a person who does the job of systems security to a level of competency that meets or exceeds that standard and who has earned a credential as testament to their knowledge and skills. It is a foundational certification, based on the knowledge and skills that people should already have when they first start out as an information security professional.

Let's *operationalize* that set of words by showing them in action:

- *Systems*—Generally, a *system* is a collection or set of elements that interconnect and interact with each other to fulfill or achieve a larger purpose or objective. In this context, we mean *information systems. Information systems* are the collected sets of hardware, software, databases, and data sets; the communications, networking, and other technologies that connect all of those elements together into a cohesive, working whole; and the people who use them and depend on them to achieve their goals and objectives.

- *Security*—Again, generally speaking, security is the set of plans, procedures, and actions that keep something safe from harm, damage, or loss, through accident, acts of nature, or deliberate actions taken by people. Applying that to information systems, we see that *information systems security* is everything we need to do during design, implementation, operational use, and maintenance to keep all aspects of an information system protected against accidental or deliberate damage; it includes keeping its information free from unauthorized changes or viewing; and it keeps those systems up and running so that the information is there when people need it to get their jobs done.

- *Certified*—The person holding this credential (or certification) has earned the right to do so by means of having demonstrated their mastery of the knowledge, skills, and attitudes that are defined to be the subject area or domain of the certification. Specifically, an SSCP has passed the certification exam and demonstrated the required work experience in the field of information security, as specified by the SSCP subject area domains.

- *Practitioner*—A person whose professional or workplace duties, responsibilities, and tasks has them using the knowledge, skills, and abilities required by the standard to have earned the certification. There's a degree of *practice* in the definition of *practitioner*, of course; as a practitioner, you are continually *doing* the stuff of your profession, and in doing so you continue to *learn it better* as well as refine, polish, and enrich the ways in which you do those tasks and fulfill those responsibilities. Practitioners get better with practice! (After all, if you've been "practicing medicine" for 20 years, we expect you are a much better medical doctor now than you were when you started.)

Note that a practitioner may be a specialist or a generalist; this is usually defined by the standards issued by the credentialing organization and reflects accepted and valued practice in the profession or industry as a whole.

# What Can We Expect of Our SSCPs?

The world of commerce, industry, and governance expects you, as an SSCP, to be a hands-on practitioner of information systems security, someone who continuously monitors information systems to safeguard against security threats, vulnerabilities, and risks while having the knowledge to apply security concepts, tools, and procedures to react to security incidents. As an SSCP, you demonstrate certain knowledge and skills, in areas such as:

- Information technology and cybersecurity theory and hands-on/technical practice
- Cybersecurity policy, procedures, standards, and guidelines
- Using simple coding or programming language techniques, in languages such as command line interface, PowerShell, Java, HTML, CSS, Python, and C#

You'll also need more than just technical skills and knowledge. As an SSCP, you'll be working with people constantly, as you assist them in securing their organization's information security needs. This takes adaptability on your part, plus strong interpersonal skills. You'll need to be a critical thinker, and to make sounds judgments; you'll have to communicate in person and in writing as you build and manage professional relationships within your organization and the larger information security community of practice. You'll build this social capital both through your problem-solving skills and by applying your emotional intelligence.

---

### Soft Skills: Very Strong Tickets to Success

Employers, clients, and others you'll work with value your technical knowledge and skills, but they desperately need to be able to work with and communicate with you as you bring that knowledge and skills to bear on their problems. The irony of calling these skills "soft" is that for some of us, it can be very hard work to improve on them. Investing in improving these skills will more than pay off for you in terms of salary and opportunities.

---

It's also natural to expect that as an SSCP, you will be continually learning about your craft. You'll keep current about the ways that threats evolve and stay informed about known vulnerabilities as they might be exploited against the systems under your care. You'll know how to apply analytical and research skills to dig deeper into what you're seeing in the way those systems are behaving, with an eye to identifying problems, recognizing that an information security incident might be under way, and responding to such incidents. This also means that you will periodically reflect on what you've been doing, how you've been doing it, and what you've been learning, and consider where improvement and growth are required to ensure continued effectiveness.

# Who Should Take the SSCP Certification Exam?

The SSCP designation is designed for individuals who desire to learn hands-on, technical, cybersecurity fundamentals. While any individual who desires to practice cybersecurity can learn the material, there are certain requirements before sitting for the exam. SSCP candidates must have at least one year of cumulative work experience in one or more of the seven domains of the (ISC)² SSCP Common Body of Knowledge (CBK). A one-year prerequisite pathway will be granted for candidates who received an accredited university degree (bachelor's or master's) in a cybersecurity program. Candidates without the required experience can take and pass the SSCP exam to earn an Associate of (ISC)² designation and will have up to two years to gain the work experience needed for the SSCP.

## Certificate vs. Certification vs. "Being Certified"

If you're new to formal certifications, these terms may seem interchangeable—but they are not!

A *certificate* is an official document or proof that displays or attests to your completion of a formal program, school, or training course. Earning a certificate may require passing a formal exam, hands-on practice, or just remaining in the course until the end. Certificate courses are designed to teach a skill and/or influence knowledge and understanding of a topic.

A *certification* goes several steps further than a certificate. Typically, certifications require a minimum period of professional experience, which may include supervision by someone who also holds that same certifications.

Certifications are established by professional organizations that serve a particular industry, and thus earning that certification means you've demonstrated what that industry needs. Certificates are defined and issued by the schools or training programs that teach them.

Typically, certifications have requirements for ongoing learning, experience, and skills development; certificates usually do not.

Finally, consider who awards you that credential. If it's the school or the training organization, it's a certificate. If it's that standards-setting body, it's a certification.

As a result, you are entitled—you have earned the right—to put the official, accepted designation of that certification after your name, when used as a part of your professional correspondence, marketing, or other communications. John Doe, SSCP, or Jayne Smith, MD, are ways that these individuals rightfully declare their earned certifications.

Academic programs increasingly offer sets of accredited university courses bundled as certificate programs; instead of completing 120 semester hours for a bachelor's degree, for example, a certificate program might only require 15 to 30 semester hours of study.

Thus, we see that "being certified" means that you've met the standards required by the professional organization that defines and controls that certification as a process and as a standard; you've earned the right to declare yourself "certified" in the domain of that standard.

# The National and International Need

We've certainly needed people who understood information security as a systems discipline since the dawn of the computer age, but it wasn't until the early 1990s that we saw national and global awareness of this need start to attract headlines and influence the ways people prepared for careers in cybersecurity. One of the results of the President's Commission on Critical Infrastructure Protection (PCCIP), created by Bill Clinton, was the recognition that the nation needed a far larger and more sustained effort focused on securing the Internet-based backbones and systems on which our society and much of the world depended upon for day-to-day business, commerce, public services, hygiene, transportation, medicine—in short, for everything! Virtually all of that infrastructure was owned and operated by private business; this was not something governments could mandate, direct, or perform.

The National Institute of Standards and Technology (NIST) took the lead in defining standards-based frameworks and approaches for identifying, managing, and controlling risks to information systems and infrastructures. As a part of this effort, NIST established the National Initiative for Cybersecurity Education (NICE). This partnership between government, academia, and the private sector works to continually define the standards and best practices that cybersecurity professional educators and trainers need to fulfill in order to produce a qualified cybersecurity workforce.

In the meantime, the Department of Defense (DoD) has continued its efforts to professionalize its workforce (both the uniformed and civilian members) and, in a series of regulations and directives, has defined its baseline set of approved certifications in various fields. One of these, DoD Directive 8140, defines the minimum acceptable certifications someone must demonstrate to hold jobs in the information assurance technical, managerial, and systems architecture job series. DoD 8140 also defines the certifications necessary to hold jobs as a cybersecurity service provider at various levels.

Internationally, the International Organization for Standardization (ISO) and the International Electrotechnical Commission (IEC) have jointly issued their own family of standards designed to help private and public organizations worldwide attain minimum acceptable standards in achieving information security, information assurance, and cybersecurity. The ISO/IEC 27000 family of standards provides best practice recommendations on information security management and the management of information risks through information security controls, within the context of an overall information security management system (ISMS). ISO/IEC 27001 is the best-known standard in the family providing requirements for an ISMS. The European Union has issued a series of regulations and policy documents that help refine and implement these ISO/IEC standards.

(ISC)[2] plays a part in helping all of these standards bodies and regulatory agencies assess the current needs of the information security community of practitioners and works to update its set of certifications to support these national, international, and global needs. As a result, the SSCP certification is recognized around the world.

# The SSCP and Your Professional Growth Path

Possibly one of the best ways to see your SSCP in the context of your professional growth and development can be seen at the CyberSeek website. CyberSeek is a partnership sponsored by NIST that brings together the current state of the job market in cybersecurity, information security, and information risk management. It combines data on job market demand for such skills, current average salaries, and even insight on the numbers of professionals holding various certifications. The real gem, however, for the new cybersecurity or information security pro is its Career Mapping tool. See this at www.cyberseek.org and use it to help navigate the options to consider and the opportunities that an earned SSCP after your name might open up.

As an international, nonprofit membership association with more than 140,000 members, (ISC)² has worked since its inception in 1989 to serve the needs for standardization and certification in cybersecurity workplaces around the world. Since then, (ISC)²'s founders and members have been shaping the information security profession and have developed the following information security certifications:

- Certified Information Systems Security Professional (CISSP): The CISSP is an experienced professional who holds the most globally recognized standard of achievement in the industry, and the first information security credential to meet the strict conditions of ISO/IEC Standard 17024. The CISSP certification has three concentrations:

    - Certified Information Systems Security Professional: Information Systems Security Architecture Professional (CISSP-ISSAP): The CISSP-ISSAP is a chief security architect, analyst, or other professional who designs, builds, and oversees the implementation of network and computer security for an organization. The CISSP-ISSAP may work as an independent consultant or other professional who provides operational guidance and direction to support business strategies.

    - Certified Information Systems Security Professional: Information Systems Security Engineering Professional (CISSP-ISSEP): The CISSP-ISSEP can effectively incorporate security into all facets of business operations.

    - Certified Information Systems Security Professional: Information Systems Security Management Professional (CISSP-ISSMP): The CISSP-ISSMP is a cybersecurity manager who demonstrates deep management and leadership skills and excels at establishing, presenting, and governing information security programs.

- Systems Security Certified Practitioner (SSCP): The SSCP is a high-value practitioner who demonstrates technical skills in implementing, monitoring, and administering IT infrastructure using information security policies and procedures. The SSCP's commitment to continuous learning and practice ensures consistent information assurance.

- Certified Cloud Security Professional (CCSP): The CCSP is a globally recognized professional who demonstrates expertise and implements the highest standards in cloud security. The certification was co-created by (ISC)² and Cloud Security Alliance—the leading stewards for information security and cloud computing security.

- Certified Authorization Professional (CAP): The CAP is a leader in information security and aligns information systems with the risk management framework (RMF). The CAP certification covers the RMF at an extensive level, and it's the only certification under the DoD 8570/DoD 8140 Approved Baseline Certifications that aligns to each of the RMF steps.

- Certified Secure Software Lifecycle Professional (CSSLP): The CSSLP is an internationally recognized professional with the ability to incorporate security practices—authentication, authorization, and auditing—into each phase of the software development lifecycle (SDLC).

- HealthCare Information Security and Privacy Practitioner (HCISPP): The HCISSP is a skilled practitioner who combines information security with healthcare security and privacy best practices and techniques.

Each of these certifications has its own requirements for documented full-time experience in its requisite topic areas.

Newcomers to information security who have not yet had supervised work experience in the topic areas can take and pass the SSCP exam and then become recognized as Associates of (ISC)$^2$. Associates then have two years to attain the required experience to become full members of (ISC)$^2$.

## The SSCP Seven Domains

(ISC)$^2$ is committed to helping members learn, grow, and thrive. The Common Body of Knowledge (CBK) is the comprehensive framework that helps it fulfill this commitment. The CBK includes all the relevant subjects a security professional should be familiar with, including skills, techniques, and best practices. (ISC)$^2$ uses the various domains of the CBK to test a certificate candidate's levels of expertise in the most critical aspects of information security. You can see this framework in the SSCP Exam Outline at www.isc2.org/-/media/ISC2/Certifications/Exam-Outlines/SSCP-Exam-Outline-Nov-1-2018.ashx.

Successful candidates are competent in the following seven domains:

**Domain 1: Access Controls** Policies, standards, and procedures that define who users are, what they can do, which resources and information they can access, and what operations they can perform on a system, such as:

    1.1 Implement and maintain authentication methods

    1.2 Support internetwork trust architectures

    1.3 Participate in the identity management lifecycle

    1.4 Implement access controls

**Domain 2: Security Operations and Administration** Identification of information assets and documentation of policies, standards, procedures, and guidelines that ensure confidentiality, integrity, and availability, such as:

    2.1 Comply with codes of ethics

    2.2 Understand security concepts

    2.3 Document, implement, and maintain functional security controls

2.4 Participate in asset management

2.5 Implement security controls and assess compliance

2.6 Participate in change management

2.7 Participate in security awareness and training

2.8 Participate in physical security operations (e.g., data center assessment, badging)

**Domain 3: Risk Identification, Monitoring, and Analysis** Risk identification is the review, analysis, and implementation of processes essential to the identification, measurement, and control of loss associated with unplanned adverse events. Monitoring and analysis are determining system implementation and access in accordance with defined IT criteria. This involves collecting information for identification of, and response to, security breaches or events, such as:

3.1 Understand the risk management process

3.2 Perform security assessment activities

3.3 Operate and maintain monitoring systems (e.g., continuous monitoring)

3.4 Analyze monitoring results

**Domain 4: Incident Response and Recovery** "The show must go on" is a well-known saying that means even if there are problems or difficulties, an event or activity must continue. Incident response and recovery ensures the work of the organization will continue. In this domain, the SSCP gains an understanding of how to handle incidents using consistent, applied approaches like business continuity planning (BCP) and disaster recovery planning (DRP). These approaches are utilized to mitigate damages, recover business operations, and avoid critical business interruption:

4.1 Support incident lifecycle

4.2 Understand and support forensic investigations

4.3 Understand and support business continuity plan (BCP) and disaster recovery plan (DRP) activities

**Domain 5: Cryptography** The protection of information using techniques that ensure its integrity, confidentiality, authenticity, and nonrepudiation, and the recovery of encrypted information in its original form:

5.1 Understand fundamental concepts of cryptography

5.2 Understand reasons and requirements for cryptography

5.2 Understand and support secure protocols

5.2 Understand public key infrastructure (PKI) systems

**Domain 6: Network and Communications Security** The network structure, transmission methods and techniques, transport formats, and security measures used to operate both private and public communication networks:

6.1 Understand and apply fundamental concepts of networking

6.2 Understand network attacks and countermeasures (e.g., DDoS, man-in-the-middle, DNS poisoning)

6.3 Manage network access controls

6.4 Manage network security

6.5 Operate and configure network-based security devices

6.6 Operate and configure wireless technologies (e.g., Bluetooth, NFC, Wi-Fi)

**Domain 7: Systems and Application Security**  Countermeasures and prevention techniques for dealing with viruses, worms, logic bombs, Trojan horses, and other related forms of intentionally created damaging code:

7.1 Identify and analyze malicious code and activity

7.2 Implement and operate endpoint device security

7.3 Operate and configure cloud security

7.4 Operate and secure virtual environments

# Using This Book

This book is structured to take you on your learning journey through all seven subject area domains that the SSCP requires. It does this one building block at a time, starting with the fundamentals involved in a particular topic or subject, and building on those to guide you toward the degree of knowledge you'll need as an SSCP. This book is structured in four major parts:

- Part 1 provides a solid foundation of how organizations use information to drive decision making, and the role of information systems and information technologies in making that information available, reliable, and useful. It then looks to the fundamental concepts of information security and assurance, using operational definitions and examples to help you apply these concepts to real-world situations you may find around you today:

    - Business and the private sector speak their own language, and organize, direct, manage, and lead their people in different ways than do governments or military services. If you haven't had experience in the private sector or have no business background, start with Chapter 1.

 **Using the Language of Business**

Chapter 1's content is valuable to every SSCP, but it is not officially a part of the SSCP domains, and is outside the scope of the SSCP certification exam. Even if you've had private sector work experience, you'll find Chapter 1 will strengthen your understanding of *why* business finds information security and assurance so important. With that as foundation, you can go on and learn *how* to make that security happen.

    - Chapter 2 provides a deep look at the fundamentals of information security and assurance.

- Part 2 takes you deep into the practice of risk management, with great emphasis on information risk management:

    - Chapter 3 defines the basic concepts of risk management and risk mitigation and familiarizes you with the processes all organizations can use to understand risks, characterize their impact on organizational objectives, and prioritize how to deal with information risks specifically.

    - Chapter 4 dives into risk mitigation. Here's where we make decisions about specific risks (or, rather, about the vulnerabilities we've discovered that could lead to such a risk becoming reality). We'll look at choices you can make, or advise your company's management to make, and how you can estimate the value of your mitigation choices as compared to the possible impacts if nothing is done.

- Part 3 gets down into the technologies of information security; we'll start each major subject area in Part 3 first by reviewing the fundamentals of various information systems technologies and how they are used, and then look to their vulnerabilities and what choices we might have to help mitigate their associated risks. Key throughout Part 3 is the need to own and manage the baseline architectures of our information systems—for without effective management of our systems, we have little hope of being able to keep them secure, much less operating correctly!

    - Chapter 5 is all about communications as a people-to-people and systems-to-systems set of processes and *protocols*. Two *protocol stacks*—the Open Systems Interconnection (OSI) 7-layer reference model and the Transmission Control Protocol over Internet Protocol (TCP/IP)—will become your highway to understanding and appreciating the different perspectives you'll need as you seek to secure networks and systems.

    - Chapter 6 considers identity management and access control, which are two sides of the same process: how do we know that users or processes asking to use our systems and our information are who they claim they are, and how do we control, limit, or deny their access to or use of any of our information, our systems, our knowledge, or our people?

    - Chapter 7 demystifies cryptography and cryptographic systems, with special emphasis on the use of symmetric and asymmetric encryption algorithms as part of our digital certificates, signatures, and public infrastructure for security.

    - Chapter 8 considers the security aspects of computing and communications hardware, and the systems software, utilities, firmware, and connections that bring that all together.

    - Chapter 9 continues on the foundation laid in Chapter 8 by investigating how we secure applications software, data, and endpoint devices. It also looks at the specific issues involved when organizations migrate their information systems to the cloud (or have developed them in the cloud from the beginning).

- Part 4 shifts the emphasis back onto the real driving, integrative force that we need to apply to our information security problems: the people power inherent in our workforce, their managers and leaders, even our customers, clients, and those we partner with or share federated systems with:

  - Chapter 10 takes us through the information security incident response process, from planning and preparation through the real-time challenges of detection, identification, and response. It then takes us through the post-response tasks and shows how attention to these can increase our organization's chances of never having to cope with making the same mistakes twice by learning from the experiences of an incident response while they're still fresh in our response team members' minds.

  - Chapter 11 addresses business continuity and disaster recovery, which are both the overriding purpose of information security and assurance and the worst-case scenario for why we need to plan and prepare if we want our organization to survive a major incident and carry on with business as usual.

  - Chapter 12 takes a look back across all chapters and highlights important issues and trends which you as an SSCP may have to deal with in the very near future. It also offers some last-minute practical advice on getting ready to take your SSCP exam and ideas for what you can do after that.

As you look at the chapters and the domains, you should quickly see that some domains fit neatly into a chapter all by themselves; other domains share the limelight with each other in the particular chapters that address their subject areas. You'll also see that some chapters focus on building foundational knowledge and skills; others build applied problem-solving skills and approaches; and some provide a holistic, integrated treatment spanning CBK domains. This is intentional—the design of this book takes you on a journey of learning and mastery of those seven CBK domains.

Risk identification, monitoring, and analysis *as a domain* is a fundamental element of two chapters (Chapters 3 and 4) almost by itself. This important topic deserves this level of attention; you might even say that the very reason we *do* information security at all is because we're trying to manage and mitigate risks to our information! Similarly, we see that Chapter 11, which focuses on the people power aspects of achieving business continuity in the face of information security incidents and disasters, must make significant use of the *domains* of access control, security operations and administration, and risk identification, monitoring, and analysis. Finally, the growing emphasis in the marketplace on data security, cloud security, endpoint security, and software lifecycle security dictates that we first build a strong foundation on hardware and systems security (Chapter 8), on which we build our knowledge and skills for applications, data, cloud, and mobile endpoint security.

# Objective Map

Table I.1 contains an objective map to show you at-a-glance where you can find each objective covered. Note that all chapters except Chapters 1 and 12 cover objectives from the SSCP exam.

**TABLE I.1**    Objective Map

| Objective | Chapter |
|---|---|
| **Domain 1: Access Controls** | |
| 1.1 Implement and maintain authentication methods | 6 |
| 1.2 Support internetwork trust architectures | 6 |
| 1.3 Participate in the identity management lifecycle | 6, 11 |
| 1.4 Implement access controls | 6 |
| **Domain 2: Security Operations and Administration** | |
| 2.1 Comply with codes of ethics | 2, 11 |
| 2.2 Understand security concepts | 2, 11 |
| 2.3 Document, implement, and maintain functional security controls | 11 |
| 2.4 Participate in asset management | 11 |
| 2.5 Implement security controls and assess compliance | 3, 4 |
| 2.6 Participate in change management | 3, 4 |
| 2.7 Participate in security awareness and training | 3, 4, 11 |
| 2.8 Participate in physical security operations (e.g., data center assessment, badging) | 3, 4 |

*(continued)*

**TABLE I.1**   Objective Map *(continued)*

| Objective | Chapter |
|---|---|
| **Domain 3: Risk Identification, Monitoring, and Analysis** | |
| 3.1 Understand the risk management process | 3, 4 |
| 3.2 Perform security assessment activities | 4 |
| 3.3 Operate and maintain monitoring systems (e.g., continuous monitoring) | 4, 10 |
| 3.4 Analyze monitoring results | 4 |
| **Domain 4: Incident Response and Recovery** | |
| 4.1 Support incident lifecycle | 10 |
| 4.2 Understand and support forensic investigations | 10 |
| 4.3 Understand and support business continuity plan (BCP) and disaster recovery plan (DRP) activities | 10 |
| **Domain 5: Cryptography** | |
| 5.1 Understand fundamental concepts of cryptography | 7 |
| 5.2 Understand reasons and requirements for cryptography | 7 |
| 5.2 Understand and support secure protocols | 7 |
| 5.2 Understand public key infrastructure (PKI) systems | 7 |
| **Domain 6: Network and Communications Security** | |
| 6.1 Understand and apply fundamental concepts of networking | 5 |
| 6.2 Understand network attacks and countermeasures (e.g., DDoS, man-in-the-middle, DNS poisoning) | 5 |
| 6.3 Manage network access controls | 6 |
| 6.4 Manage network security | 5 |
| 6.5 Operate and configure network-based security devices | 5 |
| 6.6 Operate and configure wireless technologies (e.g., Bluetooth, NFC, Wi-Fi) | 5 |

| Objective | Chapter |
|---|---|
| **Domain 7: Systems and Application Security** | |
| 7.1 Identify and analyze malicious code and activity | 8 |
| 7.2 Implement and operate endpoint device security | 8, 9 |
| 7.3 Operate and configure cloud security | 8, 9 |
| 7.4 Operate and secure virtual environments | 8, 9 |

# Earning Your Certification

Earning your SSCP requires that you take and pass the SSCP exam, of course; it also requires that you have at least one year of full-time work experience, in at least one of the seven domains of knowledge of the SSCP. A one-year prerequisite waiver will be granted by (ISC)² if you have earned a bachelor's degree or higher in a recognized cybersecurity-related discipline. The website www.isc2.org/Certifications/SSCP/Prerequisite-Pathway explains this and should be your guide. Note the requirements to be able to document your work experience.

No matter where you are on that pathway right now, put this book to work! Use it as a ready reference, as a roadmap, and as a learning tool. Let it help you broaden and deepen your knowledge base, while you sharpen your skills on the job or in your classes—or both!

## Before the Exam: Grow Your Knowledge, Skills, and Experience

The key to this or any personal and professional development you wish to achieve is to first set your goals. SMART goals can help you plan and achieve most anything you set your body, mind, heart and spirit to:

- *Specific*—What is it, *exactly,* that you want to achieve?
- *Measurable*—How will you know that you've achieved that specific goal?
- *Achievable*—Is it really within your power and ability to achieve it? Or do you need to first build other strengths, develop other talents, or align other resources to help you take this goal on?
- *Realistic*—Can you actually do this? Are there practical ways to go about accomplishing this goal?
- *Timely*—When, *exactly,* do you want or need to accomplish this goal by?

Having set SMART goals, set a plan; lay out the tasks you'll need to accomplish, and break those down, week by week, perhaps even day by day, to get to the goals of taking and passing the exam, and having the prerequisite experience or earned degree.

Start by thoroughly reading, and rereading, this study guide. Work through its review questions, not only to focus on why the *right* answers are in fact correct, but to identify and understand what's wrong with the *wrong* answers. Work through the case studies, and let them suggest other real-world issues to you as you do.

Other options to consider include:

- Volunteer, at work, school, or in your local community, to work with others on information security–related projects or tasks.

- Find a study buddy.

- Enlist the help and guidance of a mentor.

- Enroll in formal training courses for the SSCP, either face-to-face, virtual live online, or in other modes that suit you.

- Take college courses that prepare you for the SSCP or that help you master some or all of its domains of knowledge.

- Use other learning resources, such as videos, and IT and security blog sites.

If you're already working (even part-time) in an IT-related job, consider talking with your supervisor about your ambition to earn your SSCP; you might find a wealth of practical advice and assistance, right there at work!

## The SSCP Exam

The SSCP exam is a computer-based examination, which you must take at an (ISC)[2] approved testing facility. Pearson VUE is (ISC)[2]'s official and exclusive global testing partner, but be advised: not all Pearson VUE testing locations meet the special test security requirements that (ISC)[2] imposes on test-takers and proctors alike. Start by reviewing the testing terms and conditions here: www.isc2.org/Register-for-Exam.

Register early at https://home.pearsonvue.com/isc2, and select the SSCP as the certification exam you're pursuing. Check the availability of testing centers at or near locations that best suit your needs. Note that different testing centers have different schedule options, with some being more available on the weekends while others might be closed.

You don't have to pay at this step—you pay for your exam when you're ready to schedule the exam (and you're ready to schedule the exam once you know when you'll be ready to take and pass it!).

A great way to learn more about the exam process is to take a "test drive," using the exam demo and tutorial about the exam experience. You can find this on the Pearson VUE website, www.pearsonvue.com/athena/athena.asp.

Armed with driving or public transport directions and a map, find your way from home (or where you'll be coming to the test from) to the testing site of your choice. Check out how long that trip takes at the time of day you want to take the test—or at the times of day that center has a testing slot available! (Take this "test drive" a few days in advance.)

Plan ahead. Know how to get to the testing center an hour early. Be prepared!

## (ISC)² Terms and Conditions

(ISC)² requires that all candidates for certification read and accept the terms and conditions here: www.isc2.org/uploadedFiles/Certification_Programs/CBT-Examination-Agreement.pdf. Candidates who do not agree to the terms and conditions will not be permitted to sit for any (ISC)² examination.

## Nondisclosure Agreement (NDA)

You will be required to agree to the NDA that will be presented at the beginning of your exam. Failure to read/accept the agreement within the allotted 5 minutes will result in your exam ending and a forfeit of your exam fees. Please take a moment to review the agreement now so that you are familiar with it when you sit for your exam.

## Exam Fees and Payment

An exam voucher may be attained in fees paid during the scheduling process on the Pearson VUE website: https://home.pearsonvue.com/. Vouchers may be obtained in bulk on the (ISC)² website. This is ideal for companies that are scheduling several people for various exams. The more vouchers purchased, the greater the discount.

## Reschedule Policy

If you wish to reschedule your exam, you must contact Pearson VUE by phone, at least 24 hours prior to your exam appointment; if you contact them online, you must do this at least 48 hours ahead of your appointment. Rescheduling an exam less than 24 hours prior is subject to a same-day forfeit exam fee. Exam fees are also forfeited for no-shows. There is a $50 fee for exam reschedules.

## Cancellation Policy

If you wish to cancel your exam, you must contact Pearson VUE 24 hours prior to your scheduled appointment. Canceling an exam less than 24 hours prior to your appointment or missing your exam may result in forfeiting your exam fees. There is a $100 fee for cancellations.

## The Exam Structure and Format

During the SSCP exam, you will focus on recalling, recognizing, and indicating your understanding of the information and ideas presented in this study guide. The SSCP exam is *proctored*, which means you will be supervised by a neutral person (a proctor) at all times while taking the test. The exam is pass/fail.

There are 125 multiple-choice questions on the exam. Of that number, only 100 are graded, whereas the remaining 25 are evaluated by exam developers and used to inform future exams. You will not know which of the 100 questions will be graded, so be sure to answer all exam questions to the best of your ability. The questions are written to check that you remember, understand, and can apply what you've learned in the seven knowledge domains that make up the SSCP, and they are covered by this study guide. Here are some thoughts to keep in mind about these questions and the exam process itself:

- Each multiple-choice question will list four possible answers.

- There are no true or false questions.

- Expect scenario-based questions that describe a situation, then ask that you use the situation to select the correct multiple-choice answer.

- All acronyms are spelled out, such as the confidentiality, integrity, and availability (CIA) triad.

- Many questions will ask for the *most* or *least* correct answer.

- Some questions will contain logical operators, such as not, always, test, true, or false.

You are not penalized for wrong answers, so be sure to answer every question. You will need a score of 700 out of 1000 points to pass the exam. The questions are weighted. This means you may be required to have more or fewer than 70 questions answered correctly to pass the exam.

One of the benefits to candidates taking an examination via CBT is that most candidates receive their scores immediately upon completing their examination. In some cases, however, to ensure it is providing accurate and valid test results to candidates, (ISC)² must conduct periodic psychometric analyses of a group of candidates' responses before it releases their exam results. For the small number of candidates affected by this process, the candidates will receive their results within four to six weeks after taking the exam. (ISC)² apologizes in advance for this inconvenience to those candidates who will not receive their pass/fail status at the test centers, but this is an important part of (ISC)²'s quality assurance process to protect the integrity of the credentials. Candidates who are impacted by this process will be informed when they complete their tests.

## Reasonable Accommodations

If you require reasonable and appropriate accommodations for exams, you can request special accommodations through (ISC)². Once these are approved, be sure to coordinate with your chosen test center to ensure that they can meet your needs. *Work through this process early.* The on-site test administrator will not have the power to grant you an accommodation at the time of your exam if it has not been approved in advance.

(ISC)² provides reasonable and appropriate accommodations for its exams for people who have demonstrated a need for test accommodations. If you wish to request an accommodation, please visit www.isc2.org/Register-for-Exam and click Requesting Special Accommodations for information on requesting an accommodation.

Test accommodations are individualized and considered on a case-by-case basis. Once an accommodation is approved by (ISC)², they will send it to Pearson VUE Accommodations. Please allow two to three business days for Pearson VUE to get this information. Then, call Pearson VUE at 800-466-0450 so that you can schedule your exam. Please don't start by scheduling through Pearson VUE's website or through their main registration phone line. Contact (ISC)² first.

Please note that the purpose of test accommodations is to provide examinees with full access to the test. However, they are not a guarantee of improved performance or test completion.

## On the Day of the Exam

Plan to arrive at your test center at least 30 minutes before your exam start time. To check in, you'll need to

- Show two valid, unexpired forms of personal ID (examples include government-issued IDs such as a driver's license, passport, etc.). Both must have your signature, and one of the two must have your photo. For more information about acceptable IDs, please visit: www.isc2.org/Register-for-Exam, and click What You Need to Bring to the Test Center for more information.

- Provide your signature.

- Submit to a palm vein scan (unless it's prohibited by law).

- Have your photo taken. Hats, scarves, and coats may not be worn for your photo. You also can't wear these items in the test room.

- Leave your personal belongings outside the testing room. You'll have access to secure storage. Storage space is small, so plan ahead. Pearson VUE test centers do not assume responsibility for your personal belongings.

The test administrator (TA) will give you a short orientation. If you have already arranged for special accommodations for your testing, and (ISC)² and Pearson VUE have approved these, be sure to go over them with the TA. Then, the TA will escort you to a computer terminal. Upon concluding the exam, click the Finish or Submit button.

## After the Exam

The proctor will escort you out of the room. You'll receive a printed copy of your preliminary examination report by the front desk attendant. The report will congratulate you for passing the exam, or, should you fail, list the domains you need to study again from weakest to strongest.

Upon successfully passing the SSCP exam, you are not yet certified until (ISC)² approves it. You must be endorsed by another (ISC)²-certified professional before the credential can be awarded. The New Endorsement Application is located here: `https://apps.isc2.org/Endorsement/#/Home`.

An endorser can be anyone who is an active (ISC)² credential holder and can attest to your assertions regarding professional experience and education (if applicable) and that you are in good standing within the cybersecurity industry.

If you do not know an (ISC)²-certified professional, you may request (ISC)² to endorse your application.

Although you can start and save a draft application, you must pass the exam for the selected certification before you can submit your application for endorsement.

If you do not yet possess the education and/or experience required for the certification, you can request to be an Associate of (ISC)², which requires only that you pass the credential exam.

# Congratulations! You're Now an SSCP. Now What?

As a recognized member of a profession, you've voluntarily taken up the duties and obligations that come with that recognition. You also have gone through an open door to the opportunities and benefits that come with that status. Those benefits and obligations go hand in hand as you continue to grow and learn as an information systems security professional.

## Maintaining the SSCP Certification

SSCP credentials are maintained in good standing by participating in various activities and gaining professional continuing professional education credits (CPEs). CPEs are obtained through numerous methods such as reading books, attending seminars, writing papers or articles, teaching classes, attending security conventions, and participating in many other qualifying activities. Visit the (ISC)² website for additional information concerning the definition of CPEs.

Individuals are required to post a minimum of 20 CPE credits each year on the (ISC)² member website. Generally, the CPE credit post will be recognized immediately by the system, but it's also subject to random audit. Please note that any CPEs accomplished prior to being awarded the (ISC)² certification may not be claimed. If an individual accomplishes more than 20 CPEs for one year, the remainder may be carried forward to the following year. The (ISC)² website describes CPEs as items gained external to your current employment duties.

## Join a Local Chapter

As an SSCP, you've become one of over 23,000 (ISC)² members worldwide. They, like you, are there to share in the knowledge, experience, and opportunity to help accomplish the goals and objectives of being an information security professional. Many of these members participate in local area chapters, and (ISC)² has numerous local chapters around the world. You can find one in your area by visiting www.isc2.org/Chapters.

Being an active part of a local chapter helps you network with your peers as you share knowledge, exchange information about resources, and work on projects together. You can engage in leadership roles and participate in co-sponsored local events with other industry associations. You might write for or speak at (ISC)² events and help support other (ISC)² initiatives. You can also be a better part of your local community by participating in local chapter community service outreach projects.

Chapter membership earns you CPE credits and can make you eligible for special discounts on (ISC)² products and programs.

# Let's Get Started!

This book is for you. This is your journey map, your road atlas, and your handbook. Make it work for you.

Choose your own course through it, based on what you already know, what the self-assessment tells you, and what you've experienced thus far in your work or studies.

Go for it.

# Self-Assessment

1. Which statement about business continuity planning and information security is most correct?

    **A.** Plans are useful only because they start the development of detailed procedures and processes, and thus, there is no need to maintain or improve such plans.

    **B.** Planning is more important than the plans it produces.

    **C.** Plans represent significant investments and decisions and thus should be updated only when significant changes to objectives or circumstances dictate.

    **D.** Planning should continuously bring plans and procedures in tune with ongoing operational reality.

2. Which of the following statements about social engineering attacks is incorrect?

    **A.** Most targeted individuals don't see the harm in responding or in answering simple questions posed by the attacker.

    **B.** Most people believe they are too smart to fall for such obvious ploys, but they do anyway.

    **C.** Most targeted individuals and organizations have effective tools and procedures to filter out phishing and related scams, so they are now better protected from such attacks.

    **D.** Most people want to be trusting and helpful.

3. In general, what differentiates phishing from whaling attacks?

    **A.** Phishing attacks tend to be used to gain access to systems via malware payloads or by getting recipients to disclose information, whereas whaling attacks try to get responsible managers to authorize payments to the attacker's accounts.

    **B.** Phishing attacks are focused on businesses; whaling attacks are focused on high-worth individuals.

    **C.** Whaling attacks tend to offer something that ought to sound "too good to be true," whereas phishing attacks masquerade as routine business activities such as package delivery confirmations.

    **D.** Whaling attacks send out huge numbers of emails attempting to lure targeted individuals into responding or following a link; phishing attacks use telephones or other means of making personal contact with a selected target.

4. You're the only IT person at a small tool and die machine shop, which uses a LAN and cloud-hosted platforms to run the business on. The previous IT person had told your boss not to worry about the business being the target of a cyberattack. Which statement best lets you explain the real risks the company might face?

    **A.** Since we don't handle consumer-level payment cards, and we really don't have any proprietary information, we probably don't have to worry about being a target.

    **B.** We do share an extranet connection with key customers and suppliers, but it should prevent an attack on our systems that could lead to an attack on theirs.

**C.**  Our cloud systems hosting company provides most of our security, and as long as we keep our systems on the factory floor and the workstations our staff use properly updated, we should be okay.

**D.**  Since we haven't really done even a basic vulnerabilities assessment, we don't know what risks we could be facing. Let's do that much at least, and let that tell us what the next step should be. Soon.

5.  Which of these steps would *not* help you limit or prevent attacks on your systems that attempt to spoof, corrupt, or tamper with data?

**A.**  Ensure that firewalls, routers, and other network infrastructures filter for and block attempts to access network storage without authorization.

**B.**  Develop and use an organizational data model and data dictionary that contain all data-focused business logic; use them to build and validate business processes and the apps that support them.

**C.**  Implement data quality processes that ensure all data is fit for all purposes, in accordance with approved business logic.

**D.**  Implement information classification, and use access control and identity management to enforce it.

6.  Which of the following are not examples of "shadow IT" contributing to an information security problem? (Choose all that apply.)

**A.**  One user defines a format or style sheet for specific types of documents for others in the division to use.

**B.**  An end user writes special-purpose database queries and reports used to forecast sales and project production and inventory needs, which are reviewed and used at weekly division meetings.

**C.**  Several users build scripts, flows, and other processing logic to implement a customer service help desk/trouble ticket system, using its own database on a shared use/collaboration platform that the company uses.

**D.**  Users post documents, spreadsheets, and many other types of information on a company-provided shared storage system, making the information more freely available throughout the company.

7.  Which statement about privacy and data protection is the most correct and most important?

**A.**  International standards and agreements specify that personally identifiable information (PII) and information about an individual's healthcare, education, work, or credit history must be protected from unauthorized use or disclosure.

**B.**  It's up to the organization that gathers, produces, uses, or disposes of such private data to determine what protection, if any, is needed.

**C.**  Storing backup or archive copies of privacy-related information in a datacenter in another country, without doing any processing there, does not subject you to that country's data protection laws.

**D.**  Sometimes, it seems cheaper to run the risk of fines or loss of business from a data breach involving privacy-related data than to implement proper data protection to prevent such a loss. While this might make financial sense, it is not legal or ethical to do so.

8. In which phase or phases of a typical data exfiltration attack would an attacker probably not make use of phishing? (Choose all that apply.)

   **A.** Reconnaissance and characterization

   **B.** Data gathering, clumping, masking, and aggregating

   **C.** Installing and using covert command and control capabilities

   **D.** Initial access

9. When choosing your countermeasures and tactics to protect hardware and systems software, you should start with which of the following?

   **A.** Published Current Vulnerabilities and Exposures (CVE) databases

   **B.** The information systems baseline that documents the systems your organization uses

   **C.** Your organization's business impact analysis

   **D.** Your organization's IT vulnerabilities assessment

10. What kind of malware attacks can corrupt or infect device-level firmware? (Choose all that apply.)

    **A.** SNMP-based attacks that can trigger the device to download and install a firmware update remotely

    **B.** Remote or onsite device management (or mismanagement) attacks that allow a hacker to initiate a firmware update using a hacked firmware file

    **C.** Phishing or misdirection attacks that fool operators or users into initiating an upload of a hacked firmware file

    **D.** None, because firmware updates require operator intervention to download trusted updates and patch files from the manufacturer's or vendor's websites, and then initiate and monitor the update and restart of the device

11. What is a zero day exploit?

    **A.** An exploit conducted against a vulnerability within the same day as it is reported

    **B.** An exploit that impacts a system immediately, rather than having a delayed effect like ransomware or scareware does

    **C.** There are no real zero day exploits, but the mass media has exaggerated the dangers of unreported vulnerabilities

    **D.** An exploit conducted against a newly discovered vulnerability before it becomes known to the cybersecurity community or the system's vendor or owners

12. Which of the following statements best summarizes the benefits of using trusted platform modules (TPMs) as part of an organization's IT infrastructure?

    **A.** Because they have onboard hardware implementations of encryption, hashing, and key generation, they greatly simplify the use of certificate authorities and the public key infrastructure (PKI).

    **B.** As a trust root, a TPM can make hierarchies of trust more reliable.

**C.** The TPM replaces the host system's random number generators and hash routines with its hardware-accelerated, more secure versions. This enhances system security as well as runtime performance.

**D.** As a signed part of operating systems kernels, TPMs make it possible to validate software updates more reliably.

13. Which statement about how cryptography protects the meaning or content of files and messages is incorrect?

**A.** Cryptography obscures meaning by misdirection, concealment, or deception.

**B.** Cryptography obscures meaning by making it difficult or impossible for unauthorized users to access it, view it, copy it, or change it.

**C.** Cryptography transforms the meaning and content of a file or message into a unique value.

**D.** Cryptography is part of digitally signing files and messages to authenticate senders.

14. Which of the following best explains symmetric encryption?

**A.** Uses one key to encrypt blocks of text to be ciphered and another key to decrypt it back

**B.** Uses the same key or a simple transform of it to encrypt clear text into ciphertext, and then decrypt the ciphertext back into plaintext

**C.** Was used extensively in classical encryption but has since been superseded by much stronger asymmetric encryption

**D.** Is best suited to cleartext that has a very high degree of regularity to its structure and content

15. Properly used, cryptographic techniques improve all aspects of information security except:

**A.** Confidentiality

**B.** Authentication

**C.** Nonrepudiation

**D.** Accountability

16. Nonrepudiation relies on cryptography to validate that:

**A.** The sender or author of a document or file is who the recipient thinks it is

**B.** The file or message has not been tampered with during transit or storage

**C.** The file or message has not been viewed by others or copied without the sender's and named recipient's knowledge

**D.** The certificate, public key, or both associated with the sender or author match what is associated with the file or message

17. Which statement best describes how digital signatures work?

   A. The sender hashes the message or file to produce a message digest and applies the chosen encryption algorithm and their private key to it. This is the signature. The recipient uses the sender's public key and applies the corresponding decryption algorithm to the signature, which will produce a matching message digest only if the message or file is authentically from the sender.

   B. The sender hashes the message or file to produce a message digest and applies the chosen decryption algorithm and their public key to it. This is the signature. The recipient uses the sender's private key and applies the corresponding encryption algorithm to the signature, which will produce a matching message digest only if the message or file is authentically from the sender.

   C. The sender hashes the message or file to produce a message digest and applies the chosen decryption algorithm and their private key to it. This is the signature. The recipient uses the sender's public key and applies the corresponding encryption algorithm to the signature, which will produce a matching message digest only if the message or file is authentically from the sender.

   D. The sender encrypts the message or file with their private key and hashes the encrypted file to produce the signed message digest. This is the signature. The recipient uses the sender's public key and applies the corresponding decryption algorithm to the signature, which will produce a matching message digest only if the message or file is authentically from the sender.

18. Which statement about subjects and objects is not correct?

   A. Subjects are what users or processes require access to in order to accomplish their assigned duties.

   B. Objects can be people, information (stored in any fashion), devices, processes, or servers.

   C. Objects are the data that subjects want to access in order to read it, write to it, or otherwise use it.

   D. Subjects are people, devices, or processes.

19. Which statement about a reference monitor in an identity management and access control system is correct?

   A. It should be tamper-resistant.

   B. Its design and implementation should be complex so as to defeat reverse engineering attacks.

   C. It's an abstract design concept, which is not actually built into real hardware, operating systems, or access control implementations.

   D. It is part of the secure kernel in the accounting server or services provided by strong access control systems.

**20.** What kinds of privileges should be part of what your mandatory access control policies can grant or deny to a requesting subject? (Choose all that apply.)

    **A.** Any privilege relating to reading from, writing to, modifying or deleting the object in question if it was created or is owned by the requesting subject

    **B.** Reading or writing/modifying the metadata associated with an object

    **C.** Modifying access control system constraints, rules, or policies

    **D.** Reading, writing, deleting, or asking the system to load the object as an executable task or thread and run it

**21.** Which set of steps correctly shows the process of identity management?

  **1.** Proofing

  **2.** Provisioning

  **3.** Review

  **4.** Revocation

  **5.** Deletion

    **A.** 1, 2, 3, 4, and then 5

    **B.** 2, 3, 4

    **C.** 1, 2, 4, 5

    **D.** 2, 3, 5

**22.** What's the least secure way to authenticate device identity prior to authorizing it to connect to the network?

    **A.** MAC address whitelisting

    **B.** Multifactor authentication that considers device identification, physical location, and other attributes

    **C.** Verifying that the device meets system policy constraints as to software and malware updates

    **D.** Devices don't authenticate, but the people using them do.

**23.** In access control authentication systems, which is riskier, false positive or false negative errors?

    **A.** False negative, because they lead to a threat actor being granted access

    **B.** False positive, because they lead to a threat actor being granted access

    **C.** False negative, because they lead to legitimate subjects being denied access, which impacts business processes

    **D.** False positive, because they lead to legitimate subjects being denied access, which impacts business processes

**24.** Which statement about single-factor versus multifactor authentication is most correct?

   **A.** Single-factor is easiest to implement but with strong authentication is the hardest to attack.

   **B.** Multifactor requires greater implementation, maintenance, and management but can be extremely hard to spoof as a result.

   **C.** Multifactor authentication requires additional hardware devices to make authentication properly secure.

   **D.** Multifactor authentication should be reserved for those high-risk functions that require extra security.

**25.** When comparing the TCP/IP and OSI reference model as sets of protocols, which statement is most correct?

   **A.** Network hardware and systems are built on TCP/IP, whereas the OSI reference model only provides concepts and theories.

   **B.** TCP/IP only provides concepts and theories, whereas network hardware and systems are built using the OSI reference model.

   **C.** Both sets of protocols provide theories and concepts, but real hardware is built around the data, control, and management planes.

   **D.** Hardware and systems are built using both models, and both models are vital to threat assessment and network security.

**26.** Is IPv6 backward compatible with IPv4?

   **A.** No, because the differences in addressing, packet header structure, and other features would not allow an IPv4 packet to successfully travel on an IPv6 network

   **B.** No, because IPv4 packets cannot meet the new security considerations built into IPv6

   **C.** Yes, because IPv6 has services built into the protocol stacks to convert IPv4 packets into IPv6 compatible structures

   **D.** Yes, because the transport and routing protocols are the same

**27.** Which statement about subnetting is correct?

   **A.** Subnetting applies only to IPv4 networks, unless you are using classless interdomain routing.

   **B.** Both IPv4 and IPv6 provide for subnetting, but the much larger IPv6 address field makes this a lot simpler to design and manage.

   **C.** Subnetting in IPv4 involves the CIDR protocol, which runs at Layer 3; in IPv6, this protocol, and hence subnetting, is not used.

   **D.** Because the subnet mask field is so much larger in IPv6, it is easier to subnet in this newer protocol stack than in IPv4.

**28.** Which statement or statements about ports and the Internet is *not* correct? (Choose all that apply.)

    **A.** Using port numbers as part of addressing and routing was necessary during the early days of the Internet, largely because of the small size of the address field, but IPv6 makes most port usage obsolete.

    **B.** Standard ports are defined for a number of protocols, and these ports allow sender and receiver to establish connectivity for specific services.

    **C.** Standardized port assignments cannot be changed, or things won't work right, but they can be mapped to other port numbers by the protocol stacks on senders' and recipients' systems.

    **D.** Many modern devices, such as those using Android, cannot support ports, and so apps have to be redesigned to use alternate service connection strategies.

**29.** Which of the following statements about man-in-the-middle (MITM) attacks is most correct?

    **A.** Session stealing attacks are not MITM attacks.

    **B.** MITM attacks can occur at any layer and against connectionless or connection-oriented protocols.

    **C.** This basic attack strategy can be used at any layer of the protocols where there is connection-oriented, stateful communication between nodes.

    **D.** MITM attacks can work only at Layer 4.

**30.** What important role does systems monitoring perform in support of incident management?

    **A.** They are not related; monitoring is a routine task that uses trend analysis and data analytics to determine whether past systems behavior and use has been within expected bounds.

    **B.** Essential; by bringing together alert and alarm indicators from systems and their associated security controls and countermeasures, monitoring is the watchdog capability that activates incident response capabilities and plans.

    **C.** Incident response includes its own monitoring and alarms capabilities, so systems monitoring provides a good backup or alternate path to determining whether an incident is occurring.

    **D.** Ongoing, continuous monitoring is used to adjust or fine-tune alarm threshold settings so that false alarm rates can be better managed.

**31.** How might you keep a gap from becoming a blind spot in your information security defenses?

    **A.** Transfer this risk to insurers or other parties.

    **B.** Ensure that systems elements around the gap provide sufficient detection and reporting capabilities so that an event of interest occurring in the gap cannot spread without being detected.

    **C.** Ensure that other systems elements can either detect or report when an event of interest is happening within the gap.

    **D.** You can't, as by definition the gap is where you have no appreciable security coverage, and this includes having no monitoring or detection capabilities.

**32.** CVE data and your own vulnerability assessments indicate that many of your end-user systems do not include recent security patches released by the software vendors. You decide to bring these systems up to date by applying these patches. This is an example of which of the following?

   **A.** Remediating or mitigating a risk

   **B.** Transferring a risk

   **C.** Avoiding a risk

   **D.** Accepting a risk

**33.** Which of the following might be legitimate ways to transfer a risk? (Choose all that apply.)

   **A.** Recognize that government agencies have the responsibility to contain, control, or prevent this risk, which your taxes pay them to do.

   **B.** Pay insurance premiums for a policy that provides for payment of claims and liabilities in the event the risk does occur.

   **C.** Shift the affected business processes to a service provider, along with contractually making sure they are responsible for controlling that risk or have countermeasures in place to address it.

   **D.** Change the underlying business process to use more secure software and hardware systems.

**34.** Which statement correctly describes why CVE data should be part of your vulnerability assessments?

   **A.** It should provide most if not all of the vulnerability information you need to implement risk mitigation.

   **B.** Since hackers use CVE data to aid in planning their attacks, this should be the first place you look for insight as you do emergency hardening of your IT systems. Once these obvious vulnerabilities have been mitigated, a more complete vulnerability assessment should be done.

   **C.** It's a great source of information for known systems elements and known vulnerabilities associated with them, but it does nothing for vulnerabilities that haven't been reported yet or for company-developed IT elements.

   **D.** Since the vast majority of systems in use are based on Windows, if your business does not use Windows platforms you can probably avoid the expense of investigating CVE for vulnerability information.

**35.** Which of the following activities are not part of information risk mitigation?

   **A.** Implementing new systems features or capabilities to enhance product quality

   **B.** Incident management and investigation, after a suspected information security breach

   **C.** Installing and testing new firewall, switch, and router systems and settings

   **D.** Developing an information classification policy and process

36. Which of the following shows the major steps of the information risk management process in the correct order?

    A. Assess risks across the organization; identify information security and privacy risks; implement countermeasures; establish security and privacy posture; review supply chain for IT security risk elements

    B. Establish basic security posture; review risks; implement countermeasures; ongoing monitoring and assessment; testing; training

    C. Set priorities; assess risks; select controls and countermeasures; implement controls; validate correct operation; monitor

    D. Develop business impact analysis (BIA); establish risk tolerance levels; implement damage control choices; monitor

37. What is information risk?

    A. The threat that your computers, online storage, or cloud-hosted or other data could be hacked into and data stolen or changed

    B. The probability of an event occurring that disrupts your information and the business processes and systems that use it

    C. Vulnerabilities in your information systems that can be exploited by a threat actor and cause harmful impacts

    D. The probability that management and leadership's directions and communications will be misunderstood, causing the wrong actions to be taken by stakeholders, possibly causing financial loss, injury, or death

38. Which is the most correct statement as to what it means to have a proactive approach with your information security risk management plans, programs, and systems?

    A. Being proactive means that your countermeasures and controls can actively trace back to identify, locate, and characterize your attackers, which can help you both in defending against them and in potentially seeking legal redress.

    B. Senior leaders and managers in many businesses appreciate active, thoughtful, forward-looking approaches, and you will find it easier to gain their support.

    C. Proactive information security systems allow your security specialists to take real-time control of all systems elements and bring all information about events of interest into one common operational picture. This greatly enhances your ability to detect, characterize, and contain incidents.

    D. Being proactive means that you use the best knowledge you have today, including lessons learned from other organizations' experience with information risk, and you plan ahead to use these lessons to deal with these risks them, rather than wait for them to occur and then investigate how to respond to them.

**39.** What kind of information is part of an information risk assessment process? (Choose all that apply.)

   **A.** Lost revenues during the downtime caused by the risk incident, including time it takes to get things back to normal

   **B.** Damage to equipment or facilities, or injury or death to people

   **C.** Estimated costs to implement chosen solutions, remediations, controls, or countermeasures

   **D.** Total costs to create an asset that is damaged or disrupted by the risk event

**40.** There are three ways in which risk assessments can be done. Choose the option that orders them from best to least in terms of their contribution to risk management decision making.

   **A.** Qualitative, quantitative, and CVE-based

   **B.** CVE-based, quantitative, and qualitative

   **C.** There is no order; they all can and should be used, as each reveals something more about the risks you have to manage.

   **D.** Quantitative, CVE-based, and qualitative

**41.** Patsy is reviewing the quantitative risk assessment spreadsheet for her division, and she sees a number of entries where the annual loss expectancy is far greater than the single loss expectancy. This suggests that:

   **A.** The RTO is later than the RPO.

   **B.** The ARO is less than 1.

   **C.** The particular risk is assessed to happen many times per year; thus its ARO is much greater than 1.

   **D.** This looks like an error in estimation or assessment, and should be further investigated.

**42.** Which statement is incorrect as to how you should use RTO, MAO, and RPO in planning information risk management activities?

   **A.** Return to operations (RTO) is the desired time to get all business processes back into operation, whether on backup or workaround systems or on production systems brought back to normal. The recovery priority objective (RPO) sets priorities for which systems to bring up first or which business processes to get back into operation before others (of lower priority).

   **B.** Recovery point objective (RPO) establishes the maximum amount of data that is lost due to a risk event. This could be in numbers of transactions or in units of time and indicates the amount of rework of information that is acceptable to get systems back into normal operation.

   **C.** Recovery time objective (RTO) must be less than or equal to the maximum acceptable outage. MAO sets a maximum down time (outage time) before mission impact becomes unacceptable; RTO can be used to emphasize faster-than-MAO restoration.

   **D.** Maximum acceptable outage (MAO) relates to the mission or business objectives; if multiple systems support those objectives, then all of their recovery time objectives (RTOs) must be less than or equal to the MAO.

**43.** What are all of the choices we need to make when considering information risk management, and what's the correct order to do them in?

**1.** Treatment: accept, treat (fix or mitigate), transfer, avoid, recast

**2.** Damage limitation: deter, detect, prevent, avoid

**3.** Perspective: outcomes, assets, process or threat based

**4.** Impact assessment: quantitative or qualitative

    **A.** 1, 2, 3, then 4

    **B.** 3, 4, 2, then 1

    **C.** 4, 3, 2, then 1

    **D.** 2, 3, 1 then 4

**44.** What do we use protocols for? (Choose all that apply.)

    **A.** To conduct ceremonies, parades, or how we salute superiors, sovereigns, or rulers

    **B.** To have a conversation with someone, and keep disagreement from turning into hostile, angry argument

    **C.** To connect elements of computer systems together so that they can share tasks and control each other

    **D.** As abstract design tools when we are building systems, but we don't actually build hardware or software that implements a protocol

    **E.** None of the above

**45.** As an SSCP, you work at the headquarters of a retail sales company that has many stores around the country. Its training department has prepared different training materials and operations manuals for in-store sales, warehouse staff, and other team members to use in their jobs. Almost all of these describe procedures that people do as they work with each other or with customers. From an information security standpoint, which of the following statements is correct?

    **A.** Since these all describe people-to-people interactions and processes, they are not implemented by the IT department, and so they're not something that information security is concerned with.

    **B.** Most of their content is probably common practice in business and retail sales and so would not be trade secrets, company proprietary, or private to the company.

    **C.** Although these processes are not implemented in IT systems, the documents and videos themselves are hosted in company-provided IT systems, and so information security requirements apply.

    **D.** If the company has decided that the content of these training materials is proprietary or company confidential, then their confidentiality must be protected. They must also be protected from tampering or unauthorized changes and be available to staff in the stores to use when they need them if the company is to do business successfully. Therefore, information security applies.

**46.** We often hear people talk about the need for information systems to be safe and reliable. Is this the same as saying that they need to be secure?

    **A.** No, because reliability has to do with failures of equipment, errors in software design or use, or bad data used as input, whereas security is focused on keeping the systems and their data safe from intrusion or unwanted change.

    **B.** Yes, because the objective of information security is to increase our confidence that we can make sound and prudent decisions based on what those information systems are telling us and, in doing so, cause no harm.

    **C.** Yes, because all information and information systems are built by humans, and humans make mistakes, so we need strong safety rules and procedures to keep from causing harm.

    **D.** No, but they have ideas in common. For example, data integrity can lead to unsafe operation, but information security by itself cannot identify possible safety consequences.

**47.** Due diligence means which of the following?

    **A.** Pay your debts completely, on time.

    **B.** Do what you have to do to fulfill your responsibilities.

    **C.** Make sure that actions you've taken to fulfill your responsibilities are working correctly and completely.

    **D.** Read and review the reports from subordinates or from systems monitoring data.

**48.** Protection of intellectual property (IP) is an example of what kind of information security need?

    **A.** Privacy

    **B.** Confidentiality

    **C.** Availability

    **D.** Integrity

**49.** A thunderstorm knocks out the commercial electric power to your company's datacenter, shutting everything down. This impacts which aspect of information security?

    **A.** Privacy

    **B.** Confidentiality

    **C.** Integrity

    **D.** Availability

**50.** Explain the relationship between confidentiality and privacy, if any:

    **A.** Confidentiality is about keeping information secret so that we retain advantage or do not come to harm; privacy is about choosing who can enter one's life or property.

    **B.** Confidential information is information that must be kept private, so they really have similar meanings.

    **C.** Privacy laws allow criminals to hide their actions and intentions from society, but confidentiality allows for the government to protect defense-related information from being leaked to our enemies.

    **D.** Confidentiality is the freedom to choose whom we share information with; privacy refers to information that is specifically about our individual lives, activities, or interests.

# Getting Started as an SSCP

Part 1 of this book starts you on your journey toward becoming a Systems Security Certified Practitioner (SSCP).

Chapter 1 provides a solid foundation for your studies of information security within the context of the world's many different business environments and marketplaces. It presents information and information security in a *systems* context, in which people and organizations have to use information to plan, accomplish, and govern their activities to achieve their goals. It does this in the context of the world of private business (or nonprofit) organizations, by showing how decision makers need dependable, reliable information. If you've had a lot of experience in the private sector, and you're familiar with how typical businesses make decisions, you may only need to quickly skim this chapter. By itself, Chapter 1's content is not part of the SSCP test; anything that appears in Chapter 1 for the first time will be covered in greater depth, as part of the SSCP domains and modules in subsequent chapters.

Chapter 2 explores the fundamental concepts of information security, often expressed by the three pillars of confidentiality, integrity, and availability. You'll apply these concepts to a variety of situations as you learn how they are distinctly different and yet complementary; you'll also examine how vital they are in a variety of organizational mission contexts.

# Chapter 1

# The Business Case for Decision Assurance and Information Security

Why do businesses, governments, the military, or private individuals need to have "secure" information? As an SSCP, you'll have to help people and organizations identify their information security needs, build the systems to secure their information, and keep that information secure.

We'll focus your attention in this chapter on how businesses use information to get work done—and why that drives their needs for information security. In doing so, you'll see that today's global marketplaces present a far more challenging set of information security needs than even a country's government might.

To see how that all works, you'll first have to understand some fundamental concepts about information, business, governance, and security.

# Information: The Lifeblood of Business

Human beings are first and foremost *information processing* animals. We sense the world around us and inside us; we translate those sensory signals into information that our mind uses as we make decisions. We use our memories of experiences as the basis of the new thoughts that we think, and we use those thoughts as we decide what goals to strive for or which actions to take right in this immediate moment. Whether we think about a pretty sunset or a bad business decision, we are using information. All living things do this; this is not something unique to humans! And the most fundamental way in which we use information is when we look at some new thing our senses report to us and quickly decide: is it food, is it friend, is it foe, or can it be safely ignored? We stay alive because we can make that decision quickly, reliably, and repeatedly.

We also enhance our survival by learning from experience. We saw something new yesterday, and since it didn't seem to be friend or foe, we tasted a bit of it. We're still alive today, so it wasn't poisonous to us; when we see it today, we recognize it and remember our trial tasting. We have now learned a new, safe food. As we continue to gather information, we feed that new information back into our memory and our decision-making systems, as a way of continuing to learn from experience.

We also help others in their learning by making our knowledge and experience something that they can learn from. Whether we do that by modeling the right behaviors or by telling the learner directly, we communicate our knowledge and experience—we transfer information to achieve a purpose. We invented languages that gave us commonly understood ways of communicating meaning, and we had to develop ways we could agree with one another about how to carry on a conversation.

We use language and communication, loaded with information and meaning, to try to transform the behavior of others around us. We advise or guide others in their own decision making; in some situations, we can command them to do what we need or want. Each of these situations requires that we've previously worked to set the conditions so that transferring the information will lead to the effects we want. What conditions? Think of all of the things you implicitly agree to when having a conversation with someone:

- Understanding and using the same language, and using the same words and gestures for the same meanings

- Using the same rules to conduct the conversation—taking turns, alternating "sending" and "receiving"

- Signaling that the message was understood, or that it was not understood

- Signaling agreement

- Seeking additional information, either for greater understanding or to correct errors

- Agreeing to ways to terminate the conversation

Information systems builders refer to such "rules of the road" as the *protocols* by which the system operates. As humans, we've been using protocols since we learned to communicate. And as people band together in groups—families, clans, societies, businesses—those groups start with the person-to-person communications methods and languages, and then layer on their own protocols and systems to meet their special needs. It is our use of information that binds our societies together (and sometimes is used to tear them apart!).

---

### Different Conversations, Different Protocols

You've probably had a number of social conversations today, from simple greetings to chitchat with friends, family, or coworkers. Contrast those conversations with a typical call to an emergency services dispatch center. Operators typically start the conversation with a quick question:

> Operator: "911, do you need police, fire, or medical emergency service?"

Callers may be injured, frightened, angry, or near to panic; there may also be an urgent need to get the right kind of responders to the scene in order to prevent loss of life or further injury. The protocol for these kinds of calls has been designed to have the dispatch operator take charge of the conversation quickly and calmly, and guide it where it needs to go.

Do social conversations normally work that way?

---

## Data, Information, Knowledge, Wisdom...

In casual conversation, we recognize that these terms have some kind of hierarchical relationship, and yet we often use them as if they are interchangeable names for similar sets of ideas. In knowledge management, we show how each is subtly different and how by applying layers of processing and thought, we attain greater value from each layer of the knowledge pyramid (shown in Figure 1.1):

- We start with *data*—the symbols and representations of observable facts, or the results of performing measurements and estimates. Your name and personally identifiable information (PII) are data elements, which consist of many different data items (your first, middle, and surnames). *Raw data* refers to observations that come directly from some kind of sensor, recorder, or measuring device (a thermometer measures temperatures, and those measurements are the raw data). *Processed data* typically has had compensations applied to it, to take out biases or calibration errors that we know are part of the sensor's original (raw) measurement process.

- We create *information* from data when we make conclusions or draw logical inferences about that data. We do this by combining it with the results of previously made decisions, or with other data that we've collected. One example might be that we conclude that based on your PII, you are who you claim to be, or by contrast, that your PII does not uniquely separate you from a number of other people with the same name, leading us to conclude that perhaps we need more data or a better process for evaluating PII.

- We generate *knowledge* from data and information when we see that broad general ideas (or *hypotheses*) are probably true and correct based on that data and information. One set of observations by itself might suggest that there are valuable mineral or oil and gas deposits in an area. But we'll need a lot more understanding of that area's geography before we decide to dig a mine or drill for oil!

- *Wisdom* is knowledge that enables us to come to powerful, broad, general conclusions about future courses of action. Typically, we think of wisdom as drawing on the knowledge of many different fields of activity, and drawing from many different experiences within each field. This level of the knowledge pyramid is also sometimes referred to as *insight*.

**FIGURE 1.1**    The knowledge pyramid

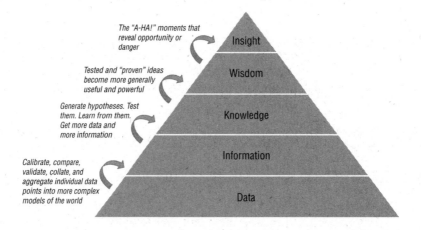

Obviously, there's a lot of room for interpretation as to whether some collection of facts, figures, ideas, or wild guesses represents "data" in its lowest form, "wisdom" in its most valuable, or any level in between on that pyramid. Several things are important for the SSCP to note as we talk about all of this:

- Each step of processing adds value to the data or information we feed into it. The results should be more valuable to the organization, the business, or the individual than the inputs alone were. This value results from the combination with other information, and from applying logic and reasoning to create new ideas.

- The value of any set of inputs, and the results of processing them, is directly in proportion to their reliability. If the data and the processing steps are not reliable, we cannot count on them as inputs to subsequent processing. If we do use them, we use them at risk of being misled or of making some other kind of mistake.

- From data to wisdom, this information can be either *tacit* (inside people's heads) or *explicit* (in some form that can be recorded, shared, and easily and reliably communicated).

Although we often see one label (such as "data") used for everything we do as we observe, think, and decide, some important distinctions must be kept in mind:

- Data should be verifiable by making other observations: either repeat the observations of the same subject, or make comparable observations of other subjects.

- *Data processing* tends to refer to applying logic and reasoning to make sure that all of the observations conform to an acceptable quality and consistency standard. This is sometimes called *data cleaning* (to remove errors and biases), *data validation* (to compare it to a known, accepted, and authoritative source), or *data smoothing* (to remove data samples that are so "out of range" that they indicate a mistaken observation and should not be used in further processing). Manually generated employee time card information, for example, might contain errors—the most common is having the wrong year written down for the first pay period after the New Year!

- *Information processing* usually is the first step in a series of actions where we apply *business logic* to the data to inform or enable the next step in a *business process*. Generating employee payroll from the time cards might require validating that the employee is correctly identified and that the dates and hours agree with the defined pay period, and then applying the right pay formula to those hours to calculate gross pay earned for that period.

As an SSCP, you may also encounter *knowledge management* activities in your business or organization. Many times, the real "know-how" of an organization exists solely inside the minds of the people who work there. Knowledge management tries to uncover all of that tacit knowledge and make it into forms that more people in the company can learn and apply to their own jobs. This is an exciting application of these basic ideas and can touch on almost every aspect of how the company keeps its information safe and secure. It is beyond the scope of the SSCP certification exam, but you do need to be aware of the basic idea of knowledge management.

---

**What's in a Name?**

Some people and businesses see very clear distinctions between the levels of the knowledge pyramid shown in Figure 1.1 and speak of each level in ways that make those distinctions plain. Others use the terms *data* or *information* to refer to all of it, even though they will then turn around and say, "That's not very wise" or "You should have known better" when you've made a serious mistake!

On the other hand, when someone says, "What does the data really say?" they are asking that you set aside your preconceptions, recognize your biases, and try to look at just what the facts are trying to show you.

As an SSCP, you'll need to appreciate that these different levels of "knowing stuff" exist, and that they shape our information-intensive world. You'll also need to know when to look for "just the facts" and when to seek knowledge and attain wisdom of your own.

But for most of what you'll deal with as an SSCP, you'll realize that *information* as a term covers everything nicely!

---

# Information Is *Not* Information Technology

As an SSCP you will regularly have to distinguish between the information you are protecting and the technologies used to acquire, process, store, use, and dispose of that information. As discussed, information is about things that people or businesses can know or learn. If that information is written on paper documents, then the pencils or pens and the paper are how that information is captured and communicated; filing cabinets become the storage technology. The postal system or a courier service becomes part of the communications processes used by that business. Look around almost any modern-day business or organization, and you see a host of information technologies in use:

- Computers and networks to connect them, and disks, thumb drives, or cloud service providers for storage and access
- Paper documents, forms to fill out, and a filing cabinet to put them in
- Printed, bound books, and the bookshelves or library spaces to keep them in
- Signs, posters, and bulletin boards
- Audio and acoustic systems, to convey voice, music, alarms, or other sounds as signals
- Furniture, office, and workspace arrangement, and the way people can or are encouraged to move and flow through the workspaces
- Organizational codes and standards for appearance, dress, and behavior

These and many more are ways in which meaning is partially transformed into symbols (text or graphics, objects, shapes or colors), the symbols arranged in messages, and the messages used to support decision making, learning, and action. Figure 1.2 demonstrates many of these different forms that information may take, in a context that many of us are all too familiar with: passenger security screening at a commercial airport.

**FIGURE 1.2**    Messaging at passenger screening (notional)

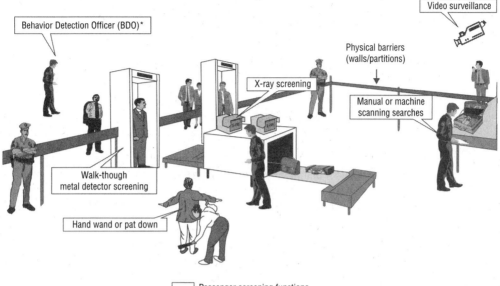

As an SSCP, you need to know and understand how your organization uses information *and* how it uses many different technologies to enable it. *As an SSCP, you protect the information as well as the technologies that make it useful and available.*

Notice how many different types of technologies are involved—and yet, "IT" as the acronym for "information technology" only seems to refer to digital, general-purpose computers and the networks, communications, peripherals, software, and other devices that make them become an "information processing system."

In the introduction, we defined the first *S* in SSCP to mean information systems. After all, an SSCP is not expected to keep the air conditioning systems in the building working correctly, even though they are a "system" in their own right. That said, note that nothing in your job description as an SSCP says "I only worry about the computer stuff."

---

### Cybersecurity, Information Assurance, or What?

There are unfortunately a lot of buzzwords in this business, and they may or may not mean what people think they mean when they use them. Let's take a look at a few of them:

- *Assurance*: Taking steps to increase confidence in the success of an activity or venture, often by managing or mitigating risks.

- *Insure*: Either the writing of an insurance policy (transferring a risk to the insurer), or another word for "assure."

*(continued)*

*(continued)*

- *Security*: Taking steps to protect people, assets, or property from harm or loss.

- *Cyber*: As a prefix, this has its origins in cybernetics, the study of control systems.

- *Cybersecurity*: Taken by many to mean (1) the security of digital, Web-based, or network-enabled information systems, particularly those that are critical to decision making, or (2) the protecting and securing of military or national command, control, communications, and intelligence (C3I) systems so that continuity of government and control of military forces can be reasonably assured.

- *Information security*: Providing security to information, and the processes (typically the people-centric processes) that use information to make decisions.

- *Information assurance*: Taking steps to provide confidence that the information you need to make decisions will be there, when you need it, where you need it, accurately enough to use to make decisions with, regardless of how you accomplish this confidence.

We do see a tendency for different segments of the marketplace to use these terms in different ways. Businesses, academics, and security professionals who are strongly aligned with national security, defense, and intelligence missions tend to think of what SSCPs are concerned with as "cybersecurity."

The other 99% of employers, working in the retail, manufacturing, educational, and services sectors, tend not to have traditional viewpoints rooted in cybernetics and control theory. Thus, they think of the SSCP's domains of interest either as information assurance (the outcome they need) or as information security (the ways to achieve information assurance).

No one view is more correct than the other. In fact, even the U.S. Department of Defense will speak in the same paragraph about cybersecurity and information assurance.

For the SSCP certification exam, you may see any of these terms as parts of questions or exam scenarios, which does reflect the reality across the many different kinds of workplaces SSCPs might find themselves in.

# Policy, Procedure, and Process: How Business Gets Business Done

As an SSCP, you might be working for a business; you might even open your own business as an information security services provider. Whatever your situation, you'll need to understand some of the basic ideas about what business *is*, how businesses organize and govern themselves and their activities, and what some of the "business-speak" is all about. Some of this terminology, and some of these concepts, may occur in scenarios or questions you'll encounter on the SSCP exam, but don't panic—you're not going to need to get a business degree first before you take that exam!

Let's get better acquainted with business by learning about the common ways in which businesses plan their activities, carry them out, and measure their success. We'll also take a brief look at how businesses make decisions.

## Who Is the Business?

As an SSCP, you will most likely be working *for* a business, or you will *create* your own business by becoming an independent consultant. Either way, "know your client" suggests that you'll need to know a bit about the "entity" that is the business that's paying your bills. Knowing this can help you better understand the business's decision processes, as you help them keep those processes and the information they depend on secure.

Businesses can in general take on several legal forms:

- A *sole proprietorship* is a business owned by one person, typically without a legal structure or framework. Usually the business operates in the name of that individual, and the bank accounts, licenses, leases, and contracts that the business executes are in the individual owner's name. One-person consulting practices, for example, and many startup businesses are run this way. When the owner dies, the business dies.

- A *corporation* is a fictitious entity—there are no living, breathing corporations, but they exist in law and have some or all of the civil and legal rights and responsibilities that people do. The oldest business still operating in the world is Hōshi Ryokan in Komatsu, Japan, which has been in business continually since the year 705 AD. In the United States, CIGNA Insurance, founded in 1792, is one of the four oldest corporations in America (three others were also formed the same year: Farmer's Almanac, the New York Stock Exchange, and the law firm of Cadwalader, Wickersham & Taft). Corporations can take many forms under many legal systems, but in general, they have a common need for a written charter, a board of directors, and executive officers who direct the day-to-day operation of the company.

- A *partnership* is another form of fictitious, legal entity that is formed by other legal entities (real or fictitious) known as the *general partners*. The partners agree to the terms and conditions by which the partnership will operate, and how it will be directed, managed, and held accountable to the partners.

Businesses also have several sets of people or organizations that have interest in the business and its successful, safe, and profitable operation:

- *Investors* provide the money or other assets that the business uses to begin operations, expand the business, and pay its expenses until the revenues it generates exceed its expenses and its debt obligations. The business uses investors' money to pay the costs of those activities, and then pays investors a *dividend* (rather like a rent payment), much as you'd pay interest on a loan. Unlike a lender, investors are partial owners in the business.

- *Stakeholders* are people or organizations that have some other interest or involvement with the business. Neighboring property owners are stakeholders to the extent that the conduct of this business might affect the value of their properties or the income they generate from their own businesses. Residential neighbors have concerns about having a peaceful, safe, and clean neighborhood. Suppliers or customers who build sizable, enduring, or otherwise strategic relationships with a business are also holding a stake in that business's success, even if they are not investors in it.

- *Employees* are stakeholders too, as they grow to depend on their earnings from their jobs as being a regular part of making their own living expenses.

- *Customers* will grow to depend on the quality, cost-effectiveness, and utility of what they buy from the business, and to some extent enjoy how they are treated as customers by the business.

- *Competitors* and other businesses in the marketplace also have good reason to keep an eye on one another, whether to learn from each other's mistakes or to help one another out as members of a community of practice.

## "What's Your Business Plan?"

You'll hear this question a lot in the business world. A *business plan* is a document that captures what the business owners want to achieve and how they intend to do that. Typically, a business plan shows planned activities over a span of time (perhaps several years), shows startup and ongoing costs of operating the business, and projects revenues from those operations. Initially, startup (or fixed) and operating costs usually exceed revenues, and the business is operating at a loss. At some point, revenues will equal the sum of startup costs and accumulated operating or recurring costs, and the business is said to "break even." From here on out, the business is operating at a profit. Within an ongoing business, new projects are often sizable enough that the business leaders require projects to have their own business plans.

The SSCP needs to deal with business plans in several ways:

- On a project basis, by estimating the costs of a given information security system versus the potential impacts to the business if the system is not implemented. This determines whether or not the proposed project is cost effective (benefits exceed the cost), as well as estimating the payback period (the time, usually in years, that the costs implementing and operating the project are exceeded by accumulated savings from impacts it helped avoid).

- At the larger, more strategic level, the business plan sets out objectives and goals, and sets priorities for them. These priorities drive which projects are well provided with funding or other resources, and which ones have to wait until resources become available. Prioritized goals also drive which information security problems should be addressed first.

We'll delve into this topic in greater depth starting in the next chapter as we look at information risk management. The more you know about how your employer plans their business, and how they know if they are achieving those plans, the better you'll be able to help assure them that the information they need is safe, secure, and reliable.

## Purpose, Intent, Goals, Objectives

There are as many reasons for going into business, it seems, as there are people who create new businesses: personal visions, ambitions, and dreams; the thoughtful recognition of a need, and of one's own abilities to address it; enjoyment at doing something that others also can benefit from. How each organization transforms the personal visions and dreams of its founders into sustainable plans that achieve goals and objectives is as much a function of the personalities and people as it is the choices about the type of business itself. As an SSCP, you should understand what the company's leaders, owners, and stakeholders want it to achieve. These goals may be expressed as "targets" to achieve over a certain time frame—opening a number of new locations, increasing sales revenues by a certain amount, or launching a new product by a certain date. Other inward-facing goals might be to improve product quality (to reduce costs from scrap, waste, and rework), improve the way customer service issues are handled, or improve the quality, timeliness, and availability of the information that managers and leaders need to make more effective decisions more reliably.

Notice that each goal or objective is quickly transformed into a plan: a statement of a series of activities chosen and designed to achieve the results in the best way the business knows how to do. The plan does not become reality without it being *resourced*—without people, money, supplies, work spaces, and time being made available to execute that plan. Plans without resource commitments remain "good ideas," or maybe they just remain as wishful thinking.

---

### CIA in Product Development

Suzette works as a database developer for a heavy equipment manufacturing company. The company sees a need in the marketplace for greater efficiency in the hydraulic systems that make most heavy equipment useful, and management has decided to form a "tiger team" to work on design concepts for new hardware subsystems elements. The team will use data from the company's computer-aided design and manufacturing (CADAM) systems, its customer relationship management (CRM) systems, and its field service support systems, as they work on their ideas.

Suzette is neither a sales engineer nor an equipment designer, but she does appreciate the power of information. She suggests to her boss, Norma, the IT director, that the company ought to set up an isolated virtual space for the tiger team to use for their design activities. Into that space, they would import copies of the current production databases and all of the software tools, and implement access controls such that no one but the team members and selected senior managers could access that space.

*(continued)*

*(continued)*

Suzette argues that this provides several important CIA benefits:

- *Confidentiality* protects the new intellectual property (IP) that the team is creating for the company. If design data is leaked or not controlled, the company may not be able to protect that IP by patenting it. This requires very strong access control and access accounting and monitoring.

- *Integrity* is necessary in both directions—the company don't want problems in the new design to be inadvertently flowing back into the customer service or product service trouble ticket systems, for example.

- *Availability* also is a two-way requirement: the design team might have to run many simulation and modeling exercises, using substantial amounts of computer time and memory, as they evaluate different ideas. That cannot be allowed to disrupt production on the factory floor or support in real time to customers and field engineers.

As an SSCP working in the IT department, Paul is tasked to help evaluate this idea. If you were Paul, what kind of questions might you have?

## Business Logic and Business Processes: Transforming Assets into Opportunity, Wealth, and Success

All businesses work by using ideas to transform one set of "inputs" into another set of "outputs"; they then provide or sell those outputs to their customers at a price that (ideally) more than pays for the cost of the inputs, pays everybody's wages, and pays a dividend back to the investors. *That set of ideas is key to what makes one business different from another.* That initial set of ideas is perhaps the "secret sauce" recipe, the better mousetrap design, or simply being the first to recognize that one particular marketplace doesn't have anybody providing a certain product or service to its customers.

That key idea must then be broken down into step-by-step sequences of tasks and procedures that the company's managers can train people to do; even if they buy or rent machines to do many of those tasks, the detailed steps still need to be identified and described in detail. Safety constraints also have to be identified so that workers and equipment aren't injured or damaged and so that wastage of time and materials is minimized. There may also be a need for decisions to be made between steps in the process, and adjustments made or sequences of steps repeated (such as "stir until thickened" or "bake the enamel at 750 degrees Fahrenheit for one hour").

But wait, there's more! That same systematic design of how to make the products also has to be spelled out for how to buy the raw materials, how to sell the finished products to customers, how to deal with inquiries from potential customers, and how to deal with customer complaints or suggestions for new or improved products. Taken together, this *business logic* is the set of ideas and knowledge that the owners and managers need in order to be able to set up the business and operate it effectively.

Business logic is intellectual property. It is a set of ideas, expressed verbally and in written form. It is built into the arrangement of jobs, tasks, and equipment, and the flow of supplies into and finished products out of the business. The business logic of a company either helps it succeed better than its competitors, or holds the company back from success in the marketplace. Knowing how to get business done efficiently—better, faster, cheaper—is a *competitive advantage*. Prudent business executives guard their business logic:

- *Trade secrets* are those parts of a company's business logic that it believes are unique, not widely known or understood in the marketplace, and not easily deduced or inferred from the products themselves. Declaring part of its business logic as a trade secret allows a company to claim unique use of it—in effect, declare that it has a monopoly on doing business in that particular way. A company can keep trade secrets as long as it wants to, as long as its own actions do not disclose those secrets to others.

- *Patents* are legal recognition by governments that someone has created a new and unique way of doing something. The patent grants a legal monopoly right in that idea, for a fixed length of time. Since the patent is a published document, anyone can learn how to do what the patent describes. If they start to use it in a business, they either must license its use from the patent holder (typically involving payment of fees) or risk being found guilty of *patent infringement* by a patents and trademarks tribunal or court of law.

As an SSCP, you probably won't be involved in determining whether an idea or a part of the company's business logic is worthy of protection as a trade secret or patentable idea, but much like the company's trademarks and copyrighted materials, you'll be part of protecting all of the company's intellectual property. That means keeping its secrets secret; keeping its expression, ideas, and supporting data free from corruption by accident or through hostile intent; and keeping that IP available when properly authorized company team members need it.

## The Value Chain

All but the simplest, most trivial business logic will require a series of steps, one after another. Michael Porter's *value chain* concept looks at these steps and asks a very important question about each one: does this step add value to the finished product, or does it only add cost or risk of loss? Figure 1.3 illustrates the basic value chain elements.

**FIGURE 1.3** The value chain

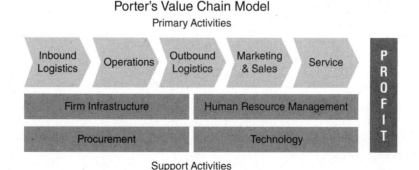

Porter's Value Chain Model
Primary Activities

| Inbound Logistics | Operations | Outbound Logistics | Marketing & Sales | Service | P R O F I T |

| Firm Infrastructure | Human Resource Management |
| Procurement | Technology |

Support Activities

Value chain analysis provides ways to do in-depth investigation of the end-to-end nature of what a business does, and how it deals with its suppliers and customers. More importantly, value chain analysis helps a company learn from its own experiences by continuously highlighting opportunities to improve. It does so by looking at every step of the value chain in fine detail. What supports this step? What inputs does it need? What outputs or outcomes does it produce? What kind of standards for quality, effectiveness, or timeliness are required of this step? How well does it measure up against those standards? Does this step have a history of failures or problems associated with it? What about complaints or suggestions for improvement by the operations staff or the people who interact with this step? Do any downstream (or upstream) issues exist that relate to this step and need our attention?

If you think that sounds like an idea you could apply to information security, and to providing a healthy dose of CIA to your company's IT systems, you're right!

Value chain analysis can be done using an *Ishikawa diagram*, sometimes called a *fault tree* or *fishbone diagram*, such as the generic one shown in Figure 1.4. The major business process is the backbone of the fish, flowing from left to right (the head and tail are optional as diagram elements); the diagonals coming into the backbone show how key elements of the business logic are accomplished, with key items or causes of problems shown in finer and finer detail as the analysis proceeds. Clearly, a fishbone or Ishikawa diagram could be drawn for each element of a complex business process (or an information security countermeasure system), and often is.

**FIGURE 1.4**    Ishikawa (or "fishbone") diagram for a value process

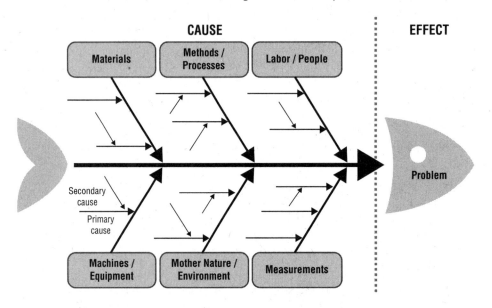

As an SSCP, you'll find that others in the business around you think in terms like *value chain* and *fault tree analysis*; they use diagrams like the fishbone as ways of visualizing problems and making decisions about how to deal with them. Think of them as just one more tool in your tool kit.

# Being Accountable

The value chain shows us that at each step of a well-designed business process, management ought to be able to measure or assess whether that step is executing properly. If that step is not working correctly, managers can do fault isolation (perhaps with a fishbone) to figure out what went wrong. *This is the essence of accountability: know what's supposed to happen, verify whether it did happen, and if it didn't, find out why.*

That may seem overly simplified, but then, powerful ideas really are simple! At every level in the company, managers and leaders have that same opportunity *and responsibility* to be accountable. Managers and leaders owe these responsibilities to the owners of the business, to its investors and other stakeholders, as well as to its customers, suppliers, and employees. These are "bills" of services that are due and payable, every day—that is, if the manager and leader want to earn their pay!

## The Three "Dues"

You will encounter these terms a lot as an SSCP, and so we'll use them throughout this book. You'll need to be able to recognize how they show up as elements of situations you'll encounter, on the job as well as on the certification exam:

- *Due care* is the responsibility to fully understand and accept a task or set of requirements, and then ensure that you have fully designed and implemented and are operating systems and processes to fulfill those requirements.

- *Due diligence* is the responsibility to ensure that the systems and processes you have implemented to fulfill a set of requirements are actually working correctly, completely, and effectively.

- *Due process* means that there is in fact a process that defines the right and correct way to do a particular task; that process specifies all of the correct steps that must be taken, constraints you must stay within, and requirements you must meet in order to correctly perform this task. Although we normally think of this as due process of law—meaning that the government cannot do something unless all of the legal requirements have been met—due process is also a useful doctrine to apply to any complex or important task.

If you talk with anyone in a safety-related profession or job, you'll often hear them say that "Safety rules are written in blood" as a testament to the people who were injured or killed, and the property that was damaged, before we were smart enough to write a good set of safety rules or regulations. In fact, most occupational safety laws and rules—and the power of commercial insurance companies to enforce them—come to us courtesy of generations of whistleblowers who risked their jobs and sometimes their lives to tell journalists and government officials about high-risk aspects of their life at work.

Due care means that you make sure you don't design tasks or processes that put your people or your company's assets in danger of harm or loss. Due diligence means you check up on those processes, making sure that they're being followed completely, *and that they still work right*. Otherwise, due process of law may shut down your business.

## Financial Accounting Standards and Practices

The Generally Accepted Accounting Principles (GAAP) provide an excellent example of putting these three "dues" to work in a business. GAAP has been developed over time by accountants, lawyers, business leaders, and government regulators to provide a common set of practices for keeping track of all of the financial aspects of a business's activities. By itself, GAAP does not have the force of law. However, many laws require different kinds of businesses to file different statements (such as tax returns) with their governments, which can be subject to audits, and the audits will be subject to GAAP standards. Insurance companies won't insure businesses whose record-keeping is not up to GAAP standards, or they will charge those businesses higher premiums on the insurance they will write. Banks and investment firms may not lend to such businesses, or will do so only at higher interest costs.

Part of GAAP includes dictating the standards and practices for how the company ensures that only the right people can create, alter, print, download, or delete the financial records of the business. As an SSCP, you'll be implementing and maintaining many of the information security systems and controls that implement those GAAP requirements.

And…you'll be auditing those information security systems too, in part as more of your duties to help the company be GAAP-compliant.

Many laws exist in many nations that go further than GAAP in dictating the need to keep detailed records of how each step in a business is done, who did it, when and where, and what the results or outcomes of that step turned out to be. These laws also spell out significant requirements for controlling who has access to all of those records, and dictate how long the company must keep what kind of records on hand to answer audits or litigation. Strangely enough, they also dictate when to safely dispose of records in order to help protect the company from spending too much time and money searching old archives of records in response to complaints! (The SSCP may have a role to play in the destruction or safe disposal of outdated business records too.)

## Ethical Accountability

Business ethics are a set of standards or codes of behaviors that most of the members of a business marketplace or the societies it serves believe or hold to be right and necessary for the safe operation of that marketplace. In many respects, the common elements of nearly every ethical code apply in business—honesty, truthfulness, integrity, and being true to one's given word or pledge on a contract or agreement are all behaviors that are vital to making business work. (As a proof, think about doing business with a company or a person who you know is not honest or truthful….)

Some marketplaces and some professions go further than the basics and will work together to agree to a more explicitly expressed code of ethics. Quite often these codes of ethics are made public so that prospective customers (and government regulators) will know that the marketplace will be self-regulating.

## Legal Accountability (Criminal and Civil)

We've mentioned a few of the many laws that can hold a business professional's feet to the fire. We're not going to mention them all! Do be aware that they fall into two broad categories that refer to the kind of punishment (or liability) you can find yourself facing if you are found guilty of violating them—namely, criminal law and civil law. Both are about violations of the law, by the way! *Criminal law* has its roots in violations of law such as physical assault or theft; the victims or witnesses inform the government, and the government prosecutor files a complaint against a defendant (who may then be subject to arrest or detainment by the police, pending the outcome of the trial). Criminal law usually has a higher standard of proof of guilt, and compared to civil law, it has tougher standards regarding the use of evidence and witness testimony by prosecution or the defendant. *Civil law* typically involves failure to fulfill your duties to society, such as failing to pay your property taxes; a civil law proceeding can foreclose on your property and force its sale in such a case, but (in most jurisdictions) it cannot cause you to be punished with time in jail. A subset of civil law known as *tort law* is involved with enforcement of private contracts (which make up the bulk of business agreements).

## The Concept of Stewardship

If you think about the concepts of the "three dues," you see an ancient idea being expressed—the idea of being a good steward. A *steward* is a person who stands in the place of an absent owner or ruler and acts in that absent person's best interests. A good steward seeks to preserve and protect the value of the business, lands, or other assets entrusted to their care, and may even have freedom to take action to grow, expand, or transform those assets into others as need and opportunity arise. You may often hear people in business refer to "being a good steward" of the information or other assets that have been entrusted to them. In many respects, the managing directors or leaders of a business are expected and required to be good stewards of that business and its assets—whether or not those same individuals might be the owners of the business.

# Who Runs the Business?

We've shown you how businesses create their business logic and build their business processes that *are* their business, and we've mentioned some of the many decision makers within a typical business. Let's take a quick summary of the many kinds of job titles you may find as you enter the world of business as an SSCP. This is not an exhaustive or authoritative list by any means—every business may create its own job titles to reflect its needs, the personalities of its founders, and the culture they are trying to inculcate into their new organization. That said, here are some general guidelines for figuring out who runs the business, and who is held accountable for what happens as they do.

## Owners and Investors

Owners or majority shareholders often have a very loud voice in the way that the company is run. In most legal systems, the more active an owner or investor is in directing day-to-day operation of the company, the more responsible (or liable) they are for damages when or if things go wrong.

## Boards of Directors

Most major investors would like a bit of distance from the operation of the company and the liabilities that can come with that active involvement, and so they will elect or appoint a group of individuals to take long-term strategic responsibility for the company. This board of directors will set high-level policy, spell out the major goals and objectives, and set priorities. The board will usually appoint the chief officers or managing directors of the company. In most cases, board membership is not a full-time job—a board member is not involved day to day with the company and the details of its operation, unless there is a special need, problem, or opportunity facing the company.

## Managing or Executive Directors and the "C-Suite"

The board of directors appoints a series of executive officers who run the company on a day-to-day basis. Typically, the top executive will be known as the managing director, the president, or the chief executive officer (CEO) of the company. In similar fashion, the most senior executives for major functional areas such as Operations, Finance, and Human Resources Management might have a title such as chief operations officer (COO) or chief financial officer (CFO). These senior directors are often collectively known as the "C-Suite," referring to the common practice of having all of their offices, desks, etc., in one common area of the company's business offices. (In cultures that use the Managing Director title instead of CEO, this area of the company's offices and the group of people who hold those roles might be known as the Directors instead.)

Other members of the "C-Suite" team that an SSCP may have more need to be aware of might include:

- Chief information officer (CIO), responsible for corporate communications, information strategy, and possibly information systems
- Chief technology officer (CTO), responsible for all of the IT and telecommunications technologies, primarily focused on the long-term strategy for their modernization and use
- Chief knowledge officer (CKO), who looks to strategies and plans to help the company grow as a learning organization
- Chief security officer (CSO), responsible for keeping all assets and people safe and secure
- Chief information security officer (CISO), whose focus is on information security, information systems security, and information technology security

Just because the word "chief" is in a duty title does not necessarily make its holder a resident of the C-Suite. This will vary company by company. A good, current organizational chart will help you know who sits where, and will give you a start on understanding how they relate to *your* duties, responsibilities, and opportunities as an SSCP.

## Layers of Function, Structure, Management, and Responsibility

It's a common experience that if one person tries to manage the efforts of too many people, at some point, they fail. This *span of control* is typically thought to hit a useful maximum of about 15 individuals; add one more to your 15-person team, and you start to have too little time to work with each person to help make sure they're working as effectively as they can, or that you've taken care of their needs well. Similarly, if as a manager you have too many "direct reports" in too many geographically separate locations, spanning too many time zones, your ability to understand their needs, problems, and opportunities becomes very limited. Organizations historically cope with this by introducing layers of management and leadership, from work unit up through groups, departments, divisions, and so on. What each of these levels of responsibility is called, and how these are grouped together, differs from company to company.

One way to look at this is with a pyramid chart, as shown in Figure 1.5. This is normally shown with the CEO or commanding general at the top, and conveys a sense that each level below is there to translate that senior leader's decisions into finer and finer detail, and pass them down to the next level. Finally, these directives get to the workers at the bottom of the pyramid—the ones who actually put tools to machines on the assembly line, or who drive the delivery trucks or take the customer orders and put them into the sales and fulfillment systems.

**FIGURE 1.5**    The organization chart as pyramid (traditional view)

Managers manage by measuring, or so they say. *Line managers*—the first level of supervisors who are accountable for the work that others do—often require a lot of visibility into the way individual workers are getting their work done. In quality management terms, the place that work actually gets done is called the *gemba*, a word the West has borrowed from the Japanese. *Walking the gemba* has in some companies become how they refer to managers walking through the work areas where the real value-added work is getting done, by the people who are hands-on making the products or operating the machines and systems that make the business of business take place. This has given rise to the inverted organizational pyramid, which sees the chief at the bottom of the picture, supporting the work of those in successive layers above him or her; finally, at the top of the pyramid is the layer of the workers at the gemba who are the ones on whom the business really depends for its survival and success. All of those managers and administrators, this view says, only exist for one reason: to organize, train, equip, and support the workers at the gemba. See Figure 1.6.

**FIGURE 1.6**    The inverted pyramid supports work at the gemba

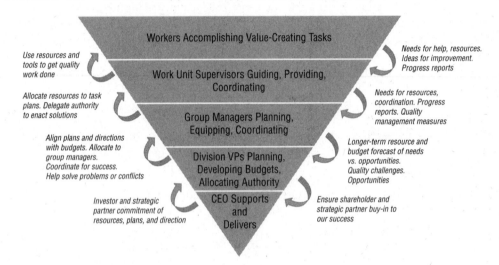

As an information technology professional, this inverted pyramid view should speak to you. You do your work as an SSCP not because your job is valuable to the company by itself, but because doing your job enables and empowers others to get *their* jobs done better. SSCPs and others in the IT security team need to have direct, open, and trustworthy lines of communication with these true "information workers" in the organization. Policy and strategy come from the pointy end of the pyramid, whereas real day-to-day operational insight comes from the people "on the firing line," doing the actual work.

## Plans and Budgets, Policies, and Directives

High-level goals and objectives are great to plan with, but they don't get business done on a day-to-day basis. The same process that translated the highest-level business logic down into steps that can be done on the assembly line or the sales floor have also allocated budget and resources to those work units; the work unit managers have to account for success or failure, and for resource expenditure. *More* business logic, in the form of policy documents, dictates how to translate those higher-level plans and budgets down to the levels of the work unit managers who actually apply those resources to get tasks accomplished. Policies also dictate how they should measure or account for expenses, and report to higher management about successes or problems.

# Summary

We've covered a lot of ground in this chapter as we've built the foundations for your growth as SSCPs and your continued study of information systems security and assurance. We put this in the context of business because the nature of competition, planning, and accountability for business can be much harsher than it is in any other arena (witness the number of small businesses that fail in their first few years). Successful businesses are the ones that can translate the hopes and dreams of their founders into solid, thoughtful business logic; and as we say, that investment in business logic can become the key to competitive advantage that a business can have in its chosen marketplace. Keeping that business logic safe and secure requires the due care and due diligence of all concerned—including the SSCPs working with the business on its information systems.

# Chapter

# 2

# Information Security Fundamentals

## THE SSCP EXAM OBJECTIVES COVERED IN THIS CHAPTER INCLUDE:

Domain 2: Security Operations and Administration

✓ 2.1: Comply with Codes of Ethics

✓ 2.2: Understand Security Concepts

What do businesses, governments, the military, or private individuals need to have "secure" information? As an SSCP, you'll have to help people and organizations identify their information security needs, build the systems to secure their information, and keep that information secure. In this chapter, you'll explore the basic concepts of information security and learn to develop a high-level view of what users need to do keep their information safe, secure, and resilient. You'll also learn how privacy is a vital element of, but is different from, information security.

We'll focus your attention in this chapter on how businesses use information to get work done—and why that drives their needs for information security.

To see how that all works, you'll first have to understand some fundamental concepts about information, business, governance, and security. You'll also need to keep information and information technology separate and distinct in your mind as you go through this chapter. *Information* focuses on what people use and what kind of security it needs; *information technology* is how we implement those needs.

# The Common Needs for Privacy, Confidentiality, Integrity, and Availability

We've looked at what information is, and what business is; we've looked at how businesses need information to make decisions and how they need *more* information to know that their decisions are being carried out effectively. Now it's time to look at key characteristics of information that directly relate to keeping it safe, secure, and reliable. Let's define these characteristics now, but we'll do this from simplest to most complex in terms of the ideas that they represent.

And in doing so, we're going to have to get personal.

## Privacy

For a little more than 200 years, Western societies have had a clearly established legal and ethical concept of privacy as a core tenet of how they want their societies to work. *Privacy*, which refers to a person (or a business), is the freedom from intrusion by others into one's own life, place of residence or work, or relationships with others. Privacy means that you have the freedom to choose who can come into these aspects of your life and what they can know about you. Privacy is an element of *common law*, or the body of unwritten legal principles that are just as enforceable by the courts as the written laws are in many countries. It starts with the privacy rights and needs of one person and grows to treat families, other organizations, and other relationships (personal, professional, or social) as being free from unwarranted intrusion.

Businesses create and use *company confidential* or *proprietary* information almost every day. Both terms declare that the business owns this information; the company has paid the costs to develop this information (such as the salaries of the people who thought up these ideas or wrote them down in useful form for the company), which represents part of the business's competitive advantage over its competitors. Both terms reflect the legitimate business need to keep some data and ideas *private to the business*.

---

**Unwarranted?**

Note the dual meaning of this very important term to you as an SSCP and as a citizen. An *unwarranted action* is one that is either:

(1) Without a warrant, a court order, or other due process of law that allows the action to take place

(2) Has no reasonable cause; serves no reasonable purpose; or exceeds the common sense of what is right and proper

---

Staying in a hotel room demonstrates this concept of privacy. You are renting the use of that room on a nightly basis; the only things that belong to you are what you bring in with you. Those personal possessions and the information, books, papers, and files on your phone or laptop or thumb drives are your personal property and by law are under *your* control. No one has permission or legal authority to enter your hotel room without your consent. Of course, when you signed for the room, you signed a contract that gave your express permission to designated hotel staff to enter the room for regular or emergency maintenance, cleaning, and inspection. This agreement does not give the hotel permission to search through your luggage or your belongings, or to make copies or records of what they see in your room. Whether it is just you in the room, or whether a friend, family member, or associate visits or stays with you, is a private matter, unless of course your contract with the hotel says "no guests" and you are paying the single occupancy rate. The hotel room is a *private space* in this regard—one in which you can choose who can enter or observe.

This is key: privacy can be enforced both by contracts and by law.

## Privacy: In Law, in Practice, in Information Systems

Public law enforces these principles. Laws such as the Fourth and Fifth Amendments to the U.S. Constitution, for example, address the first three, whereas the Privacy Act of 1974 created restrictions on how government could share with others what it knew about its citizens (and even limited sharing of such information within government). Medical codes of practice and the laws that reflect them encourage data sharing to help health professionals detect a potential new disease epidemic, but they also require that personally identifiable information in the clinical data be removed or anonymized to protect individual patients.

The European Union has enacted a series of policies and laws designed to protect individual privacy as businesses and governments exchange data about people, transactions, and themselves. The latest of these, General Data Protection Regulation 2016/679 (GDPR), is a law that applies to all persons, businesses, or organizations doing anything involving the data related to an EU person. The GDPR's requirements meant that by May 2018, businesses had to change the ways that they collected, used, stored, and shared information about anyone who contacted them (such as by browsing to their website); they also had to notify such users about the changes and gain their informed consent to such use. Many news and infotainment sites hosted in the United States could not serve EU persons until they implemented changes to become GDPR compliant.

In some jurisdictions and cultures, we speak of an inherent right to privacy; in others, we speak to a requirement that people and organizations protect the information that they gather, use, and maintain when that data is about another person or entity. In both cases, the right or requirement exists to prevent harm to the individual. Loss of control over information about you, or about your business, can cause you grave if not irreparable harm.

It's beyond the scope of this book and the SSCP exam to go into much depth about the GDPR's specific requirements, or to compare its unified approach to the collection of federal, state, and local laws, ordinances, and regulations in the United States. Regardless, it's important that as an SSCP you become aware of the expectations in law and practice for the communities that your business serves in regard to protecting the confidentiality of data you hold about individuals you deal with.

## Private and Public Places

Part of the concept of privacy is connected to the *reasonable expectation* that other people can see and hear what you are doing, where you are (or where you are going), and who might be with you. It's easy to see this in examples; walking along a sidewalk, you have every reason to think that other people can see you, whether they are out on the sidewalk as well or looking out the windows of their homes and offices, or from passing vehicles. The converse is that when out on that *public* sidewalk, out in the open spaces of the town or city, you have no reason to believe that you are *not* visible to others. This helps us differentiate between *public places* and *private places:*

- Public places are areas or spaces in which anyone and everyone can see, hear, or notice the presence of other people, and observe what they are doing, intentionally or unintentionally. There is little to no degree of control as to who can be in a public place. A city park is a public place.

- Private places are areas or spaces in which, by contrast, you as owner (or the person responsible for that space) have every reason to believe that you can control who can enter, participate in activities with you (or just be a bystander), observe what you are doing, or hear what you are saying. You choose to share what you do in a private space with the people you choose to allow into that space with you. By law, this is your reasonable expectation of privacy, because it is "your" space, and the people you allow to share that space with you share in that reasonable expectation of privacy.

Your home or residence is perhaps the prime example of what we assume is a private place. Typically, business locations can be considered private in that the owners or managing directors of the business set policies as to whom they will allow into their place of business. Customers might be allowed onto the sales floor of a retail establishment but not into the warehouse or service areas, for example. In a business location, however, it is the business owner (or its managing directors) who have the most compelling reasonable expectation of privacy, in law and in practice. Employees, clients, or visitors cannot expect that what they say or do in that business location (or on its IT systems) is private to them, and not "in plain sight" to the business. As an employee, you can reasonably expect that your pockets or lunch bag are private to you, but the emails you write or the phone calls you make while on company premises are not necessarily private to you. This is not clear-cut in law or practice, however; courts and legislatures are still working to clarify this.

The pervasive use of the Internet and the World Wide Web, and the convergence of personal information technologies, communications and entertainment, and computing, have blurred these lines. Your smart watch or personal fitness tracker uplinks your location and exercise information to a website, and you've set the parameters of that tracker and your Web account to share with other users, even ones you don't know personally. Are you doing your workouts today in a public or private place? Is the data your smart watch collects and uploads public or private data?

"Facebook-friendly" is a phrase we increasingly see in corporate policies and codes of conduct these days. The surfing of one's social media posts, and even one's browsing histories, has become a standard and important element of prescreening procedures for job placement, admission to schools or training programs, or acceptance into government or military service. Such private postings on the public Web are also becoming routine elements in employment termination actions. The boundary between "public" and "private" keeps moving, and it moves because of the ways we think about the information, and not because of the information technologies themselves.

The GDPR and other data protection regulations require business leaders, directors, and owners to make clear to customers and employees what data they collect and what they do with it, which in turn implements the separation of that data into public and private data. As an SSCP, you probably won't make specific determinations as to whether certain kinds of data are public or private, but you should be familiar with your organization's privacy policies and its procedures for carrying out its data protection responsibilities. Many of the information security measures you will help implement, operate, and maintain are vital to keeping the dividing line between public and private data clear and bright.

# Confidentiality

Often thought of as "keeping secrets," confidentiality is actually about *sharing* secrets. Confidentiality is both a legal and ethical concept about *privileged communications* or *privileged information.* Privileged information is information you have, own, or create, and that you share with someone else with the agreement that they cannot share that knowledge with anyone else without your consent, or without due process in law. You place your trust and confidence in that other person's adherence to that agreement. Relationships between professionals and their clients, such as the doctor-patient or attorney-client ones, are prime examples of this privilege in action. Except in very rare cases, courts cannot compel parties in a privileged relationship to violate that privilege and disclose what was shared *in confidence.*

### Privacy Is Not Confidentiality

As more and more headline-making data breaches occur, people are demanding greater protection of personally identifiable information (PII) and other information about them as individuals. Increasingly, this is driving governments and information security professionals to see *privacy* as separate and distinct from *confidentiality.* While both involve keeping close-hold, limited-distribution information safe from inadvertent disclosure, we're beginning to see that they may each require subtly different approaches to systems design, operation and management to achieve.

Confidentiality refers to how much we can trust that the information we're about to use to make a decision has not been seen by unauthorized people. The term *unauthorized people* generally includes anybody or any group of people who could learn something from our confidential information, and then use that new knowledge in ways that would thwart our plans to attain our objectives or cause us other harm.

Confidentiality needs dictate who can read specific information or files, or who can download or copy them. This is very different from who can modify, create, or delete those files.

One way to think about this is that integrity violations *change what we think we know*; confidentiality violations *tell others what we think is our private knowledge.*

## Integrity

Integrity, in the most common sense of the word, means that something is whole and complete, and that its parts are smoothly joined together. People with high personal integrity are ones whose actions and words consistently demonstrate the same set of ethical principles. You know that you can count on them and trust them to act both in ways they have told you they would and in ways consistent with what they've done before.

Integrity for information systems has much the same meaning. Can we rely on the information we have and trust in what it is telling us?

This attribute reflects two important decision-making needs:

- First, is the information accurate? Have we gathered the right data, processed it in the right ways, and dealt with errors, wild points, or odd elements of the data correctly so that we can count on it as inputs to our processes? We also have to have trust and confidence in those processes—do we know that our business logic that combined experience and data to produce wisdom actually works correctly?

- Next, has the information been tampered with, or have any of the intermediate steps in processing from raw data to finished "decision support data" been tampered with? This highlights our need to trust not only how we get data, and how we process it, but also how we communicate that data, store it, and how we authorize and control changes to the data *and* the business logic and software systems that process that data.

Integrity applies to three major elements of any information-centric set of processes: to the people who run and use them, to the data that the people need to use, and to the systems or tools that store, retrieve, manipulate, and share that data. We'll look at all of these concepts in greater depth in later chapters, but it's important here to review what Chapter 1 said about DIKW, or data, information, knowledge, and wisdom:

- Data are the individual facts, observations, or elements of a measurement, such as a person's name or their residential address.

- Information results when we process data in various ways; information is data plus conclusions or inferences.

- Knowledge is a set of broader, more general conclusions or principles that we've derived from lots of information.

- Wisdom is (arguably) the insightful application of knowledge; it is the "a-ha!" moment in which we recognize a new and powerful insight that we can apply to solve problems with or to take advantage of a new opportunity—or to resist the temptation to try!

You also saw in Chapter 1 that professional opinion in the IT and information systems world is strongly divided about *data* versus *D-I-K-W*, with nearly equal numbers of people holding that they are the same ideas, that they are different, and that the whole debate is unnecessary. As an SSCP, you'll be expected to combine experience, training, and the data you're observing from systems and people in real time to *know* whether an incident of interest is about to become a security issue, whether or not your organization uses knowledge management terminology like this. This is yet another example of just how many potentially conflicting, fuzzy viewpoints exist in IT and information security.

## Availability

Is the data there, when we need it, in a form we can use?

We make decisions based on information; whether that is new information we have gathered (via our data acquisition systems) or knowledge and information we have in our memory, it's obvious that if the information is not where we need it, when we need it, we cannot make as good a decision as we might need to:

- The information might be in our files, but if we cannot retrieve it, organize it, and display it in ways that inform the decision, then the information isn't available.

- If the information has been deleted, by accident, sabotage, or systems failure, then it's not available to inform the decision.

These might seem obvious, and they are. Key to availability requirements is that they specify what information is needed; where it will need to be displayed, presented, or put in front of the decision makers; and within what span of time the data is both available (displayed to the decision makers) and meaningful. Yesterday's data may not be what we need to make today's decision.

---

### CIA in Real Estate Development

Suppose you work in real estate, and you've come to realize that a particular area outside of town is going to be a "path of progress" for future development. That stretch of land is in the right place for others to build future housing areas, business locations, and entertainment attractions; all it needs is the investment in roads and other infrastructure, and the willingness of other investors to make those ideas become real projects. The land itself is unused scrub land, not even suitable for raising crops or cattle; you can buy it for a hundredth of what it might sell for once developers start to build on this path to progress.

- *Confidentiality:* Note how your need for confidentiality about this changes with time. While you're buying up the land, you really don't need or want competitors who might drive up the prices on your prime choices of land. Once you've established your positions, however, you need to attract the attention of other investors and of developers, who will use their money and energy to make your dreams come true. This is an example of the time value of confidentiality—nothing stays secret forever, but while it stays secret, it provides advantage.

- *Integrity:* In that same "path of progress" scenario, you have to be able to check the accuracy of the information you've been gathering from local landowners, financial institutions, and business leaders in the community. You have to be able to tell whether one of those sources is overly enthusiastic about the future and has exaggerated the potential for growth and expansion in the area. Similarly, you cannot misrepresent or exaggerate that future potential when you entice others to come and buy land from you to develop into housing or business properties that they'll sell on to other buyers.

- *Availability:* You'll need to be able to access recorded land titles and descriptions, and the legal descriptions of the properties you're thinking of buying and then holding for resale to developers. The local government land registry still uses original paper documents and large paper "plat" maps, and a title search (for information about the recorded owners of a piece of land, and whether there are any liens recorded against it) can take a considerable amount of time. If that time fits into your plans, the data you need is available; if you need to know faster than the land registry can answer your queries, then it is not available.

## Privacy vs. Security, or Privacy and Security?

It's easy to trivialize this question by trotting out the formal definitions: privacy is freedom from intrusion, and security is the protection of something or someone from loss, harm, or injury, now or in the future. This reliance on the formal definitions alone hasn't worked in the past, and it's doubtful that a logical debate will cool down the sometimes overly passionate arguments that many people have on this topic.

Over the last 20 years, the increasing perception of the threat of terrorist attacks has brought many people to think that strong privacy encourages terrorism and endangers the public and our civilization. Strong privacy protections, these people claim, allow terrorists to "hide in plain sight" and use the Internet and social media as their command, control, communications, and intelligence systems. "If you've got nothing to hide," these uber-security zealots ask, "why do you need any privacy?"

But is this privacy-versus-security dilemma real or imagined? Consider, for example, how governments have long argued that private citizens have no need of encryption to protect their information; yet without strong encryption, there would be no way to protect online banking, electronic funds transfers, or electronic purchases from fraud. Traffic and security CCTV and surveillance systems can help manage urban problems, dispatch first responders more effectively, and even help identify and detain suspects wanted by the police. But the same systems can easily be used by almost anyone to spy on one's neighbors, know when a family is not at home, or stalk a potential victim. The very systems we've paid for (with our taxes) become part of the threat landscape we have to face!

We will not attempt to lay out all of this debate here. Much of it is also beyond the scope of the SSCP exam. But as an SSCP, you need to be aware of this debate. More and more, we are moving our private lives into the public spaces of social media and the Web; as we do this, we keep shifting the balance between information that needs to be protected and that which ought to be published or widely shared. At the technical level, the SSCP can help people and organizations carry out the policy choices they've made; the SSCP can also advise and assist in the formulation of privacy and security policies, and even help craft them, as they grow in professional knowledge, skills, and abilities.

---

### "If You've Got Nothing to Hide..."

This is not a new debate. In ancient Greece, even the architecture of its homes and the layout of the city streets helped make private spaces possible, as witnessed by the barbed criticism of Socrates:

*"For where men conceal their ways from one another in darkness rather than in light, there no man will every rightly gain either his due honor or office or the justice that is befitting."*

Socrates seems to argue for the *transparent society*, one in which every action, anywhere, anytime, is visible to anyone in society.

Take a look at Greg Ferenstein's "The Birth and Death of Privacy: 3,000 Years of History Told Through 46 Images," at https://medium.com/the-ferenstein-wire/the-birth-and-death-of-privacy-3-000-years-of-history-in-50-images-614c26059e, to put this debate into context.

*(continued)*

> *(continued)*
>
> The problem seems to be that for most of history, this transparency has been in only one direction: the powerful and wealthy, and their government officials, can see into everyone else's lives and activities, but the average citizen cannot see up into the doings of those in power.
>
> *Who watches the watchers?*
>
> —*Juvenal,* Satire VI, *lines 347–348, late first century/early second century AD.*

Whether it's the business of business, the functions of government, or the actions and choices of individuals in our society, we can see that information is what makes everything *work*. Information provides the context for our decisions; it's the data about price and terms that we negotiate about as buyers or sellers, and it's the weather forecast that's part of our choice to have a picnic today at the beach. Three characteristics of information are key to our ability to make decisions about anything:

- If it is publicly known, we must have confidence that everybody knows it or can know it; if it is private to us or those we are working with, we need to trust that it stays private or *confidential*.

- The information we need must be reliable. It must be accurate enough to meet our needs and come to us in ways we can trust. It must have *integrity*.

- The information must be there when we need it. It must be *available*.

Those three attributes or characteristics—the confidentiality, integrity, and availability of the information itself—reflect the needs we all have to be reasonably sure that we are making well-informed decisions, when we have to make them, and that our competitors (or our enemies!) cannot take undue or unfair advantage over us in the process. Information security practitioners refer to this as the CIA of information security. Every information user needs *some* CIA; for some purposes, you need a *lot* of it; for others, you can get by with more uncertainty (or "less CIA").

## CIA Needs of Individuals

Each of us has a private life, which we may share with family, friends, or loved ones. We expect a reasonable degree of security in that private life. As taxpayers and law-abiding members of our societies, whether we realize it or not, we have agreed to a social compact—a contract of sorts between each of us as an individual and the society as a whole. We fulfill our duties to society by obeying the laws, and society keeps us safe from harm. Society defends us against other nations that want to conquer or destroy us; society protects us against criminals; and society protects us against the prospects of choking on our own garbage, sewage, or exhaust. In English, *safety* and *security* are two different words for two concepts we usually keep separate; in Spanish, one word, *seguridad*, embraces both ideas equally.

People may be people, but they can take on many different roles in a society. For example:

- Government officials or officers of the government have been appointed special authorities and responsibilities in law and act in the name of the government and the people of their jurisdiction. They must conduct their jobs in accordance with applicable laws and regulations, as well as be held to standards of conduct set by the government.

- Licensed professionals, such as doctors, engineers, lawyers, or the clergy or priesthood, are recognized (issued a license) by the government to provide services to people and organizations within the bounds of their profession. Those professions set standards for their practice and their conduct, which may or may not be reinforced by applicable law.

- Corporate officers and officials, business owners, and other key people in the operation of a business (or even a nonprofit organization) are responsible by law and in practice for due care and due diligence in the conduct of their business.

- Celebrities, such as entertainment or sports personalities, are typically private people whose choice of work or avocation has made them famous. Their particular business may be self-regulating, such as when Major League Baseball sanctions (punishes) a player for misusing performance-enhancing substances.

- Journalists, reporters, and those in the news and information media are believed to be part of keeping society informed and thus should be held to standards of objectivity, honesty, and fairness. Those standards may be enforced by their employers or the owners of the news media that they work for.

- *Whistleblowers* are individuals who see something that they believe is wrong, and then turn to people outside of their own context to try to find relief, assistance, or intervention. Historically, most whistleblowers have been responsible for bringing public pressure to bear to fix major workplace safety issues, child labor abuses, graft and corruption, or damage to the environment, in circumstances where the responsible parties could harass, fire, or sometimes even physically assault or kill the whistleblower.

- Private citizens are, so to speak, anybody who doesn't fall into any of those categories. Private citizens are subject to law, of course, and to the commonly accepted ethical and behavioral standards of their communities.

It's not hard to see how societies benefit as a whole when the sum total of law, ethics, and information security practices provide the right mix of CIA for each of these kinds of individuals.

## Private Business's Need for CIA

The fundamental fact of business life is competition. Competition dictates that decisions be made in timely ways, with the most reliable information available at the time. It also means that even the consideration of alternatives—the decisions the business is *thinking* about making—need to be kept out of the eyes and ears of potential competitors. Ethical concepts like *fair play* dictate that each business be able to choose where and when it will make its decisions known to their marketplaces, to the general public, and to its competitors.

## Government's Need for CIA

Government agencies and officers of the government have comparable needs for availability and integrity of the information that they use in making decisions. As for confidentiality, however, government faces several unique needs.

First, government does have a responsibility to its citizens; as it internally deliberates upon a decision, it needs to do so confidentially to avoid sending inappropriate signals to businesses, the markets, and the citizens at large. Governments are made up of the people who serve in them, and those people do need reasonable time in which to look at all sides of complex issues. One example of this is when government is considering new contracts with businesses to supply goods and services that government needs. As government contracts officers evaluate one bidder's proposal, it would be inappropriate and unfair to disclose the strengths and weaknesses of that proposal to competitors, who might then (unfairly!) modify their own proposals.

The law enforcement duties of government, for example, may also dictate circumstances in which it is inappropriate or downright dangerous to let the identity of a suspect or a key witness be made public knowledge.

## The Modern Military's Need for CIA

Military needs for confidentiality of information present an interesting contrast. Deterrence—the strategy of making your opponents fear the consequences of attacking you, and so leading them to choose other courses of action—depends on your adversary having a good idea of just what your capabilities are and believing that you'll survive their attack and be able to deal a devastating blow to them regardless. Yet you cannot let them learn too much, or they may find vulnerabilities in your systems and strategies that they can exploit.

Information integrity and availability are also crucial to the modern military's decision making. The cruise missile attack on the offices of the Chinese Embassy in Belgrade, Yugoslavia, during the May 1999 NATO war against the Yugoslavian government illustrates this. NATO and USAF officials confirmed that the cruise missile went to the right target and flew in the right window on the right floor to destroy the Yugoslavian government office that was located there—except, they say, they used outdated information and didn't realize that the building had been rented out to the Chinese Embassy much earlier. Whether this was a case of bad data availability in action—right place, wrong tenant at wrong time—or whether there was some other secret targeting strategy in action depends on which Internet speculations you wish to follow.

## Do Societies Need CIA?

Whether or not a society is a functioning democracy, most Western governments and their citizens believe that the people who live in a country are responsible for the decisions that their government makes and carries out in their names. The West holds the citizens of other countries responsible for what they let their governments do; so, too, do the enemies of Western societies hold the average citizens of those societies responsible.

Just as with due care and due diligence, citizens cannot meet those responsibilities if they are not able to rely on the information that they use when they make decisions. Think about the kind of decisions you can make as a citizen:

- Which candidates do I vote for when I go to the polls on Election Day? Which party has my best interests at heart?

- Is the local redevelopment agency working to make our city, town, or region better for all of us, or only to help developers make profits at the taxpayers' expense?

- Does the local water reclamation board keep our drinking water clean and safe?

- Do the police work effectively to keep crime under control? Are they understaffed or just badly managed?

Voters need information about these and many other issues if they are going to be able to trust that their government, at all levels, is doing what they need done.

Prior to the Internet, many societies kept their citizens, voters, investors, and others informed by means of what were called the *newspapers of record*. Sometimes this term referred to newspapers published by the government (such as the *Moscow Times* during the Soviet era); these were easily criticized for being little more than propaganda outlets. Privately owned newspapers such as *The New York Times*, *Le Figaro*, and the *Times of London* developed reputations in the marketplace for separating their reporting of verifiable facts about newsworthy events from their editorial opinions and explanations of the meanings behind those facts. With these newspapers of record, a society could trust that the average citizen knew enough about events and issues to be able to place faith and confidence in the government, or to vote the government out at the next election as the issues might demand.

Radio, and then television, gave us further *broadcasting* of the news—as with the newspapers, the same story would be heard, seen, or read by larger and larger audiences. With multiple, competing newspapers, TV, and radio broadcasters, it became harder for one news outlet to outright lie in its presentation of a news story. (It's always been easy to ignore a story.)

Today's analytics-driven media and the shift to "infotainment" has seen *narrowcasting* replace broadcasting in many news marketplaces. Machine learning algorithms watch your individual search history and determine the news stories you might be interested in—and quite often don't bother you with stories the algorithms think you are not interested in. This makes it much more difficult for people who see a need for change to get their message across; it also makes it much easier to suppress the news a whistleblower might be trying to make public.

Other current issues, such as the outcry about "fake news," should raise our awareness of how nations and societies need to be able to rely on readily available news and information as they make their daily decisions. It's beyond the scope of the SSCP exam to tackle this dilemma, but as an SSCP, you may be uniquely positioned to help solve it.

# Training and Educating Everybody

"The people need to know" is more than just "We need a free press." People in all walks of life need to know more about how their use of information depends on a healthy dose of CIA and how *they* have both the ability and responsibility to help keep it that way.

You've seen by now that whether we're talking about a business's leaders and owners, its workers, its customers, or just the individual citizens and members of a society, everybody needs to understand what CIA means to them as they make decisions and take actions throughout their lives. As an SSCP, you have a significant opportunity to help foster this learning, whether as part of your assigned job or as a member of the profession and the communities you're a part of.

In subsequent chapters, we'll look more closely at how the SSCP plays a vital role in keeping their business information systems safe, secure, and resilient.

# SSCPs and Professional Ethics

"As an SSCP" is a phrase we've used a lot so far. We've used it two different ways: to talk about the opportunities facing you, and to talk about what you will have to know as you rise up to meet those opportunities.

There is a third way we need to use that phrase, and perhaps it's the most important of them all. Think about yourself *as a Systems Security Certified Professional* in terms of the "three dues." What does it mean to you to live up to the responsibilities of due care and due diligence, and thus ensure that you meet or exceed the requirements of due process?

(ISC)² provides us a Code of Ethics, and to be an SSCP you agree to abide by it. It is short and simple. It starts with a preamble, which we quote in its entirety:

> The safety and welfare of society and the common good, duty to our principals, and to each other, requires that we adhere, and be seen to adhere, to the highest ethical standards of behavior.

> Therefore, strict adherence to this Code is a condition of certification.

Let's operationalize that preamble—take it apart, step by step, and see what it really asks of us:

1. Safety and welfare of society: Allowing information systems to come to harm because of the failure of their security systems or controls can lead to damage to property, or injury or death of people who were depending on those systems operating correctly.

2. The common good: All of us benefit when our critical infrastructures, providing common services that we all depend on, work correctly and reliably.

3. Duty to our principals: Our duties to those we regard as leaders, rulers, or our supervisors in any capacity.

4. Our duty to each other: To our fellow SSCPs, others in our profession, and to others in our neighborhood and society at large.

5.  Adhere and be seen to adhere to: Behave correctly and set the example for others to follow. Be visible in performing our job ethically (in adherence with this Code) so that others can have confidence in us as a professional and learn from our example.

The code is equally short, containing four canons or principles to abide by:

> Protect society, the common good, necessary public trust and confidence, and the infrastructure.
>
> Act honorably, honestly, justly, responsibly, and legally.
>
> Provide diligent and competent service to principals.
>
> Advance and protect the profession.

The canons do more than just restate the preamble's two points. They show us *how* to adhere to the preamble. We must take action to protect what we value; that action should be done with honor, honesty, and justice as our guide. Due care and due diligence are what we owe to those we work for (including the customers of the businesses that employ us).

The final canon addresses our continued responsibility to grow as a professional. We are on a never-ending journey of learning and discovery; each day brings an opportunity to make the profession of information security stronger and more effective. We as SSCPs are members of a worldwide *community of practice*—the informal grouping of people concerned with the safety, security, and reliability of information systems and the information infrastructures of our modern world.

In ancient history, there were only three professions—those of medicine, the military, and the clergy. Each had in its own way the power of life and death of individuals or societies in its hands. Each as a result had a significant burden to be the best at fulfilling the duties of that profession. Individuals felt the calling to fulfill a sense of duty and service, to something larger than themselves, and responded to that calling by becoming a member of a profession.

This, too, is part of being an SSCP.

---

### EXERCISE 2.1

### Nuclear Medicine and CIA

In 1982, Atomic Energy of Canada Limited (AECL) began marketing a new model of its Therac line of X-ray treatment machines to hospitals and clinics in Canada, the United States, and Latin American countries. Previous models had used manually set controls and mechanical safety interlocks to prevent patients or staff from being exposed to damaging or lethal radiation levels. The new Therac-25 used a minicomputer and software to do all of these functions. But inadequate software test procedures, and delays in integrating the software and the X-ray control systems, meant that the Therac-25 went to market without rigorously demonstrating these new computer-controlled safety features worked correctly. In clinical use in the U.S., Canada, and other countries, patients were being killed or seriously injured by the machine; AECL responded slowly if at all to requests for help from clinicians and field support staff. Finally, the problems became so severe that the system was withdrawn from the market. Wikipedia provides a good

*(continued)*

place to get additional information on this famous case study, which you can see at
https://en.wikipedia.org/wiki/Therac-25. This is a well-studied case, and the
Web has many rich information sources, analyses, and debates that you can (and
should) learn from.

Without going into this case in depth, how would you relate the basic requirements for
information security (confidentiality, integrity, availability) to what happened? Does this
case demonstrate that safety and reliability, and information security, are two sides of the
same coin? Why or why not?

If you had been working at AECL as an information security professional, what would
have been your ethical responsibilities, and to whom would you have owed them?

# Summary

Our Internet-enabled, e-commerce-driven world simply will not work without trustworthy,
reliable information exchanges. Trust and reliability, as we've seen, stem from the right mix
of confidentiality, privacy, and integrity in the ways we gather, process, use and share information. It's also clear that if reliable, trustworthy information isn't where we need it, when
we need it, we put the decisions we're about to make at risk; without availability, our safe
and secure information isn't *useful*; it's not *reliable*. These needs for trustworthy, reliable
information and information systems are equally important to governments and private
businesses; and they are vitally important to each of us as individuals, whether as citizens
or as consumers.

These fundamental aspects of information security—the CIA triad plus privacy—tie
directly into our responsibilities in law and in ethics as information systems security professionals. As SSCPs, we have many opportunities to help our employers, our clients, and our
society achieve the right mix of information security capabilities and practices.

From here, we move on to consider risk—what it is and how to manage and mitigate it,
and why it's the central theme as we plan to defend our information from all threats.

# Exam Essentials

**Know how to differentiate between data, information, knowledge, and wisdom.**    This
hierarchy of data to knowledge represents the results of taking the lower-level input (i.e.,
data) and processing it with business logic that uses other information you've already
learned or processed so that you now have something more informative, useful, or valuable.
Data might be the individual parts of a person's home address; when you get updates to this

data, and compare it to what you have on file, you conclude that they have moved to a new location (thus, you have created information). You might produce knowledge from information like this if you look across all of your contact information and see that a lot of people change their address two or three times per year. Perhaps they're "snowbirds," moving with the seasons. Longer, deeper looks at such knowledge can produce powerful conclusions that you could apply in new situations.

**Explain the difference between information, information systems, and information technology systems.**   Information is what people use, think with, create, and make decisions with. Information systems are the business logic or processes that people use as they do this, regardless of whether the information is on paper, in electronic form, or only tacit (in their own minds). Information technologies such as paper and pen, computers, and punch cards are some of the ways you record information and then move, store, or update those recordings to achieve some purpose.

**Explain the difference between due care and due diligence.**   Due care is making sure that you have designed, built, and used all the necessary and prudent steps to satisfy all of your responsibilities. Due diligence is continually monitoring and assessing whether those necessary and prudent steps are achieving required results and that they are still necessary, prudent, and sufficient.

**Know the difference between confidentiality and privacy.**   Privacy is defined in law and ethics as the freedom from intrusion by others into your life, your possessions, your place of work, or where you live. By controlling who can come into (or view) such private activities or places, you control what they can know about you and your activities. Confidentiality is defined in law and ethics as the requirement you place on another when you share information with them that you wish to keep private or in confidence; further disclosure by that person you share with cannot happen without your express consent.

**Know how to explain confidentiality, integrity, and availability as they pertain to information security needs.**   Confidentiality is about protecting the investment we have made in obtaining or producing information and the competitive advantage that information investment gives us so that others cannot take the information away from us and neutralize our advantage. Integrity means that the information as a set is reliable, complete, and correct, and has been created, modified, or used only by people and processes that we trust. Availability means that the information can be extracted, produced, displayed, or output where we need it, when we need it, in the form or format we need it in, to support our decision-making needs. Note that if information systems cannot assure integrity, the data that is produced (i.e., available) is not reliable, and in fact could be hazardous to use in making decisions.

**Explain what business logic is and its relationship to information security.**   Business logic is the set of rules that dictate or describe the processes that a business uses to perform the tasks that lead to achieving the required results, goals, or objectives. Business logic is often called *know-how*, and it may represent insights into making better products or being more efficient than is typical, and as such, generates a competitive advantage for the business. It is prudent to protect business logic so that other unauthorized users, such as competitors, do not learn from it and negate its advantage to the business.

**Explain what intellectual property is and how it relates to information security.** Intellectual property consists of sets of ideas, designs, procedures, and data expressed in forms that can be used to implement business logic. Typically, a business invests considerable effort in creating its intellectual property (IP) so that it will have a significant competitive advantage over others in the marketplace. As such, that investment is worthy of protection.

**Explain the apparent conflict between privacy and security.** Criminals, terrorists, and law-abiding citizens can all use powerful encryption, virtual private networks, and other information security technologies to protect their information and their activities from prying eyes. This causes some people to believe that protecting the privacy of the innocent is exposing others to harm. Yet these same people want *their* medical or financial information kept safe and securely out of the hands of criminal hackers.

**Explain the roles of CEOs or managing directors in a modern business.** CEOs or managing directors are the most senior, responsible individuals in a business. They have ultimate due care and due diligence responsibility for the business and its activities. They have authority over all activities of the company and can direct subordinate managers in carrying out those responsibilities. They may report to a board of directors, whose members have long-term, strategic responsibility for the success of the business.

**Explain what a stakeholder is in the context of a business.** A stakeholder is a person or organization that has an interest in or dependence on the successful operation of the business. Stakeholders could be investors; employees of the business; its strategic partners, vendors, or customers; or even its neighbors. Not all interests are directly tied to profitable operation of the business—neighbors, for example, may have a stake in the company operating safely and in ways that do not cause damage to their own properties or businesses.

**Explain the difference between legal, regulatory, and ethical obligations or responsibilities as they pertain to information security.** Legal responsibilities are defined in criminal or civil law, and they are enforced by government authorities, typically in a court of law. Regulatory responsibilities are established by government agencies that specify rules and procedures for business activities. They may have the force of law, but they were not written as laws by the legislature. Ethical responsibilities are the ideas about right and wrong behavior widely held in the society and marketplace where the business is located or functions.

**Explain why everybody needs to know about information security.** We all make decisions, whether as employees, students, family members, or members of our society. We must put some measure of trust and confidence into the information we use when we make those decisions, and therefore, we must be able to trust where we get information from. This means holding our sources accountable and cooperating with them in their efforts to protect information by keeping it confidential, preserving its integrity, and making it available to us. We are all parts of communities of trust.

**Compare safety and security for information systems.** Safety means operating a system in ways that do no harm, either to the system, its users, and bystanders, or to their property. Security means operating a system in ways that ensure that the information used in that system is available, of high integrity, and has been kept confidential as required. Systems with low information integrity are most likely unsafe to use or be around when they are used.

**Explain the preamble of the (ISC)$^2$ Code of Ethics.**   The preamble reminds us that everyone's safety and welfare depends on keeping information systems safe and secure from harm, misuse, or incorrect operation. As information systems security professionals, we have the opportunity and responsibility to ensure the safe and correct operation of these systems. As professionals, we have an obligation to one another and to society to have our actions be the standard others should aspire to.

**Explain the canons of the (ISC)$^2$ Code of Ethics.**   Protect society and the infrastructures it depends on; act honorably and with integrity; provide correct, complete, professional service to those we work for and with; and help grow and maintain our profession.

**Justify why you should follow the (ISC)$^2$ Code of Ethics.**   When you decide to be an information systems security professional, you are agreeing to the principles of the preamble and canons of that code. *Not* following the code places you in a contradiction—you cannot honestly protect an information system if you knowingly give incorrect, incomplete, or unprofessional advice to its owners, for example.

# Review Questions

1. How do you turn data into knowledge?

   **A.** These are both names for the same concepts, so no action is required.

   **B.** You use lots of data to observe general ideas and then test those ideas with more data you observe, until you can finally make broad, general conclusions. These conclusions are what are called knowledge.

   **C.** You apply data smoothing and machine learning techniques, and the decision rules this produces are called knowledge.

   **D.** You have to listen to the data to see what it's telling you, and then you'll know.

2. Which is more important to a business—its information or its information technology?

   **A.** Neither, since it is the business logic and business processes that give the business its competitive advantage.

   **B.** The information is more important, because all that the information technology does is make the information available to people to make decisions with.

   **C.** The information technology is more important, because without it, none of the data could be transformed into information for making decisions with.

   **D.** Both are equally important, because in most cases, computers and communications systems are where the information is gathered, stored, and made available.

3. As the IT security director, Paul does not have anybody looking at systems monitoring or event logging data. Which set of responsibilities is Paul in violation of?

   **A.** Due care

   **B.** Due diligence

   **C.** None of the above

   **D.** Both due care and due diligence

4. Explain the relationship between confidentiality and privacy, if any.

   **A.** Confidentiality is about keeping information secret so that we retain advantage or do not come to harm; privacy is about choosing who can enter into one's life or property.

   **B.** Confidential information is information that must be kept private, so they really have similar meanings.

   **C.** Privacy laws allow criminals to hide their actions and intentions from society, but confidentiality allows for the government to protect defense-related information from being leaked to enemies.

   **D.** Confidentiality is the freedom to choose with whom you share information; privacy refers to information that is specifically about individuals' lives, activities, or interests.

5. Jayne discovers that someone in the company's HR department has been modifying employee performance appraisals. If done without proper authorization, this would be what kind of violation?

   **A.** Integrity

   **B.** Confidentiality

   **C.** Availability

   **D.** Privacy

6. At a job interview, Fred is asked by the interviewer about activities, pictures, and statements he's made by posting things on his Facebook and LinkedIn pages. This question by the interviewer:

   **A.** Is a violation of Fred's right to privacy, as those posts were done on Fred's private pages

   **B.** Doesn't worry Fred, as the conversation with the interviewer is confidential

   **C.** Is a legitimate one, since these pages are published by Fred, and therefore they are speech he has made in public places

   **D.** Doesn't worry Fred, as he took those pages down yesterday and closed those accounts

7. A thunderstorm knocks out the commercial electric power to your company's datacenter, shutting down everything. This impacts which aspect of information security?

   **A.** Privacy

   **B.** Confidentiality

   **C.** Integrity

   **D.** Availability

8. Business logic is:

   **A.** A set of tasks that must be performed to achieve an objective within cost and schedule constraints

   **B.** The set of rules and constraints that drive a business to design a process that gets business done correctly and effectively

   **C.** Software and data used to process transactions and maintain accounts or inventories correctly

   **D.** The design of processes to achieve an objective within the rules and constraints the business must operate within

**9.** How does business logic relate to information security?

   **A.** Business logic represents decisions the company has made and may give it a competitive advantage over others in the marketplace; it needs to be protected from unauthorized disclosure or unauthorized change. Processes that implement the business logic need to be available to be run or used when needed. Thus, confidentiality, integrity, and availability apply.

   **B.** Business logic for specific tasks tends to be common across many businesses in a given market or industry; therefore, there is nothing confidential about it.

   **C.** Business logic should dictate the priorities for information security efforts.

   **D.** Business logic is important during process design; in daily operations, the company uses its IT systems to get work done, so it has no relationship to operational information security concerns.

**10.** Your company uses computer-controlled machine tools on the factory floor as part of its assembly line. This morning, you've discovered that somebody erased a key set of machine control parameter files, and the backups you have will need to be updated and verified before you can use them. This may take most of the day to accomplish. What information security attribute is involved here?

   **A.** Confidentiality

   **B.** Integrity

   **C.** Availability

   **D.** Due care

**11.** Protection of intellectual property (IP) is an example of what kind of information security need?

   **A.** Privacy

   **B.** Confidentiality

   **C.** Availability

   **D.** Integrity

**12.** John works as the chief information security officer for a medium-sized chemical processing firm. Which of the following groups of people would not be stakeholders in the ongoing operation of this business?

   **A.** State and local tax authorities

   **B.** Businesses in the immediate neighborhood of John's company

   **C.** Vendors, customers, and others who do business with John's company

   **D.** The employees of the company

**13.** When you compare safety to security for information systems, which of the following statements are correct? (Choose all that apply.)

   **A.** When information security measures fail to keep critical data available and correct, the resulting system malfunctions could lead to loss of revenue, property damage, injury, or death.

   **B.** Operating a system in an unsafe manner could introduce information that further corrupts the system, violates its integrity, or leads to it crashing, which violates availability needs.

   **C.** Keeping a system safe also means "safe from harm," and thus means much the same as keeping it secure.

   **D.** Safe system operation is the responsibility of its designers, builders, and operators; the information security people have no role in that, and thus safety and security are unrelated concepts.

**14.** Why is the preamble to (ISC)²'s Code of Ethics important to us as SSCPs?

   **A.** It is vital to understand the code because it sets purpose and intention; it's our mission statement as professionals.

   **B.** It sounds like it ought to be important, but it just states personal values; the canons tell us what to do and why that matters.

   **C.** It's not that important, since it only provides a context for the canons, which are the real ethical responsibilities that we have.

   **D.** It sets the priorities for us to address, highest to lowest, starting with the profession, the organization, the people we work for or our customers, and then society as a whole.

**15.** Due diligence means:

   **A.** Paying your debts completely, on time

   **B.** Doing what you must do to fulfill your responsibilities

   **C.** Making sure that actions you've taken to fulfill your responsibilities are working correctly and completely

   **D.** Reading and reviewing the reports from subordinates or from systems monitoring data

**16.** Suppose that you work for a business or have a business as your client. As an SSCP, which of the following groups do you have responsibilities to? (Choose all that apply.)

   **A.** Coworkers, managers, and owners of the business that employs you (or is your client)

   **B.** Competitors of the business that employs you or is your client

   **C.** Customers, suppliers, or other companies that work with this business

   **D.** People and groups that have nothing to do with this business

**17.** We often hear people talk about the need for information systems to be safe and reliable. Is this the same as saying that they need to be secure?

**A.** No, because reliability has to do with failures of equipment, errors in software design or use, or bad data used as input, whereas security is focused on keeping the systems and their data safe from intrusion or unwanted change.

**B.** Yes, because the objective of information security is to increase our confidence that we can make sound and prudent decisions based on what those information systems are telling us, and in doing so cause no harm.

**C.** Yes, because all information and information systems are built by humans, and humans make mistakes, so we need strong safety rules and procedures to keep from causing harm.

**D.** No, but they have ideas in common. For example, data integrity can lead to unsafe operation, but information security by itself cannot identify possible safety consequences.

**18.** As an SSCP, you work at the headquarters of a retail sales company that has many stores around the country. Its training department has prepared different training materials and operations manuals for in-store sales, warehouse staff, and other team members to use in their jobs. Most of these describe procedures that people do as they work with one another or with customers. From an information security standpoint, which of the following statements are correct?

**A.** Since these all describe people-to-people interactions and processes, they are not implemented by the IT department, and so they're not something that information security is concerned with.

**B.** Most of their content is probably common practice in business and retail sales and so would not be trade secrets, company proprietary, or private to the company.

**C.** Although these processes are not implemented in IT systems, the documents and videos themselves are hosted in company-provided IT systems, and so information security requirements apply.

**D.** If the company has decided that the content of these training materials is proprietary or company confidential, then their confidentiality must be protected. They must also be protected from tampering or unauthorized changes and be available to staff in the stores to use when they need them, if the company is to do business successfully. Therefore, information security applies.

**19.** What do we use protocols for? (Choose all that apply.)

**A.** To conduct ceremonies, parades, or how we salute superiors, sovereigns, or rulers

**B.** To have a conversation with someone and keep disagreement from turning into a hostile, angry argument

**C.** To connect elements of computer systems together so that they can share tasks and control each other

**D.** As abstract design tools when we are building systems, although we don't actually build hardware or software that implements a protocol

**E.** None of the above

**20.** Do the terms *cybersecurity*, *information assurance*, and *information security* mean the same thing? (Choose all that apply.)

**A.** No, because *cyber* refers to control theory, and therefore *cybersecurity* is the best term to use when talking about securing computers, computer networks, and communications systems.

**B.** Yes, but each finds preference in different markets and communities of practice.

**C.** No, because cybersecurity is about computer and network security, information security is about protecting the confidentiality and integrity of the information, and information assurance is about having reliable data to make decisions with.

**D.** No, because different groups of people in the field choose to interpret these terms differently, and there is no single authoritative view.

# Integrated Risk Management and Mitigation

Part 2 provides you with a roadmap toward a *proactive defense*. You'll see how to manage risks to the confidentiality, integrity, and availability of the information assets your organization depends on. This requires you to have a solid understanding of what risk is (and is not!). We'll show how *information risk management* is all about providing a cost-effective *integrated defense*—a set of interlocking, layered strategies; tactical procedures; and operational details that reduce the potential impact of the occurrence of information risks. Integrating all elements of your information defense posture and strategy is key to making defense in depth work—and not allowing it to become an outmoded and easily avoided set of point defenses. Being *proactive* means that you take a continuous, forward-looking attitude, mindset, and stance toward information risk; you think ahead of the adversary, think ahead of the risk, and plan, do, check, and act to keep your information systems secure, safe, and resilient. We'll do this by taking the SSCP's perspective, as if you as a practitioner have just joined an organization's information security team. You'll be learning the ropes for today's tasks, while examining the larger organizational context that your actions must support. With time, you'll learn more about the organization's priorities, challenges, and information risks. We will broadly follow the outline and structure of NIST Special Publication (SP) 800-37 Rev. 2, Information Systems Security and Privacy Risk Management Framework (RMF), throughout Part 2.

Chapter 3 shows you integrated information risk management in action from the SSCP's perspective. We'll look at how different perspectives on risk lead to making critical risk management decisions and how real-world constraints guide and limit what you can do to manage risks. This broadly reflects NIST SP 800-37's first two steps.

Chapter 4 will zoom into greater detail as we look at risk mitigation technologies and processes; it will also show how these fit within larger layers of planning, decision making, implementation, monitoring, and adaptation. We'll use NIST SP 800-37 Rev. 2's Steps 3 through 7 as our guide.

# Chapter 3

# Integrated Information Risk Management

---

## SSCP EXAM OBJECTIVES COVERED IN THIS CHAPTER INCLUDE:

**Domain 3: Risk Identification, Monitoring, and Analysis**

✓ 3.1: Understand the Risk Management Process

Defense is a set of strategies, management is about making decisions, and mitigation is a set of tactics chosen to implement those decisions. *Integrated information risk management* is about protecting what's important to the organization. It's about what to protect and why; risk mitigation addresses how. Some outcomes, processes, or assets are by their nature much more critical to organizational success (and survival!) than others. By the same token, some threats pose more danger to the organization and its vulnerabilities than others do. The CIA triad of cybersecurity needs prevails, and the SSCP can fill many important roles in shaping an effective integrated information defense strategy, as you'll see in this chapter. We'll also borrow from NIST Special Publication 800-37 Rev. 2, Information Systems Security and Privacy Risk Management Framework (RMF), to look at what leadership and management have to do to start the risk management process.

We are also going to challenge your thinking about defense—specifically about an idea called *defense in depth*. Some cybersecurity systems vendors claim that defense in depth is "dead," whereas many others in the industry continue to strongly recommend it. You'll see that the difference between whether defense in depth is very much alive and well, or on its way to the scrap heap, can be found in one word: *integrated*. Let's see what this means.

# It's a Dangerous World

Let's face it: your organization's systems, its information, its very existence is in danger. Your money, your capital equipment, supplies, and inventory all are at risk of theft or damage. Your information assets are at risk of being stolen, and your trade secrets, customer information, and business practices, even your talented people, are "up for grabs" if hackers can get into your files. Perhaps most important, your organization's *reputation* for honesty, reliability, and quality could be ruined by hostile action by such *threat actors* as these, or just by your own failure to quickly and prudently deal with accidental or natural disruptions to your business activities.

The key to risk and risk management is simple: *it's about making decisions in reliable ways* and using the CIA triad to help you know when the decision you're about to make is a reliable one...and when it is a blind leap into the dark. From the SSCP's perspective, information security is necessary because it enables more decisions to be made on time and on target. Reliable decision making is as much about long-range planning as it is about incident response. This means that you can rely on the following:

- Your individual and organizational memory (the information and knowledge you think you already have, know, and understand)

- New information that you've gathered, processed, and used as inputs to this decision

- Your ability to deliberate, examine, review, think, and then to decide, free from disruption

- Your ability to communicate our decision (the "new marching orders") to those elements of your organization and systems that have to carry them out

Each element of that basic decision cycle must be *reliable* if you want to count on your decisions being the right decisions at the right time. Each of those elements has its own CIA set of needs. By controlling or managing information risk, the SSCP helps the organization manage its decision risk, and thereby manage its overall exposure to risk while it decides and acts to achieve its goals and objectives.

The good news is that neither the SSCP nor the organizational leaders and stakeholders she works for have to figure out how to do all of this from scratch. Universities, businesses, and governments have for generations been compiling "lessons learned" about organizational management and leadership, especially on topics such as risk management. The dawn of the computer age highlighted the need to bring even more talent and expertise to bear, to find even better ways to manage and mitigate information risk and decisions risk. Since the 1990s, governments, private business, and academia have been collaborating to develop what organizations large and small need to be able to deal with information systems risk. They've produced risk management frameworks as well as highly technical standards, practices, and recommendations for the nitty-gritty work of hardening your information systems and defending them in prudent and effective ways.

A *risk management framework* is a management tool kit that you can use to bring these kinds of risks (and others) under control. One such framework, published by the U.S. Department of Commerce, National Institute of Standards and Technology, provides what it calls "a systems life cycle approach for security and policy." We'll use its overall approach to introduce the concepts of risk, defensive strategies, and responses; then we'll look more closely at how organizations manage risk and attain some control over it.

But first, let's look at what we mean by *risk* and, more specifically, *information risk*.

## What Is Risk?

Earlier in this chapter, we gave a formal definition of what we mean by risk. A *risk* is the possibility that an event can occur that can disrupt or damage the organization's planned activities, assets, or processes, which may impact the organization's ability to achieve some or all of its goals and objectives. This involves a threat (an actor, or a force of nature) acting on an asset's vulnerabilities so as to cause undesired or unplanned results.

Let's take our definition apart, piece by piece, and see how we can *operationalize* it—turn it into something we can make part of day-to-day, task-level operational steps we must accomplish to achieve it. We'll do that from the inside out, as shown in Figure 3.1.

**FIGURE 3.1**   Vulnerability leads to failure, which leads to impact

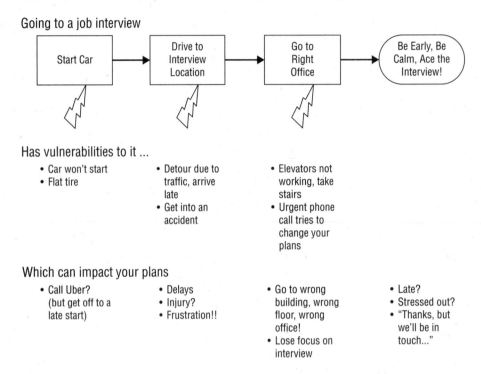

Going to a job interview

Has vulnerabilities to it ...

- Car won't start
- Flat tire

- Detour due to traffic, arrive late
- Get into an accident

- Elevators not working, take stairs
- Urgent phone call tries to change your plans

Which can impact your plans

- Call Uber? (but get off to a late start)

- Delays
- Injury?
- Frustration!!

- Go to wrong building, wrong floor, wrong office!
- Lose focus on interview

- Late?
- Stressed out?
- "Thanks, but we'll be in touch..."

Start by recognizing that vulnerabilities exist in everything we do, in everything we build—even in each of us. A bulletproof vest cannot stop heavy machine gun fire; structure fires can melt "fireproof" document safes, or even be so hot that safe actually burns. Parts wear out; mechanisms overheat; anything that runs on electricity can (and will) have that electrical supply fail. Humans make errors as we design, build, and use these systems. And to add insult to injury, the physical world is a *noisy* place—data gets corrupted, messages get garbled, and the result is often that what we thought we said is not what others think we meant.

Fortunately, each of these weaknesses is not occurring on a nonstop basis. Risks are "if something happens." We talk about a vulnerability becoming an event when something goes wrong—when a part fails, when a message doesn't get through, when a person makes a mistake, or when somebody exploits that vulnerability to cause an unwanted or poorly anticipated event to actually occur. Vulnerabilities by themselves do not cause harmful or disruptive events; it is only when some action is taken (or a required action is not taken) that such an event occurs. Even then, not all events that occur are events of interest to information security professionals. Two recent events are still making headline news illustrate this difference.

Our first example is one of a classical "non-zero day" exploit gone horribly viral in scale. On September 7, 2017, Equifax announced that millions of individual consumer credit report files might have been subject to an "unauthorized disclosure" due to a breach in the security of the company's systems. Since this initial announcement, continued reporting shows that more than 148 million consumers worldwide might have had their credit history, government identification, and other private data stolen from Equifax by the attackers. In the weeks that followed Equifax's announcement, an all-too-familiar sequence of events was revealed.

First, an exploitable software vulnerability was detected in the Apache Struts web software, used by Equifax and many others, by a security researcher in Shanghai, China; he reported his discovery immediately to the Apache Software Foundation, which then published the vulnerability and a fix on March 6, 2017. One day later, the vulnerability showed up in Metasploit, one of the most popular exploitation tool suites used by black hat and white hat hackers alike. By March 10, reconnaissance probes by hackers started to hit the Equifax servers. By early May, attackers exploited these vulnerabilities to gain access to multiple database applications served by many Equifax web pages, and then systematically "exfiltrated" (that is, *stole*) data from Equifax. Data from a U.S. Government Accountability Office (GAO) report indicates that hackers ran nearly 9,000 unauthorized queries over 76 days, many of which simply blended in with "normal" activity levels, and used standard encryption protocols to further disguise this traffic.

Equifax detected these exfiltrations on July 30, waited a day to verify that these were in fact unauthorized accesses leading to a data breach, and then shut down the affected servers. Equifax waited until September 7 to report the data losses to the U.S. Federal Trade Commission and to the public, claiming it had no legal obligation to report sooner.

What were the outcomes of the Equifax data breach? Equifax did spend, by some reports, up to $200 million on improving its systems security measures, and its board of directors did ask the chief executive officer and chief information security officer to retire early—with up to $500 million in retirement and severance benefits intact. As of March 2018, actual claims by consumers totaled $275 million; these are expected to rise to at least $600 million before all claims have been fully resolved.

---

### Zero Day Exploits

We can look at the lifecycle of an exploitable vulnerability in terms of key events in its life:

- First discovery

- Notification to the builder or vendor about the vulnerability

- Public notification and reporting of the vulnerability, such as in common vulnerabilities and exploits (CVE) databases

- First release by the builder or vendor of a fix (to correct it) or a patch (to provide a workaround to avoid it)

- Widespread adoption of the fix or patch throughout the marketplace

*(continued)*

---

*(continued)*

Throughout that lifecycle, attackers exploiting that vulnerability have varying degrees of surprise and success.

A *zero day exploit* is an exploitation of a newly discovered vulnerability before that vulnerability is discovered by or reported to the developers, vendors, or users of the affected system. The term suggests that the system's defenders have zero time to prepare for such an exploit, since they are not aware of the vulnerability or the potential for an attack based on it.

In the Equifax case, for example, there seem to have been at most a few days between discovery of the Apache Struts exploitable errors by a Chinese researcher and his reporting to Apache Software Foundation. From the day he reported it on, exploits using that vulnerability were no longer "zero day."

Regrettably, we lack such colorful names as "zero day" for exploits once they've taken on a degree of notoriety and thus have lost the element of surprise.

---

By contrast, consider numerous data systems failures that have caused significant losses to the companies involved. Delta Airlines, for example, had to cancel hundreds of flights in January 2017 due to multiple systems crashes at its Atlanta, Georgia, operations center; this was after its datacenter crashed the previous August when its (supposedly) uninterruptible electrical power systems failed. This cost Delta more than $150 million and inconvenienced tens of thousands of travelers. Yet, by all reports, this event was not of interest to IT security professionals; it was simply a cascading set of errors leading to otherwise preventable failures. Not all risks are information security risks, even if they impact the availability of information systems to support decision making. In retrospect, we see that choosing whether an event is a security concern or not is largely a judgment call we may have to make.

Two important questions must be asked about such failures or risk occurrences as incidents:

- First, how predictable are incidents like these? How often do the sorts of mistakes that lead to such incidents happen? When might they happen? If we can predict how often such circumstances might occur, or identify conditions that increase the likelihood of such mistakes or failures, we might gain insight into ways to prevent them. In risk management terms, this asks us to make reasonable assumptions that help us estimate the *frequencies of occurrence* and *probabilities of occurrence* for such events.

- Second, how much impact do they have on the organization, its goals and objectives, and its assets, people, or reputation? What did this *cost* us, in terms of money, lost business, real damages, injuries or deaths, and loss of goodwill among our customers and suppliers?

These answers suggest that if something we do, use, or depend on *can fail*, no matter what the cause, then we can start to look at the *how* of those failures—but we let those frequencies, probabilities, and possible impacts guide us to prioritize which risks we look at first, and which we can choose to look at later.

# Risk: When Surprise Becomes Disruption

We care about risks because when they occur (when they become an incident), they disrupt our plans. Incidents disrupt us in two ways:

- They break our chain of thought. They interrupt the flow of decision making that we "normally" would be using to carry out our planned, regular, normal activities.

- They cause us to react to their occurrence. We divert time, labor, money, effort, and decision making into responding to that incident.

Consider, for example, a simple daily set of activities like driving to work. As you back your car out of the driveway, a sudden noise and an impact suggests that you've run over something (hopefully not someone!). You stop the car, get out, and look; you find a child's bicycle had been left in the driveway behind your car. The damage to bicycle and car is minor but not zero; money, time, and effort are required to fix them. You've got to decide when and how to get those repairs done, in ways that don't completely disrupt your plans for the day. And you're probably both upset (why didn't you look better first?) and relieved (no one got hurt).

Most of the time, we think of risks as "bad news." Things break; opportunities are lost; systems or property is damaged; people get hurt or killed. If we stop and think about this, we see that risk can be good news but still disruptive to our plans. An unexpected opportunity appears (a surprising offer of a dream job, halfway across the country), but to take advantage of it, you must divert resources to do what's necessary.

The occurrence of a risk, therefore, takes our preplanned, previously evaluated, deliberated decisions and action plans and tosses them aside. And it does this because either new information (the bicycle behind your car, the new job) was not *anticipated* as you put your original decisions together, or your decision process was not set up to deal with that new information without derailing your train of thought.

 **Real World Scenario**

**Case Study: Voter Registration**

Throughout this chapter, we'll look at the information processing needs of modern democracies as a recurring theme. We'll see that some of the information risks that voting systems face are clearly linked to the information technologies they use, whereas many other risks are linked to choices about information management and operation of those systems.

We'll start with a case study on voter registration processes. Many countries use voting systems to empower their citizens to choose elected representatives or other officials and to express opinion about issues. Voter registration systems provide ways to identify lawful, authorized voters by associating *personally identifying information* (PII) with location

*(continued)*

*(continued)*

information, thus registering a specific person as eligible to vote at a particular local polling place. The process typically works:

1.  The voter establishes a lawful residence within a voting district.

2.  The voter registers with the election authority by providing proof of identification (the PII) and proof of residency within the district.

3.  The election authority validates the PII, verifies the address information, and then adds the voter to the election rolls (the database of registered voters).

When it's time for an election, the election authority provides each polling place with a validated list of those registered voters eligible to vote. The polling place officials use this list to ensure that only registered voters vote and that each registered voter votes only one time in only one polling place during that election.

How does CIA apply to this process? In most voting processes:

- Confidentiality is required by law; voters cast their votes anonymously, protecting their freedom to make their own choices without coercion or pressure from the government or from anyone else.

- Integrity of voter registration data is required to ensure that vote fraud does not occur (that is, that only registered voters actually vote, and that no one who was ineligible to be a registered voter was allowed to register).

- Availability of the voter registration system affects each step in the registration and balloting processes. This means that at any time during the process, failures or errors in that system must not deny any voter the opportunity to register. Once registered, the use of registration systems and information during the election must not deny any registered voter the opportunity to actually cast their ballot.

Disruption to an election can occur if failures in the voter registration systems prevent citizens from registering to vote or prevent registered voters from actually being able to vote on Election Day. If either of these risks becomes an incident, the general public or significant subgroups of voters can lose faith and confidence not only in the results of this one election, but also in the electoral process as a whole. This can (and has!) led to civil unrest, demonstrations, and revolutions.

All because a nation could not keep track of who was eligible to vote...

# Information Security: Delivering Decision Assurance

Everything people and human organizations do is a series of steps, and each step is a series of substeps; our lives and our businesses run on layers upon layers of tasks and subtasks. You go to work in the morning, but that in itself requires steps (like waking up), and all of those steps contain or are made up of substeps. Businesses get things done in step-by-step ways; these *business processes* are often chained together, the results of one process becoming the inputs to the next. Within each process we often find many subprocesses, as well as many decision points that affect the way each particular process is applied to each particular set of input conditions, day in and day out. This is why sometimes we say that all work is actually *decision work*, since even the simplest task you do requires you to decide "Should I do this next?" before starting; "Am I doing this right?" while you're doing it; and "Did I finish it correctly?" when you think it's time to stop.

Each step in a process is a decision. That's the number one most powerful lesson of *cybernetics*, the study of control systems. The most powerful lesson from 10,000 years of warfare and conflict between nations is that first, you defeat the way your adversary *thinks*. By defeating his strategy, you may not even need to engage his armies on the field—or you will spend far less effort in actual combat if you must nonetheless! By outthinking your opponent in this way, you are much more able to win through to your own goals, often at much lower costs to you. We call this *getting inside the opponent's decision cycle*. And for the same 10,000 years, this same lesson has shaped the way marketplaces work and thus shapes the way that businesses compete with one another.

Every one of those decisions, large or small, is an opportunity for somebody or something to "mess with" what you had planned and what you want and need to accomplish:

- Competitors can learn what you're planning to do.

- Customer requests can be mishandled, misrouted, or ignored, which may lead to customers taking their business elsewhere.

- Costs can be erroneously increased, and revenues can be lost.

---

### Booking an Airline Flight

The following figure illustrates the typical decision flow that many of us have experienced when we wish to make travel arrangements via a commercial airline. In this (greatly simplified) flow, you see how the different actors—the customer and the airline—have to interact with each other and provide information that leads to decisions. Each of the links connecting the actions and decisions show the transfer of information between these actors. When those links fail to work correctly, the entire transaction can be put at risk of failure.

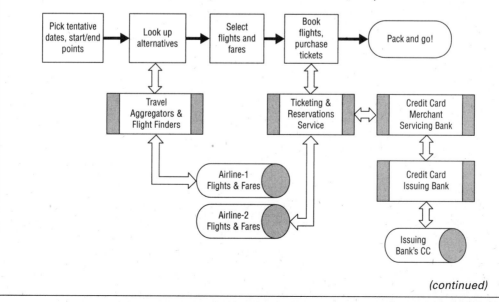

*(continued)*

*(continued)*

Let's look at this from the standpoint of how failures to assure confidentiality, integrity, and availability of the underlying information can cause the airline to lose business:

- Information about flights between destinations, timetables and schedules, and available fares is typically published (or "public-facing"), whether on websites, travel agency systems, or printed travel brochures. It's freely available to anyone, competitors included. But it does have to be correct, and it does have to be there when prospective travelers are shopping around or contemplating a voyage. (Integrity and availability are required, but there's no need for confidentiality).

- Once a traveler contacts the airline and begins to put trip plans together, confidentiality covers two essential needs. First, it protects the *customer* from loss of control of their PII, their travel plans, or their payment information. Next, it protects the *airline* from its competitors, who might wish to lure the customer away from them by making a better offer (in terms of price, service, schedule, or other benefits). The *customer* can always "shop aggressively" by sharing whatever information they want to with competing travel providers, but very few businesses can survive long if they tell their competitors the price and terms of transactions they've just made or that are "on hold" while the customer shops around!

- Quality of customer service indicators, such as the total time required to make a reservation, confirm it, and receive payment for it, tell the airline how well its business processes work. Should its competitors gain this information, it may reveal opportunities for them to do these processes faster, better, or cheaper, and thus gain a competitive advantage. Once again, the details of the customer service interaction need some degree of confidentiality to protect the airline's know-how.

- Picture the situation if it takes six months or so to turn today's badly served and unhappy customer encounter into useful, insightful quality-of-service information. How many customers might the airline have lost if it takes six months to learn what causes each former customer to leave? Availability of process quality information is key here; if that information is not produced in a timely manner, the company is seriously limited in its ability to improve.

Note that even an everyday business transaction such as booking an airline reservation not only contains (or requires) numerous decisions but also generates information that can and should be used to make other decisions.

*Decision assurance*, then, consists of protecting the availability, reliability, and integrity of the four main components of the decision process:

- The knowledge we already have (our memory and experience), including knowledge of our goals, objectives, and priorities
- New information we receive from others (the marketplace, customers, others in the organization, and so on)

- Our cognitive ability to think and reason with these two sets of information and to come to a decision

- Taking action to carry out that decision or to communicate that decision to others, who will then be responsible for taking action

From our CIA perspective, integrity and availability affect all four components of every decision we make (including the ones we have machines make on our behalf). Whether confidentiality is required for a particular decision, its inputs, its decision logic, or the actions or communications that are the result of making the decision, is something that the decision maker needs to decide about as well.

One of the most powerful decision assurance tools that managers and leaders can use at almost any organizational level is to "sanity-check" the inputs, the thinking, and the proposed actions with other people before committing to a course of action. "Does this make sense?" is a question that experience suggests ought to be asked often but isn't. For information security specialists, checking your facts, your stored knowledge, your logic, and your planning with others can take many different forms:

- Sharing or pooling risk management information with others in your marketplace, with insurers or re-insurers, or with key stakeholders

- Actively participating in threat and risk reduction communities of practice, information exchanges, and community emergency response planning groups, which might include representation from local and national government authorities

- Using "anti-groupthink" processes and techniques to prevent your decision processes from stifling new voices or contrary views

- Finding ways to be "surprise-tolerant" so that unanticipated observations about day-to-day operational events can generate possible new insight

- Building, maintaining, and using mentors, peer groups, and trusted advisory groups, both from within the organization and from outside

## "Common Sense" and Risk Management

It's important to remember that most of what makes human organizations (and individual efforts) successful is our ability to recognize, think, and decide at many levels—some of which we are not consciously aware of. "Common sense," for example, teaches us many "lessons learned" from experience: you don't leave your car unlocked with packages on the seats if you want to come back and find those packages still in the car. You don't leave your house or apartment unlocked when you go on vacation. You don't leave the default user IDs of "admin" and "password" enabled on your laptops, phones, routers, switches, modems, and firewalls. (You don't, do you?)

Risk management *includes* this kind of prudent use of common sense. Risk management recognizes that before we can do anything else, we need to make sure that the blindingly obvious safety precautions, the common-sense computing hygiene measures, have already been put in place and are being used conscientiously.

The one drawback to common sense, as Voltaire said, is that it isn't so common. Sometimes this is because what we call "common sense" turns out to be that we've made decisions intuitively, without consciously thinking them through. Other times, we've probably read or heard the "lessons learned" by others, but right at the moment we make a decision, we're not using them explicitly. If those lessons lead to writing a problem-solving checklist (like a fault isolation diagram), then "common sense" becomes documented, common *practice* for us. As you've seen in earlier chapters, *due care* is applying common sense to ensure that the right processes, with the right steps and safeguards, have been put in place to achieve a set of goals. *Due diligence* is the follow-through that continually verifies those processes are still working right *and* that they are still necessary and sufficient to meet what's needed.

Common sense can and often does suggest that there are still reasonable, prudent actions that we can take to make sure that an appropriate set of information security measures are in place and effective. Information security best practices suggest a good minimum set of "when in doubt" actions to ensure that the organization:

- Physically protects and secures information systems, information storage (paper or electronic), and supporting infrastructure
- Controls access by all users, visitors, and guests, such as with usernames and passwords, for all computer systems
- Controls disclosure and disposal of information and information systems
- Trains all staff (or anyone with access) on these minimum security measures

This "safe computing" or *computing hygiene* standard, is a proven place for any organization to start with. If you don't have at least this much going for your information security program, you're just asking for trouble!

You are going to need to go beyond common sense in dealing with information risks, and that means you'll need to *manage* those risks. This means you must augment your guesswork and intuition with informed judgment, measurement, and accountability.

---

### Where's the C3 in That Commonsense Approach?

Probably the most often-overlooked element of information security is what the military calls the *command, control, and communications* (or C3, sometimes written with an exponent as $C^3$) element. Who notices that something has happened or that something has changed? Whom do they tell? How quickly? *Why?* Then who decides to have other people take what kind of action? *How quickly* must all of those conversations happen so that the organization can adapt fast enough when the risk happens, prevent or contain damage, and take the right steps to get back to normal? In other words, where is the decision assurance about risks and incidents as they occur?

In the absence of a good, well-considered information risk C3 strategy and set of procedures, your coworkers could be innocently assuming that "somebody else" noticed the problems on the system or that "some other department" was handling those issues. In the face of these assumptions, nobody pays attention to the alarms or the quirks in the systems; nobody knows that something needs investigating. Nobody calls for help.

This is the number one killer of "classic defense in depth," which surrounds our valuable information assets, systems, and processes with lots of point defense tools *that don't talk very well with one another*. Industry has created products such as security information management (SIM) systems, security event management (SEM) systems, and security information and event management (SIEM) systems to try to address this need, but they all fall far short of what's required.

# The Four Faces of Risk

Risk, as we stated earlier, is about a *possible* occurrence of an event that leads to loss, harm, or disruption. Individuals and organizations face risk, and are confronted by its possibilities of impact, in four basic ways, as Figure 3.2 illustrates. Three observations are important here, so important that they are worth considering as rules in and of themselves:

- Rule 1: All things will end. Systems will fail; parts will wear out. People will get sick, quit, die, or change their minds. Information will never be complete or absolutely accurate or true.

- Rule 2: The best you can do in the face of Rule 1 is spend money, time, and effort making *some* things more robust and resilient at the expense of others, and thus trade off the risk of one kind of failure for another.

- Rule 3: There's nothing you can do to avoid Rule 1 and Rule 2.

**FIGURE 3.2**     Four faces of risk, viewed together

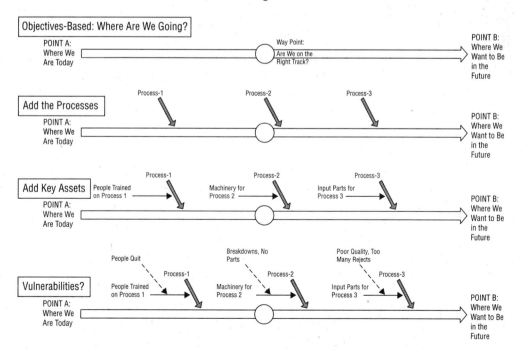

You may recognize these as the Three Laws of Thermodynamics, also expressed in song as "You Can't Win, You Can't Break Even, and You Can't Get Out of the Game," sung by Michael Jackson in the movie *The Wiz*.

Risk management, then, is trading off effort and resources *now* to reduce the possibility of a risk occurring *later*, and if it does occur, in limiting the damage it can cause to us or those things, people, and objectives we hold important. The impact or loss that can happen to us when a risk goes from being a possibility to a real occurrence—when it becomes an incident—is often looked at first in terms of how it affects our organization's goals, objectives, systems, and our people. This provides four ways of looking at risk, no one of which is the one best right way. All of these perspectives have something to reveal to us about the information risks our organization may be facing.

Think back to the Ishikawa, or fishbone, diagram we introduced in Chapter 1, "The Business Case for Decision Assurance and Information Security." The "tail" and "head" of the fishbone and the central left-to-right arrow of the backbone demonstrate the outcomes-based viewpoint. The major inputs of materials, methods, measurements, people, and machines are assets. The environment is where external threats (natural, accidental, or deliberate) can strike from. Internal threats can be visualized as the failure of any connecting arrow to "deliver the goods"—make good on the promised on-time, on-target delivery of a service, set of information, materials, labor, or other outcomes to the steps in the process that need them.

---

### "Bases" or "Faces"?

What's the right way to think about outcomes, processes, assets, or vulnerabilities? Are they *perspectives* or are they *bases*? Both terms make sense.

In accounting and business terms, we talk about a *basis* as being the foundation or starting point of a chain of decisions about the value of an asset. We've purchased a new computer, and that purchase price establishes its value for tax, inventory control, and accounting terms. That value is called its *basis*.

---

When we make an *estimate*, we are predicting a future outcome of a set of choices. That same computer has a purchase value, but to estimate what its useful life is, we have to make assumptions about how often it is used, how routine maintenance and repairs are done, and how often such machines break down under comparable use. Those assumptions, plus that purchase value, are the basis of estimate we can then calculate the useful life with.

By calling these the *faces of risk*, we highlight the need for you as the SSCP to be conscious of how you *look* at things and how you perceive a situation. And that, of course, depends a lot on where you stand.

# Outcomes-Based Risk

This face of risk looks at *why* people or organizations do what they do or set out to achieve their goals or objectives. The *outcomes* of achieving those goals or objectives are the tangible or intangible results we produce, the harvest we reap. Passing the SSCP examination and earning your SSCP credential is an objective, yes, and the achievement of it is an outcome in and of itself. But in doing so, you enable or enhance your ability to be a more effective information security practitioner, which can enable you to achieve other, more strategic goals. A severe illness or injury could disrupt your ability to study for, take, and pass the examination; a family emergency could lead you to abandon that objective altogether. These are risks to the outcome (or objective) itself, and they are largely independent of the ways in which you had planned to achieve the outcome.

Here's a hypothetical example: Search Improvement Engineering (SIE) is a small software development company that makes and markets web search optimization aids targeted to mobile phone users. SIE's chief of product development wants to move away from in-house computers, servers, and networks and start using cloud-based integrated development and test tools instead; this, she argues, will reduce costs, improve overall product quality and sustainability, and eliminate risks of disruption that owning (and maintaining) their own development computer systems can bring. The *outcome* is to improve software product quality, lower costs, and enable the company to make new products for new markets. This further supports the higher-level outcomes of organizational survival, financial health, growth, and expansion. One outcomes-based risk would be the disclosure, compromise, or loss of control over SIE's designs, algorithms, source code, or test data to other customers operating on the cloud service provider's systems. (We'll look at how to evaluate and mitigate that risk in later chapters.)

# Process-Based Risk

Everything we want to achieve or do requires us to take some action; action requires us to make a decision. Even if it's only one action that flows from one decision, that's a *process*. In organizational terms, a *business process* takes a logical sequence of purpose, intention, conditions, and constraints and structures them as a set of systematic actions and decisions in order to carry them out. This *business logic*, and the business processes that implement it, also typically provide indicators or measurements that allow operators and managers to monitor the execution of the process, assess whether key steps are working correctly, signal completion of the process (and thus perhaps trigger the next process), or issue an alarm to indicate that attention and action are required. When a task (a process step) fails to function properly, this can either stop the process completely or lead to erroneous results.

If we look further at our hypothetical SIE, we see that the company has several major sets of business processes. Human resources management processes support hiring, training, and providing salary and benefits for workers; financial processes ensure that bills are paid and invoices are issued, both of which are accurately reflected in the accounting ledgers ("the books" as the chief financial officer calls them). Software development processes define, track, and manage how customer needs and market research ideas translate into new functional requirements for products and the development and testing of those products. Customer relationship management (CRM) processes bring everything from "who is" a customer, to "What do they like to buy from us?" together with credit rating, market share, and many other factors to help SIE know how important one customer is versus another. Process-based risks to this last set of processes could be that complaints or concerns from important customers aren't recognized quickly, properly investigated, and acted on in ways that help customers decide to stay with SIE for their search optimization software needs.

Note that in this example, the *outcome* of using the processes is where we feel the *impact* of the risk becoming an incident—but it is the process that we're focused on as we investigate "what can go wrong" as we wonder "Why are customers leaving us?"

## Asset-Based Risk

Broadly speaking, an asset is anything that the organization (or the individual) has, owns, uses, or produces as part of its efforts to achieve some of its goals and objectives. Buildings, machinery, or money on deposit in a bank are examples of hard, or *tangible assets*. The people in your organization (including you!), the knowledge that is recorded in the business logic of your business processes, your reputation in the marketplace, the intellectual property that you own as patents or trade secrets, and every bit of information that you own or use are examples of soft, or *intangible assets*. Assets are the tools you use to perform the steps in your business processes; without assets, the best business logic cannot do anything.

Lots of information risk management books start with *information assets*—the information you gather, process, and use, and the business logic or systems you use in doing that—and *information technology assets*—the computers, networks, servers, and cloud services in which that information moves, resides, and is used. The unstated assumption in nearly all cases is that if the information asset or IT asset exists, it must therefore be *important* to the company or organization, and therefore, the possibility of loss or damage to that asset is a risk worth managing. This assumption may or may not still hold true. Assets also lose value over time, reflecting their decreasing usefulness, ongoing wear and tear, obsolescence, or increasing costs of maintenance and ownership. A good example of an obsolete IT asset would be a mainframe computer purchased by a university in the early 1970s for its campus computer center, perhaps at a cost of over a million dollars. By the 1990s, the growth in personal computing and network capabilities meant that students, faculty, and staff needed far more capabilities than that mainframe computer center could provide, and by 2015, it was probably far outpaced by the capabilities in a single smartphone connected to the World Wide Web and its cloud-based service provider systems. Similarly, an obsolete information asset might be the paper records of business transactions regarding products the company no longer sells, services, or supports. At some point, the *law of diminishing returns* says that it costs more to keep it and use it than the value you receive or generate in doing so.

## Threat-Based (or Vulnerability-Based) Risk

These are two sides of the same coin, really. *Threat actors* (natural or human) are things that can cause damage and distruction leading to loss. *Vulnerabilities* are weaknesses within systems, processes, assets, and so forth that are points of potential failure. When (not if) they fail, they result in damage, disruption, and loss. Typically, threats or threat actors exploit (make use of) vulnerabilities. Threats can be natural (such as storms or earthquakes), accidental (failures of processes or systems due to unintentional actions or normal wear and tear, causing a component to fail), or deliberate actions taken by humans or instigated by humans. Such intentional attackers have purposes, goals, or objectives they seek to accomplish; Mother Nature or a careless worker does not intend to cause disruption, damage, or loss.

As an example, consider a typical small office/home office (SOHO) IT network, consisting of a modem/router, a few PCs or laptops, and maybe a network attached printer and storage system. A thunderstorm can interrupt electrical power; the lack of a backup power supply is a weakness or vulnerability that the thunderstorm unintentionally exploits. By contrast, the actions of the upstairs neighbors or passers-by who try to "borrow some bandwidth" and make use of the SOHO network's wireless connection will most likely degrade service for authorized users, quite possibly leading to interruptions in important business or personal tasks. This is deliberate action, taken by threat actors, that succeeds perhaps by exploiting poorly configured security settings in the wireless network, whether its intention was hostile (e.g., willful disruption) or merely inconsiderate.

Think back to what we just discussed about process-based risks. It's quite common for an organization to have some of its business processes contain steps for which there are no easy, affordable alternative ways to get results when that step fails to function properly. These steps are said to be "on the *critical path*" from start to finish, and thus a set of processes containing such a critical step is a critical path in and of itself. Almost without exception, critical paths and the critical steps on them are *vulnerabilities* in the business logic and the business processes that the company depends upon.

It's perhaps natural to combine the threat-based and vulnerability-based views into one perspective, since they both end up looking at vulnerabilities to see what impacts can possibly disrupt an organization's information systems. The key question that the threat-based perspective asks, at least for human threat actors, is *why*. What is the motive? What's the possible advantage the attacker can gain if they exploit this vulnerability? What overall gains an attacker might achieve by an attack on our information systems at all? Many small businesses (and some quite large ones) do not realize that a successful incursion into *their* systems by an attacker may only be a step in that attacker's larger plan for disruption, damage, or harm to *others*.

Note that whether you call this a "threat-based" or a "vulnerability-based" approach or perspective, you end up taking much the same action: you identify the vulnerabilities on the critical path to your high-priority objectives, and then decide what to do about them in the face of a possible threat becoming a reality and turning into an incident.

---

### 🌐 Real World Scenario

#### Case Study, Continued: Voter Registration and Risk Perspectives

Let's use the four faces of risk to take a closer look at the voter registration and Election Day processes. We'll build our own fishbone diagram to help us visualize and understand all of the moving parts in this real-world problem.

An outcomes-based view of voter registration and voting looks at what the citizens want their democracy to achieve as a functioning democracy (and not the issues or candidates being voted on themselves). Typical outcomes that such voter registration and election processes should achieve include:

- Citizen confidence in their elected officials and system of government, which translates into their willingness to obey the laws, pay their taxes, and participate in civic processes in general

- Fair and equitable participation of each voting demographic in the registration and election processes

- Compliance with legal and regulatory information confidentiality, integrity, and availability requirements

- The enhancement, or at least preservation, of the reputation of the local or regional government's management and delivery of voter registration and election services

- No basis for a court-ordered rerun of the election or significant recount of votes

- Voter registration and election costs, both direct and indirect, that are kept within budget, if not minimized

- A political process—the final outcome of the election—that functions equitably and transparently to meet the needs of the citizens

Note that each required or intended outcome can easily be inverted to identify the risk we wish to avoid. (We'll leave these to you to formulate as an exercise in logic.)

Process-based risk assessment starts by identifying key processes, which, if they fail, could cause the overall system of voter registration and the elections dependent upon it to fail:

- How are citizens and residents in the region informed of their rights and the requirements they need to fulfill to be able to register and to vote?

- How do citizens apply to register to vote?

- What other sources of information are used to validate that PII or residence information, provided by the applicant, is true and correct?

- What legal requirements or constraints limit how applicant information can be shared, used, or published, even in aggregate?

- How is registration information used on Election Day to control the voting process?

- How is voting done, and how are individual votes cast by voters tabulated to produce election results?

- How do we validate that election results accurately reflect the individual voters' ballots?

Asset-based risk assessment first needs to identify the list of assets involved in voter registration and voting itself. Without these assets being available and reliable, one or more processes in voter registration, balloting, and tabulating election results cannot happen. Typically, we think of three groups of assets—information assets, technology assets (or systems assets), and people:

- Information assets might include the registration applicant files, additional files used in the validation of registration applications, and the voter rolls themselves (lists of registered voters sent to each polling place for use during voting).

- Information technology assets could include physical documents, as well as the containers, cabinets, boxes, or bags used to organize, store, transport, and put them to use in voting and counting of the votes. Even a simple cardboard or wooden ballot box is an asset. Computer-aided or fully computerized registration and voting systems also need machines to input, process, store, transport, and use voter registration files, voter rolls, and the ballots themselves. The communications links used to bring the voter rolls to each polling station, and to bring each station's results together to produce the final election results, are also key assets.

- Don't forget the people who make all of this work! Government employees (or contractors) process registration applications, validate applicant-provided information, and update registration records; they make sure that voter rolls are available at the polling stations. They supervise the ballot-counting processes, which a senior government official must certify as true and correct before the results are made public. Each person involved in the process is an asset, and like all assets, they have their own unique characteristics—some of which may impact their reliability!

Finally, a threat-based or vulnerability-based perspective would look at each of the other three faces of risk. What can go wrong? Where are the vulnerabilities in our systems, our processes, or our people, that might represent a chance for accident or willful mischief to corrupt our voter registration and election processes?

- An individual clerk could make a mistake, or willfully decide to "misplace" some voter registration records, and thus disenfranchise many citizens by preventing them from registering in time to vote.

*(continued)*

*(continued)*

- Paper-based registration systems could be damaged by a fire, a leaky pipe, or other natural hazard; if the problem is not discovered in time, the voter rolls prepared for an election may be incomplete, also leading to disenfranchising some citizens.

- Voting machines can be tampered with, or may accidentally malfunction due to poor maintenance, power fluctuations, and so forth. Paper ballots can be falsified, tampered with, or "lost" at the polling station or on their way to central tabulating centers.

- Small, easily overlooked but vital items—like special-purpose electrical power cords—can fail to show up with the voting machines that need them, causing delays and disruption at polling places (as apparently happened in precincts in Georgia on Election Day 2018).

- Voters can be intimidated or prevented from entering a polling station, or otherwise believe that their individual choice is not secret.

- Polling stations can be disrupted or forced to close early due to bad weather or civil disobedience, and thus prevent some people from voting.

What this case study reveals is that protecting the processes of voter registration and voting itself requires us to think long and deep. We need a "cradle to grave" view, considering every event on the path from start to finish. This is how we answer the risk manager's three big questions: what we need to defend, against what, and how we do that.

# Getting Integrated and Proactive with Information Defense

Imagine for a moment a typical walled city in medieval Europe. Within the city was the castle, sitting on higher ground and surrounded by a moat, trenches, and a wall of its own. When threatened by an attacking army, farmers and villagers in the surrounding area retreated inside the city's walls, and if the attackers breached the walls, they'd further retreat inside the castle keep itself. This layered defense had both static elements, such as the walls, moat, and trenches, as well as dynamic elements (troops could be moved about within the city). The assets being defended (the people, their livestock, food supplies, etc.) could be moved inward layer by layer as the threat increased. Watchmen, captains of the guard, and other officials would use runners to carry messages to the city's leaders, who'd send messages back to each element of the defense.

Continued advances in warfighting technology, of course, meant that static walls of stone quickly became obsolete. Yet this layered defense concept, when combined with an active, flexible command, control, and communications architecture, still dominates our thinking when we look to implement information risk management and mitigations strategies. *As well it should.* We use a layered or "top-down" approach when we design, build, and operate a business and the processes and systems that support it. Why not use that same "layers upon layers" perspective to look at how to defend it, preserve it, and keep it safe?

We see by now that several ideas interact with each other, as we look to what the SSCP can do to help the organization achieve the right mix of information security, performance, and cost. Let's start by examining how our process for designing our information defense systems mirrors the way we design, build, and operate our organization's business processes and the IT systems that serve its needs.

Consider a layered or structural approach to your organization's information security needs. Whether you are trying to ensure that new business objectives can be developed, launched, and operated successfully, or you're just trying to protect the data and systems in use today, you can look at the organization, the risks it faces, *and your opportunities to secure and defend it* in a layered fashion, as Figure 3.3 illustrates. From the inner, most vital center of the organization on out, you might see these layers as follows:

- Core functions, assets, and information are vital to the survival of the organization.

- Key business processes allow trusted members of the organization to use core functions, assets, and information in the performance of their duties.

- Surrounding those key business processes are a variety of support processes, tasks, systems, (and people!); their work may not be vital to survival, but it does facilitate success.

- At the boundary to the outside world, one or more gateway functions control who has access, what they can bring in with them, what they can do as they interact with the organization and its information systems, and what they can take back outside with them when they leave.

- Other boundary points interface with service providers, whether as infrastructures (like power, water, or transportation) or to deliver products as services (accountants, lawyers, etc.).

- Other gateway functions monitor, control, or fulfill mandatory reporting and compliance needs, such as filing and paying taxes and paying bills.

- Public-facing boundary points provide prospective customers or partners, the news media, neighbors, and the general public with ways to learn about the organization, ask questions of it, or offer ideas or suggestions.

**FIGURE 3.3**    The layered view

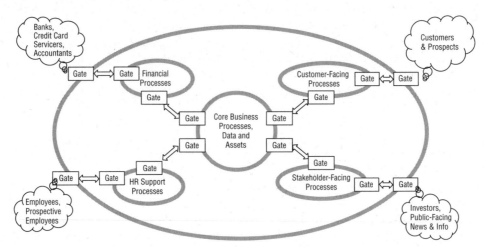

As SSCPs, we have to defend those layers of function against risk; failure to do so exposes the organization to unmanaged risks, which leaves us unable to predict what might go wrong or to plan how to respond when it does. Natural systems (such as the immune system in our bodies) and human-built systems have long recognized a few key principles when planning for defense:

- Understand your environment so that you can identify possible potential attackers and differentiate hostile actions from non-hostile ones.

- Deter potential attackers by having a visible, credible defensive capability and posture.

- Monitor potential attackers for signs that they are preparing to attack.

- Avoid or prevent the attack, either by means of effective deterrence, negotiation, or by other means.

- Detect attacks as they begin, and monitor them as they progress (or when they terminate).

- Deflect or delay attacks where and when possible.

- Degrade an attacker's capabilities by wearing them down (attrition), stalling them (barricades, obstacles), or destroying their attack forces.

- Defeat the attack by sufficiently degrading deflecting, or destroying the attacking force's units, weapons, and capabilities.

Note how these concepts apply equally, whether you are considering nonintentional threats, such as "acts of Nature," accidents, or deliberate, hostile attacks on your organization, its assets, and its interests. For example:

- A business located in a "hurricane alley" (an area known for severe storms) should learn about historic weather patterns, storm severity, and local physical, logistical, and administrative design practices that can be used in combination to survive the worst of the storms with minimal damage. Storm shelters, offsite backup capabilities, and disaster recovery plans are some of the tools the business might use.

- The same business, if located in a high-crime area, might use a mix of strong physical security measures, strong relationships with law enforcement and emergency services, and neighborhood outreach and engagement to provide a broad-spectrum approach to reduce the risk of being seen by local criminal elements as a "legitimate" or "easy" target.

These layers of function may take physical, logical, and administrative forms throughout every human enterprise:

- *Physical systems elements* are typically things such as buildings, machinery, wiring systems, and the hardware elements of IT systems. The land surrounding the buildings, the fences and landscaping, lighting, and pavements are also some of the physical elements you need to consider as you plan for information risk management. The physical components of infrastructures, such as electric power, water, sewer, storm drains, streets and transportation, and trash removal, are also important. What's missing from this list? *People.* People are of course physical (perhaps illogical?) elements that should not be left out of our risk management considerations!

- *Administrative elements* are the policies, procedures, training, and expectations that we spell out for the humans in the organization to follow. These are typically the first level at which legal and regulatory constraints or directives become a part of the way the organization functions.

- *Logical elements* (sometimes called *technical elements*) are the software, firmware, database, or other control systems settings that you use to make the physical elements of the organization's IT systems obey the dictates and meet the needs of the administrative ones

We no doubt used a top-down systems engineering approach when we designed our business, our business logic and its processes, and its IT infrastructures; let's apply the same process to designing the defense of those layers of systems and functions. In doing so, let's borrow a page or two from our history books and notice what the number one critical failing of most defenses (layered or not) turns out to be.

Classical "defense-in-depth" thinking (that is, old-fashioned ideas that probably don't work anymore) taught that each layer protected what was inside from what was outside. Oftentimes it was not very successful at defending against the threats from within—such as a trusted insider who had revealed to outsiders information about critical weaknesses in that defense, or a saboteur who had created such an exploitable weakness for an outside attacking force to take advantage of. More to the point, the classical approach *was* point by point; it looked at a specific weakness, chose a control and applied it, and in doing so often ignored a system-level need for integrated awareness, command, and control. We might say that a current defense-in-depth system is "classical" to the degree it implemented point-wise due care but failed to look at system-level due diligence needs.

This lack of systems thinking encourages three critical failures on our part. We're far too willing to ignore "blind spots" in our defenses; to blindly trust in our systems, processes, and people; and then *not check up on them* to see if they're actually working correctly. This three-part peril is what kills most classical defense-in-depth approaches.

## Trust, but Verify

In everyday life, we have many tactics, techniques, and procedures for keeping ourselves and those we care for safe and sound. We make sure our homes have proper smoke alarms in them; we have doors and windows we can lock. We trust in these components and even in the overall design of our home and the emergency response systems in our neighborhoods to take care of us. But how often do we *verify* that this trust is well placed? Do we check the batteries in the smoke alarms, or check that all of the windows and doors are secured before we go to bed each night? Do we have our family do "fire drills" to make sure that each family member knows what to do if and when the alarms go off?

This might lead you to think that the weakest link in any proactive, integrated defense system is actually the one you haven't recently verified is still working properly—and you'd be right to think so! Our organizations will develop requirements for information security, and as SSCPs we'll do our part to use those requirements to build in features and procedures to keep our systems safe. Those requirements must include how we plan to verify that what we built, installed, and trained people to use is actually doing the job we trust it to do. That verification is not just done at "acceptance testing" time, when we turn the systems over to the users; it must be continuous. Chapter 4, "Operationalizing Risk Mitigation," will delve into this topic in greater depth and show you how to design and carry out both acceptance testing and ongoing monitoring and assessment activities.

## Due Care and Due Diligence: Whose Jobs Are These?

This is a very important question! Legally, the doctrines of due care and due diligence provide a powerful framework in which to view how organizations, their leaders and managers, their stakeholders, and all of their employees or members have to deal with the total set of responsibilities they have agreed to fulfill. Due care and due diligence are two burdens that you willingly take on as you step into a leadership, managerial, or other responsible role in an organization. And a piece of these burdens flows down to each member of that organization, and that includes customers, suppliers, or other outsiders who deal with it.

What does it mean, in a business sense, to fulfill your responsibilities? Suppose you want to open a retail business. You go to friends or family and ask them to invest money or other resources in your business. When you accept those investments, you and your investors agree that you will use them prudently, properly, legally, and effectively to set up and operate the business to achieve the goals you've agreed to with the investors.

You take *due care* of those responsibilities, and your investors' expectations and investments, when you set up the business, its business logic and processes, and all of its facilities, equipment, people, and supplies so that it can operate. The burden of due care requires you not only to use common sense, but also to use best practices that are widely known in the marketplace or the domain of your business. Since these represent the lessons learned through the successes or failures of others, you are being careful when you consider these; you are perhaps acting recklessly when you ignore them.

As a business leader, owner, or stakeholder, you exercise *due diligence* by inspecting, auditing, monitoring, and otherwise ensuring that the business processes, people, and systems are working correctly and effectively. This means you must check that those processes and people are doing what they were set up to do and that they are performing these tasks correctly. More than that, you must also verify that they are achieving their share of the business's goals and objectives in efficient and effective ways—in the best ways possible, in fact!

Everybody in the organization has a piece of the due care and due diligence burden to carry—including the customers! Consider your relationship with your bank; you would be careless indeed if you never checked your bank balance or looked at transactions (online or on a periodic statement) and verified that each one was legitimate. In fact, under many banking laws, if the customer fails to provide timely notice to the bank of a possible fraudulent transaction, this can relieve the bank of its responsibilities to resolve it (and to reimburse the customer for any loss they suffered).

Because the concepts of due care and due diligence first developed in business communities, we often think that this means that government officials somehow do not have these same burdens of responsibilities, either in law or in practice. This is not true! It is beyond the scope of this book to go into this further, but as an SSCP, you do need to be aware that everyone has a share of these burdens. By being willing to be a certified professional, you step up and accept the burden of due care by pledging to do the best job possible in designing, building, operating, and maintaining information security systems. You accept the burden of due diligence by accepting the need to ensure that such systems continue to work effectively, correctly, and efficiently, by means of monitoring their actions, analyzing the log data they produce, and keeping the organization's leadership and management properly informed.

## Be Prepared: First, Set Priorities

Preparedness means we have to assume that some attackers will win through to their targets and that some damage will happen. Even for natural threats, such as earthquakes or hurricanes, all it takes is one "perfect storm" to wipe out our business completely—if we are not prepared for it. So how do we limit our risk—that is, not keep all of our eggs in one basket to be smashed by a single hazardous event? How do we contain it, perhaps by isolating damage so that a fire in one building does not spread to others?

We should always start with a *current* set of priorities for our goals and objectives. Many organizations (and most human beings!) do the things they do and have the things they have because of decisions that they made quite some time ago. "We've always done it this way," or "It's always been my dream to own a big house on the beach" may have *been* our goals; the question is, are these *still* our most important goals today?

By focusing on today's priorities, we can often find tasks we are doing that no longer matter. Sometimes the hardest question for people or organizations to answer is, "Why are we doing this particular business *process*?" In large, established organizations, history and momentum have a lot to do with how business gets done; "We've always done it this way" can actually be a *good* practice, when you can be sure that the process in question is the best way to reach your organization's *goal* or target outcome. But market conditions change, technologies evolve, people grow and learn, and more often than not, processes become outmoded, unproductive, or otherwise obsolete.

Even our sense of the threats we face, or the vulnerabilities inherent to who we are (as a business) or what we do, are subject to change.

Thus, the first step in defense is to know yourself (as an individual or as a business) *right now*. Know who and what you want to become. Prioritize what it takes to achieve *today's* plan and not fall back on yesterday's strategies. On the basis of that knowledge, look at what you need, what you have to do, and what obstacles or threats have to be faced today and in the near term—and if outcomes, objectives, processes, or assets you currently have don't serve those priorities, then those are probably not worthy of extensive efforts to mitigate risks against them.

# Risk Management: Concepts and Frameworks

Recall that a *risk management framework* is a set of concepts, tools, processes, and techniques that help organize information about risk. As you've no doubt started to see, the job of managing risks to your information is a set of many jobs, layered together. More than that, it's a set of jobs that changes and evolves with time as the organization, its mission, and the threats it faces evolve.

Let's start by taking a quick look at NIST Special Publication 800-37, Risk Management Framework (RMF) for Information Systems and Organizations: A System Life Cycle Approach for Security and Privacy. In its May 2018 draft updated form, this RMF establishes a broad, overarching perspective on what it calls the fundamentals of information systems risk management. Organizational leadership and management must address these areas of concern, shown conceptually in Figure 3.4:

1. Organization-wide risk management
2. Information security and privacy
3. System and system elements
4. Control allocation
5. Security and privacy posture
6. Supply chain risk management

You can see that there's an expressed top-down priority or sequence here. It makes little sense to worry about your IT supply chain (which might be a source of malware-infested hardware, software, and services) if leadership and stakeholders have not first come to consensus about risks and risk management at the broader, strategic level. (You should also note that in NIST's eyes, the big-to-little picture goes from strategic, to operational, to tactical, which is how many in government and the military think of these levels. Business around the world, though, sees it as strategic, to tactical, to day-to-day operations.)

**FIGURE 3.4**   NIST RMF areas of concern

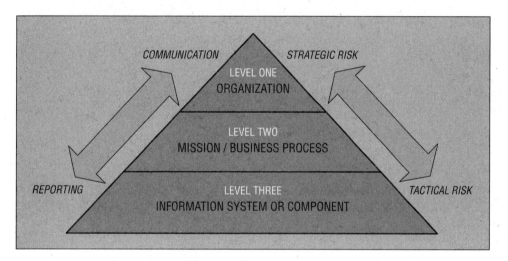

The RMF goes on by specifying seven major phases (which it calls *steps*) of activities for information risk management:

1. Prepare

2. Categorize

3. Select

4. Implement

5. Assess

6. Authorize

7. Monitor

It is tempting to think of these as step-by-step sets of activities—for example, once all risks have been categorized, you then start selecting which are the most urgent and compelling to make mitigation decisions about. Real-world experience shows, though, that each step in the process reveals things that may challenge the assumptions we just finished making, causing us to reevaluate what we thought we knew or decided in that previous step. It is perhaps more useful to think of these steps as overlapping sets of attitudes and outlooks that frame and guide how overlapping sets of people within the organization do the data gathering, inspection, analysis, problem solving, and implementation of the chosen risk controls. Figure 3.5 shows that there's a continual ebb and flow of information, insight, and decision between and across all elements of these "steps."

**FIGURE 3.5**    NIST RMF phased approach

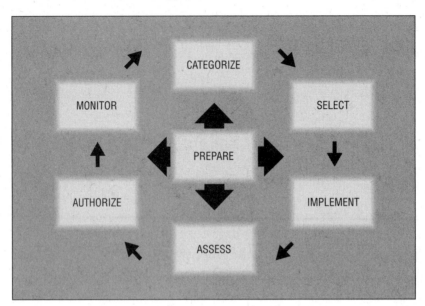

Although NIST publications are directive in nature for U.S. government systems, and indirectly provide strong guidance to the IT security market in the United States and elsewhere, many other information risk management frameworks are in widespread use around the world. For example, the International Organization for Standardization publishes ISO Standard 31000:2018, Risk Management Guidelines, in which the same concepts are arranged in slightly different fashion. First, it suggests that three main tasks must be done (and in broad terms, done in the order shown):

1. Scope, Context, Criteria
2. Risk Assessment, consisting of Risk Identification, Risk Analysis, and Risk Evaluation
3. Risk Treatment

   Three additional, broader functions support or surround these central risk mitigation tasks:
4. Recording and Reporting
5. Monitoring and Review
6. Communication and Consultation

As you can see in Figure 3.6, the ISO RMF also conveys a sense that on the one hand, there is a sequence of major activities, but on the other hand, these major steps or phases are closely overlapping.

**FIGURE 3.6** ISO 31000:2018 Conceptual RMF

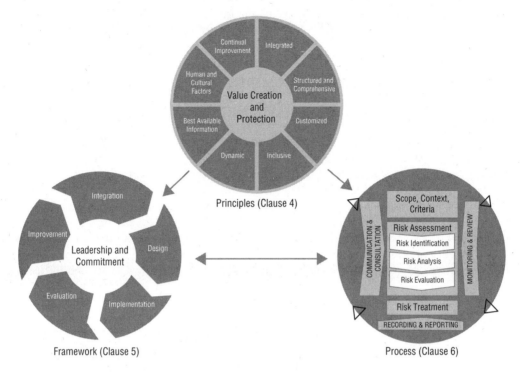

Principles (Clause 4)

Framework (Clause 5)

Process (Clause 6)

It's wise to bear in mind that each major section of these RMFs gives rise to more detailed guidance, instructions, and "lessons learned" advice. For example, NIST Special Publication 800-61 Rev. 2, Computer Security Incident Handling Guide, looks more in-depth at what happens when an information risk actually occurs and becomes an incident. Its phases of Preparation, Detection, Analysis, Containment, Eradication, Recovery, and Post-Incident Activities parallel those found in the RMF, which looks at the larger picture of information risk management. We'll explore these in greater detail in Chapter 10, "Incident Response and Recovery."

# The SSCP and Risk Management

As an SSCP, you'll have two major opportunities to help your organization or your business keep its information and information systems safe, secure, and reliable, as these risk management frameworks suggest. At one level, you'll be working as a technical specialist to help implement information risk controls. You'll be doing the day-to-day operational tasks that treat risk, ensuring that the chosen risk treatment procedures are delivering the required level of safety and security; you'll also be part of the team that responds when risk treatments fail. As you continue to grow in your profession and gain experience and insight, you'll be able to offer technical insight and informed opinion to your managers. It's important, then, to see how the technical, operational details that deliver information security and decision assurance, day by day, fit within the context of the management decisions that create the risk management plans that you and others carry out.

For the SSCP exam, you'll need to have a broad awareness of the existence of standards such as these, but you won't need to be conversant with their details. You will, however, need to be able to keep track of the context the question or issue comes up in, and be able to recognize when to shift your thinking from bigger-picture "information risk management" to more detailed, finer-grain "information security incident response" and back again.

To help you in that shift of thinking, we'll split the managerial and leadership portions of risk management and mitigation off from the technical, operational, and administrative where it makes sense. The rest of this chapter, for example, will show how SSCPs support leadership and management as they prepare the organization to manage its risks, perform its information risk assessments, and use them to develop the business impact analysis (BIA). An effective BIA provides a solid transition from understanding the risks to mitigating them. We will briefly outline the remaining steps, but use Chapter 4 to get into the technical, administrative, and operational details of risk mitigation.

We'll also translate the somewhat bureaucratic language that is used in the NIST RMF, and in ISO 31000:2018, into the sort of terms you're more likely to hear and use within the workplace.

So let's get started!

## Plan, Do, Check, Act

The Project Management Institute and many other organizations talk about the basic cycle of making decisions, taking steps to carry out those decisions, monitoring and assessing the outcomes, and taking further actions to correct what's not working and strengthen or improve what is.

One important idea to keep in mind is that these cycles of Plan, Do, Check, Act (PDCA) don't just happen one time—they repeat, they chain together in branches and sequels, and they nest one inside the other, as you can see in Figure 3.7. Note too that planning is a forward-looking, predictive, thoughtful, and deliberate process. We plan our next vacation *before* we put in for leave or make hotel and travel arrangements; we plan how to deal with a major disruption due to bad weather *before* the tornado season starts!

The SSCP applies this framework at the daily operational level. What must you accomplish today? How will you do it? What will you need? Then, *do* those tasks. Check to see if you did them correctly *and* that you got the desired outcomes as a result. If not, take corrective action if you can, or seek help and guidance if you cannot.

**FIGURE 3.7**    PDCA cycle diagram (simple), with subcycles

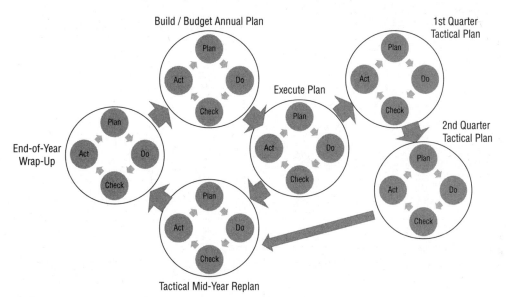

We'll see this PDCA cycle in action here as we look at risk assessment and the decisions that come from it; Chapter 4 will then show PDCA in action as we look at ways to mitigate selected risks. Let's take a closer look at these four steps:

- *Planning* is the process of laying out the step-by-step path we need to take to go from "where we are" to "where we want to be." It's a natural human activity; we do this every moment of our lives. Our most potent tools for planning are what Kipling called his "six honest men"—asking what, why, when, how, where, and who of almost everything we are confronted with and every decision we have to make. As an SSCP, you need those six honest teammates with you at all times!

- *Doing* encompasses everything it takes to accomplish the plan. From the decisions to "execute the plan" on through all levels of action, this phase is where we see people using new or different business processes to achieve what the plan needs to accomplish, using the steps the plan asks for.

- *Checking* is part of conducting due diligence on what the plan asked us to achieve and how it asked us to get it done. We check that tasks are getting done, on time, to specification; we check that errors or exceptions are being handled correctly. And of course, we gather this feedback data and make it available for further analysis, process improvement, and leadership decision making.

- *Acting* involves making decisions and taking *corrective* or *amplifying* actions based on what the *checking* activities revealed. In this phase, leaders and managers may agree that a revised plan is needed, or that the existing plan is working fine but some individual processes need some fine-tuning to achieve better results.

As with many theoretical or "school-house" models, PDCA looks simple in concept and suggests clean, well-defined breakpoints between each of its four elements. In reality, these four steps flow into and out of one another; sometimes checking will lead right back to some "modified doing," or the day-to-day urgencies may dictate that we "get doing" before the planning is done or the checking of the actions we took based on the last version of the plan! For you as an SSCP, it's important to recognize these separate "thought models" for dealing with situations and to recognize when you might be *doing* when you haven't actually *planned* what to do—which would, after all, be somewhat risky behavior in itself.

# Risk Assessment

Risk assessment is a systematic process of identifying risks to achieving organizational priorities. There are many published handbooks, templates, and processes for doing risk assessment, and they all have several key elements that you should not lose sight of while trying to implement the chosen framework of the day.

At the heart of a risk assessment process must be the organizational goals and objectives, suitably prioritized. Typically, the highest priorities are *existential* ones—ones that relate to the continued existence and health of the organization. These often involve significant threats to continued operation or significant and strategic opportunities for growth. Other priorities may be vitally important in the near term, but other options may be available if the chosen favorite fails to be successful. The "merely nice to have" objectives may fall lower in the risk assessment process. This continual reevaluation of priorities allows the risk assessment team to focus on the most important, most compelling risks first.

The next major element of risk assessment is to thoroughly examine and evaluate the processes, assets, systems, information, and other elements of the organization as they relate to or support achieving these prioritized goals and objectives. This linkage of "what" and "how" with "why" helps narrow the search for system elements or process steps that, if they fail or are vulnerable to exploitation, could put these goals in jeopardy.

Most risk assessment processes typically summarize their findings in some form of BIA. This relates costs (in money, time, and resources) to the organization that *could* be faced if the risk events do occur. It also takes each risk and assesses how frequently it might occur. The *expected cost* of these risks (their costs multiplied by their frequencies and probabilities of occurrences, across the organization) represents the anticipated financial impact of that risk, over time; this is a key input to making risk mitigation or control choices.

Let's see what it takes to put this kind of risk assessment process and thinking into action.

## Establish Consensus about Information Risk

Preparing the organization to *manage* its information risk requires that senior leadership, key stakeholders, and others develop and establish key working relationships and processes that focus on risk management in general and on information risk management in particular. These key individuals will need to focus attention on the relationships between organizational priorities on the one hand, and the business processes and information systems that have been built and are being used to meet those priorities on the other. This consensus should align resource allocations with those priorities.

A critical task during this first step is ensuring a common understanding of the organization's context and culture. Doing so involves reaching a consensus on *risk appetite*, or the willingness of the organization to accept risk, and on how leadership make decisions about risk. (This is sometimes referred to as the organization's *risk tolerance*.) It is also important at this point to understand how the organization controls changes to its business processes and systems, particularly to its information technology systems.

We also begin to see at this point that the organization might have a bias, or a customary way of considering risk—that is, does it view risk in terms of outcomes, processes, assets, or threats? Asset-focused risk thinkers, for example, will probably drive the organization to build its risk assessments (and its BIA) in terms of asset values and damages to those assets. Threat-based thinkers, by contrast, may try to drive the assessment conversation more in the direction of threat modeling. The key is that *all perspectives* have something of value to contribute at this stage; the wiser organizations will use outcomes, processes, assets, and threats as the points to ponder as they perform their information risk assessments. No one "face of risk" is the most correct.

Risk management frameworks such as NIST SP 800-37 and ISO 31000:2018 provide top-down guidance to organizations in setting the organizational attitude and mindset in ways that support building this consensus. These RMFs also provide specific recommendations, often in step-by-step fashion, that organizations large and small can learn from. NIST SP 800-37 calls this step "Prepare" as a way to emphasize how important it is to establish a common ground of understanding within the organization. The "movers and shakers" who drive the business forward have to agree, and they have to speak with a common set of words and meanings when they engage with the people who will actually do the hard work of managing and mitigating information risk. ISO 31000:2018 perhaps says this more clearly by focusing on the key *outcomes* of this step. First, we agree to where the boundaries are—what do we own and operate, and what do we count on outsiders to do on our behalf? Next, we look at context; finally, we must agree to our thresholds for accepting risk or our willingness to pay to mitigate it.

The SSCP exam does not go into either RMF in great detail; nor, for that matter, would an SSCP be expected to have in-depth expertise on applying part of an RMF on the job. That said, these RMFs can help the SSCP recognize the context that their day-to-day operational duties support—and maybe help them in spotting when there are weak spots in the organization's overall information risk management approach.

## Information Risk Impact Assessment

What happens when an organization's information is lost, compromised by disclosure to unauthorized parties, or corrupted? These questions (which reflect the CIA triad) indicate what the organization stands to *lose* if such a breach of information security happens. Let's illustrate with a few examples:

**Personally identifying information (PII)**   Loss or compromise can cause customers to take their business elsewhere and can lead to criminal and civil penalties for the organization and its owners, stakeholders, leaders, and employees.

**Company financial data, and price and cost information**   Loss or compromise can lead to loss of business, to investors withdrawing their funds, or to loss of business opportunities as vendors and partners go elsewhere. Can also result in civil and criminal penalties.

**Details about internal business processes**   Loss could lead to failures of business processes to function correctly; compromise could lead to loss of competitive advantage, as others in the marketplace learn how to do your business better.

**Risk management information**   Loss or compromise could lead to insurance policies being canceled or premiums being increased, as insurers conclude that the organization cannot adequately fulfill its *due diligence* responsibilities.

When we view information in such terms—as "What does it cost us if we lose it?"—we decide how vital the information is to us. What this categorization or classification really does is tell us *how important it is to protect that information, based on possible loss or impact.* We categorize our possible losses, in terms of severity of damage, impact, or costs; we also categorize them in terms of outcomes, processes, and assets they have or depend on. Finally, we categorize them by threat or common vulnerabilities. This kind of risk analysis can help us identify critical locations, elements, or objectives that could be putting the entire organization at risk; in doing so, that focuses our risk analysis further.

Risk analysis is a complex undertaking and often involves trying to sort out what can cause a risk to become an incident. *Root cause analysis* looks to find what the underlying vulnerability or mechanism of failure is that leads to the incident, for example. By contrast, *proximate cause analysis* asks, "What was the last thing that happened that caused the risk to occur?" (This is sometimes called the "last clear opportunity to prevent" the incident, a term that insurance underwriters and their lawyers often use.) Our earlier example of backing your car out of the driveway, only to run over a child's bicycle left in the wrong place, illustrates these ideas. You could have looked first, maybe even walked around the car before you got in and started to drive; you had the last clear opportunity to prevent damage, and thus your actions were the proximate cause. (You failed in your due diligence, in other words.) Your child, however, is the one who left the bicycle in the wrong place; the root of the problem may be the failure to help your child learn and appreciate what his responsibility of due care for his bicycle requires. And who was responsible for teaching due care to your child? (A word of advice: don't say "My spouse.")

We've looked at a number of examples of risks becoming incidents; for each, we've identified an *outcome* that describes what might happen (customers go to our competitors; we must get our car and the bicycle repaired). Outcomes are part of the *basis of estimate* with which we can make two kinds of *risk assessments*: quantitative and qualitative.

## Quantitative Risk Assessment: Risk by the Numbers

*Quantitative assessments* use simple techniques (like counting possible occurrences, or estimating how often they might occur) along with estimates of the typical cost of each loss:

- *Single loss expectancy (SLE)*: Usually measured in monetary terms, SLE is the total cost you can reasonably expect should the risk event occur. It includes immediate and delayed costs, direct and indirect costs, costs of repairs, and restoration. In some circumstances, it also includes lost opportunity costs, or lost revenues due to customers needing or choosing to go elsewhere.

- *Annual rate of occurrence (ARO)*: ARO is an estimate of how often during a single year this event could reasonably be expected to occur.

- *Annual loss expectancy (ALE)*: ALE is the total expected losses for a given year and is determined by multiplying the SLE by the ARO.

- *Safeguard value*: This is the estimated cost to implement and operate the chosen risk mitigation control. You cannot know this until you've chosen a risk control or countermeasure and an implementation plan for it; we'll cover that in the next chapter.

Other numbers associated with risk assessment relate to how the business or organization deals with time when its systems, processes, and people are not available to do business. This "downtime" can often be expressed as a mean (or average) allowable downtime, or a maximum downtime. Times to repair or restore minimum functionality, and times to get everything back to normal, are also some of the numbers the SSCP will need to deal with. For example:

- The *maximum acceptable outage (MAO)* is the maximum time that a business process or task cannot be performed without causing intolerable disruption or damage to the business. Sometimes referred to as the *maximum tolerable outage (MTO)*, or the *maximum tolerable period of disruption (MTPOD)*, determining this maximum outage time starts with first identifying *mission-critical outcomes*. These outcomes, by definition, are vital to the ongoing success (and survival!) of the organization; thus, the processes, resources, systems, and no doubt people they require to properly function become *mission-critical resources*. If only *one* element of a mission-critical process is unavailable, and no immediate substitute or workaround is at hand, then the MAO clock starts ticking.

- The *mean time to repair (MTTR)*, or *mean time to restore*, reflects our average experience in doing whatever it takes to get the failed system, component, or process repaired or replaced. The MTTR must include time to get suitable staff on scene who can diagnose the failure, identify the right repair or restoration needed, and draw from parts or replacement components on hand to effect repairs. MTTR calculations should also include time to verify that the repair has been done correctly *and that the repaired system works correctly*. This last requirement is very important—it does no good at all to swap out parts and say that something is fixed if you cannot assure management and users that the repaired system is now working the way it needs to in order to fulfill mission requirements.

These types of quantitative assessments help the organization understand what a risk can do when it actually happens (becomes an incident) and what it will take to get back to normal operations and clean up the mess it caused. One more important question remains: *how long to repair and restore is too long?* Two more "magic numbers" shed light on this question:

- The *recovery time objective (RTO)* is the amount of time in which system functionality or ability to perform the business process must be back in operation. Note that the RTO must be less than or equal to the MAO (if not, there's an error in somebody's thinking). As an *objective*, RTO asks systems designers, builders, maintainers, and operators to strive for a better, faster result. But be careful what you ask for; demanding too rapid an RTO can cause more harm than it deflects by driving the organization to spend far more than makes bottom-line sense.

- The *recovery point objective (RPO)* measures the *data loss* that is tolerable to the organization, typically expressed in terms of how much data needs to be loaded from backup systems in order to bring the operational system back up to where it needs to be. For example, an airline ticketing and reservations system takes every customer request as a transaction, copies the transactions into log files, and processes the transactions (which causes updates to its databases). Once that's done, the transaction is considered completed. If the database is backed up in its entirety once a week, let's say, then if the database crashes five days after the last backup, that backup is reloaded and then five days' worth of transactions must be reapplied to the database to bring it up to where customers, aircrew, airport staff, and airplanes expect it to be. Careful consideration of an RPO allows the organization to balance costs of routine backups with time spent reapplying transactions to get back into business.

We'll go into these numbers (and others) in greater depth in Chapter 10 as you learn how to help your organization plan for and manage its response to actual information security and assurance incidents. It's important that you realize that these numbers play three critical roles in your integrated, proactive information defense efforts. All of these quantitative assessments (plus the qualitative ones as well) help you achieve the following:

- Establish the "pain points" that lead to information security requirements that can be measured, assessed, implemented, and verified.

- Shape and guide the organization's thinking about risk mitigation control strategies, tactics, and operations, and keep this thinking within cost-effective bounds.

- Dictate key business continuity planning needs and drive the way incident response activities must be planned, managed, and performed.

One final thought about the "magic numbers" is worth considering. The organization's leadership have their stakeholders' personal and professional fortunes and futures in their hands. Exercising due diligence *requires* that management and leadership be able to show, by the numbers, that they've fulfilled that obligation and brought it back from the brink of irreparable harm when disaster strikes. Those stakeholders—the organization's investors, customers, neighbors, and workers—need to trust in the leadership and management team's ability to meet the bottom line every day. Solid, well-substantiated numbers like these help the stakeholders trust, but verify, that their team is doing their job.

## Calculating Quantitative Risks for a Small Business

Jayne owns a small 3D-printing facility that provides custom parts for various design and engineering firms. She deals with customers across the nation via the Internet. Her business is located in an earthquake zone, and a sufficiently strong earthquake could devastate her facility and damage or destroy her 3D-printing machines. It would cost up to $500,000 to replace her facility or to rebuild it in a new location after such a disaster. It could take six months to get new equipment installed in a new or repaired facility and get back in business. This could lead to a loss of $200,000 in revenues. Official government estimates suggest that such a devastating earthquake might happen once every 50 years. Jayne needs to appreciate how much she stands to lose if such an earthquake strikes her business.

First, how much does she expect to lose altogether if such an earthquake occurs? This is her *single loss expectancy*, which is the sum of all costs she incurs plus all lost business revenues because of the earthquake. This is calculated as follows:

> Single loss expectancy = (replacement costs) + (lost revenue)
> SLE = $500,000 + $200,000 = $700,000

Next, let's look at how often Jayne might expect or anticipate such a loss to occur. For natural events such as earthquakes or storms, governments usually publish data about expected rates of occurrence. In Jayne's case, the published annual rate of occurrence for such an earthquake is once in each 50-year period; we must normalize that to show number of occurrences anticipated in any single year:

> ARO = (number of occurrences) / (number of years)
> ARO = 1/50 = 0.02

Now Jayne wants to know how much of a loss, in any given year, she can anticipate because of such a major earthquake. She gets this annual loss expectancy (ALE) by simply multiplying the loss on a single event by the probability of that event occurring in any given year:

> Annual loss expectancy = SLE * ARO
> ALO = $700,000 * 0.02 = $14,000

One possible risk mitigation strategy would be to sign a "warm standby" agreement with another 3D-printing firm, one using similar equipment and software systems but located away from the earthquake-prone area where Jayne's business is located. The safeguard value here might be minimal (the costs of negotiating the agreement); it could also lead to Jayne having an inexpensive "surge" capacity for her business. But she now has to worry if the warm standby provider will actually be there in case of an earthquake and be able to meet her customers' needs on time.

*(continued)*

---

*(continued)*

Jayne also has to worry about electrical power outages due to storms; 3D printing is spoiled if power is lost any time during the print-and-cure operation cycle, making the product unusable. Typically about four hours of lost time is involved to clean up the printers and reset them to restart the spoiled job. The costs of scrapping the current print job, cleaning up, and resetting can reach about $250 in materials and staff time. Her production schedule normally provides sufficient slack time for one rework cycle per customer job, so she hasn't lost revenues because of such outages (yet!). During the business day, Jayne has noticed that such storms cause power outages about four times per month during the rainy season, which lasts three months; in other months she's experienced no power outages. How would Jayne assess this risk in terms of expected impacts to her business?

SLE = _____ + _____

ARO = _____ / _____

ALE = _____ * _____

With a single loss expectancy of $250, and an annual loss rate of 12 times per year (four times per month during three rainy months), Jayne can expect up to $3,000 in annual losses due to weather-induced electrical power interruptions. Common sense might suggest that an uninterruptible power supply might be a prudent investment!

---

## Qualitative Risk Assessment

*Qualitative assessments* focus on an inherent quality, aspect, or characteristic of the risk as it relates to the outcome(s) of a risk occurrence. "Loss of business" could be losing a few customers, losing many customers, or closing the doors and going out of business entirely!

So, which assessment strategy works best? The answer is *both*. Some risk situations may present us with things we can count, measure, or make educated guesses about in numerical terms, but many do not. Some situations clearly identify *existential threats* to the organization (the occurrence of the threat puts the organization completely out of business); again, many situations are not as clear-cut. Senior leadership and organizational stakeholders find both qualitative and quantitative assessments useful and revealing.

Qualitative assessment of information is most often used as the basis of an *information classification system*, which labels broad categories of data to indicate the range of possible harm or impact. Most of us are familiar with such systems through their use by military and national security communities. Such simple hierarchical information classification systems often start with "Unclassified" and move up through "For Official Use Only," "Confidential," "Secret," and "Top Secret" as their way of broadly outlining how severely the nation would be impacted if the information was disclosed, stolen, or otherwise compromised. Yet even these cannot stay simple for long.

Businesses, private organizations, and the military have another aspect of data categorization in common: the concept of *need to know*. Need to know limits who has access to read, use, or modify data based on whether their job functions require them to do so. Thus, a school's purchasing department staff have a need to know about suppliers, prices, specific purchases, and so forth, but they do not need to know any of the PII pertaining to students, faculty, or other staff members. Need-to-know leads to *compartmentalization of information* approaches, which create procedural boundaries (administrative controls) around such sets of information. (We'll discuss this more in Chapter 6, "Identity and Access Control.")

## The Risk Register

At this point, the organization or business needs to be building a *risk register*, a central repository or knowledge bank of the risks that have been identified in its business and business process systems. This register should be a living document, constantly refreshed as the company moves from risk identification through mitigation to the "new normal" of operations after instituting risk controls or countermeasures.

As an internal document, a company's risk register is a compendium of its weaknesses and should be considered as closely held, confidential, proprietary business information. It provides a would-be attacker, competitors, or a disgruntled employee with powerful insight into ways that the company might be vulnerable to attacks. This need to protect the confidentiality of the risk register becomes even more acute as the risk register is updated from first-level outcomes or process-based identification through impact assessments, and then linked (as you'll see in the next chapter, "Operationalizing Risk Mitigation") with systems vulnerability or root cause/proximate cause assessments.

There is no one agreed or best format or structure for a risk register, although many vendors provide platforms and systems to assist businesses in organizing all of their risk management information and processes. These details are beyond the scope of the SSCP exam, but you'll need to be aware of the role that a risk register should play in planning and conducting information risk management efforts.

## Common Vulnerabilities

Many nations conduct or sponsor efforts to collect and publish information about system vulnerabilities that are commonly found in commercial-off-the-shelf (COTS) IT systems and elements or that result from common design or system production weaknesses. In the United States, the Mitre Corporation maintains its database of Common Vulnerabilities and Exposures (or CVE) information as a public service. Mitre is one of several federally funded research and development corporations (FFRDCs) that research science and technology topics in the national interest; many of its findings are made available as published reports or databases. Mitre operates the National Cybersecurity FFRDC (NCF), which as of this writing is the only federally funded research center for cybersecurity and vulnerability assessment. Its website, https://cve.mitre.org/, has a rich set of information and resources that SSCPs should become familiar with. In the United States, the National Institute of Standards and Technologies (NIST) operates the National Vulnerability Database, https://nvd.nist.gov/; in the United Kingdom, these roles are provided by the Government Communications Headquarters (GCHQ, which is roughly equivalent to the U.S. National Security Agency), which you can find at its National Cyber Security Centre at www.ncsc.gov.uk.

## The Business Impact Analysis

The business impact analysis (BIA) is where the rubber hits the road, so to speak. Risk management must be a balance of priorities, resources, probabilities, and impacts, as you've seen throughout this chapter. All this comes together in the BIA. As its name implies, the BIA is a consolidated statement of how different risks could impact the prioritized goals and objectives of an organization.

The BIA reflects a combination of due care and due diligence in that it combines "how we do business" with "how we know how well we're doing it."

There is no one right, best format for a BIA; instead, each organization must determine what its BIA needs to capture and how it has to present it to achieve a mix of purposes:

- BIAs should inform, guide, and shape risk management decisions by senior leadership.

- BIAs should provide the insight to choose a balanced, prudent mix of risk mitigation tactics and techniques.

- BIAs should guide the organization in accepting residual risk to goals, objectives, processes, or assets in areas where this is appropriate.

- BIAs may be required to meet external stakeholder needs, such as for insurance, financial, regulatory, or other compliance purposes.

You must recognize one more important requirement at this point: to be effective, a BIA must be *kept up to date*. The BIA must reflect today's set of concerns, priorities, assets, and processes; it must reflect today's understanding of threats and vulnerabilities. Outdated information in a BIA could at best lead to wasted expenditures and efforts on risk mitigation; at worst, it could lead to failures to mitigate, prevent, or contain risks that could lead to serious damage, injury, or death, or possibly put the organization out of business completely.

At its heart, making a BIA is pretty simple: you identify what's important, estimate how often it might fail, and estimate the costs to you of those failures. You then rank those possible impacts in terms of which basis for risk best suits your organization, be that outcomes, processes, assets, or vulnerabilities. For all but the simplest and smallest of organizations, however, the amount of information that has to be gathered, analyzed, organized, assessed, and then brought together in the BIA can be overwhelming. The BIA is one of the most critical steps in the information risk management process, end to end; it's also perhaps the most iterative, the most open to reconsideration as things change, and the most in need of being kept alive, current, and useful. Most of that is well beyond the scope of the SSCP examination, and so we won't go into the mechanics of the business impact analysis process in any further detail. As an SSCP, however, you'll be expected to continue to grow your knowledge and skills, thus becoming a valued contributor to your organization's BIA.

## From Assessments to Information Security Requirements

Two sets of information provide a rich source of information security requirements for an organization. The first is the legal, regulatory, and cultural context in which the organization must exist. As stated before, failure to fulfill these obligations can put the organization out of existence, and its leaders, owners, stakeholders (and even its employees) at risk of civil or criminal prosecution. The second set of information that should drive the synthesis of information security requirements is the organization's BIA.

There are typically two major ways that information security requirements take form or are expressed or stated within an organization. The first is to write a system requirements specification (SRS), which is a formal document used to capture high-level statements of function, purpose, and intent. An SRS also contains important system-level constraints. It guides or directs analysts and developers as they design, build, test, deploy, and maintain an information; it also drives end-user training activities.

Organizations also write and implement policies and procedures that state what the information security requirements are and what the people in the organization need to do to fulfill them and comply with them:

- *Policies* are broad statements of direction and intention; in most organizations, they establish direction and provide constraints to leaders, managers, and the workforce. Policies direct or dictate what should be done, to what standards of compliance, who does it, and why they should do it. Policies are usually approved ("signed out") by senior leadership, and are used to guide, shape, direct, and evaluate the performance of the people who are affected by the policies; they are thus considered administrative in nature.

- *Procedures* take the broad statements expressed in policies and break them down into step-by-step detailed instructions to those people who are assigned responsibility to perform them. Procedures state how a task needs to be performed and should also state what constraints or success criteria apply. As instructions to people who perform these tasks, procedures are administrative in nature.

You might ask which should come first, the SRS or the policies and procedures. Once senior leadership agrees to a statement of need, it's probably faster to publish a policy and a new procedure than it is to write the SRS, design the system, test it, deliver it, and train users on the right ways to use it. But be careful! It often takes a *lot* of time and effort for the people in an organization to operationalize a new policy and the procedures that come with it. Overlooking this training hurdle can cause the new policy or procedures to fail.

---

### FERPA: From Law Through Policy to Requirements

In the United States, the Family Educational Rights and Privacy Act (FERPA) provides the legal requirements pertaining to the collection, storage, use, sharing, and disposal of individual educational records. Schools, training companies, and other organizations that must meet FERPA's requirements have to ensure that their people who have access to "FERPA-protected information" are trained to understand their legal responsibilities (their *due care* burdens). Records systems, whether automated or not, have to meet various access control standards and practices. FERPA-protected information cannot be disclosed to other persons or organizations except in specific circumstances as defined in law.

*(continued)*

*(continued)*

Suppose a school is converting its paper-based records system over to a cloud-hosted system using a platform-as-a-service (PAAS) approach. The "platform" would be a database product with built-in functions that implement student admission, registration, enrollment, grading, transcripts, attendance, or other functions. As the school shops around for such a PAAS provider, one key question the school should ask is, "How does your platform ensure FERPA compliance?" The school might also want to thoroughly understand how the PAAS provider will upload its paper records into the new system, and make sure that this process does not involve any opportunities for FERPA-protected information to "leak" outside of the hands of those who are trained to protect it.

In the meantime, the school needs to have written policies and procedures in place that dictate who can access the records (who has keys to the filing cabinets, for example), as well as who has to approve release of information from those records to someone who is not a FERPA-certified school official.

By the way, it's important to note that many other nations, as well as the European Union, have their own "FERPA-like" legal requirements. How might these impact a company that provides online educational resources, classes and support for home-study children who might live abroad?

# Four Choices for Limiting or Containing Damage

Four strategic choices exist when we think of how to protect prioritized assets, outcomes, or processes. These choices are at the strategic level, because just the nature of them is comparable to "life-or-death" choices for the organization. A strategic risk might force the company to choose between abandoning a market or opportunity and taking on a fundamental, gut-wrenching level of change throughout its ethics, culture, processes, or people, for example. We see such choices almost before we've started to think about what the alternatives might cost and what they might gain us. These strategic choices are often used in combination to achieve the desired level of assurance against risk. As an SSCP, you'll assist your organization in making these choices across strategic, tactical, and operational levels of planning, decision making, and actions that people and the organization must take. Note that each of these choices is a verb; these are things that you *do*, actions you perform. This is key to understanding which ones to choose and how to use them successfully. We'll look at each individually, and then take a closer look at how they combine and mutually reinforce each other to attain greater protective effect.

There are choices at the strategic and tactical level that seem quite similar and are often mistaken as identical. The best way to keep them separate in your mind might be as follows:

- If you've just completed the risk assessment and BIA, your strategic choices are about *operational risk mitigation planning* and which risks to deal with in other ways. This is the strategic choice (as you'll see) of deterring, detecting, preventing, or avoiding a risk altogether. Note that prevent, deter, and detect will probably involve choices of risk mitigation controls, but you cannot make those choices until after you've done the architectural and vulnerability assessments.

- If you've already done the architectural and vulnerability assessments, as we'll cover in Chapter 4, you're ready to start making hard *mitigation* choices for the risks you're not going to avoid altogether. These are *tactical* choices you'll be making, as they will dictate how, when, and to what degree of completeness you implement operational (day-to-day), functional choices in the ways you try to control risks.

Having identified the risks and prioritized them, what next? What realistic options exist? One (more!) thing to keep in mind is that as you delve into the details of your architecture, and find, characterize, and assess its vulnerabilities against the prioritized set of risks, you will probably find some risks you thought you could and should "fix" that prove far too costly or disruptive to attempt to do so. *That's okay.* Like any planning process, risk management and risk mitigation taken together are a living, breathing, dynamic set of activities. Let these assessments shed light on what you've already thought about, as well as what you haven't seen before.

---

### "Operational" or "Tactical" as the Day-to-Day?

What's the right way to look at this hierarchy of broad, longer-term to fine-grain day-to-day detail? The definitions we've given you reflect how the *business* community speaks about planning and conducting business operations, with the smallest of day-to-day tasks as operations. Another way to think of this is to say that *tactics* transform strategies into processes you can use day by day to *operate* the business. If you're familiar with military planning and operations, you'll note that almost without exception, the world's military thinkers, planners, and doctrine authors have flipped the roles of tactical and operational art and decision making. Operational art, for example, refers to the larger scale of maneuvering and positioning forces to achieve an objective, whereas tactics dictate how to train individual foot soldiers to lay down different patterns of small-arms fire in support of steps in that operational plan. Many agencies in the U.S. federal government, as well as those in Western Europe, also quite frequently talk tactics at the lowest level of this hierarchy of definitions.

"The customer is always right" is perhaps the key to keep in mind. Usually you can tell from the context; when in doubt, ask!

---

So what are these strategic choices?

# Deter

To *deter* means to discourage or dissuade someone from taking an action because of their fear or dislike of the possible consequences. Deterring an attacker means that you get them to change their mind and choose to do something else instead. Your actions and your posture convince the attacker that what they stand to gain by launching the attack will probably not be worth the costs to them in time, resources, or other damages they might suffer (especially if they are caught by law enforcement!). Your actions do this by working on the attacker's decision cycle. Why did they pick you as a target? What do they want to achieve? How probable is it that they can complete the attack and escape without being caught? What does it cost them to prepare for and conduct the attack? If you can cast sufficient doubt into the attacker's mind on one or more of these questions, you may erode their confidence; at some point, the attacker gives up and chooses not to go through with their contemplated or planned attack.

By its nature, deterrence is directed onto an active, willful threat actor. Try as you might, you cannot deter an accident, nor can you command the tides not to flood your datacenter. You do have, however, many different ways of getting into the attacker's decision cycle, demotivating them, and shaping their thinking so that they go elsewhere:

- Physical assets such as buildings (which probably contain or protect other kinds of assets) may have very secure and tamper-proof doors, windows, walls, or rooflines that prevent physical forced entry. Guard dogs, human guards or security patrols, fences, landscaping, and lighting can make it obvious that an attacker has very little chance to approach the building without being detected or prevented from carrying out their attack.

- Strong passwords and other access control technologies can make it visibly difficult for an attacker to hack into your computer systems (be they local or cloud-hosted).

- Policies and procedures can be used to train your people to make them less vulnerable to social-engineering attacks.

Deterrence can be passive, active, or a combination of the two. Fences, the design of parking, access roads and landscaping, and lighting tend to be passive deterrence measures; they don't take actions in response to the presence of an attacker, for example. Active measures give the defender the opportunity to create doubt in the attacker's mind: Is the guard looking my way? Is anybody watching those CCTV cameras?

# Detect

To *detect* means to notice or consciously observe that an event of interest is happening. Notice the built-in limitation here: you have to *first* decide what set of events to "be on the lookout for" and therefore which events you possibly need to make action decisions about in real time. While you're driving your car down a residential street, for example, you know you have to be watching for other cars, pedestrians, kids, dogs, and others darting out from between parked cars—but you normally would "tune out" watching the skies to see if an airplane was about to try to land on the street behind you. You also need to decide what to do about false alarms, both the false positives (that alarm when an event of interest hasn't occurred) and the false negatives (the absence of an alarm when an event is actually happening).

If you think of how many false alarms you hear every week from car alarms or residential burglar alarms in your neighborhood, you might ask why we bother to try to detect that an event of interest might possibly be happening. Fundamentally, you cannot respond to something if you do not know it is happening. Your response might be to prevent or disrupt the event, to limit or contain the damage being caused by it, or to call for help from emergency responders, law enforcement, or other response teams. You may also need to activate alternative operations plans so that your business is not severely disrupted by the event. Finally, you do need to know what actually happened so that you can decide what corrective actions (or remediation) to take—what you must do to repair what was damaged and to recover from the disruption the incident has caused.

## Prevent

To *prevent* an attack means to stop it from happening or, if it is already underway, to halt it in its tracks, thus limiting its damage. A thunderstorm might knock out your commercial electrical power (which is an *attack*, even if a nondeliberate one), but the uninterruptible power supplies keep your critical systems up and running. Heavy steel fire doors and multiple dead-bolt locks resist all but very determined attempts to cut, pry, or force an entry into your building. Strong access control policies and technologies prevent unauthorized users from logging into your computer systems. Fire-resistant construction of your home's walls and doors is designed to increase the time you and your family have to detect the fire and get out safely before the fire spreads from its source to where you're sleeping. (We in the computer trades owe the idea of a *firewall* to this pre-computer-era, centuries-old idea of keeping harm on one side of a barrier from spreading through to the other.)

Preventive defense measures provide two immediate paybacks to the defender: they limit or contain damage to that which you are defending, and they cost the attacker time and effort to get past them. Combination locks, for example, are often rated in terms of how long it would take someone to just "play with the dial" to guess the combination or somehow sense that they've started to make good guesses at it. Fireproof construction standards aim to prevent the fire from burning through (or initiating a fire inside the protected space through heat transfer) for a desired amount of time.

Note that we gain these benefits whether we are dealing with a natural, nonintentional threat, an accident, or a deliberate, intentional attack.

## Avoid

To *avoid* an attack means to change what you do, and how you do it, in such ways as to not be where your attacker is expecting you to be when they try to attack you. This can be a temporary change to your planned activities or a permanent change to your operations. In this way, you can reduce or eliminate the possible disruptions or damages of an attack from natural, accidental, or deliberate causes:

- Physically avoiding an attack might involve relocating part of your business or its assets to other locations, shutting down a location during times of extremely bad weather, or even closing a branch location that's in too dangerous a market or location.

- Logically avoiding an attack can be done by using cloud service providers to eliminate your business's dependence on a specific computer system or set of services in a particular place. At a smaller scale, you do this by making sure that the software, data, and communications systems allow your employees to get business done from any location or while traveling, without regard to where the data and software are hosted. Using a virtual private network (VPN) to mask your IP and Media Access Control (MAC) addresses is another example of using logical means to avoid the possible consequences of an attack on your IT infrastructure and information systems.

- A variety of administrative methods can be used, usually in conjunction with physical or logical ones such as those we've discussed. Typically they will be implemented in policies, procedural documents, and quite possibly contracts or other written agreements.

---

### Ignoring or Accepting a Risk

One additional choice is available to you as a risk manager: choose to ignore or accept a risk and its possible consequences. This is not strictly a "risk treatment" option, since it does nothing to reduce the possible impact or loss if the risk should occur. However, it does allow you to decide that in some specific cases, the cost of not pursuing the goal or objective because of that risk is just too much of an *opportunity cost* to bear. Consider the collision damage insurance on your personal car, for example. At some point in time, the premiums you pay to cover the possibility of damage to your car in an accident exceed the actual market value of your car—you pay more to insure it than your insurer will pay to repair it, even if the car is "totaled" or damaged beyond repair. So, by becoming *self-insuring* for collision damage, you accept the risk (or choose to ignore its possibilities) when you stop paying collision damage premiums, sign a waiver of coverage with your insurer, and use the money you save for some other opportunity.

---

Like everything in risk management and risk mitigation, these basic elements of choice can be combined in a wide variety of ways:

- Alarms combine detection and notification to users and systems owners; by alerting the attacker that they've been spotted "in the act," the sound of the alarms may motivate the attacker to stop the attack and leave the scene (which is a combination of preventing further damage while it deters and prevents continued or repeated attack).

- Strong protective systems can limit or contain damage during an attack, which prevents the attack from spreading; to the degree that these protective systems are visible to the attacker, they may also deter the attack by raising the costs to the attacker to commence or continue the attack. They may also raise the attacker's fear of capture, arrest, or other losses and thus further deter attack.

- Most physical and logical attack avoidance methods require a solid policy and procedural framework, and they quite often require users and staff members to be familiar with them and even trained in their operational use.

This last point bears some further emphasis. Organizations will often spend substantial amounts of money, time, and effort to put physical and even logical risk management systems into use, only to then put minimal effort into properly defining the who, what, when, where, how, and why of their use, maintenance, and ongoing monitoring. The money spent on a strong, imposing fence around your property will ultimately go to waste without routinely inspecting it and keeping it maintained. (Has part of it been knocked down by frost heave or a fallen tree? Has someone cut an opening in it? You'll never know if you don't walk the fence line often.)

This suggests that *continuous follow-through* is in fact the weakest link in our information risk management and mitigation efforts. We'll look at ways to improve on this in the remainder of this book.

---

### Defending Your Bank Accounts at the ATM

As a retail (consumer) bank customer, you typically can withdraw or deposit money into your bank account in one of several ways. Deposits can be done by postal mail, at an ATM, by online deposit of a check, or by transfer from another account (yours or someone else's). Withdrawals can be done by writing a check, using a debit or credit card for a purchase, withdrawing cash at an ATM, or doing a transfer to another account. As a retail customer, you expect your bank to:

- Detect all attempts to access your bank accounts, and information about you and your accounts at the bank.

- Notify you immediately of any attempts that seem unauthorized. Keep records of all attempts, whether successful or not, to access your accounts and bank information.

- Prevent any unauthorized transfers of funds into or out of your accounts.

Note that you don't really expect your bank to *avoid* unauthorized attempts to access your accounts or withdraw funds; you expect it to *prevent* them. (Why would that make sense to you?)

*(continued)*

*(continued)*

Let's look more closely at one aspect of your relationship with your bank: account access via an ATM. To fulfill its due diligence responsibilities, the bank must ensure that the ATM is installed, maintained, protected, and monitored, perhaps by requiring that

- All of its ATMs are in well-lighted, indoor areas, with sufficient surveillance to make it very unlikely that a threat actor could attach card skimmers, micro-cameras, or similar devices in an attempt to capture your card information, PIN, etc.

- Surveillance of its ATMs is visible and obvious, making it seem unlikely that someone could assault a customer during or after they do an ATM transaction.

- The ATM machines themselves, and their communications links, are physically and logically protected so as to make it difficult, time-consuming, and costly for an attacker to gain access to the ATM control mechanisms, customer data, transaction data, or cash in the machine.

Would you expect or require anything else from your bank?

Which of your expectations (or requirements) are part of the bank's due care responsibilities? Which are part of its due diligence responsibilities?

Let's go a step further into the real world. This is all well and good for ATMs that the bank owns or operates under contract, but what about network ATMs, possibly located around · the world, operated and maintained by many different companies in many different legal jurisdictions?

# Summary

Every organization, large or small, public or private, faces an almost limitless sea of risks—things that can go wrong or at least occur in unanticipated ways. Risk management is about the possibilities of future events upsetting or disrupting our plans of today, and the systems and business processes we use today. At its heart, risk management is about ensuring that decisions can be made reliably, on time, and on target; thus we see that information security is really about delivering decision assurance; it's about increasing our confidence that the decisions we make (large or small) are ones we can count on.

Risk management is the responsibility of the organization's leaders and stakeholders; they have the primary burdens of due care (to ensure that they're doing business correctly and effectively) and of due diligence (to continuously monitor and assess how well their business is working and whether it could work *better*). Since we cannot address every risk, and in fact cannot usually address any specific risk perfectly and completely, we've seen that risk management is the art of compromise. As SSCPs, we must balance the organization's tolerance for risk against its ability and willingness to spend money, time, effort, and other assets to contain, control, or limit the impacts those risks might have if they actually occur.

Risk management frameworks can provide us the managerial structures and the organized knowledge of experience that we need to plan and conduct our risk management and mitigation activities. If risk management is making decisions about risk, risk mitigation is carrying out those decisions.

The interplay between management and mitigation, between decision making and implementation, is continuous. We can, however, see that some actions and decisions are strategic, affecting the very survival or long-term success of the organization. Many others are directly involved in day-to-day business operations; and in between, tactical decisions, plans, and actions translate strategic needs and decisions into the world of the day to day.

The bridge between risk management and risk mitigation is the BIA, the business impact analysis. This analysis combines the organizational priorities and an in-depth understanding of business processes, along with their vulnerabilities. In doing so, it provides the starting point for the next set of hard work: implementing, testing, and operationally using the right set of risk mitigation controls, which we'll explore in Chapter 4.

# Exam Essentials

**Explain the information risk management process.**   Information risk management is a process that guides organizations through identifying risks to their information, information systems, and information technology systems; characterizing those risks in terms of impacts to prioritized goals and objectives; making decisions about which risks to treat, accept, transfer, or ignore; and then implementing risk treatment plans. As an ongoing management effort, it requires continuous monitoring of internal systems and processes, as well as constant awareness of how threats and vulnerabilities are evolving throughout the world.

**Explain information risk and its relationship to information systems and decision making.** You need information to make any decision, and if you cannot trust in that information's confidentiality, integrity, and availability when you must make a decision, then your decision is at risk. Information systems implement the processes that gather data, process it, and help you generate new information; risks that cause these processes to suffer a compromise of confidentiality, integrity, or availability are thus information systems risks. These information systems risks further reduce your confidence that you can make on-time, accurate decisions.

**Differentiate between outcomes-based, process-based, asset-based, and threat-based views of risk.**   Each of these provides alternative ways to view, think about, or assess risks to an organization, and they apply equally to information risks or any other kind of risk. Outcomes-based starts with goals and objectives and what kind of risks can impact your ability to achieve them. Process-based looks at your business processes and how different risks can impact, disrupt, or block your ability to run those processes successfully and correctly. Asset-based risks looks at any tangible asset (hardware, machinery, buildings, people) or intangible asset (knowledge, business know-how, or information of any kind) and asks how risks can decrease the value of the asset or make it lose usefulness to the business. Threat-based, also called vulnerability-based, focuses on how things go wrong—what the root and proximate causes of risks might be—whether natural, accidental, or deliberately caused.

**Explain why information risk management needs to be integrated and proactive.** Information security managers and incident responders need to know the status, state, and health of all elements of the information system, including its risk controls or countermeasures, in order to make decisions about dealing with an *incident of interest*. The timeliness and integrity of this information is critical to detecting an incident, characterizing it, and containing it before it causes widespread damage or disruption. Integrating all elements of your information risk management systems brings this information together rapidly and effectively to enable timely incident management. To be proactive requires that you think ahead to possible outcomes of risk events, and devise ways to deter, detect, prevent, contain, or avoid the impacts of such events, rather than merely being reactive—waiting until an event happens to learn from it, and only then instituting risk controls for the *next* time such an event occurs.

**Differentiate due care from due diligence for information risk management.** Due care and due diligence both aim to strike a prudent, sensible balance between "too little" and "too much" when it comes to implementing any set of responsibilities. Due care requires identifying information risks to high-priority goals, objectives, processes, or assets; implementing controls, countermeasures, or strategies to limit their possible impacts; and operating those controls (and the systems themselves) in prudent and responsible ways. Due diligence requires ongoing monitoring of these controls as well as periodic verification that they still work correctly and that new vulnerabilities or threats, changes in business needs, or changes in the underlying systems have not broken some of these risk control measures.

**Know how to conduct an information risk assessment.** Start with a prioritized list of outcomes, processes, assets, threats, or a mix of these; it is important to know that you're assessing possible risks in decreasing order of their importance or concern to leadership and management. The next step is to gather data to help make quantitative and qualitative assessments of the impact of each risk to the organization and its information, should such a risk event occur. Data from common vulnerabilities and exploitations registries (national and international) can assist by pointing out things to look for. As part of this, build a risk registry, a database or listing of the risks you have identified, your impact assessments, and what you've learned about them during your investigation. This combined set of information feeds into the BIA process.

**Know what a business impact analysis is, and explain its role in information risk management.** The BIA brings together everything that has been learned in the information risk assessment process and organizes it in priority order, typically by impact (largest to smallest, soonest versus later in time, highest-priority business objective, etc.). It combines quantitative and qualitative assessments to characterize the impacts these risks might cause if they became incidents. Typically, the BIA will combine risk perspectives so that it characterizes the impacts of a risk to high-interest goals and objectives as well as to costs, revenues, schedules, goodwill, or other stakeholder interests.

**Know the role of a risk register in information risk management.** A risk register is a document, database, or other knowledge management system that brings together everything the organization learns about risks, as it's learned. Ideally it is organized in ways that capture analysis results, management decisions, and updates as controls and countermeasures are implemented and put to use. Like the BIA, it should be a living document or database.

**Know the difference between qualitative and quantitative assessments and their use.** Quantitative assessments attempt to arithmetically compute values for the probability of occurrence and the single loss expectancy. These assessments typically need significant insight into costs, revenues, usage rates, and many other factors that can help estimate lost opportunities, for example. Qualitative assessments, by contrast, depend on experienced people to judge the level or extensiveness of a potential impact, as well as its frequency of occurrence. Both are valuable and provide important insight; quite often, management and leadership will not have sufficient data to support a quantitative assessment, or enough knowledge and wisdom in an area of operations to make a qualitative judgment.

**Know how to calculate the key elements of a quantitative risk assessment.** The single loss expectancy (SLE) is the total of all losses that could be incurred as a result of one occurrence of a risk. Typically expressed in monetary terms, it includes repair and restoration costs for hardware, software, facilities, data, people, loss of customer goodwill, lost business opportunity, or other costs directly attributable to the event. The annual rate of occurrence (ARO) is an estimate of how many times per year a particular risk is considered likely to occur. An ARO of 0.5, for example, says that this risk is expected to occur no more often than once every two years. The annual loss expectancy (ALE) is the product of the SLE multiplied by the ARO, and it represents the yearly expected losses because of this one risk.

**Know how to determine the safeguard value.** The safeguard value is the total cost that may be incurred to specify or design, acquire, install, operate, and maintain a specific risk mitigation control or countermeasure. You need to first complete vulnerabilities assessments in order to know what to fix, control, or counter, however.

**Explain what MAO, RTO, and RPO mean.** The maximum acceptable outage (MAO) is the time limit to restore all mission-essential systems and services so as to avoid impact to the mission of the organization. Recovery time objectives (RTOs) are established for each system that supports the organization and its missions. Organizations may set more aggressive needs for recovery, and if so, they may be spending more than is necessary to achieve these shorter RTOs. All RTOs must be shorter than the MAO that they support; otherwise, the MAO cannot be achieved. Recovery point objectives (RPOs) relate to the maximum data loss that the organization can tolerate because of a risk event; they can be expressed as numbers of transactions or in units of time. Either way, the RPO represents work that has to be accomplished again, and is paced by what sort of backup and restore capabilities are in place.

**Explain threat modeling and its use in information risk assessment.** Threat modeling starts with the premise that all systems have an external boundary that separates what the system owner, builder, and user own, control, or use, from what's not part of the system (that is, the rest of the world and the Internet). Systems are built by putting together other systems or elements, each of which has its boundary. Thus, there are internal boundaries inside every system. Crossing any boundary is an opportunity to ask security-driven questions—whether this attempt is authorized, for an authorized purpose, at this time, for example. The external boundary of a system is thus called its threat surface, and as you identify every way that something or someone can cross a boundary, you are identifying, characterizing, and learning about (modeling) the threats with respect to that surface. The outermost threat surface can (and should) be known without needing to delve into system internal design and construction, but the real payoff is when, layer by layer, these boundaries are examined for possible trapdoors, Trojan horse "features," or other easily exploitable weaknesses.

**Know the basic choices for limiting or containing damage from risks.**    The choices are deter, detect, prevent, and avoid. Deter means to convince the attacker that costs they'd incur and difficulties they'd encounter by doing an attack are probably far greater than anticipated gains. Detecting that an attack is imminent or actually occurring is vital to taking any corrective, evasive, or containment actions. Prevention either keeps an attack from happening or contains it so that it cannot progress further into the target's systems. Avoiding the possible damage from a risk requires terminating the activity that incurs the risk, or redesigning or relocating the activity to nullify the risk.

**Know what a risk management framework is and what organizations can gain by using one or tailoring one to their needs.**    Risk management frameworks (RMFs) are compendiums of guidance based on experience in identifying, characterizing, managing, and mitigating risks to public and private organizations. RMFs, typically, are created by government agencies or international standards organizations, and they may be directive or advisory for an organization depending on the kind of business it's in. RMFs provide rich sets of management processes that you can select from and tailor to the needs of your particular business.

**Explain the role of organizational culture and context in risk management.**    Organizations have their own "group personalities," which may or may not resemble those of their founders or current senior leaders, managers, or stakeholders. How decisions get made, whether quantitative assessments are preferred (or not) over qualitative ones, and how the appetite for risk is determined are just some of the key elements of culture that set the context for information risk management planning and implementation.

**Describe the basic steps of the NIST Special Publication 800-37 Rev. 2 RMF.**    This RMF describes seven major steps to information and privacy risk management: Prepare, Categorize, Select, Implement, Assess, Authorize, and Monitor. As these names, expressed as verbs, suggest, the actions that organizational leadership, management, and security or risk management specialists should take start at the broad cultural or context level, move through understanding information risk impacts, and choose, build, install, and activate new risk controls or countermeasures. Once activated, these controls are assessed for effectiveness, and senior leadership then declares them part of the new operational baseline. Ongoing monitoring ensures due diligence.

**Explain what a zero day exploit means.**    A zero day exploit involves a vulnerability discovered but not reported to the affected system's builders, vendors, or users, or the information security community at large. Between the time of its discovery and such reporting and notification, attackers who know of the vulnerability can create an exploit with which they can attack systems affected by that vulnerability. The term suggests that the system's defenders have zero time to prepare for such an exploit, since they are not aware of the vulnerability or the potential for an attack based on it.

# Review Questions

1. Which of the following shows the major steps of the information risk management process in the correct order?

   A. Assess risks across the organization; identify information security and privacy risks; implement countermeasures; establish security and privacy posture; review supply chain for IT security risk elements

   B. Establish basic security posture; review risks; implement countermeasures; perform ongoing monitoring and assessment, testing, and training

   C. Set priorities; assess risks; select controls and countermeasures; implement controls; validate correct operation; monitor

   D. Develop business impact analysis; establish risk tolerance levels; implement damage control choices; monitor

2. What is information risk?

   A. The threat that data on your computers, online storage, local or cloud-hosted data, or other data could be hacked into, stolen, or changed

   B. The probability of an event occurring that disrupts your information and the business processes and systems that use it

   C. Vulnerabilities in your information systems that can be exploited by a threat actor and cause harmful impacts

   D. The probability that management's and leadership's directions and communications will be misunderstood, causing the wrong actions to be taken by stakeholders, possibly causing financial loss, injury, or death

3. How does information risk relate to information systems risk or information technology risk?

   A. These three terms all mean much the same thing, although with a greater or lesser degree of emphasis on securing the underlying computers and networks.

   B. They express the logical flow of making decisions about risk: first, what information do you need; second, how you get it, use it, and share it with others in the decision process; and third, what technologies help make all of that happen. The probability of an event causing a disruption to any step of that decision process is a risk.

   C. They reflect the need to think about risks in outcomes-based, process-based, asset-based, or threat-based terms.

   D. They suggest the levels of organizational leadership and management that need to be part of managing each risk: senior leaders with information risk, tactical unit managers with information systems risks, and the IT department with information technology risks.

4. Which statement about risk perspectives or views is most correct?

    A. Outcomes-based risk assessment is best, because it focuses attention on the highest-priority goals and objectives of the organization as the places to start risk identification and assessment.

    B. Asset-based risk assessment is best, because it focuses attention on where your sunk costs or remaining book value of capital assets is greatest, and thus most expensive to repair or replace if a risk occurs.

    C. Threat-based risk management is best, because it keeps you looking at rapidly evolving exploits and forces you to realize that somebody, somewhere, has their own reasons for stealing every stray bit of information or computer power from you.

    D. Each of these provides great insight as you start your risk management planning and implementation efforts; no one approach by itself covers everything a good risk management strategy must do.

5. What does it mean to have an integrated information risk management system?

    A. You choose controls and countermeasures that provide all-risk coverage, have graceful degradation or fallback capabilities, and provide end-to-end visibility and management via built-in command, control, and communications capabilities.

    B. You avoid point defense countermeasures or controls, as they tend to make you overlook gaps between them.

    C. You provide the communications capabilities to bring status, state, and health information from all countermeasures and controls, and all systems elements, to information security managers, who can then direct timely changes in these controls in real time as required to respond to an incident.

    D. Vendors of security information and event managers claim that their products are "integrated," but they often do not clearly say what this means or help customers achieve greater security because of this.

6. Which is the most correct statement as to what it means to have a proactive approach with your information security risk management plans, programs, and systems?

    A. Being proactive means that your countermeasures and controls can actively trace back to identify, locate, and characterize your attackers, which can help you both in defending against them and in potentially seeking legal redress.

    B. Senior leaders and managers in many businesses appreciate active, thoughtful, forward-looking approaches, and you will find it easier to gain their support.

    C. Proactive information security systems allow your security specialists to take real-time control of all system elements, and bring all information about events of interest into one common operational picture. This greatly enhances your ability to detect, characterize, and contain incidents.

    D. Being proactive means that you use the best knowledge you have today, including lessons learned from other organizations' experience with information risk, and you plan ahead to deal with them, rather than wait for them to occur and then investigate how to respond to them.

**7.** Tom is the chief information security officer for a medium-sized business. It's been brought to his attention that the company has been storing its backup systems images and database backups in an offsite facility that has no alarm system and no way of knowing whether there were any unauthorized persons entering that facility. Which of the following might apply to this situation?

**A.** This could be a failure of due care in that security requirements for the backup information should have been specified and implemented in the storage plan and contracts.

**B.** Since there are no records to check to see if any unauthorized persons had access to these backups, there has been no due diligence lapse.

**C.** This is at least a failure of due diligence, since there seems to have been no systematic or periodic check of the storage facility or the backup media stored in it.

**D.** This could be a case of failing to perform both due care and due diligence.

**8.** What kind of information is part of an information risk assessment process? (Choose all that apply.)

**A.** Lost revenues during the downtime caused by the risk incident, including the time it takes to get things back to normal

**B.** Damage to equipment or facilities, or injury or death to people

**C.** Estimated costs to implement chosen solutions, remediations, controls, or countermeasures

**D.** Total costs to create an asset that is damaged or disrupted by the risk event

**9.** The acronym BIA refers to which of the following?

**A.** A document identifying all of the impacts to the business due to the risks it has chosen to assess; forms the basis for risk mitigation planning and implementation

**B.** The basic information security needs to provide for the privacy, integrity, and availability of business information

**C.** The budgeted implementation and accreditation plan for information security, often required by insurers and financial authorities of businesses dealing with sensitive or safety-related information

**D.** The budgeted cost of information availability, which when compared with the actual cost of information availability, lets management assess planned versus actual success of their information risk management programs

**10.** There are three ways in which risk assessments can be done. Choose the answer that orders them from best to least in terms of their contribution to risk management decision making.

**A.** Qualitative, quantitative, and CVE-based

**B.** CVE-based, quantitative, and qualitative

**C.** There is no order; they all can and should be used, as each reveals something more about the risks you have to manage.

**D.** Quantitative, CVE-based, and qualitative

**11.** Terri has recently been assigned to the information security team as a risk assessment analyst. As she goes through the files (on paper and in the company's cloud-based information systems) that the company already has, she realizes that they are inconsistent in format and hard to use to perform analysis, and that there are no controls over who in the company can access these files. Does any of this present an information security concern? (Choose all that apply.)

**A.** No, because the company would have chosen a cloud systems provider that fully protects any unauthorized persons or outsiders from accessing any company data.

**B.** Yes, because the data in these files could represent significant vulnerabilities of company systems, and its inadvertent or deliberate disclosure could be very damaging to the company.

**C.** Yes, because the lack of controls on access and use suggests that data integrity is lacking or cannot be assessed.

**D.** Yes, because conflicting formats and content might make much of the data unusable for analysis and decision making without a lot of effort, impacting whether that data can support decision making in a timely manner.

**12.** Patsy is reviewing the quantitative risk assessment spreadsheet for her division, and she sees a number of entries where the annual loss expectancy is far greater than the single loss expectancy. This suggests that:

**A.** The RTO is later than the RPO.

**B.** The ARO is less than 1.

**C.** The particular risk is assessed to happen many times per year; thus its ARO is much greater than 1.0.

**D.** This looks like an error in estimation or assessment, and it should be further investigated.

**13.** How do you use RTO, MAO, and RPO in planning information risk management activities? Select the statements that are correct.

**A.** Return to operations (RTO) is the desired time to get all business processes back into operation, whether on backup or workaround systems or on production systems. The recovery point objective (RPO) sets priorities for which systems to bring up first, or for which business processes to get back into operation before others (of lower priority).

**B.** The recovery point objective (RPO) establishes the maximum amount of data that is lost due to a risk event. This could be in numbers of transactions or in units of time, and it indicates the amount of rework of information that is acceptable to get systems back into normal operation.

**C.** The recovery time objective (RTO) must be less than or equal to the maximum acceptable outage. The MAO sets a maximum downtime (outage time) before mission impact becomes unacceptable; the RTO can be used to emphasize faster than MAO restoration.

**D.** The maximum acceptable outage (MAO) relates to the mission or business objectives; if multiple systems support those objectives, then all of their recovery time objectives (RTOs) must be less than or equal to the MAO.

**14.** Threat modeling and threat assessment:

   **A.** Should be done during risk management so that the threat modeling and assessment can drive the detailed work of risk mitigation planning

   **B.** Refer to the boundaries of a system and look to identify, understand, assess, and manage anything that attempts to cross that boundary as a way to identify possible threats

   **C.** Involves highly mathematical approaches, such as predictive code analysis, to produce meaningful results

   **D.** Is best done using modeling and simulation tools

**15.** What are all of the choices you need to make when considering information risk management, and what's the correct order to do them in?

   **1.** Treatment: accept, treat (fix or mitigate), transfer, avoid, recast

   **2.** Damage limitation: deter, detect, prevent, avoid

   **3.** Perspective: outcomes, assets, process or threat based

   **4.** Impact assessment: quantitative or qualitative

   **A.** 1, 2, 3, then 4

   **B.** 3, 4, 2, then 1

   **C.** 4, 3, 2, then 1

   **D.** 2, 3, 1 then 4

**16.** Jill has recently joined a software development startup company as an information risk analyst, and she notices that the company does not make use of any risk management frameworks. Which is the best advice you could give to Jill?

   **A.** As a new employee, she'd be speaking out of turn to say anything just yet. Watch and learn.

   **B.** As an SSCP, Jill knows that risk management frameworks can offer valuable lessons to learn from as organizations start to plan and conduct risk management (and information risk management) activities. Jill should talk with her supervisor, and perhaps propose that she draft a concept for how to select, tailor, and use one of the widely accepted RMFs.

   **C.** Jill should suggest to her supervisor that key stakeholders, perhaps even the board of directors, would not be pleased to see that the company is "reinventing this wheel" on its own. Perhaps the organization should adapt an RMF to its needs, she suggests.

   **D.** Most RMFs really do not add value to small, entrepreneurial firms just starting out. Jill can keep the use of RMFs in the back of her mind, and maybe find small elements of these large, complex frameworks to introduce, bit by bit, to her company's security processes and posture.

**17.** Why do SSCPs need to appreciate the culture of the organization they are working with in order to be effective as information risk managers? (Choose all that apply.)

   **A.** Organizational culture determines how willingly managers and workers at all levels will accept greater responsibilities and accountability, which can severely limit the SSCP's ability to get a risk management plan enacted.

   **B.** "Old-boy" networks and informal information and decision paths may make anything written down in business processes, manuals, and so forth somewhat suspect.

    **C.** Privately held companies tend to be run more loosely than publicly held ones, because shareholder protection law and regulations dictate limits on what executives and board members can do or how they can do it.

    **D.** Larger companies have probably had more different people in key positions over time, and so the effect of one domineering personality (as might happen in small entrepreneurial organizations) is probably not as pronounced.

18. As chief risk officer, you are asked if ignoring a risk is the same thing as accepting it. Which of the following might be part(s) of your reply?

    **A.** Yes, because in both cases you have decided to do nothing different and just keep on with business as usual.

    **B.** No, because quite often you choose to ignore something without first really understanding it or assessing its possible impacts to you.

    **C.** No, because in ignoring a risk you may be violating your own responsibilities for due care or due diligence.

    **D.** Yes, because as the responsible manager, you still have due care and due diligence responsibilities here.

19. When we call an attack a "zero day exploit," we mean that:

    **A.** The attack exploited a vulnerability within the first 24 hours of its discovery.

    **B.** The attack exploited a vulnerability within the first 24 hours of its being announced by the affected systems or software vendor, or when it was posted in the CVE.

    **C.** This term is meaningless hyperbole, invented by the popular press.

    **D.** The attack exploited a previously unreported vulnerability before the affected systems or software vendor recognized and acknowledged it, reported or disclosed it, or provided warning to its customers.

20. Kim manages risk for an online publishing company on the island of St. Kitts, which currently uses an on-premises datacenter as its content development facility; it e-ships content to customers who are then responsible for hosting it wherever they want. Kim's division vice president is concerned about risks, and so Kim has done some estimating. The datacenter has enough backup power supply capacity to do a graceful shutdown, but normal round-the-clock, seven-day-per-week development operations must have commercial power available. Recent experience shows that at least once per month, a brownout or blackout lasting at least eight hours occurs. Each disruption costs the company an additional two hours to restore operations. Which statements about risk assessment are not correct? (Choose all that apply.)

    **A.** Risk appetite should determine the MAO, which can then be used as part of estimating SLE.

    **B.** If the SLE exceeds the safeguard value, Kim should advise that the company implement that safeguard.

    **C.** If the ALE exceeds the safeguard value, Kim should advise that the company implement that safeguard.

    **D.** Once she has estimated the ALE, Kim can assess different safeguards to see how long their payback period might be so that she can advise her management regarding these alternatives.

# Chapter

# 4

# Operationalizing Risk Mitigation

---

## THE SSCP EXAM OBJECTIVES COVERED IN THIS CHAPTER INCLUDE:

**Domain 2: Security Operations and Administration**

✓ **2.4: Participate in Asset Management**

✓ **2.5: Implement Security Controls and Assess Compliance**

✓ **2.6: Participate in Change Management**

✓ **2.7: Participate in Security Awareness and Training**

✓ **2.8: Participate in Physical Security Operations (e.g., Data Center Assessment, Badging)**

**Domain 3: Risk Identification, Monitoring, and Analysis**

✓ **3.2: Perform Security Assessment Activities**

✓ **3.3: Operate and Maintain Monitoring Systems (e.g., Continuous Monitoring)**

✓ **3.4: Analyze Monitoring Results**

*Risk management* decides what risks to try to control; *risk mitigation* is how SSCPs take those decisions to the operational level. Senior leadership and management must drive this activity, supporting it with both resources and their attention span. These stakeholders, the business's or organization's leadership and decision makers, must lead by setting priorities and determining the acceptable cost–benefits trade. SSCPs, as they grow in knowledge and experience, can provide information, advice, and insight to organizational decision makers and stakeholders as they deliberate the organization's information risk strategy and needs. Chapter 3, "Integrated Information Risk Management," showed that this is a strategic set of choices facing any organization.

*Risk mitigation* is what SSCPs do, day in and day out. This is a tactical activity, as well as a set of tasks that translate tactical planning into operational processes and procedures. Risk mitigation delivers on the decision assurance and information security promises made by risk management, and SSCPs make those promises and expectations become operational reality. SSCPs participate in this process in many ways, as you'll see in this chapter. First, we'll focus on the "what" and the "why" of integrated defense in depth and examine how SSCPs carry out its tactics, techniques, and procedures. Then we'll look in more detail at how organizational leadership and management need the SSCP's assistance in planning, managing, administering, and monitoring ongoing risk mitigation efforts as part of carrying out the defense-in-depth strategic plan (discussed in Chapter 3). The SSCP's role in developing, deploying, and sustaining the "people power" component of organizational information security will then demonstrate how all of these seemingly disparate threads can and should come together. We'll close by looking at some of the key measurements used to plan, achieve, and monitor risk management and mitigation efforts.

# From Tactical Planning to Information Security Operations

Chapter 3 showed how organizations can use risk management frameworks, such as NIST SP 800-37 Rev. 2 or ISO 31000:2018, to guide their assessment of risks that face the organization's information and information technology systems. Making such assessments guides the organization from the strategic consideration of longer-term goals and objectives to the tactical planning necessary to implement information risk mitigation as a vital part of the organization's ongoing business processes. One kind of assessment, the *impact assessment*, characterizes how important and vital some kinds of information are to the organization. This prioritization may be because of the outcomes, assets, or processes that use or produce that information, or because of how certain kinds of threats or vulnerabilities inherent in those information processes put the organization itself at risk.

The next step in the assessment process is seeking out the critical vulnerabilities and determining what it takes to mitigate the risks they pose to organizational goals, objectives, and needs. This vulnerability assessment is not to be confused with having a "vulnerability-based" or "threat-based" perspective on risks overall. The impact assessment has identified outcomes, processes, or assets that must be kept safe, secure, and resilient. Even if we started the impact assessment by thinking about the threats, or the kinds of vulnerabilities (in broad terms) that such threats could exploit, we now have to roll up our sleeves and get into the details of just how the information work actually gets done day by day, week by week. Four key ideas helps SSCPs keep a balanced perspective on risk as she looks to translate strategic thinking about information risk into action plans that implement, operate, and assess the use of risk management controls:

- First, we make strategic choices about which risks to pay attention to—to actively work to detect, deter, avoid, or prevent. In doing so, we also quite naturally choose which risks to just accept or ignore. These choices are driven by our sense of what's important to the survival of the organization, its growth, or its other longer-term objectives. Then we decide what to "cure" or "fix" somehow.

- Second, we must remember that many words we use to talk about risk—such as *mitigation*—have multiple meanings as we shift from strategic, through tactical, and into day-to-day operations. *Mitigate* and *remediate*, for example, can often be used to refer to applying patches to a system, or even to replacing components or subsystems with ones of completely different design; other times, we talk about mitigating a risk by taking remedial (curative, restorative) actions.

- Third, all of these processes constantly interact with one another; there are no clean boundaries between one "step" of risk management and the next.

- Finally, we must accept that we are never finished with information risk management and mitigation. We are always chasing residual risk, whether to keep accepting it or to take actions to mitigate or remedy it.

Chapter 3 also showed something that is vital to the success of information security efforts: they must be integrated and proactive if they are to be even reasonably successful when facing the rapidly evolving threat space of the modern Internet-based, Web-enabled world. By definition, an integrated system is one that its builders, users, and maintainers *manage*. More succinctly: *unmanaged systems are highly vulnerable to exploitation; well-managed systems are still vulnerable, but less so*. We'll look further into this paradigm both here and in subsequent chapters.

We are now ready to cross the boundary between strategic risk management and tactical risk mitigation. For you to fully grasp the speed and agility of thought that this requires, let's borrow some ideas from the way military fighter pilots train to think and act in order to survive and succeed.

# Operationally Outthinking Your Adversaries

Let's focus on the key difference between planning and operations. Planning is a deliberate, thoughtful process that we engage in *well in advance* of the time we anticipate we'll need to do what our plans prescribe. It asks us to investigate; gather data; understand the stated and unstated assumptions, needs, constraints, and ideals—all of which we try to bring together into our plan. Planning is a balancing act; we identify tasks we need to do; we estimate the people, money, material, and time we'll need to accomplish those tasks; and then we trim our plan to fit the resources, time, and people available to us. It's an optimization exercise. Planning *prepares* us to take action; as Dwight D. Eisenhower, 34th president of the United States and Supreme Allied Commander, Europe, during World War II, famously said, "Plans are worthless, but planning is indispensable." Making plans, reviewing them, exercising them, and evaluating and modifying them trains your mind to think about how tasks and resources, time, and space fit together. By planning, replanning, reviewing, and updating your plans as part of your "security normal," you build an innate sense of how to make that "fit" achieve your objectives—and what to do when things just don't fit!

Plans *should* lead to process engineering and design tasks, in which we thoughtfully create the procedures, processes, and tools that our workforce will use day to day. Planning should reveal the need for training and human resources development. Planning should bring these needs together and show us how to recognize the moment in which all of the physical, logical, and administrative steps have been taken, our people are trained, and testing has verified that we're ready to open our doors and start doing business. Once that "initial operational capability" milestone has been reached, and once we've *delivered* the "minimum operational increment of capability" that our users can accept, we switch from planning to operations. We *do* what's been planned.

## No Plan Survives Contact with Reality

Plans are a set of predictions that rest on assumptions. Plans address the future, and to date, none of us has 100% perfect foresight. Think about all of the assumptions made during the business impact analysis (BIA) process, which we worked through in Chapter 3, and ask, "What if most of them are wrong?" A clear case in point is the underlying assumption of cryptography; we can protect our information *today* by encoding it in ways that will take far more time, money, and effort than adversaries will find it worth their while to attempt to crack. (This is sometimes called "sprinkling a little crypto dust" over your systems, as if by magic, it will fix everything.) Your super-secure password that *might* take a million years of CPU time just might crack on the first guess! (It's not very probable…but not impossible!) Your thorough audit of your IT infrastructure just might miss a backdoor that a developer or engineer put in and "forgot" to tell you about. Your penetration testing contractor might have found a few more vulnerabilities than they've actually told you about. The list of surprises like this is, quite frankly, endless.

Since your plans cannot be perfect, you have to be able to *think* your way through a surprising situation. This requires you to take the time to think, especially in the heat of battle during an IT security incident.

And if your adversary can deny you that "thinking time," if they can push you to *react* instead of thoughtfully considering the situation and the facts on hand *and* considering the situation in the context of your own objectives, you fall prey to your adversary outthinking *you*.

How do you avoid this?

## Observe, Orient, Decide, Act

The four steps of observe, orient, decide, and act, known as the *OODA loop*, provide a process by which you can keep from overreacting to circumstances. First observed in studies conducted by Colonel John Boyd, USAF, of U.S. combat fighter pilots during the Vietnam War, it has become a fundamental concept in fields as diverse as law enforcement training, business and leadership, cybernetics and control systems design, artificial intelligence, and information systems design and use. If you can master the OODA loop and make it part of your day-to-day operational kit bag, you can be the kind of SSCP who "keeps their head, when all about you are losing theirs and blaming it on you," as Kipling put it so adroitly.

Figure 4.1 shows the OODA loop, its four major steps, and the importance of feedback loops within the OODA loop itself. It shows how the OODA loop is a continually learning, constantly adjusting, forward-leaning decision-making and control process.

**FIGURE 4.1**   John Boyd's OODA loop

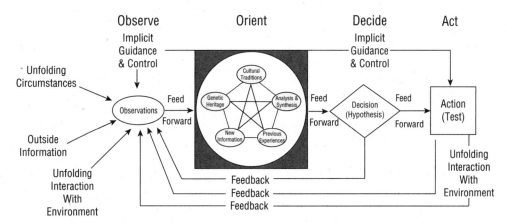

- *Observe*: Look around you! Gather information about what is happening, right now, and what's been happening very recently. Notice how events seem to be unfolding; be sensitive to what might be cause and effect being played out in front of you. Listen to what people are saying, and watch what they are doing. Look at your instruments, alarms, and sensors. Gather the data. Feed all of this into the next step.

- *Orient*: Apply your memory, your training, and your planning! Remember why you are here—what your organization's goals and objectives are. Reflect upon similar events you've seen before. Combine your observations and your orientation to build the basis for the next step.

- *Decide*: Make an educated guess as to what's going on *and what needs to be done about it*. This hypothesis you make, based on having oriented yourself to put the "right now" observations in a proper mental frame or context, suggests actions you should take to deal with the situation *and continue toward your goals*.

- *Act*: Take the action that you just decided on. Make it so! And go right back to the first step and *observe* what happens! Assess the newly unfolding situation (what was there plus your *actions*) to see if your hypothesis was correct. Check your logic. Correct your decision logic if need be. Decide to make other, different observations.

## Getting Inside the Other Side's OODA Loop

Think about Figure 4.1 in the context of two or more decision systems working in the same decision space, such as a marketplace. Suppliers and purchasers all are using OODA loops in their own internal decision making, whether they realize it or not. When the OODA loops of customers and suppliers harmonize with one another, the marketplace is in balance; no one party has an information advantage over the other. Now imagine if the customers can observe the actions of multiple suppliers, maybe even ones located in other marketplaces in other towns. If such customers can observe more information and think "around their OODA loop" more quickly than the suppliers can, the customers can spot better deals and take advantage of them faster than the suppliers can change prices or deliveries to the markets.

Let's shift this to a less-than-cooperative situation and look at a typical adversary intrusion into an organization's IT systems. On average, the IT industry worldwide reports that it takes businesses about 220 days to first observe that a threat actor has discovered previously unknown or unreported vulnerability and exploited it to gain unauthorized access to the business's systems. It also takes about 170 days, on average, to find a vulnerability, develop a fix (or *patch*) for it, apply the fix, and validate that the fix has removed or reduced the risk of harm that the vulnerability could allow to occur. Best case, one cycle around the OODA loop takes the business from observing the penetration to fixing it; that's 220 plus 170 days, or 13 months of being at the mercy of the intruder! By contrast, the intruder is probably running on an OODA loop that might take a few days to go from initially seeking a new target, through initial reconnaissance, to choosing to target a specific business. Once inside the target's systems, the decision cycle time to seek information assets that suit the attacker's objectives, to formulate actions, to carry out those actions, and then to cover their tracks might run into days or weeks. It's conceivable that the attacker could have executed multiple exploits per week over those 13 months of "once-around-the-OODA" that the business world seems to find acceptable.

It's worth emphasizing this aspect of the zero day exploit in OODA loop terms. The attacker does not need to *find* the vulnerability before anybody else does; she needs to develop a way to *exploit* it, against your systems, before that vulnerability has been discovered *and reported* through the normal, accepted vulnerability reporting channels, *and* before the defenders have had reasonable opportunity to become aware of its existence. Once you, as one of the white hats, *could* have known about it, it's no longer a zero day exploit—just one you hadn't implemented a control for yet.

## Defeating the Kill Chain

In Chapter 2, "Information Security Fundamentals," we introduced the concept of the value chain, which shows each major set of processes a business uses to go from raw inputs to finished products that customers have bought and are using. Each step in the value chain creates value—it creates greater economic worth, or creates more of something else that is important to customers. Business uses what it knows about its methods to apply energy (do work) to the input of each stage in the value chain. The value chain model helps business focus on improving the individual steps, the lag time or latency within each step and between steps, and the wastage or costs incurred in each step. But business and the making of valuable products is not the only way that value chain thinking can be applied.

Modern military planners adapted the value chain concept as a way to focus on optimally achieving objectives in warfare. The *kill chain* is the set of activities that show, step by step, how one side in the conflict plans to achieve a particular military objective (usually a "kill" of a target, such as neutralizing the enemy's air defense systems). The defender need not defeat every step in that kill chain—all they have to do is interrupt it enough to prevent the attacker from achieving their goals, when their plans require them to.

It's often said that criminal hackers and cyber threat actors only have to be lucky once, in order to achieve their objectives, but that the cyber defender must be lucky every day to prevent all attacks. This is no doubt true if the defender's OODA loops run slower than those of their attackers. As you'll see, it takes more than just choosing and applying the right physical, logical, and administrative risk treatments or controls to achieve this.

---

### What Does Your IT Security Team Need to Make Its OODA Loops Effective?

Think about what this implies for your information security organization. To have its own OODA loops working properly, the information security team needs to be well informed by the systems it's protecting and by the people who use them. The team needs to have a clear understanding of the goals and objectives, as well as the plans and processes that have been put in place to achieve those objectives. The team also needs to appreciate the larger context—how the world of information technology is changing every day, and how the world of the threat actors is changing, too.

How would you further refine those broad, general statements into specific, actionable needs? How would you go about setting specific criteria for success?

---

# Operationalizing Risk Mitigation: Step by Step

Let's start by taking apart our definition of risk mitigation (from Chapter 3), and see what it reveals in the day-to-day of business operations.

*Risk mitigation* is the process of implementing risk management decisions by carrying out actions that contain, transfer, reduce, or eliminate risk to levels the organization finds acceptable, which can include accepting a risk when it simply is not practical to do anything else about it.

Figure 4.2 shows the major steps in the risk mitigation process we'll use here, which continues to put the language of NIST SP 800-37 and ISO 31000:2018 into more pragmatic terms. These steps are:

1. Assess the information architecture and the information technology architectures that support it.

2. Assess vulnerabilities, and conduct threat modeling as necessary.

3. Choose risk treatments and controls.

4. Implement risk mitigation controls.

5. Verify control implementations.

6. Engage and train users as part of the control.

7. Begin routine operations with new controls in place.

8. Monitor and assess system security with new controls in place.

**FIGURE 4.2** Risk mitigation major steps

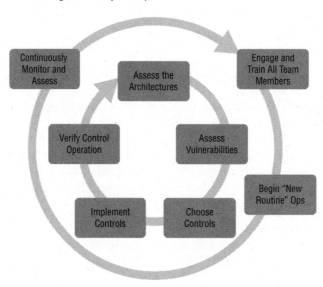

The boundary between planning and doing, as we cross from Step 3 into Step 4, is the point where the SSCP helps the organization fit its needs for risk treatment and control into its no-doubt very constrained budget of people, money, resources, and time. In almost all circumstances, the SSCP will have to operate within real constraints. No perfect solution will exist; after all of your effort to put in place the best possible risk treatments and controls, there will be residual risk that the organization has by default chosen to accept. If you and your senior leaders have done your jobs well, that residual risk should be within the company's risk tolerance. If it is not, that becomes the priority for the *next* round of risk mitigation planning!

## Step 1: Assess the Existing Architectures

Let's continue to peel the onion of defense in depth back, layer by layer, as we put information risk mitigation in action. We started with context and culture; now, we need to draw a key distinction between the organization's *information architecture* (how people share information to make decisions and carry them out) and the *information technology architecture* (the hardware, software, and communications tools) that supports that people-centric sharing of information and decision.

Other chapters will look in greater technical and operational depth at specific layers of the information architecture or the technologies they depend on. In Chapter 5, "Communications and Network Security," you'll learn how the SSCP needs to address both the human and technological aspects of these important infrastructures. In Chapter 7, "Cryptography," you'll see how to apply and manage modern cryptographic techniques to almost every element of an information architecture. Chapter 8, "Hardware and Systems Security," provides a closer look at systems security.

But before we get into the technological details, we first must map out the systems, processes, and information assets that are in use, right now, today, within our organization. All of those elements taken together are what we call the information architecture of the organization or business. Whether that architecture was well planned using the best design standards and templates, or it grew organically or haphazardly as users responded to changing needs and opportunities, is beside the point. *The information architecture is what exists, and you as the SSCP must know it and understand it if you are to protect and preserve it.* And if this statement holds for the *information* architecture, for that set of purposes, plans, ideas, and data, it holds doubly so for the underlying *information technology architectures* (note that many organizations don't realize how many such architectures they really have!) that embody, support, and enable it.

### Assessing the Information Architecture: People and Processes

The information architecture largely consists of the human and administrative processes that are the culture, context, process, and even the personality of the organization. You learned in Chapter 3 how vital it is to get this human-centric information architecture focused on the issue of information risk management. Now we need to consider how to take the *results* of that preparation activity, make them useful, and put them to use as we start developing risk mitigation plans.

## Organizational Political and Cultural Context

No organization exists in a vacuum. It is a player in a marketplace; it is subject to written and unwritten norms and expectations that govern, shape, or constrain its actions and its choices. Laws and regulations also dictate what the organization can and cannot do, especially when it comes to how it keeps its information and decision systems safe, reliable, and secure. Laws and regulations may also *require* reporting or public disclosure of information, including information about information security incidents.

*Organizational culture* is the sum of all of the ways, written and unwritten, in which organizations make decisions and carry them out. Quite often, the organizational culture reflects the personalities and personal preferences of its founders, stakeholders, leaders, or key investors. Two key aspects of organizational culture that affect information security planning and operations are its willingness to accept or take risks and its need for control.

Being *risk-averse* or *risk-tolerant* is a measure of an appetite for risk, whether that risk is involved with trying something new or with dealing with vulnerabilities or threats. The higher the *risk appetite*, the more likely the organization's decision makers are to accept risk or to accept higher levels of residual risk.

The need for control shows up in how organizations handle decision making. Hierarchically structured, top-down, tightly controlled organizations may insist that decisions be made "at the top" by senior leaders and managers, with rigidly enforced procedures dictating how each level of the organization carries out its parts of making those decisions happen. By contrast, many organizations rely on senior leaders to make strategic decisions, and then delegate authority and responsibility for tactical and operational decision making to those levels where it makes best sense. It is within the C-suite of officials (those with duty titles such as chief executive officer, chief financial or operations or human resources officer, or chief information officer) where critical decisions can and must be made if the organization is to attempt to manage information and information systems risk—let alone successfully mitigate those risks. The SSCP may advise those who advise the C-suite; more importantly, the SSCP will need to know what decisions were made and have some appreciation as to the logic, the criteria, and the assumptions that went into those decisions. Some of that may be documented in the BIA; some may not.

## The Information Architecture: Business Processes and Decision Flow

Let's look at this topic by way of an example. Suppose you're working for a manufacturing company that makes hydraulic actuators and mechanisms that other companies use to make their own products and systems. The company is organized along broad functional lines—manufacturing, sales and marketing, product development, purchasing, customer services, finance, and so on.

The company may be optimized along "just-in-time" lines so that purchasing doesn't stockpile supplies and manufacturing doesn't overproduce products in excess of reasonable customer demand forecasts. Nevertheless, asks the SSCP, should that mean that sales and marketing have information systems access to directly control how the assembly line equipment is manufacturing products today?

Let's ask that question at the next level down—by looking at the information technologies that the organization depends on to make its products, sell them, and make a profit.

One approach might be that the company makes extensive use of computer-aided design and manufacturing systems and integrated planning and management tools to bring information together rapidly, accurately, and effectively. This approach can optimize day-to-day, near-term, and longer-term decision making, since it improves efficiency.

Another information architecture approach might rely more on departmental information systems that are not well integrated into an enterprise-level information architecture. In these situations, organizations must depend on their people as the "glueware" that binds the organization together.

Once again, the SSCP is confronted with needing insight and knowledge about what the organization does, how it does it, and why it does it that way—and yet much of that information is not written down. For many reasons, much of what organizations really *do* in the day-to-day of doing their business isn't put into policies, procedures, or training manuals; it's not built into the software that helps workers and managers get jobs done. This tacit, implied knowledge of who to go to and how to get things done can either make or break the SSCP's information security plans and efforts. The SSCP is probably not going to be directly involved in what is sometimes called *business process engineering*, as the company tries to define (or redefine) its core processes. Nor will the SSCP necessarily become a knowledge engineer, who tries to get the *tacit knowledge* inside coworkers' heads out and transform it into documents, procedures, or databases that others can use (and thereby transform it into *explicit knowledge*). It's possible that the BIA provides the insights and details about major elements of the information technology architecture, in which case it provides a rich starting point to begin mitigation planning. Nonetheless, any efforts the company can make in these directions, to get what everybody knows actually written down into forms that are useful, survivable, and repeatable, will have a significant payoff. Such process maturity efforts can often provide the jumping-off point for innovation and growth. It's also a lot easier to do process vulnerability assessments on explicit process knowledge than it is to do them when that knowledge resides only inside someone's mind (or muscle memory).

With that "health warning" in mind, let's take a closer look at what the organization uses to get its jobs done. In many respects, the SSCP will need to *reverse engineer* how the organization does what it does—which, come to think of it, is exactly what threat actors will do as they try to discover exploitable vulnerabilities that can lead to opportunities to further *their* objectives, and then work their way up to choosing specific attack tools and techniques.

## Assessing the IT Architecture: Systems, Networks, and Service Providers

The information technology architecture of an organization is more than just the sum of the computers, networks, and communications systems that the business owns, leases, or uses. The IT architecture is first and foremost a plan—a strategic and tactical plan—that defines how the organization will translate needs into capabilities; capabilities into hardware, software, systems, and data; and then manage how to deliver, support, and secure those systems and technologies. Without that plan—and without the commitment of senior leadership to keep that plan up to date and well supported—the collection of systems, networks, and data is perhaps little more than a hobby shop of individually good choices that more or less work together.

The development of an IT architecture (as a plan and as a system of systems) is beyond the scope of what SSCPs will need to know; there are, however, a few items in many IT architectures and environments that are worthy of special attention from the SSCP.

One good way of understanding what the organization's real IT architecture is would be to do a special kind of inventory of all the hardware, software, data, and communications elements of that architecture, paying attention to how all those elements interact with one another and the business processes that they support. Such an *information technology baseline* provides the foundation for the *information security baseline*—in which the organization documents its information security risks, its chosen mitigation approaches, and its decisions about residual risk. The good news is that many software tools can help the SSCP discover, identify, and validate the overall shape and elements of the information technology baseline, and from that start to derive the skeleton of your information security baseline. The bad news? There will no doubt be *lots* of elements of both baselines that you will have to discover the old-fashioned way: walk around, look everywhere, talk with people, take notes, and ask questions.

Key elements of the IT architecture that this baseline inventory should address would include:

- End-user IT equipment and systems, including applications installed on those systems

- Key services that directly support business functions and business processes

- Centralized (shared) servers for processing, data storage, and communications

- Key business applications (sometimes called *platforms*) that provide integrated sets of services and the databases that they use and support

- Network, communications, and other interfaces that connect elements of the organization (and the IT systems that they use) together

- External service providers, partners, or other organizations that interface with, use, or make up a part of the organization's IT architecture

- All software, whether licensed, unlicensed (*freeware*), or developed in-house

- Backup and recovery capabilities

- Archival storage

Whether the SSCP is building the organization's first-ever IT architecture baseline or updating a well-established one, the key behavior that leads to success is *asking questions*. What is it? Where is it? Why is it here (which asks, "How does it support which business process")? Who is responsible for it? Who uses it? What does it connect to? When is it used? Who built it? Who maintains it? What happens when it breaks?

Let's take a closer look at some of the special cases you may encounter as you build or update your organization's IT architectural baseline.

## Special Case 1: Standalone Systems and "Shadow IT"

Many organizations consider all of their IT assets, systems, software, and tools to be part of one large system, regardless of whether they are all plugged in together into one big system or network. Other organizations will have their IT systems reflect the way that work groups, departments, and divisions interact with one another. How the organization manages that system of systems often reflects organizational culture, decision-making styles, and control needs. Sadly, many organizational systems just grow organically, changing to meet the needs, whims, and preferences of individual users, departments, and stakeholders.

Let's look at two classes of systems that might pose specific information risks:

- *Standalone systems* exist to meet some specific business need but are not as integrated into organizational systems planning, management, and control as other systems are. Some of these loosely coupled (or poorly integrated) systems may be kept apart for valid reasons, such as to achieve a more cost-effective solution to data protection needs or to support product, software, or systems development and testing. Oftentimes, *legacy systems* are only loosely coupled to the main IT systems. These older systems, possibly based on obsolete technologies, have been literally inherited from earlier business ventures or organizational structures, or because of a lack of investment funding to modernize them. Users may have to carry data manually, on tapes or disks, to and from the main IT environment to these legacy systems, for example. This can introduce any number of vulnerabilities and thereby increase the exposure to risk.

- *Shadow IT* is the somewhat pejorative term used by many IT departments to refer to data and applications programs that are outside of the IT department's areas of responsibilities and control. Organizations that are large enough to have an IT department often rely on well-defined, managed sets of software, data, and tools that they provide to users across the organization. In doing so, the IT department also can be better poised to support those formally deployed systems. The so-called *shadow IT* applications and systems are created by talented (or merely well-intended) users on their own, often using the powerful applications programs that come with modern office and productivity suites. One user might build a powerful spreadsheet model, for example, that other users want to use; they in turn generate other spreadsheets, or other versions of the original one, to meet their needs. Their needs may serve legitimate business needs, but their design approach of one spreadsheet after another often becomes unsustainable. As shadow IT applications proliferate and become unsustainable, they expose the organization to an ever-increasing risk that key data will become unavailable, unreliable, lost, or exposed to the wrong set of eyes.

## Special Case 2: Networks

Chapter 5 will address the key technical concepts and protocols involved with modern computer and communications networks. At this point, the key concept that SSCPs should keep in mind is that networks exist because they allow one computer, at one location, to deliver some kind of *service* to users at other locations. Those users may be people, software tasks running on other computers, or a combination of both people and software. Collectively, we refer to anything requesting a service from or access to an information asset as a *subject*; the service or asset they are requesting we call an *object*.

This idea or model of subjects requesting services is fundamental to all aspects of modern information technology systems—even standalone computers that support only a single person's needs make use of this model. Once an organization is providing services over a network, the problem of knowing who is requesting what be done, when and how, and with what information assets, becomes quite complicated.

### Special Case 3: Clouds, Service Bureaus, Other External IT Systems Providers

End users need to get work done to satisfy the needs of the organization. End users rely on services that are provided and supported by the IT architecture; that architecture is made up of service providers, who rely on services provided by other levels of providers, and on it goes. ("It's services all the way down," you might say.) Over time, many different business models have been developed and put into practice to make the best use of money, time, people, and technology when meeting all of these service needs.

The IT architecture baseline needs to identify any external person, agency, company, or organization that fulfills a service provider role. Most of these external relationships should have written agreements in place that specify responsibilities, quality of service, costs, billing, and support for problem identification, investigation, and resolution. These agreements, whether by contract, memoranda of understanding, or other legal forms, should also lay out each party's specific information security responsibilities. In short, every external provider's C-I-A roles and responsibilities should be spelled out, in writing, so that the SSCP can include them in the security baseline, monitor their performance and delivery of services, *and* audit for successful implementation and compliance with those responsibilities.

### Virtual or "Software-Defined" Service Provision

"Doing it in the cloud" is the most recent revolution in information technology, and like many such revolutions, it's about ideas and approaches as much as it is about technologies and choices. At the risk of oversimplifying this important and complex topic just now, let's consider that everything we do with information technology is about getting services performed. Furthermore, all services involve using software (which runs on some hardware, somewhere) to make other software (running on some other hardware, perhaps) to do what we need done, and give us back the results we need. We'll call this the *service provision* model, and it is at the heart of how everything we are accustomed to when we use the Web actually works. Let's operationalize that model to see how it separates what the end user cares about from the mere details of making the service happen.

Users care most about the C-I-A aspects of the service, seen strictly from their own point of view:

- Can only authorized users or subjects ask for it?

- Is the service delivered on time, when I need it?

- Does the service work accurately, reliably, and repeatedly?

- When it fails, does the service go through *graceful degradation* or fail in some kind of safe mode so that errors in input or stored data do not lead to misleading or harmful results?

- Are unauthorized users prevented from seeing the results of the service?

By contrast, the *service provider* has to care about C-I-A from both its users' perspective and its own internal needs:

- Can I keep unauthorized subjects from accessing this service, its internal data or logic, or its outputs?

- Where are the computers, storage facilities, and communications or networks that I need to host the service, run it when needed, and accept inputs from and deliver outputs to the authorized user?

- Can I validate to users that the service is accurate and reliable?

This brings us to consider the "as-a-service" set of buzzwords, which we can think of in increasing order of how much business logic they implement or provide to the organization:

- IaaS can mean *infrastructure as a service*. Infrastructures are sets of common services and their delivery mechanisms that are used by many different kinds of end users. Whether we are homeowners, hoteliers, or helicopter maintenance depot operators, we all use electric power, need clean drinking water, and depend on sewer and garbage disposal services to keep things clean and safe. These services come to us much like any commodity (a gallon of water is a gallon of water, anywhere we go), and if the service delivery meets published administrative and technical standards, we call it an infrastructure service.

- IaaS can also mean *identity as a service*, with which individuals, organizations, and even software processes can have sets of credentials established that attest to their identity. The goal of identity as a service is to provide organizations (and people) with increasingly more reliable ways to unambiguously confirm that a user, business, or software agent is in fact who they claim to be. (We'll see how this works and how we use this service in Chapter 6, "Identity and Access Control.")

- SaaS, or *software as a service*, typically involves using general-purpose software systems or suites, such as Microsoft Office or Open Office, without having to directly install them on each end user's hardware. Although almost all businesses write many of the same kinds of documents, their individual corporate business logic takes form as they *use* these software suites and exists outside of the software products themselves.

- PaaS, or *platform as a service*, usually refers to a large, complex set of business functions implemented as a complete system (such as an insurance company's claims submission and processing system). Some PaaSs provide generalized features, such as customer relationship management capabilities, that can be highly tailored to meet an individual company's needs; others reflect the predominant business logic of an entire industry and provide near-turn-key capabilities that need little modification by most users. One example might be a medical office billing, accounts management, and insurance processing PaaS, suitable for clinical practices in the U.S. marketplace. (It probably wouldn't work very well in the United Kingdom, or in Colombia, without extensive tailoring to local needs.)

We'll examine this topic in more detail in Chapter 9, "Applications, Data, and Cloud Security"; for right now, it's important to remember that ultimately, the responsibilities of due care and due diligence always remain with the owners, managing directors, or chief executives of the organization or business. For the purposes of building and updating the

IT architecture baseline, it's important to be able to identify and specify where, when, how, and by whom these buzzwords are implemented in existing service provider relationships.

With the baseline in hand, the SSCP is ready to start looking at *vulnerability assessments*.

# Step 2: Assess Vulnerabilities and Threats

We've looked at *how badly it will hurt* when things go wrong; now, let's look at *how things go wrong*.

The IT architecture baseline links IT systems elements to business processes; the planning we've done so far then links key business processes to prioritized business goals and objectives. That linking of priorities to architectural elements helps the SSCP focus on which *information assets* need to be looked at first to discover or infer what possible vulnerabilities may be lurking inside. It's time for you as the SSCP to use your technical insight and security savvy to look at systems and ask, "How do these things usually fail? And then what happens?"

"How do things fail?" should be asked at two levels: how does the business process fail, and how does the underlying IT element or information asset fail to support the business process, and thus cause that business process to fail?

This phase of risk mitigation is very much like living the part of a detective in a whodunit. The SSCP will need to interview people who operate the business process, as well as the people who provide input to it and depend on its outputs to do their own jobs. Examining any trouble reports (such as IT help ticket logs) may be revealing. Customer service records may also start to show some patterns or relationships—broken or failing processes often generate customer problems, and out-of-the-ordinary customer service needs often stress processes to the breaking point.

It's all about finding the cause-and-effect logic underneath the "what could go wrong" parts of our systems. Recall from Chapter 3 our discussion of proximate cause and root cause:

- Finding the *root cause* of a vulnerability helps us focus on what to fix so that we can eliminate or reduce the likelihood of that component or system failing.

- Finding the *proximate cause* helps us find better ways to detect failures while they are starting to happen, contain the damage that they can cause, and offers an opportunity to take corrective action before the damage gets worse.

Both are valuable ideas to keep in mind as we look through our systems for "Where can it break and why?"

---

**Keeping "How Things Work" Separate from "Why Things Fail"**

It's tempting to combine this step and the previous one, since both involve a lot of investigative work and probably interviewing a lot of the people who use different IT and information processes to get their jobs done. You will, after all, need to correlate what people and data reveal about the purpose and design of information architectures, and the IT that supports and enables them, with the information you discover about how they fail, what happens when they fail, and what happens when such failures are reported to management. As the information risk analyst in all of this, you as an SSCP need to be able to find the connections between all of these disparate, often contradictory data sets and perspectives.

However...

Think about the two very different frames of mind, or the different emotional perspectives, your interview subjects might be in. People often respond to "How does this work?" kinds of questions by offering information and insight; people naturally want to be helpful, and quite often they will want to show their pride in their mastery of particular parts of their jobs. Now consider coming to that same person and asking, "How does this process fail? What breaks in it? What happens when it fails?" These kinds of questions put people on the defensive; subconsciously, they will believe you are actually asking them, "What did you do that broke it?"

How do you avoid putting people on the defensive when you're asking, "Why does it break when you use it?" kinds of questions? Most of this can be done by the way in which you plan your information-gathering efforts, in particular by spelling out detailed questions you wish to ask each person you speak with. The rest of it is, however, subject to your own personal approach and mannerisms when you're dealing with someone who just might become defensive or hostile to your inquiries. And all of that is beyond the scope of this book and the SSCP exam.

## Vulnerability Assessment as Quality Assurance

In many respects, vulnerability assessment is looking at the as-built set of systems, processes, and data and discovering where and how quality design was *not* built into them in the first place! As a result, a lot of the same tools and processes we can use to verify correct design and implementation can help us identify possible vulnerabilities:

- *Data quality assurance* looks end-to-end at everything involved in the way the organization acquires external data, how it generates its own data internally, and what it does with the data. It captures the business logic that is necessary to say that a given input is correct in content, in meaning, and in format. Then it enforces business logic that restricts the use of that data to valid, authorized processes and further specifies who in the organization can use those processes. In addition, data quality can and should identify exceptions—cases where an unforeseen combination of data values requires human (supervisory or managerial) decisions regarding what, if anything, to do with such exceptions. Data quality management plans, procedures, detailed implementation notes, and the underlying data models themselves are important inputs to the vulnerability assessment. We'll cover this in more detail in Chapter 9.

- *Software quality assurance* also is (or should be!) an end-to-end process, which starts with the system functional requirements that document what the software needs to do to properly implement business logic and deliver the correct results to the end users. Software development processes should ensure that all required functions are met by the software, *and that it does nothing else.* "Side effects," or "undocumented features," quite often end up becoming the next set of zero day exploits. Software design walk-throughs and reviews, software testing, and end-user acceptance testing are some of the processes that organizations should use to control the risk that the software they are building is correct, complete, safe to use, reliable, and resilient. End-user operational documentation also provides a great opportunity for the organization to get its software used correctly. All of these processes produce information—meeting minutes, inspection or walk-through logs, trouble tickets or help desk complaints, and requests for change; all of these should be examined as part of the vulnerability assessment. Chapter 9 will go into this in more detail.

- Software source code, the builds and controls libraries that support assembling it into finished products, and the finished executable systems can also be analyzed with a wide variety of tools, as you'll see in Chapter 9.

- Communications and network systems should have suitable features built in and turned on so that usage can be monitored and controlled. Whether it's simply to prevent staff members from surfing too many YouTube videos on company time, or to prevent the exfiltration of critical, private data out of the organization, control of how the company-provided communications assets are used is vital to information security.

Even the company suggestion box should be examined for possible signs that particular business processes don't quite work right or are in need of help.

That's a *lot* of information sources to consider. You can see why the SSCP needs to use prioritized business processes as the starting point. A good understanding of the information architecture and the IT architectures it depends on may reveal some critical paths—sets of processes, software tools, or data elements that support many high-priority business processes. The software, procedural, data, administrative, and physical assets that are on those critical paths are excellent places to look more deeply for evidence of possible vulnerabilities.

## Sharing Vulnerability and Risk Insight: A Community of Practice Approach

As you saw in Chapter 2, you and your organization are not alone in the effort to keep your information systems safe, secure, resilient, and reliable. There are any number of communities of practice with which you can share experience, insight, and knowledge:

- Critical infrastructure protection and assurance communities, such as InfraGard in the United States, bring together public agencies, law enforcement and national security specialists, and private sector businesses in ways that encourage trust and dialogue.

- The Computer Society of the Institute of Electrical and Electronics Engineers sponsor many activities, such as their Center for Secure Design. See `https://cybersecurity .ieee.org/center-for-secure-design/` for ideas and information that might help your business or organization.

- Many local universities and community colleges work hand-in-hand with government and industry to achieve excellence in cybersecurity education and training for people of all ages, backgrounds, and professions.

You also have resources such as Mitre's Common Vulnerabilities and Exposures (CVE) system and NIST's National Vulnerability Database that you can draw upon as you assess the vulnerabilities in your organization's systems and processes. Many of these make use of the *Common Vulnerability Scoring System* (CVSS), which is an open industry standard for assessing a wide variety of vulnerabilities in information and communications systems. CVSS makes use of the C-I-A triad of security needs (introduced in Chapter 1, "The Business Case for Decision Assurance and Information Security") by providing guidelines for making quantitative assessments of a particular vulnerability's overall score. Scores run from 0 to 10, with 10 being the most severe of the CVSS scores. Although the details are beyond the scope of the SSCP exam, it's good to be familiar with the approach CVSS uses—you may find it useful in planning and conducting your own vulnerability assessments.

As you can see at `https://nvd.nist.gov/vuln-metrics/cvss`, CVSS consists of three areas of concern:

- Base metrics, which assess qualities intrinsic to a particular vulnerability. These look at the nature of the attack, the attack's complexity, and impacts to confidentiality, integrity, and availability.

- Temporal metrics, which characterize how a vulnerability changes over time. These consider whether exploits are available in the wild, and what level of remediation exists; they also consider the level of confidence in the reporting about a vulnerability and exploits related to it.

- Environmental metrics, which assess dependencies on particular implementations or systems environments. These include assessments of collateral damage, what percent of systems in use might be vulnerable, and the severity of impact of an exploit (ranging from minimal to catastrophic).

Each of these uses a simple scoring process—impact assessment, for example, defines four values from Low to High (and "not applicable or not defined"). Using CVSS is as simple as making these assessments and totaling up the values.

Note that during reconnaissance, hostile threat actors use CVE and CVSS information to help them find, characterize, and then plan their attacks. The benefits we gain as a community of practice by sharing such information outweighs the risks that threat actors can be successful in exploiting it against our systems *if* we do the rest of our jobs with due care and due diligence.

---

### Start with the CVE?

An obvious question is, "Should I start my vulnerabilities assessment by rounding up what published CVE data says about my systems and their components?" Two concerns ought to be recognized before you make this leap of faith:

- The less complete your information and IT architectures are, and the more unknown elements you have in those systems, the greater the chance that a "CVE first" approach will cover what you need.

*(continued)*

*(continued)*

- Too much reliance on CVE as your source of insight can lull you into missing out on vulnerabilities your business has unwittingly built into or papered over in its business logic and business processes.

Think about the "I" in "C-I-A" for a moment. The software tools you've installed and the business is using may be "CVE-free," but if you feed suspect data into them, their algorithms will work just fine but produce results that might be harmful to your business. This is the *garbage in, garbage out (GIGO)* problem that has plagued humankind since the invention of the first business process.

It's also fair to say that the absence of a reported vulnerability is not proof of the absence of that vulnerability. Zero day exploits are great examples of this; a hacker discovers a new vulnerability and exploits it before anyone is aware that the vulnerability existed in the first place.

So, by all means—gather published CVE data on every known systems element, component, installed software product, and everything else you can find. But don't stop there as you investigate or consider how things might break.

## A Word about Threat Modeling

If you picture a diagram of your information architecture (or IT architecture), you'll notice that you probably can draw boundaries around groups of functions based on the levels of trust you must require all people and processes to have in order to cross that boundary and interact with the components inside that space. The finance office, for example, handles all employee payroll information, company accounting, and accounts payable and receivable, and would no doubt be the place you'd expect to have access to the company's banking information. That imaginary line that separates "here there be finance office functions" from the larger world is the threat surface—a boundary that threats (natural, accidental, or deliberate) have to cross in order to access the "finance-private" information inside the threat surface. The threat surface is the sum total of all the ways that a threat can cross the boundary:

- A *physical threat surface* might be the walls, doors, locks on the doors, and other physical barriers that restrict the movement of people and information into and out of the finance office. A wiretap on a phone or a USB device plugged into a computer in the finance office would be examples of threats crossing that physical threat surface.

- A *logical threat surface* might be the user authentication and authorization processes that control who can access, use, extract, or change finance office information. A hacker who found a backdoor on a finance office computer would be violating the logical threat surface.

- An *administrative threat surface* would be the set of policies, procedures, and instructions that separate proper, authorized use from unauthorized use. Such a policy might ban the use or entry of smartphones, USB thumb drives, and so forth in the finance office; blocking all of the USB ports on the devices, or having pat-down inspections of people going in and out to prevent them from carrying in a smartphone, would be physical implementations of that administrative control. Failing to search the janitor's trash bags to ensure that they're not "inadvertently" throwing away payroll records, would be an example of a threat crossing this physical threat surface.

You see the dilemma here: authorized users and uses cross the threat surface all the time, and in fact, you cannot achieve the "A" in C-I-A without providing that right of way. Yet the threat actors (again, natural, accidental, or deliberate) need to be detected when they try to cross the threat surface and prevented from getting across it—and if prevention fails, you need to limit how much damage they can do.

*Threat modeling* is the broad, general term given to the art and science of looking at systems and business processes in this way. It brings a few thoughts into harmony with one another in ways that the SSCP should aware of. First, it encourages you to encapsulate complex functions inside a particular domain, boundary, or threat surface. In doing so, it also dictates that you look to minimize ways that anything can cross a threat surface. It then focuses your attention on how you can detect attempts to cross, validate the ones that are authenticated and authorized, and prevent the ones that aren't. Threat modeling also encourages you to account for such attempts and to use that accounting data (all of those log files and alarms!) both in real-time alert notification and incident response, and as a source of analytical insight.

As you grow as an SSCP, you'll need to become increasingly proficient in seeing things at the threat surface.

## How Does the SSCP Assess the Human Components?

"Trust, but verify" applies to the human element of your organization's information processes too! You need to remember that every organization, large or small, can fall afoul of the disgruntled employee, the less-than-honorable vendor or services provider, or even the well-intended know-it-all on its staff who thinks that they don't need to follow all of those processes and procedures that the rest of the team needs. The details of how such a *personnel reliability program* should be set up and operated are beyond the scope of the SSCP exam or this book. Part of this is what information security practitioners call the "identity and access control problem," and Chapter 6 will delve into this in greater depth. From a vulnerability assessment perspective, a few key points are worth highlighting now.

The information security impact assessment is the starting point (as it is for all vulnerability assessments). It should drive the design of jobs so that users do not have capabilities or access to information beyond what they really need to have and use. In doing so, it also indicates the trustworthiness required for each of those jobs; a scheduling clerk, for example, would not have access to company proprietary design information or customer financial data, and so may not need to be as trustworthy as the firm's intellectual property lawyers or its accountants. With the job defining the need for capabilities and information, the processes designed for each job should have features that enforce these constraints and notify information security officials when attempts to breach those constraints occur. The log files, alerts, and alarms or other outputs that capture these violations must be inspected, analyzed, and assessed in ways that give timely opportunity for a potential security breach (deliberate or accidental) to be identified and corrected before it is harmfully exploited.

Beyond (but hand in hand with) separation of duties, the business process owners and designers must ensure that no task is asking more of any system component—especially the human one—than it can actually be successful with. As with any computer-based part of your business logic, tasks that systems designers allocate to humans to perform must be something humans can learn how to do. The preconditions for the task, including the human's training, prior knowledge, and experience, must be identified and achievable. Any required tools (be they hammers or database queries) must be available; business logic for handling exceptions, out-of-limits conditions, or special needs have to be defined and people trained in their use. Finally, the saying "if you can't measure it, you can't manage it" applies to assessing the reliability of the human component as much as it does to the software, systems, and other components of a business process.

This combination of ingredients—separation of duties, proper task design, meaningful performance monitoring and assessment, and ongoing monitoring to detect errors or security concerns—reduces the risks that an employee is overstressed, feels that they are undervalued, or is capable of taking hostile action if motivated to do so.

Chapter 9 will address other aspects of how the human resources the organization depends on can be more active and effective elements in keeping the organization's information safe, secure, and resilient.

### Don't Forget the Administrative Controls!

The administrative controls—the people-facing policies and procedures that dictate what should be done, how it should be done, why, and by whom—are often overlooked when conducting a vulnerability assessment. Since most of the headline-grabbing IT systems breaches and information security incidents exploit administrative process vulnerabilities and human frailties, it should be painfully obvious that SSCPs need to pay as close attention to vulnerabilities in the people-driven processes as they do the ones in the hardware, software, and data elements of the information architectures that drive and support the organization.

Key vulnerabilities can exist in the processes used for management and control of all information assets, systems, and baselines. Configuration management and change control, user account provisioning, new IT or information systems project planning and management, and especially the help desk processes throughout the organization should be key parts of your vulnerability assessment activities.

Each such vulnerability in these people-powered processes is an opportunity to increase the level of security awareness, and to strengthen the culture of security accountability across the organization's work force. It's also a great opportunity to get management and leadership to visibly support such a *security hygiene* mind set and culture.

As SSCPs, we have a burden of due care and due diligence to actively find and exploit such opportunities.

## Gap Analysis

Even the most well-designed information system will have *gaps*—places where the functions performed by one element of the system do not quite meet the expectations or needs of the next element in line in a process chain. When we consider just how many varied requirements we place on modern IT systems, it's no wonder there aren't *more* gaps rather than fewer! In general terms, *gap analysis* is a structured, organized way to find these gaps. In the context of information systems security, you do gap analysis as part of vulnerability assessment.

Several different kinds of activities can generate data and insight that feed into a gap analysis:

- Review and analysis of systems requirements, design, and implementation documentation

- Software source code inspection (manual or automated)

- Review of software testing procedures and results

- Inspections, audits, and reviews of procedures, facilities, logs, and other documentation, including configuration management or change control systems and logs

- Penetration testing

- Interviews with end users, customers, managers, as well as bystanders at the workplace

This last brings up an interesting point about the human element: as any espionage agency knows, it's quite often the lowest-level employees in the target organization who possess the most valuable insight into its vulnerabilities. Ask the janitors, or the buildings and grounds maintenance staff; talk with the cafeteria workers or other support staff who would have no official duties directly involved in the systems you're doing the gap analysis for. Who knows what you may find out?

A strong word of caution is called for: the results of your gap analysis could be the most sensitive information that exists in the company! Taken together, it is a blueprint for attack—it makes targets of opportunity easily visible and may even provide a step-by-step pathway through your defenses. You'd be well advised to gain leadership's and management's agreement to the confidentiality, integrity, and availability needs of the gap analysis findings *before* you have to protect them.

---

 **Real World Scenario**

### Gap Analysis: Voting on Election Day

At a typical polling place on Election Day, we see a sequence of activities something like this:

First, we see the initialization sequence:

1. Equipment, furniture, etc., is positioned, set up, and tested as required. Phone lines, power, and other communications are also verified to be connected and working. Building security is verified to be working.

2. Staff are selected and trained.

3. Voter rolls are provided to the polling place.

*(continued)*

*(continued)*

Next comes Election Day:

1. Staff arrive, open the facility, and get it ready for voting to begin.

2. Polls open, and voters can enter to vote.

3. On a per-voter basis, registration is verified against identity, and the voter votes. The voter leaves.

4. Polls close, and the staff begin the process of securing the ballots and generating their counts and any reports.

5. Ballot materials are secured for transport to a central election commission facility.

Once Election Day is over, and if no recount is needed, the polling place is decommissioned; equipment is removed, communications services are disconnected, and keys to the doors are given back to the facility owner or manager as required.

Gap analysis could be done in several ways:

- Design reviews might find that there are ways to take blank ballot sheets and "vote" them fraudulently, or that logs and counts maintained throughout the day have enough procedural errors in them that we cannot rule out the "ghost vote."

- Penetration testing could be done to see if voting machines, polling places, or even staff can be hacked into or suborned.

- Post-election audits could demonstrate that voter registration rolls, numbers of ballots cast, and other data indicate a potential for fraud.

Many nations are relying increasingly on Internet-enabled electronic voting systems, which may not be as reliable, safe, or secure as we need them to be. At the July 2017 DEFCON convention, for example, it took less than 90 minutes for teams of hackers to crack open 30 different computerized ballot box systems.

"It takes a thief to catch a thief" doesn't mean that you have to hire untrustworthy felons to be part of your security team. You should, though, learn to *think like a thief* and do gap analysis like a hacker would. Do the virtual equivalent of walking around the building on the *outside*, trying all of the doors and windows and looking for places that the security cameras probably can't see you; run your own network scanners to look for unsecured ports, and fingerprint the systems to see if they're running old, outdated, unpatched software that's known to be prey to exploits. Bring your Wi-Fi scanner, too, and see what kind of unsecured or poorly secured connections might be possible.

**WARNING**    Make sure that you have the system owner's *written permission* for any gap analysis or penetration testing you're doing. Otherwise, instead of trying to break *in*, you may be needing a way out, and there aren't very many "get out of jail free" cards that work in the wild!

# Step 3: Select Risk Treatment and Controls

We've mentioned before that the SSCP needs to help the organization find cost-effective solutions to its risk mitigation needs. Here's where that happens. Let's look at our terms more closely first.

*Risk treatment* involves all aspects of taking an identified risk and applying a set of chosen methods to eliminate or reduce the likelihood of its occurrence, the impacts it has on the organization when (not if) it occurs, or both. Note that we say "eliminate or reduce," both for probability of occurrence and for the impact aspects of a given risk. The set of methods taken together constitute the risk controls that we are applying to that particular risk.

Unfortunately, the language about dealing with risks is not very precise. Many different books, official publications, and even widely accepted risk management frameworks like NIST SP 800-37 can leave some confusion. Let's see if some simple language can help un-muddy these waters:

- We decide what to do about a risk by selecting a risk treatment strategy or approach— such as to accept, avoid, treat, or transfer the risk.

- When we decide to treat a risk, we may also choose a variety of physical, logical, or administrative control techniques.

- When we're done applying those controls, what's left over from the original risk is the residual risk. We'll deal with it another time, perhaps in next year's plan and budget, or after the next major systems upgrade.

## Risk Treatment Strategies

Risk treatment strategies, tactics, or methods fall into the following broad categories.

### Accept

This risk treatment strategy means that you simply decide to do nothing about the risk. You recognize it is there, but you make a conscious decision to do nothing differently to reduce the likelihood of occurrence or the prospects of negative impact. This is known as being *self-insuring*—you assume that what you save on paying risk treatment costs (or insurance premiums) will exceed the annual loss expectancy over the number of years you choose to self-insure or accept this risk.

The vast majority of vulnerabilities in the business processes and context of a typical organization involve negligible damages, very low probabilities of occurrence, or both. As a result, it's just not prudent to spend money, time, and effort to do anything about such risks. In some cases, however, the vulnerabilities can be extensive and the potential loss significant, even catastrophic, to the organization, but the costs involved to deal with the risk by means of mitigation or transfer are simply unachievable.

Another, more practical example can be found in many international business situations. Suppose your company chooses to open wholesale supply operations in a developing country, one in which telecommunications and transportation infrastructures can be unreliable. When these infrastructures deliver the services you need, your organization makes a profit and earns political and community support as nontangible rewards. That reliable delivery doesn't happen all of the time, however. You simply cannot spend the money to install and operate your own alternative infrastructures. Even if you could afford to do it, you would risk alienating the local infrastructure operators and the larger political community, and you need all the goodwill from these people that you can get! As a result, you just decide to accept the risk.

Note that accepting a risk is not taking a gamble or betting that the risks won't ever materialize. That would be *ignoring* the risk. A simple example of this is the risk of having your business (or your hometown!) completely destroyed by a meteor falling in from outer space. We know it *could* happen; we've even had some spectacular near misses in recent years, such as what happened over Chelyabinsk, Russia in February 2013. The vast majority of us simply choose to ignore this risk, believing it to be of vanishingly small probability of occurrence. We do not gather any data; we do not estimate probabilities or losses; we don't even make a qualitative assessment about it. We simply ignore it, relegate it to the realm of big-box-office science fiction thrillers, and go on with our lives with nary another thought about it.

Proper risk acceptance is an informed decision by organizational leaders and stakeholders.

## Transfer

Transferring a risk means that rather than spend our own money, time, and effort to reduce, contain, or eliminate the risk, we assign responsibility for it to someone else. For example:

- Insuring your home against fire or flood transfers the risk of repairing or replacing your home and possessions to the insurance company. You take no real actions to decrease the likelihood of fire, or the extent to which it could damage your home and possessions, beyond what is normally reasonable and prudent to do. You don't redesign the home to put in more fire-retardant walls, doors, or floor coverings, for example. You paid for this via your insurance premiums.

- In the event of a fire in your home, you have transferred the responsibility for dealing with the fire to the local emergency responders, the fire department, and even the city planners who required the builders to put water mains and fire hydrants throughout your neighborhood. You paid for this risk to be assumed by the city and the fire department as part of your property taxes, and perhaps even a part of the purchase price (or rent you pay) on your home.

- You know that another nation might go to war with your homeland, causing massive destruction, death, injury, and suffering. Rather than taking up arms yourself, you pay taxes to your government to have it raise armed forces, train and equip them, and pursue strategies of deterrence and foreign relations to reduce the likelihood of an all-out war in our times.

Other ways of transferring risk might involve taking the process itself (the one that could incur the risk) and transferring it to others to perform as a service. Pizza tonight? Carry-out pizza incurs the risk that you might get into an accident while driving to or from the pizza parlor, but having the pizza delivered transfers that risk of accident (and injury or damage) to the pizza delivery service.

In almost all cases, transferring a risk is about transforming the risk into something somebody else can deal with for you. You save the money, time, and effort you might have spent to treat the risk yourself and instead pay others to assume the risk and deal with it.

There is a real moral hazard in some forms of risk transference, and the SSCP should be on alert for these. Suppose your company says that it doesn't need to spend a lot of money dealing with information security, because it has a really effective liability insurance plan that covers it against losses. If thousands (or millions!) of customers' personally identifying information is stolen by a hacker, this insurance policy may very well pay for losses that the company entails; the customers would need to sue the company or otherwise file a claim against it to recover from their direct losses to having their identity compromised or stolen. The insurance may pay all of those claims or only a portion of them, but only after each customer discovers the extent of the damages they've suffered and goes through the turmoil, effort, and expense of repairing the losses they've suffered, and then of filing a claim with the company. Perhaps the better, more ethical (and usually far less costly!) solution would have been to find and fix the vulnerabilities that could be exploited in ways that lead to such a data breach in the first place.

## Remediate or Mitigate (Also Known as Reduce or Treat)

Simply put, this means that we find and fix the vulnerabilities to the best degree that we can; failing that, we put in place other processes that shield, protect, augment, or bridge around the vulnerabilities. Most of the time this is *remedial* action—we are repairing something that either wore out during normal use or was not designed and built to be used the way we've been using it. We are applying a remedy, a cure, either total or partial, for something that went wrong.

Do not confuse taking remedial action to mitigate or treat a risk with making the repairs to a failed system itself. Mitigating the risk is something you aim to do *before* a failure occurs, not after! Such remediation measures might therefore include the following:

- Designing acceptable levels of redundancy into systems so that when components or elements fail, it does not cause critical business processes to halt or behave in harmful ways

- Designing acceptable fail-safe or graceful degradation features into systems so that when something fails, a cascade of failures leading to a disaster cannot occur

- Identifying acceptable amounts of downtime (or service disruption levels) and using these times to dictate design for services that detect and identify the failure, correct it, and restore full service to normal levels

- Pre-positioning backup or alternate operations capabilities so that critical business functions can go on (perhaps at a reduced capacity or quality)

- Identifying acceptable amounts of time by which all systems and processes must be restored to normal levels of performance, throughput, quality, or other measures of merit

Some vulnerabilities are best mitigated or treated by applying the right corrective fix—for example, by updating a software package to the latest revision level so that you are reasonably assured that it now has all the right security features and fixes included in it. Providing uninterruptible power supplies or power conditioning equipment may eliminate or greatly reduce the intermittent outages that plague some network, communications, and computing systems. The first (applying the software update) might be directly treating the vulnerability (by replacing a faulty algorithm with a more robustly designed one); providing power conditioning equipment is making up for shortcomings in the quality and reliability of the commercial power system and is a good example of bridging around or augmenting a known weakness.

**When in Doubt, What's the Requirement Say?**

We talked earlier about "common sense" approaches to information systems risk management and mitigation. Common sense might dictate simple solutions such as physical locks on the doors or an uninterruptible power supply; it usually cannot tell you the *performance criteria* that you should use to choose those locks or how much you should spend on that UPS. Those numbers come from having first done the analysis to determine what the real needs are, and then estimating the costs to purchase, install, verify, operate, and maintain the risk mitigation controls.

The written information security requirements documents should capture what you need to know in order to decide whether your chosen risk control is cost-effective.

## Avoid or Eliminate

The logical opposite of accepting a risk is to make the informed decision to stop doing business in ways or in places that expose you to that risk. Closing a store in a neighborhood with a high crime rate eliminates the exposure to risk (a store you no longer operate cannot be robbed, and your staff who no longer work there are no longer at risk of physical assault during such a robbery).

You avoid a risk either by eliminating the activity that incurs the risk or moving the affected assets or processes to locations or facilities where they are not exposed to the risk. Suppose you work for a small manufacturing company in which the factory floor has some processing steps that could cause fire, toxic smoke, and so forth to spread rapidly through the building. The finance office probably does not need to be in this building—avoid the risks to your accountants, and avoid the possible financial disruption of your business, by moving those functions and those people to another building. Yet the safety systems that are part of your manufacturing facility probably can't be moved away from the equipment they monitor and the people they protect; at some point, the business may have to decide that the risk of injury, death, destruction, and litigation just aren't worth the profits from the business in the long run.

## Recast

This term refers to the never-ending effort to identify risks, characterize them, select the most important ones to mitigate, and then deal with what's left. As we've said before, most risk treatments won't deal with 100% of a given risk; there will be some *residual risk* left over. Recasting the risk usually requires that first you clearly state what the new *residual* risk is, making it more clearly address what still needs to be dealt with. From the standpoint of the BIA, the original risk has been reduced—its nature, frequency, impact, and severity have been recast or need to be described anew so that future cycles of risk management and mitigation can take the new version of the risk into consideration.

## Residual Risk

This has been defined as the risk that's left over, unmitigated, after you have applied a selected risk treatment or control. Let's look at this more closely via the following example.

 **Real World Scenario**

### Residual Risk to PII in the Medical Insurance Industry

Suppose you work for a company that provides medical insurance claims processing support in the United States; the company has patient account records for upward of 6 million individual patients who file claims on private and public insurance providers. It uses Web-based front-end applications to support patient claims processing; care provider billing and accounts management; and claims status, accounting, and reporting for the insurance providers, along with all of the related tax and other regulatory filings that are needed. One identified risk is that somebody could conceivably download the entire patient/claimant database and extract PII or other valuable information from it without your knowledge or consent.

Mitigation 1: Separate testing and software development systems so that "live" patient/claimant data cannot be used on test systems and test data cannot be used on the production systems. This reduces the risk that poorly tested software could lead to a data breach. This provides assurance that test data won't be used to pay (or deny) real patient claims, nor will the software designers and testers be potentially capable of leaking the client database outside of the company's control. But it does nothing to ensure that the design of the current production system doesn't already contain an exploitable vulnerability, one that could lead to such a breach.

Mitigation 2: Ensure that the host facility for the production system uses rigorous access controls to authenticate users and processes trying to access it; log all access attempts. This includes authorized systems administrators who need to generate database backups for shipment to an offsite (cold or warm) standby facility to support continuity-of-operations needs. But those media themselves are subject to loss, misdirection, or unauthorized use if your physical logistics processes aren't suitably robust.

Mitigation 3: Ensure that all data in the system is encrypted when at rest, in motion, and in use. Thus, the backups generated for off-site storage are encrypted when they are generated. This does have a residual (remaining) risk that if the backup media were lost

*(continued)*

*(continued)*

or stolen, even their encrypted content is subject to decryption attacks. The manner in which the company controls encryption key distribution, certificate use, and so forth could also mean that the "strong" encryption used to protect the client data files was not as strong as you were led to believe.

At each step, you see that the total set of risks involved with loss of an entire patient/client database and the PII within it is reduced, either by reducing the threat surface around that database system or by protecting the information itself against misuse. Other risks remain, however.

## Risk Treatment Controls

Once again, you see the trio of physical, logical, and administrative (PLA) actions as possible controls you can apply to a given risk or set of risks. You'll see in Chapter 6 that this same trio have important roles to play as you strive to ensure that only authenticated users are authorized to take actions with your information systems. In that respect, a physical *access* control, such as a locked door requiring multifactor identification to be verified to permit entry, is also a physical *risk* control.

### Physical Controls

Physical controls are combinations of hardware, software, electrical, and electronic mechanisms that, taken together, prevent, delay, or deter somebody or something from physically crossing the threat surface around a set of system components you need to protect. Large-scale architectural features, such as the design of buildings, their location in an overall facility, surrounding roads, driveways, fences, perimeter lighting, and so forth, are visible, real, and largely static elements of physical control systems. You must also consider where within the building to put high-value assets, such as server rooms, wiring closets, network and communication provider points of presence, routers and Wi-Fi hotspots, library and file rooms, and so on. Layers of physical control barriers, suitably equipped with detection and control systems, can both detect unauthorized access attempts and block their further progress into your safe spaces within the threat surface.

Network and communications wiring, cables, and fibers are also physical system components that need some degree of physical protection. Some organizations require them to be run through steel pipes that are installed in such a way as to make it impractical or nearly impossible to uncouple a section of pipe to surreptitiously tap into the cables or fibers. Segmenting communications, network, and even power distribution systems also provides a physical degree of isolation and redundancy, which may be important to an organization's C-I-A needs.

Note the important link here to other kinds of controls. Physical locks require physical keys; multifactor authentication requires logical and physical systems; both require "people power" to create and then run the policies and procedures (the administrative controls) that glue it all together, and keep all of the parts safe, secure, and yet available when needed.

### Logical (or Technical) Controls

Here is where you use software and the parameter files or databases that direct that software to implement and enforce policies and procedures that you've administratively decided are important and necessary. It is a bit confusing that a "policy" can be a human-facing set of rules, guidelines, and instructions, and a set of software features and their control settings. Many modern operating systems, and identity-as-a-service provisioning systems, refer to these internal implementations of rules and features as *policy objects*, for example. So we write our administrative "acceptable use" policy document, and use it to train our users so that they know what is proper and what is not; our systems administrators then "teach" it to the operating system by setting parameters and invoking features that implement the software side of that human-facing policy.

### Administrative Controls

In general terms, anything that human organizations write, state, say, or imply that dictates how the humans in that organization should do business (and also what they should *not* do) can be considered an administrative control. Policy documents, procedures, process instructions, training materials, and many other forms of information all are intended to guide, inform, shape, and control the way that people act on the job (and to some extent, too, how they behave *off* the job!).

Administrative controls are typically the easiest to create—but sometimes, because they require the sign-off of very senior leadership, they can be ironically the most difficult to update in some organizational cultures. It usually requires a strong sense of the underlying business logic to create good administrative controls.

Administrative controls can cover a wide range of intentions, from informing people about news and useful information, to offering advice, and from defining the recommended process or procedure to dictating the one accepted way of doing a task or achieving an objective.

### Choosing a Control

For any particular risk mitigation need, an organization may face a bewildering variety of competing alternative solutions, methods, and choices. Do we build the new software fix in house or get a vendor to provide it? Is there a turn-key hardware/software system that will address a lot of our needs, or are we better off doing it internally one risk at a time? What's the right mix of physical, logical, and administrative controls to apply?

It's beyond the scope of this book, and the SSCP exam, to get into the fine-grain detail of how to compare and contrast different risk mitigation control technologies, produces, systems, or approaches. The technologies, too, are constantly changing. As you gain more experience as an SSCP, you'll have the opportunity to become more involved in specifying, selecting, and implementing risk mitigation controls.

## Step 4: Implement Controls

Controls, also called *countermeasures*, are the active steps we take to put technologies, features, and procedures in place to help prevent a vulnerability from being exploited and causing a harmful or disruptive impact. We must remember that with each new control we install or each new countermeasure we adopt, we must also make it part of the command, control, and communications capabilities of our integrated information security and assurance systems. For example:

- Physical systems technologies, such as buildings, locks, cabinets, fire detection and suppression systems, and even exterior and interior lighting, all can play multiple roles. They can prevent or deter unwanted activities; they can contain damage; they can either directly generate an alarm (and thus notify responders) or indicate that something has happened because of a change in their appearance or condition. (A broken window clearly indicates something has gone wrong; you ignore it at your peril!) Getting our money's worth of security out of our physical systems' elements usually requires human monitoring, whether by on-site inspection or remote (CCTV or other) monitoring.

- Logical systems technologies can and should provide the connectivity, information sharing, and analytical capabilities that keep everyone informed and enable assured decision making in the event of an incident. Getting everybody out of a building in the event of a fire requires the integrated capability to detect the fire and then notify building occupants about it; occupants have to be trained to recognize that the alarm is directing them to evacuate. Signage and other building features, such as emergency lighting and crash-bar door locks (that allow keyless exit), are also part of the end-to-end safety requirement, as is the need to notify first responders and organizational leadership. These provide the communications element of the C3 system.

- Administrative systems dictate the command and control aspects of integrated and proactive systems. By translating our planning results into people-facing products, we inform, advise, and direct our team how to plan, monitor, and act when faced with various circumstances. Administrative procedures delegate authority to incident managers (individual people or organizational units), for example; without this authoritative statement of delegation, all we can do is hope that somebody will keep their head when an incident actually happens, and that the right, knowledgeable head will take charge of the scene.

In many organizations, a spiral development process is used to manage risk mitigation efforts. A few high-priority risks are identified, and the systems that support them are examined for underlying vulnerabilities. Suitable risk mitigation controls are chosen and implemented; they are tested to ensure proper operation and correct results. End users are trained about the presence, purpose, and use of these controls, and they are declared operational. Then the next set of prioritized risks, and perhaps residual risks from this first set, are implemented in much the same way.

Note that even in this spiral or cyclic fashion, there really is a risk mitigation implementation plan! It may only exist as an agreed-to schedule by which the various builds or releases of risk mitigation controls will be specified, installed, tested, and made operational. The SSCP assists management by working to ensure that each increment of risk mitigation (each set of mitigation controls being installed, tested, and delivered to operational use) is logically consistent, that each control is installed correctly, and that users and security personnel know what to expect from it.

As with any implementation project, the choice to implement a particular set of risk mitigation controls should carry with it the documented need it is fulfilling. What is this new control required to actually *do* once we start using it? This statement of functional requirements forms the basis for verification and validation of our implementation, and it is also a basis for ongoing system security monitoring and assessment. The risk mitigation implementation plan should address these issues.

The implementation plan should also show how you'll engage with the routine configuration management and change control processes that are used in the business. In many businesses and organizations, policies direct that changes to business processes, operational software, or security systems have to be formally requested and then reviewed by the right set of experts, who then recommend to a formal change control board that the request be approved. Configuration management board approval usually includes the implementation plan and schedule so that this change can be coordinated with other planned activities throughout the organization.

This step includes all activities to get the controls into day-to-day routine operational use. User training and awareness needs identified in the implementation plan must be met; users, security personnel, and the rest of the IT staff must be aware of the changes and how to deal with anything that seems strange in the "new normal" that the new controls bring with them. In most organizations, some level of senior leadership or management approval may be required to declare that the new controls are now part of the regular operational ways of doing business.

Detailed implementation of specific controls will be covered in subsequent chapters. For example, Chapter 5 will go into greater depth about technologies and techniques to use when securing voice, video, and public and internal social media, as well as how physical and logical segmentation of networks and systems should be achieved.

## Communications

Keep in mind that "control" is just the middle element of command, control, and communications. The control devices or procedural elements have to communicate with the rest of the system so that we know what is going on. Some types of data that *must* be shared include but are not limited to:

- Status, state, and health information of the control, subsystem, or element. This tells systems operators and support staff if a component that has stopped working has entered a fail-safe state—or if it's been disconnected from the system altogether! Systems health information can be routinely sent by each system component to a central management system; that management system can also poll each system component or direct special queries to a systems element that seems to be behaving oddly. TCP/IP networks, for example, support the Simple Network Management Protocol (SNMP) and other protocols that allow network elements to broadcast, report centrally, or directly query other elements of the network.

- Alarm indications need to be promptly communicated by the element that first senses them; alarm conditions cannot and should not wait for routine polling to get around to discovering that something has gone out of limits, is about to fail, or has possibly been tampered with. (Think about your Windows computer telling you that "a network device or cable is unplugged," or when Outlook reports that it "cannot communicate with the server" as examples of alarm conditions being detected by one systems element—the NIC, or the TCP/IP protocol software stack, perhaps—and reporting it to another systems element—you, the user.)

- Routine operational protocol handshaking is also a vital, but often overlooked, element of information security management systems. Virtually every element of every system works by means of cycles of exchanges of signals. These handshakes make it possible for systems elements to each do their part in making the overall system support and achieve the user's needs and requirements. These protocol or housekeeping messages probably make up the bulk of what we actually see in our network traffic. They are what make general-purpose capabilities such as TCP/IP able to deliver so many types of services to meet almost any user need.

All of those types of control data must be exchanged between systems elements, if the system is to accomplish its assigned tasks. Even systems that are purely people-powered exchange information as part of the protocols that bring those people together to form a team. (Think about a baseball game: the catcher signals to the pitcher, but the runner on second is trying to see the signals too, to see if now's the time to attempt to steal third base.)

## Command and Control

Recall that *command* is the process of deciding what to do and issuing directives or orders to get it done; *control*, on the other hand, takes commands and breaks them down into the step-by-step directions to work units, while it monitors those work units for their performance of the assigned task. All systems have some kind of command and control function, and the OODA loop model presented earlier in this chapter provides a great mental model of such control systems. Most human-built systems exist to get specific jobs done or needs met, but those systems also have to have internal control processes that keep the system operating smoothly, set off alarms when it cannot be operated safely, or initiate corrective actions if they can. We can think of command and control of systems as happening at three levels of abstraction: getting the job done, keeping the system working effectively, and keeping it safe from outside corruption, damage, or attack.

Industrial control systems give us a great opportunity to see the importance of effective command, control, and communications in action at the first two levels. Most industrial machinery is potentially dangerous to be around—if it moves the wrong way at the wrong time, things can get broken and people can be killed. Industrial control system designers and builders have wrestled with this problem for almost three centuries, such as those that control an oil refinery or an electric power generating station. Command systems translate current inputs (such as demands for electricity and price bids for its wholesale purchase) into production or systems throughput goals; then they further refine those into device-by-device, step-by-step manipulation of elements of the overall system. Most of the time, this is done by exchanging packets of parameter settings, rather than device commands specifically (such as "increase temperature to 450 degrees F" rather than "open up the gas valve some more"). Other control loops keep the system and its various subsystems operating within well-understood safety constraints. These *Supervisory Control and Data Acquisition (SCADA)* systems are a special class of network and systems devices for data sharing, command, and control protocols used throughout the world for industrial process control. Much of this marketplace is dominated by special-purpose computers known as *programmable logic controllers* (PLCs), although many Internet of Things devices and systems are becoming more commonplace in industrial control environments.

NIST Special Publication 800-82 Rev. 2, Guide to Industrial Control System (ICS) Security, is an excellent starting point for SSCPs who need to know more about ICS security challenges and how they relate to information system risk management concepts in broader terms. It also helps map ICS or SCADA vulnerability information into the National Vulnerability Database (NIST Publication 800-53 Rev. 4).

Since the early 1990s, however, more and more industrial equipment operators and public utility organizations have had to deal with a third kind of command, control, and communications need: the need to keep their systems safe when faced with deliberate attacks directed at their SCADA or other command, control, and communications systems. It had become painfully clear that the vast majority of the lifeblood systems that keep a modern nation alive, safe, secure, well fed, and in business were hosted on systems owned and operated by private business, most of them using the Internet or the public switched telephone network (PSTN) as the backbone of their command, control, and communications system. In the United States, the *President's Commission on Critical Infrastructure Protection (PCCIP)* was created by President Bill Clinton to take on the job of awakening the nation to the need for this third level of C3 systems—the ones that keep modern information-driven economies working correctly and safe from hostile attacks via those information infrastructures. In many respects, the need for SSCPs and the standards we need people to uphold as SSCPs was given birth by the PCCIP.

**The Three Laws of Robotics as C3 or C-I-A?**

Science fiction author and scientist Dr. Isaac Asimov first published these "laws" in 1942. These laws, Asimov's characters claimed, fundamentally shaped and controlled what artificially intelligent robotic machines could and should do, and what they could not. The first and highest law concerned the safety of human life; the second law dictated obedience to human-directed purpose; the third law directed self-preservation so that the robot could always be there to answer human needs. As a student of history, military history, astronomy, control theory, and just about every other field of endeavor, Asimov expressed the 1940s systems engineering view of risk management very succinctly.

Suppose you work with a team that is designing the next generation of autonomous robots for industrial use—ones that have far greater latitude to make decisions about what to do next, based on their own internal OODA loops and their knowledge of their local environment, than machines in use today can do. We've talked a lot, as SSCPs, about the needs for confidentiality, integrity, and availability as they support our decision assurance needs. Yet many of our machine-learning systems today make decisions that we as humans do not understand and cannot prove are correct. Although this is all well beyond the current bounds of this text and the SSCP certification itself, we have some important questions to ask ourselves here. How do *we*, as humans, have decision assurance, if our systems are making decisions by themselves in ways we cannot understand?

Can our analytics systems or our robots follow the Three Laws? Should they? Or is a healthy dose of C-I-A sufficient?

### Step 5: Authorize: Senior Leader Acceptance and Ownership

As we said in Chapter 3, risk management must start with the senior leaders of the organization taking full responsibility for everything related to risk management. "The captain goes down with the ship" may not literally require that the ship's commander drown when the ship sinks, but it *does* mean that no matter what happens, when it happens, ultimately that captain or commander has full responsibility. Captains of ships or captains of industry (as we used to call such senior leaders) may share their due care and due diligence responsibilities, and they usually must delegate the authority and responsibility to achieve them. Regardless, the C-suite and the board of directors are the ones who operate the business in the names of the owners and stakeholders. They "own" the bad news when due diligence fails to protect the stakeholder's interests

This has two vital spin-offs for risk management programs, plans, and processes:

1.  It requires senior leadership to set the priorities, establish the success criteria, and then fund, staff, and resource the risk management plans in line with those priorities.

2.  It requires senior leadership to celebrate the successes of these risk management programs and processes, as well as own up to their failures and shortcomings.

That last does need a bit of clarification. Obviously, the best way to keep a secret is to not share it with anyone; the next-best way is to not tell anyone else that you *have* a secret. If senior leaders or stakeholders are making a lot of public noise about "our successful efforts to eliminate information risk," for example, that might be just the attractive nuisance that a threat actor needs to come and do a little looking around for something exploitable that's been overlooked or oversold.

Statements by senior leaders, and their appearance at internal and external events, all speak loudly. Having the senior leaders formally sign off on acceptance testing results or on the results of audits and operational evaluation testing are opportunities to confirm to everyone that these things are *important*. They're important enough to spend the senior leadership's time and energy on. The CEO and the others in the C-suite do more than care about these issues. They get involved with them; they *lead* them. That's a very powerful silver bullet to use internally; it can pay huge dividends in gaining end-user acceptance, understanding, and willing compliance with information security measures. It can open everyone's eyes—maybe just a little; perhaps just enough to spot something out of the ordinary before it becomes an exploited vulnerability.

# The Ongoing Job of Keeping Your Baseline Secure

There's been a lot of hard work accomplished to get to where a set of information risk controls have been specified, acquired (or built), installed, tested, and signed off by the senior leaders as meeting the information security needs of the business or organization. The job thus far has been putting in place countermeasures and controls so that the organization can roll with the punches, and weather the rough seas that the world, the competition, or the willful threat actors out there try to throw at it. Now it's on to the *really* hard part of the job—keeping this information architecture and its IT architectures safe, secure, and resilient so that confidentiality, integrity, and authorization requirements are met and stay met. How do we know all of those safety nets, countermeasures, and control techniques are still working the way we intended them to *and* that they're still adequate to keep us safe?

The good news is that this is no different than the work we did in making our initial security assessments of our information architecture, the business logic and business processes, and the IT architectures and systems that make them possible. The bad news is that this job never ends. We must continually monitor and assess the effectiveness of those risk controls and countermeasures, and take or recommend action when we see they no longer are adequate. Putting the controls in place was taking due care; due diligence is achieved through constant vigilance.

More good news: the data sources you used originally, to gain the insight you needed to make your first assessments, are still there, just waiting for you to come around, touch base, and ask for an update. Let's take a closer look at some of them.

## Build and Maintain User Engagement with Risk Controls

As you selected and implemented each new or modified information risk mitigation control, you had to identify the training needs for end users, their managers, and others. You had to identify what users and people throughout the organization needed to know and understand about this control and its role in the bigger picture. Achieving this minimum set of awareness and understanding is key to *acceptance* of the control by everyone concerned. This need for acceptance is continual, and depending on the nature of the risk control itself, the need for ongoing refresher training and awareness may be quite great. Let's look at how different risks might call for different approaches to establish initial user awareness and maintain it over time:

- Suppose your organization has adopted a policy that prohibits end users from installing their own software onto company-provided computer systems. Your IT department has established logical controls throughout all computers to enforce this. Initial user training communicates and gains new employees' acknowledgment of this. Annual employee performance reviews are opportunities to reaffirm the importance of this policy and the need for employees to comply.

- Some users in your organization need to access company information systems and networks via their personal computers or smartphones. This means that the risk of commingling personal data and company data on these employee-owned devices is very real. You determine that currently available mobile device management technologies don't quite fit your circumstances, but even if they did, mobile or personal device users need to appreciate that the risks of data compromise, device loss or theft, misuse of the device by a family member, or conflicts between company-approved software and personal-use software on these devices could pose additional risks. Getting these mobile or personal device users to be actively part of keeping company data and systems secure is a daily challenge.

The key to keeping users engaged with risk management and risk mitigation controls is simple: align their own, individual interests with the interests the controls are supporting, protecting, or securing. Chapter 11, "Business Continuity via Information Security and People Power," will show you some strategies and techniques for achieving and maintaining this alignment by bringing more of your business's "people power" to bear on everybody's C-I-A needs.

## Participate in Security Assessments

By this time, our newly implemented risk mitigation controls have gone operational. Day by day, users across the organization are using them to stay more secure, (hopefully) achieving improved levels of C-I-A in their information processing tasks. The SSCP and the information security team now need to shift their mental gears and look to ongoing monitoring and assessment of these changes. In one respect, this seems easy; the identified risk, and therefore the related vulnerability, focused us on changing something in our physical, logical, or administrative processes so that our information could be more secure, resilient, reliable, and confidential; our decisions should now be more assured.

Are they?

The rest of the world did not stand still while we were making these changes. Our marketplace continued to grow and change; no doubt other users in other organizations were finding problems in the underlying hardware, software, or platforms we use; and the vendors who build and support those systems elements have been working to make fixes and patches available (or at least provide a procedural workaround) to resolve these problems. Threat actors may have discovered new zero day exploits. And these or other threat actors have been continuing to ping away at our systems.

We do need to look at whether this new fix, patch, control, or procedural mitigation is working correctly, but we've got to do that in the context of *today's* system architecture and the environment it operates in…and not just in the one in which we first spotted the vulnerability or decided to do something about the risk it engendered.

The SSCP may be part of a variety of ongoing security assessment such as *penetration testing* or *operational test and evaluation* (OT&E) activities, all intended to help understand what the security posture of the organization is at the time that the tests or evaluations are conducted. Let's take a closer look at some of these types of testing. This kind of test and evaluation is not to be confused with the acceptance testing or verification that was done when a new control was implemented—that verification test is necessary to prove that you did that fix correctly. It should also be kept distinct in your mind from regression testing, the verification that a fix to one systems element did not break others. Ongoing security test and evaluation is looking to see if things are *still* working correctly now that the users—and the threat actors—have had some time to put the changes and the total system through their paces.

**Remember the PLA!**

Your ongoing security assessments should always take the opportunity to assess the entire set of information risk controls—be they physical, logical, or administrative in nature.

## Adding a Security Emphasis to OT&E

OT&E, in its broadest sense, is attempting to verify that a given system and the people-powered processes that implement the overall set of business logic and purpose actually get work done correctly and completely, when seen from the end users' or operators' perspective. That may sound straightforward, but quite often, it is a long, complex process that produces some insight rather than clear, black-and-white "succeed" or "fail" scorecard results. Without going into too much detail, this is mainly because unavoidable differences exist between the system that business analysts thought was needed and what operational users in the organization are actually *doing*, day by day, to get work done. Some of those differences are caused by the passage of time; if it takes months to analyze a business's needs, and more months to build the systems, install, test, and deliver them, the business has continued to move on. Some reflect different perceptions or understanding about the need; it's difficult for a group of systems builders to understand what a group of systems users actually have to do in order to get work done. (And quite often, users are not as clear and articulate as they think they are when they try to tell the systems analysts what they need from the new system. Nor are the analysts necessarily the good listeners that they pride themselves on being.)

OT&E in security faces the same kind of lags in understanding, since quite often the organization doesn't know it has a particular security requirement until it is revealed (either by testing and evaluation, or by enemy action via a real incident). This does create circular logic: we think we have a pretty solid system that fulfills our business logic, so we do some OT&E on it to understand how well it is working and where it might need to be improved—but the OT&E results cause us (sometimes) to rethink our business logic, which leads to changes in the system we just did OT&E on, and in the meantime, the rest of the world keeps changing around us.

The bottom line is that operational test and evaluation is one part of an ongoing learning experience. It has a role to play in continuous quality improvement processes; it can help an organization understand how mature its various business processes and systems are. And it can offer a chance to gain insight into potentially exploitable vulnerabilities in systems, processes, and the business logic itself.

*Ethical Penetration Testing* is security testing focused on trying to actively find and exploit vulnerabilities in an organization's information security posture, processes, procedures, and systems. *Pen-testing*, as it's sometimes called, often looks to use "ethical hackers" who attempt to gain access to protected, secure elements of those systems. There are some significant legal and ethical issues that the organization and its testers must address, however, before proceeding with even the most modest of controlled pen-testing. In most jurisdictions around the world, it is illegal for anyone to attempt to gain unauthorized entry into someone else's information systems without their express written permission; even with that permission in hand, mistakes in the execution of pen-testing activities can expose the requesting company or the penetration testers to legal or regulatory sanctions.

The first major risk to be considered in pen-testing is that first and foremost, pen testers are trying to actively and surreptitiously find exploitable vulnerabilities in your information security posture and systems. This activity could disrupt normal business operations, which in turn could disrupt your customers' business operations. For this reason, the scope of pen-testing activities should be clearly defined. Reporting relationships between the people doing the pen-testing, their line managers, and management and leadership within your own organization must be clear and effective.

Another risk comes into play when using external pen-testing consulting firms to do the testing, analyze the results, and present these results to you as the client. Quite often, pen-testing firms hire reformed former criminal hackers (or hackers who narrowly escaped criminal prosecution), because they've got the demonstrated technical skills and hacker mindset to know how to conduct all aspects of such an attack. Yet, you are betting your organization's success, if not survival, on how trustworthy these hackers might be. Can you count on them actually telling you about everything they find? Will they actually turn over all data, logs, and so forth that they capture during their testing and not retain any copies for their own internal use? This is not an insurmountable risk, and your contract with the pen-testing firm should be adamant about these sorts of risk containment measures. That said, it is not a trivial risk.

The SSCP exam will not go into much detail as it pertains to operational testing and evaluation or to penetration testing. You should, however, understand what each kind of ongoing or special security assessment, evaluation, and testing activities might be; have a realistic idea of what they can accomplish; and be aware of some of the risks associated with them.

## Assessment-Driven Training

Whether security assessments are done via formalized penetration testing, as part of normal operational test and evaluation, or by any of a variety of informal means, each provides the SSCP an opportunity to identify ways to make end users more effective in the ways they contribute to the overall information security posture. Initial training may instill a sense of awareness, while providing a starter set of procedural knowledge and skills; this is good, but as employees or team members grow in experience, they can and should be able to step up and do more as members of the total information security team.

End user questions and responses during security assessment activities, or during debriefs of them, can illuminate such opportunities to improve awareness and effectiveness. Make note of each "why" or "how" that surfaces during such events, during your informal walk-arounds to work spaces, or during other dialogue you have with others in the organization. Each represents a chance to improve awareness of the overall information security need; each is an opportunity to further empower teammates be more intentional in strengthening their own security hygiene habits.

A caution is in order: some organizational cultures may believe that it's more cost-effective to gather up such questions and indicators, and then spend the money and time to develop and train with new or updated training materials when a critical mass of need has finally arisen. You'll have to make your own judgment, in such circumstances, whether this is being penny-wise but pound-foolish.

# Manage the Architectures: Asset Management and Configuration Control

Think back to how much work it was to discover, understand, and document the information architecture that the organization uses, and then the IT architectures that support that business logic and data. Chances are that during your discovery phase, you realized that a lot of elements of both architectures could be changed or replaced by local work unit managers, group leaders, or division directors, all with very little if any coordination with any other departments. If that's the case, you and the IT director, or the chief information security officer and the CIO, may have an uphill battle on your hands as you try to convince everyone that proper stewardship does require more central, coordinated change management and control than the company is accustomed to.

The definitions of these three management processes are important to keep in mind:

- *Asset management* is the process of identifying everything that could be a key or valuable asset and adding it to an inventory system that tracks information about its acquisition costs, its direct users, its physical (or logical) location, and any relevant licensing or contract details. Asset management also includes processes to periodically verify that *tagged property* (items that have been added to the formal inventory) are still in the company's possession and have not disappeared, been lost, or been stolen. It also includes procedures to make changes to an asset's location, use, or disposition.

- *Configuration management* is the process by which the organization decides what changes in controlled systems baselines will be made, when to implement them, and the verification and acceptance needs that the change and business conditions dictate as necessary and prudent. Change management decisions are usually made by a configuration management board, and that board may require impact assessments as part of a proposed change.

- *Configuration control* is the process of regulating changes so that only authorized changes to controlled systems baselines can be made. Configuration control implements what the configuration management process decides and prevents unauthorized changes. Configuration control also provides audit capabilities that can verify that the contents of the controlled baseline in use today are in fact what they should be.

## What's at Risk with Uncontrolled and Unmanaged Baselines?

As an SSCP, consider asking (or looking yourself for the answers to!) the following kinds of questions:

- How do we know when a new device, such as a computer, phone, packet sniffer, etc., has been attached to our systems or networks?

- How do we know that one of our devices has gone missing, possibly with a lot of sensitive data on it?

- How do we know that someone has changed the operating system, updated the firmware, or updated the applications that are on our end users' systems?

- How do we know that an update or recommended set of security patches, provided by the systems vendor or our own IT department, has actually been implemented across all of the machines that need it?

- How do we know that end users have received updated training to make good use of these updated systems?

If you're unable to get good answers to those kinds of questions, from policy and procedural directives, from your managers, or from your own investigations, you may be working in an environment that is ripe for disaster.

## Auditing Controlled Baselines

To be effective, any management system or process must collect and record the data used to make decisions about changes to the systems being managed; they must also include ways to audit those records against reality. For most business systems, we need to consider three different kinds of baselines: recently archived, current operational, and ongoing development. Audits against these baselines should be able to verify that:

- The recently archived baseline is available for fallback operations if that becomes necessary. If this happens, we also need to have an audited list of what changes (including security fixes) are included in it and which documented deficiencies are still a part of that baseline.

- The current operational baseline has been tested and verified to contain proper implementation of the changes, including security fixes, which were designated for inclusion in it.

- The next ongoing development baseline has the set of prioritized changes and security fixes included in its work plan and verification and test plan.

Audits of configuration management and control systems should be able to verify that the requirements and design documentation, source code files, builds and control systems files, and all other data sets necessary to build, test, and deploy the baseline contain authorized content and changes only.

We'll address this in more detail in Chapters 9 and 10.

# Ongoing, Continuous Monitoring

Prudent risk managers have been doing this for thousands of years. Guards would patrol the city and randomly check to see that doors were secured at the end of the workday and that gates were closed and barred. Tax authorities would select some number of taxpayers' records and returns for audit, to look for both honest mistakes and willful attempts to evade payment. Merchants and manufacturers, shipping companies, and customers make detailed inventory lists and compare those lists after major transactions (such as before and after a clearance sale or a business relocation). Banks and financial institutions keep detailed transaction ledgers and then balance them against statements of accounts. These are all examples of regular operational use, inspection, audit, and verification that a set of risk mitigation controls are still working correctly.

We monitor our risk mitigation controls so that we can conclude that either we are safe or we are not. Coming to a well-supported answer to that question requires information and analysis, and that can require a lot of data just to answer "Are we safe today?" Trend analysis (to see if safety or security has changed over time, with an eye to discovering why) requires even more data. The nature of our business, our risk appetite (or tolerance), and the legal and regulatory compliance requirements we face may also dictate how often we have to collect such data and for how long we have to keep it available for analysis, audit, or review.

Where does the monitoring data come from? This question may seem to have an obvious answer, but it bears thinking about the four main types of information that we deliberately produce with each step of a business process:

- First, we produce the outputs or results we require for business reasons. We calculate the new throttle setting; we transact the sale of an airline ticket; we post a debit to an account balance. Those are examples of required outputs that help achieve required outcomes of the business logic.

- Next, we produce verification outputs—additional information that lets the end user and their quality management processes look at the primary process outputs so that they can verify that the process steps have run correctly. This verification is a routine part of the business logic. An example might be where the business logic requires a confirmation (of a credit or debit card transaction by the card processing agent) before it allows the next step to proceed.

- Third, we look at safety and security requirements that add additional steps to our business logic. Administrative policy might require valid authentication and authorization of a user before they can access a customer file, and our access control systems enforce those policies. But it is the *audit* or accounting requirements that drive access control builders to log all attempts by all processes or people to access protected resources. From a safety perspective, we might have requirements that dictate systems are built with interlocks—hardware or software components that do not permit a potentially hazardous step being initiated if all of the safety prerequisite steps have not been met. If nobody else requires it, our liability insurers probably want us to keep good log information on each hazardous step—who initiated it, were all initial conditions correct, and what happened?

- Finally, we consider diagnostic information, sometimes called *fault detection and fault isolation (FDFI)* information. Most hardware systems have features built into their design that facilitate finding failed hardware. Sometimes these *built-in test equipment* (BITE) systems use industry-standard communications and data protocols, such as what we see in modern computer-controlled automotive systems. Other times they use proprietary protocols and interfaces. Software, too, will often have test features built into its source code so that during development testing, the programmers can demonstrate that the software functions correctly. All of these debug features can be rich sources of systems security monitoring and assessment information.

Notice one important fact: no useful data gets generated unless somebody, somewhere, decided to create a process to get the data generated by the system, output in a form that is useful, and then captured in some kind of document, log file, or other memory device. When we choose to implement controls and countermeasures, we choose systems and components that help us deal with potential problems *and* inform us when problems occur.

 **Real World Scenario**

**Ongoing Monitoring at Small State University's East of Ealing Campus**

Pete works as the campus director at the East of Ealing campus at Small State University. The campus has a dozen classrooms and five administrative, staff, and faculty offices, all in one small building. It serves about 2,000 students in a variety of online and face-to-face classes and has about 40 faculty members and four part-time and full-time staff. Academic and administrative IT capabilities are all cloud-hosted by the main university organization. On site, classrooms and offices are equipped with Windows 10 systems (desktop, laptop, or tablet), all with a centrally supported standard set of operating systems, utilities, applications, and data resources. They are connected via managed switches that provide access to the Internet and the public switched telephone network; these switches are managed by university IT staff on the main campus. The building has a security alarm system that provides for intrusion detection, fire, and smoke and carbon monoxide event alarms, and is key-card controlled for after-hours entry and exit by faculty and staff.

What kind of monitoring data is generated? Where is that data kept? How is that data collected, collated, and used, and for what purposes?

> The building security and fire alarm system is operated by a central office security firm, which maintains records of events (such as authorized or unauthorized access attempts). This central office has policies for when to use alarm data to send out a private patrol firm for onsite inspection or to notify emergency responders. It also has procedures for contacting university officials for specific kinds of events.
>
> The communications and network systems, and the university-owned computers, are able to be remotely managed by university IT staff members. Log data (such as Windows Security Event logs or activity and security logs produced by the managed switches) can be used by IT staff on an as-required basis, but they are not routinely collected or aggregated by university IT.
>
> University faculty and staff members have been given administrative instructions to "keep their eyes open" and report to the head of the local campus team if they detect anything unusual.

One morning, Pete comes into the office and boots up his university laptop, and something strikes him as odd. A bit of investigating reveals that a whole folder tree of data files has disappeared; the folders contained student admissions and enrollment data, all of which is considered by the Family Educational Records Privacy Act (FERPA) as private data requiring protection. Pete is pretty confident that the folder tree and files were there the night before, when he logged off, shut down, and (since there were no night classes scheduled) secured the building.

You are a member of the university IT team, and you get a somewhat panicky call from Pete. Where might you look for telltale information to help you determine whether this is an accidental deletion or a data breach incident?

Pete, by the way, has just read a book about cybersecurity, and he is asking you whether all of the elements and systems in the university's cybersecurity systems make that system integrated and proactive. What do you think?

## Exploiting What Monitoring and Event Data Is Telling You

All of that monitoring data does you absolutely no good at all unless you actually *look at it*. Analyze it. Extract from it the stories it is trying to tell you. This is perhaps the number one large-scale set of tasks that many cybersecurity and information security efforts fail to adequately plan for or accomplish. *Don't repeat this mistake.*

Mistake number two is to not have somebody on watch to whom the results of monitoring and event data analysis are sent to so that *when* (not if) a potentially emergency situation is developing, the company doesn't find out about it until the Monday morning after the long holiday weekend is over. Those watch-standers can be on call (and receive alerts via SMS or other mobile communications means) or on site, and each business will make that decision based on their mission needs and their assessment of the risks. *Don't repeat this mistake either.*

Mistake number three is to not look at the log data at all unless some other problem causes you to think, "Maybe the log files can tell me what's going on."

These three mistakes suggest that we need what emergency medicine calls a *triage* process: a way to sort out patients with life-threatening conditions needing immediate attention from the ones who can wait a while (or should go see their physician during office hours).

Let's look at the analysis problem from the point of view of those who need the analysis done and work backward from there to develop good approaches to the analytical tasks themselves. But let's not repeat mistake number four, often made by the medical profession—that more often than not, when the emergency room triage team sends you back home and says "See your doctor tomorrow," their detailed findings don't go to your doctor with you.

### What the Alert Team Needs

The alert team is watching over the deployed, in-use operational IT systems and support infrastructures. That collection of systems elements is probably supporting ongoing customer support, manufacturing, shipping, billing and finance operations, and website and public-facing information resources, as well as the various development and test systems used by different groups in the company. Their job is to know the status, state, and health of these in-use IT systems, but not necessarily the details of how or for what purpose any particular end user or organization is using those systems.

Who is the alert team? It might be a part of the day shift help desk team, the people everybody calls whenever any kind of IT issue comes up. In other organizations, the alert team is part of a separate IT security group, and their focus is on IT security issues and not normal user support activities.

What does this alert team do? The information security alert team has as their highest priority being ready and able to receive alerts from the systems they monitor and respond accordingly. That response typically includes the following:

- Receive and review alarm, alert, and systems performance reporting data in real time.
- Identify and characterize alarms as emergency or non-emergency, based on predetermined criteria.
- Take immediate corrective or containment action as dictated by predetermined procedures, if any are required for the alarm in question.
- Notify designated emergency responders, such as police, fire, and so forth, if required.
- Notify designated technical support staff, or the internal *computer emergency response team* (CERT), if required.
- Notify designated point of contact in management and leadership, if required.
- Log this alarm event, and their disposition of it, in the alert team's own logs.

What we can see from that list of alert team tasks is that we're going to need the help of our systems designers, builders, and maintainers to help figure out

- What data to look for in the monitoring and event data outputs
- What logic to apply to the data to determine that an alarm state requiring urgent action is indicated
- What, if any, immediate action is required or recommended

The immediacy of the alert team's needs suggests that lots of data has to be summarized up to some key indicators, rather like a dashboard display in an automobile or an airplane. There are logical places on that dashboard for "idiot lights," the sort of red-yellow-green indicators designed to get the operator's attention and then direct them to look at other displays to be better informed. There are also valid uses on this dashboard for indicator gauges, such as throughput measures on critical nodes and numbers of users connected.

The alert team may also need to be able to see the data about an incident shown in some kind of timeline fashion, especially if there are a number of systems elements that seem to be involved in the incident. Timeline displays can call attention to periods that need further investigation and may even reveal something about cause and effect.

Before we jump to a conclusion and buy a snazzy new security information management dashboard system, however, take a look at what the *other* monitoring and event data analysis customers in our organization might need.

## What IT Support Staff Need

The IT support team is actually looking at a different process: the process of taking user needs, building systems and data structures to meet those needs, deploying those systems, and then dealing with user issues, problems, complaints, and ideas for improvements with them. That process lends itself to a fishbone or Ishikawa diagram that takes the end users' underlying value chain and reveals all of the inputs, the necessary preconditions, the processing steps, the outputs, and how outputs relate to outcomes. This process may have many versions of the information systems and IT baselines that it must monitor, track, and support at any one time. In some cases, some of those versions may be subsets of the entire architecture, tailor-made to support specific business needs. IT and the configuration management and control board teams will be controlling these many different product baseline versions, which includes keeping track of which help desk tickets or requests for changes are assigned to (scheduled to be built into) which delivery. The IT staff must also monitor and be able to report on the progress of each piece of those software development tasks.

Some of those "magic metrics" may lend themselves to a dashboard-style display. For large systems with hundreds of company-managed end-user workstations, for example, one such status indicator could be whether all vendor-provided updates and patches have been applied to the hardware, operating systems, and applications platform systems. Other indicators could be an aggregate count of the known vulnerabilities that are still open and in need of mitigation and the critical business logic affected by them.

Trend lines are also valuable indicators for the IT support staff. Averages of indicators such as system uptime, data or user logon volumes, accesses to key information assets, or transaction processing time can be revealing when looked at over the right timeframe—and when compared to other systems, internal, or external events to see if cause-and-effect relationships exist.

## What End Users Need

What end users require may vary a lot depending on the needs of the organization and which users are focused on which parts of its business logic. That said, end users tend to need traffic-light kind of indications that tell them whether systems, components, platforms, or other elements they need are ready and available, down for maintenance, or in a "hands-off" state while a problem is being investigated. They may also appreciate being able to see the scheduled status of particular changes that are of interest to them. *Transparent* change management systems are ones in which end users or other interested parties in the business have this visibility into the planned, scheduled builds and the issues or changes allocated to them.

## What Leadership and Management Need

We might rephrase "What do leadership and management need?" and ask how the analysis of monitoring and event data can help management and leadership fulfill their due care and due diligence responsibilities. Depending on the management and leadership style and culture within the organization, the same dashboard and summary displays used by the alert team and IT support staff may be just what they need. (This is sometimes called a "high-bandwidth-in" style of management, where the managers need to have access to lots of detailed data about what's going on in the organization.) Other management and leadership choose to work with high-level summaries, aggregates, or alarm data as their daily feeds.

One key lesson to remember is suggested by the number of alert team tasks that lead to notifying management and leadership of an incident or alarm condition. Too many infamous data breach incidents became far too costly for the companies involved because the company culture discouraged late-night or weekend calls to senior managers for "mere" IT systems problems. (The data breach at retail giant Target, in 2013, suffered in part from this failure to properly notify and engage senior leadership *before* such incidents happen so that the company could respond properly *when* one occurred.)

 **Real World Scenario**

### How Much Monitoring Data?

Roy works for a typical medium-sized private university, which serves about 32,000 students with a staff and faculty team of about 2,000 people in 32 states across the United States. Each of those people use the university's online resources throughout the day to participate in classes, build course material, manage student data, or just keep the university's bills paid.

Let's assume for planning purposes that each person has a typical Windows 10 computer. By a combination of university IT policy and manufacturer defaults, event logging for hardware, operating systems, security management, and applications are all turned on. These might generate up to 250 events (across multiple types of logs) every hour that the user is actively using the computer, whether for work or leisure.

When users access university online resources, every aspect of what they do is logged, both for security monitoring and transaction backup purposes. Logs are generated in all of the communications devices (modems, routers, switches, firewall systems, etc.) as well as within the servers themselves. Thus a typical online user might cause logging of up to another 1,000 events per hour of intensive work, scattered across dozens of machines.

Students are online an average of four hours per day; staff and faculty an average of eight hours per day. Students might be anywhere on Earth, and while most staff and faculty are within the United States, a good number of them are located in other time zones as well. Peak usage of systems by staff might be during normal working hours (in their own home time zones), whereas student peak usage will probably be in their evenings and weekends.

How many events are logged, on average, across a typical week?

Suppose an incident has occurred in which a number of students, staff, and faculty seem to have been able to access and redistribute files and email messages that according to administrative policy they should not have had access to or the right to share with others. How much event log data might Roy have to examine to be able to investigate who might have done what?

## Incident Investigation, Analysis, and Reporting

At some point, the SSCP must determine that an *incident of interest* has occurred. Out of the millions of events that a busy datacenter's logging and monitoring systems might take note of every 24 hours, only a handful might be worthy of sounding an alarm:

- Unplanned shutdown of any asset, such as a router, switch, or server
- Unauthorized attempts to elevate a user's or process's privilege state to systems owner or root level
- Unauthorized attempts to extract, download, or otherwise exfiltrate restricted data from the facility
- Unauthorized attempts to change, alter, delete, or replace any data, software, or other controlled elements of the baseline system
- Unplanned or unauthorized attempts to initiate system backup or recovery tasks
- Unplanned or unauthorized attempts to connect a device, cable, or process to the system
- Unauthorized attempts to access system resources of any kind as part of trying to cause any of these events to occur, or to hide, alter, or mask data that would reveal these attempts
- Alarms or alerts from malware, intrusion detection, or other defensive systems

That's a pretty substantial list, but in a well-managed and well-secured datacenter, most of those kinds of incidents shouldn't happen often. When they do (not if they do), several important things have to occur properly and promptly:

1. Alarm or notify the right first responders, whether they are normal IT staff, IT security staff, or a specialized CERT.
2. Perform immediate steps to characterize the incident and determine whether affected users should cease business operations as normal (but not log off or shut down their systems without IT responder direction!).
3. Alert appropriate management and leadership in case they need to make other decisions as part of responding to the incident.

Part of that initial triage kind of response involves determining whether the incident is sufficiently serious or disruptive that the organization should activate its incident response plans and procedures. We'll cover these in Chapter 11 in more detail; for now, recognize that businesses have an abiding due diligence responsibility to think through what to do in an emergency *well before* that emergency first occurs!

Immediate response to an incident may mean that the first person to notice it has to make an immediate decision: is this an emergency that threatens life or property and thus requires initiating emergency alarms and procedures? Or is it "merely" an information systems incident not requiring outside emergency responders? Before you take on operational responsibilities, make sure you know how your company wants to handle these decisions.

# Reporting to and Engaging with Management

We said at the onset of this book that the commitment by senior business leadership and management is pivotal to the success of the company's information risk management and mitigation efforts. As an SSCP, you and the rest of the team went to great efforts to get those senior leaders involved, gain their understanding, and acceptance of your risk assessments. You then gained their pledges to properly fund, staff, and support your risk mitigation strategies, as well as your chosen risk countermeasures and controls.

Much like any other accountable, reportable function in the company, information security must make regular reports to management and leadership. The good news (no incidents of interest) as well as the bad news about minor or major breaches of security must be brought to the attention of senior leaders and managers. They need to see that their investments in your efforts are still proving to be successful—and if they are not, then they need to understand why, and be informed to consider alternative actions to take in the face of new threats or newly discovered vulnerabilities.

Management and leadership may also have legal and regulatory reporting requirements of their own to meet, and your abilities to manage security systems event data, incident data, and the results of your investigations may be necessary for them to meet these obligations. These will, of course, vary as to jurisdiction; a multinational firm with operating locations in many countries may face a bewildering array of possibly conflicting reporting requirements in that regard.

Whatever the reporting burden, the bottom line is that the information security team must report its findings to management and leadership. Whether those findings are routine good news about the continued secure good health of the systems or dead-of-night emergency alarms when a serious incident seems to be unfolding, management and leadership have an abiding and enduring need to know.

No bad news about information security incidents will ever get better by waiting until later to tell management about it.

# Summary

We've spent Chapters 3 and 4 learning how to defend our information, our information systems (the business logic that uses information), and our information technology architectures from harm due to accident, Mother Nature, or hostile action by insiders or external actors alike. That has taken us from risk management through risk mitigation, as we've seen how the leadership, management, systems, and security teams must work together to make smart trade-offs between the possible pain of a risk becoming reality and the real costs incurred to purchase, install, and operate a control or countermeasure that prevents or reduces that possible loss.

Throughout, we have applied the basic concepts of confidentiality, integrity, and availability as the characteristics by which we assess our information security measures. In broad terms, this C-I-A triad helps us manage the risks. We've seen that without knowing and controlling our systems baselines, we have very little opportunity to detect a vulnerability becoming a disruptive event; thus, we've seen how managing our systems baselines and exerting a reasonable amount of change control keeps them safer. The underlying software and hardware of an unmanaged and uncontrolled system may have the same vulnerabilities as a well-managed, tightly controlled system using the same technologies; it is that lack of people-centric management and control processes that expose the unmanaged systems to greater probability of occurrence of an exploitation being attempted or succeeding.

Finally, we've seen that the understanding and involvement of all levels of organizational leadership and management are vital to making risk management pay off. Risk management is not free; it takes valuable staff time, intellectual effort, and analysis to pull all of the data; understand the business logic, processes, and architecture; and find the high-priority vulnerabilities. It takes more money, time, and effort to make changes that contain, fix, or eliminate the risks that those vulnerabilities bring with them. But by the numbers, we see that there are ways to make quantitative as well as qualitative assessments about risks, and which ones to manage or mitigate.

# Exam Essentials

**Know the major activities that are part of information risk mitigation.** Risk mitigation is the set of activities that take identified risks and deal with them in ways management finds reasonable and prudent. Its input is the BIA, which characterizes identified risks and their likely impacts to the business. Risk mitigation planning next assesses the information and IT architectures the business depends on; assesses vulnerabilities in those architectures; and then recommends risk treatments. This leads to creating the risk mitigation implementation plan, which captures decisions as to risk treatments, implementation schedules, and verification testing needs. Once the chosen treatments (also called controls or countermeasures) are shown to be working correctly, the new security baseline (preexisting baseline plus risk reductions due to mitigations) is approved by senior leadership. Ongoing operational use is monitored, and logs and other data are reviewed, to determine the continued correct operation of the system and to maintain vigilance for new or heretofore unnoticed risks. Risk mitigation planning also identifies potential incidents of interest (which might be risks becoming reality), and the needs for alerts and alarms to initiate emergency responses and other management actions.

**Know the important security differences between the information architecture and the information technology architecture.**    The information architecture focuses on how people use information to accomplish business objectives; thus, its principal security issues are involved with guiding, shaping, or constraining human behavior. Well-considered work-force education and training programs that align business objectives with information security and decision assurance needs are solid investments to make. By contrast, the IT architecture is perceived as needing predominantly logical or technical controls that require significant expertise and knowledge to deploy and maintain effectively. This perception is true as far as it goes, but it must be driven by the needs for technical security support to the security needs of the information architecture.

**Know how to conduct an architecture assessment.**    The architecture assessment is both an inventory of all systems elements and a map or process flow diagram that shows how these elements are connected to form or support business processes and thereby achieve the needs of required business logic. This requires a thorough review and analysis of existing physical asset/equipment inventories, network and communications diagrams, contracts with service providers, software and systems change control logs, error reports, and change requests. It also should include data-gathering interviews with end users and support personnel.

**Explain the purpose and value of a systems or architecture baseline for security purposes.**    The systems or architecture baseline, which the assessment documents, is both the reality we have to protect and the model or description of that reality. The baseline as documentation reflects the as-built state of the system today, and versions of the baseline can reflect the "build-to" state of the system for any desired set of changes that are planned. These provide the starting point for vulnerability assessments, change control audits, and problem analysis and error correcting.

**Explain the importance of assessing "shadow IT" systems, standalone systems, and cloud-hosted services as part of a security assessment.**    Many organizations are more dependent on IT systems elements that are not in their direct configuration management and control. As such, formal IT management may not have detailed design information, and hence vul-nerability insight, about such systems elements. The information security assessment needs to identify each instance of such systems elements, and based on the BIA, determine how much inspection, investigation, or analysis of these systems (and contracts related to them, if any) need to be part of the security assessment.

**Know how to perform a vulnerabilities assessment.**    The vulnerabilities assessment gath-ers data about the information architecture and the IT architecture, including Common Vulnerabilities and Exposures (CVE) data from public sources. This data is analyzed in the context of the BIA's prioritized impacts to determine critical vulnerabilities in these archi-tectures. Threat modeling may also be useful in this process. The result is a list of known or suspected vulnerabilities, collated with the BIA's priorities, for use in risk mitigation implementation planning.

**Explain the role of threat modeling in vulnerability assessment.**    Threat modeling focuses your attention on the boundaries that separate systems from one another, and from the outside world, and thus on how any request for access, service, or information can cross such boundaries. These crossing points are where legitimate users and threat actors can conceivably enter your systems. These may be tunnels (VPN or maintenance trapdoors) left open by accident, for example. Threat modeling is an important component in a well-balanced vulnerability assessment.

**Know how to include human elements in the architecture and vulnerability assessments.**    As the vulnerability assessment reviews business processes and the systems elements that support them, this may indicate process steps where end-user, manager, or other staff actions present vulnerabilities. These may be due to training deficiencies, or to weaknesses in administrative controls (such as a lack of policy direction and guidance), or they may indicate significant risks in need of physical or logical controls and countermeasures.

**Explain the basic risk treatment options of accept, transfer, remediate, avoid, and recast.**    Once you've identified a vulnerability, you deal with (or treat) its associated risk with a combination of control options as required. Accepting the risk means you choose to go ahead and continue doing business in this way. Transferring the risk usually involves paying someone else to take on the work of repairs, reimbursements, or replacement of damaged systems if the risk event occurs. Remediation includes repairing or replacing the vulnerable system and is often called "fixing" or "mitigating" the risk. Avoiding a risk means to change a business process so that the risk no longer applies. The application of any risk controls may reduce the probability of occurrence or the nature of the impact of the risk, and thus you have recast (reassessed) the risk.

**Know how to determine residual risk and relate it to information security gap analysis.**    Residual risk is the risk remaining after applying treatment options, and thus it is a recasting of the original risk. Residual risks are in essence gaps in our defenses; gap analysis uses the same approach as vulnerability assessment but is focused on these gaps to see which if any present unacceptable levels of exposure to risk.

**Know how and why to perform an information security gap analysis.**    A gap analysis is similar to auditing a system's requirements list against the as-built implementation; both seek to discover any needs (requirements) that are not addressed by an effective combination of system features, functions, and elements. An information security gap analysis can reveal missing or inadequate security coverage, and it is useful during vulnerability assessment and after mitigations have been implemented. It is performed by reviewing the baselined set of information security requirements (which should meet or exceed BIA requirements) against the baseline information and IT architectures, noting any unsatisfied or partially satisfied requirements.

**Know how the physical, logical, and administrative aspects of risk controls work together.**    Each of these types of controls takes a decision about security policy and practice and implements it so that people, information technology, and physical systems behaviors fit within security-approved manners. An acceptable use policy, for example, may state that employee-owned devices cannot be brought into secure work areas; a physical search of handbags and so forth might enforce this, and logical controls that detect such devices when they attempt to connect to the networks are a further layer of detection and prevention. Almost all security starts with making decisions about risks; we then write requirements, objectives, plans, or other administrative (people-facing) documents to cause those decisions to be carried out and to monitor their effectiveness.

**Explain the requirements for integrated command, control, and communications of risk treatments and countermeasures.**   Each element of our controls and countermeasures needs to be part of an interlocking, self-reinforcing whole in which elements constantly communicate information about their status, state, and health, or about any alert or alarm-worthy conditions. Systems security managers should have near-seamless, real-time visibility into this information, as well as the ability to remotely manage or command systems elements in response to a suspected or actual information security event. Without this, gaps become blind spots.

**Explain the various uses of testing and verification for information assurance and security.**   Testing and verification are intended to verify that systems meet specified requirements. Testing is typically conducted in test environments, whereas verification can involve observations collected during testing or during ongoing operational use. Security testing and verification aim to establish how completely the information security requirements are satisfied in the deployed systems, including any risk mitigations, controls, or countermeasures that have been added to them since deployment. It validates that the confidentiality, integrity, and availability of the information systems meets or exceeds requirements in the face of ongoing risks and threats. It can also indicate that new threats, vulnerabilities, or risks are in need of attention, decision making, and possibly mitigation.

**Know why we gather, analyze, and interpret event and monitoring data.**   Almost all systems are built around the principle of "trust, but verify." Due diligence requires that we be able to monitor, inspect, or oversee a process and be able to determine that it is working correctly—and when it is not, to be able to make timely decisions to intervene or take corrective action. Due diligence dictates that systems be built in such ways that they provide not only outputs that serve the needs of business logic but also suitable diagnostic, malfunction, or other alarm indicators. Much of these are captured in event log files by the systems themselves. IT security personnel need to gather these event logs and other monitoring data and collate, analyze, and assess it to (a) be able to recognize that an event of interest is occurring or has occurred, and (b) verify that interventions or responses to this incident are having the desired effect.

**Know the importance of elevating alerts and findings to management in a timely manner.**   Two time frames of interest dictate how information security teams elevate alerts and findings to management. The first is in real time or near-real time, when an event of possible interest is being detected and characterized. If such an event requires emergency responses, which quite often are disruptive to normal business operations, then the right levels of management should be engaged in this decision. When not faced with an emerging situation, management needs to be apprised when ongoing monitoring, assessment, or analysis suggests that the systems are behaving either in abnormal ways or in ways indicative of previously unrecognized risks. Further investigation may involve additional staff or other resources or be disruptive to normal operations; thus, management should be engaged in a timely manner.

**Explain the role of incident management in risk mitigation.** Risks express a probability of an event whose outcome we will likely find disruptive, if not damaging, to achieving our goals and objectives. Risk mitigation attempts to limit or contain risks and to notify us when a risk event seems to be imminent or is occurring. Incident management provides the ability in real time to decide when and how to intervene to prevent further damage, halt the incident, restore operational capabilities, and possibly request support from other emergency responders. All of those incident management actions help mitigate the effects of risk on our organization and its business processes.

# Review Questions

1.  Which of the following activities are not part of information risk mitigation?

    **A.** Implementing new systems features or capabilities to enhance product quality

    **B.** Incident management and investigation after a suspected information security breach

    **C.** Installing and testing new firewall, switch, and router systems and settings

    **D.** Developing an information classification policy and process

2.  An architecture assessment includes which of the following activities? (Choose all that apply.)

    **A.** Review of risk mitigation plans and risk countermeasure log files

    **B.** Ongoing monitoring of systems performance, event logs, and alert data

    **C.** Review of problem reports, change requests, and change management information

    **D.** Review of network and communications connectivity, diagrams, wiring closets, etc.

3.  Which statement(s) about information architectures and IT architectures are most correct?

    **A.** Securing the IT architecture first provides the fastest path to a prudent security posture; once that is achieved, a vulnerability assessment of the information architecture can be done to reveal other residual risks.

    **B.** Business needs should drive administrative security policies based on the information architecture; the IT architecture then needs to have its administrative, logical, and physical controls driven to support the information architecture's security needs.

    **C.** The IT architecture's security is primarily dependent on technical or logical controls; these need to be determined first, and then they will inform policy writers as they create or update administrative security requirements for the information architecture.

    **D.** Without effective education and training of all members of the organization, the IT architecture cannot be made secure or kept secure.

4.  How should IT services such as PaaS, IaaS, and SaaS be evaluated as part of a security assessment?

    **A.** Since terms-of-service agreements cover your business's use of these services, this transfers all of the information security risk to the cloud service provider and makes the security assessment a lot easier.

    **B.** PaaS security needs should be adequately covered by the platform services provider, whereas IaaS may or may not provide strong enough security measures to meet your needs and thus should be avoided if possible.

    **C.** The BIA and the architectural baselines should make clear what risks are transferred to the cloud services provider either in whole or in part, or where their services are assumed to be parts of the mitigation strategy. The security assessment should clearly identify this to as great a detail as it can, particularly for the risks identified in the BIA as of greatest concern.

    **D.** Penetration testing, with the consent of the cloud services provider, would be the most reliable way of assessing the security of these services.

**5.** Why are shadow IT systems or elements a concern to information security specialists? (Choose all that apply.)

   **A.** These are exploits and malware found on the dark Web and, as such, must be considered hostile to your organization's goals and objectives. They should be banned from the business and its systems by policy.

   **B.** Most are written by well-intended users and may be widely used by people in the organization, but quite often they are not subjected to even the most basic software quality assurance measures and are outside of configuration management and control. Hence, they pose potential risks to the IT architecture.

   **C.** The more complex and dynamic these shadow systems become, the less confidence management should have in the reliability, integrity, and confidentiality of the results they produce.

   **D.** As long as common vulnerabilities have been addressed (for example, by blocking the use of unsigned macros in Microsoft Office), shadow IT components are no more likely to introduce risks than other IT systems.

**6.** Which statement correctly describes the usefulness of CVE data as part of your risk mitigation planning?

   **A.** It should provide most, if not all, of the vulnerability information you need to implement risk mitigation.

   **B.** Since hackers use CVE data to aid in planning their attacks, this should be the first place you look for insight as you do emergency hardening of your IT systems. Once these obvious vulnerabilities have been mitigated, a more complete vulnerability assessment should be done.

   **C.** It's a great source of information for known systems elements and known vulnerabilities associated with them, but it does nothing for vulnerabilities that haven't been reported yet or for company-developed IT elements.

   **D.** Since the vast majority of systems in use are based on Windows, if your business does not use Windows platforms you can probably avoid the expense of investigating CVE for vulnerability information.

**7.** What is the role of threat modeling in performing a vulnerability assessment?

   **A.** Threat modeling involves creating models of systems, their vulnerabilities, and possible exploits, as well as modeling or simulating attacks to determine which vulnerabilities are in fact most severe. This drives mitigation planning.

   **B.** Threat modeling focuses attention on boundaries between systems elements and the outside world, and this may help you discover poorly secured VPN or maintenance features or tunnels installed by malware.

   **C.** Threat modeling can be used to validate that your risk mitigation controls and countermeasures have been successfully implemented, and so it comes after the vulnerability assessment.

   **D.** Threat modeling is a useful first step when planning penetration testing.

**8.** How should the SSCP assess the human elements in a system as part of vulnerability assessments? (Choose all that apply.)

   **A.** Since the human user is the weakest element in any IT security system, the vulnerability assessment should start by examining all manual data entry, manipulation, or process interaction steps for possible vulnerabilities.

   **B.** The organizational culture and context should determine whether senior leaders and managers create a climate of trust and empowerment or one of rigidly enforced controls and constraints. This sets the bounds within which the SSCP can examine manual interaction with and use of the IT systems for possible vulnerabilities.

   **C.** Every step in every process, whether performed by people or machines, is a potential vulnerability and should be assessed in accordance with the BIA's established priorities.

   **D.** If the vulnerability assessment indicates that no amount of user training or administrative controls can reduce the risk of an incorrect human action to accessible levels, then further physical or logical controls, or a process redesign, may be needed.

**9.** What does it mean to accept a risk?

   **A.** Accepting a risk is when management has reviewed and approved the vulnerability assessment prior to authorizing mitigation to proceed.

   **B.** Accepting a risk means that management knows and understands the probability of occurrence, the possible impacts, and the possible costs of mitigation but chooses nonetheless to not make any changes to business processes or systems. This approach is, in effect, self-insuring against the risk.

   **C.** Accepting a risk means that management has decided to get insurance coverage that will compensate for loss or damages if the risk event actually occurs.

   **D.** Accepting a risk means the same thing as ignoring it.

**10.** Which of the following might be legitimate ways to transfer a risk? (Choose all that apply.)

   **A.** Recognize that government agencies have the responsibility to contain, control, or prevent this risk, which your taxes pay them to do.

   **B.** Pay insurance premiums for a policy that provides for payment of claims and liabilities in the event the risk does occur.

   **C.** Shift the affected business processes to a service provider, along with contractually making sure they are responsible for controlling that risk or have countermeasures in place to address it.

   **D.** Change the underlying business process to use more secure software and hardware systems.

**11.** What are some of the reasons you might recommend that risks be avoided? (Choose all that apply.)

   **A.** It might cost more to mitigate or control a risk than the business stands to gain by operating with the risk in place.

   **B.** Replacing a vulnerable set of processes with ones that are less vulnerable can be more effective and less costly than attempting to redesign or repair the vulnerable steps or elements.

 **C.** In most cases, very few risks can be avoided; you really end up accepting them, ignoring them, or fixing things so that the risks are far less likely to occur or are less damaging if they do.

 **D.** Avoidance means that you're refusing to face the facts and trying to ignore what experience is showing you. This is much like ignoring a risk, which makes sense only for risks that are truly beyond the ordinary.

**12.** CVE data and your own vulnerability assessments indicate that many of your end-user systems do not include recent security patches released by the software vendors. You decide to bring these systems up to date by applying these patches. This is an example of which of the following?

 **A.** Remediating or mitigating a risk

 **B.** Transferring a risk

 **C.** Avoiding a risk

 **D.** Accepting a risk

**13.** How do physical, logical, and administrative controls interact with one another?

 **A.** Usually, the only way these controls can interact is via postevent analysis.

 **B.** Administrative controls should direct and inform people; logical controls implement those directions in the IT architecture; physical controls reinforce by preventing or deterring disruptions to the hardware, systems, and support infrastructures themselves.

 **C.** After determining the physical security and asset protection needs and controls, the administrative and logical controls can be tailored to eliminate or reduce gaps in risk mitigation coverage.

 **D.** It may seem like these should harmonize well, but in practice, that rarely happens since administrators seldom appreciate what IT security needs actually entail.

**14.** How might you keep a gap from becoming a blind spot in your information security defenses? (Choose all that apply.)

 **A.** Transfer this risk to insurers or other parties.

 **B.** Ensure that systems elements around the gap provide sufficient detection and reporting capabilities so that an event of interest occurring in the gap cannot spread without being detected.

 **C.** Ensure that other systems elements can either detect or report when an event of interest is happening within the gap.

 **D.** You can't, as by definition the gap is where you have no appreciable security coverage, and this includes having no monitoring or detection capabilities.

**15.** What roles do testing and verification play in information security? (Choose all that apply.)

 **A.** Provide continued confidence in the security of the information systems under test and verification

 **B.** Highlight the need for further risk mitigation, controls, and countermeasures

 **C.** Confirm that countermeasures and controls are still achieving the required degree of protection

 **D.** Verify that penetration testing subcontractors have satisfactorily fulfilled their contract with the business

**16.** Which of the following most correctly address whether penetration testing is suitable for use during systems security verification or is best suited to ongoing monitoring and assessment? (Choose all that apply.)

**A.** Penetration testing is most revealing when performed against a baseline already in use for some time, because the risks of people becoming complacent and mitigation controls becoming out of date increase with time.

**B.** Penetration testing is not useful during verification testing or systems assessment, because by its nature penetration testing is a somewhat covert attempt to simulate a hostile attack, whereas verification testing is a formalized, planned, and monitored activity.

**C.** Penetration testing has a valid and valuable contribution to make at any point in the lifecycle of a system, from initial systems analysis throughout its deployed operational use.

**D.** Penetration testing is normally used during postdeployment systems assessment and starts with current knowledge of how threat actors attempt to reconnoiter, surveil, select, and penetrate a target; verification starts with a functional security requirements baseline and confirms (via audit, test, or inspection) that each requirement in that baseline still functions properly. Both techniques complement each other during ongoing operational assessment.

**17.** How do we perform ongoing monitoring of our IT systems to ensure that all risk mitigation controls and countermeasures are still protecting us? (Choose all that apply.)

**A.** Periodically, gather up all of the event logs and monitoring log files, collate them, and see if potential events of interest are apparent.

**B.** Routinely poll or ask users if abnormal systems behaviors have been noted.

**C.** Review systems performance parameters, such as throughputs, systems loading levels, resource utilization, etc., to see if they meet with expectations.

**D.** Review current postings in CVE and NVD systems to determine if the vulnerability assessment is still effective.

**18.** What important role does systems monitoring perform in support of incident management?

**A.** They are not related—monitoring is a routine task that uses trend analysis and data analytics to determine if past systems behavior and use have been within expected bounds.

**B.** The role is essential; by bringing together alert and alarm indicators from systems and their associated security controls and countermeasures, monitoring is the watchdog capability that activates incident response capabilities and plans.

**C.** Incident response includes its own monitoring and alarms capabilities, so systems monitoring provides a good backup or alternate path to determining whether an incident is occurring.

**D.** Ongoing, continuous monitoring is used to adjust or fine-tune alarm threshold settings so that false alarm rates can be better managed.

**19.** How are dashboards used as part of systems monitoring or incident response?

    **A.** Dashboards typically display highly summarized key performance indicators, which are suitable for long-term business planning; as such, they're not useful in real-time systems monitoring or incident response.

    **B.** Dashboards can be useful in systems monitoring; they can flag IT staff when events are occurring that may indicate systems loading issues or even failures of systems components. But they are not usually suitable for detecting security incidents.

    **C.** By summarizing systems status, such as which elements are healthy and which are nonresponsive, dashboards can be helpful in incident response decisions. But the details below the level of the dashboard are what ongoing monitoring depends on.

    **D.** By combining highly summarized key performance parameters with ongoing and recent event data, systems managers can see at a glance whether systems are behaving within expected limits, detect whether subsystems have failed (or are under attack), and drill down to get further data to inform incident response decision making.

**20.** What is the role of incident response and management in risk mitigation and risk management?

    **A.** Incident response and management are vital to risk mitigation; they provide the timely detection, notification, and intervention capabilities that contain the impact of a risk event and manage efforts to recover from it and restore operations to normal.

    **B.** Although it comes after the risk assessment and mitigation planning, implementation, and verification, incident response is not part of risk mitigation or risk management.

    **C.** Incident management is a part of risk mitigation but not part of risk management.

    **D.** Incident management is a part of risk management, but not of risk mitigation.

# The Technologies of Information Security

Part 3 takes us further into the technical details that SSCPs need to be able to implement many of the risk mitigation controls and countermeasures we examined in Part 2 and keep them running.

Chapter 5 shows us what we need to secure in our communications and computer networking systems and protocols and how to do it. It uses the concept of the *endpoint* as boundary or demarcation between how our devices talk with each other, and how we (and our businesses, organizations, and society) get work done by talking with each other. You'll use the Open Systems Interconnection (OSI) 7-layer network protocol stack, plus a few extras, to refresh your networking basics, see the threat landscape, and secure your networks from many different classes of threats.

Chapter 6 deals with two sides of the same coin: identity and access control. The essence of information risk mitigation is ensuring that only the right people and processes can read, view, use, change, or remove any of our sensitive information assets, or use any of our most important information-based business processes. You'll learn how to authenticate that a subject user (be that a person or a software process) is who they claim to be; use predetermined policies to decide if they are authorized to do what they are attempting to do; and build and maintain accounting or audit information that shows you who asked to do what, when, where, and how. Chapter 6 combines decades of theory-based models and ideas with cutting-edge how-to insight; both are vital to an SSCP on the job.

Chapter 7 dives deep into cryptography, the art and science of hiding plain meaning so that it is kept away from the wrong set of eyes or ears. Cryptographic techniques have become so commonplace in our modern world that we even have digital, virtual money—the cryptocurrencies—that theoretically make it all but impossible to counterfeit or fake a financial transaction. Chapter 7 will show us how to deploy and manage a variety of cryptographically powered processes, from secure email to trusted software update mechanisms.

Chapter 8 shows us how to protect and secure the hardware and software systems that provide the backbone of infrastructures modern organizations must have to survive and succeed. From computing hardware and operating systems, to cloud-based infrastructures, SSCPs will learn important concepts and techniques pertaining to these core levels of our IT-enabled world.

Chapter 9 goes one further technology layer out and shows how we can ensure the confidentiality, integrity, and availability needs of the applications software systems, databases, and storage systems, as well as the "glueware" that binds them all together. It looks at securing the endpoints, whether the data, apps, and infrastructure that support them reach back into the clouds or just to a local area network. It also provides an end-to-end view of all of these technologies, and in doing so enables the SSCP to see that most (if not all) information security problems touch on every one of these technologies—so there's a part of the solution you'll need in each one of them as well.

Let's get started!

# Chapter

# 5

# Communications and Network Security

---

## THE SSCP EXAM OBJECTIVES COVERED IN THIS CHAPTER INCLUDE:

**Domain 6: Network and Communications Security**

✓ **6.1: Understand and Apply Fundamental Concepts of Networking**

✓ **6.2: Understand Network Attacks and Countermeasures (e.g., DDoS, Man in the Middle, DNS Poisoning)**

✓ **6.3: Manage Network Access Controls**

✓ **6.4: Manage Network Security**

✓ **6.5: Operate and Configure Network-Based Security Devices**

✓ **6.6: Operate and Configure Wireless Technologies (e.g., Bluetooth, NFC, Wi-Fi)**

How do we build trust and confidence into the globe-spanning communications that our businesses, our fortunes, and our very lives depend on? Whether by in-person conversation, videoconferencing, or the World Wide Web, people and businesses *communicate*. Communications, as we saw in earlier chapters, involves exchanging ideas to achieve a common pool of understanding—it is *not* just about data or information. Effective communication requires three basic ingredients: a system of symbols and protocols, a medium or a channel in which those protocols exchange symbols on behalf of senders and receivers, and *trust*. Not that we always trust every communications process 100%, nor do we need to!

We also have to grapple with the *convergence* of communications and computing technologies. People, their devices, and their ways of doing business no longer accept old-fashioned boundaries that used to exist between voice, video, TXT and SMS, data, or a myriad of other computer-enabled information services. This convergence transforms what we trust when we communicate and how we achieve that trust. As SSCPs, we need to know how to gauge the trustworthiness of a particular communications system, keep it operating at the required level of trust, and improve that trustworthiness if that's what our stakeholders need. Let's look in more detail at how communications security can be achieved and, based on that, get into the details of securing the network-based elements of our communications systems.

To do this, we'll need to grow the CIA trinity of earlier chapters—confidentiality, integrity, and availability—into a more comprehensive framework that adds two key ideas to our stack of security needs. This is just one way you'll start thinking in terms of protocol stacks—as system descriptors, as roadmaps for diagnosing problems, and as models of the threat and risk landscape.

# Trusting Our Communications in a Converged World

It's useful to reflect a bit on the not-too-distant history of telecommunications, computing, and information security. Don't panic—we don't have to go all the way back to the invention of radio or the telegraph! Think back, though, to the times right after World War II and what the communications and information systems of that world were like. Competing private companies with competing technical approaches, and very different business models, often confounded users' needs to bring local communications systems into harmony with ones in another state, in another country, or on a distant continent. Radio and telephones didn't connect very well; mobile two-way radios and their landside systems were complex, temperamental, and expensive to operate. Computers didn't talk with each other, except via parcel post or courier delivery of magnetic tapes or boxes of punched cards. Mail was not electronic.

By the 1960s, however, many different factors were pushing each of the different communications technologies to somehow come together in ways that would provide greater capabilities, more flexibility, and growth potential, and at lower total cost of ownership. Communications satellites started to carry hundreds of voice-grade analog channels, or perhaps two or three broadcast-quality television signals. At the same time, military and commercial users needed better ways to secure the contents of messages, and even secure or obscure their routing (to defeat traffic analysis attacks). The computer industry centered on huge mainframe computers, which might cost a million dollars or more—and which sat idle many times each day, and especially over holiday weekends! Mobile communications users wanted two-way voice communication that didn't require suitcase-sized transceivers that filled the trunk of their cars.

Without going too far into the technical, economic, or political, what transformed all of these separate and distinct communications media into one world-spanning Web and Internet? In 1969, in close cooperation with these (and other) industries and academia, the U.S. Department of Defense Advanced Research Projects Agency started its ARPANet project. By some accounts, the scope of what it tried to achieve was audacious in the extreme. The result of ARPANet is all around us today, in the form of the Internet, cell phone technology, VOIP, streaming video, and everything we take for granted over the Web and the Internet. And so much more.

One simple idea illustrates the breadth and depth of this change. Before ARPANet, we all thought of communications in terms of calls we placed. We set up a circuit or a channel, had our conversation, then took the circuit down so that some other callers could use parts of it in their circuits. ARPANet's packet-based communications caused us all to forget about the channel, forget about the circuit, and focus on the messages themselves. (You'll see that this had both good and bad consequences for information security later in this chapter.)

One of the things we take for granted is the convergence of all of these technologies, and so many more, into what seems to us to be a seamless, cohesive, purposeful, reliable, and sometimes even secure communications infrastructure. The word *convergence* is used to sum up the technical, business, economic, political, social, and perceptual changes that brought so many different private businesses, public organizations, and international standards into a community of form, function, feature, and intent. What we sometimes ignore, to our peril, is how that convergence has drastically changed the ways in which SSCPs need to think about communications security, computing security, and information assurance.

Emblematic of this change might be the Chester Gould's cartoon character Dick Tracy and his wristwatch two-way radio, first introduced to American readers in 1946. It's credited with inspiring the invention of the smartphone, and perhaps even the smartwatches that are becoming commonplace today. What Gould's character didn't explore for us were the information security needs of a police force whose detectives had such devices—nor the physical, logical, and administrative techniques they'd need to use to keep their communications safe, secure, confidential, and reliable.

To keep those and any other communications trustworthy, think about some key ingredients that we find in any communications system or process:

- *Purpose or intent.* Somebody has something they want to accomplish, whether it is ordering a pizza to be delivered or commanding troops into battle. This intention *should* shape the whole communication process. With a clear statement of intent, the sender can better identify who the target audience is, and whether the intention can be achieved by exchanging one key idea or a whole series of ideas woven together into some kind of story or narrative.

- *Senders and recipients.* The actual people or groups on both ends of the conversation or the call; sometimes called the *parties* to the communication.

- *Protocols* that shape how the conversation or communication can start, how it is conducted, and how it is brought to a close. Protocols include a choice of language, character or symbol set, and maybe even a restricted domain of ideas to communicate about. Protocols provide for ways to detect errors in transmission or receipt, and ways to confirm that the recipient both received and understood the message as sent. Other protocols might also verify whether the true purpose of the communication got across as well.

- *Message content*, which is the ideas we wish to exchange encoded or represented in the chosen language, character or symbol sets, and protocols.

- A *communications medium*, which is what makes transporting the message from one place to another possible. Communications media are *physical*—such as paper, sound waves, radio waves, electrical impulses sent down a wire, flashes of light or puffs of smoke, or almost anything else.

For example, a letter or holiday greeting might be printed or written on paper or a card, which is placed in an envelope and mailed to the recipient via a national or international postal system. Purpose, the communicating parties, the protocols, the content, and the medium all have to work together to convey "happy holidays," "come home soon," or "send lawyers, guns, and money" if the message is to get from sender to receiver with its meaning intact.

At the end of the day (or at the end of the call), both senders and receivers have two critical decisions to make: how much of what was communicated was trustworthy, and what if anything should they do as a result of that communication? The explicit content of what was exchanged has a bearing on these decisions, of course, but so does all of the *subtext* associated with the conversation. Subtext is about context: about "reading between the lines," drawing inferences (or suggesting them) regarding what was *not* said by either party.

The risk that subtext can get it wrong is great! The "Hot Line" illustrates this potential for disaster. During the Cold War, the "Hot Line" communications system connected the U.S. national command authority and their counterparts in the Soviet Union. This system was created to reduce the risk of accidental misunderstandings that could lead to nuclear war between the two superpowers. Both parties insisted that this be a plain text teletype circuit, with messages simultaneously sent in English and Russian, to prevent either side from trying to read too much into the voice or mannerisms of translators and speakers at either end. People and organizations need to worry about getting the subtext wrong or missing it altogether. So far, as an SSCP, you won't have to worry about how to "secure the subtext."

Communications security is about data in motion—as it is going to and from the endpoints and the other elements or nodes of our systems, such as servers. It's not about data at rest or data in use, per se. Chapter 8, "Hardware and Systems Security," and Chapter 9, "Applications, Data, and Cloud Security," will show you how to enhance the security of data at rest and in use, whether inside the system or at its endpoints. Chapter 11, "Business Continuity via Information Security and People Power," will also look at how we keep the people layer of our systems communicating in effective, safe, secure, and reliable ways, both in their roles as users and managers of their company's IT infrastructures, but also as people performing their broader roles within the company or organization and its place in the market and in society at large.

## Introducing CIANA

Chapter 2, "Information Security Fundamentals," introduced the concepts of confidentiality, integrity, and availability as the three main attributes or elements of information security and assurance. We also saw that before we can implement plans and programs to achieve that triad, we have to identify what information must be protected from disclosure (kept confidential), its meaning kept intact and correct (ensure its integrity), and that it's where we need it, when we need it (that is, the information is available). As we dig further into what information security entails, we'll have to add two additional and very important attributes to our CIA triad: nonrepudiation and authentication.

To *repudiate* something means to attempt to deny an action that you've performed or something you said. You can also attempt to deny that you ever received a particular message or didn't see or notice that someone else performed an action. In most cases, we repudiate our own actions or the actions of others so as to attempt to deny responsibility for them. "They didn't have my informed consent," we might claim; "I never got that letter," or "I didn't see the traffic light turn yellow." Thus, *nonrepudiation* is the characteristic of a communications system that prevents a user from claiming that they never sent or never received a particular message. This communications system characteristic sets limits on what senders or receivers can do by restricting or preventing any attempt by either party to repudiate a message, its content, or its meaning.

Authentication, in this context, also pertains to senders and receivers. *Authentication* is the verification that the sender or receiver is who they claim to be, and then the further validation that they have been granted permission to use that communications system. Authentication might also go further by validating that a particular sender has been granted the privilege of communicating with a particular sender. These privileges—use of the system, and connection with a particular party—can also be defined with further restrictions, as we'll see later in Chapter 6, "Identity and Access Control." Authentication as a process has one more "A" associated with it, and that is *accountability*. This requires that the system keep records of who attempts to access the system, who was authenticated to use it, and what communications or exchanges of messages they had with whom.

Thus, *CIANA*: confidentiality, integrity, availability, nonrepudiation, and authentication.

Recall from earlier chapters that our CIA triad (now expanded to CIANA) crystallizes our understanding of what information needs what kinds of protection. Most businesses and organizations find that it takes several different but related thought processes to bring this all together in ways that their IT staff and information security team can appreciate and carry out. Several key sets of ideas directly relate to, or help set, the information classification guidelines that should drive the implementation of information risk reduction efforts:

- *Strategic plans* define long-term goals and objectives, identify key markets or target audiences, and focus on strategic relationships with key stakeholders and partners.

- The *business impact analysis* (BIA) links high-priority strategic goals, objectives, and outcomes with the business logic, processes, and information assets vital to achieving those outcomes.

- A *communications strategy* guides how the organization talks with its stakeholders, customers, staff, and other target audiences so that mutual understanding leads to behaviors that support achieving the organization's strategic goals.

- Risk management plans, particularly information and IT risk management plans, provide the translation of strategic thinking into near-term tactical planning.

The net result *should* be that the organization combines those four viewpoints into a cohesive and effective information risk management plan, which provides the foundation for "all things CIANA" that the information security team needs to carry out. This drives the ways that SSCPs and others on that information security team conduct vulnerability assessments, choose mitigation techniques and controls, configure and operate them, and monitor them for effectiveness.

## Threat Modeling for Communications Systems

With that integrated picture of information security needs, it's time to do some threat modeling of our communications systems and processes. Chapter 4, "Operationalizing Risk Mitigation," introduced the concepts of threat modeling and the use of boundaries or threat surfaces to segregate parts of our systems from each other and from the outside world. Let's take a quick review of the basics:

- Notionally, the total CIANA security needs of information assets *inside* a threat surface is greater than what actors, subjects, or systems elements *outside* of that boundary should enjoy.

- *Subjects* access objects to use or change them; *objects* are information assets (or people or processes) that exist for subjects to use, invoke, or otherwise interact with. A person reads from a file, possibly by invoking a display process that accesses that file, and presents it on their endpoint device's display screen. In that case, the display process is both an object (to the person invoking it) and a subject (as it accesses the file).

- The *threat surface* is a boundary that encapsulates objects that require a degree of protection to meet their CIANA needs.
- *Controlled paths* are deliberately created by the system designers and builders and provide a channel or gateway that subjects on one side of the threat surface use to access objects on the other side. Such paths or portals should contain features that authenticate subjects prior to granting access.

Note that this subject-object access can be bidirectional; there are security concerns in both reading and writing across a security boundary or threat surface. We'll save the theory and practice of that for Chapter 6.

The threat surface thinks of the problem from the defensive perspective: what do I need to protect and defend from attack? By contrast, threat modeling also defines the *attack surface* as the set of entities, information assets, features, or elements that are the focus of reconnaissance, intrusion, manipulation, and misuse, as part of an attack on an information system. Typically, attack surfaces are at the level of vendor-developed systems or applications; thus, Microsoft Office Pro 2016 is one attack surface, while Microsoft Office 365 Home is another. Other attack surfaces can be specific operating systems, or the hardware and firmware packages that are our network hardware elements. Even a network intrusion detection system (NIDS) can be an attack surface!

Applying these concepts to the total set of organizational communications processes and systems could be a daunting task for an SSCP. Let's peel that onion a layer at a time, though, by separating it into two major domains: that which runs on the internal computer networks and systems, and that which is really people-to-people in nature. We'll work with the people-to-people more closely in Chapter 11.

For now, let's combine this concept of threat modeling with the most commonly used sets of protocols, or protocol *stacks*, that we use in tying our computers, communications, and endpoints together.

# Internet Systems Concepts

As an SSCP, you'll need to focus your thinking about networks and security to one particular kind of networks—the ones that link together most of the computers and communications systems that businesses, governments, and people use. This is "the Internet," capitalized as a proper name. It's almost everywhere; almost everybody uses it, somehow, in their day-to-day work or leisure pursuits. It is what the World Wide Web (also a proper noun) runs on. It's where we create most of the value of e-commerce, and where most of the information security threats expose people and business to loss or damage. This section will introduce the basic concepts of the Internet and its protocols; then, layer by layer, we'll look at more of their innermost secrets, their common vulnerabilities, and some potential countermeasures you might need to use. The OSI 7-layer reference model will be our framework and guide along the way, as it reveals some critical ideas about vulnerabilities and countermeasures you'll need to appreciate.

> If you already have a solid understanding of TCP/IP and the OSI 7-layer model, the most commonly used protocols and services that make them tick, and how to consider threats at each layer of both protocol stacks, then feel free to skip this section and dive right into "CIANA at Layer 1."

Communications and network systems designers talk about *protocol stacks* as the layers or nested sets of different protocols that work together to define and deliver a set of services to users. An individual protocol or layer defines the specific characteristics, the form, features, and functions that make up that protocol or layer. For example, almost since the first telephone services were made available to the public, The Bell Telephone Company in the U.S. defined a set of connection standards for basic voice-grade telephone service; today, one such standard is the RJ-11 physical and electrical connector for four-wire telephone services. The RJ-11 connection standard says nothing about dial tones, pulse (rotary dial), or Touch-Tone dual-tone multiple frequency signaling, or how connections are initiated, established, used, and then taken down as part of making a "telephone call" between parties. Other protocols define services at those layers. The "stack" starts with the lowest level, usually the physical interconnect standard, and layers each successively higher-level standard onto those below it. These higher-level standards can go on almost forever; think of how "reverse the charges," advanced billing features, or many caller ID features need to depend on lower-level services being defined and working properly, and you've got the idea of a protocol stack.

This is an example of using *layers of abstraction* to build up complex and powerful systems from subsystems or components. Each component is abstracted, reducing it to just what happens at the interface—how you request services of it, provide inputs to it, and get services or outputs from it. What happens behind that curtain is (or should be) none of your concern, as the external service user. (The service *builder* has to fully specify how the service behaves internally so that it can fulfill what's required of it.) One important design imperative with stacks of protocols is to isolate the impact of changes; changes in physical transmission of signals should not affect the way applications work with their users, nor should adding a new application require a change in that physical media.

A protocol stack is a document—a set of ideas or design standards. Designers and builders *implement* the protocol stack into the right set of hardware, software, and procedural tasks (done by people or others). These implementations present the features of the protocol stack as *services* that can be requested by subjects (people or software tasks).

## Datagrams and Protocol Data Units

First, let's introduce the concept of a datagram, which is a common term when talking about communications and network protocols. A *datagram* is the unit of information used by a protocol layer or a function within it. It's the unit of measure of information in each individual transfer. Each layer of the protocol stack takes the datagram it receives from the layers above it and repackages it as necessary to achieve the desired results. Sending a message via flashlights (or an Aldiss lamp, for those of the sea services) illustrates the datagram concept:

- An on/off flash of the light, or a flash of a different duration, is one bit's worth of information; the datagrams at the lamp level are bits.

- If the message being sent is encoded in Morse code, then that code dictates a sequence of short and long pulses for each datagram that represents a letter, digit, or other symbol.

- Higher layers in the protocol would then define sequences of handshakes to verify sender and receiver, indicate what kind of data is about to be sent, and specify how to acknowledge or request retransmission. Each of those sequences might have one or more message in it, and each of those messages would be a datagram at that level of the protocol.

- Finally, the captain of one of those two ships dictates a particular message to be sent to the other ship, and *that* message, captain-to-captain, is itself a datagram.

Note, however, another usage of this word. The User Datagram Protocol (UDP) is an alternate data communications protocol to Transmission Control Protocol, and both of these are at the same level (Layer 3, Internetworking) of the TCP/IP stack. And to add to the terminological confusion, the OSI model (as we'll see in a moment) uses *protocol data unit* (PDU) to refer to the unit of measure of the data sent in a single protocol unit and datagram to UDP. Be careful not to confuse UDP and PDU!

Table 5.1 may help you avoid some of this confusion by placing the OSI and TCP/IP stacks side by side. We'll examine each layer in greater detail in a few moments.

**TABLE 5.1**   OSI and TCP/IP side by side

| Types of layers | Typical protocols | OSI layer | OSI protocol data unit name | TCP/IP layer | TCP/IP datagram name |
|---|---|---|---|---|---|
| Host layers | HTTP, HTTPS, SMTP, IMAP, SNMP, POP3, FTP, ... | 7. Application | Data | *(Outside of TCP/IP model scope)* | Data |
| | Characters, MPEG, SSL/TLS, compression, S/MIME, ... | 6. Presentation | | | |
| | NetBIOS, SAP, session handshaking connections | 5. Session | | | |
| | TCP, UDP | 4. Transport | Segment, except: UDP: datagram | Transport | Segment |

*(continued)*

**TABLE 5.1**   OSI and TCP/IP side by side *(continued)*

| Types of layers | Typical protocols | OSI layer | OSI protocol data unit name | TCP/IP layer | TCP/IP datagram name |
|---|---|---|---|---|---|
| Media layers | IPv4 / IPv6 IP address, ICMP, IPSec, ARP, MPLS, … | 3. Network | Packet | Network (or Internetworking) | Packet |
| | Ethernet, 802.1, PPP, ATM, Fibre Channel, FDDI, MAC address | 2. Link | Frame | Data Link | Frame |
| | Cables, connectors, 10BaseT, 802.11x, ISDN, T1, … | 1. Physical | Symbol | Physical | Bits |

# Handshakes

We'll start with a simple but commonplace example that reveals the role of handshaking to control and direct how the Internet handles our data communications needs. A *handshake* is a sequence of small, simple communications that we send and receive, such as hello and goodbye, ask and reply, or acknowledge or not-acknowledge, which control and carry out the communications we need. Handshakes are defined in the protocols we agree to use. Let's look at a simple file transfer to a server that I want to do via File Transfer Protocol (FTP) to illustrate this:

1. I ask my laptop to run the file transfer client app.

2. Now that it's running, my FTP client app asks the OS to connect to the FTP server.

3. The FTP server accepts my FTP client's connection request.

4. My FTP client requests to upload a file to a designated folder in the directory tree on that server.

5. The FTP server accepts the request, and says "start sending" to my FTP client.

6. My client sends a chunk of data to the server; the server acknowledges receipt, or requests a retransmission if it encounters an error.

7. My client signals the server that the file has been fully uploaded, and requests the server to mark the received file as closed, updating its directories to reflect this new file.

8. My client informs me of successfully completing the upload.

9. With no more files to transfer, I exit the FTP app.

It's interesting to note that the Internet was first created to facilitate things like simple file transfers between computer centers; email was created as a higher-level protocol that used FTP to send and receive small files that were the email notes themselves.

To make this work, we need ways of physically and logically connecting end-user computers (or smartphones or smart toasters) to servers that can support those endpoints with functions and data that users want and need. What this all quickly turned into is the kind of infrastructure we have today:

- End-user devices (much like "endpoints" in our systems) hand off data to the network for transmission, receive data from other users via the network, and monitor the progress of the communications they care about. In most systems, a *network interface card* (NIC, or chip), acts as the go-between. (We'll look at this in detail later.)

- An *Internet point of presence* is a physical place at which a local *Internet service provider (ISP)* brings a physical connection from the Internet backbone to the user's NIC. Contractually, the user owns and is responsible for maintaining their own equipment and connections to the point of presence, and the ISP owns and maintains from there to the Internet backbone. Typically, a modem or combination modem/router device performs both the physical and logical transformation of what the user's equipment needs in the way of data signaling into what the ISP's side needs to see.

- The *Internet backbone* is a mesh of Internet working nodes and high-capacity, long-distance communications circuits that connect them to each other and to the ISPs.

The *physical* connections handle the electronic (or electro-optical) signaling that the devices themselves need to communicate with each other. The *logical* connections are how the right pair of endpoints—the user NIC and the server or other endpoint NIC—get connected with each other, rather than with some other device "out there" in the wilds of the Internet. This happens through *address resolution* and *name resolution*.

## Packets and Encapsulation

Note in that FTP example earlier how the file I uploaded was broken into a series of chunks, or *packets*, rather than sent in one contiguous block of data. Each packet is sent across the Internet by itself (wrapped in header and trailer information that identifies the sender, recipient, and other important information we'll go into later). Breaking a large file into packets allows smarter trade-offs between actual throughput rate and error rates and recovery strategies. (Rather than resend the entire file because line noise corrupted one or two bytes, we might need to resend just the one corrupted packet.) However, since sending each packet requires a certain amount of handshake overhead to package, address, route, send, receive, unpack, and acknowledge, the smaller the packet size, the less efficient the overall communications system can be.

Sending a file by breaking it up into packets has an interesting consequence: if each packet has a unique serial number as part of its header, as long as the receiving application can put the packets back together in the proper order, we don't need to care what order they are sent in or arrive in. So if the receiver requested a retransmission of packet number 41, it can still receive and process packet 42, or even several more, while waiting for the sender to retransmit it.

Right away we see a key feature of packet-based communications systems: we have to add information to each packet in order to tell both the recipient *and* the next layer in the protocol stack what to do with it! In our FTP example earlier, we start by breaking the file up into fixed-length chunks, or packets, of data—but we've got to wrap them with data that says where it's from, where it's going, and the packet sequence number. That data goes in a header (data preceding the actual segment data itself), and new end-to-end error correcting checksums are put into a new trailer. This creates a new datagram at this level of the protocol stack. That new, *longer* datagram is given to the first layer of the protocol stack. That layer probably has to do something to it; that means it will encapsulate the datagram it was given by adding another header and trailer. At the receiver, each layer of the protocol unwraps the datagram it receives from the lower layer (by processing the information in *its* header and trailer, and then removing them), and passes this *shorter* datagram up to the next layer. Sometimes, the datagram from a higher layer in a protocol stack will be referred to as the *payload* for the next layer down. Figure 5.1 shows this in action.

**FIGURE 5.1**   Wrapping: layer-by-layer encapsulation

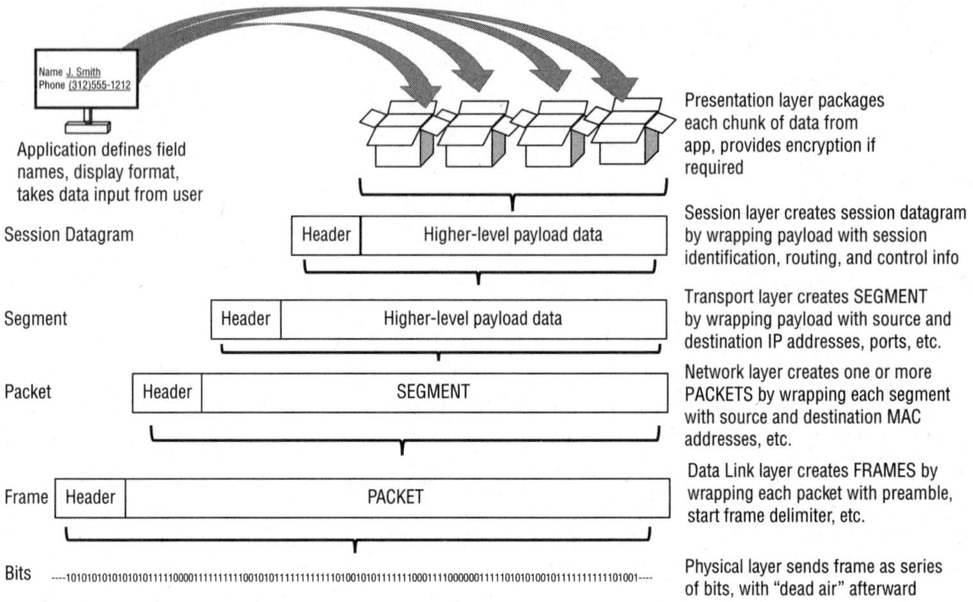

The flow of wrapping, as shown in Figure 5.1, illustrates how a higher-layer protocol *logically* communicates with its opposite number in another system by having to first wrap and pass its datagrams to lower-layer protocols in its own stack. It's not until the Physical layer connections that signals actually move from one system to another. (Note that this even holds true for two virtual machines talking to each other over a software-defined network that connects them, even if they're running on the same bare metal host!) In OSI 7-layer reference model terminology, this means that layer $n$ of the stack takes the service data unit (SDU) it receives from layer $n+1$, processes and wraps the SDU with its layer-specific header and footer to produce the datagram at its layer, and passes this new datagram as an SDU to the next layer down in the stack.

We'll see what these headers look like, layer by layer, in a bit.

## Addressing, Routing, and Switching

In plain old telephone systems (POTS), your phone number uniquely identified the pair of wires that came from the telephone company's central office switches to your house. If you moved, you got a new phone number, or the phone company had to physically disconnect your old house's pair of wires from its switch at that number's terminal, and hook up your new house's phone line instead. From the start (thanks in large part to the people from Bell Laboratories and other telephone companies working with the ARPANet team), we knew we needed something more dynamic, adaptable, and easier to use. What they developed was a way to define both a logical address (the IP or Internet Protocol address), the physical address or identity of each NIC in each device (its *media access control* or *MAC address*), and a way to map from one to the other while allowing a device to be in one place today and another place tomorrow. From its earliest ARPANet days until the mid-1990s, the Internet Assigned Numbers Authority (IANA) handled the assignment of IP addresses and address ranges to users and organizations who requested them.

*Routing* is the process of determining what path or set of paths to use to send a set of data from one endpoint device through the network to another. In POTS, the route of the call was static—once you set up the circuit, it stayed up until the call was completed, unless a malfunction interrupted the call. The Internet, by contrast, does not route calls—it routes individually addressed packets from sender to recipient. If a link or a series of communications nodes in the Internet itself go down, senders and receivers do not notice; subsequent packets will be dynamically rerouted to working connections and nodes. This also allows a node (or a link) to say "no" to some packets as part of load-leveling and traffic management schemes. The Internet (via its protocol stack) handles routing as a distributed, loosely coupled, and dynamic process—every node on the Internet maintains a variety of data that help it decide which of the nodes it's connected to should handle a particular packet that it wants to forward to the ultimate recipient (no matter how many intermediate nodes it must pass through to get there).

*Switching* is the process used by one node to receive data on one of its input ports and choose which output port to send the data to. (If a particular device has only one input and one output, the only switching it can do is to pass the data through or deny it passage.) A simple switch depends on the incoming data stream to explicitly state which path to send the data out on; a router, by contrast, uses routing information and routing algorithms to decide what to tell its built-in switch to properly route each incoming packet.

Another way to find and communicate with someone is to know their *name* and then somehow look that name up in a directory. By the mid-1980s, the Internet was making extensive use of such naming conventions, creating the *Domain Name System (DNS)*. A domain name consists of sets of characters joined by periods (or "dots"); "bbc.co.uk" (pronounced as "bee-bee-bee dot co dot uck," by the way) illustrates the higher-level domain ".co.uk" for commercial entities in the United Kingdom, and "bbc" is the name itself. Taken together that makes a fully qualified domain name. The DNS consists of a set of servers that resolve domain names into IP addresses, registrars that assign and issue both IP addresses and the domain names associated with them to parties who want them, and the regulatory processes that administer all of that.

## Network Segmentation

*Segmentation* is the process of breaking a large network into smaller ones. "The Internet" acts as if it is one gigantic network, but it's not. It's actually many millions of *internet segments* that come together at many different points to provide seamless service. An *internet segment* (sometimes called "an internet," lowercase) is a network of devices that communicate using TCP/IP and thus support the OSI 7-layer reference model. This segmentation can happen at any of the three lower layers of our protocol stacks, as we'll see in a bit. Devices within a network segment can communicate with each other, but which layer the segments connect on, and what kind of device implements that connection, can restrict the outside world to seeing the connection device (such as a router) and not the nodes on the subnet below it.

Segmentation of a large internet into multiple, smaller network segments provides a number of practical benefits, which affect the choice of how to join segments and at which layer of the protocol stack. The switch or router that runs the segment, and its connection with the next higher segment, are two single points of failure for the segment. If the device fails or the cable is damaged, no device on that segment can communicate with the other devices or the outside world. This can also help isolate other segments from failure of routers or switches, cables, or errors (or attacks) that are flooding a segment with traffic.

*Subnets* are different than network segments. We'll take a deep dive into the fine art of *subnetting* after we've looked at the overall protocol stack.

## URLs and the Web

In 1990, Tim Berners-Lee, a researcher at CERN in Switzerland, confronted the problem that researchers were having: they could not find and use what they already knew or discovered, because they could not effectively keep track of everything they wrote and where they put it! CERN was drowning in its own data. Berners-Lee wanted to take the much older idea of a hyperlinked or hypertext-based document one step further. Instead of just having links to points within the document, he wanted to have documents be able to point to other documents anywhere on the Internet. This required that several new ingredients be added to the Internet:

- A unique way of naming a document that included where it could be found on the Internet, which came to be called a *locator*

- Ways to embed those unique names into another document, where the document's creator wanted the *links* to be (rather than just in a list at the end, for example)

- A means of identifying a computer on the Internet as one that stored such documents and would make them available as a service

- Directory systems and tools that could collect the addresses or names of those document servers

- Keyword search capabilities that could identify what documents on a server contained which keywords

- Applications that an individual user could run that could query multiple servers to see if they had documents the user might want, and then present those documents to the user to view, download, or use in other ways

- Protocols that could tie all of those moving parts together in sensible, scalable, and maintainable ways

By 1991, new words entered our vernacular: *webpage, Hypertext Transfer Protocol (HTTP), Web browser, Web crawler,* and *URL,* to name a few. Today, all of that has become so commonplace, so ubiquitous, that it's easy to overlook just how many powerfully innovative ideas had to come together all at once. Knowing when to use the right *uniform resource locators (URLs)* became more important than understanding IP addresses. URLs provide us with an unambiguous way to identify a protocol, a server on the network, and a specific asset on that server. Additionally, a URL as a command line can contain values to be passed as variables to a process running on the server. By 1998, the business of growing and regulating both IP addresses and domain names grew to the point that a new nonprofit, nongovernmental organization was created, the Internet Corporation for Assigned Names and Numbers (ICANN, pronounced "eye-can").

The rapid acceptance of the World Wide Web and the HTTP concepts and protocols that empowered it demonstrates a vital idea: the layered, keep-it-simple approach embodied in the TCP/IP protocol stack and the OSI 7-layer model *works.* Those stacks give us a strong but simple foundation on which we can build virtually any information service we can imagine.

## Topologies

I would consider putting in drawings with each topology. Some people are visual learners & need to see it to understand it.

The brief introduction (or review) of networking fundamentals we've had thus far brings us to ask an important question: how do we hook all of those network devices and endpoints together? We clearly cannot build one switch with a million ports on it, but we can use the logical design of the Internet protocols to let us build more practical, modular subsystem elements and then connect them in various ways to achieve what we need.

A *topology,* to network designers and engineers, is the basic logical geometry by which different elements of a network connect together. Topologies consist of nodes and the links that connect them. Experience (and much mathematical study!) gives us some simple, fundamental topologies to use as building blocks for larger systems:

- *Point-to-point* is the simplest topology: two nodes, with one link between them. This is sometimes called *peer-to-peer* if the two nodes have relatively the same set of privileges and responsibilities with respect to each other (that is, neither node is in control of the other). If one node fails, or the connection fails, the network cannot function; whether the other node continues to function normally or has to abnormally terminate processes is strictly up to that node (and its designers and users).

- *Bus* topologies or networks connect multiple nodes together, one after the other, in series, as shown in Figure 5.2. The bus provides the infrastructure for sending signals to all of the nodes, and for sending addressing information (sometimes called *device select*) that allows each node to know when to listen to the data and when to ignore it. Well-formed bus designs should not require each node to process data or control signals in order to pass them on to the next node on the bus. *Backplanes* are a familiar implementation of this; for example, the industry-standard PCI bus provides a number of slots that can take almost any PCI-compatible device (in any slot). A *hot-swap bus* has special design features that allow one device to be powered off and removed without requiring the bus, other devices, or the overall system to be shut down. These are extensively used in storage subsystems. Bus systems typically are limited in length, rarely exceeding three meters overall.

**FIGURE 5.2**　Bus topology

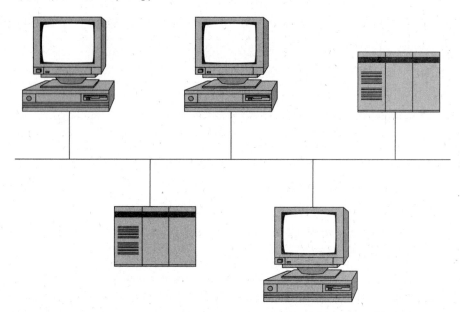

- *Ring networks* are a series of point-to-point-to-point connections, with the last node on the chain looped back to connect to the first, as shown in Figure 5.3. As point-to-point connections, each node has to be functioning properly in order to do its job of passing data on to the next node on the ring. This does allow ring systems nodes to provide *signal conditioning* that can boost the effective length of the overall ring (if each link has a maximum 10 meter length, then 10 nodes could span a total length of 50 meters out and back). Nodes and connections all have to work in order for the ring to function. Rings are designed to provide either a unidirectional or bidirectional flow of control and data.

**FIGURE 5.3**    Ring network topology

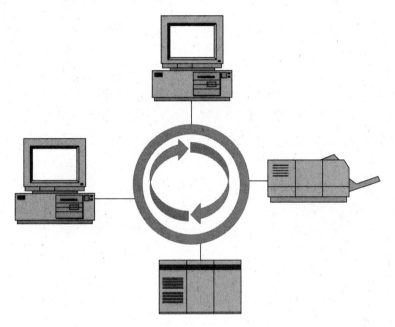

- *Star* networks have one central node that is connected to multiple other nodes via point-to-point connections. Unlike a point-to-point network, the node in the center has to provide (at least some) services to control and administer the network. The central node is therefore a *server* (since it provides services to others on the star network), and the other nodes are all *clients* of that server. This is shown in Figure 5.4.

**FIGURE 5.4**    Star (or tree) network topology

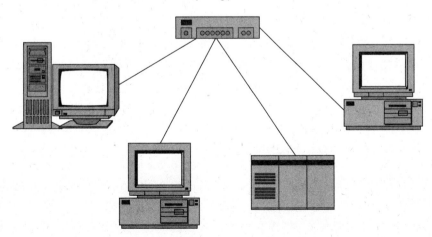

- *Mesh* networks in general provide multiple point-to-point connections between some or all of the nodes in the mesh, as shown in Figure 5.5. Mesh designs can be uniform (all nodes have point-to-point connections to all other nodes), or contain subsets of nodes with different degrees of interconnection. As a result, mesh designs can have a variety of client-server, server-to-server, or peer-to-peer relationships built into them. Mesh designs are used in datacenters, since they provide multiple paths between multiple CPUs, storage controllers, or Internet-facing communications gateways. Mesh designs are also fundamental to supercomputer designs, for the same reason. Mesh designs tend to be very robust, since normal TCP/IP alternate routing can allow traffic to continue to flow if one or a number of nodes or connections fail; at worst, overall throughput of the mesh and its set of nodes may decrease until repairs can be made.

**FIGURE 5.5**    Mesh network topology (*fully connected*)

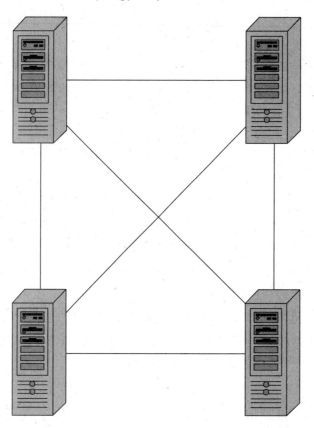

With these in mind, a typical SOHO (small office/home office) network at a coffee house that provides Wi-Fi for its customers might use a mix of the following topology elements:

- A simple mesh of two point-to-point connections via ISPs to the Internet to provide a high degree of availability

- Point-to-point from that mesh to a firewall system
- Star connections to support three subnets: one for retail systems, one for store administration, and one for customer or staff Wi-Fi access. Each of these would be its own star network.

# "Best Effort" and Trusting Designs

The fundamental design paradigm of TCP/IP and OSI 7-layer stacks is that they deliver "best-effort" services. In contract law and systems engineering, *a best efforts basis* sets expectations for services being requested and delivered; the server will do what is reasonable and prudent, but will not go "beyond the call of duty" to make sure that the service is performed, day or night, rain or shine! There are no guarantees. Nothing asserts that if your device's firmware does things the "wrong" way its errors will keep it from connecting, getting traffic sent and received correctly, or doing any other network function. Nothing also guarantees that your traffic will go where you want it to, *and nowhere else*, that it will *not* be seen by anybody else along the way, and will not suffer any corruption of content. Yes, each individual packet does have parity and error correction and detection checksums built into it. These may (no guarantees!) cause any piece of hardware along the route to reject the packet as "in error," and request the sender retransmit it. An Internet node or the NIC in your endpoint might or might not detect conflicts in the way that fields within the packet's wrappers are set; it may or may not be smart enough to ask for a resend, or pass back some kind of error code and a request that the sender try again.

Think about the idea of routing a segment in a best-effort way: the first node that receives the segment will *try* to figure out which node to forward it on to, so that the packet has a pretty good chance of getting to the recipient in a reasonable amount of time. But this depends on ways of one node asking other nodes if they know or recognize the address, or know some other node that does.

The protocols do define a number of standardized error codes that relate to the most commonly known errors, such as attempting to send traffic to an address that is unknown and unresolvable. A wealth of information is available about what might cause such errors, how participants might work to resolve them, and what a recommended strategy is to recover from one when it occurs. What this means is that the burden for managing the *work* that we want to accomplish by means of using the Internet is not the Internet's responsibility. That burden of plan, do, check, and act is allocated to the higher-level functions within application programs, operating systems, and NIC hardware and device drivers that are using these protocols, or the people and business logic that actually invokes those applications in the first place.

In many respects, the core of TCP/IP is a trusting design. The designers (and the Internet) *trust* that equipment, services, and people using it will behave properly, follow the rules, and use the protocols in the spirit and manner in which they were written. Internet users and their equipment are expected to *cooperate* with each other, as each spends a fragment of their time, CPU power, memory, or money to help many other users achieve what they need.

One consequence we need to face head on of this trusting, cooperative, best-efforts nature of our Internet: *security becomes an add-on*. We'll see how to add it on, layer by layer, later in this chapter.

# Two Protocol Stacks, One Internet

Let's look at two different protocol stacks for computer systems networks. Both are published, public domain standards; both are widely adopted around the world. The "geekiest" of the standards is *TCP/IP*, the Transmission Control Protocol over Internet Protocol standard (two layers of the stack right there!). Its four layers define how we build up networks from the physical interconnections up to what it calls the Transport layer, where the heavy lifting of turning a file transfer into Internet traffic starts to take place. TCP/IP also defines and provides homes for many of the other protocols that make addressing, routing, naming, and service delivery happen.

By contrast, the OSI 7-layer reference model is perhaps the most "getting-business-done" of the two stacks. It focuses on getting the day-to-day business and organizational tasks done that really are why we wanted to internetwork computers in the first place. This is readily apparent when we start with its topmost, or application, layer. We use application programs to handle personal, business, government, and military activities—those applications certainly need the operating systems that they depend on for services, but no one does their online banking just using Windows 10 or Red Hat Linux alone!

Many network engineers and technicians may thoroughly understand the TCP/IP model, since they use it every day, but they have little or no understanding of the OSI 7-layer model. They often see it as too abstract or too conceptual to have any real utility in the day-to-day world of network administration or network security. Nothing could be further from the truth! As you'll see, the OSI's top three levels provide powerful ways for you to think about information systems security—beyond just keeping the networks secure. In fact, many of the most troublesome information security threats that SSCPs must deal with occur at the upper layers of the OSI 7-layer reference model—beyond the scope of what TCP/IP concerns itself with. As an SSCP, you need a solid understanding of how TCP/IP works—how its protocols for device and port addressing and mapping, routing, and delivery, and network management all play together. You will also need an equally thorough understanding of the OSI 7-layer model, how it contrasts with TCP/IP, and what happens in its top three layers. Taken together, these two protocols provide the infrastructure of all of our communications and computing systems. Understanding them is the key to understanding why and how networks can be vulnerable—and provides the clues you need to choose the right best ways to secure those networks.

## Complementary, Not Competing, Frameworks

Both the TCP/IP protocol stack and the OSI 7-layer reference model grew out of efforts in the 1960s and 70s to continue to evolve and expand both the capabilities of computer networks and their usefulness. While it all started with the ARPANet project in the United States, international business, other governments, and universities worked diligently to develop compatible and complementary network architectures, technologies, and systems. By the early 1970s, commercial, academic, military, and government-sponsored research networks were already using many of these technologies, quite often at handsome profits.

**Historical Note**

ARPA initiated its ARPANet project in large part to provide a means for the governance functions of the United States to be able to survive a general, widespread nuclear attack on the US by the Soviet Union. Many of the features of what we now know and love as the Internet exist because ARPA's designers simply could not count on any particular subset of the network's nodes or links continuing to operate during or after such an attack.

*Transmission Control Protocol over Internet Protocol (TCP/IP)* was developed during the 1970s, based on original ARPANet protocols and a variety of competing (and in some cases conflicting) systems developed in private industry and in other countries. From 1978 to 1992, these ideas were merged together to become the published TCP/IP standard; ARPANet was officially migrated to this standard on January 1, 1993; since this protocol became known as "the Internet protocol," that date is as good a date to declare as the "birth of the Internet" as any. TCP/IP is defined as consisting of four basic layers. (We'll see why that "over" is in the name in a moment.)

The decade of the 1970s continued to be one of incredible innovation. It saw significant competition between ideas, standards, and design paradigms in almost every aspect of computing and communications. In trying to dominate their markets, many mainframe computer manufacturers and telephone companies set de facto standards that all but made it impossible (contractually) for any other company to make equipment that could plug into their systems and networks. Internationally, this was closing some markets while opening others. Although the courts were dismantling these near-monopolistic barriers to innovation in the United States, two different international organizations, the International Organization for Standardization (ISO) and the International Telegraph and Telephone Consultative Committee (CCITT), both worked on ways to expand the TCP/IP protocol stack to embrace higher-level functions that business, industry, and government felt were needed. By 1984, this led to the publication of the International Telecommunications Union (ITU, the renamed CCITT) Standard X.200 and ISO Standard 7498.

This new standard had two major components, and here is where some of the confusion among network engineers and IT professionals begins. The first component was the Basic Reference Model, which is an abstract (or conceptual) model of what computer networking is and how it works. This became known as the *Open Systems Interconnection Reference Model*, sometimes known as the OSI 7-layer model. (Since ISO subsequently developed more reference models in the open systems interconnection family, it's preferable to refer to this one as the OSI 7-layer reference model to avoid confusion.) The other major component was a whole series of highly detailed technical standards.

In many respects, both TCP/IP and the OSI 7-layer reference model largely agree on what happens in the first four layers of their model. But while TCP/IP doesn't address how things get done beyond its top layer, the OSI reference model does. Its three top layers are all dealing with information stored in computers as bits and bytes, representing both the data that needs to be sent over the network and the addressing and control information needed to make that happen. The bottommost layer has to transform computer representations of data and control into the actual signaling needed to transmit and receive across the network. (We'll look at each layer in greater depth in subsequent sections as we examine its potential vulnerabilities.)

---

### Traffic on the Internet vs. Calls Between Layers

As an SSCP, you've got to keep two eyes on how your networks are built, managed, and kept secure. One eye looks to the data streaming by on the network itself—bits, frames, packets, and so on, containing user payload data and control information, as you'll see later. You watch this data flow with test tools like packet sniffers, protocol analyzers, and port mappers. The other eye has to look at how the software and systems people on your team manage the software that uses those protocol stacks. Both eyes together get involved in bird-dogging the way your organization exerts configuration management and control over all the settings that control your networks and their security.

In the next section, you'll see the formats of the data streaming by on the network, and learn how that traffic marks itself layer by layer, protocol by protocol.

These protocol stacks are built into your systems as libraries of software routines, with each routine having a well-defined interface that other programs use to request a service. The lowest level device driver software handles the interface to the NIC, for example; it gets invoked (or called) to perform a service, which might be "notify me when a new incoming frame starts to arrive." *Sockets* are the software interfaces to many of the services provided by an implementation of a protocol stack. Sockets provide the applications developer with well-defined ways to access each service individually. The application design then reflects which services are needed in what order to meet its users' needs.

Each of those boundaries between layers is a threat surface—as a systems security specialist, you would not want just anybody to write a device driver or an app that makes calls directly to lower-level functions (would you?). Access control settings allow *trusted applications* to make such calls; untrusted (or normal user-level applications) can call those trusted applications, which will authenticate and authorize the request.

Finally, within each application itself, its developer builds in the logic that enables it to take user-level inputs and commands and turn them into interactions with the higher levels of the protocol stack. That FTP example illustrates this: the builders of my file transfer client had to anticipate what I'd want to do; specify those needs as requirements; and design, build, test, and deploy a client app with that logic built in.

For the SSCP exam, you won't need to get into the details of those libraries full of sockets or know all of the services involved in typical systems that implement networking. But you should be quite comfortable using your binocular vision to look simultaneously at the network traffic itself and the management and control of the software (and hardware) that keeps it secure—or opens it up to attack.

Let's use the OSI 7-layer reference model, starting at the physical level, as our roadmap and guide through internetworking. Table 5.2 shows a simplified side-by-side comparison of the OSI and TCP/IP models and illustrates how the OSI model's seven layers fit within a typical organization's use of computer networks. You'll note the topmost layer is "layer 8," the layer of people, business, *purpose*, and *intent*. (Note that there are many such informal "definitions" of the layers above layer 7, some humorous, some useful to think about using.) As we go through these layers, layer by layer, you'll see where TCP/IP differs in its approach, its naming conventions, or just where it and OSI have different points of view. With a good overview of the protocols layer by layer, we'll look in greater detail at topics that SSCPs know more about, or know how to *do* with great skill and cunning!

**TABLE 5.2**   OSI 7-layer model and TCP/IP 4-layer model in context

| System components | OSI layer | TCP/IP, protocols and services (examples) | Key address element | Datagrams are called... | Role in the information architecture |
|---|---|---|---|---|---|
| People | | | Name, building and room, email address, phone number, ... | Files, reports, memos, conversations, ... | Company data, information assets |
| Application software + people processes, gateways | 7 – Application | HTTP, email, FTP, ... | URL, IP address + port | Upper-layer data | Implement business logic and processes |
| | 6 – Presentation | SSL/TSL, MIME, MPEG, compression | | | |
| | 5 – Session | | | | |
| Load balancers, gateways | 4 – Transport | TCP, UDP | IP address + port | Segments | Implement connectivity with clients, partners, suppliers, ... |
| Routers, OS software | 3 – Network | IPv4, IPv6, IPSec, ICMP, ... | IP address + port | Packets | |
| Switches, hubs, routers | 2 – Data Link | 802.1X, PPP, ... | MAC address | Frames | |
| Cables, antenna, ... | 1 - Physical | | Physical connection | Bits | |

# Layer 1: The Physical Layer

*Layer 1, the Physical layer*, is very much the same in both TCP/IP and the OSI 7-layer model. The same standards are used in both. It typically consists of hardware devices and electrical devices that transform computer data into signals, move the signals to other nodes, and transform received signals back into computer data. Layer 1 is usually embedded in the NIC and provides the physical handshake between one NIC and its connections to the rest of the network. It does this by a variety of services, including the following:

- Transmission media control, controlling the circuits that drive the radio, fiber-optic, or electrical cable transmitters and receivers. This verifies that the fiber or cable or Wi-Fi system is up and operating and ready to send or receive. In point-to-point wired systems, this is the function that tells the operating system that "a network cable may have come unplugged," for example. (Note that this can be called *media control* or *medium control*; since most NICs and their associated interface circuits probably support only one kind of media, you might think that *medium* is the preferred term. Both are used interchangeably.)

- Collision detection and avoidance manages the transmitter to prevent it from interfering with other simultaneous transmissions by other nodes. (Think of this as waiting until the other people stop talking before you start!)

- The physical plug, socket, connector, or other mechanical device that is used to connect the NIC to the network transmission medium. The most standard form of such interconnection uses a Bell System RJ-45 connector and eight-wire cabling as the transmission medium for electrical signals. The eight wires are twisted together in pairs (for noise cancellation reasons) and can be with or without a layer of metalized Mylar foil to provide further shielding from the electromagnetic noise from power lines, radio signals, or other cabling nearby. Thus, these systems use either UTP (unshielded twisted pair) or STP (shielded twisted pair) to achieve speed, quality, and distance needs.

- Interface with the Data Link layer, managing the handoff of datagrams between the media control elements and the Data Link layer's functions

Multiple standards, such as the IEEE 802 series, document the details of the various physical connections and the media used at this layer.

At Layer 1, the datagram is the bit. The details of how different media turn bits (or handfuls of bits) into modulated signals to place onto wires, fibers, radio waves, or light waves are (thankfully!) beyond the scope of what SSCPs need to deal with. That said, it's worth considering that at Layer 1, addresses don't really matter! For wired (or fibered) systems, it's that physical path from one device to the next that gets the bits where they need to go; that receiving device has to receive all of the bits, unwrap them, and use Layer 2 logic to determine if that set of bits was addressed to it.

This also demonstrates a powerful advantage of this layers-of-abstraction model: nearly everything interesting that needs to happen to turn the user's data (our payload) into transmittable, receivable physical signals can happen with absolutely zero knowledge of how that transmission or reception actually happens! This means that changing out a 10BaseT physical media with Cat6 Ethernet gives your systems as much as a thousand-time increase in throughput, with no changes needed at the network address, protocol, or applications layers. (At most, very low-level device driver settings might need to be configured via operating systems functions, as part of such an upgrade.)

It's also worth pointing out that the physical domain defines both the collision domain and the physical segment. A *collision domain* is the physical or electronic space in which multiple devices are competing for each other's attention; if their signals out-shout each other, some kind of collision detection and avoidance is needed to keep things working properly. For wired (or fiber-connected) networks, all of the nodes connected by the same cable or fiber are in the same collision domain; for wireless connections, all receivers that can detect a specific transmitter are in that transmitter's collision domain. (If you think that suggests that typical Wi-Fi usage means lots of overlapping collision domains, you'd be right!) At the physical level, that connection is also known as a *segment*. But don't get confused: we *segment* (chop into logical pieces) a network into logical sub-networks, which we'll call *subnets*, at either Layer 2 or Layer 3, but not at Layer 1.

## Layer 2: The Data Link Layer

*Layer 2, the Data Link layer*, performs the data transfer from node to node of the network. As with Layer 2 in TCP/IP, it manages the *logical* connection between the nodes (over the link provided by Layer 1), provides flow control, and handles error correction in many cases. At this layer, the datagram is known as a *frame*, and frames consist of the data passed to Layer 2 by the higher layer, plus addressing and control information.

The IEEE 802 series of standards further refine the *concept* of what Layer 2 in OSI delivers by setting forth two sublayers:

- The Media Access Control (MAC) sublayer uses the unique MAC addresses of the NICs involved in the connection as part of controlling individual device access to the network and how devices use network services. The MAC layer grants permission to devices to transmit data as a result.

- The Logical Link Control (LLC) sublayer links the MAC sublayer to higher-level protocols by encapsulating their respective PDUs in additional header/trailer fields. LLC can also provide frame synchronization and additional error correction.

The MAC address is a 48-bit address, typically written (for humans) as six octets—six 8-bit binary numbers, usually written as two-digit hexadecimal numbers separated by dashes, colons, or no separator at all. For example, 3A-7C-FF-29-01-05 is the same 48-bit address as 3A7CFF290105. Standards dictate that the first 24 bits (first three hex digit pairs) are the organizational identifier of the NIC's manufacturer, and 24 bits (remaining three hex digit pairs) are a NIC-specific address. The IEEE assigns the organizational identifier, and the manufacturer assigns NIC numbers as it sees fit. Each

24-bit field represents over 16.7 million possibilities, which for a time seemed to be more than enough addresses; not anymore. Part of IPv6 is the adoption of a larger, 64-bit MAC address, and the protocols to allow devices with 48-bit MAC addresses to participate in IPv6 networks successfully.

Note that one of the bits in the first octet (in the organizational identifier) flags whether that MAC address is universally or locally administered. Many NICs have features that allow the local systems administrator to overwrite the manufacturer-provided MAC address with one of their own choosing. This does provide the end-user organization with a great capability to manage devices by using their own internal MAC addressing schemes, but it can be misused to allow one NIC to impersonate another one (so-called *MAC address spoofing*).

Let's take a closer look at the structure of a frame, shown in Figure 5.6. As mentioned, the payload is the set of bits given to Layer 2 by Layer 3 (or a layer-spanning protocol) to be sent to another device on the network. Conceptually, each frame consists of:

- A preamble, which is a 56-bit series of alternating 1s and 0s. This synchronization pattern helps serial data receivers ensure that they are receiving a frame and not a series of noise bits.

- The *Start Frame Delimiter* (SFD), which signals to the receiver that the preamble is over and that the real frame data is about to start. Different media require different SFD patterns.

- The destination MAC address.

- The source MAC address.

- The Ether Type field, which indicates either the length of the payload in octets or the protocol type that is encapsulated in the frame's payload.

- The payload data, of variable length (depending on the Ether Type field).

- A *Frame Check Sequence* (FCS), which provides a checksum across the entire frame, to support error detection.

The inter-packet gap is a period of dead space on the media, which helps transmitters and receivers manage the link and helps signify the end of the previous frame and the start of the next. It is not, specifically, a part of either frame, and it can be of variable length.

**FIGURE 5.6**    Data Link layer frame format

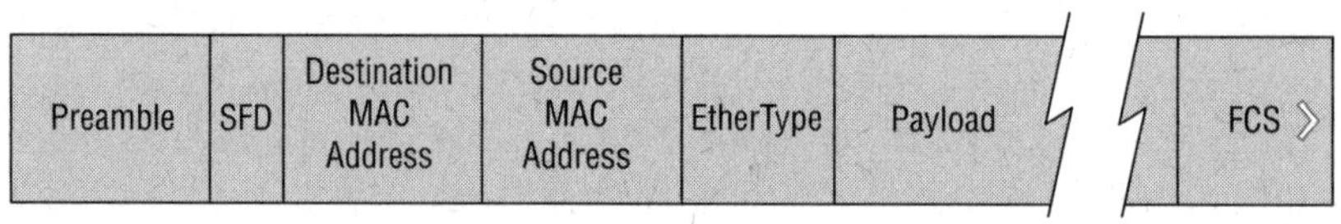

Layer 2 devices include bridges, modems, NICs, and switches that don't use IP addresses (thus called *Layer 2 switches*). Firewalls make their first useful appearance at Layer 2, performing rule-based and behavior-based packet scanning and filtering. Datacenter designs can make effective use of Layer 2 firewalls.

## Layer 3: The Network Layer

*Layer 3, the Network layer*, is defined in the OSI model as the place where variable-length sequences of fixed-length packets (that make up what the user or higher protocols want sent and received) are transmitted (or received). Routing and switching happens at Layer 3. Logical paths between two hosts are created; data packets are routed and forwarded to destinations; packet sequencing, congestion control, and error handling occur here. Layer 3 is where we see a lot of the Internet's "best efforts" design thinking at work, or perhaps, *not* at work; it is left to individual designers who build implementations of the protocols to decide how Layer 3–like functions in their architecture will handle errors at the Network layer and below.

ISO 7498/4 also defines a number of network management and administration functions that (conceptually) reside at Layer 3. These protocols provide greater support to routing, managing multicast groups, address assignment (at the Network layer), and other status information and error handling capabilities. Note that it is the job of the payload— the datagrams being carried by the protocols—that make these functions belong to the Network layer, and not the protocol that carries or implements them.

The most common device we see at Layer 3 is the router; combination bridge-routers, or *brouters*, are also in use (bridging together two or more Wi-Fi LAN segments, for example). Layer 3 switches are those that can deal with IP addresses. Firewalls also are a part of the Layer 3 landscape.

Layer 3 uses a packet. Most of the details of these packet headers are beyond the scope of the SSCP exam, but there are a few fields worth taking a closer look at; see Figure 5.7. For now, let's focus on the IP version 4 format, which has been in use since the 1970s and thus is almost universally used:

- Both the source and destination address fields are 32-bit IPv4 addresses.

- The Identification field, Flags, and Fragment Offset participate in error detection and reassembly of packet fragments.

- The Time To Live (or TTL) field keeps a packet from floating around the Internet forever. Each router or gateway that processes the packet decrements the TTL field, and if its value hits zero, the packet is discarded rather than passed on. If that happens, the router or gateway is supposed to send an *Internet Control Message Protocol* (ICMP) packet to the originator with fields set to indicate which packet didn't live long enough to get where it was supposed to go. (The tracert function uses TTL in order to determine what path packets are taking as they go from sender to receiver.)

- The Protocol field indicates whether the packet is using ICMP, TCP, Exterior Gateway, IPv6, or Interior Gateway Routing Protocol (IGRP).

- Finally, the data (or payload) portion.

**FIGURE 5.7** IPv4 packet format

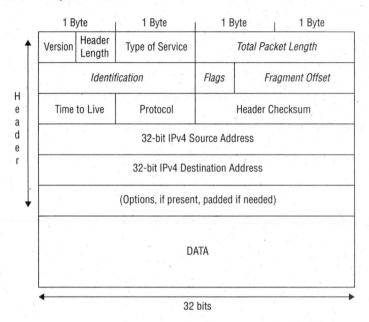

You'll note that we went from MAC addresses at Layer 2, to IP addresses at Layer 3. This requires the use of Address Resolution Protocol (ARP), one of several protocols that span multiple layers. We'll look at those together after we examine Layer 7.

## Layer 4: The Transport Layer

Now that we've climbed up to Layer 4, things start to get a bit more complicated. This layer is the home to many protocols that are used to transport data between systems; one such protocol, the Transport Control Protocol, gave its name (TCP) to the entire protocol stack! Let's first look at what the layer does, and then focus on some of the more important transport protocols.

*Layer 4, the Transport layer,* is where variable-length data from higher-level protocols or from applications gets broken down into a series of fixed-length packets; it also provides quality of service, greater reliability through additional flow control, and other features. In TCP/IP, Layer 4 is where TCP and UDP work; the OSI reference model goes on to define five different connection-mode transport protocols (named TP0 through TP4), each supporting a variety of capabilities. It's also at Layer 4 that we start to see tunneling protocols come into play.

Transport layer protocols primarily work with *ports*. Ports are software-defined labels for the connections between two processes, usually ones that are running on two different computers. The source and destination port, plus the protocol identification and other protocol-related information, are contained in that protocol's header. Each protocol defines what fields are needed in its header and prescribes required and optional actions that receiving nodes should take based on header information, errors in transmission, or other conditions.

Ports are typically bidirectional, using the same port number on sender and receiver to establish the connection. Some protocols may use multiple port numbers simultaneously.

Over time, the use of certain port numbers for certain protocols became standardized. Important ports that SSCPs should recognize when they see them are shown in Table 5.3, which also has a brief description of each protocol.

 Questions about these common protocols often appear on the certification exam!

**TABLE 5.3**  Common TCP/IP ports and protocols

| Protocol | TCP/UDP | Port number | Description |
|---|---|---|---|
| File Transfer Protocol (FTP) | TCP | 20/21 | FTP control is handled on TCP port 21, and its data transfer can use TCP port 20 as well as dynamic ports, depending on the specific configuration. |
| Secure Shell (SSH) | TCP | 22 | Used to manage network devices securely at the command level; secure alternative to Telnet, which does not support secure connections. |
| Telnet | TCP | 23 | Teletype-like unsecure command line interface used to manage network device. |
| Simple Mail Transfer Protocol (SMTP) | TCP | 25 | Transfers mail (email) between mail servers, and between end user (client) and mail server. |
| Domain Name System (DNS) | TCP/UDP | 53 | Resolves domain names into IP addresses for network routing. Hierarchical, using top-level domain servers (.com, .org, etc.) that support lower-tier servers for public name resolution. DNS servers can also be set up in private networks. |
| Dynamic Host Configuration Protocol (DHCP) | UDP | 67/68 | DHCP is used on networks that do not use static IP address assignment (almost all of them). |
| Trivial File Transfer Protocol (TFTP) | UDP | 69 | TFTP offers a method of file transfer without the session establishment requirements that FTP has; using UDP instead of TCP, the receiving device must verify complete and correct transfer. TFTP is typically used by devices to upgrade software and firmware. |

*(continued)*

**TABLE 5.3**   Common TCP/IP ports and protocols *(continued)*

| Protocol | TCP/UDP | Port number | Description |
|---|---|---|---|
| Hypertext Transfer Protocol (HTTP) | TCP | 80 | HTTP is the main protocol that is used by Web browsers and is thus used by any client that uses files located on these servers. |
| Post Office Protocol (POP) v3 | TCP | 110 | POP version 3 provides client–server email services, including transfer of complete inbox (or other folder) contents to the client. |
| Network Time Protocol (NTP) | UDP | 123 | One of the most overlooked protocols is NTP. NTP is used to synchronize the devices on the Internet. Most secure services simply will not support devices whose clocks are too far out of sync, for example. |
| NetBIOS | TCP/UDP | 137/138/139 | NetBIOS (more correctly, NETBIOS over TCP/IP, or NBT) has long been the central protocol used to interconnect Microsoft Windows machines. |
| Internet Message Access Protocol (IMAP) | TCP | 143 | IMAP version 3 is the second of the main protocols used to retrieve mail from a server. While POP has wider support, IMAP supports a wider array of remote mailbox operations that can be helpful to users. |
| Simple Network Management Protocol (SNMP) | TCP/UDP | 161/162 | SNMP is used by network administrators as a method of network management. SNMP can monitor, configure, and control network devices. SNMP traps can be set to notify a central server when specific actions are occurring. |
| Border Gateway Protocol (BGP) | TCP | 179 | BGP is used on the public Internet and by ISPs to maintain very large routing tables and traffic processing, which involve millions of entries to search, manage, and maintain every moment of the day. |
| Lightweight Directory Access Protocol (LDAP) | TCP/UDP | 389 | LDAP provides a mechanism of accessing and maintaining distributed directory information. LDAP is based on the ITU-T X.500 standard but has been simplified and altered to work over TCP/IP networks. |

| Protocol | TCP/UDP | Port number | Description |
|---|---|---|---|
| Hypertext Transfer Protocol over SSL/TLS (HTTPS) | TCP | 443 | HTTPS is used in conjunction with HTTP to provide the same services but does it using a secure connection that is provided by either SSL or TLS. |
| Lightweight Directory Access Protocol over TLS/SSL (LDAPS) | TCP/UDP | 636 | LDAPS provides the same function as LDAP but over a secure connection that is provided by either SSL or TLS. |
| FTP over TLS/SSL (RFC 4217) | TCP | 989/990 | FTP over TLS/SSL uses the FTP protocol, which is then secured using either SSL or TLS. |

It's good to note at this point that as we move down the protocol stack, each successive layer adds additional addressing, routing, and control information to the data payload it received from the layer above it. This is done by *encapsulating* or wrapping its own header around what it's given by the layers of the protocol stack or the application-layer socket call that asks for its service. Thus, the datagram produced at the Transport layer contains the protocol-specific header and the payload data. This is passed to the Network layer, along with the required address information and other fields; the Network layer puts that information into its IPv4 (or IPv6) header, sets the Protocol field accordingly, appends the datagram it just received from the Transport layer, and passes that on to the Data Link layer. (And so on...)

Most of the protocols that use Layer 4 either use TCP/IP as a stateful or connection-oriented way of transferring data or use UDP, which is stateless and not connection oriented. TCP bundles its data and headers into *segments* (not to be confused with segments at Layer 1), whereas UDP and some other Transport layer protocols call their bundles *datagrams*:

- *Stateful communications processes* have sender and receiver go through a sequence of steps, and sender and receiver have to keep track of which step the other has initiated, successfully completed, or asked for a retry on. Each of those steps is often called the *state* of the process at the sender or receiver. Stateful processes require an unambiguous identification of sender and recipient, and some kind of protocols for error detection and requests for retransmission, which a connection provides.

- *Stateless communication processes* do not require sender and receiver to know where the other is in the process. This means that the sender does not need a connection, does not need to service retransmission requests, and may not even need to validate who the listeners are. Broadcast traffic is typically both stateless and connectionless.

Layer 4 devices include gateways (which can bridge dissimilar network architectures together, and route traffic between them) and firewalls.

From here on up, the two protocol stacks conceptually diverge. TCP/IP as a standard stops at Layer 4 and allocates to users, applications, and other unspecified higher-order logic the tasks of managing what traffic to transport and how to make business or organizational sense of what's getting transported. The OSI 7-layer reference model continues to add further layers of abstraction, and for one very good reason: because each layer adds clarity when taking business processes into the Internet or into the cloud (which you get to through the Internet, of course). That clarity aids the design process and the development of sound operational procedures; it is also a great help when trying to diagnose and debug problems.

We also see that from here on out, almost all functions except perhaps that of the firewall and the gateway are hosted either in operating systems or applications software, which of course is running on servers or endpoint devices.

---

### Does TCP/IP Have Layers above the Transport Layer?

Although some websites and books suggest that the TCP/IP protocol stack looks at other layers beyond the Transport layer, this is not technically correct. Some systems vendors, for example, will state that the Transport and Session layers combine to create a "host-to-host" communications layer; on top of this, Presentation and Application combine into a "process" layer.

There are also some people who refer to such layers above Transport, or those above Layer 7 in the OSI model, as the "office politics," "money," "cultural," or even "religious" layers, the last perhaps referring to organizations where beliefs are so zealously held that new ideas just "can't happen here..."

As an SSCP, you may find that your company or organization, or its IT systems vendors and engineers, may use such terms; that's okay. Take the conversation the next level down to help identify what specific protocols are involved, rather than try to split hairs about the name of a bundle of services.

---

## Layer 5: The Session Layer

*Layer 5, the Session layer*, is where the overall dialogue or flow of handshakes is controlled in order to support a logically related series of tasks that require data exchange. Sessions typically require initiation, ongoing operation, adjournment, and termination; many require checkpointing to allow for graceful fallback and recovery to earlier points within the session. Think of logging onto your bank's webpages to do some online banking; from the moment you start to log on, you're initiating a session; a session can contain many transactions as steps you seek to perform; finally, you log off (or time out or disconnect) and end the session. Sessions may be also need full-duplex (simultaneous activity in both directions), half-duplex (activity from one party to the other, a formal turnaround, and then activity in the other way), or simplex (activity in one direction only). Making a bank deposit requires half-duplex operation: the bank has to completely process the deposit steps, then update your account balance, before it can turn the dialogue around and update the display of account information on your endpoint. The OSI model also defines Layer 5 as responsible for gracefully bringing sessions to a close and for providing session checkpoint and recovery capabilities (if any are implemented in a particular session's design).

Newer protocols at the Session layer include Session Description Protocol (SDP) and Session Initiation Protocol (SIP). These and related protocols are extensively used with VOIP (voice over IP) services. Another important protocol at this layer is Real-Time Transport Protocol (RTP). RTP was initially designed to satisfy the demands for smoother delivery of streaming multimedia services and rides over UDP (at the Transport layer). Other important uses are in air traffic control and data management systems, where delivery of flight tracking information must take place in a broadcast or multicast fashion but be in real time—imagine the impact (pardon the pun) if flight tracking updates on an inbound flight consistently come in even as little as a minute late!

## Layer 6: The Presentation Layer

*Layer 6, the Presentation layer,* supports the mapping of data in terms and formats used by applications into terms and formats needed by the lower-level protocols in the stack. The Presentation layer handles protocol-level encryption and decryption of data (protecting data in motion), translates data from representational formats that applications use into formats better suited to protocol use, and can interpret semantical or metadata about applications data into terms and formats that can be sent via the Internet.

This layer was created to consolidate both the thinking and design of protocols to handle the wide differences in the ways that 1970s-era systems formatted, displayed, and used data. Different character sets, such as EBCIDIC, ASCII, or FIELDATA, used different number of bits; they represented the same character, such as an uppercase A, by different sets of bits. Byte sizes were different on different manufacturers' minicomputers and mainframes. The presentation of data to the user, and the interaction with the user, could take many forms: a simple chat, a batch file input and printed output of the results, or a predefined on-screen form with specified fields for data display and edit. Such a form is one example of a data structure that presentation must consider; others would be a list of data items retrieved by a query, such as "all flights from San Diego to Minneapolis on Tuesday morning."

Sending or receiving such a data structure represents the need to *serialize* and *deserialize* data for transmission purposes. To the application program, this table, list, or form may be a series of values stored in an array of memory locations. Serializing requires an algorithm that has to first "walk" the data structure, field by field, row by row; retrieve the data values; and output a list of coordinates (rows and fields) and values. Deserializing uses the same algorithm to take an input list of coordinates and values and build up the data structure that the application needs.

There are several sublayers and protocols that programmers can use to achieve an effective Presentation-layer interface between applications on the one hand and the Session layer and the rest of the protocol stack on the other. HTTP is an excellent example of such a protocol.

NetBIOS (the Network Basic Input/Output System) and Server Message Block (SMB) are also very important to consider at the Presentation layer. NetBIOS is actually an application programming interface (API) rather than a formal protocol per se. From its roots in IBM's initial development of the personal computer, NetBIOS now runs over TCP/IP (or NBT, if you can handle one more acronym!) or any other transport mechanism. Both NetBIOS and SMB allow programs to communicate with each other, whether they are on the same host or different hosts on a network.

Keep in mind that many of the cross-layer protocols, apps, and older protocols involved with file transfer, email, and network-attached file systems and storage resources (such as the Common Internet File System [CIFS] protocol) all "play through" Layer 6.

## Layer 7: The Application Layer

*Layer 7, the Application layer,* is where most end users and their endpoints interact with and are closest to the Internet, you might say. Applications such as Web browsers, VOIP or video streaming clients, email clients, and games use their internal logic to translate user actions—data input field-by-field or selection and action commands click-by-click into application-specific sets of data to transfer via the rest of the protocol stack to a designated recipient address. Multiple protocols, such as FTP and HTTP, are in use at the Application layer, yet the logic that must determine what data to pass from user to distant endpoint and back to user all resides in the application programs themselves. None of the protocols, by themselves, make those decisions for us.

There are various mnemonics to help remember the seven OSI layers. Two common mnemonics, and their correspondence with the OSI protocol stack, are shown in Figure 5.8. Depending upon your tastes, you can use:

- "Please Do Not Throw Sausage Pizza Away"
- "All People Seem to Need Data Processing"

**FIGURE 5.8**    Easy OSI mnemonics

| Read Going Up | Layer | Read Going Down |
| --- | --- | --- |
| Away | Application | All |
| Pizza | Presentation | People |
| Sausage | Session | Seem |
| Throw | Transport | To |
| Not | Network | Need |
| Do | Datalink | Data |
| Please | Physical | Processing |

Look back to Figure 5.1, which demonstrates the OSI reference model in action, in simplified terms, by starting with data a user enters into an application program's data entry screen. The name and phone number entered probably need other information to go with them from this client to the server so that the server knows what to do with these values; the application must pass all of this required information to the Presentation layer, which stuffs it into different fields in a larger datagram structure, encrypting it if required.

## Cross-Layer Protocols and Services

But wait...remember, both TCP/IP and the OSI reference model are *models*, models that define and describe in varying degrees of specificity and generality. OSI and TCP/IP both must support some important functions that cross layers, and without these, it's not clear if the Internet would work very well at all! The most important of these are:

- *Dynamic Host Configuration Protocol (DHCP)* assigns IPv4 (and later IPv6) addresses to new devices as they join the network. This set of handshakes allows DHCP to accept or reject new devices based on a variety of rules and conditions that administrators can use to restrict a network. DHCP servers allow subscriber devices to lease an IP address, for a specific period of time (or indefinitely); as the expiration time reaches its half-life, the subscribing device requests a renewal.

- *Address Resolution Protocol (ARP)* is a discovery protocol, by which a network device determines the corresponding IP address for a given MAC address by (quite literally) asking other network devices for it. On each device, ARP maintains in its cache a list of IP address and MAC address pairs. Failing to find the address there, ARP seeks to find either the DHCP that assigned that IP address, or some other network device whose ARP cache knows the desired address.

  ARP has several variations that are worth being knowing a bit about:

  - *Reverse ARP* (RARP), which lets a machine request its IP address from other machines on the LAN segment. RARP preceded the creation of DHCP, and is considered obsolete by many networking specialists. It is, however, showing up as a component of some modern protocols such as Cisco's Overlay Transport Virtualization (OTV).

  - *Inverse ARP* (InARP), similar to RARP, is very useful in configuring remote devices.

  - *Proxy ARP* allows subnets joined via a router to still resolve MAC addresses, by having the router act as proxy.

  - *Gratuitous ARP* supports advanced networking scenarios in a variety of ways. Properly used, they can detect IP address conflicts, and can help update the ARP tables in other machines on the network. Gratuitous ARPs are also sent by NICs and other interfaces as they power up or reset, in order to preload their own ARP tables.

- *Domain Name Service (DNS)* works at Layer 4 and Layer 7 by attempting to resolve a domain name (such as isc2.org) into its IP address. The search starts with the requesting device's local DNS cache, then seeks "up the chain" to find either a device that knows of the requested domain, or a domain name server that has that information. Layer 3 has no connection to DNS.

- *Network management functions* have to cut across every layer of the protocol stacks, providing configuration, inspection, and control functions. These functions provide the services that allow user programs like ipconfig to instantiate, initiate, terminate, or monitor communications devices and activities. Simple Network Management Protocol (SNMP) is quite prevalent in the TCP/IP community; Common Management Information Protocol (CMIP) and its associated Common Management Information Service (CMIS) are more recognized in OSI communities.

- *Cross MAC and PHY (or physical) scheduling* is vital when dealing with wireless networks. Since timing of wireless data exchanges can vary considerably (mobile devices are often moving!), being able to schedule packets and frames can help make such networks achieve better throughput and be more energy-efficient. (Mobile customers and their device batteries appreciate that.)

- *Network Address Translation (NAT)*, sometimes known as Port Address Translation (PAT), IP masquerading, NAT overload, and many-to-one NAT, all provide ways of allowing a routing function to edit a packet to change (translate) one set of IP addresses for another. Originally, this was thought to make it easier to move a device from one part of your network to another without having to change its IP address. As we became more aware of the IPv4 address space being exhausted, NAT became an incredibly popular workaround, a way to sidestep running out of IP addresses. Although it lives at Layer 3, NAT won't work right if it cannot reach into the other layers of the stack (and the traffic) as it needs to.

## IP and Security

As stated, the original design of the Internet assumed a trustworthy environment; it also had to cope with a generation of computing equipment that just did not have the processing speed or power, or the memory capacity, to deal with effective security, especially if that involved significant encryption and decryption. Designers believed that other layers of functionality beyond the basic IP stack could address those issues, to meet specific user needs, such as by encrypting the contents of a file before handing it to an application like FTP for transmission over the Internet. Rapid expansion of the Internet into business and academic use, and into international markets, quickly demonstrated that the innocent days of a trusting Internet were over. In the late 1980s and early 1990s, work sponsored by the U.S. National Security Agency, U.S. Naval Research Laboratory, Columbia University, and Bell Labs came together to create Internet Protocol Security, or IPsec as it came to be known.

*IPSec* provides an open and extensible architecture that consists of a number of protocols and features used to provide greater levels of message confidentiality, integrity, authentication, and nonrepudiation protection:

- The IP Security Authentication Header (AH) protocol uses a secure hash and secret key to provide connectionless integrity and a degree of IP address authentication.

- Encapsulating Security Payloads (ESP) by means of encryption supports confidentiality, connectionless integrity, and anti-replay protection, and authenticates the originator of the data (thus providing a degree of nonrepudiation).

Security associations (or SAs) bundle together the algorithms and data used in securing the payloads. ISAKMP, the Internet Security Association and Key Management Protocol, for example, provided the structure, framework, and mechanisms for key exchange and authentication. IPSec implementations depend upon authenticated keying materials. Since IPSec preceded the development and deployment of PKI, it had to develop its own infrastructure and processes to support users in meeting their key management needs. This could be either via Internet Key Exchange (IKE and IKEv2), the Kerberized Internet Negotiation of Keys (KINK, using Kerberos services), or using an IPSECKEY DNS record exchange.

The mechanics of how to implement and manage IPSec are beyond the scope of the SSCP exam itself; however, SSCPs do need to be aware of IPSec and appreciate its place in the evolution of Internet security.

IPSec was an optional add-in for IPv4 but is a mandatory component of IPv6. IPSec functions at Layer 3 of the protocol stacks, as an internetworking protocol suite; contrast this with TLS, for example, which works at Layer 4 as a transport protocol.

## Layers or Planes?

If you stand alongside of those protocol stacks and think in more general terms, you'll quickly recognize that every device, every protocol, and every service has a role to play in the three major functions we need networks to achieve: movement of data, control of that data flow, and management of the network itself. If you were to draw out those flows on separate sheets of paper, you'd see how each provides a powerful approach to use when designing the network, improving its performance, resolving problems with the network, and protecting it. This gives rise to the three *planes* that network engineers speak of quite frequently:

- The *data plane* is the set of functions, processes, and protocols that move or forward frames and packets from one interface to another.

- The *control plane* provides all of the processes, functions, and protocols for switching, routing, address resolution, and related activities.

- The *management plane* contains all of the processes, functions, and protocols that administrators use to manage, configure, and control the network.

Hardware designers use these concepts extensively as they translate the protocol stacks into real router, switch, or gateway devices. For example, the movement of data itself ought to be as fast and efficient as possible, either by specifically designed high-speed hardware, firmware, or software. Control functions, which are the heart of all the routing protocols, still need to run pretty efficiently, but this will often be done by using separate circuits and data paths within the hardware. System management functions involve either collecting statistical and performance data or issuing directives to devices, and for system integrity reasons, designers often put these in separate paths in hardware and software as well.

As we saw with the OSI reference model, the concept of separating network activity into data, control, and management planes is both a sound theoretical idea and a tangible design feature in the devices and networks all around us. (Beware of geeks who think that these planes, like the 7-layer model, are just some nice ideas!)

### Identity as a Control Plane?

More and more, we see that identity management and access control are absolutely vital to achieving and maintaining information security. Microsoft, among others, has started to emphasize this by referring to identity as "the new control plane." Keep an eye open to see how this concept of a fourth plane gains traction across the information security marketplace of ideas.

## Software-Defined Networks

As the name suggests, software-defined networks (SDNs) use network management and virtualization tools to completely define the network in software. SDNs are most commonly used in cloud systems deployments, where they provide the infrastructure that lets multiple virtual machines communicate with each other in standard TCP/IP or OSI reference model terms. Cloud-hosted SDNs don't have their own *real* Physical layer, for they depend on the services of the bare metal environment that is hosting them to provide these. That said, the protocol stacks at Layer 1 still have to interact with device drivers that are the "last software port of call," you might say, before entering the land of physical hardware and electrical signals.

It might be natural at this point to think that all but the smallest and simplest of networks are software defined, since as administrators we use software tools to configure the devices on the network. This is true, but in a somewhat trivial sense. Imagine a small business network with perhaps a dozen servers, including dedicated DNS, DHCP, remote access control, network storage, and print servers. It might have several Wi-Fi access points and use another dozen routers to segment the network and support it across different floors of a building or different buildings in a small office park. Each of these devices is configured first at the physical level (you connect it with cables to other devices); then, you use its built-in firmware functions via a Web browser or terminal link to configure it by setting its control parameters. That's a lot of individual devices to configure! Network management systems can provide integrated ways to define the network and remotely configure many of those devices.

# Virtual Private Networks

Virtual private networks (VPNs) were developed initially to provide businesses and organizations a way to bring geographically separate LAN segments together into one larger private network. Prior to using VPN technologies, the company would have to use private communications channels, such as leased high-capacity phone circuits or microwave relays, as the physical communications media and technologies within the Physical layer of this extended private network. (Dial-up connections via modem were also examples of early VPN systems.) In effect, that leased circuit tunneled under the public switched telecommunications network; it was a circuit that stayed connected all the time, rather than one that was established, used, and torn down on a per-call basis.

VPNs tunnel under the Internet using a combination of Layer 2 and Layer 3 services. They provide a secure, encrypted channel between VPN connection "landing points" (not to be confused with *endpoints* in the laptop, phone, or IoT device sense!). As a Layer 2 service, the VPN receives *every* frame or packet from higher up in the protocol stack, encrypts it, wraps it in its own routing information, and lets the Internet carry it off to the other end of the tunnel. At the receiving end of the tunnel, the VPN service unwraps the payload, decrypts it, and passes it up the stack. Servers and services at each end of the tunnel have the normal responsibilities of routing payloads to the right elements of that local system, including forwarding them on to LAN or WAN addresses as each packet needs.

Most VPN solutions use one or more of the following security protocols:

- IPSec
- TLS
- Datagram Transport Layer Security (DTLS)
- Microsoft Point-to-Point Encryption, or Microsoft Secure Socket Tunneling Protocol, used with Point-to-Point Tunneling Protocol
- Secure Shell VPN
- Multiprotocol Label Switching (MPLS)
- Other proprietary protocols and services

Mobile device users (and systems administrators who need to support mobile users) are increasingly turning to VPN solutions to provide greater security.

On the one hand, VPNs bring some powerful security advantages home, both to business and individual VPN customers alike. From the point in your local systems where the VPN starts tunneling, on to the tunnel's landing point, PKI-driven encryption is preventing anybody from knowing what you're trying to accomplish with that data stream. The only traffic analysis they can glean from monitoring your data is that you connect to a VPN landing point.

On the other hand, this *transfers* your trust to your VPN service provider and the people who own and manage it. You have to be confident that their business model, their security policies (administrative and logical), and their reputation support your CIANA needs. One might rightly be suspicious of a VPN provider with "free forever" offers with no clear up-sell strategy; if they don't have a way of making honest money with what they are doing, due diligence requires you to think twice before trusting them.

Do keep in mind that if your VPN landing point server fails, so does your VPN. Many SOHO VPN clients will allow the user to configure the automatic use of alternate landing sites, but this can still involve service interruptions of tens of seconds.

## A Few Words about Wireless

Wireless network systems are the history of the Internet in miniature: first, let's make them easy to use, right out of the shrink-wrap! Then, we'll worry about why they're not secure and whether we should do something about that.

In one respect, it's probably true to say that wireless data communication is first and foremost a Layer 1 or Physical layer set of opportunities, constraints, issues, and potential security vulnerabilities. Multiple technologies, such as Wi-Fi, Bluetooth, NFC, and infrared and visible light LED and photodiode systems, all are important and growing parts of the way organizations use their network infrastructures. (Keep an eye open for Li-Fi as the next technology to break our trains of thought. *Li-Fi* is the use of high-frequency light pulses from LEDs used in normal room or aircraft cabin illumination systems.)

Regardless of the technologies used, wireless systems are either a part of our networks, or they are not. These devices either use our TCP/IP protocols, starting with the physical layer on up, or use their own link-specific sets of protocols. Broadly speaking, though, no matter what protocol stack or interface (or interfaces, plural!) they are using, the same risk management and mitigation processes should be engaged to protect the organization's information infrastructures.

Key considerations include the following:

- Access control and identity management, both for the device and the user(s) via that device.
- Location tracking and management; it might be too risky, for example, to allow an otherwise authorized user to access company systems from a heretofore unknown or not-yet-approved location.
- Link protection, from the physical connection on up, including appropriate use of secure protocols to protect authentication and payload data.
- Congestion and traffic management.
- Software and hardware configuration management and control, for both the mobile device's operating system and any installed applications.

Chapter 8, "Hardware and Systems Security," goes into many of these issues in greater depth.

## Wi-Fi

Wi-Fi, which actually does *not* mean "wireless fidelity," is probably the most prevalent and pervasive wireless radio technology currently in use. Let's focus a moment longer on protecting the data link between the endpoint device (such as a user's smartphone, laptop, smartwatch, etc.) and the wireless access point, which manages how, when, and which wireless subscriber devices can connect at Layer 1 and above. (Note that a wireless access point can also be a wireless device itself!) Let's look at wireless security protocols:

- Wired Equivalency Protocol (WEP) was the first attempt at securing Wi-Fi. As the name suggests, it was a compromise intended to make some security easier to achieve, but it proved to have far too many security flaws and was easily circumvented by attackers. Its encryption was vulnerable to passive attacks, such as traffic analysis. Unauthorized mobile stations could easily use a known plaintext attack or other means to trick the WEP access point, leading to decrypting the traffic. Perhaps more seriously, it was demonstrated that about a day's worth of intercepted traffic could build a dictionary (or rainbow table) with which real-time automated decryption could be done by the attacker. Avoid its use altogether if you can.

- Wi-Fi Protected Access (WPA) was an interim replacement while the IEEE 802.11i standard was in development. It used preshared encryption keys (PSKs, sometimes called "WPA Personal") while providing Temporal Key Integrity Protocol (TKIP, pronounced *"tee-kip"*) for encryption. WPA Enterprise uses more robust encryption, an authentication server, or PKI certificates in the process.

- Wi-Fi Protected Access Version 2 (WPA2) took this the next step when IEEE 802.11i was released in 2004. Among other improvements, WPA2 brings Advanced Encryption Standard (AES) algorithms into use.

## Bluetooth

*Bluetooth* is a short-range wireless radio interface standard, designed to support wireless mice, keyboards, or other devices, typically within 1 to 10 meters of the host computer they are being used with. Bluetooth is also used to support data synchronization between smartwatches and fitness trackers with smartphones. Bluetooth has its own protocol stack, with one set of protocols for the controller (the time-critical radio elements) and another set for the host. There are 15 protocols altogether. Bluetooth does not operate over Internet Protocol networks.

In contrast with Wi-Fi, Bluetooth has four security modes:

- Mode 1, Unsecure, bypasses any built-in authentication and encryption (at host or device). This does not prevent other nearby Bluetooth devices from pairing up with a host. This mode is supported only through Bluetooth Version 2.0 plus Enhanced Data Rate (EDR) and should not be used with later versions of Bluetooth.

- Mode 2, centralized security management, which provides some degree of authorization, authentication, and encryption of traffic between the devices.

- Mode 3, device pairing, looks to the remote device to initiate encryption-based security using a separate secret link (secret to the paired devices). This too is supported only by version 2.0 + EDR systems.

- Mode 4, key exchange, supports more advanced encryption algorithms, such as elliptic-curve Diffie-Hellman.

Bluetooth is prone to a number of security concerns, such as these:

- Bluejacking, the hijacking of a Bluetooth link to get the attacker's data onto an otherwise trusted device

- Bluebugging, by which attackers can remotely access a smartphone's unprotected Bluetooth link and use it as an eavesdropping platform, collect data from it, or operate it remotely

- Bluesnarfing, the theft of information from a wireless device through a Bluetooth connection

- Car whispering, which uses software to allow hackers to send and receive audio from a Bluetooth-enabled car entertainment system

Given these concerns, it's probably best that your mobile device management solution understand the vulnerabilities inherent in Bluetooth, and ensure that each mobile device you allow onto your networks (or your business premises!) can be secured against exploitations targeted at its Bluetooth link.

## Near-Field Communication

Near-field communication (NFC) provides a secure radio-frequency communications channel that works for devices within about 4 cm (1.6 inches) of each other. Designed to meet the needs of contactless, card-less payment and debit authorizations, NFC uses secure on-device data storage and existing radio frequency identification (RFID) standards to carry out data transfers (such as phone-to-phone file sharing) or payment processing transactions.

Multiple standards organizations work on different aspects of NFC and its application to problems within the purview of each body.

NFC is susceptible to man-in-the-middle attacks at the physical Data Link layer and is also susceptible to high-gain antenna interception. Relay attacks, similar to man-in-the-middle, are also possible. NFC as a standard does not include encryption, but like TCP/IP, it will allow for applications to layer on encrypted protection for data and routing information.

---

 **Design Scenario**

**Gateway to E.T.?**

You may recall the 1996 science-fiction blockbuster movie *Independence Day*, in which our earthly protagonists hack into an invading alien space armada's command and control networks, inject a malware payload, and in doing so save what's left of Earth and humankind. It's probably reasonable to assume that a direct level-for-level correspondence did not exist between our hero's laptop computer and the extraterrestrials' systems.

Would this be where you'd need a gateway? What would it have to do? And how might you know it's working correctly?

# IP Addresses, DHCP, and Subnets

Now that we've got an idea of how the layers fit together conceptually, let's look at some of the details of how IP addressing gets implemented within an organization's network and within the Internet as a whole. As it's still the dominant ecosystem on almost all of our networks, we'll use IPv4 addresses to illustrate. Recall that an IPv4 address field is a 32-bit number, represented as four octets (8-bit chunks) written usually as base 10 numbers.

Let's start "out there" in the Internet, where we see two kinds of addresses: static and dynamic. *Static IP addresses* are assigned once to a device, and they remain unchanged; thus, 8.8.8.8 has been the main IP address for Google since, well, *ever*, and it probably always will be. The advantage of a static IP address for a server or webpage is that virtually every layer of ARP and DNS cache on the Internet will know it; it will be quicker and easier to find. By contrast, a *dynamic IP address is assigned each time that device connects to the network*. ISPs most often use dynamic assignment of IP addresses to subscriber equipment, since this allows them to manage a pool of addresses better. Your subscriber equipment (your modem, router, PC, or laptop) then need a DHCP server to assign them an address.

It's this use of DHCP, by the way, that means that almost everybody's SOHO router can use the same IP address *on the LAN side*, such as 192.168.2.1 or 192.168.1.1. The router connects on one side (the wide area network [WAN]) to the Internet by way of your ISP, and on the other side to the devices on its local network segment. Devices on the LAN segment can see other devices on that segment, but they cannot see "out the WAN side," you might say, without using network address translation, which we'll look at in a moment.

It's almost guaranteed that you'll encounter questions about address classes and subnetting on the SSCP exam, so it's good to get **very** familiar with these concepts. Practice calculating subnets and CIDRs, and check your work with any of the free subnet calculators available online. Just because IPv6 seems to have made subnetting "old hat" does not mean it's gone away—nor will it, any time soon!

## IPv4 Address Classes

IPv4's addressing scheme was developed with classes of addresses in mind. These were originally designed to be able to split the octets so that one set represented a node within a network, while the other octets were used to define very large, large, and small networks. At the time (1970s), this was thought to make it easier for humans manage IP addresses. Over time, this has proven impractical. Despite this, IPv4 address class nomenclature remains a fixed part of our network landscape, and SSCPs need to be familiar with the defined address classes:

- Class A addresses used the first octet to define such very large networks (at most 128 of them), using 0 in the first bit to signify Class A address or some other address type. IBM, for example, might have required all 24 bits' worth of the other octets to assign IP addresses to all of its nodes. Think of Class A addresses as looking like <net>.<node>.<node>.<node>.

- Class B addresses used two octets for the network identifier and two for the node, or <net>.<net>.<node>.<node>. The first 2 bits of the address would be 10.

- Class C addresses used the first three octets for the network identifier: <net>.<net>.<net>.node, giving smaller organizations networks of at most 256 addresses; the first 3 bits of the first octet were 110.

- Class D and Class E addresses were reserved for experimental and other purposes.

These address classes are summarized in Table 5.4.

**TABLE 5.4**   IPv4 address classes

| Class | Leading bits | Size of Network Number field | Size of Node Number field | Number of networks | Number of nodes per network | Start address | End address |
|-------|------|------|------|------|------|------|------|
| A | 0 | 8 | 24 | 128 | 16,777,216 | 0.0.0.0 | 127.255.255.255 |
| B | 10 | 16 | 16 | 16,384 | 65,536 | 128.0.0.0 | 191.255.255.255 |
| C | 110 | 24 | 8 | 2,097,152 | 256 | 192.0.0.0 | 223.255.255.255 |

There are, as you might expect, some special cases to keep in mind:

- 127.0.0.1 is commonly known as the *loopback address*, which apps can use for testing the local IP protocol stack. Packets addressed to the local loopback are sent only from one part of the stack to another ("looped back" on the stack), rather than out onto the Physical layer of the network. Note that this means the entire range of the addresses starting with 127 are so reserved, so you could use any of them.

- 169.254.0.0 is called the *link local address*, which is used to auto-assign an IP address when there is no DHCP server that responds. In many cases, systems that are using the link local address suggest that the DHCP server has failed to connect with them, for some reason.

In Windows systems this is known as the *Auto-IP Address* (APIPA) because it is generated by Windows when a DHCP server does not respond to requests; regardless of what you call it, it's good to recognize this IP address when trying to diagnose why you've got no Internet connection.

The node address of 255 is reserved for broadcast use. *Broadcast messages* go to all nodes on the specified network; thus, sending a message to 192.168.2.255 sends it to all nodes on the 192.168.2 network, and sending it to 192.168.255.255 sends it to a lot more nodes! Broadcast messages are blocked by routers from traveling out onto their WAN side. By contrast, multicasting can provide ways to allow a router to send messages to other nodes beyond a router, using the address range of 224. 255.255.255 to 239.255.255.255. *Unicasting* is what happens when we do not use 255 as part of the node address field—the message goes only to the specific address. Although the SSCP exam won't ask about the details of setting up and managing broadcasts and multicasts, you should be aware of what these terms mean and recognize the address ranges involved.

## Subnetting in IPv4

Subnetting seems to confuse people easily, but in real life, we deal with sets and subsets of things all the time. We rent an apartment, and it has a street address, but the building is further broken down into individual sub-addresses known as the apartment number. This makes postal mail delivery, emergency services, and just day-to-day navigation by the residents easier. Telephone area codes primarily divide a country into geographic regions, and the next few digits of a phone number (the city code or exchange) divide the area code's map further. This, too, is a convenience feature, but first for the designers and operators of early phone networks and switches. (Phone number portability is rapidly erasing this correspondence of phone number to location.)

Subnetting allows network designers and administrators ways to logically group a set of devices together in ways that make sense to the organization. Suppose your company's main Class B IP address is 163.241, meaning you've got 16 bits' worth of node addresses to assign. If you use them all, you have *one* subgroup, 0.0 to 254.254 (remember that broadcast address!). Conversely:

- Using the last two bits gives you three subgroups.
- Using the last octet gives you 127 subgroups.
- And so on.

Designing our company's network to support subgroups requires we know three things: our address class, the number of subgroups we want, and the number of nodes in each subgroup. This lets us start to create our subnet masks. A subnet mask, written in IP address format, shows which bit positions (starting from the right or least significant bit) are allocated to the node number within a subnet. For example, a mask of 255.255.255.0 says that the last 8 bits are used for the node numbers within each of 254 possible subnets (if this were a Class B address). Another subnet mask might be 255.255.255.128, indicating two subnets on a Class C address, with up to 127 nodes on each subnet. (Subnets do not have to be defined on byte or octet boundaries, after all.)

Subnets are defined using the full range of values available for the given number of bits (minus 2 for addresses 0 and 255). Thus, if we require 11 nodes on each subnet, we still need to use 4 bits for the subnet portion of the address, giving us address 0, node addresses 1 through 11, and 15 for all-bits-on; two addresses are therefore unused.

This did get cumbersome after a while, and in 1993, Classless Inter-Domain Routing (CIDR) was introduced to help simplify both the notation and the calculation of subnets. CIDR appends the number of subnet address bits to the main IP address. For example, 192.168.1.168/24 shows that 24 bits are assigned for the *network* address, and the remaining 8 bits are therefore available for the node-within-subnet address. (Caution: don't get those backward!) Table 5.5 shows some examples to illustrate.

**TABLE 5.5**  Address classes and CIDR

| Class | Number of network bits | Number of node bits | Subnet mask | CIDR notation |
|-------|------------------------|---------------------|-------------|---------------|
| A | 9 | 23 | 255.128.0.0 | /9 |
| B | 17 | 15 | 255.255.128.0 | /17 |
| C | 28 | 4 | 255.255.255.240 | /28 |

Unless you're designing the network, most of what you need to do with subnets is to *recognize* subnets when you see them and interpret both the subnet masks and the CIDR notation, if present, to help you figure things out. CIDR counts bits starting with the leftmost bit of the IP address; it counts left to right. What's left after you run out of CIDR are the number of bits to use to assign addresses to nodes on the subnet (minus 2).

Before we can look at subnetting in IPv6, we first have to deal with the key changes to the Internet that the new version 6 is bringing in.

## Running Out of Addresses?

By the early 1990s, it was clear that the IP address system then in use would not be able to keep up with the anticipated explosive growth in the numbers of devices attempting to connect to the Internet. At that point, Version 4 of the protocol (or IPv4 as it's known) used a 32-bit address field, represented in the familiar four-octet address notation (such as 192.168.2.11). That could only handle about 4.3 billion unique addresses; by 2012, we already had 8 billion devices connected to the Internet, and had invented additional protocols such as NAT to help cope. According to the IETF, 2011 was the year we started to see address pool exhaustion become realit; one by one, four of the five Regional Internet Registries (RIRs) exhausted their allocation of address blocks not reserved for IPv6 transition between April 2011 and September 2015. Although individual ISPs continue to recycle IP addresses no longer used by subscribers, the bottom of the bucket has been reached. Moving to IPv6 is becoming imperative. IPv4 also had a number of other faults that needed to be resolved. Let's see what the road to that future looks like.

# IPv4 vs. IPv6: Key Differences and Options

Over the years we've used it, we've noticed that the design of IPv4 has a number of short-comings to it. It did not have security built into it; its address space was limited, and even with workarounds like NAT, we still don't have enough addresses to handle the explosive demand for IoT devices. (Another whole class of Internet users are the *robots*, smart software agents, with or without their hardware that let them interact with the physical world. Robots are using the Internet to learn from each other's experiences in accomplishing different tasks.)

IPv6 brings a number of much-needed improvements to our network infrastructures:

- Dramatic increase in the size of the IP address field, allowing over 18 quintillion (a billion billions) nodes on each of 18 quintillion networks. Using 64-bit address fields each for network and node addresses provides for a billion networks of a billion nodes or hosts on each network.

- More efficient routing, since ISPs and backbone service providers can use hierarchical arrangements of routing tables, while reducing if not eliminating fragmentation by better use of information about maximum transmission unit size.

- More efficient packet processing by eliminating the IP-level checksum (which proved to be redundant given most Transport layer protocols).

- Directed data flows, which is more of a multicast rather than a broadcast flow. This can make broad distribution of streaming multimedia (sports events, movies, etc.) much more efficient.

- Simplified network configuration, using new autoconfigure capabilities.

- Simplified end-to-end connectivity at the IP layer by eliminating NAT. This can make services such as VOIP and quality of service more capable.

- Security is greatly enhanced, which may allow for greater use of ICMP (since most firewalls block IPv4 ICMP traffic as a security precaution). IPSec as defined in IPv4 becomes a mandatory part of IPv6 as a result.

This giant leap of changes from IPv4 to IPv6 stands to make IPv6 the clear winner, over time, and is comparable to the leap from analog video on VHS to digital video. To send a VHS tape over the Internet, you must first convert its analog audio, video, chroma, and synchronization information into bits, and package (encode) those bits into a file using any of a wide range of digital video encoders such as MP4. The resulting MP4 file can then transit the Internet.

IPv6 was published in draft in 1996 and became an official Internet standard in 2017. The problem is that IPv6 is not backward compatible with IPv4; you cannot just flow IPv4 packets onto a purely IPv6 network and expect anything useful to happen. Everything about IPv6 *packages* the user data differently and flows it differently, requiring different implementations of the basic layers of the TCP/IP protocol stack. Figure 5.9 shows how these differences affect both the size and structure of the IP Network layer header.

**FIGURE 5.9** Changes to the packet header from IPv4 to IPv6

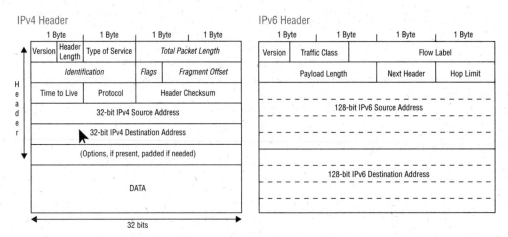

For organizations setting up brand-new network infrastructures, there's a lot to be gained by going directly to an IPv6 implementation. Such systems may still have to deal with legacy devices that operate only in IPv4, such as "bring your own devices" users. Organizations trying to transition their existing IPv4 networks to IPv6 may find it worth the effort to use a variety of "dual-rail" approaches to effectively run both IPv4 and IPv6 at the same time on the same systems:

- Dual stack, in which your network hardware and management systems run both protocols simultaneously, over the same Physical layer.

- Tunnel, by encapsulating one protocol's packets within the other's structure. Usually, this is done by encapsulating IPv6 packets inside IPv4 packets.

- NAT-PT, or network address translation–protocol translation, but this seems best done with Application layer gateways.

- Dual-stack Application layer gateways, supported by almost all major operating systems and equipment vendors, provide a somewhat smoother transition from IPv4 to IPv6.

- MAC address increases from EUI-48 to EUI-64 (48 to 64 bit).

With each passing month, SSCPs will need to know more about IPv6 and the changes it is heralding for personal and organizational Internet use. This is our future!

# CIANA Layer by Layer

We've come a long way thus far in showing you how Internet protocols work, which should give you both the concepts and some of the details you'll need to rise to the real challenge of this chapter. As an SSCP, after all, you are not here to learn how to design, build, and administer networks—you're here to learn how to *keep networks safe, secure, and reliable*!

As we look at vulnerabilities and possible exploits at each layer, keep in mind the concept of the *attack surface*. This is the layer of functionality and features, usually in software, that an attacker has to interact with, defeating or disrupting its normal operation as part of a reconnaissance or penetration attempt. This is why so many attacks that involve lower layers of the OSI or TCP/IP stacks actually start with attacks on applications, because apps can often provide the entry path the attacker needs to exploit.

For all layers, it is imperative that your organization have a well-documented and well-controlled information technology baseline, so that it knows what boxes, software, systems, connections, and services it has or uses, down to the specifics about make, model, and version! This is your starting point to find the *Common Vulnerabilities and Exposures* (CVE) data about all of those systems elements.

It's time now to put our white hats firmly back on, grab our vulnerability modeling and assessment notes from Chapter 4, and see how the OSI 7-layer reference model can also be our roadmap from the physical realities of our networks up through the Application Layer—and beyond!

## CIANA at Layer 1: Physical

In all technologies we have in use today, data transmission at its root has to use a physical medium that carries the datagrams from Point A to Point B. Despite what Marshall McLuhan said, when it comes to data transmission, *the medium is not the message.* (McLuhan was probably speaking about messages at Layer 7…) And if you can do something in the physical world, something else can interfere with it, block it, disrupt or distort it.

Or…somebody else can snoop your message traffic, at the physical level, as part of their target reconnaissance, characterization, and profiling efforts.

### Vulnerabilities

In Chapter 8, you'll work with a broader class of physical systems, their vulnerabilities, and some high-payoff countermeasures. That said, let's take a closer look at the Physical layer from the perspective of reliable and secure data transmission and receipt. We need to consider two kinds of physical transmission: *conduction* and *radiation*.

- Electrical wires, fiber optics, even water pipes provide physical channels through which electrons, photons, or pulses of water (or air) can travel. Modems turn those flows into streams of datagrams (1s or 0s, and in some cases synchronization patterns or *S-tones*).

- Radiated signals in most data communications are either radio waves (such as Wi-Fi or microwave) or light (using lasers, flashlights, etc.). Radiated signals travel through air, the vacuum of space, and solid objects.

Conducted and radiated signals are easy prey to a few other problems:

- Spoofing happens when another transmitter acts in ways to get a receiver to mistake it as the anticipated sender. This can happen accidentally, such as when the RFI (radio frequency interference) from a lightning strike is misinterpreted by an electronic device as some kind of command or data input. More often, spoofing is deliberate.

- Large electrical motors, and electric power systems, can generate electromagnetic interference (EMI); this tends to be very low frequency but can still disrupt some Layer 1 activities.

- Interception happens when a third party is able to covertly receive and decode the signals being sent, without interrupting the flow from sender to receiver.

- Jamming occurs when a stronger signal (generated deliberately, accidentally, or naturally) drowns out the signal from the transmitter.

Finally, consider the physical vulnerabilities of the Layer 1 equipment itself—the NIC, the computer it's in, the router and modem, the cabling, and fiber optic elements that make Layer 1 possible. Even the free space that Wi-Fi or LiFi (LEDs used as part of medium data rate communications systems) are part of the system! The walls of a building or vehicle can obstruct or obscure radiated signals, and every electrical system in the area can generate interference. Even other electrical power customers in the same local grid service area can cause electrical power quality problems that can cause modems, routers, switches, or even laptops and desktops to suffer a variety of momentary interruptions.

All of these kinds of service disruptions at Layer 1 can for the most part be either intermittent, even bursty in nature, or they can last for minutes, hours, or even days.

## The Exploiter's Tool Kit

For hostile (deliberate) threat actors, the common attack tools at Layer 1 start with physical access to your systems:

- Cable taps (passive or with active repeaters)
- Cables plugged into unused jacks on your switches, routers, or modems
- Tampering with your local electrical power supply system

Wi-Fi reconnaissance can be easily conducted from a smartphone app, and this can reveal exploitable weaknesses in your systems at Layer 1 and above. This can aid an attacker in tuning their own Wi-Fi attack equipment to the right channel and pointing it in the right spots in your Wi-Fi coverage patterns, to find potential attack vectors.

### A SOHO Apartment Office: Layer 1 Concerns?

Sean lives in a seventh-floor apartment in a reasonably modern building in a major city. He uses a 100 MB/second fiber connection from his local ISP to drive a SOHO network of two routers providing several Wi-Fi and Cat 5 or Cat 6 hardwired LAN connections, which support a variety of laptops and smartphones. He's noticed that most weekdays, from about 11 a.m. to maybe 2 or 3 p.m. local, certain applications like Skype for Business just cannot stay online; on really bad days, even simple Web surfing cannot connect to reliable sites. Inspection of various diagnostic information, such as router and modem logs, and systems and application logs, doesn't reveal anything obvious.

The wireless routers do occasionally notice a lot of unknown device connection attempts, which are all blocked by the routers (could this be workers or residents in neighboring buildings, or in the park across the street, seeking a free Wi-Fi connection at lunch or afternoon tea-time?); this doesn't seem to be the culprit. The elevator hoist motors are four floors above—four steel and concrete floors, that is—so EMI from the motors themselves doesn't seem to be the issue.

This has been going on for several years now. So far, the only reasonably fool-proof remedy has been a cold reboot (power off, then power on) of the fiber modem/router, then the other router.

Sean asks for your advice. What else might he look at, to try to identify why this keeps happening, and what might he do to reduce the risk of further ongoing disruption?

## Countermeasure Options

Without getting far too technical (for an SSCP or for the exam), the basics of the medium should provide *some* degree of protection against some source of interference, disruption, or interception. Signal cables can be contained in rigid pipes, and these are buried in the ground or embedded in concrete walls. This reduces the effect of RFI while also reducing the chance of the cable being cut or tapped into. Radio communications systems can be designed to use frequency bands, encoding techniques, and other measures that reduce accidental or deliberate interference or disruption. Placing Layer 1 (and other) communications systems elements within physically secured, environmentally stabilized physical spaces should always be part of your risk mitigation thinking.

This also is part of placing your physical infrastructure under effective configuration management and change control.

Power conditioning equipment can also alleviate many hard-to-identify problems. Not every electronic device behaves well when its AC power comes with bursts of noise, or with voltage drops or spikes that aren't severe enough to cause a shutdown (or a blown surge suppressor). Some consumer or SOHO routers, and some cable or fiber modems provided by ISPs to end users, can suffer from such problems. Overheating can also cause such equipment to perform erratically.

Note that most IPS and IDS products and approaches don't have any real way to reach down into Layer 1 to detect an intrusion. What you're left with is the old-fashioned approach of inspection and audit of the physical systems against a controlled, well-documented baseline.

## Residual Risk

In general terms, the untreated Layer 1 risks end up being passed on to Layer 2 and above in the protocol stacks, either as interruptions of service, datagram errors, faulty address and control information, or increased retry rates leading to decreased throughput. Monitoring and analysis of monitoring data may help you identify an incipient problem, especially if you're getting a lot of red flags from higher layers in the protocol stack.

Perhaps the worst residual risk at Layer 1 is that you won't detect trespass at this level. Internet-empowered systems can lull us into complacency; they can let us stop caring about where a particular Cat 5 or Cat 6 cable actually goes, because we're too worried about authorized users doing the wrong thing or unauthorized users hacking into our systems or our apps. True, the vast majority of attacks happen remotely and involve no physical access to your Layer 1 systems or activities.

How would you make sure that you're not the exception to that rule?

# CIANA at Layer 2: Data Link

Attackers at this level have somehow found their way past your logical safeguards on the Physical layer. Perhaps they've recognized the manufacturer's default broadcast SSID of your wireless router, used that to find common vulnerabilities and exploits information, and are now attacking it with one or more of those exploits to see if they can spoof their way into your internet. Note how some of the attack surfaces involve layer-spanning protocols like ARP or DHCP, so we'll address them here first.

## Vulnerabilities and Assessment

A number of known vulnerabilities in Layer 2 systems elements can lead to a variety of attack patterns, such as:

- MAC address–related attacks, MAC spoofing (command line accessible), CAM (content addressable memory) table overflow
- DHCP lease-based denial of service attack (also called IP pool starvation attack)
- ARP attacks, attacker sending IP/MAC pairs to falsify IP address for known MAC, or vice versa
- VLAN attacks: VLAN hopping via falsified (spoofed) VLAN IDs in packets

- Denial of service by looping packets, as a spanning tree protocol (STP) attack
- Reconnaissance attacks against Data Link layer discovery protocols
- SSID spoofing as part of man-in-the-middle attacks

These may lead to denial or disruption of service or degraded service (if your network systems have to spend a lot of time and resources detecting such attacks and preventing them). They may also provide an avenue for the attacker to further penetrate your systems and achieve a Layer 3 access. Attacks at this layer can also enable an attacker to reach out through your network's nodes and attack other systems.

## Countermeasure Options

A variety of steps can be taken to help disrupt the kill chain, either by disrupting the attacker's reconnaissance efforts or the intrusion attempts themselves:

- Secure your network against external sniffers via encryption.
- Use SSH instead of unsecure remote login, remote shell, etc.
- Ensure maximum use of SSL/TLS.
- Use secured versions of email protocols, such as S/MIME or PGP.
- Use network switching techniques, such as dynamic ARP inspection or rate limiting of ARP packets.
- Control when networks are operating in promiscuous mode.
- Use whitelisting of known, trusted MAC addresses.
- Use blacklisting of suspected hostile MAC addresses.
- Use honeynets to spot potential DNS snooping.
- Do latency checks, which may reveal that a potential or suspect attacker is in fact monitoring your network.
- Monitor what processes and users are actually using network monitoring tools, such as Netmon, on your systems; when in doubt, one of those might be serving an intruder!

---

### Where Has Your Print Queue Gone Today?

If tasks in your systems take longer than seems reasonable, it's probably a sign that something needs investigating. In one case, a user who was tired of complaining about long delays in getting files printed on a network printer right outside of his office was able to determine that the print queue had been rerouted to an IP address in Russia; the files were then sent back to the print server for printing, as a way of masking the data exfiltration.

## Residual Risk

Probably the most worrisome residual risk of an unresolved Layer 2 vulnerability is that an intruder has now found a way to gain Layer 3 access or beyond on your network.

# CIANA at Layer 3: Network

One of the things to keep in mind about IP is that it is a *connectionless* and therefore stateless protocol. By itself, it does not provide any kind of authentication. Spoofing IP packets, launching denial of service attacks, or other attacks have quite literally become the child's play of script kiddies worldwide. ICMP, the other major protocol at this layer, is also pretty easy to use to gather reconnaissance information or to launch attacks with.

Attacks at any layer of the protocol stacks can be either hit-and-run or very persistent. The hit-and-run attacker may need to inject only a few bad packets to achieve their desired results. This can make them very hard to detect. The persistent threat requires more continuous action be taken to accomplish the attack.

## Vulnerabilities and Assessment

Typical attacks seen at this level, which exploit known common vulnerabilities or just the nature of IP networks, can include:

- IP spoofing.
- Routing (RIP) attacks.
- ICMP attacks, including Smurf attacks, which use ICMP packets in a DDoS attack against the victim's spoofed IP address.
- Ping flood.
- Ping of Death attack (ICMP datagram exceeding maximum size: if the system is vulnerable to this, it will crash); most modern OSs are no longer vulnerable.
- Teardrop attack (false offset information into fragmented packets: causes empty or overlapping spots during reassembly, leading to receive system/app instability).
- Packet sniffing reconnaissance.

## Countermeasure Options

First on your list of countermeasure strategies should be to implement IPSec if you've not already done so for your IPv4 networks. Whether you deploy IPSec in tunnel mode or transport mode (or both) should be driven by your organization's impact assessment and CIANA needs. Other options to consider include these:

- Securing ICMP
- Securing routers and routing protocols with packet filtering (and the ACLs this requires)
- Provide ACL protection against address spoofing

## Residual Risk

For the most part, strong protection via router ACLs and firewall rules, combined with a solid IPSec implementation, should leave you pretty secure at this layer. You'll need to do a fair bit of ongoing traffic analysis yourself, combined with monitoring and analysis of the event logs from this layer of your defense, to make sure.

The other thing to keep in mind is that attacks at *higher* levels of the protocol stack could wend their way down to surreptitious manipulation, misuse, or outright disruption of your Layer 3 systems.

# CIANA at Layer 4: Transport

Layer 4 is where packet sniffers, protocol analyzers, and network mapping tools pay big dividends for the black hats. For the white hats, the same tools—and the skill and cunning needed to understand and exploit what those tools can reveal—are essential in vulnerability assessment, systems characterization and fingerprinting, active defense, and incident detection and response. Although it's beyond the scope of the SSCP exam or this book to make you a protocol wizard, it's *not* beyond the scope of the SSCP's ongoing duties to take on, understand, and master what happens at the Transport layer.

Let's take a closer look.

## Vulnerabilities and Assessment

How much of this applies to your site or organization?

- SYN flood (can defend with SYN cookies)
- Injection attacks (guessing/forcing reset of sequence numbers to jump your packet in ahead of a legitimate one); also called TCP hijacking
- Opt-Ack attack (attacker convinces target to send quickly, in essence a self-inflicted DoS)
- TLS attacks (tend to be attacks on compression, cryptographics, etc.)
- Bypass of proper certificate use for mobile apps
- TCP port scans, host sweeps, or other network mapping as part of reconnaissance
- OS and application fingerprinting, as part of reconnaissance

## Countermeasure Options

Most of your countermeasure options at Layer 4 involve better identity management and access control, along with improved traffic inspection and filtering. Start by considering the following:

- TCP intercept and filtering (routers, firewalls)
- DoS prevention services (such as Cloudflare, Prolexic, and many others)
- Blacklisting of attackers' IP addresses

- Whitelisting of known, trusted IP addresses
- Better use of SSL/TLS and SSH
- Fingerprint scrubbing techniques

## Residual Risk

One vulnerability that may remain, after taking all of the countermeasures that you can, is that your traffic itself is still open to being monitored and subjected to traffic analysis. *Traffic analysis* looks for patterns in sender and recipient address information, protocols or packet types, volumes and timing, and just plain coincidences. Even if your data payloads are well encrypted, someone willing to put the time and effort into capturing and analyzing your traffic may find something worthwhile.

# CIANA at Layer 5: Session

More and more, we are seeing attacks that try to take advantage of session-level complexities. As defensive awareness and response has grown, so has the complexity of session hijacking and related Session layer attacks. Many of the steps involved in a session hijack can generate other issues, such as ACK storms, in which both the spoofed and attacking host are sending ACKs with correct sequence numbers and other information in the packet headers; this might require an attacker to take further steps to silence this storm so that it's not detectable as a symptom of a possible intrusion.

## Vulnerabilities and Assessment

How much of this applies to your site or organization?

- Session hijacking.
- Man-in-the-middle (MITM).
- ARP poisoning.
- DNS poisoning.
- Local system hosts file corruption or poisoning.
- Blind hijacking (attacker injects commands into the communications stream but cannot see results, such as error messages or system response directly).
- Man-in-the-browser attacks, which are similar to MITM but via a Trojan horse that manipulates calls to/from stack and browser. Browser helper objects, extensions, API hooking, and Ajax worms can inadvertently facilitate these types of attacks.
- Session sniffing to gain a legitimate session ID and then spoof it.
- SSH downgrade attack.

## Countermeasure Options

As with the Transport layer, most of the countermeasures available to you at the Session layer require some substantial sleuthing around in your system. Problems with inconsistent applications or systems behavior, such as not being able to consistently connect to websites or hosts you frequently use, might be caused by errors in your local hosts file (containing your ARP and DNS cache). Finding and fixing those errors is one thing; investigating whether they were the result of user error, applications or systems errors, or deliberate enemy action is quite another set of investigative tasks to take on!

Also, remember that your threat modeling should have divided the world into those networks you can trust, and those that you cannot. Many of your DoS prevention strategies therefore need to focus on that outside, hostile world—or, rather, on its (hopefully) limited connection points with your trusted networks.

Countermeasures to consider include the following:

- Replace weak password authentication protocols such as PAP, CHAP, and NT LAN Manager (NTLM), which are often enabled as a default to support backward compatibility, with much stronger authentication protocols.

- Migrate to strong systems for identity management and access control.

- Use PKI as part of your identity management, access control, and authentication systems.

- Verify correct settings of DNS servers on your network and disable known attack methods, such as allowing recursive DNS queries from external hosts.

- Use tools such as SNORT at the Session layer as part of an active monitoring and alarm system.

- Implementation and use of more robust IDSs or IPSs.

### Residual Risk

As you lock down your Session layer defenses, you may find situations where some sessions and the systems that support them need a further layer of defense (or just a greater level of assurance that you've done all that can be done). This may dictate setting up proxies as an additional boundary layer between your internal systems and potential attackers.

## CIANA at Layer 6: Presentation

Perhaps the most well-known Presentation layer attacks have been those that exploit vulnerabilities in NetBIOS and SMB; given the near dominance of the marketplace by Microsoft-based systems, this should not be a surprise.

More importantly, the cross-layer protocols, and many older apps and protocols such as SNMP, FTP, and such, all work through or with Layer 6 functionality.

### Vulnerabilities and Assessment

Vulnerabilities at this layer can be grouped broadly into two big categories: attacks on encryption or authentication, and attacks on the apps and control logic that support Presentation layer activities. These include:

- Attacks on encryption used, or on weak protection schemes
- Attacks on Kerberos or other access control at this layer
- Attacks on known NetBIOS and SMB vulnerabilities

### Countermeasure Options

Building on the countermeasures you've taken at Layer 5, you'll need to look at the specifics of how you're using protocols and apps at this layer. Consider replacing insecure apps, such as FTP or email, with more secure versions.

### Residual Risk

Much of what you can't address at Layer 6 or below will flow naturally up to Layer 7, so let's just press on!

# CIANA at Layer 7: Application

It's just incredible when we consider how many application programs are in use today! Unfortunately, the number of application-based or Application layer attacks grows every day as well. Chapter 9 addresses many of the ways you'll need to help your organization secure its applications and the data they use from attack, but let's take a moment to consider two specific cases a bit further:

- Voice, POTS, and VOIP: Plain old telephone service and voice-over IP all share a common security issue: how do you provide the "full CIANA" of protection to what people *say* to each other, regardless of the channel or the technology they use?

- Collaboration systems: LinkedIn, Facebook Workspace, Microsoft Teams, and even VOIP systems like Skype provide many ways in which people can organize workflows, collaborate on developing information (such as books or software), and have conversations with each other. Each of these was designed with the goal of empowering users to build and evolve their own patterns of collaboration with each other.

These are just two such combinations of ubiquitous technologies and the almost uncontrollable need that people have to *talk* with each other, whether in the course of accomplishing the organization's mission and goals or not. When we add in any possible use of a Web browser… Pandora's box is well and truly open for business, you might say.

### Vulnerabilities and Assessment

Many of these attacks are often part of a protracted series of intrusions taken by more sophisticated attackers. Such *advanced persistent threats* may spend months, even a year or more, in their efforts to crack open and exploit the systems of a target business or organization in ways that will meet the attacker's needs. As a result, *constant vigilance* may be your best strategy. Keep your eyes and IPS/IDS alert and on the lookout for the following:

- SQL or other injection
- Cross-site scripting (XSS)
- Remote code execution (RCE)
- Format string vulnerabilities
- Username enumeration
- HTTP floods

- HTTP server resource pool exhaustion (Slowloris, for example)
- Low-and-slow attacks
- Get/post floods
- DoS/DDoS attacks on known server vulnerabilities
- NTP amplification
- App-layer DoS/DDoS
- Device, app, or user hijacking

## Countermeasure Options

It's difficult to avoid falling into a self-imposed logic trap and see applications security separate and distinct from network security. These two parts of your organization's information security team have to work closely together to be able to spot, and possibly control, vulnerabilities and attacks. It will take a concerted effort to do the following:

- Monitor website visitor behavior.
- Block known bad bots.
- Challenge suspicious/unrecognized entities with a cross-platform JavaScript tester such as jstest (at `http://jstest.jcoglan.com`); for cookies, use privacy-verifying cookie test Web tools, such as `https://www.cookiebot.com/en/gdpr-cookies`. Add challenges such as CAPTCHAs to determine if the entity is a human or a robot trying to be one.
- Use two-factor/multifactor authentication.
- Use Application layer IDS and IPS.
- Provide more effective user training and education focused on attentiveness to unusual systems or applications behavior.
- Establish strong data quality programs and procedures (see Chapter 9).

## Residual Risk

Most of what you've dealt with in Layers 1 through 7 depends on having trustworthy users, administrators, and software and systems suppliers and maintainers. Trusting, helpful people, willing to go the extra mile to solve a problem, are perhaps *more* important to a modern organization than their network infrastructure and IT systems are. But these same people are prone to manipulation by attackers. You'll see how to address this in greater depth when we get to Chapter 11.

# Securing Networks as Systems

Looking at the layers of a network infrastructure—by means of TCP/IP's four layers, or the OSI 7-layer reference model's seven layers—provides many opportunities to recognize vulnerabilities, select and deploy countermeasures, and monitor their ongoing operation.

It's just as important to take seven giant steps back and remember that to the rest of the organization, that infrastructure is a system in and of itself. So how does the SSCP refocus on networks as systems, and plan for and achieve the degree of security for them that the organization needs?

Let's think back to Chapters 3 and 4, and their use of risk management frameworks. One key message those chapters conveyed, and that frameworks like NIST's embody, is the need to take a cohesive, integrated, end-to-end and top-to-bottom approach. That integrated approach needs to apply across the systems, equipment, places, faces, and time-frames that your organization needs to accomplish its mission.

*Timeframes* are perhaps most critical to consider as we look at systems security. Other chapters have looked at the planning, preparation, and deployment phases; Chapter 10, "Incident Response and Recovery," will look at incident response, which in effect is dealing with things *after* an event of interest has mushroomed into something worse.

What about the *now*?

# A SOC Is Not a NOC

Your organization or business may already have a *network operations center (NOC)*; this could be either a physically separate facility or a work area within the IT support team's workspaces. NOCs perform valuable roles in maintaining the day-to-day operation of the network infrastructure; in conjunction with the IT support help desk, they investigate problems that users report, and respond to service requests to install new systems, configure network access for new users, or ensure updates to servers and server-based applications get done correctly. You might say that the NOC focuses on getting the network to work, keeping it working, and modifying and maintaining it to meet changing organizational needs.

The *security operations center (SOC)* has an entirely different focus. The SOC focuses on deterring, preventing, detecting, and responding to network security events. The SOC provides real-time command and control of all network-related monitoring activities, and it can use its device and systems management tools to further drill down into device, sub-system, server, or other data as part of its efforts to recognize, characterize, and contain an incident. It integrates all network-security related activities and information so as to make informed, timely, and effective decisions to ensure ongoing systems' reliability, availability, and security. The SOC keeps organizational management and leadership apprised of developing and ongoing information security incidents and can notify local law enforcement or other emergency responders as required. Let's look more closely at this important set of tasks we're chartering our SOC to perform:

- Real-time command and control: The SOC has to be able to "reach out and touch" any element of the organization's network infrastructure, be that element part of the people, hardware, or software parts of the infrastructure. Within the span of assigned information security duties, the SOC has to be able to tell people, hardware, and software to take specific actions, or to *stop* taking certain actions; to report additional information; or to execute preplanned contingency actions.

- Management tools: Systems such as people-facing communications tools like phones, pagers, and email, through ICPM and on up to integrated security event information management systems (SEIMs), are the heavy lifters of the SOC. They provide the SOC with the means to gather information, request additional information, ask for a set of diagnostic steps to be performed, or invoke analysis tools to review data already on hand at the SOC. Management tools should provide a real-time status—a state and health display of each element of the network infrastructure.

- Recognize, characterize, and contain: These are the most urgent and time-critical tasks that a SOC must perform. (Once contained, disaster recovery or business continuity efforts will probably take command of the incident and direct company assets and people in the recovery tasks.)

- Integrated: The SOC has to bring everything together so that the SOC team and their systems have the best and complete total awareness of the organization's information infrastructure.

- Keep management informed: Organizational policy and procedure should clearly spell out what decisions the SOC team can make in real time and which need to have senior leadership or management participate in or direct the decision. Leadership and management must also be kept informed, since they may have to engage with other organizational units, external stakeholders, or legal authorities in order to fulfill due diligence and reporting responsibilities.

- Notify and request support from local emergency responders: The SOC's first priority of course is safety of life, and in some cases, an information security event may have the potential of involving risk to lives and property on site or nearby.

It's important to note that a separate, dedicated, fully staffed, and fully equipped SOC can be difficult, expensive, and time-consuming to set up and get operating; it will continue to be a nontrivial cost to the organization. The organization should build a very strong business case to set up such a separate SOC (or ISOC, information security operations center, to distinguish it from a physical or overall security operations center). Such a business case may be called for to protect highly sensitive data, or if law, government regulation, or industry rules dictate it. If that is the case, one hopes that the business impact analysis (BIA) provides supporting analysis and recommendations!

Smaller organizations quite often combine the functions of NOC and SOC into the same (smaller) set of people, workspaces, systems, and tools. There is nothing wrong with such an approach—but again, the business case, supported by the BIA, needs to make the case to support this decision.

## Tools for the SOC and the NOC

It doesn't take a hard-nosed budget analyst to realize that many of the tools the NOC needs to configure, manage, and maintain the network can also address the SOC's needs to recognize, characterize, and contain a possible intrusion. These tools span the range of physical, logical, and administrative controls. For example:

- Administrative network management starts with understanding the organization's needs, translating that into design, and then managing the build-out of the network itself. Network design tools, including network simulation and modeling suites, can help designers focus on data, control, or management issues separately; view specific network usage scenarios; or evaluate proposed changes, all without having to disturb the current operational network infrastructure.

- Physical controls can include the placement of security devices, such as firewalls, proxies or gateways, or the segmentation of the network into more manageable subnetworks that are easier to defend. Physical design of the network can also be a powerful ingredient in isolating and containing the damage from an intruder, an accident, or an act of nature. Don't forget to ensure that these physical devices are also physically protected from the range of threats indicated by your vulnerability analysis.

- Logical network management translates the administrative and physical design characteristics into the actual software and data configuration that brings the network to life.

Combinations of these three control (and management) strategies can also support both the SOC and the NOC:

- Traffic management and load management systems, which can be hardware, software, or both, provide valuable insight about normal and abnormal network usage. This can help in determining whether congestion is caused by design flaws, legitimate changes in operational patterns of usage, component or subsystem failures, or hostile action.

- Network-based security devices, such as NIDSs and NIPSs, as well as network management systems and tools, help enforce network management policy decisions or generate warnings or alarms for out-of-limits or suspicious activity, and they can participate in incident characterization, containment, and recovery.

## Integrating Network and Security Management

Chapter 3, "Integrated Information Risk Management," stressed the need for integrated command and control of your company's information systems security efforts; we see this in the definition of the SOC as well. So what is the secret sauce, the key ingredient that brings all of these very different concerns, issues, talents, capabilities, functions, hardware, software, data, and physical systems together and *integrates* them?

System vendors quickly offer us products that claim to provide "integrated" solutions. Some of these systems, especially in the security information and event management (SIEM) marketplace, go a long way in bringing together the many elements of a geographically dispersed, complex network infrastructure. In many cases, such SIEM products as platforms require significant effort to tailor to your organization's existing networks and your security policies. As your team gains experience using them, you'll see a vicious circle of learning take place; you learn more about security issues and problems, but this takes even more effort to get your systems configured to respond to what you've just learned, which causes more residual issues, which...

You'll also have the chance for a *virtuous* circle of learning, in which experience teaches you stronger, more efficient approaches to meet your constantly evolving CIANA needs. SIEM as an approach, management philosophy, and as a set of software and data tools can help in this regard.

The key ingredient remains the *people plane*, the set of information security and network technology people that your organization has hired, trained, and invested in to make NOC-like and SOC-like functions serve and protect the needs of the organization.

 **Real World Scenario**

### Integrating Information Security at an Online University

I spoke recently with Sean, who is an information security operations team lead for a major university's online campus, supporting tens of thousands of students around the world. In their SOC, they use a variety of tools, dashboard displays, and monitoring systems to keep an eye on the status, state, and health of the university's systems and users. These may range from a "threat candy" display (with animated arrows flying around the map, showing current intrusion attempts from known or suspect hostile IPs or regions), to pie and bar charts, to long, scrolling lists of event logs, status information, and other key indicators.

Some of those displays alert the SOC watch team to a possible situation worthy of investigation, something that might become an event of interest in information security terms. More often than not, it is the near-nonstop human monitoring—the eyeballs on multiple, detailed logs and activity indicators—that tips off the experienced SOC watch team member.

I asked him what integrates this. "People," he said.

They have a team of five people focused on SOC monitoring and alerting activities. They work extensively throughout the business day with software and systems maintainers, developers, and support staff. They work with the systems and network engineers and maintainers, as well as teams that keep major business platforms and student-facing platforms and systems up and running. Nearly all of those are cloud-hosted applications, platforms, and services, so at times, the SOC watch team has to interface directly with the cloud hosting or platform technical and security support teams as well.

Team members primarily work daytime with an on-call watch officer assigned; their department chief has key SOC dashboards and alert panels running continuously on a PC or laptop when he's at home, and he and the team have alarm apps on their smartphones as well. They pride themselves on their responsiveness.

As with many functions, there's probably a right-sizing balance to be made when standing up a SOC team. How would you do this? What questions would you ask, of your organization and of a SIEM, network monitoring system (NMS), or other network security systems vendor, to help you find the right balance?

# Summary

Since the Internet has become the de facto standard for e-commerce, e-business, and e-government, it should be no surprise that as SSCPs, we need to understand and appreciate what makes the Internet work and what keeps it working reliably and securely. By using the OSI 7-layer reference model as our roadmap, we've reaffirmed our understanding of the protocol stacks that are theory and the practice of the Internet. We've ground lots of those details under our fingernails as we've dug into how those protocols work to move data, control that data flow, and manage the networks, all at the same time. This foundation paves our way to Chapter 6, where we'll dive deep into identity management and access control.

We've seen how three basic conceptual models—the TCP/IP protocol stack, the OSI 7-layer reference model, and the idea of the data, control, and management plane—are powerful tools for thinking about networks *and* physical, real design features that make most of the products and systems we build our networks with actually *work*. In doing so, we've also had a round-up review of many of the classical and current threat vectors or attacks that intruders often use against every layer of our network-based business or organization and its mission.

We have not delved deep into specific protocols, nor into the details of how those protocols can be hacked and corrupted as part of an attack. But we've laid the foundations you can use to continue to learn those next layers down as you take on more of the role of a network defender. But that, as we say, is a course beyond the scope of this book or the SSCP exam itself, so we'll have to leave it for another day.

# Exam Essentials

**Explain the relationship between the TCP/IP protocol and the OSI 7-layer reference model.** Both the TCP/IP protocol, established by the Internet Engineering Task Force, and the OSI reference model, developed by the International Organization for Standardization (ISO), lay out the fundamental concepts for networking and the details of how it all comes together. Both use a layers-of-abstractions approach, and to a large degree, their first four layers (Physical, Data Link, Network, and Transport) are nearly identical. TCP/IP stops there; the OSI reference model goes on to define the Session, Presentation, and Application layers. Each layer establishes a set of services, delivered by other protocols, which perform functions that *logically* relate to that layer—however, a number of important functions must be cross-layer in design to actually make important functions work effectively. TCP/IP is often thought of as the designer's and builder's choice for hardware and network systems, as a bottom-up set of standards (from Physical on up to Transport). The OSI reference model provides a more cohesive framework for analyzing and designing the total information flow that gets user-needed purposes implemented and carried out. SSCPs need to be fluent in both.

**Explain why IPv6 is not directly compatible with IPv4.**   Users of IPv4 encountered a growing number of problems as the Internet saw a many-fold increase in number of attached devices, users, and uses. First was IPv4's limited address space, which needed the somewhat cumbersome use of Network Address Translation (NAT) as a workaround. The lack of built-in security capabilities was making far too many systems far too vulnerable to attack. IPv4 also lacked built-in quality of service features. IPv6 resolves these and a number of other issues, but it essentially is a completely different network. Its packet structures are just not compatible with each other—you need to provide a gateway-like function to translate IPv4 packet streams into IPv6 ones, and vice versa. Using both systems requires one of several alternative approaches: tunneling, "dual-stack" simultaneous use, address and packet translation, or Application layer gateways. As of 2018, many large systems operators run both in parallel, employ tunneling approaches (to package one protocol inside the other, packet by packet), or look to Application layer gateways as part of their transition strategy.

**Compare and contrast the basic network topologies.**   A network topology is the shape or pattern of the way nodes on the network are connected with each other. The basic topologies are point-to-point, bus, ring, star, and mesh; larger networks, including the world-spanning Internet, are simply repeated combinations of these smaller elements. A bus connects a series of devices or nodes in a line and lets each node choose whether or not it will read or write traffic to the bus. A ring connects a set of nodes in a loop, with each node receiving a packet and either passing it on to the other side of the ring or keeping it if it's addressed to the node. Meshes provide multiple bidirectional connections between most or all nodes in the network. Each topology's characteristics offer advantages and risks to the network users of that topology, such as whether a node or link failure causes the entire network to be inoperable, or whether one node must take on management functions for the others in its topology. Mesh systems, for example, can support load leveling and alternate routing of traffic across the mesh; star networks do load leveling, but not alternate routing. Rings and point-to-point cannot operate if all nodes and connections aren't functioning properly; bus systems can tolerate the failure of one or more nodes but not of the backplane or system of interconnections. Note that the beauty of TCP/IP and the OSI 7-layer reference model as layers of abstraction enable us to use these topologies at any layer, or even across multiple layers, as we design systems or investigate issues with their operation and performance.

**Explain the different network roles of peer, client, and server.**   Each node on a network interacts with other nodes on the network, and in doing so they provide services to each other. All such interactions are governed by or facilitated by the use of handshake protocols. If two interconnected nodes have essentially equal roles in those handshakes—one node does not control the other or have more control over the conversation—then each node is a *peer*, or equal, of the other. Simple peer-to-peer service provision models are used for file, printer, or other device sharing, and they are quite common. When the service being provided requires more control and management, or the enforcement of greater security measures (such as identity authentication or access control), then the relationship is more appropriately a client-server relationship. Here, the requesting client node has to make a request to the server node (the one providing the requested services); the server has to recognize the request, permit it to proceed, perform the service, and then manage the termination of the service request. Note that even in simple file or print sharing, the *sharing* may be peer-to-peer, but the actual use of the shared resource almost always involves a *service* running on the node that possesses that file or printer, which carries out the sharing of the file or the printing of the requesting node's data.

**Explain how IPv4 addressing and subnetting works.**   An IPv4 address is a 32-bit number, which is defined as four 8-bit portions, or *octets*. These addresses in human-readable form look like 192.168.2.11, with the four octets expressed as their base 10 values (or as two hexadecimal digits), separated by dots. In the packet headers, each IP address (for sender and recipient) occupies one 32-bit field. The address is defined to consist of two parts: the network address and the address of a node on that network. Large organizations (such as Google) might need tens of thousands of node addresses on their network; small organizations might only need a few. This has given rise to address classes: Class A uses the first octet for organization and the other three for node. Class B uses two octets each for organization and node. Class C uses three octets for organization and the fourth for node on the Internet; Class D and E are reserved for special purposes. Subnetting allows an organization's network designers to break a network into segments by logically grouping addresses: the first four devices in one group, the next four in another, and so on. This effectively breaks the node portion of the address into a subnet portion and a node-on-the-subnet portion. A subnet mask is a 32-bit number in four-octet IP address format, with 0s in the rightmost bit positions that indicate bits used to assign node numbers: 255.255.255.240 shows the last 4 bits are available to support 16 subnet addresses. But since all networks reserve address 0 and "all bits on" for special purposes, that's really only 14 node addresses available on this subnet. Classless Inter-Domain Routing (CIDR) simplifies the subnetting process and the way we write it: that same address would be 255.255.255.240/28, showing that 28 bits of the total address specify the network address.

**Explain the differences between IPv4 and IPv6 approaches to subnetting.**   IPv4's use of a 32-bit address field meant that you had to assign bits from the address itself to designate a node on a subnet. IPv6 uses a much larger address field of 128 bits, which for unicast packets is broken into a 48-bit host or network field, 16 bits for subnet number, and 64 bits for the node address on that network segment. No more borrowing bits!

**Explain the role of port numbers in Internet use.**   Using software-defined port numbers (from 0 to 65535) allows protocol designers to add additional control over routing service requests: the IP packets are routed by the network between sender and recipient, but adding a port number to a Transport layer or higher payload header ensures that the receiving system knows which set of services to connect (route) that payload to. Standardized port number assignments make application design simpler; thus, port 25 for email, port 80 for HTTP, and so on. Ports can be and often are remapped by the protocol stacks for security and performance reasons; sender and recipient need to ensure that any such mapping is consistent, or connections to services cannot take place.

**Describe the man-in-the-middle attack, its impacts, and applicable countermeasures.** In general terms, the man-in-the-middle (MITM) attack can happen when a third party can place themselves between the two nodes and either insert their own false traffic or modify traffic being exchanged between the two nodes, in order to fool one or both nodes into mistaking the third party for the other (legitimate) node. This can lead to falsified data entering company communications and files, the unauthorized disclosure of confidential information, or disruption of services and business processes. Protection at every layer of the protocol stack can reduce or eliminate the exposure to MITM attacks. Strong Wi-Fi encryption, well-configured and enforced identity management and access control, and use of secure protocols as much as possible are all important parts of a countermeasure strategy.

**Describe cache poisoning and applicable countermeasures.** Every node in the network maintains a local memory or cache of address information (MAC addresses, IP addresses, URLs, etc.) to speed up communications—it takes far less time and effort to look it up in a local cache than it does to re-ask other nodes on the network to re-resolve an address, for example. Cache poisoning attacks attempt to replace legitimate information in a device cache with information that could redirect traffic to an attacker, or fool other elements of the system into mistaking an attacker for an otherwise legitimate node. This sets the system up for a man-in-the-middle attack, for example. Two favorite targets of attackers are ARP and DNS caches. A wide variety of countermeasure techniques and software tools are available; in essence, they boil down to protecting and controlling the server and using whitelisting and blacklisting techniques, but these tend not to be well suited for networks undergoing rapid growth or change.

**Explain the need for IPSec, and briefly describe its key components.** The original design of the Internet assumed that nodes connecting to the net were trustworthy; any security provisions had to be provided by user-level processes or procedures. For the 1960s, this was reasonable; by the 1980s, this was no longer acceptable. Multiple approaches, such as access control and encryption techniques, were being developed, but these did not lead to a comprehensive Internet security solution. By the early 1990s, *IPSec* was created to provide an open and extensible architecture that consists of a number of protocols and features used to provide greater levels of message confidentiality, integrity, authentication, and non-repudiation protection. It does this first by creating security associations, which are sets of protocols, services, and data that provide encryption key management and distribution services. Then, using the IP Security Authentication Header (AH), it establishes secure, connectionless integrity. The Encapsulating Security Payloads (ESP) protocol uses these to provide confidentiality, connectionless integrity, and anti-replay protection, and authenticates the originator of the data (thus providing a degree of nonrepudiation).

**Explain how physical placement of security devices affects overall network information security.** Physical device placement of security components determines the way network traffic at Layer 1 can be scanned, filtered, blocked, modified, or allowed to pass unchanged. It also directly affects what traffic can be monitored by the security system as a whole. For wired and fiber connections, devices can be placed inline—that is, on the connection from a secured to a non-secured environment. All traffic therefore flows through the security device. Placement of the device in a central segment of the network (or anywhere else) not only limits its direct ability to inspect and control traffic as it attempts to flow through, but may also limit how well it can handle or inspect traffic for various subnets in your over-all LAN. This is similar to host-based versus LAN-based antimalware protection. Actual placement decisions need to be made based on security requirements, risk tolerance, afford-ability, and operability considerations.

**Describe the key security challenges with wireless systems and control strategies to use to limit their risk.**   Wireless data communication currently comes in three basic sets of capa-bilities: Wi-Fi, Bluetooth, and near-field communication (NFC). All share some common vulnerabilities. First, wireless devices of any type must make a connection to some type of access point, and then be granted access to your network, to affect your own system's secu-rity. Second, they can be vulnerable to spoofing attacks in which a hostile wireless device can act as a man-in-the-middle to create a fake access point or directly attack other users' wireless devices. Third, the wireless device itself is very vulnerable to loss or theft, allowing attackers to exploit everything stored on the device. Mobile device management (MDM) solutions can help in many of these regards, as can effective use of identity management and access control to restrict access to authorized users and devices only.

**Explain the use of the concept of data, control, and management planes in network security.**   All networks exist to move data from node to node; this requires a control function to handle routing, error recovery, and so forth, as well as an overall network man-agement function that monitors the status, state, and health of network devices and the system as a whole. Management functions can direct devices in the network to change their operational characteristics, isolate them from some or all of the network, or take other maintenance actions on them. These three sets of functions can easily be visualized as three map overlays, which you can place over the diagram of the network devices themselves. Each *plane* (or overlay) provides a way to focus design, operation, troubleshooting, incident detection, containment, and recovery in ways best suited to the task at hand. This is not just a logical set of ideas—physical devices on our networks, and the software and firm-ware that run them, are built with this concept in mind.

**Describe the role that network traffic shaping and load balancing can play in information security.**   Traffic shaping and load balancing systems attempt to look at network traffic (and the connections it wants to make to systems resources) and avoid overloading one set of links or resources while leaving others unused or under-utilized. They may use static parameters, preset by systems administrators, or dynamically compute the parameters they need to accomplish their tasks. Traffic shaping is primarily a bandwidth management approach, allocating more bandwidth for higher-priority traffic. Load balancing tries to spread workloads across multiple servers. This trending and current monitoring informa-tion could be useful in detecting anomalous system usage, such as a distributed denial-of-service attack or a data exfiltration taking place. It may also provide a statistical basis for what is "normal" and what is "abnormal" loading on the system, as another indication of a potential security event of interest in the making. Such systems can generate alarms for out-of-limits conditions, which may also be useful indicators of something going wrong.

# Review Questions

1. When comparing the TCP/IP and OSI 7-layer reference model as sets of protocols, which statement is most correct?

   **A.** Network hardware and systems are actually built on TCP/IP, whereas the OSI reference model provides only concepts and theories.

   **B.** TCP/IP provides only concepts and theories, whereas network hardware and systems are actually built using the OSI reference model.

   **C.** Both sets of protocols provide theories and concepts, but real hardware is built around the data, control, and management planes.

   **D.** Hardware and systems are built using both models, and both models are vital to threat assessment and network security.

2. Is IPv6 backward compatible with IPv4?

   **A.** No, because the differences in addressing, packet header structure, and other features would not allow an IPv4 packet to successfully travel on an IPv6 network.

   **B.** No, because IPv4 packets cannot meet the new security considerations built into IPv6.

   **C.** Yes, because IPv6 has services built into the protocol stacks to convert IPv4 packets into IPv6-compatible structures.

   **D.** Yes, because the transport and routing protocols are the same.

3. Which basic network topology best describes the Internet?

   **A.** Star

   **B.** Mesh

   **C.** Ring

   **D.** Bus

4. Which relationship between nodes provides the greatest degree of control over service delivery?

   **A.** VPN tunnel

   **B.** Peer-to-peer

   **C.** Client-server

   **D.** Peer-to-server

5. Which statement about subnetting is correct?

   **A.** Subnetting applies only to IPv4 networks, unless you are using Classless Inter-Domain Routing (CIDR).

   **B.** Both IPv4 and IPv6 provide for subnetting, but the much larger IPv6 address field makes this a lot simpler to design and manage.

   **C.** Subnetting in IPv4 involves the CIDR protocol, which runs at Layer 3; in IPv6, this protocol, and hence subnetting, is not used.

   **D.** Because the subnet mask field is so much larger in IPv6, it is easier to subnet in this newer protocol stack than in IPv4.

6. Which of the following transmission media presents the greatest security challenges for a network administrator?

   **A.** Twisted-pair wiring

   **B.** Fiber optic

   **C.** Radio frequency wireless

   **D.** Light waves, either infrared or visible, but not in a fiber

7. Which statement (or statements) about ports and the Internet is/are not correct? (Choose all that apply.)

   **A.** Using port numbers as part of addressing and routing was necessary during the early days of the Internet, largely because of the small size of the address field, but IPv6 makes most port usage obsolete.

   **B.** Standard ports are defined for a number of protocols, and these ports allow sender and receiver to establish connectivity for specific services.

   **C.** Standardized port assignments cannot be changed or things won't work right, but they can be mapped to other port numbers by the protocol stacks on the sender's and recipient's systems.

   **D.** Many modern devices, such as those using Android, cannot support ports, and so apps have to be redesigned to use alternate service connection strategies.

8. Which of the following statements about man-in-the-middle (MITM) attacks is most correct?

   **A.** Session stealing attacks are not MITM attacks.

   **B.** MITM attacks can occur at any layer and against connectionless or connection-oriented protocols.

   **C.** This basic attack strategy can be used at any layer of the protocols where there is connection-oriented, stateful communication between nodes.

9. Which statement about cache poisoning is most correct?

   **A.** The cache on a user's local machine is immune from being poisoned by an attacker.

   **B.** Privately maintained DNS servers are the most lucrative targets of attackers, and thus the best strategy is to use commercial DNS service providers with proven security and reliability records.

   **C.** Almost every device on the network, from a smartphone or laptop on up, has address and DNS cache on it; these can be poisoned in a variety of ways, exposing the user and the network to various attacks.

   **D.** Cache poisoning can be prevented by encrypting the cache.

10. What happens to datagrams as they are passed through the protocol stack from the Data Link layer to the Transport layer?

    **A.** They get shorter as the headers and footers are removed as the datagrams move from one layer to the next.

    **B.** They get longer as more header and footer information is wrapped around the datagram.

**C.** They get converted from character or graphic information and formatting into byte formats.

**D.** If an encryption protocol is being used, they get encrypted.

**11.** Which layer of the OSI protocol stack does IPSec function?

**A.** Layer 2

**B.** Layer 3

**C.** Layer 4

**D.** Layer 5

**12.** You're trying to diagnose why a system is not connecting to the Internet. You've been able to find out that your system's IP address is 169.254.0.0. Which of the following statements correctly suggests the next best step?

**A.** It sounds like you've got a corrupted local DNS cache, which you should flush and then reset the connection.

**B.** Try connecting via another browser.

**C.** Check the DHCP server on your LAN to see if it's functioning correctly.

**D.** Check to see if any router and modem between your system and your ISP are functioning correctly; you may need to do a hardware (cold) reset of them.

**13.** Your IT team has a limited budget for intrusion detection and prevention systems and wants to start with a central server and a small number of remote IDS / IPS devices. Your team lead asks you where you think the remote devices should go. Which answer would you suggest?

**A.** Place them in the datacenter on the key access paths to its switch fabric.

**B.** Place them on the links between your ISP's point of presence and your internal systems.

**C.** Identify the links between high-risk internal systems (such as software development) and mission-critical systems (such as customer order processing, manufacturing control, or finance), and put them on the links between those systems.

**D.** The central server is a good start, and you can save even more money by skipping the remote devices for right now.

**14.** Which measures would you recommend be used to reduce the security risks of allowing Wi-Fi, Bluetooth, and NFC devices to be used to access your company's networks and information systems? (Choose all that apply.)

**A.** MDM systems

**B.** Effective access control and identity management, including device-level control

**C.** Because the Physical layer is wireless, there is no need to protect anything at this layer.

**D.** Whitelisting of authorized devices

**15.** You've been asked to investigate a possible intrusion on your company's networks. Which set of protocols or design concepts would you find most valuable, and why? Choose the most correct statement.

**A.** Start with the TCP/IP protocol stack; you don't need anything else.

**B.** The OSI 7-layer reference model may help you understand the nature of the intrusion to a layer or set of layers; next, you can use the TCP/IP protocol to help investigate the details with a protocol analyzer.

**C.** The data, control, and management planes aren't going to be useful to you now; they're only a high-level design concept.

**D.** You'll most likely need TCP/IP, the OSI 7-layer reference model, and the data, control, and management diagrams and information about your company's networks to fully understand and contain this incident.

**16.** What can traffic shaping, traffic management, or load balancing systems do to help identify or solve information security problems? (Choose all that apply.)

**A.** Nothing, since they work autonomously to accomplish their assigned functions.

**B.** Log data they generate and keep during operation may provide some useful insight after an incident, but nothing in real time would be helpful.

**C.** Such tools usually can generate alarms on out-of-limits conditions, which may be indicative of a system or component failure or an attack or intrusion in progress.

**D.** Given sufficient historical data, such systems may help network administrators see that greater-than-normal systems usage is occurring, which may be worthy of closer attention or investigation.

**17.** What is the risk of leaving the default settings on the access control lists in routers or firewalls?

**A.** Since the defaults tend to allow any device, any protocol, any port, any time, you risk leaving yourself wide open to any attacker or reconnaissance probes. Thus, the risk is very great.

**B.** The default settings tend to have everything locked down tightly until the network administrator deliberately opens up apps, time periods, or ports to access and use. Thus, the risk is very low.

**C.** Although the default settings leave everything wide open, the normal access control and identity management you have in place on systems, servers, and other resources is all that you need; the risk is very low.

**D.** As long as you've changed the administrator login ID and password on the device, you have nothing to worry about.

**18.** Which of the following is the best form of Wi-Fi security to use today?

**A.** WEP

**B.** WPA

**C.** WPA TKIP

**D.** WPA2

**19.** Your team chief is worried about all of those Bluetooth devices being used at the office; she's heard they are not very secure and could be putting the company's information and systems at great risk. How might you respond?

    **A.** Even with a maximum range of 10 meters (30 feet), you shouldn't have to worry about eavesdroppers or hackers out in the parking lot. Look to how you control visitor access instead.

    **B.** Bluetooth devices don't have a lot of bandwidth, so it's very unlikely that they present a data exfiltration or an intrusion threat.

    **C.** The biggest threat you might face is that Bluetooth on most of your staff's smartphones is probably not secure; talk with your MDM service provider and see if they can help reduce that exposure.

    **D.** You're right, chief! Bluephishing is fast becoming a social engineering threat, and you need to figure out a strategy to deal with it.

**20.** Which of the following statements about a NOC and a SOC is correct? (Choose all that apply.)

    **A.** Both perform essentially the same functions.

    **B.** With the increased emphasis on security, senior managers and stakeholders may feel that not having a security operations center is not taking the risks seriously enough.

    **C.** The focus of a NOC is different than that of a SOC.

    **D.** It's usually a mistake to try to overload the NOC with the security functions the SOC has to take on.

# Chapter

# 6

# Identity and Access Control

---

## THE SSCP EXAM OBJECTIVES COVERED IN THIS CHAPTER INCLUDE:

**Domain 1: Access Controls**

✓ 1.1: Implement and Maintain Authentication Methods

✓ 1.2: Support Internetwork Trust Architectures

✓ 1.3: Participate in the Identity Management Lifecycle

✓ 1.4: Implement Access Controls

Chapter 6 deals with two sides of the same coin: identity management and access control. The essence of information risk mitigation is ensuring that only the right people and processes can read, view, use, change, or remove any of our sensitive information assets, or use any of our most important information-based business processes. We also require the ability to prove who or what touched what information asset and when, and what happened when they did. We'll see how to authenticate that a subject user (be that a person or a software process) is who they claim to be; use predetermined policies to decide if they are authorized to do what they are attempting to do; and build and maintain accounting or audit information that shows us who asked to do what, when, where, and how. Chapter 6 combines decades of theory-based models and ideas with cutting-edge how-to insight; both are vital to an SSCP on the job.

# Identity and Access: Two Sides of the Same CIANA Coin

At the heart of all information security (whether Internet-based or not) is the same fundamental problem. Information is not worth anything if it doesn't move, get shared with others, and get combined with other information to make decisions happen. But to keep that information safe and secure, to meet all of our company's CIANA needs, we usually cannot share that information with just anybody! The flip side of that also tells us that in all likelihood, any one person will not have valid "need to know" for all of the information our organization has or uses. Another way to think about that is that if you do not know *who* is trying to access your information, you don't know *why* to grant or deny their attempt.

Each one of the elements of the CIANA security paradigm—which embraces confidentiality, integrity, availability, nonrepudiation, and authentication—has this same characteristic. Each element must look at the entire universe of people or systems, and separate out those we trust with access to our information from those we do not, while at the same time deciding what to let those trusted people or systems *do* with the information we let them have access to.

What do we mean by "have access to" an object? In general, access to an object can consist of being able to do one or more of the following kinds of functions:

- Read part or all of the contents of the object

- Read metadata about the object, such as its creation and modification history, its location in the system, or its relationships with other objects

- Write to the object or its metadata, modifying it in whole or part

- Delete part or all of the object, or part or all of its metadata

- Load the object as an executable process (as an executable program, a process, process thread, or code injection element such as a dynamic link library [DLL file])

- Receive data or metadata from the object, if the object can perform such services (i.e., if the object is a server of some kind)

- Read, modify, or delete security or access control information pertaining to the object

- Invoke another process to perform any of these functions on the object

- And so on…

This brings us right to the next question: *who*, or *what*, is the thing that is attempting to access our information, and how do we know that they are who they claim to be? It used to be that this identity question focused on people, software processes or services, and devices. The incredible growth in Web-based services complicates this further, and we've yet to fully understand what it will mean with Internet of Things (IoT) devices, artificial intelligences, and robots of all kinds joining our digital universal set of *subjects*—that is, entities requesting access to objects.

Our organization's CIANA needs are at risk if unauthorized subjects—be they people or processes—can execute any or all of those functions in ways that disrupt our business logic:

- *Confidentiality* is violated if any process or person can read, copy, redistribute, or otherwise make use of data we deem private, or of competitive advantage worthy of protection as trade secrets, proprietary, or restricted information.

- *Integrity* is lost if any person or process can modify data or metadata, or execute processes out of sequence or with bad input data.

- *Authorization*—the granting of permission to use the data—cannot make sense if there is no way to validate to whom or what we are granting that permission.

- *Nonrepudiation* cannot exist if we cannot validate or prove that the person or process in question is in fact who they claim to be and that their identity hasn't been spoofed by a man-in-the-middle kind of attacker.

- *Availability* rapidly dwindles to zero if nothing stops data or metadata from unauthorized modification or deletion.

One more key ingredient needs to be added as we consider the vexing problems of managing and validating identities and protecting our information assets and resources from unauthorized use or access: the question of *trust*. In many respects, that old adage needs to be updated: it's not *what* you know, but *how you know how much you can trust what you think you know*, that becomes the heart of identity and access management concerns.

# Identity Management Concepts

We need a way to associate an *identity*, in clear and unambiguous ways, with exactly one such person, device, software process or service, or other subject, whether a part of our system or not. In legal terms, we need to avoid the problems of *mistaken identity*, just because of a coincidental similarity of name, location, or other information related to two or more people, processes, or devices. It may help if we think about the process of *identifying* such a subject:

1. We ask (or the device offers) a *claim* as to who or what it is.

2. The claimant offers further supporting information that attests to the truth of that claim.

3. We verify the believability (the credibility or trustworthiness) of that supporting information.

4. We ask for additional supporting information, or we ask a trusted third party to *authenticate* that information.

5. Finally, we conclude that the subject is whom or what it claims to be.

So how do we create an identity? It's one thing for your local government's office of vital records to issue a birth certificate when a baby is born, or a manufacturer to assign a MAC address to an Internet-compatible hardware device. How do systems administrators manage identities?

## Identity Provisioning and Management

The *identity management lifecycle* describes the series of steps in which a subject's identity is initially created, initialized for use, modified as needs and circumstances change, and finally retired from authorized use in a particular information system. These steps are typically referred to as provisioning, review, and revocation of an identity:

- *Provisioning* starts with the initial claim of identity and a request to create a set of credentials for that identity; typically, a responsible manager in the organization must approve requests to provision new identities. (This demonstrates separation of duties by preventing the same IT provisioning clerk from creating new identities surreptitiously.) Key to this step is *identity proofing*, which separately validates that the evidence of identity as submitted by the applicant is truthful, authoritative, and current. Once created, the identity management functions have to deploy that identity to all of the access control systems protecting all of the objects that the new identity will need access to. Depending on the size of the organization, the complexity of its IT systems, and even how many operating locations around the planet the organization has, this "push" of a newly provisioned identity can take minutes, hours, or maybe even a day or more. Many larger organizations will use regularly scheduled update and synchronization tasks, running in the background, to bring all access control subsystems into harmony with each other. An urgent "right-now" push of this information can force a near-real-time update, if management deems it necessary.

- *Review* is the ongoing process that checks whether the set of access privileges granted to a subject are still required or if any should be modified or removed. Individual human subjects are often faced with changes in their job responsibilities, and these may require that new privileges be added and others be removed. *Privilege creep* happens when duties have changed and yet privileges that are no longer actually needed remain in effect for a given user. For example, an employee might be temporarily granted certain administrative privileges in order to substitute for a manager who has suddenly taken medical retirement, but when the replacement manager is hired and brought on board, those temporary privileges should be reduced or removed.

- *Revocation* is the formal process of terminating access privileges for a specific identity in a system. Such revocation is most often needed when an employee leaves the organization (whether by death, retirement, termination, or by simply moving on to other pastures). Employment law and due diligence dictate that organizations have policies in place to handle both preplanned and sudden departures of staff members, to protect systems and information from unauthorized access after such departure. Such unplanned departures might require immediate actions be taken to terminate all systems privileges within minutes of an authorized request from management.

---

### Revoking vs. Deleting an Identity

It's vital that we keep these two concepts separate and distinct. Think of all of the information associated with a typical user:

- Their identity itself, and the supporting information that was used to initially create it

- Files created, modified, or maintained by them on company systems, whether for personal use, business use, or both

- Records containing information about that identity or user, which were created in other files in the company's systems; these might be payroll, training, personnel management, or workflow control settings

- Metadata, systems event logs, and other information that attests to what information the user has accessed, used, modified, or attempted to access

- Emails sent or received by the user, or with message text pertaining to that user

- Archive or backup copies of those files, records, metadata, or systems that contain it

*Revoking* the identity blocks it from further access but changes no other data pertaining to that identity, no matter where it might be stored in your systems. *Deleting* that identity could mean a catastrophic loss of information, if the company ever has to answer a digital discovery request (about a wrongful termination, for example).

---

The identity management lifecycle is supported by a wide range of processes and tools within a typical IT organization. At the simplest level, operating systems have built-in features that allow administrators to create, maintain, and revoke user identities and privileges. Most OS-level user creation functions can also create roaming profiles, which can allow one user identity to have access privileges on other devices on the network, including any tailoring of those privileges to reflect the location of the user's device or other conditions of the access request. What gets tricky is managing access to storage, whether on local devices or network shared storage, when devices and users can roam around. This can be done at the level of each device using built-in OS functions, but it becomes difficult if not impossible to manage as both the network and the needs for control grow. At some point, the organization needs to look at ways to manage the identity lifecycle for *all* identities that the organization needs to care about. This will typically require the installation and use of one or more servers to provide the key elements of identity and access control.

## Identity and AAA

SSCPs often need to deal with the "triple-A" of identity management and access control, which refers to *authentication, authorization,* and *accounting.* As stated earlier, these are all related to identities, and are part of how our systems decide whether to grant access (and with which privileges) or not—so in that sense they sit on the edge of the coin between the two sides of our CIANA coin. Let's take a closer look at each of these important functions.

Authentication is where everything must start. *Authentication* is the act of examining or testing the identity credentials provided by a subject that is requesting access, and based on information in the access control list, either granting (accepts) access, denying it, or requesting additional credential information before making an access determination:

- Multifactor identification systems are a frequent example of access control systems asking for additional information: the user completes one sign-on step, and is then challenged for the second (or subsequent) factor.

- At the device level, access control systems may challenge a user's device (or one automatically attempting to gain access) to provide more detailed information about the status of software or malware definition file updates, and (as you saw in Chapter 5, "Communications and Network Security") deny access to those systems not meeting criteria, or route them to restricted networks for remediation.

Once an identity has been authenticated, the access control system determines just what capabilities that identity is allowed to perform. Authorization requires a two-step process:

- *Assigning privileges during provisioning.* Prior to the first access attempt, administrators must decide which permissions or privileges to grant to an identity, and whether additional constraints or conditions apply to those permissions. The results of those decisions are stored in access control tables or access control lists in the access control database.

- *Authorizing a specific access request.* After authenticating the identity, the access control system must then determine whether the specifics of the access request are allowed by the permissions set in the access control tables.

At this point, the access request has been granted in full; the user or requesting subject can now go do what it came to our systems to do. Yet, in the words of arms control negotiators during the Cold War, *trust, but verify*. This is where our final *A* comes into play. *Accounting* gathers data from within the access control process to monitor the lifecycle of an access, from its initial request and permissions being granted through the interactions by the subject with the object, to capturing the manner in which the access is terminated. This provides the audit trail by which we address many key information security processes, each of which needs to ascertain (and maybe prove to legal standards) who did what to which information, using which information:

- Software or system anomaly investigation

- Systems hardening, vulnerability mitigation, or risk reduction

- Routine systems security monitoring

- Security or network operations center ongoing, real-time system monitoring

- Digital forensics investigations

- Digital discovery requests, search warrants, or information requested under national security letters

- Investigation of apparent violations of appropriate use policies

- Incident response and recovery

- The demands of law, regulation, contracts, and standards for disclosure to stakeholders, authorities, or the public

Obviously, it's difficult if not impossible to accomplish many of those tasks if the underlying audit trail wasn't built along the way, as each access request came in and was dealt with.

Before we see how these AAA functions are implemented in typical information systems, we need to look further into the idea of permissions or capabilities.

# Access Control Concepts

Access control is all about *subjects* and *objects* (see Figure 6.1). Simply put, *subjects* try to perform an action upon an object; that action can be reading it, changing it, executing it (if the object is a software program), or doing anything to the object. *Subjects* can be anything that is requesting access to or attempting to access anything in our system, whether data or metadata, people, devices, or another process, for whatever purpose. Subjects can be people, software processes, devices, or services being provided by other Web-based systems. *Subjects* are trying to *do something* to or with the *object* of their desire. *Objects* can be collections of information, or the processes, devices, or people that have that information and act as gatekeeper to it. This subject-object relationship is fundamental to your understanding of access control. It is a one-way relationship: objects *do not* do anything to a subject.

Don't be fooled into thinking that two subjects interacting with each other is a special case of a bidirectional access control relationship. It is simpler, more accurate, *and much more useful* to see this as two one-way subject-object relationships. It's also critical to see that every task is a chain of these two-way access control relationships.

**FIGURE 6.1** Subjects and objects

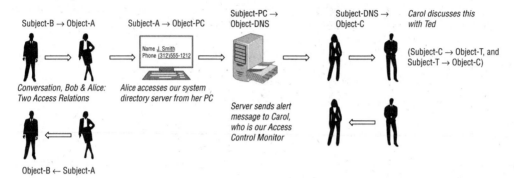

As an example, consider the access control system itself as an *object*. It is a lucrative target for attackers who want to get past its protections and into the soft underbellies of the information assets, networks, and people behind its protective moat. In that light, hearing these functions referred to as *datacenter gatekeepers* makes a lot of sense. Yet the access control system is a *subject* that makes use of its own access control tables, and of the information provided to it by requesting subjects. (You, at sign-on, are a subject providing a bundle of credential information as an object to that access control process.)

---

### Subjects Can Be Objects? And Objects Can Be Subjects?

This can sound confusing, but perhaps a social engineering example will help keep it clear for you. As a user of your company's systems, you have in your possession knowledge of your user ID, password, and the proper ways to log on and access certain information assets. You log on *as a subject* when you access that information.

An attacker tries to get you to disclose your user ID and password to her. The attacker is now the subject, and *you* are the object—she wants what you know!

Subjects access objects; an object, as a subject, can access other objects; and on and on.

Keep in mind as well that both subjects and objects have their own *identities*. You might think of that as needing to make sure that the right subject is authenticated and authorized to access exactly the right object, and no other.

# Subjects and Objects—Everywhere!

Let's think about a simple small office/home office (SOHO) LAN environment, with an ISP-provided modem, a Wi-Fi router, and peer-to-peer file and resource sharing across the half a dozen devices on that LAN. The *objects* on this LAN would include:

- Each hardware device, and its onboard firmware, configuration parameters, and device settings, and its external physical connections to other devices

- Power conditioning and distribution equipment and cabling, such as an UPS

- The file systems on each storage device, each computer, and each subtree and each file within each subtree

- All of the removable storage devices and media, such as USB drives, DVDs, and CDs used for backup or working storage

- Each installed application on each device

- Each defined user identity on each device, and the authentication information that goes with that user identity, such as username and password

- Each person who is a user, or is attempting to be a user (whether as *guest* or otherwise)

- Accounts at all online resources used by people in this organization, and the access information associated with those accounts

- The random-access memory (RAM) in each computer, as free memory

- The RAM in each computer allocated to each running application, process, process thread, or other software element

- The communications interfaces to the ISP, plain old telephone service, or other media

- And so on...

Note that third item: on a typical Windows 10 laptop, with 330 GB of files and installed software on a 500 GB drive, that's *only* half a million files—and *each* of those, and each of the 100,000 or so folders in that directory space, is an *object*. Those USB drives, and any cloud-based file storage, could add similar amounts of objects for each computer; mobile phones using Wi-Fi might not have quite so many objects on them to worry about. A conservative upper bound might be 10 million objects.

What might our population of *subjects* be, in this same SOHO office?

- Each human, including visitors, clients, family, and even the janitorial crew

- Each user ID for each human

- Each hardware device, including each removable disk

- Each mobile device each human might bring into the SOHO physical location with them

- Each *executing* application, process, process thread, or other software element that the operating system (of the device it's on) can grant CPU time to
- Any software processes running elsewhere on the Internet, which establish or can establish connections to objects on any of the SOHO LAN systems
- And so on…

That same Windows 10 laptop, by the way, shows 8 apps, 107 background processes, 101 Windows processes, and 305 services currently able to run—loaded in memory, available to Windows to dispatch to execute, and almost every one of them connected by Windows to events so that hardware actions (like moving a mouse) or software actions (such as an Internet Control Message Protocol packet hitting our network interface card will wake them up and let them run. That's 521 pieces of *executing* code. And as if to add insult to injury, the one live human who is using that laptop has caused 90 *user identities* to be currently active. Many of these are associated with installed services, but each is yet another subject in its own right.

Multiply that SOHO situation up to a medium-sized business, with perhaps 500 employees using its LANs, VPNs, and other resources available via federated access arrangements, and you can see the magnitude of the access control management problem.

## Data Classification and Access Control

Next, let's talk layers. No, not layers in the TCP/IP or OSI 7-layer reference model sense! Instead, we need to look at how permissions layer onto each other, level by level, much as those protocols grow in capability layer by layer.

Previously, you learned the importance of establishing an information classification system for your company or organization. Such systems define broad categories of protection needs, typically expressed in a hierarchy of increasing risk should the information be compromised in some way. The lowest level of such protection is often called *unclassified*, or *suitable for public release*. It's the information in press releases or in content on public-facing webpages. Employees are not restricted from disclosing this information to almost anyone who asks. Next up this stack of classification levels might be *confidential* information, followed by *secret* or *top secret* (in military parlance). Outside of military or national defense marketplaces, however, we often have to deal with *privacy-related* information, as well as company proprietary data.

For example, the US-CERT (Computer Emergency Readiness Team) has defined a schema for identifying how information can or cannot be shared among the members of the US-CERT community. The Traffic Light Protocol (TLP) can be seen at www.us-cert.gov/tlp and appears in Figure 6.2. It exists to make sharing of sensitive or private information easier to manage so that this community can balance the risks of damage to the reputation, business, or privacy of the source against the needs for better, more effective national response to computer emergency events.

**FIGURE 6.2** US-CERT Traffic Light Protocol for information classification and handling

| Color | When should it be used? | How may it be shared? |
|---|---|---|
| **TLP:RED**  Not for disclosure, restricted to participants only. | Sources may use TLP:RED when information cannot be effectively acted upon by additional parties, and could lead to impacts on a party's privacy, reputation, or operations if misused. | Recipients may not share TLP:RED information with any parties outside of the specific exchange, meeting, or conversation in which it was originally disclosed. In the context of a meeting, for example, TLP:RED information is limited to those present at the meeting. In most circumstances, TLP:RED should be exchanged verbally or in person. |
| **TLP:AMBER**  Limited disclosure, restricted to participants' organizations. | Sources may use TLP:AMBER when information requires support to be effectively acted upon, yet carries risks to privacy, reputation, or operations if shared outside of the organizations involved. | Recipients may only share TLP:AMBER information with members of their own organization, and with clients or customers who need to know the information to protect themselves or prevent further harm. **Sources are at liberty to specify additional intended limits of the sharing: these must be adhered to.** |
| **TLP:GREEN**  Limited disclosure, restricted to the community. | Sources may use TLP:GREEN when information is useful for the awareness of all participating organizations as well as with peers within the broader community or sector. | Recipients may share TLP:GREEN information with peers and partner organizations within their sector or community, but not via publicly accessible channels. Information in this category can be circulated widely within a particular community. TLP:GREEN information may not be released outside of the community. |
| **TLP:WHITE**  Disclosure is not limited. | Sources may use TLP:WHITE when information carries minimal or no foreseeable risk of misuse, in accordance with applicable rules and procedures for public release. | Subject to standard copyright rules, TLP:WHITE information may be distributed without restriction. |

Note how TLP defines both the conditions for use of information classified at the different TLP levels, but also any restrictions on how a recipient of TLP-classified information can then share that information with others.

Each company or organization has to determine its own information security classification needs and devise a structure of categories that support and achieve those needs. They all have two properties in common, however, which are called the *read-up* and *write-down* problems:

- *Reading up* refers to a subject granted access at one level of the data classification stack, which then attempts to read information contained in objects classified at higher levels.

- *Writing down* refers to a subject granted access at one level that attempts to write or pass data classified at that level to a subject or object classified at a lower level.

Shoulder-surfing is a simple illustration of the read-up problem, because it can allow an unauthorized person to masquerade as an otherwise legitimate user. A more interesting example of the read-up problem was seen in many login or sign-on systems, which would first check the login ID, and if that was correctly defined or known to the system, then solicit and check the password. This design inadvertently confirms the login ID is legitimate; compare this to designs that take both pieces of login information, and return "user name or password unknown or in error" if the input fails to be authenticated.

Writing classified or proprietary information to a thumb drive, and then giving that thumb drive to an outsider, illustrates the write-down problem. Write-down also can happen if a storage device is not properly zeroized or randomized prior to its removal from the system for maintenance or disposal.

Having defined our concepts about subjects and objects, let's put those read-up and write-down problems into a more manageable context by looking at privileges or capabilities. Depending on whom you talk with, a subject is granted or defined to have permission to perform certain functions on certain objects. The backup task (as subject) can read and copy a file, and update its metadata to show the date and time of the most recent backup, but it does not (or should not) have permission to modify the *contents* of the file in question, for example. Systems administrators and security specialists determine broad categories of these permissions and the rules by which new identities are allocated some permissions and denied others.

## Bell-LaPadula and Biba Models

Let's take a closer look at CIANA, in particular the two key components of confidentiality and integrity. Figure 6.3 illustrates a database server containing proprietary information and an instance of a software process that is running at a level not approved for proprietary information. (This might be because of the person using the process, the physical location or the system that the process is running on, or any number of other reasons.) Both the server and the process act as subjects *and* objects in their different attempts to request or perform read and write operations to the other. As an SSCP, you'll need to be well acquainted with how these two different models approach confidentiality and integrity:

- *Protecting confidentiality* requires that we prevent attempts by the process to *read* the data from the server, but we also must prevent the server from attempting to *write* data to the process. We can, however, allow the server to read data inside the process or associated with it. We can also allow the process to write its data, at a lower classification level, up into the server. This keeps the proprietary information safe from disclosure, while it assumes that the process running at a lower security level can be trusted to write valid data up to the server.

- *Protecting integrity* by contrast requires just the opposite: we must prevent attempts by a process running at a lower security level from writing into the data of a server running at a higher security level.

**FIGURE 6.3**   Bell-LaPadula (a) vs. Biba access control models (b)

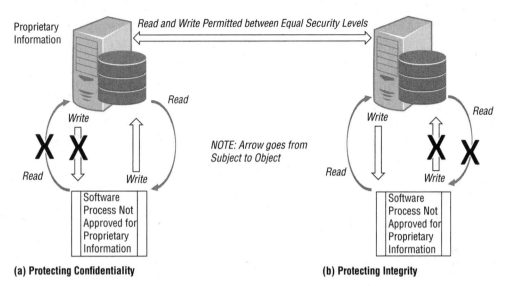

**(a) Protecting Confidentiality**          **(b) Protecting Integrity**

The first model is the Bell-LaPadula model, developed by David Bell and Leonard LaPadula for the Department of Defense in the 1970s, as a fundamental element of providing secure systems capable of handling multiple levels of security classification. Bell-LaPadula emphasized protecting the confidentiality of information—that information in a system running at a higher security classification level must be prevented from leaking out into systems running at lower classification levels. Shown in Figure 6.3(a), Bell-LaPadula defines these controls as:

- The *simple security property (SS)* requires that a subject may not read information at a higher sensitivity (i.e., no "read up").

- The * *(star) security property* requires that a subject may not write information into an object that is at a lower sensitivity level (no "write-down").

The *discretionary security property* requires that systems implementing Bell-LaPadula protections must use an access matrix to enforce discretionary access control

Remember that in our examples in Figure 6.2, the process is both subject *and* object, and so is the server! This makes it easier to see that the higher-level subject can freely *read from* (or be written into) a lower-level process; this does not expose the sensitive information to something (or someone) with no legitimate need to know. Secrets stay in the server.

Data integrity, on the other hand, isn't preserved by Bell-LaPadula; clearly, the lower-security-level process could disrupt operations at the proprietary level by altering data that it cannot read. The other important model, developed some years after Bell-LaPadula, was expressly designed to prevent this. Its developer, Kenneth Biba, emphasized data integrity over confidentiality; quite often the non-military business world is more concerned about preventing unauthorized modification of data by untrusted processes, than it is about protecting the confidentiality of information. Figure 6.3(b) illustrates Biba's approach:

- The *simple integrity property* requires that a subject cannot read from an object which is at a lower level of security sensitivity (no "read-down").

- The * *(star) Integrity property* requires that a subject cannot write to an object at a higher security level (no "write-up").

Quarantine of files or messages suspected of containing malware payloads offers a clear example of the need for the "no-read-down" policy for integrity protection. Working our way down the levels of security, you might see that "business vital proprietary," privacy-related, and other information would be much more sensitive (and need greater *integrity* protection) than newly arrived but unfiltered and unprocessed email traffic. Blocking a process that uses privacy-related data from reading from the quarantined traffic could be hazardous! Once the email has been scanned and found to be free from malware, other processes can determine if its content is to be elevated (written up) *by some trusted process* to the higher level of privacy-related information.

As you might imagine, a number of other access models have been created to cope with the apparent and real conflicts between protecting confidentiality and assuring the integrity of data. You'll probably encounter Biba and Bell-LaPadula on the SSCP exam; you may or may not run into some of these others:

- The Clark-Wilson model considers three things together as a set: the subject, the object, and the kind of transaction the subject is requesting to perform upon the object. Clark-Wilson requires a matrix that only allows transaction types against objects to be performed by a limited set of trusted subjects.

- The Brewer and Nash model, sometimes called the "Chinese Wall" model, considers the subject's recent history, as well as the role(s) the subject is fulfilling, as part of how it allows or denies access to objects.

- Non-interference models, such as Gogun-Meseguer, use security domains (sets of subjects), such that members in one domain cannot interfere with (interact with) members in another domain.

- The Graham-Denning model also use a matrix to define allowable boundaries or sets of actions involved with the secure creation, deletion, and control of subjects, and the ability to control assignment of access rights.

All of these models provide the foundational theories or concepts behind which access control systems and technologies are designed and operate. Let's now take a look at other aspects of how we need to think about *managing* access control.

---

### Star or Simple? Which Way?

Biba and Bell-LaPadula define properties (sometimes called *axioms, principles,* or *rules*) that can easily be gotten backward if you don't look at the next word in the property name. Always ask "what are we protecting?" and let that need for confidentiality or integrity tell you which directions you can read or write in!

# Role-Based

*Role-based access control (RBAC)* grants specific privileges to subjects regarding specific objects or classes of objects based on the duties or tasks a person (or process) is required to fulfill. Several key factors should influence the ways that role-based privileges are assigned:

- *Separation of duties* takes a business process that might logically be performed by one subject and breaks it down into subprocesses, each of which is allocated to a different, separate subject to perform. This provides a way of compartmentalizing the risk to information security. For example, retail sales activities will authorize a sales clerk to accept cash payments from customers, put the cash in their sales drawer, and issue change as required to the customer. The sales clerk cannot initially load the drawer with cash (for making change) from the vault, or sign off the cash in the drawer as correct when turning the drawer in at the end of their shift. The cash manager on duty performs these functions, and the independent counts done by sales clerk and cash manager help identify who was responsible for any errors.

- *Need to know*, and therefore need to access, should limit a subject's access to information objects strictly to those necessary to perform the tasks defined as part of their assigned duties, and no more.

- *Duration, scope or extent of the role* should consider the time period (or periods) the role is valid over, and any restrictions as to devices, locations, or factors that limit the role. Most businesses, for example, do not routinely approve high-value payments to others after business hours, nor would they normally consider authorizing these when submitted (via their approved apps) from a device at an IP address in a country with which the company has no business involvement or interests. Note that these types of attributes can be associated with the subject (such as role-based), the object, or the conditions in the system and network at the time of the request.

Role-based access has one strategic *administrative* weakness. *Privilege creep*, the unnecessary, often poorly justified, and potentially dangerous accumulation of access privileges no longer strictly required for the performance of one's duties, can inadvertently put an employee and the organization in jeopardy. Quality people take on broader responsibilities to help the organization meet new challenges and new opportunities; and yet, as duties they previously performed are picked up by other team members, or as they move to other departments or functions, they often retain the access privileges their former jobs required. To contain privilege creep, organizations should review each employee's access privileges in the light of their currently assigned duties, not only when those duties change (even temporarily!) but also on a routine, periodic basis.

# Attribute-Based

*Attribute-based access control (ABAC)* systems combine multiple characteristics (or attributes) about a subject, an object, or the environment to authorize or restrict access. ABAC uses Boolean logic statements to build as complex a set of rules to cover each *situation* as the business logic and its information security needs dictate. A simple example might be the case of a webpage designer who has limited privileges to upload new webpages into a beta test site in an extranet authorized for the company's community of beta testers but is denied (because of their role) access to update pages on the production site. Then, when the company prepares to move the new pages into production, they may need the designer's help in doing so and thus (temporarily) require the designer's ability to access the production environment. Although this could be done by a temporary change in the designer's subject-based RBAC access privileges, it may be clearer and easier to implement with a logical statement such as:

> IF (it's time for move to production) AND (designer-X) is a member of (production support team Y) THEN (grant access to *a, b, c...*)

Attribute-based access control can become quite complex, but its power to tailor access to exactly what a situation requires is often worth the effort. As a result, it is sometimes known as *externalized, dynamic, fine-grained,* or *policy-based* access control or authorization management.

## Subject-Based

Subject-based access control looks at characteristics of the subject that are not normally expected to change over time. For example, a print server (as a subject) should be expected to have access to the printers, the queue of print jobs, and other related information assets (such as the LAN segment or VLAN where the printers are attached); you would not normally expect a print server to access payroll databases directly! As to human subjects, these characteristics might be related to age, their information security clearance level, or their physical or administrative place in the organization. For example, a middle school student might very well need separate roles defined as a student, a library intern, or a software developer in a computer science class, but because of their age, in most jurisdictions they cannot sign contracts. The webpages or apps that the school district uses to hire people or contract with consultants or vendors, therefore, should be off limits to such a student.

## Object-Based

Object-based access control uses characteristics of each object or each class of objects to determine what types of access requests will be granted. The simplest example of this is found in many file systems, where objects such as individual files or folders can be declared as read-only. More powerful OS file structures allow a more granular approach, where a file folder can be declared to have a set of attributes based on classes of users attempting to read, write, extend, execute, or delete the object. Those attributes can be further defined to be inherited by each object inside that folder, or otherwise associated with it, and this inheritance should happen with every new instance of a file or object placed or created in that folder.

## Mandatory vs. Discretionary Access Control

One question about access control remains: now that your system has authenticated an identity and authorized its access, what capabilities (or privileges) does that subject have when it comes to passing along its privileges to others? The "write-down" problem illustrates this issue: a suitably cleared subject is granted access to read a restricted, proprietary file; creates a copy of it; and then writes it to a new file that does not have the restricted or proprietary attribute set. Simply put, *mandatory (or nondiscretionary) access control* uniformly enforces policies that prohibit any and all subjects from attempting to change, circumvent, or go around the constraints imposed by the rest of the access control system. Specifically, mandatory or nondiscretionary access prevents a subject from:

- Passing information about such objects to any other subject or object

- Attempting to grant or bequeath its own privileges to another subject

- Changing any security attribute on any subject, object, or other element of the system

- Granting or choosing the security attributes of newly created or modified objects (even if this subject created or modified them)

- Changing any of the rules governing access control

*Discretionary access control*, on the other hand, allows the systems administrators to tailor the enforcement of these policies across their total population of subjects. This flexibility may be necessary to support a dynamic and evolving company, in which the IT infrastructure as well as individual roles and functions are subject to frequent change, but it clearly comes with some additional risks.

# Network Access Control

Connecting to a network involves performing the right handshakes at all of the layers of the protocols that the requesting device needs services from. Such connections either start at Layer 1 with physical connections, or start at higher layers in the TCP/IP protocol stack. Physical connections require either a cable, fiber, or wireless connection, and in all practicality, such physical connections are *local* in nature: you cannot really plug in a Cat 6 cable without being there to do it. By contrast, remote connections are those that skip past the Physical layer and start the connection process at higher layers of the protocol stack. These might also be called logical connections, since they assume the physical connection is provided by a larger network, such as the Internet itself.

Let's explore these two ideas by seeing them in action. Suppose you're sitting at a local coffee house, using your smartphone or laptop to access the Internet via their free Wi-Fi customer network. You start at the Physical layer (via the Wi-Fi), which then asks for access at the Data Link layer. You don't get Internet services until you've made it to Layer 3, probably by using an app like your browser to use the "free Wi-Fi" password and your email address or customer ID as part of the logon process. At that point, you can start doing the work you want to do, such as checking your email, using various Transport layer protocols or Application layer protocols like HTTPS. The connection you make to your bank or email server is a *remote* connection, isn't it? You've come to their access portal by means of traffic carried over the Internet, and not via a wire or wireless connection.

Network access control is a fundamental and vital component of operating any network large or small. Without network access control, every resource on your network is at risk of being taken away from you and used or corrupted by others. The Internet connectivity you need, for business or pleasure, won't be available if your neighbor is using it to stream their own videos; key documents or files you need may be lost, erased, corrupted, or copied without your knowledge. "Cycle-stealing" of CPU and GPU time on your computers and other devices may be serving the needs of illicit crypto-currency miners, hackers, or just people playing games. You lock the doors and windows of your house when you leave because you don't want uninvited guests or burglars to have free and unrestricted access to the network of rooms, hallways, storage areas, and display areas for fine art and memorabilia that make up the place you call home. (You *do* lock up when you leave home, don't you?) By the same token, unless you want to give everything on your network away, you need to lock it up and keep it locked up, day in and day out.

*Network access control (NAC)* is the set of services that give network administrators the ability to define and control what devices, processes, and persons can connect to the network or to individual subnetworks or segments of that network. It is usually a distributed function involving multiple servers within a network. A set of NAC protocols define ways that network administrators translate business CIANA needs and policies into compliance filters and settings. Some of the goals of NAC include:

- Mitigation of non-zero day attacks (that is, attacks for which signatures or behavior patterns are known)
- Authorization, authentication, and accounting of network connections
- Encryption of network traffic, using a variety of protocols
- Automation and support of role-based network security
- Enforcement of organizational security policies
- Identity management

At its heart, network access control is a *service* provided to multiple devices and other services on the network; this establishes many client-server relationships within most networks. It's important to keep this client-server concept in mind as we dive into the details of making NAC work.

A quick perusal of that list of goals suggests that an organization needs to define and manage all of the names of people, devices, and processes (all of which are called *subjects* in access control terms) that are going to be allowed some degree of access to some set of information resources, which we call *objects*. Objects can be people, devices, files, or processes. In general, an *access control list (ACL)* is the central repository of all the identities of subjects and objects, as well as the verification and validation information necessary to authenticate an identity and to authorize the access it has requested. By *centralized*, we don't suggest that the entire ACL has to live on one server, in one file; rather, for a given organization, *one* set of cohesive security policies should drive its creation and management, even if (especially if!) it is physically or logically is segmented into a root ACL and many subtree ACLs.

Network access control is an example of the need for an integrated, cohesive approach to solving a serious problem. Command and control of the network's access control systems is paramount to keeping the network secure. Security operations center (SOC) dashboards and alarm systems need to know *immediately* when attempts to circumvent access control exceed previously established alarm limits so that SOC team members can investigate and respond quickly enough to prevent or contain an intrusion.

## IEEE 802.1X Concepts

IEEE 802.1X provides a port-based standard by which many network access control protocols work, and does this by defining the Extensible Authentication Protocol (EAPOL). Also known as "EAP over LAN," it was initially created for use in Ethernet (wired) networks, but later extended and clarified to support wired and wireless device access control, as well as the Fiber Distributed Data Interface (ISO standard 9314-2). Further extensions provide for secure device identity and point-to-point encryption on local LAN segments.

This standard has seen implementations in every version of Microsoft Windows since Windows XP, Apple Macintosh systems, and most distributions of Linux.

EAPOL defines a four-step authentication handshake, the steps being *initialization*, *initiation*, *negotiation*, and *authentication*. We won't go into the details here, as they are beyond the scope of what SSCPs will typically encounter (nor are they detailed on the exam), but it's useful to know that this handshake needs to use what the standard calls an *authenticator* service. This authenticator might be a RADIUS client (more on that in a minute), or almost any other IEEE 802.1X-compatible authenticators, of which many can function as RADIUS clients.

Let's look a bit more closely at a few key concepts that affect the way NAC as systems, products, and solutions is often implemented.

- *Preadmission vs. postadmission* reflects whether designs authenticate a requesting endpoint or user before it is allowed to access the network, or deny further access based on postconnection behavior of the endpoint or user.

- *Agent vs. agentless* design describes whether the NAC system is relying on trusted agents within access-requesting endpoints to reliably report information needed to support authentication requests, or whether the NAC does its own scanning and network inventory, or uses other tools to do this. An example might be a policy check on the verified patch level of the endpoint's operating system; a trusted agent, part of many major operating systems, can report this. Otherwise, agentless systems would need to interrogate, feature by feature, to check if the requesting endpoint meets policy minimums.

- *Out-of-band vs. inline* refers to where the NAC functions perform their monitoring and control functions. Inline solutions are where the NAC acts in essence as a single (inline) point of connection and control between the protected side of the network (or threat surface!) and the unprotected side. Out-of-band solutions have elements of NAC systems, typically running as agents, at many places within the network; these agents report to a central control system and monitoring console, which can then control access.

- *Remediation* deals with the everyday occurrence that some legitimate users and their endpoints may fail to meet all required security policy conditions—for example, the endpoint may lack a required software update. Two strategies are often used in achieving remediation:

  - *Quarantine networks* provide a restricted IP subnetwork, which allows the endpoint in question to have access only to a select set of hosts, applications, and other information resources. This might, for example, restrict the endpoint to a software patch and update management server; after the update has been successfully installed and verified, the access attempt can be reprocessed.

  - *Captive portals* are similar to quarantine in concept, but they restrict access to a select set of webpages. These pages would instruct the endpoint's user how to perform and validate the updates, after which they can retry the access request.

---

### Careful with That Quarantine!

In malware or antivirus terminology, *quarantine* involves the placing of a file suspected to be infected into a secured area in file storage; only trusted processes and their users can then read, examine, or possibly execute those files to see if they are or are not malware in disguise. Keep this distinct in your mind from the *quarantine network*, which limits endpoints and their users to a restricted set of hosts, software, and services. Both quarantines are based on the same idea of carving off a safe space in which those suspected of or actually carrying a disease are restricted from leaving, and only known, trusted agents (i.e., medical professionals or care workers) can enter.

---

## RADIUS Authentication

*Remote Authentication Dial-In User Service (RADIUS)* provides the central repository of access control information and the protocols by which access control and management systems can authenticate, authorize, and account for access requests. Its name reflects its history, but don't be fooled—RADIUS is *not* just for dial-in, telephone-based remote access to servers, either by design or use. It had its birth at the National Science Foundation, whose NSFNet was seeing increasing dial-up customer usage and requests for usage. NSF needed the full AAA set of access control capabilities—authenticate, authorize, and accounting— and in 1991 asked for industry and academia to propose ways to integrate its collection of proprietary, in-house systems. From those beginnings, RADIUS has developed to where commercial and open source server products exist and have been incorporated into numerous architectures. These server implementations support building, maintaining, and using that central access control list that we discussed earlier.

Without going into the details of the protocols and handshakes, let's look at the basics of how endpoints, network access servers, and RADIUS servers interact and share responsibilities:

- The network access server is the *controlling* function; it is the gatekeeper that will block any nonauthorized attempts to access resources in its span of control.

- The RADIUS server receives an authentication request from the network access server—which is thus a RADIUS *client*—and either accepts it, challenges it for additional information, or rejects it. (Additional information might include PINs, access tokens or cards, secondary passwords, or other two-factor access information.)

- The network access server (if properly designed and implemented) then allows access, denies it, or asks the requesting endpoint for the additional information requested by RADIUS.

RADIUS also supports *roaming*, which is the ability of an authenticated endpoint and user to move from one physical point of connection into the network to another. Mobile device users, mobile IoT, and other endpoints "on the move" typically cannot tolerate the overhead and wall-clock time consumed to sign in repeatedly, just because the device has moved from one room or one hotspot to another.

RADIUS, used by itself, had some security issues. Most of these are overcome by encapsulating the RADIUS access control packet streams in more secure means, much as HTTPS (and PKI) provide very secure use of HTTP. When this is not sufficient, organizations need to look to other AAA services such as Terminal Access Controller Access-Control System Plus (TACACS+) or Microsoft's Active Directory.

Once a requesting endpoint and user subject have been allowed access to the network, other access control services such as Kerberos and Lightweight Directory Access Protocol (LDAP) are used to further protect information assets themselves. For example, as a student you might be granted access to your school's internal network, from which other credentials (or permissions) control your use of the library, entry into online classrooms, and so forth; they also restrict your student logon from granting you access to the school's employee-facing HR information systems.

A further set of enhancements to RADIUS, called Diameter, attempted to deal with some of the security problems pertaining to mobile device network access. Diameter has had limited deployment success in the 3G (third-generation) mobile phone marketplace, but inherent incompatibilities still remain between Diameter and network infrastructures that fully support RADIUS.

## TACACS and TACACS+

The *Terminal Access Controller Access Control System* (TACACS, pronounced "tack-axe") grew out of early Department of Defense network needs for automating authentication of remote users. By 1984, it started to see widespread use in Unix-based server systems; Cisco Systems began supporting it and later developed a proprietary version called

Extended TACACS (XTACACS) in 1990. Neither of these were open standards. Although they have largely been replaced by other approaches, you may see them still being used on older systems.

*TACACS+* was an entirely new protocol based on some of the concepts in TACACS. Developed by the Department of Defense as well, and then later enhanced, refined, and marketed by Cisco Systems, TACACS+ splits the authentication, authorization, and accounting into separate functions. This provides systems administrators with a greater degree of control over and visibility into each of these processes. It uses TCP to provide a higher-quality connection, and it also provides encryption of its packets to and from the TACACS+ server. It can define policies based on user type, role, location, device type, time of day, or other parameters. It integrates well with Microsoft's Active Directory and with LDAP systems, which means it provides key functionality for *single sign-on (SSO)* capabilities. TACACS+ also provides greater command logging and central management features, making it well suited for systems administrators to use to meet the AAA needs of their networks.

# Implementing and Scaling IAM

The most critical step in implementing, operating, and maintaining identity management and access control (IAM) systems is perhaps the one that is often overlooked or minimized. Creating the administrative policy controls that define information classification needs, linking those needs to effective job descriptions for team members, managers, and leaders alike, has to precede serious efforts to plan and implement identity and access management. As you saw in Chapters 3 and 4, senior leaders and managers need to establish their risk tolerance and assess their strategic and tactical plans in terms of information and decision risk. Typically, the business impact analysis (BIA) captures leadership's deliberations about risk tolerance and risk as it is applied to key objectives, goals, outcomes, processes, or assets. The BIA then drives the vulnerability assessment processes for the information architecture and the IT infrastructure, systems, and apps that support it.

---

 **Real World Scenario**

**Migrating from "Simple SOHO"**

Let's start by looking at a typical SOHO deployment scenario. Tami owns a small content production business, with about five employees, which she's recently moved to a small office space in a retail park. She's been running on a LAN using a single SOHO grade wireless router, a few wireless laptops, and a wireless printer supported directly by the router. She's recently added a network-attached storage device to their router so that it can serve all users on their LAN. Having read Chapter 5, she's at least gone so far as to

---

implement device-level access control in the router by whitelisting MAC addresses and shutting off unnecessary services, ports, and protocols. She's also using cloud-hosted business platforms for internal business functions and looking toward expanding her business to include a presence on the Web.

Up to this point, however, Tami hasn't not had an integrated plan or process for access control and identity management. Like many small organizations, everybody knows each other; the concept of restricting access to certain information just doesn't seem to come up in office conversation. At least, it hasn't yet.

Tami contacts you for help. As an SSCP, she'd like your help in developing a business migration plan and business information security plan for her business, including making smart choices about access control and identity management as the business scales.

What are the first three tasks you'd recommend? Why?

What would you recommend as the next set of steps?

Assuming your organization has gone through those processes, it's produced the information classification guidelines, as well as the administrative policies that specify key roles and responsibilities you'll need to plan for as you implement an IAM set of risk mitigation controls:

- Who determines which people or job roles require what kind of access privileges for different classification levels or subsets of information? Who conducts periodic reviews, or reviews these when job roles are changed?

- Who can decide to override classification or other restrictions on the handling, storage, or distribution of information?

- Who has organizational responsibility for implementing, monitoring, and maintaining the chosen IAM solution(s)?

- Who needs to be informed of violations or attempted violations of access control and identity management restrictions or policies?

# Choices for Access Control Implementations

Two more major decisions need to be made before you can effectively design and implement an integrated access control strategy. Each reflects in many ways the decision-making and risk tolerance culture of your organization, while coping with the physical realities of its information infrastructures. The first choice is whether to implement a centralized or decentralized access control system:

- *Centralized access control* is implemented using one system to provide all identity management and access control mechanisms. This system is the one-stop-shopping point for all access control decisions; every request from every subject, throughout the organization, comes to this central system for authentication, authorization, and accounting. Whether this system is a cloud-hosted service, or operates using a single local server or a set of servers, is not the issue; the organization's logical space of subjects and objects is not partitioned or segmented (even if the organization has many LAN segments, uses VPNs, or is geographically spread about the globe) for access control decision-making. In many respects, implementing centralized access control systems can be more complex, but use of systems such as Kerberos, RADIUS, TACACS, and Active Directory can make the effort less painful. Centralized access control can provide greater payoffs for large organizations, particularly ones with complex and dispersed IT infrastructures. For example, updating the access control database to reflect changes (temporary or permanent) in user privileges is done once, and pushed out by the centralized system to all affected systems elements.

- *Decentralized access control* segments the organization's total set of subjects and objects (its access control problem) into partitions, with an access control system and its servers for each such partition. Partitioning of the access control space may reflect geographic, mission, product or market, or other characteristics of the organization and its systems. The individual access control systems (one per partition) have to coordinate with each other, to ensure that changes are replicated globally across the organization. Windows Workgroups are examples of decentralized access control systems, in which each individual computer (as a member of the workgroup) makes its own access control decisions, based on its own local policy settings. Decentralized access control is often seen in applications or platforms built around database engines, in which the application, platform, or database uses its own access control logic and database for authentication, authorization, and accounting. Allowing each Workgroup, platform, or application to bring its own access control mechanisms to the party, so to speak, can be simple to implement, and simple to add each new platform or application to the organization's IT architecture; but over time, the maintenance and update of all of those disparate access control databases can become a nightmare.

The next major choice that needs to be made reflects whether the organization is delegating the fine-grained, file-by-file access control and security policy implementation details to individual to users or local managers, or is retaining (or enforcing) more global policy decisions with its access control implementation:

- *Mandatory access control (MAC)* denies individual users (subjects) the capability to determine the security characteristics of files, applications, folders, or other objects within their IT work spaces. Users cannot make arbitrary decisions, for example, to share a folder tree if that sharing privilege has not been previously granted to them. This implements the mandatory security policies as defined previously, and results in highly secure systems.

- *Discretionary access control (DAC)* allows individual users to determine the security characteristics of objects, such as files, folders, or even entire systems, within their IT work spaces. This is perhaps the most common access control implementation methodology, as it comes built-in to nearly every modern operating system available for servers and endpoint devices. Typically, these systems provide users the ability to grant or deny the privileges to read, write (or create), modify, read and execute, list contents of a folder, share, extend, view other metadata associated with the object, and modify other such metadata.

- *Nondiscretionary access control (NDAC)* allow the organization to choose when and how to make access control decisions based upon a wide range of specific needs. By using role-based access control, for example, it can (in effect) levy mandatory access control policies on one set of subjects, under one set of roles and conditions, but allow those same subjects to enjoy more of a discretionary access control under other conditions. Various strategies, based on role, subject, object, or attribute, can provide the required degree of flexibility and control.

Having made those decisions, based on your organization's administrative security policies and information classification strategies, and with roles and responsibilities assigned, you're ready to start your IAM project.

## "Built-in" Solutions?

Almost every device on your organization's networks (and remember, a device can be both subject *and* object) has an operating system and other software (or firmware) installed on it. For example, Microsoft Windows operating systems provide *policy objects*, which are software and data constructs that the administrators use to enable, disable, or tune specific features and functions that the OS provides to users. Such policies can be set at the machine, system, application, user, or device level, or for groups of those types of subjects. Policy objects can enforce administrative policies about password complexity, renewal frequency, allowable number of retries, lockout upon repeated failed login attempts, and the like. Many Linux distributions, as well as Apple's operating systems, have very similar functions built into the OS. All devices ship from the factory with most such policy objects set to "wide open," you might say, allowing the new owner to be the fully authorized systems administrator they need to be when they first boot up the device. As administrator/owners, we're highly encouraged to use other built-in features, such as user account definitions and controls, to create "regular" or "normal" user accounts for routine, day-to-day work. You then have the option of tailoring other policy objects to achieve the mix of functionality and security you need.

 Windows and other operating systems often come with specific user identities built in, as part of how the OS protects itself from accidental or malicious tampering. The *trusted installer* identity, for instance, is what gets invoked to install software updates, new apps, or patches to the OS; this happens when you click Yes to that "This task wants to make changes to your computer" prompt.

For a small home or office LAN, using the built-in capabilities of each device to implement a consistent *administrative* set of policies may be manageable. But as you add functionality, your "in-house sysadmin" job jar starts to fill up quickly. That new NAS or personal cloud device probably needs you to define per-user shares (storage areas), and specify which family users can do what with each. And you certainly don't want the neighbors next door to be able to see that device, much less the existence of any of the shares on it! If you're fortunate enough to have a consistent base of user devices—everybody in the home is using a Windows 10 or macOS Mojave laptop, and they're all on the same make and model smartphone—then you think through the set of policy object settings once and copy (or *push*) them to each laptop or phone. At some point, keeping track of all of those settings overwhelms you. You need to centralize. You need a *server* that can help you implement administrative policies into technical policies, and then have that server treat all of the devices on your network as clients.

Before we look at a client-server approach to IAM, let's look at one more built-in feature in the current generation of laptops, tablets, smartphones, and phablets, which you may (or may not) wish to utilize "straight from the shrink wrap."

## Multifactor Authentication

As mentioned at the start of this chapter, authentication of a subject's claim to an identity may require multiple steps to accomplish. We also have to separate this problem into two categories of identities: human users, and everything else. First, let's deal with human users. Traditionally, users have gained access to systems by using or presenting a user ID (or account ID) and a password to go with it. The user ID or account ID is almost public knowledge—there's either a simple rule to assign one based on personal names or they're easily viewable in the system, even by nonprivileged users. The password, on the other hand, was intended to be kept secret by the user. Together, the user ID and password are considered one *factor*, or subject-supplied element in the identity claim and authentication process.

In general, each type of factor is something that the user has, knows, or is; this applies to single-factor and multifactor authentication processes:

- *Things the user has*: These would normally be physical objects that users can reasonably be expected to have in their possession and be able to produce for inspection as part of the authentication of their identity. These might include identification cards or documents, electronic code-generating identity devices (such as key fobs or apps on a smartphone), or machine-readable identity cards. Matching of scanned images of documents with approved and accepted ones already on file can be done manually or with image-matching utilities, when documents do not contain embedded machine-readable information or OCR text.

- *Information the user knows*: Users can know personally identifying information such as passwords, answers to secret questions, or details of their own personal or professional life. Some of this is presumed to be private, or at least information that is not widely known or easily determined by examining other publicly available information.

- *What the user is*: As for humans, users are their physical bodies, and biometric devices can measure their fingerprints, retinal vein patterns, voice patterns, and many other physiological characteristics that are reasonably unique to a specific individual and hard to mimic. Each type of factor, by itself, is subject to being illicitly copied and used to attempt to spoof identity for systems access.

Use of each factor is subject to false positive errors (acceptance of a presented factor that is not the authentic one) or false negative errors (rejection of authentic factors), and can be things that legitimate users may forget (such as passwords, or leaving their second-factor authentication device or card at home). As you add more factors to user sign-on processes, you add complexity and costs. User frustration can also increase with additional factors being used, leading to attempts to cheat the system.

There is also a potential privacy concern with all of these factors. In order for authentication systems to work, the system has to have a reference copy of the documents, the information, or the biometric measurements. Access to these reference copies needs to be controlled and accounted for, for any number of legal and ethical reasons. It might seem obvious that the reference copies be stored in an encrypted form, and then have the endpoint device that accepts this information encrypt it for transmission to the identity management system for comparison with the encrypted copies on file. This may make it difficult or impossible to determine whether the endpoint's data has an acceptable amount of error in it (the document was not properly aligned with the scanner, or the finger was not aligned the same way on the fingerprint reader). As an SSCP, you do not need to know how to solve these problems, but you should be aware of them and take them into consideration as you plan for identity authentication.

All of the foregoing applies whether your systems are using single-factor or multifactor authentication processes.

Multifactor authentication requires the use of more than one factor in authenticating the legitimacy of the claimed identity. The underlying presumption is that with more factors being checked, the likelihood that the subject's claim to the identity is invalid decreases.

Three cautions may be worth some attention at this point with regard to the use of built-in biometric and image identification systems in the current generations of laptops, phablets, and smartphones.

First, these may be challenging to scale, if your organization needs to allow for roaming profiles (which enable the same user to log on from different devices, perhaps even in different locations around the world).

Second, there's the risk that a third party could compel or inveigle your user into using the biometrics to complete an access attempt. Legally, a growing number of jurisdictions have the authority to compel someone to unlock devices in their possession, such as when crossing borders. Pickpockets, too, have been known to steal someone's smartphone, immediately try to unlock it, and turn and point the camera at its owner to complete the photo-based authentication challenge. Although many businesses may never have to worry about these concerns, the one that you work for (or help create) just might.

Finally, we must consider that as with any instrumentation or control system and process, errors do happen. The false negative, false rejection, or Type 1 error, happens when a legitimate, trusted access request by a subject is denied in error. Type 2 errors, also known as false acceptance or false positive errors, occur when an unauthorized or unrecognized subject is mistakenly allowed access. Biometric authentication technologies, for example, must frequently cope with errors induced by their users' physical health, ambient noise, lighting, or weather conditions, or electrical noise that affects the sensors at the endpoint device. The important question becomes how much error in today's measurements you can tolerate, when compared to the on-file (baseline) biometric data, before you declare that the readings do not match the baseline:

- Tolerate too little error, which increases your *false rejection rate*, and you increase the chance of false negatives or Type 1 errors (denying legitimate access requests).

- Tolerate too much error, which increases your *false acceptance* rate, and you increase the chance of false positives or Type 2 errors (accepting as a match, and thereby allowing access that should have been denied).

**What Are We Testing For?**

Remember, access control is testing whether a subject should be allowed past the gate that isolates the object of his desires from him. A *positive* result means a green light for access; a *negative* means a red light, no access allowed. Thus a false positive is giving the black hat attacker a green light to enter your system.

## Server-Based IAM

In the vast majority of IT infrastructures, companies and organizations turn to server-based identity management and access control systems. They scale much more easily than node-by-node, device-by-device attempts at solutions, and they often provide significantly greater authentication, authorization, and accounting functions in the bargain. Although seemingly more complex, they are actually much easier to configure, operate, maintain, and monitor. Let's take a closer look.

Conceptually, an identity management and access control system provides a set of services to client processes, using a centralized repository to support authentication of identity claims and grant or deny access, and accounting for successful and unsuccessful attempts at access. Different systems designs may use one server or multiple servers to perform those functions. These servers can of course either be dedicated hardware servers, be job streams that run on hardware servers along with other jobs (such as print sharing or storage management), or be running on virtual machines in a public, private, or hybrid cloud environment. In any case, careful attention must be paid to how those servers are connected to each other, to the rest of your networks and systems, and to the outside world.

In particular, notice that different access control systems are modeled around different transmission protocols. As you saw in Chapter 5, UDP and TCP deliver very different error detection and correction opportunities for systems designers. RADIUS is an example of an access control system built around UDP, and so its basic flow of control and data is prone to data loss or error. TACACS, and systems based on its designs, are built around TCP, which provides better control over error detection and retransmission.

On the other hand, different access control designs provide different mixes of authentication, authorization, and accountability functionality. RADIUS implementations tend to provide richer accounting of access activities than TACACS, for example.

Server-based IAM systems (integrated or not) may also make use of multiple information repositories, as well as multiple servers performing some or all of the AAA tasks. This is particularly helpful in enterprise architectures, where an organization might have business units in multiple locations around the globe. Performance, reliability, and availability would dictate a local IAM server and repository, which synchronizes with the repositories at other locations as often as business logic requires it to.

---

 **Real World Scenario**

**Migrating to an IAM Server Approach**

Thanks in part to your wise counsel, Tami now recognizes that her business needs to move to a server-based approach for identity management and access control. She's completed the information classification guide and policy, which (somewhat belatedly) recognized that she needed better protection for employee data files, contracts with clients, drafts of business plans, and proposals for new customers or for additional projects with existing ones. She also wants to plan ahead, or at least provide the growth opportunity to use collaboration platforms in which individual client organizations and her team can work together on a project-by-project basis.

Clearly, your client Tami is looking forward to getting a draft proposal for an identity management and access system from you.

What questions would you want to ask Tami about this? What topics need further analysis or investigation? Or are you ready to put together a strawman concept now? If so, what do you propose?

---

# Integrated IAM systems

As organizations grow more complex in their information needs, they usually need more powerful ways to bring together different aspects of their identity management and access control systems. A typical mid-sized company might need any number of specific platforms for logically separated tasks, such as human resources management, finance and accounting, customer relations management, and inventory. In the past, users had to first sign on to their local client workstation, then sign on to the corporate intranet, and then present yet another set of credentials to access and use each software platform and the data associated with it. Each application might have been built by different vendors, and each might be using different approaches to end-user identification authentication and access authorization. When the business further expands and needs to share information resources or provide (limited subsets of) platform access to partners, clients, or vendors, its identity and access management functions become more complicated. We need to share authorization information across related but separate applications, platforms, and systems, including systems that aren't under our direct control or management.

One approach is to use a directory system as the repository for identity authentication and access authorization information (or *credentials*), and then ensure that each time an application needs to validate an access request or operation, it uses that same set of credentials. This would require a server for that repository, and an interface by which client systems can request such services. The International Telecommunications Union (ITU) first published the X.500 Directory Specification in the late 1980s, and since then it has become the standard used by almost all access control and identity management systems. It included a full-featured Directory Access Protocol (DAP), which needed all of the features of the OSI 7-layer protocol stack. Broader use of X.500 by TCP/IP implementations was spurred by the development at MIT of LDAP.

## Single Sign-On

Single sign-on (SSO) was the first outgrowth of needing to allow one user identity with one set of authenticated credentials to access multiple, disparate systems to meet organizational needs. SSO is almost taken for granted in the IT world—cloud-based service providers that do not support an SSO capability often find that they are missing a competitive advantage without it. On the one hand, critics observe that if the authentication servers are not working properly (or aren't available), then the SSO request fails and the user can do nothing. This may prompt some organizations to ensure that each major business platform they depend on has its own sign-on capability, supported by a copy of the central authentication server and its repository. SSO implementations also require the SSO server to internally store the authenticated credentials and reformat or repackage them to meet the differing needs of each platform or application as required. Because of this, SSO is sometimes called *reduced sign-on*.

---

### Single Sign *Off?*

Single sign-off is not an access control issue or capability per se. It doesn't have to gain permission from the IAM systems to log off or shut down, but it also can't just hang up the phone and walk away, so to speak.

Single sign-off depends on the host operating system gathering information about all of the applications, platforms, systems, and information assets that a user or subject has established access to, and at the click of the "sign off" button, it walks through that list, terminating applications, closing the files the apps had open, and releasing resources back to the system. As each task in the sign-off completes, the operating system that supports it notifies the access control accounting functions and makes notes in its own event logs as dictated by local policy settings.

In most cases, single sign-off is a local machine or local host activity. Active sessions created by the user or subject are usually not considered by single shut-off, and in most cases, they are presumed to have a timeout feature that will close them down in an orderly fashion after a period of inactivity, regardless of the reason. In other cases, there may be powerful business reasons for keeping those sessions running even if the initiating subject has logged off and gone away on vacation!

Thus, single sign-*on* can enable far more connections to information assets than single sign-*off* will automatically disconnect and close down.

## Identity as a Service (IDaaS)

A number of third-party solutions now provide cloud-based as ways of obtaining subscription-based identity management and access control capabilities. Some of these product offerings are positioned toward larger organizations, with 500 or more users' worth of identity and access information needing to be managed. When the vendors in question have well-established reputations in the identity and access management marketplace, then using IDaaS may be a worthwhile alternative to developing and fielding your own in-house solutions (even if your chosen server architectures end up being cloud-based). This marketplace is almost 10 years old at this writing, so there should be a rich vein of lessons learned to pore over as you and your organization consider such an alternative.

IDaaS should not be confused with digital identity platforms, such as provided by using a Microsoft, Google, or other account. These digital identity platforms can provide alternate ways to authenticate a user, but you should be cautious: you're trusting that digital identity platform has done its job in proofing the identity information provided by the user to the degree that *your* information security needs require.

## Federated IAM

Generally speaking, a *federated* system is one built up from stand-alone systems that collaborate with each other in well-defined ways. In almost every industry, federations of businesses, nonprofit or civic organizations, and government agencies are created to help address shared needs. These federations evolve over time as needs change, and many of them fade away when needs change again. Federated identity management and access control systems can serve the needs of those organizational federations when they require identities to be portable across the frontiers between their organizations and their IT infrastructures.

Federated identity management systems provide mechanisms for sharing identity and access information, which makes identity and access portable, allowing properly authorized subjects to access otherwise separate and distinct security domains. Federated access uses open standards, such as the OASIS Security Assertion Markup Language (SAML), and technologies such as OAuth, OpenID, various security token approaches, Web service specifications, Windows Identity Foundation, and others. Federated access systems typically use Web-based SSO for user access (which is not to be confused with SSO within an organization's systems). Just as individual platform or system access is logically a subset of SSO, SSO is a subset of federated access.

One outgrowth of federated IAM approaches has been to emphasize the need for better, more reliable ways for entities to be able to assert their identity as a part of an e-business transaction or operation. Work to develop an identity assurance framework is ongoing, and there are efforts in the US, UK, and a few other nations to develop standards and reference models to support this.

## Trust Frameworks

One of the key considerations in federating access between or across systems is the way that trust relationships do or do not transfer. One example might be a humanitarian relief operation that involves a number of nonprofit, nongovernmental organizations (NGOs) from different countries, sharing a consolidated planning, coordination, and information system platform operated by a major aid agency. Some of the NGOs might trust aid agency employees with shared access to their information systems; others might not. There might also be local organizations, working with some of the NGOs, who are not known to the international aid agency; even host nation government agencies might be a part of this puzzle. The aid agency might wish to grant only a limited set of accesses to some of the NGOs and their staff and maybe no access at all to a few of the NGOs. This demonstrates several types of trust relationships:

- One-way trust relationships exist where organization A trusts its users and trusts the users of organization B, but while B trusts its own people as users, it does not fully trust the users in organization A and must limit their access to B's systems and information resources.

- Two-way trust relationship exist when both organizations have the same level of trust in all of the users in the other's domain. This does not have to be as high a level of trust as what they repose in their own people but just a symmetric or matching degree of trust.

- Transitive trust happens when organization A trusts organization B, and B trusts C, and because of that A can trust C.

As the complexity of the relationships between organizations, their systems and platforms, and the domains of user subjects (and objects) associated with those platforms increases, trust relationships can start to matrix together sometimes in convoluted ways. This could quickly overwhelm efforts by each organization's systems administrators to manage locally. Federated approaches to identity and access management are not by themselves simple, but they can be easier to manage, especially when the social or organizational context and trust relationships are not simple and straightforward. Federated systems also allow for much quicker, cleaner disconnects, such as when the relief operation ends or when one agency's systems are found to be less secure than can be tolerated by others in the federation.

Solutions to situations like this might contain elements of the following:

- Advanced firewall technologies

- Gateways and proxies as interface control points

- VLANs and restricted VLANs

- Public access zones

- Extranets for datacenter access

- Extensive Authentication Protocol (EAP)

- Whitelisting of applications, with application visibility and control functions to monitor and enforce whitelisting policies

- Multifactor authentication of subjects

- Behavior and posture monitoring, such as enforcing device update status and using remediation or quarantine to enforce updates or limit access
- Network segmentation to include zero trust architectures where required

This last needs some explanation and discussion.

# Zero Trust Architectures

From some perspectives, the normal conventions for designing and implementing network security implicitly or explicitly assume that once a subject has been granted access to the network, they are trusted to do what they were granted access to do. This is a little bit like registering as a hotel guest, and the key card you're given lets you use the elevator to access the floors the guest rooms are on or go into the fitness center. Your key card will not, however, let you into other guests' rooms or into areas restricted to the staff. Even in the hotel, the question must be asked: do you have legitimate business on floors where your room is not located?

Zero trust network design and access control reflect the need to counter the more advanced persistent threats and the increasing risk of data exfiltration associated with many of them. This shifts the security focus from the perimeter to step-by-step, node-by-node movement and action within the organization's information infrastructure. Instead of large, easily managed networks or segments, zero trust designs seek to micro-segment the network. Fully exploiting the capabilities of attribute-based access control, the zero trust approach promises to more effectively contain a threat, whether an outsider or insider, and thus limit the possibility of damage or loss.

You might at first think that zero trust architectures, and their attitude of "never trust, always verify," are incompatible with federated identity management and access control systems. Federated systems seem to encourage us to make one giant, trusting community of collaboration and sharing, with which we can break down the walls between companies, departments, and people; how can zero trust play a role in this? It does this by increasing the levels of *decision assurance* within the organization. Zero trust architectures add to the CIANA payback via:

- Ensuring that all accesses to all objects, by all subjects, are fully authenticated and authorized each time; this limits the opportunity for a process to misbehave and start corrupting other data or processes.

- Combining attributes about subjects, objects, and types of access (and the business task being performed) with time of day, location, or other environmental or context information; this limits the exposure to abnormal events.

- Adopting and enforcing a least-privilege strategy ensures that step by step, task by task, subjects and the processes they run are doing just what they need to *and nothing else.*

- Segmenting the network and infrastructure into clearly defined zones of trust, and inspecting, verifying, and logging both the traffic crossing that demarcation point and blocked attempts to cross it.

- Increasing the use of additional authentication methods, such as those needed to thwart credential-based attacks.

Never trust, always authenticate access requests fully, and always track and account for all activity, authorized or not. Analyze and assess those accounting records; seek the anomalies and investigate them.

This may sound like rampant paranoia, but the truth is, the advanced persistent threats are not just "out there" somewhere. They are probably already in your systems. Perhaps now's the time to replace "trust, but verify" with *constant vigilance* as your watchwords.

# Summary

Two major themes tie everything in this chapter together with Chapter 5's deep dive into network architectures and the protocol stacks that make them work. The first of those themes is the need to systematically and rigorously manage and control the creation, maintenance, and use of *identities* as they relate to subjects claiming the right to access our systems and our information. Identities are not, of course, the subjects, no more than you are your name. Nor are you the information needed to authenticate your claim that you are you when you try to access your online bank or your employer's information system. That brings us to the second of those themes, which involves the "triple A" of authenticating a claim to an identity by a subject, authorizing that subject's access to an object, and keeping detailed accounting records of every activity involved in that process and in the subject's use of the object.

Three forces have come together to make the SSCP's job even more demanding when it comes to this combined set of topics we call identity and access management. Organizations have grown in complexity internally and externally, as they take on both temporary and long-term relationships with partners, vendors, clients, and others in their markets. This combines with the natural tendency to want *more* data, *better* data, to support more decisions made more quickly, resulting in ever more complex patterns of information access and use within the organization and across its federated ecosystem of other, hopefully like-minded organizations and individuals. Finally, we have to acknowledge the growing sophistication of the advanced persistent threat actors, and their willingness and ability to take months to infiltrate, scout out valuable information assets to steal a copy of, and then complete their attack by exfiltrating their prize. All three of these trends are forcing us to take on more complex, powerful, flexible approaches to network security, identity management, and access control.

# Exam Essentials

**Compare and contrast single-factor and multifactor authentication.**   Typically, these refer to how human users gain access to systems. Each factor refers to something that the user has, knows, or is. Users can have identification cards or documents, electronic code-generating identity devices (such as key fobs or apps on a smartphone), or machine-readable identity cards. Users can know personally identifying information such as passwords, answers to secret questions, or details of their own personal or professional life. Users are their physical bodies, and biometric devices can measure their fingerprints, retinal vein patterns, voice patterns, or many other physiological characteristics that are reasonably unique to a specific individual and hard to mimic. Each type of factor, by itself, is subject to being illicitly copied and used to attempt to spoof identity for systems access. Use of each factor is subject to false positive errors (acceptance of a presented factor that is not the authentic one) and false negative errors (rejection of authentic factors), and they can be things that legitimate users may forget (such as passwords or leaving their second-factor authentication device or card at home). As you add more factors to user sign-on processes, you add complexity and costs. User frustration can also increase with additional factors being used, leading to attempts to cheat the system.

**Explain the advantages and disadvantages of single sign-on architectures.**   Initially, the design of systems and platform applications required users to present login credentials each time they attempted to use each of these different systems. This is both cumbersome and frustrating to users and difficult to manage from an identity provisioning and access control perspective. SSO (single sign-on) allows users to access an organization's systems by only having to do one sign-on—they present their authentication credentials once. It uses an integrated identity and access control management (IAM) systems approach to bring together all information about all subjects (people or processes) and all objects (people, processes, and information assets, including networks and computers) into one access control list or database. SSO then generates a ticket or token, which is the authorization of that subject's access privileges for that session. This can be implemented with systems like XTACACS, RADIUS, Microsoft Active Directory, and a variety of other products and systems, depending on the degree of integration the organization needs. SSO eliminates the hassle of using and maintaining multiple, platform-specific or system-specific sign-on access control lists; it does bring the risk that once into the system, users can access anything, including things outside of the scope, purview, or needs of their authorized duties and privileges. Properly implemented access control should provide that next level of "need to know" control and enforcement.

**Explain why we need device authentication for information security, and briefly describe how it works.**   Access to company or organizational information assets usually requires physical and logical access, typically via the Physical, Data Link, and Network layers of a protocol stack such as TCP/IP. The CIANA needs of the organization will dictate what information needs what kinds of protection, and in most cases, this means that only trusted, authorized subjects (people, processes, or devices) should be authorized to access this information. That requires that the subject first authenticate its identity. Device authentication depends on some hardware characteristic, such as a MAC address, and may also depend on authentication of the software, firmware, or data stored on the device; this ensures that trusted devices that do not have required software updates or malware definition file updates, for example, are not allowed access. Further constraints might restrict even an authorized device from attempting to access the system from new, unknown, and potentially untrustworthy locations, times of day, etc. The authentication process requires the device to present such information, which the access control system uses to either confirm the claimed identity and authorize access, request additional information, or deny the request.

**Compare and contrast single sign-on and federated access.**    SSO, by itself, does not bridge one organization's access control systems with those of other organizations, such as strategic partners, subcontractors, or key customers; this requires a federated identity and access management approach. Just as individual platform or system access is logically a subset of SSO, SSO is a subset of federated access. Federated identity management systems provide mechanisms for sharing identity and access information, which makes identity and access portable, allowing properly authorized subjects to access otherwise separate and distinct security domains. Federated access uses open standards, such as the OASIS Security Assertion Markup Language (SAML), and technologies such as OAuth, OpenID, various security token approaches, Web service specifications, Windows Identity Foundation, and others. Federated access systems typically use Web-based SSO for user access.

**Explain what is meant by the evolution of identity and its impact on information security.**    Traditionally, identity in information systems terms was specific to human end users needing access to systems objects (such as processes, information assets, or other users); this was user-to-applications access, since even a system-level application (such as a command line interpreter) is an application program per se. This has evolved to consider applications themselves as subjects, for example, and in Web service or service-oriented architectures (SOA), this involves all layers of the protocol stack. Privacy and the individual civil rights of users also are driving the need to provide a broad, integrated approach to letting users manage the information about themselves, particularly the use of personally identifying information (PII) as part of identity and access management systems. Fortunately, this evolution is occurring at a time when open and common standards and frameworks, such as the Identity Assurance Framework, are becoming more commonly used and are undergoing further development. The concept of identity will no doubt continue to involve as we embrace both the Internet of Things and greater use of artificial intelligence systems and robots.

**Describe what internetwork trust architectures are and how they are used.**    When two or more organizations need their physically and logically separate networks to collaborate together, this requires some form of sharing of identity and access control information. Internetwork trust architectures are the combination of systems, technologies, and processes used by the two organizations to support this interorganizational collaboration. This will typically require some sort of federated access system.

**Explain what a zero trust network is and its role in organizational information security.**
Zero trust network design and access control reflect the need to counter the more advanced persistent threats and the increasing risk of data exfiltration associated with many of them. This shifts the security focus from the perimeter to step-by-step, node-by-node movement and action within the organization's information infrastructure. Instead of large, easily managed networks or segments, zero trust designs seek to micro-segment the network. Fully exploiting the capabilities of attribute-based access control, the zero trust approach promises to more effectively contain a threat, whether an outsider or insider, and thus limit the possibility of damage or loss. It's sometimes called the "never trust, always verify" approach, and for good reason.

**Explain how one-way, two-way, and transitive trust relationships are used in a chain of trust.** It's simplest to start with one-way trust: node A is the authoritative source of trusted information about a topic, and since the builders of node B know this, node B can trust the information it is given by node A. This would require that the transmission of information from node A to B meets nonrepudiation and integrity requirements. Two-way trust is actually the overlap of two separate one-way trust relationships: node A is trusted by node B, which in turn is trusted by node A. Now, if node C trusts node B, then transitivity says that node C also trusts node A. This demonstrates a simple chain of trust: node A is trusted by B, which is trusted by C. This chain of trust concept is fundamental to certificates, key distribution, integrated and federated access control, and a host of other processes critical to creating and maintaining the confidentiality, integrity, authorization, nonrepudiability, and availability of information.

One-way and two-way trust are most often applied to domains of users: organization A trusts its users and trusts the users of its strategic partner B, but organization B does not have the same level of trust for organization A's users. This often happens during mergers, temporary partnerships or alliances, or the migration of subsets of an organization's users from one set of platforms to another.

**Describe the use of an extranet and important information security considerations with using extranets.** An extranet is a virtual extension to an organization's intranet (internal LAN) system, which allows outside organizations to have a greater degree of collaboration, information sharing, and use of information and systems of both organizations. For example, a parts wholesaler might use an extranet to share wholesale catalogs, or filtered portions thereof, with specific sets of key customers or suppliers. Extranets typically look to provide application-layer shared access and may do this as part of a SOA approach. Prior to the widespread adoption of VPN technologies, organizations needed significant investment in additional hardware, network systems, software, and personnel to design, deploy, maintain, and keep their extranets secure. In many industries, the use of industry-focused applications provided as a service (SaaS or PaaS cloud models, for example) can take on much of the implementation and support burden of a traditional extranet. As with any network access, careful attention to identity management and access control is a must!

**Explain the role of third-party connections in trust architectures.** In many trust architectures, either one of the parties is the anchor of the trust chain, and thus issues trust credentials for others in the architecture to use, or a trusted third party, not actually part of the architecture per se, is the provider of this information. One such role is that of a credential service provider (CSP), which (upon request) generates and provides an object or data structure that establishes the link between an identity and its associated attributes, to a subscriber to that CSP. Other examples of third parties are seen in the ways that digital certificates and encryption keys are generated, issued, and used.

**Describe the key steps in the identity management or identity provisioning lifecycle.**   In an information systems context, an identity is a set of credentials associated with (or bound to) an individual user, process, device, or other entity. The lifecycle of an identity reflects the series of events as the entity joins the organization, needs to be granted access to its information systems, and how those needs change over time; finally, the entity leaves the organization (or no longer exists), and the identity needs to be terminated to reflect this. Typically, these steps are called provisioning, review, and revocation. Provisioning creates the identity and distributes it throughout the organization's identity and access control systems and data structures, starting with management's review and approval of the access request, the identifying information that will be used, and the privileges requested. Pushing the identity out to all elements of the organization's systems may take a few minutes to a number of hours; often, this is done as part of overnight batch directory and integrated access management system updates. Review should be frequent and be triggered by changes in assigned roles as well as changes in organizational needs. Privilege creep, the accumulation of access privileges beyond that strictly required, should be avoided. When the employee (or entity) is no longer required by the organization to have access—when they are fired or separated from the organization, for example—their identity should first be blocked from further use, and then finally removed from the system after any review of their data or an audit of their access accounting information.

**Explain the role of authentication, authorization, and accounting in identity management and access control terms.**   These three processes (the "AAA" of access control) are the fundamental functions of an access control system. Authentication examines the identity credentials provided by a subject that is requesting access, and based on information in the access control list, either grants (accepts) access, denies it, or requests additional credential information, such as an additional identification factor. Next, the access control system authorizes (grants permission to) the subject, allowing the subject to have access to various other objects in the system. Accounting is the process of keeping logs or other records that show access requests, whether those were granted or not, and a history of what resources in the system that subject then accessed. Accounting functions may also be carried out at the object level, in effect keeping a separate set of records as to which subjects attempted access to a particular object, when, and what happened as a result. Tailoring these three functions allows the SSCP to meet the particular CIANA needs of the organization by balancing complexity, cost, and runtime resource utilization.

**Explain the role of identity proofing in identity lifecycle management.**   Proofing an identity is the process of verifying the correctness and the authenticity of the supporting information used to demonstrate that a person (or other subject) is in fact the same entity that the supporting information claims that they are. For example, many free email systems require an applicant to provide a valid credit or debit card, issued in the applicant's name, as part of the application process. This is then tested (or "proofed") against the issuing bank, and if the card is accepted by that bank, then at least this one set of supporting identity information has been found acceptable. The degree of required information security dictates the degree of trust placed in the identity (and your ability to authenticate it), and this then places a greater trust in the proofing of that identity. For individual (human) identities, a growing number of online identity proofing systems provide varying levels of trust and confidence to systems owners and operators that job applicants, customers, or others seeking access to their systems are who (or what) they claim to be.

**Compare and contrast discretionary and nondiscretionary access control policies.**   Mandatory (also called nondiscretionary) policies are rules that are enforced uniformly across all subjects and objects within a system's boundary. This constrains subjects granted such access (1) from passing information about such objects to any other subject or object; (2) attempting to grant or bequeath its own privileges to another subject; (3) changing any security attribute on any subject, object, or other element of the system; (4) granting or choosing the security attributes of newly created or modified objects (even if this subject created or modified them); and (5) changing any of the rules governing access control. Discretionary access policies are also uniformly enforced on all subjects and objects in the system, but depending on those rules, such subjects or objects may be able to do one or more of the tasks that are prohibited under a mandatory policy.

**Explain the different approaches that access control systems use to grant or deny access.**   *Role-based access control (RBAC)* systems operate with privileges associated with the organizational roles or duties assigned, typically to individual people. For example, a new employee working in the human resources department would not be expected to need access to customer-related transaction histories. Similarly, chief financial officers (CFOs) may have to approve transactions above a certain limit, but they probably should not be originating transactions of any size (using separation of duties to preclude a whaling attack, for example). *Attribute-based access control* systems look at multiple characteristics (or attributes) of a subject, an object, or the environment to authorize or restrict access. That said, CFOs might be blocked from authorizing major transactions outside of certain hours, on weekends, or if logged on from an IP address in a possibly untrustworthy location. Subject-based access control is focused on the requesting subject and applying roles or attributes as required to grant or deny access. *Subject-based* and *object-based* access control systems associate attributes and constraint checking against them with each subject and with each object, respectively.

**Describe the different privileges that access control systems can authorize to subjects.**   Subjects attempt to do something with or to an object, learn something about it, or request a service from it. Access control has to compare the privileges already assigned to the subject with the conditions, constraints or other factors pertaining to the object and type of access requested, to determine whether to grant access or deny it. These privileges may involve requests to read data from it, or read metadata kept in the system about the object; modify its contents, or the metadata; delete or extend it (that is, request that additional systems resources, such as space in memory or in storage, be allocated to it); load it as an executable process or thread for execution by a CPU; assign privileges or attributes to it; read, change, or delete access control system criteria, conditions, or rules associated with the object; pass or grant permissions to the object; copy or move it to another location; or even ask for historical information about other access requests made about that object. In systems that implement subject ownership of objects, passing ownership is also a privilege to control. Each of these kinds of operations may be worth considering as a privilege that the access control system can either grant or deny.

**Describe the key attributes of the reference monitor in access control systems.**  In abstract or conceptual terms, the reference monitor is a subject (a system, machine, or program) that performs all of the functions necessary to carry out the access control for an information system. Typically, it must be resistant to tampering, must always be invoked when access is requested or attempted, and must be small enough to allow thorough analysis and verification of its functions, design, and implementation in hardware, software, and procedures. It can be placed within hardware, operating systems, applications, or anywhere we need it to be, as long as such placement can meet those conditions. The security kernel is the reference monitor function within an operating system; the trusted computing base is the hardware and firmware implementation of the reference monitor (and other functions) in a processor or motherboard.

**Explain how Biba and Bell-LaPadula, as access control models, contribute to information security.**  Each of these models is focused on a different information security attribute or characteristic. Bell-LaPadula was designed to meet the Department of Defense's need for systems that could handle multiple levels of classified information; it focuses on confidentiality by providing restrictions on "read up"—that is, accessing information at a higher level than the process is cleared for—or "write-down" of classified information into a process or environment at a lower security level. Biba is focused on protecting data integrity, and so it restricts higher-level tasks from reading from lower-level tasks (to prevent the higher-level task from possibly being contaminated with incorrect data or malware), while allowing reads from lower-level to higher-level tasks.

**Explain Type 1 and Type 2 errors and their impacts in an identity management and access control context.**  Type 1 errors are *false negatives*, also called a *false rejection*, which incorrectly identify a legitimate subject as an intruder; this can result in delays or disruptions to users getting work done or achieving their otherwise legitimate system usage accomplished. Type 2 errors are *false positives* or *false acceptances*, in which unknown subjects, or authorized users or subjects exceeding their privileges, are incorrectly allowed access to systems or objects. Type 2 errors can allow unauthorized subjects (users or tasks) to access system information resources, take action, exfiltrate data, or take other harmful actions.

**Explain the roles of remediation and quarantine in network access control.**  Network access control systems can be programmed to inspect or challenge (interrogate) devices that are attempting to connect to the network, which can check for a deficiency such as software updates not applied, malware definitions not current, or other conditions. Systems with otherwise legitimate, trusted credentials that fail these checks can be routed to remediation servers, which only allow the user access to and execution/download of the required fixes. For network access control, quarantine (which is also called *captive portals*) is similar in concept but deals with client systems attempting an HTTP or HTTPS connection that fails such tests. These are restricted to a limited set of webpages that provide instructions on how to remediate the client's shortcomings.

**Describe the use of TACACS, RADIUS, and other network access control technologies.**    Network access control systems use authentication methods to validate that a subject (device or user) is whom or what they claim to be and that they are authorized to conduct access requests to sets of systems resources, and to account for such access requests, authorization, and resource use. Different access control technologies do these "AAA" tasks differently, achieving different levels of information security. Access control systems need a database of some sort that contains the information about authorized subjects, their privileges, and any constraints on access or use; this is often called an access control list (ACL). (Keep separate in your mind that routers and firewalls are often programmed with filter conditions and logic, as part of access control, by means of ACLs contained in the router's control memory. Two kinds of ACLs, two different places, working different aspects of the same overall problem.)

Terminal Access Controller Access Control System (TACACS) was an early attempt to develop network access capabilities, largely for Unix-based systems. (The "terminal" meant either a "dumb" CRT-keyboard terminal, a very thin client, or a remote card reader/printer job entry system.) XTACACS, or extended TACACS, was a Cisco proprietary extension to TACACS. TACACS+ grew out of both efforts, as an entirely new set of protocols that separate the authentication, authorization, and accounting functions, which provides greater security and control.

Remote Authentication Dial-In User Service (RADIUS) started with trying to control access to hosts by means of dial-in connections, typically using dumb terminals and thin clients. It works with (not in place of) a network access control server, which maintains the ACL information, to validate the request, deny it, or ask for additional information from the requestor. RADIUS has continued to be popular and effective, especially as it supports roaming for mobile end-user devices. An enhanced version of RADIUS, called Diameter, never gained momentum in the marketplace.

# Review Questions

1. Which statement about single-factor vs. multifactor authentication is most correct?

    **A.** Single-factor is easiest to implement but with strong authentication is the hardest to attack.

    **B.** Multifactor requires greater implementation, maintenance, and management, but it can be extremely hard to spoof as a result.

    **C.** Multifactor authentication requires additional hardware devices to make properly secure.

    **D.** Multifactor authentication should be reserved for those high-risk functions that require extra security.

2. Multifactor authentication means that our systems validate claims to subject identity based on:

    **A.** Third-party trusted identity proofing services

    **B.** Digital identity platforms

    **C.** Some aspect of what the subject is, knows, or has

    **D.** Two different biometric measurements

3. In access control authentication systems, which is riskier, false positive or false negative errors?

    **A.** False negatives, because they lead to a threat actor being granted access

    **B.** False positives, because they lead to a threat actor being granted access

    **C.** False negatives, because they lead to legitimate subjects being denied access, which impacts business processes

    **D.** False positives, because they lead to legitimate subjects being denied access, which impacts business processes

4. Your IT department head wants to implement SSO, but some of the other division heads think it adds too much risk. She asks for your advice. Which statement best helps her address other managers' concerns?

    **A.** They're right; by bridging multiple systems together with one common access credential, you risk opening everything to an attacker.

    **B.** Yes and no; single sign-on by itself would be risky, but thorough and rigorous access control at the system, application, and data level, tied to job functions or other attributes, should provide one-stop login but good protection.

    **C.** Single sign-off involves very little risk; you do, however, need to ensure that all apps and services that users could connect to have timeout provisions that result in clean closing of files and task terminations.

    **D.** Since support for single sign-on is built into the protocols and operating systems you use, there's very little risk involved in implementation or managing its use.

5. What's the most secure way to authenticate device identity prior to authorizing it to connect to the network?

   A.  MAC address whitelisting

   B.  Multifactor authentication that considers device identification, physical location, and other attributes

   C.  Verifying that the device meets system policy constraints as to software and malware updates

   D.  Devices don't authenticate, but the people using them do.

6. Which statement about federated access systems is most correct?

   A.  SSO and federated access provide comparable capabilities and security.

   B.  By making identity more portable, federated access allows multiple organizations to collaborate, but it does require greater attention to access control for each organization and its systems.

   C.  Once you've established the proper trust architecture, federated access systems are simple to implement and keep secure.

   D.  Most federated access systems need to use a digital identity platform or IDaaS to provide proper authentication.

7. Which statement about extranets and trust architectures is most correct?

   A.  Proper implementation of federated access provides safe and secure ways to bring an extranet into an organization's overall network system; thus an internetwork trust architecture is not needed.

   B.  Extranets present high-risk ways for those outside of an organization to collaborate with the organization and thus need to be kept separate from the trust architecture used for other internetwork activities.

   C.  Extranets provide extensions to an organization's intranet and thus need to use the same trust architecture as implemented in the main organizational network.

   D.  Trust architectures are the integrated set of capabilities, connections, systems, and devices that provide different organizations safe, contained, and secure ways to collaborate together by sharing networks, platforms, and data as required; thus, extranets are an example of a trust architecture.

8. What role should zero trust architectures play in your organization's information security strategy, plans, and programs?

   A.  None just yet; this is a theoretical concept that is still being developed by the IETF and government-industry working groups.

   B.  If you've done your threat modeling and vulnerability assessment correctly, you don't need the added complexity of a zero trust architecture.

   C.  By guiding you to micro-segment your networks and systems into smaller, finer-grain zones of trust, you focus your attention on ensuring that any attempts to cross a connection between such zones has to meet proper authentication standards.

   D.  Since the protocols you need to support zero trust do not work on IPv4, you need to wait to include zero trust architectures until you've transitioned your systems to IPv6.

9.  Which statement about trust relationships and access control is most correct?

    **A.**  One-way trust relationships provide the infrastructure for SSO architectures.

    **B.**  Transitive trust relationships are similar to trust chains but for individual users rather than digital certificates.

    **C.**  Trust relationships describe the way different organizations are willing to trust each other's domain of users when developing federated access arrangements.

    **D.**  Transitive trust relationships cannot be supported by federated access technologies.

10. Which set of steps correctly shows the process of identity management?

    **1.**  Proofing

    **2.**  Provisioning

    **3.**  Review

    **4.**  Revocation

    **5.**  Deletion

    **A.**  1, 2, 3, 4, and then 5

    **B.**  2, 3, 4

    **C.**  1, 2, 4, 5

    **D.**  2, 3, 5

11. Which statements about AAA in access control are correct? (Choose all that apply.)

    **A.**  Accounting provides the authorization to access resources as part of chargeback systems.

    **B.**  Analysis, auditing, and accounting are the services provided by an access control system's server.

    **C.**  Authorization checks to see if an identity has the right(s) to access a resource, while authentication validates that the identity is what it claims to be. Accounting tracks everything that is requested, approved, or denied.

    **D.**  Authentication checks to see if an identity has been granted access privileges, using the access control tables in the central repository; authorization validates the identity is allowed to access the system. Accounting keeps track of all requests, approvals, and denials.

12. Which of the following are allowed under mandatory access control policies?

    **A.**  Passing information about the object to another subject

    **B.**  Changing or creating new security attributes for an object or another subject

    **C.**  Granting privileges to another subject

    **D.**  None of these are allowed under mandatory access control policies.

13. Which of the following statements are true about discretionary access control policies? (Choose all that apply.)

    **A.** Subjects cannot be allowed to pass information about the object to another subject.

    **B.** Changing or creating new security attributes for an object or another subject can only be done by the access control system.

    **C.** Subjects can change rules pertaining to access control but only if this is uniformly permitted across the system for all subjects.

    **D.** Subjects can be permitted to pass on or grant their own privileges to other subjects.

14. Which form of access control depends on well-defined and up-to-date job descriptions?

    **A.** Role-based

    **B.** Subject-based

    **C.** Object-based

    **D.** Attribute-based

15. Which form of access control is probably best for zero trust architectures to use?

    **A.** Role-based

    **B.** Subject-based

    **C.** Object-based

    **D.** Attribute-based

16. What kinds of privileges should not be part of what your mandatory access control policies can grant or deny to a requesting subject? (Choose all that apply.)

    **A.** Any privilege relating to reading from, writing to, modifying, or deleting the object in question, if it was created or is owned by the requesting subject

    **B.** Reading or writing/modifying the metadata associated with an object

    **C.** Modifying access control system constraints, rules, or policies

    **D.** Reading, writing, deleting, or asking the system to load the object as an executable task or thread and run it

17. Which statements about a reference monitor in an identity management and access control system are correct?

    **A.** It should be tamper-resistant.

    **B.** Its design and implementation should be complex so as to defeat reverse engineering attacks.

    **C.** It's an abstract design concept, which is not actually built into real hardware, operating systems, or access control implementations.

    **D.** It is part of the secure kernel in the accounting server or services provided by strong access control systems.

**18.** A key employee seems to have gone missing while on an overseas holiday trip. What would you recommend that management do immediately, with respect to identity management and access control, for your federated access systems? Choose the most appropriate statement.

  **A.** Deprovision the employee's identity.

  **B.** Suspend all access privileges for the employee's identity, except for email, in case the employee tries to use it to contact the company for help.

  **C.** Suspend all access privileges for the employee's identity, and notify all federated systems partners to ensure that they take similar steps.

  **D.** Suspend all access privileges for devices normally used by the employee, such as their laptop, phablet, or phone (employee-owned, company-provided, or both). If possible, quickly establish a captive portal or quarantine subnet to route access attempts from these devices to.

**19.** What is the role of third parties in identity management and access control? (Choose all that apply.)

  **A.** Third parties are those who have access to your systems via federated access, and as such, are part of your trust architectures.

  **B.** Credential service can be provided by third parties or by internal services as part of your systems.

  **C.** Identity proofing can be provided by external third parties.

  **D.** Identity as a service, usually via a cloud or Web-based service, is provided by numerous third parties.

**20.** Which statement about subjects and objects is not correct?

  **A.** Subjects are what users or processes require access to in order to accomplish their assigned duties.

  **B.** Objects can be people, information (stored in any fashion), devices, processes, or servers.

  **C.** Objects are the data that subjects want to access in order to read it, write to it, or otherwise use it.

  **D.** Subjects are people, devices, or processes.

**21.** John has talked with his IT director about getting an upgrade to their network access control tools that will allow them to implement remediation and quarantine measures. His director thinks this is unnecessary because their enterprise antimalware system provides for quarantine. Is John's director correct? Which of the following should John share with his director?

  **A.** No, because malware quarantine moves infected files into safe storage where they cannot be executed or copied by users; network access control quarantine prevents devices that are not up-to-date with software updates or other features from connecting to the Internet without performing required updates.

  **B.** Yes, because both kinds of technologies can support quarantine of suspect or questionable systems.

C. No, because network access quarantine prevents HTTP or HTTPS connection attempts from systems that do not meet policy requirements by restricting them to webpages with update instructions; malware quarantine puts infected or suspected files out of reach of users to prevent inadvertent or deliberate execution or read attempts on them.

D. Yes, because the antimalware system will prevent devices that are infected from accessing any systems resources, whether files, other CPUs, or other nodes on the network.

22. Your IT director has asked you for a recommendation about which access control standard your team should be looking to implement. He's suggested either Diameter or XTACACS, as they used those in his last job. Which of the following gives you the best information to use in replying to your boss?

A. The standard is IEEE 802.1X; Diameter and XTACACS are implementations of the standard.

B. Diameter is an enhanced RADIUS and has been quite successful.

C. XTACACS replaced TACACS+, which could be a good solution for you.

D. RADIUS is the standard to work with.

23. Why do we need IPSec?

A. Now that IPv6 is here, we don't, since its built-in functions replace IPsec, which was for IPv4.

B. Since more and more apps are moving to PKI for encryption of data on the move, we no longer need IPSec.

C. IPSec provides key protocols and services that use encryption to provide confidentiality, authentication, integrity, and nonrepudiation at the packet level; without it, many of the Layer 2, 3, and 4 protocols are still unprotected from attack.

D. Since IPv6 encrypts all traffic at all layers, once you've transitioned your systems to IPv6, you won't need IPSec, except for those legacy IPv4 systems you communicate with.

# Chapter

# 7

# Cryptography

---

## THE SSCP EXAM OBJECTIVES COVERED IN THIS CHAPTER INCLUDE:

**Domain 5: Cryptography**

✓ 5.1: Understand the Fundamental Concepts of Cryptography

✓ 5.2: Understand the Reasons and Requirements for Cryptography

✓ 5.3: Understand and Support Secure Protocols

✓ 5.4: Understand Public Key Infrastructure (PKI) Systems

Information at rest; information in use; information in motion. This defines our information security problem in a nutshell and dictates our consistent, integrated use of any and every means possible to protect that information. Cryptography is one such set of techniques, and it has its roots in the fundamental ways that humans represent ideas with symbols. We often think that cryptography is all about making messages secret, but as you'll see in this chapter, almost every aspect of modern information systems technologies depends on cryptography in some manner.

We'll also have to confront the fundamental conundrum of cryptography: to keep something secret, you have to use *another* secret—but at the same time, you have to *publish*.

# Cryptography: What and Why

"Is it secret? Is it safe?"

Gandalf asks that about the One Ring (in J. R. R. Tolkien's masterpiece *The Lord of the Rings*), and yet that same set of questions is asked many times a day about critical information assets vital to businesses, organizations, and individuals. That question *seems* to focus on the confidentiality and integrity aspects of the CIA triad, but as you saw in Chapter 5, "Communications and Network Security," keeping communications and network systems truly safe and secure requires we add nonrepudiation and authentication to that triad: thus CIANA becomes our watchword. Let's see how to use cryptography to keep our systems safe, secure, and available; to prevent valid messages from being repudiated (or denied); and to authenticate actions requested by subjects throughout our systems.

Since the earliest days of written languages, people have been using "secret writing" for two important purposes: to protect the confidentiality of the message and to authenticate that the message came from whom the sender claimed to be. The earliest known use of cryptography dates from 1500 BC, in which a craftsman in Mesopotamia encrypted his recipe for a pottery glaze (the world's first known trade secret, perhaps?).

For most of the last 3,500 years, cryptography has been primarily based on *lexical analysis*—the study of the properties of a language and the ways in which people use it. It was not until the late nineteenth century CE that mathematics, number theory, and formal logic started to play a greater role in creating new cryptographic systems (and in breaking them). Ancient Greeks using their scytale to implement rail fence ciphers might not recognize the mathematics of twenty-first century cryptography, but they probably would recognize the basic elements: starting with plaintext, an algorithm, keys, and seed or salt values, they too built systematic procedures for encrypting their secrets, transmitting them (by couriers), and then decrypting them at the receiving end. They faced the same challenges we face today: keeping the content secret, protecting its authenticity, and yet getting the secret conveyed and understood in timely ways.

Cryptography brings many capabilities to the information systems designer, builder, user, and owner:

- *Confidentiality:* Protect the meaning of information and restrict its use to authorized users.

- *Utility*: Map very large sets of possible messages, values, or data items to much smaller, more useful sets.

- *Uniqueness*: Generate and manage identifiers for use in access control and privilege management systems.

- *Identity*: Validate that a person or process is who and what they claim to be.

- *Privacy*: Ensure that information related to the identity of a person or process is kept confidential, and its integrity is maintained throughout.

- *Nonrepudiation*: Provide ways to sign messages, documents, and even software executables so that recipients can be assured of their authenticity.

- *Integrity*: Ensure that the content of the information has not been changed in any way except by authorized, trustworthy processes.

The concept of privacy being a separate and distinct information security need from confidentiality is relatively new; part of the challenge has been gaining acceptance of the fact that modern digitally-enabled identity theft can be far more damaging to the individual than more traditional forms of impersonation (such as forging someone's signature onto a check drawn on their bank account) has been. Changes in law and in attitudes were necessary to make identity theft a separate and distinct form of crime. Another way that our thinking about privacy has evolved quite recently is to view it in aggregate, such as when two different companies have their separate customer files merged, or the individual customer data records commingled, perhaps by a third party service provider. The integrity of each company's data as a complete and separate set has thus been compromised, even if each individual customer record remains unchanged.

Before we can get into the details and see how modern cryptography works, let's first define some starting points. Cryptography is a terminology-rich environment—some might even say that the terms we use to talk about cryptography or explain it are themselves encrypted, as a way of keeping its inner secrets to those who have the real need to know. Don't panic—we'll break that secret code for you step by step.

 **Real World Scenario**

**If You Can Solve Kryptos, You Can Skip This Chapter!**

Cryptographers are puzzle addicts. This was most famously demonstrated when in 1990, American sculptor Jim Sanborn placed one large copper sculpture and several smaller elements in the gardens by the entrance of the Central Intelligence Agency at McClean, Virginia. Named *Kryptos*, with the theme of "Intelligence Gathering," the structure consists of four long ciphertext messages. As of this writing, three of these have been broken (with some help from clues by the artist); the fourth remains a mystery.

*(continued)*

---

*(continued)*

Sanborn worked with Ed Scheidt, who had retired from his post as chairman, CIA Office of Communications, to develop the cryptographs used on the sculpture.

A Vigenère cipher is used on the first two panels, and a transposition cipher on the third; and the encryption used on the fourth is unknown.

Visit `https://en.wikipedia.org/wiki/Kryptos` to start your quest to break the secret of *Kryptos*. And if you succeed, you can probably skip the rest of this chapter.

---

## Codes and Ciphers: Defining Our Terms

Think back to the data-information-knowledge-wisdom pyramid we discussed in Chapter 1, "The Business Case for Decision Assurance and Information Security." That pyramid represents levels of abstraction about ideas and how people share those ideas to accomplish their goals and objectives. It also shows that every idea in *your* mind has to first be represented as a set of symbols *before* you can even attempt to communicate that idea to someone else. We *encode* ideas into a set of symbols by using rules or protocols that make our encoding regular and repeatable. The encoded idea is the message we send to the receiver. The receiver then needs to *decode* that idea, translating it back from symbols to meaning in order for their own mind to make sense of the idea, interpret it, and then use it or reject it. This process of encoding and decoding messages is at the heart of every communication process and, every conversation. Natural human languages have rules of *syntax*, which define the grammar and structure of words, sentences, paragraphs, and so on; they also have rules of *semantics*, which define how we use the symbols and the syntax to express meaning. Without both sender and receiver understanding the rules of syntax and semantics in much the same way, the message may get sent and received, but it probably won't be understood.

*Encode* and *decode* seem to suggest secret codes, and unfortunately, people throughout history have been pretty sloppy with how they talk about "codes." Morse code, for example, is an open, worldwide standard way to represent letters of the alphabet and other symbols by a series of long and short signals, and yet, anyone can read a message encoded in Morse. During both World Wars I and II, American forces used "code talkers," elite units of Native Americans who spoke "in the clear," unencrypted, over voice-grade radio systems—but they spoke in Choctaw, Creek, or Navaho, which no one but an other bilingual listener might have been able to intercept and translate.

---

 **Design Scenario**

**The Prisoner's Code**

For many years—probably as long as there have been prisons—prisoners have communicated with one another with tap codes of various forms. Where this started is conjecture; modern militaries have long trained their personnel to use such simple codes to help maintain morale and unit cohesion with fellow prisoners of war. Tapping on the bars of their cell, on the walls, or on drain pipes, they could send simple but effective messages to one another encoded as pulses of sound or vibration

Tap codes use a table in which the alphabet has been placed—for Roman alphabets, a five row by five column table is sufficient (if C and K double up in one square). The first row holds A, B, C/K, D and E, and it goes on from there. Sending a message is done by first tapping the row, then the column number, with a short pause between row and column, and a longer one between letters. Thus "water" is sent as 5 taps, 2 taps; 1 tap, 1 tap; 4 taps, 4 taps; 1 tap, 5 taps; 4 taps, 2 taps. You can see this and explore other aspects of tap codes at `https://wikivisually.com/wiki/Tap_code`.

Training can also prepare prisoners to encrypt such messages, using talk-around code words or phrases as substitutes for sensitive, classified, or critical information. Thus, "mbf" might be a pre-agreed substitute term for "my big friend," a helicopter search and rescue operator, known in Western military circles as a "Jolly Green Giant" unit. Frequent use of the same talk-around code can easily be detected and broken by a prisoner's captors.

Why this code and not Morse code? The long and short sounds (dash and dot) of Morse would require somehow banging out two different, easily distinguishable sounds. This is probably a lot harder to do in captivity than the simple sequences of the same sound or signal pulse.

By contrast, "keeping it safe and secret" requires us to take our ideas, encoded as plaintext (or cleartext) and somehow hide their real meaning from those we do not wish to see or understand. This is where cryptography comes into play.

*Encryption* is the process of taking a message written in one set of symbols (and its syntax and semantics) and hiding or obscuring its meaning by changing the way the message is written. *Decryption* is then the process of unobscuring or revealing the meaning of an encrypted message and restoring it so that its original meaning is intact and revealed. The original *plaintext* message or information is encrypted into *ciphertext*, which is then decrypted back to its plaintext form and meaning.

## Plaintext or Cleartext?

Depending upon where you look, these terms can either mean the same thing or have different meanings:

- Plaintext is the original, unencrypted form of the data, in a form where its meaning or value is readily apparent. Whether it is human-readable characters or binary object code, plaintext is the data that we ultimately use. (This meaning will be used throughout this chapter.)

*(continued)*

---

*(continued)*

- Cleartext can either mean (a) plaintext or (b) data that is never intended to be transmitted, stored, or used in anything but an unencrypted form with its meaning and value available to anyone to read.

This distinction between data that we must protect, and data that is always "in the clear," is important. For example, the name of a business (like IBM or Microsoft) would always be cleartext (able to be read and recognized) on websites.

Note that you'll often see these terms—and many other information security terms—written in hyphenated form, as single words, or as compound nouns. This minor inconsistency can show up across many different documentation products in your organization. Don't let it throw you.

As an SSCP, be aware of how the other information security team members in your organization may use these terms...with or without a hyphen.

---

*Cryptographic algorithms* are the formal definition of the processes we use to encrypt plaintext into ciphertext and then decrypt ciphertext back to plaintext. In many cases, these algorithms require a set of control parameters, such as seeds, salts, keys, block size, and cycle or chain (iteration) values, all of which we'll look at in detail later. Both sender and (intended) receiver must agree to use a mutually consistent set of algorithms and control parameters if they are to successfully use cryptographic processes to send and receive information.

Figure 7.1 shows these basic concepts of encoding, decoding, encrypting, and decrypting in action. Many details are missing from this basic picture, which we'll cover in a bit.

**FIGURE 7.1**   The basics of encoding, encrypting, decrypting, and decoding

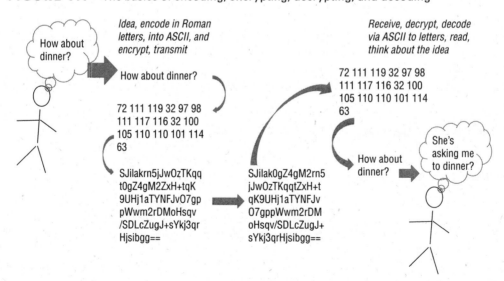

At its heart, all cryptography uses substitution and transposition to take the input plaintext and rewrite it in a different set of symbols so that its meaning is hidden. Simple substitution encrypts by replacing every occurrence of one symbol in the plaintext with its cipher value (from a table); the symbols can be individual letters, digits, short fixed-length strings of characters, or entire words. Decryption takes each symbol in the ciphertext and uses the same table to look up its plaintext value. Transposition changes the order of symbols in the plaintext message (as in the scytale cipher used in ancient Greece). Substitution and transposition are illustrated in Figure 7.2.

**FIGURE 7.2**     Substitution and transposition

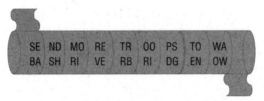

| Plaintext | D | I | N | N | E | R | T | I | M | E |
|-----------|---|---|---|---|---|---|---|---|---|---|
| Substitution Cipher | E | 8 | H | H | 3 | 4 | 5 | 8 | J | 3 |

| Plaintext | D | I | N | N | E | R | T | I | M | E |
|-----------|---|---|---|---|---|---|---|---|---|---|
| Substitution Cipher | I | D | N | N | R | E | I | T | E | M |

| SE | ND | MO | RE | TR | OO | PS | TO | WA |
|----|----|----|----|----|----|----|----|----|
| BA | SH | RI | VE | RB | RI | DG | EN | OW |

Resulting Cipher: SEBANDSHMORIREVETRRBOORIPSDGTOENWAOW

Substitution and transposition are often done in a series of steps to help make the encryption harder to break. Classical encryption used elements of natural languages—letters, words, and even sentence fragments—as the units to substitute and transpose. Modern cryptography uses advanced concepts in mathematics to first treat the plaintext as if it were a series of numbers and then applies much more complex techniques to compute the corresponding ciphertext value, rather than just look it up in a table. The key (if you pardon the pun) is in how each cryptographic system defines its rules for doing this.

Notice that a vital element of encryption and decryption is that the original meaning of the plaintext message is returned to us—encrypting, transmitting, and then decrypting it did not change its meaning or content. The ciphertext version of information can be used as a signature of sorts—a separate verification of the authenticity or validity of the plaintext version of the message. Digital signatures use encryption techniques to provide this separate validation of the content of the message, file, or information they are associated with.

Finally, we can define what cryptography is! *Cryptography* is the art and science of transforming plaintext information by means of suitable encryption techniques into ciphertext, which can then be decrypted back into matching plaintext. What we *use* cryptography for is not part of the definition, nor should it be.

A *cryptographic system* is the sum total of all the elements we need to make a specific application of cryptography be part of our information systems. It includes the algorithm for encrypting and decrypting our information; the control parameters, keys, and procedural information necessary to use the algorithm correctly and any other specialized support hardware, software, or procedures necessary to make a complete solution.

---

### A Sidebar on Sets and Functions

The simple concepts of sets and functions make cryptography the powerful concept that it is. As an SSCP, you should have a solid, intuitive grasp of both of these ideas. The good news? As a human being, your brain is already 90% of the way to where you need to go!

*Sets* provide for grouping of objects or items based on characteristics that they have in common. It's quite common to represent sets as Venn diagrams, using nested or overlapping shapes (they don't always have to be circles). In the following figure, part (a) shows an example of proper subsets—one set is entirely contained within the one outside it—and of subsets, where not all members of one set are part of another (they simply overlap). Part (b) of the figure shows a group of people who've earned one or more computer security-related certifications; many only hold one, some hold two, and a few hold all three, as shown in the overlapping regions. If a subset contains all elements of another subset, it is called an *improper subset*.

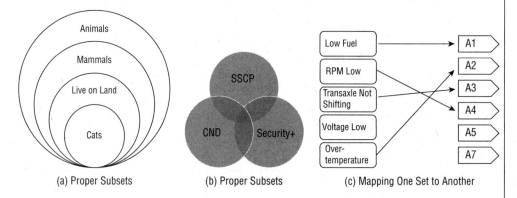

| (a) Proper Subsets | (b) Proper Subsets | (c) Mapping One Set to Another |

*Functions* are mathematical constructs that apply a given set of operations to a set of input values, producing an output value as the result. We write this as

$$f(x) = y \text{ or } f(x) \rightarrow y$$

The second form, written as a production function, shows that by applying the function $f$ to the value $x$, we *produce* the value $y$.

Note that for any given value of *x*, there can be only one *y* as a result.

One powerful application of functions is to consider them as mapping one set to another. The previous function says that the set of all values of *x* is mapped to the set *y*. This is shown in part (c) of the figure, which shows how a list of out-of-limit conditions is mapped to a list of alarms. (This looks like a table lookup function.) If you wanted any of a set of conditions to trigger the same alarm, you wouldn't use a function; you'd end up with something like the "check engine" light in automobiles, which loses more meaning than it conveys!

Not all mappings have to map every element of the source set into the destination set, nor do they use every element in the destination; some of these pairs (*x*,*y*) are just undefined. For example, the division function *f(x) = y/x* is undefined when *x* = 0 but not when *y* = 0.

This is just a brief refresher on sets and functions. You'll need to be acquainted with the concepts as an SSCP and as you prepare for the exam.

## Cryptography, Cryptology, or...?

There are many different names for very different aspects of how we study, think about, use, and try to crack "secret writing" systems. Some caution is advised, and as an SSCP you need to understand the context you're in to make sure you're using the right terms for the right sets of ideas.

For example, as Wikipedia and many others point out, a lot of people, agencies, and academics use the terms *cryptography* and *cryptology* interchangeably, as if they mean the same things. Within the U.S. military and intelligence communities, however:

- *Cryptography* refers specifically to the use and practice of cryptographic techniques.
- *Cryptanalysis* refers to the study of vulnerabilities (theoretical or practical) in cryptographic algorithms and systems and the use of exploits against those vulnerabilities to break such systems.
- *Cryptology* refers to the combined study of cryptography (the secret writing) and cryptanalysis (trying to break other people's secret writing systems or find weaknesses in your own).
- *Cryptolinguistics*, however, refers to translating between human languages to produce useful information, insight, or actionable intelligence (and has little to do with cryptography).

You may also find that other ways of hiding messages in plain sight, such as steganography, are sometimes included in discussions of cryptography or cryptology.

Note, though, that cryptograms are not part of this field of study or practice—they are games, like logic puzzles, which present ciphers as challenges to those who want something more than a crossword puzzle to play with.

# Building Blocks of Digital Cryptographic Systems

Digital systems represent all information as a series of numbers; by contrast, analog systems represent information as a continuously variable physical value. When you make a voice-over-IP (VOIP) call, the sender's speech (and background sounds) must be transformed from the digital form sent over the Internet into acoustic waves in the air that your ears can detect and process; the signal fed into that acoustic device (the headphone) is an analog electrical wave. There are many ways to encrypt and decrypt analog signals—which we won't go into here, since they're beyond what most of us in computing and networking ever encounter. (They're also well beyond the scope of the SSCP's job or the exam.) So we'll confine our studies to digital information systems and the cryptographic techniques that work with them.

---

 **Real World Scenario**

**Identifying Cryptographic Needs in E-Voting**

In previous chapters we've looked at e-voting, online voter registration, and related processes as ways to sharpen our skills as SSCPs. Let's continue with these important civic systems by taking on their cryptographic needs.

Recall that the basic process flow is that citizens first apply to register to vote; once their identity is authenticated, they are entered into the voter rolls for their local, regional, and national election commission. When an election is to be held, those rolls must be transferred to individual polling stations for use in validating that only properly registered voters can vote.

Considering your own experiences as a citizen and voter, and as an SSCP, think about the following questions:

1. What kind of events in your life would cause your voter registration information to change and hence require an update prior to the next election?

2. How can the information you initially provide, and any updates to it, be provided in ways that are self-authenticating? What does this require of the originators of that information?

3. Which other individuals or government offices need to see, use, process, or manipulate the information you provide to prove your identity and residence?

4. Which other individuals or government offices only need to know that you are legitimately registered as a voter?

Now, build a use case or user story that shows how the information about you is created, authenticated, shared, stored, used, and then destroyed as you and your information travel through the registration process. Use this document to help you identify users or functions (as in question 3) who need to know that you are you and do not have access to the details of that proof.

How might you see this use case or user story leading to your recommendations to use cryptographic solutions for parts of the voter registration and e-voting needs of your society?

All digital cryptographic systems embody certain basic concepts, albeit in many different ways. We start with defining how they will process the input plaintext, and this has to take the use of the plaintext into account:

- *Character or symbol ciphers* use individual symbols in the plaintext as the unit to encrypt and decrypt, much like the simple, classical substitution and transposition ciphers did.

- *Block ciphers* take the input plaintext as a stream of symbols and break it up into fixed-length blocks; each block is then encrypted and decrypted as if it was a single (larger) symbol. A block of 64 bits (8 eight-bit bytes) can be thought of as a 64-digit binary number, which is what the encryption algorithm would then work on. Block ciphers typically have to pad the last block of a fixed-length plaintext message (such as a file or an email) so that each block has the required length.

- *Stream ciphers* are symmetric encryption processes that work on a single byte (sometimes even a single bit!) of plaintext at a time, but they use a pseudorandom string (or *keystream*) of cipher digits to encrypt the input plaintext with. Stream ciphers typically use simple operations, such as *exclusive-or*, to encrypt each bit or byte. These operations run very fast (perhaps each encryption taking a few nanoseconds). Stream ciphers by design can work on any length of input plaintext. The keystream generator is a function (implemented in hardware, software, or both) that uses a seed value (the encryption key itself) as input, producing encryption values to be combined with each bit or byte of the input plaintext. Stream ciphers like RC4 find widespread use in mobile communications systems such as cell phones, Wi-Fi, and others, in which the plaintext input is often of unbounded length.

## Cryptographic Algorithms

A *cryptographic algorithm* defines or specifies a series of steps—some mathematical, some logical, some grouping or un-grouping of symbols, or other kinds of operations—that must be being applied, in the specified sequence, to achieve the required operation of the system. Think of the algorithm as the total set of swap rules that you need to use, *and the correct order to apply those rules in*, to make the cryptographic system work properly.

(Note, too, that we sometimes use *cryptographic algorithm* and *encryption algorithm* as interchangeable terms.) We mentioned before that the basic processes of substitution and transposition can be repetitively or iteratively applied in a given cryptographic process. The *number of rounds* that an algorithm iterates over is a measure of this repetition. A combination of hardware and software features can implement this repetition.

Encryption and decryption processes can suffer from what we call a *collision*, which can render them unusable. This can occur if one of the following happens:

- Two different plaintext phrases should not map (encrypt) to the same ciphertext phrase; otherwise, you lose the difference in meaning between the two plaintext phrases.

- Two different ciphertext phrases should not map (decrypt) to the same plaintext phrase; otherwise, you have no idea which plaintext meaning was intended.

As a case in point, consider translating from English into Spanish and back again. The English language uses two distinct words, *safety* and *security*, to refer to two very different but related set of ideas. Both safety and security are about preventing injury, damage, or other loss, but (as you saw in Chapter 2, "Information Security Fundamentals") they each approach different aspects of systems design and use. In Spanish, a single word—*seguridad*—encompasses both ideas. Encrypting an English sentence that uses both *safety* and *security* into Spanish, and then translating the resultant Spanish sentence back into English, would probably lose what English-speaking SSCPs consider as the important distinction between safety and security.

Virtually all cryptographic algorithms perform such a substitution—they replace a symbol, word, or phrase in the plaintext set with a corresponding element in the cipher-text set—our choice of algorithm has to take this potential for collision into account. The details of how this is done is beyond the scope of this book or the SSCP exam, but as an SSCP, you need to be aware that no matter what algorithm your system is using, it has its limits.

## Cryptographic Keys

Cryptographic keys provide the "secret sauce" that makes a cryptographic algorithm work. Typically, other algorithms (that are part of the overall cryptographic system) are used to generate new key values. Many things have been used throughout history as a source of keys:

- Published books, such as a specific edition of Shakespeare's *Romeo and Juliet*, *Caesar's Commentaries*, or even holy scriptures can provide a lookup table for either substitution or transposition operations. Bob, for example, could use such a book to encrypt a message by starting on a pre-agreed page, substituting the first letter in his plaintext for the first letter of the first line on the page. Carol would decrypt his message by using the same print edition of the book and go to the same pre-agreed page.

- *One-time pads* are a variation of using published books (and predate the invention of movable type). The key generator writes out a series of key words or phrases, one per sheet of paper, and makes only one copy of this set of sheets. Carol encrypts her message using the first sheet in the one-time pad *and then destroys that sheet*. Alice decrypts the ciphertext she receives from Carol using that same sheet and then destroys that sheet.

- *Pseudorandom numbers* of various length are also commonly used as keys. Senders and recipients each have a copy of the same pseudorandom number generator algorithm, which uses a seed value to start with. A sequence of pseudorandom numbers from such an algorithm provide either a one-time pad of encryption keys, or a keystream for stream cipher use.

- Hardware random number generators, combined with software functions, can also generate keys or keystreams. The latest of these use quantum computing technologies to generate unique keystreams.

It is not the algorithm, however, that provides us the degree of security we require—it is the key that does this! We talk about the *key strength* as a way to measure or assert how much effort would be required to break (illicitly decrypt) a cleartext message encrypted by a given algorithm using such a key. In most cases, this is directly related to the key size, defined as how many bits make up a key. Another way to think of this is that the key strength determines the size of the *key space*—the total number of values that such a key can take on. Thus, an 8-bit key can represent the decimal numbers 0 through 255, which is like saying that an 8-bit key space has 256 unique values in it. SSL uses a 256-bit key as its session key (to encrypt and decrypt all exchanges of information during a session), which would mean that someone trying to brute force crack your session would need to try $2^{256}$ possible values (that's a 78-digit base-10 number!) of a key to decrypt packets they've sniffed from your session. With 1 million zombie botnet computers each trying a million key values per second, they would still need $10^{59}$ *years* to go through all values. (If you're thinking of precomputing all such values, how many petabytes might such a *rainbow table* take up?)

*Key distribution and management* become the biggest challenges in running almost any cryptographic system. *Keying material* is a term that collectively refers to all materials and information that govern how keys are generated and distributed to users in a cryptographic system, and how those users validate that the keys are legitimate. *Key management* processes govern how long a key can be used and what users and systems managers must do if a key has been compromised (presumably by falling into the wrong hands). *Key distribution* describes how newly generated keys are issued to each legitimate user, along with any updates to the rules for their period of use and their safe disposal. Consider the three typical topologies from a key distribution and management perspective. The simple one-time pad system connects only two users; only one pair of pads is needed. Most real-world needs for secure communication require much larger sets of users, however. For a given set of $n$ users, the star topology requires $n$ pairs of keys to keep traffic between each user and the central site secure and private—from all other users as well as from outsiders. A full-mesh system requires $(n(n-1))$ sets of keys to provide unique and secure communication for each pair of users on this mesh.

The term *cryptographic protocols* can refer to two different sets of processes and techniques. The first is the use of cryptography itself in the operation of a cryptographic system, which typically can refer to key management and key distribution techniques. The second usage refers to the use of cryptographic systems and techniques to solve a particular problem. Secure email, for example, can be achieved in a variety of ways using different protocols, each of which uses different cryptographic techniques. We'll look at these more closely later in this chapter.

One more term we can define: a *cryptographic module* (according to Federal Information Processing Standards [FIPS] publication 140) is any combination of hardware, firmware, or software that implements cryptographic functions. What's interesting about FIPS 140 is that it directly addresses the security of an information systems supply chain with respect to its cryptographic elements. To earn certification as a cryptographic module, vendors must submit their works to the Cryptographic Module Validation Program (CMVP) for testing.

## Hashing as One-Way Cryptography

Hashing provides a way to take a very large set of expressions (messages, names, values, etc.) and map them down to a much smaller set of values. A good example of this is the Dewey Decimal Classification (DDC) system used in libraries, which gives librarians a reasonably uniform way to put nonfiction books on the shelves *and* makes it easy for patrons to find what they want. First created in 1873 and now maintained by the Library of Congress in the United States, this system assigns nonfiction subject areas to numbers from 000 to 999, with as many extra digits to the right of the decimal point as might be needed. For example, the 500 series holds all the natural science and mathematics subjects; 510 is the mathematics subset, and within that 516 is geometry, and so on. Once the main subject matter of a book is determined, its Dewey Decimal number can be assigned. Note that there might be thousands of books that all fit within a single DDC number like 516; 10 books on exactly the same subject (fundamental concepts of analytic geometry, for example) would all have the same Dewey Decimal number. Libraries were in existence long before we had digital computers, and they have often had such a large set of possible values of book *subjects* that they had to map ("show where to put them") to a space-constrained set of physical bookshelves. As businesses started to use automated information systems (such as punched cards) to maintain parts lists and inventories, this concept was reinvented and tailored to industry's needs.

Hashing provides many advantages in information systems design that stem from its ability to uniquely generate a numeric value that can represent arbitrary alphanumeric data (such as individual names or street addresses, part numbers, or drug names). These hash values can be stored in tables as relative offsets or pointers into very large files, eliminating the need to read every record to see if it's the one you actually need to use. Hashing the entire contents of a file produces a long-form error detection and correction code by reapplying the hash function and comparing that resultant hash value to the one stored with the file; a mismatch indicates the file may have been corrupted or changed. These are sometimes called *digital fingerprints* or *checksums* when used to detect (and possibly correct) errors in file storage or transmission. Hashing can also be applied to an entire message, producing a secure message hash or message digest. Since messages are typically of variable length, the message digest is fixed length, which makes them easy to use in file systems, communications systems, and security systems.

## Hash Algorithm Basics

Hash algorithms transform the long key into a hash key or short key, where the long keys can be drawn from some arbitrarily large set of values (such as personal names) and the short key or hash key needs to fit within a more constrained space. The hash key, also called the hash, the hash value, the hash sum, or other term, is then used in place of the long key as a pointer value, an index, or an identifier. Two main properties of hash functions are similar to those of a good encryption function:

- The hash function must be one way: there should be no computationally feasible way to take a hash value and back-compute or derive the long key from which it was produced.

- The hash function must produce unique values for all possible inputs; it should be computationally infeasible to have two valid long keys as input that produce the same hash value as a result of applying the hash function.

Compare these two requirements with the two main requirements for any kind of encryption system, which we do in Figure 7.3. Notice that both hashing and encryption must be one-to-one *mappings* or *functions*—no two input values can produce the same output value. But encryption *must* be able to decrypt the ciphertext back into one and only one plaintext (the identical one you started with!); if it can't, you're hashing, aren't you?

**FIGURE 7.3**   Comparing hashing and encryption as functions

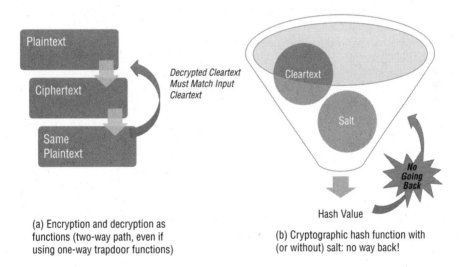

(a) Encryption and decryption as functions (two-way path, even if using one-way trapdoor functions)

(b) Cryptographic hash function with (or without) salt: no way back!

Like encryption algorithms, hash algorithms need to deal with *collisions* (situations where two different long key inputs can hash to the same hash value). These are typically addressed with additional processing stages to detect and resolve the collision.

Hash algorithms may make use of a salt value to initialize the calculations. This is typically a random (well, pseudorandom) value that is included with the input long key; if the hash algorithm is dealing with a 256-byte long key, a two-byte salt value effectively has the algorithm work on 258 bytes. This offers significant protection against rainbow table or dictionary-based attacks on hashes by making the attacker have to precompute a significantly larger table of hashed values. (We'll look at this more when we examine vulnerabilities, attacks, and defenses.)

A number of published standards define secure hash functions for use in various kinds of information security systems. The SHA series of Secure Hash Algorithms, published by the NSA, is one such series; the original SHA-0 and SHA-1 standards have been shown to be vulnerable to collision attacks and are being disbanded for use with SSL.

The details of how hashing functions work internally is beyond the scope of this book and typically not something an SSCP would need to know about on the job (or for the exam).

## Pseudorandom and Determinism

The science of probability gives us a strong definition of what we mean by *random*. A random event is one whose outcome cannot be determined in advance with 100% certainty. Flipping a perfect coin or rolling a perfect pair of dice are good examples—in which *perfect* means that no one has tampered with the coin or the dice and the way that they are flipped, rolled, or tossed offers no means of controlling where they land and come to rest with the desired outcome showing. One hundred perfect tosses of a perfect coin will produce 100 random outcomes (heads or tails) for that sequence of 100 events. But despite our intuition as gamblers and humans, the fact that 100 heads have been flipped in a row has no bearing whatsoever on what the outcome of the next flip will be as long as we are perfectly flipping a perfect coin. So the sequence of outcomes is said to have a random distribution of values—any one value has the same likelihood of occurring at any place in the sequence.

In computing, it is difficult to compute purely random numbers via software alone. Specialized hardware can, for example, trigger a signal when a cosmic ray hits a detector, and these natural events are pretty close to being perfectly randomly distributed over time. The beauty of computing is that once you write an algorithm, it is *deterministic*—given the same input and series of events, it always produces the same result. (Think what it would mean if computers were *not* deterministic!)

If we look at a very large set of numbers, we can calculate the degree of statistical randomness that set represents. There are lots of ways to do this, which are (blissfully!) well beyond the scope of what SSCPs need in the day-to-day of their jobs. If we use a deterministic algorithm to produce this set of numbers, using a seed value as a key input, we call such sets of numbers *pseudorandom*: the set as a whole exhibits statistical randomness, but given the $n$th value of the sequence and knowing the algorithm and the seed, the next element of the sequence—the $(n + 1)$th value—can be determined. (You can visualize this by imagining what happens when you drop a family-sized container of popcorn across your dark blue living room carpet. It's incredibly difficult to precompute and predict where each bit of popcorn will end up; but look at the patterns. A spray pattern would reveal that you threw the container across the room while standing in one location; other patterns might indicate a stiff breeze was coming in through the windows or the doorway, or that you lofted the container upward rather than waved it about in a side-to-side way. A purely random popcorn spill would not have any patterns you could detect.)

Modern operating systems use such pseudorandom number generators for many purposes, some of which involve encryption of identity and access control information. In 2007, it was shown that the CryptGenRandom function in Windows 2000 was not so random after all, which led to exploitable vulnerabilities in a lot of services (such as Secure Socket Layer) when supported by Windows 2000. The math behind this claim is challenging, but the same pseudorandom number generator was part of Windows XP and Vista.

*Entropy* is a measure of the randomness of a system; this term comes from thermodynamics and has crossed over into software engineering, computer science, and of course cryptography. A simple Web search on "entropy and cryptography" will give you a taste of how rich this vein of ideas is.

 **Real World Scenario**

**Digital Identification?**

It might be argued that a national identification system could take all of the data about *you* and hash it down into a suitably long hash value—your "ID number," so to speak. Clearly, this would not be something you'd memorize—you'd have to present some digital form of it, which could then be (somehow) validated as (a) being on file in an authoritative place, and (b) actually matching the person presenting it.

Suppose you are part of a team asked to implement such a system. What key considerations might you need to address? What design assumptions might you have to make? Is a "simple" cryptographic hash of all of your PII, including biometrics, going to be sufficient and effective? Why or why not?

# A Race Against Time

You need it kept safe and secret. For how long?

In general, organizations incur one-time costs to produce a set of information; ongoing costs to store it and keep it safe and secure; and disposal costs when the information has finally outlived its useful life. At the end of that useful life, however, that information could still harm your business if it fell into the wrong hands. As an example, consider a local police department's detectives, who rely on various informers to help them build successful cases against suspected criminals. When too much time has gone by, a cold case cannot be brought to prosecution, but if the identity of those informants is inadvertently disclosed, they could be at significant risk of retaliation.

On the other hand, some information has zero *value* to you or to others after a certain point in time. New product or marketing plans, for example, need to be kept confidential up until the product is released to the marketplace; after that, secrecy no longer adds value or reduces risk to the company's new products or plans.

Think back to what we saw earlier about the key strength of a cryptographic system. If it takes billions and billions (and more billions!) of years to try all values of a 256-bit key, how then can we ever say that cyber *defense* has to be lucky all of the time while the criminal hacker has to be lucky only once? More to the point, since the first 256-bit key was put into general use, we've seen key lengths increased to 512-, 1024-, and even 2048-bit lengths. If it takes longer than the lifetime of the universe for an attacker to try every possible key, why isn't that good enough? If all that an attacker can do is a brute force attack—sequentially trying each possible key—then it's purely a matter of chance whether they succeed with the first such trial key or the last one. But attackers are not limited to just plain brute force means. Without getting too mathematically rigorous, several factors conspire to make the useful lifetime of any given key length be just a few years and not centuries. First, of course, is that the pseudorandomness in the numbers used as control parameters narrows the key space to a fraction of its hypothetical size. Next, all algorithms have weaknesses in them that can be exploited to narrow that search space even further. Finally, *dumb luck* can and often does triumph over the skill and cunning of cryptosystems designers.

We must consider that it is still often easier to steal or surreptitiously copy the keys in use by a target's cryptosystems than it is to attempt to crack them. And recent surveys by (ISC)[2], the EC-Council, and others demonstrate that social engineering is the root cause of most information security systems breaches. Social engineering could, for example, reveal exploitable weaknesses in the way your organization uses cryptography, how it generates and manages keys, or how it responds when keys are compromised.

This brings us to an important consideration, which we might sum up as follows. There are two kinds of cryptographic keys in this world: those that have been compromised and those that haven't yet been compromised.

## "The Enemy Knows Your System"

Shannon's maxim—"The enemy knows your system"—rather bluntly restates Kerckhoff's principle from 1883. Whether by burglary, spies, analysis, or just dumb luck, Kerckhoff first summed up the growing sense of mathematicians and cryptographers by saying that the secrecy of the messages—the real secrets you want to protect—cannot depend on keeping your cryptographic system and its algorithms and protocols secret. The one thing that determines whether your secrets are safe is the strength of the cryptographic key that you use. If this key can be guessed, reversed-engineered from analysis of your ciphertext, stolen, or otherwise compromised, your secrets become known to the attacker.

This leads inexorably to key management—the processes we use to generate, distribute, and use cryptologic keying materials, and how we retire them from use and destroy them.

# Keys and Key Management

From the first uses of cryptography in ancient times, up until the middle 1970s, virtually all cryptologic systems depended on physically transporting keying materials from their point of origination to each user. Paper lists, books, punched paper tape, programmable read-only memory chips, and many other technologies have been used to record the values of the keys and the parameters that determine how those keys would be used. The physical security measures necessary to keep keying materials from going astray or falling into the wrong hands have had to be quite stringent, and despite this, many famous examples of espionage involve the surreptitious copying or theft of keying materials. Prudence dictates that keys be changed frequently, simply because it is comparatively easy to bribe, blackmail, or steal one's way to a copy of a set of keys; similarly, prudence suggests that using your encrypted communications systems to transmit the next set of keys is a risk not to be taken lightly.

Many nations, their military and intelligence services, and private businesses have wrestled with this problem. Pre-positioning several sets of keying material at all user sites does allow for a short "change keys" broadcast message or a similar message that overrides the default key change schedule. In doing so, this puts multiple sets of keys (today's, next week's, etc.) at risk of loss or compromise.

Symmetric encryption algorithms have the greatest challenges with key management and key distribution. Symmetric encryption not only uses the same key (or a simple transform of that key) for encryption and decryption; it also provides no *forward secrecy*—which means that when (not if!) a key is compromised, that compromised key can always be used to decrypt any ciphertext that was produced with that key.

As you'll see later, asymmetric encryption still uses keys; those keys still must be protected. And even though you publish your public key (when using hybrid encryption systems and the public key infrastructure for key exchange), your private key still represents the single most important secret that you must keep.

## Key Storage and Protection

For these and other reasons, cryptologic keying materials have to be protected at least as zealously as the secret plaintext they are being used to encrypt. This has often dictated that organizations must do the following:

- Provide hardened storage containers (safes, vaults, etc.) for the storage of keying material.
- Restrict access to encryption equipment, preventing unauthorized persons from inspecting it and observing its use.
- Control the manufacture, purchase, shipment, installation, maintenance, movement, and onward disposal of cryptologic equipment and materials.
- Require stringent personnel reliability standards for all persons who can access, use, or deal with cryptologic materials, systems, designs, etc.

Despite those precautions, cryptologic materials, keys, and systems have suffered from disclosure and compromise.

## Key Revocation and Zeroization

Any cryptographic system has to deal with *key revocation*—informing all users that a particular key is no longer valid and that it should not continue to be used. This process starts with a decision that a particular key should be revoked—either at a fixed time interval (key expiration schedule) or because a potential or actual incident has occurred that compromises the key in question. Next, a key revocation message must be broadcast to all authorized users of the system of which that key is a component. Each user must then clean house and make sure that the revoked key is removed from operational use and then disposed of in agreed-to ways.

Key revocation often has to happen when a user leaves the network that the cryptologic system services. Users may leave because they are no longer employed or a part of the organization; in wartime, they may be a unit or a location that has or is about to be over-run by the enemy. Keying materials on board aircraft, ships, or in other vessels are also subject to disasters (natural and man-made), which could lead to keying materials being compromised.

*Zeroization* (as the NSA calls it) is the process by which cryptologic systems are cleared of all keying materials, plaintext, ciphertext, control parameters, and sometimes even their software and firmware. This process serves two main purposes: it restores the device to a clean initial state, and it removes any information that might possibly be used to break the encryption scheme, decrypt previously encrypted messages, or derive the encryption key to use for later decryption of subsequent messages.

Originally, such a system reset was done by writing zeros into all memory locations, but even in the 1950s, it was known that writing zeros onto magnetic media (or printing pages of zeros on a printer to clean print impressions from the ink ribbon) would not make previous content unreadable. Many randomization techniques were developed and used instead, often tailored to the specific hardware technology that needed to be wiped or cleared.

Returning a system (including its cryptographic elements) to a clean initial state is necessary during systems test and development; it's also mandatory when the system is going to be used to process sensitive or classified information for a different user or one at a different level of information classification.

This leads many secure systems operators to establish routine "clobber" procedures, in which no hardware is damaged but all information, settings, programs, operational logs, and so forth are thoroughly erased from the system, and all systems elements are inspected to ensure nothing has been left behind that might possibly leak information from one compartment (one user) to another.

*Emergency zeroization* is often necessary to protect cryptologic systems used by the military, intelligence services, or law enforcement. During such an emergency, the goal is to assure that no cryptologic materials can be recovered by an adversary if they are attempting to seize or take control of the system. In such circumstances, rapid physical destruction is often the last choice of methods but one that is often built into such systems just in case it is needed. (The crew of the *USS Pueblo*, a signals intelligence ship captured by North Korea in 1968, attempted to destroy all of the classified and cryptologic materials onboard the ship. But there was just too much of it to destroy in two hours—partly due to bad housekeeping before the ship sailed with far too many copies of near-obsolete materials on board!) You might need to think about emergency zeroization for your business, if one of your locations is at risk of a "hostile takeover" by protesters or others.

---

**What Depths Will We Go To?**

In 1968, the Soviet ballistic missile submarine *K-129* sank in the Western Pacific, coming to rest at a depth of over 16,500 feet. The U.S. Central Intelligence Agency spent over $350 million to have Howard Hughes's Global Marine Development Corp. build the *Glomar Explorer*, ostensibly a deep-sea drilling platform, to attempt to retrieve not only the submarine itself, its missiles, and nuclear warheads, but also its communications and cryptographic systems. The salvage attempt nearly succeeded—the sub broke in two during the lift—but two missiles, their warheads, and some cryptographic systems were recovered.

Ironically, the cover story was that Hughes was interested in deep ocean floor mining and that the *Glomar Explorer* was evaluating the recovery of manganese modules from such depths. Since Howard Hughes was a self-made billionaire in many fields (including aircraft, semiconductors, and space systems), other adventurers followed his lead. As a result of this "deep cover" espionage operations, deep ocean floor mining is now a growth industry!

---

But these concerns over zeroization are not just for the national security and counter-espionage communities—consumers of secure chat, VOIP and email systems need to be wary as well! As Michael Cobb writes in TechTarget SearchSecurity, in September 2018, the *Telegrab* malware targets users of the Russian *Telegram* secure chat system in an attempt to collect keying material, keys, plaintext and ciphertext chat remnants, and other information that might be used (presumably by Russian security services) to break the encryption used and decrypt the user's chats. It's not immediately clear if normal computing hygiene practices will solve such a data remanence problem; if not, perhaps there's a market for a personal remanence-removal app.

# Modern Cryptography: Beyond the "Secret Decoder Ring"

The current practice of cryptography consists of many related subfields of study and application. We'll look at several of these areas in greater depth; note that all of them provide rich avenues by which you as an SSCP can apply your practical hands-on savvy as you continue to grow your knowledge and experience.

## Symmetric Key Cryptography

Symmetric key cryptography uses the same key to encrypt and decrypt the data being exchanged or protected. The algorithms and processes used can still be quite complex, and they may even include variations in which the sender's and recipient's keys are different but one is easy to compute from the other. The algorithms for symmetric key cryptography typically run very fast—this type is suitable for encrypting high data rate streaming services, for example, or for protecting very large databases at rest or in motion. (The name *symmetric* refers to the use of the same key, or a simple transform of the key, for encryption and decryption.)

Key distribution and key management are the Achilles' heel of symmetric key encryption strategies. Every sender-receiver pair needs to exchange keys, which means for *n* users in a key exchange system you have $n^2$ key exchanges to manage—and to update when you have to retire one key and replace it with another. With so many keys in motion, it becomes probable that keys may be intercepted and surreptitiously copied in transit, storage, or use. Brute force or other computational techniques can defeat these encryption schemes given sufficient computing resources.

## Asymmetric Key (or Public Key) Cryptography

The asymmetric key (or public key) cryptographic set of algorithms and systems uses one key for encrypting the plaintext, and a very different key for decrypting the resultant ciphertext back to useful plaintext. This typically means that very different algorithms are used to encrypt and decrypt. The strength of asymmetric key cryptography rests on the assertion that it is computationally infeasible to use the encryption key to calculate the decryption key or to use the decryption key to calculate the encryption key, even if the details of the algorithms are known! (Remember Shannon's maxim.) By this, we mean that the amount of supercomputer CPU time, memory, and so forth necessary to run through all of the calculations required to assure a successful break of these keys would take far, far too long. (Some key strength estimator tools express this in terms of thousands of years—or even millions of years—of computing time needed to break the key in question!) As a result, the asymmetric encryption algorithms are often called *trapdoor functions*, in that you can fall down through an open trapdoor, but you cannot fall backup through it!

As you might imagine, the actual mathematics involved in developing an asymmetric key algorithm—and then in trying to prove or assess how "strong" it is—goes well beyond what the typical SSCP needs to have as on-the-job math skills. Just the names of some of these mathematically hard problems alone are daunting: elliptical curves, very large integer factorization, discrete logarithms, and modular exponentiation and multiplication are just a few that are in use today or being implemented in newer cryptosystems.

Public key distribution systems rely on the near impossibility of computing one of a pair of keys given the other. This lets users publish (or make publicly available) one key (the public key) while keeping the corresponding key secret and protected (or private). In the 1970s, several sets of authors worldwide published papers on such *public key exchange protocols*, and in 1994, the Government Communications Headquarters (GCHQ) published papers that showed how its staff, working in secret, had invented many of these same concepts in the early 1970s. (GCHQ fulfills a similar role in the United Kingdom as the NSA does in the United States.)

We'll take a deeper dive into public key infrastructures, and how they have revolutionized the way we keep everything much more secure, later in this chapter.

## Hybrid Cryptosystems

Hybrid cryptosystems use multiple approaches to encrypt and decrypt the plaintext they are protecting. The most common hybrid systems are ones that combine asymmetric and symmetric algorithms. Recall that asymmetric algorithms provide exceptionally strong protection but are compute-intensive; symmetric algorithms use much less compute power (and are thus more runtime efficient) but are vulnerable to attacks against their keys. This leads to using

- *Key encapsulation* processes, which are typically built with public key infrastructures (PKIs) to handle key exchange
- *Data (or payload) encapsulation* processes, which use more runtime-efficient symmetric key algorithms

Most of the protocols we'll look at use some variation of this approach. As we examine these, keep the OSI protocol stack in mind. Somewhere in that stack, the user, an application, or a lower-level service has to be able to initiate a secure exchange with a host, negotiate with that host, control the secure session's exchange of information, and then cleanly terminate the session. The protocols we'll examine in some detail support these tasks.

## Design and Use of Cryptosystems

So far, we've been focusing primarily on using cryptosystems to protect information in transit—messages exchanged between two parties. As you saw in an earlier chapter, we need to protect information while it is at rest, whether on our own computer systems, those at a service bureau, or in a public cloud provider's systems. Encrypting that stored copy of the information protects it over *time*—what we strongly encrypt and store today is still encrypted weeks or years from now and quite probably has not been compromised. The design and effective operation of such cryptosystems has played a powerful role in the explosive growth of cloud computing (for without effective cryptographic security, everything in the cloud would effectively be public knowledge!).

## Cryptanalysis (White Hat and Black Hat)

*Cryptanalysis* is the science of analyzing encryption systems, plaintext, and ciphertext to determine the relative strength and weaknesses of those systems. Cryptanalysis also refers to using analytical techniques to break an encryption system—that is, to allow for the recovery of and access to the plaintext without properly authorized use of the decryption keys and algorithms. Recall that the *white hats* are people working with us, with our knowledge and consent, to help us make our systems more secure and resilient; the *black hats* are any unauthorized persons or entities that try to access our systems and the information in them. White hat cryptanalysis can help pinpoint weaknesses in key generation, key management and distribution, or even in the algorithms themselves. This might lead us to redesign these systems and processes or to provide other processes to reduce the risk of harm if we cannot affordably strengthen our cryptosystems. Black hats may use many of the same tools and techniques and read many of the same technical journals, wiki pages, and books that the white hats depend on as they try to find and exploit vulnerabilities in our cryptosystems and their use. Motivation and authorization are the only significant things that separate these two sets of cryptanalysts.

## Cryptographic Primitives

In most fields of study, and in most systems engineering practice, primitives are the basic building blocks that are used in design, development, testing, analysis and use of such systems. *Cryptographic primitives* are mathematical or other elements that exhibit some kind of cryptographic property in ways that can relate to real cryptographic problems. Much of the theoretical work being done in cryptography is done with these cryptographic primitives. Cryptographic primitives become the building blocks from which we design and build complex, powerful, and practical cryptographic systems. It is interesting to see how some of these cryptographic primitives compare to problems at the heart of other sciences (such as genetics or quantum physics). Mathematical functions such as one-way functions, and pseudorandom functions are often part of the study of cryptographic primitives. And as we've seen in other areas of information systems security, our use of this term is not always clean and precise. We sometimes see algorithms referred to as primitives or as complete cryptosystems in their own right.

## Cryptographic Engineering

If the study of cryptographic primitives is about the underlying theory, cryptographic engineering is the science and engineering practice of building, optimizing, deploying, using, and strengthening cryptographic systems. As you've seen, a lot of manipulation of the plaintext is needed to produce strongly encrypted ciphertext, and then more compute capability is needed to decrypt it at the receiving end. Runtime efficiency is the number one reason that the strongest of cryptographic systems—those using asymmetric algorithms—are used sparingly.

One of the biggest and perhaps most urgent problems facing cryptographic engineers is what some companies, such as IBM, call *pervasive cryptography*. Pervasive cryptography seeks to keep the data fully encrypted throughout its creation, data quality, transport, storage, retrieval, use, display, and disposal. It also seeks to protect data against threats like covert paths or aggregation—especially when the human mind is in the middle of those potential threats.

# "Why Isn't All of This Stuff Secret?"

At this point, you might be thinking that if we use cryptography to protect our deepest, darkest, and most vital secrets, then shouldn't everything about cryptography *itself* be a deep, dark, and vital secret? Well, yes and no.

It may seem hard to reconcile publishing virtually every detail of modern cryptography with the traditional view that encryption technologies and keying materials were some of the most potent secrets a nation could have. It's not that long ago that famous espionage cases involving the sale or wrongful disclosure of such crypto-secrets were making headlines, after all. People have been hung, faced firing squads, or are spending multiple life sentences in maximum security for such crimes of espionage. How, then, can the *government* have open, public debate about the subtle mathematical nuances of cryptographic algorithms, or have challenge contests that seek new approaches (or new hacks against current ones)? Several important changes in the last few decades have combined to make this change in attitude, practice, and perception happen:

- Cryptography draws its strength from the underlying sciences it is based on—set theory, discrete math, information theory, and operations research, to name but a few. These are widely known and have been written about, published, debated, and discussed across the world. Every human society has been studying these fields, and most of those societies have then applied them to the problem of keeping information secret and safe. The algorithms—the basic cryptographic primitives—are too much a part of the ways that humans think and learn just about *everything*. This is what Kerckhoff (and later Shannon) meant; the internals of your cryptographic systems and algorithms have already been discovered by others, independent of your efforts and despite your wish to keep them secret. The genie of cryptographic knowledge, you might say, isn't going back into the secret bottle any time soon.

- Despite this, governments have throughout history attempted to criminalize the private or nongovernment-sponsored use of cryptography by businesses or individuals. In some countries, using "secret writing" was considered prima fascia evidence of intent to commit espionage. After World War II, the United States and other NATO countries attempted to restrict the export of cryptographic systems, algorithms, or elements to foreign countries by placing them on the Militarily Critical Technologies List (MCTL). The irony of this, however, was that in many ways, the enemy—largely the Soviet Union and other Communist countries—already had comparable technical expertise and systems; all they needed were the keys to the West's systems.

- In the mid-1970s, several forces in the marketplace collided to make further restriction of cryptography almost impossible. The convergence of landline telephone systems, computer systems, computer networks, and even mobile telephony made it plain that the average American was already "transmitting in code" whenever they used touch-tone or encoded text messages in ASCII (or other character sets). (This had been criminalized by the passage of the Communications Act of 1934, after law enforcement's painful experiences with organized crime's use of encrypted radio to coordinate the smuggling of alcohol during Prohibition. Women working at NSA's forerunner organization were the front line of cryptologic law enforcement during this time.) By the 1980s, the trend was inescapable: hobbyists, college students, entrepreneurs, and of course businesses large and small were using encryption in big ways. Finally, the number of published papers and conference proceedings that described systems like public key infrastructures, asymmetric encryption algorithms, and digital signatures forced a decision. If the United States (and other NATO countries) would hamstring their own communications and computing industries by tightly restricting their export of cryptographic products, those industries would lose customers to other nations who had no such export restrictions in place. With the death of *key escrow* and legally mandated trapdoors in commercial encryption products (in the U.S. market only), the market's mandate had been heard loud and clear.

Finally, we have to consider the equally explosive growth in two distinct populations—the black hat cryptographers and the white hat ones. By the middle 1970s and the end of the Vietnam War, there were perhaps 10,000 people in the United States and its NATO allies who we could say were cryptologists—who knew how all of this stuff worked, and who could build and defend cryptosystems as a result. Depending on how you count up the adversaries—Communist bloc nations, organized crime, other nonaligned but not very friendly countries—perhaps there were two or three times that number of black hats. Today? Estimates vary widely, but it would not be a stretch to say that there are *millions* of white hat cryptographers, from students and hobbyists to government scientists, from businesspeople to academics, and there are probably twice that many black hats out there.

Millions of minds talk, share, write, publish, blog, and post what they learn. This incredibly powerful open peer review capability is what finds the vulnerabilities and shares that knowledge with all who need to quickly work around the next zero day exploit based on a cryptographic weakness.

That's probably the best reason to keep everything but the keys themselves public, open, and published.

---

 **Real World Scenario**

**What's Still "Classified" in the E-Voting Project?**

Part of the requirements for any public-facing project is that it must clearly communicate how the public's concerns are protected, especially when that involves ostensibly private information about individual citizens. In particular, since most democracies pride themselves on having *secret* ballots, with no official record made of how each voter actually votes, the issues of accountability, recounts, and voter fraud are lightning rods for public concern and journalistic exposure and debate.

How would you address this? What would your information classification guide look like for this project? How would you use it to assure the public that their secrets remain safe, yet fraudsters and ghosts cannot vote? And how do you make such a "reveal" to the public without revealing too much to would-be attackers?

---

# Cryptography and CIANA

Some of the applications of cryptography to the five tenets of information security are easy to recognize; others may not be. We'll go into these in greater detail in a bit, but for now, let's explore these important uses of cryptography. We'll do this starting from the most obvious uses and proceed to those that might not come to mind so readily.

## Confidentiality

Suitably encrypting cleartext information makes it difficult for unauthorized readers to view, understand, or use the meaning contained in that plaintext. Encrypting information provides for its confidentiality at rest or in motion. If the information must be decrypted for use, other means must be employed to protect the information where and when it is in use.

# Authentication

As you recall from Chapter 5, any request by a subject (be that a person or a process) for access to or use of an information asset needs to be authenticated. We must be able to prove that the subject is who (or what) they claim to be, and then compare that to our controlled and protected lists or rosters of capabilities and privileges. In almost all circumstances, doing so requires the subject to send credentialing information of some kind to our systems; while in transit, that information can be intercepted for later reuse by an otherwise unauthorized subject. It can also be altered while in transit. Credentialing information is also stored (in some form) by subjects and by our authentication systems; encrypting that stored information provides protection at rest.

We don't have to decrypt the credentials in order to validate that they are correct. If our authentication system stores *only* the encrypted (ciphertext) versions of the credentials, then a simple comparison of the ciphertext sent by the subject to the ciphertext kept on file validates or invalidates the identity of the subject. This use of digital signatures in their ciphertext form provides information protection while in use.

# Integrity

Every communications or information storage technology is subject to error, and yet every purpose for which we use communication and information requires that information to be as error-free as possible. This fact has led to developing error detection and correction techniques—adding a parity bit to each byte or calculating a checksum digit for a block of symbols, for example. As data blocks (or messages or files) get larger and larger, error correction code (ECC) must become more complex if it is to comprehensively provide information integrity assurance. ECC can identify where an error in the associated data has occurred—which bit got flipped from a 1 to a 0, or which symbol was changed into another symbol—and then show us what the correct bit or symbol ought to be. ECC works by having the sender calculate the ECC ciphertext value of the message, transmitting it along with the message content (in plaintext). The receiver calculates their own ECC ciphertext value, using the same agreed-to protocol or algorithm for that ECC process, and compares it to the ECC sent with the message. Differences in sent and received ECC can then be used to find and fix the error (often by notifying the sender to resend the block).

We use different names to refer to this use of cryptography to protect (or validate) the integrity of information, whether that information is at rest, in transit, or in use:

- *Hashing* is the general process of using an algorithm to compute a smaller, unique value that represents the contents of the plaintext in some way. This hash value can have many uses, depending on our needs. Database systems, for example, often need to take very long strings of text (such as personal names) and *map* or convert them to a logical record number in a file.

- A *digital signature* asserts that the file or message it is associated with is in fact what its name or circumstances claim it to be. Digital signatures attest to the integrity of software distribution files, for example. Digital signatures can be generated using hash algorithms or more complex encryption techniques; recipients then use the same agreed-to algorithms to validate that the signature and the file agree with each other.

## Nonrepudiation

As you saw in Chapter 5, we often need to be able to block any attempts to deny that somebody took an action, sent a message, or agreed to something in a document. Virtually every transaction in business, and many interpersonal transactions, depend on being able to prove that both parties to the transaction actually participated in it. (Imagine trying to buy a house, and having the seller claim that they never agreed to the signed offer and acceptance contract!) Nonrepudiation provides us all the confidence that having reached an agreement, one party or another cannot back away from the agreement by claiming that they never agreed to it. In most cases, this requires building a set of evidence that attests to the transaction or the agreement, the identity of the parties involved, and even to the process they went through to reach agreement. In many nations, business and government agreements are literally bound up with special colored ribbons, riveted fasteners, and seals so that visibly and physically the agreement and all of its supporting evidence are in one package. This package can be audited, placed in protected storage (such as an official records office), and used as evidence if the parties have to seek enforcement or relief in a court of law.

Generalizing this, we see that nonrepudiation requires that

- The identities of all parties have been authenticated.
- All parties have proven that they have the authority or privilege to participate in the transaction.
- The terms and conditions of the transaction exist in a form that can be recorded.
- All of this information can be collectively or separately verified and validated to be true and correct, free from any attempts to tamper with or alter it.

Nonrepudiation and integrity of information are strongly linked. We believe that the bank notes or coins we spend are *legal tender*, able to be lawfully used to pay for goods and services, because we believe in the integrity of the coins and paper notes themselves and that the issuing government won't turn around and say, "Those are no longer valid."

## "But I Didn't Get That Email..."

Let's consider one of the most common examples of the failure to provide reliable nonrepudiation—the use of typical email systems. Although email protocols provide ways for senders and recipients to exchange delivery and read receipts, these fail in nearly all circumstances to provide any proof that what one party claims was sent in an email was received and opened by the intended recipients. Within an organization (that is, when on a single, unified email server), delivery and read receipts are somewhat reliable, but no one relies on them as legally acceptable evidence or proof. It's also trivially easy for senders or recipients to edit the email after it's been sent or received, falsifying address, delivery, or content information in the process. Recipients can easily claim that they never received the email in question, and this lack of verified receipt and viewing of an email can give rise to deception or fraud.

Postal mail systems have long used registered and certified mail delivery processes to provide legally acceptable proof that a letter or package sent by one party to another was in fact delivered to the recipient and received by them. These processes require proof of identification of sender and recipient, and in the case of certified mail they record every step along the delivery path. Courts of law have long recognized that these processes, and similar ones offered by private document or package courier companies, provide acceptable evidence of delivery and receipt. Of course, the U.S. Postal Service cannot prove that the envelope containing the letter was opened, or that the letter was read or understood by the addressee—but by denying the opportunity to claim "I never received that letter," many contract disputes or simple misunderstandings can be quickly resolved.

There are several examples of commercial service providers that offer something conceptually similar to registered mail for email and e-documents. Many national postal authorities around the world have started to offer these "registered email" services to their individual, business, and government customers. The European Union set standards in place via the European Electronic Commerce Directive 2000/31/EC, for example, which specifies the technical standards such proof-of-receipt systems must meet so as to provide legally acceptable evidence of delivery and receipt. One of these systems, provided by RPost, uses a number of cryptographic techniques to provide these capabilities. The U.S. Department of Defense and other NATO nations have long used proprietary systems to ensure that when electronic messages are sent by one command to another, or to a subordinate unit, the recipient cannot ignore that message simply by claiming that "we never got that order." These systems, too, make extensive use of cryptographic techniques. Key to all of these systems is that strong identity verification, authentication, and information integrity protection measures must work together.

 The vast majority of emails sent every day are sent in the clear—with no attempt to protect their content from being snooped by hackers, neighbors, your employers, or your government.

## Availability

We assess the availability of an information system (in security terms) at two levels:

- Is the *system* itself, and the services it provides, available and ready to perform when subjects (users or processes at their behest) request objects or other services?

- Is the information needed by the user or requesting subject available when needed, and can it be completely and correctly output, displayed, or provided to that user or subject?

You've already seen how cryptography supports both of these functional needs by providing for stronger authentication and information integrity control systems. Cryptography directly contributes to making the requested information available where it is needed, when it is needed, without compromise or loss of integrity. This offers protection for information at rest and in motion.

Cryptography also contributes to overall systems availability, typically as a component of strong access controls. It prevents or limits resources being exhausted (as in a denial of service attack) and can protect key systems functions by making it much harder for unauthorized subjects to perform disruptive actions.

 **Real World Scenario**

### CIANA and E-Voting

You're still working on the city's e-voting and e-registration systems design concepts. Your project manager at the City Election Commissioner's office asks how you can summarize the needs for information security and information risk management that this project has to face. CIANA clearly jumps to your mind.

How have your initial user stories and information classification ideas evolved as you've gone further into this project? Update those to reflect a stakeholder-friendly CIANA-style audit of the issues, risks, and recommendations.

What bottom lines does that bring you to?

### Classical vs. Modern Cryptography

As mentioned previously, most of the cryptographic algorithms used prior to the dawn of the computer age relied on alphabetic substitution and transposition to encrypt human-readable plaintext messages. Since most of these messages were in words and sentences, written in a particular human language, they were subject to attacks based on known statistical information about the language being used. For example, the letter "e" is the most frequently used letter in English; thus, you could look at ciphertext and possibly guess that the most frequently occurring symbol was an encrypted "e." Similarly, pattern recognition could be used as part of an attack.

In World War II, the British built upon earlier work by Polish mathematicians and cryptographers to break the Enigma encryption used by Nazi Germany and Fascist Italy, in part because most of the radio intercepts showed very similar blocks of ciphertext at their start and end. Guessing that this might be standard salutations (like "Heil Hitler!"), date/time stamps or even weather forecast information allowed Alan Turing's team of cryptanalysts to dramatically narrow down their search through the space of all possible ciphertexts. Human language also contains many redundancies, which mean that small errors in the original plaintext may not confound the meaning of the message—and just as likely, small errors made in decrypting the ciphertext (by authorized or unauthorized recipients) may still allow the intended meaning to be understood.

These lexically derived cryptographic algorithms have little ability to deal with the fact that many messages written by humans for other humans to read exhibit strong statistical patterns. The first paragraph in this sidebar, for example, is by no means a random string of letters or words. The phrase "used prior to" is most likely going to be followed by a phrase that asserts or suggests a period of time, for example. Google Translate and other machine translation systems work on this same statistical principle.

Before you dismiss the study of classical cryptography from your mind, consider that someone may in fact be using them as part of their attacks on your systems, or as part of their data exfiltration efforts, simply because they aren't sophisticated enough techniques to be a credible threat. You should also consider that many software developers attempt to protect sensitive data by using simple, symmetric encryption embedded in their source code—often with the keys plainly visible in that code! You won't be tested on the Caesar, Vigenère, or Saint-Cyr Slide algorithms when you take your SSCP exam, but thinking about how these ciphers work may sharpen your mind regardless.

# Public Key Infrastructures

Three main factors separate the modern from the classical era of cryptography. The first is the switch from lexical analysis as the focus of cryptography to computationally hard problems—problems that are fairly easy to compute in one direction (given an $x$, find the corresponding $y$), but very difficult if not impossible to do in the reverse (given that $y$, find the $x$ that would generate it). The second is the near-simultaneous development, in the United States and United Kingdom, of what have been called *public key exchange protocols*. The third and perhaps most significant factor has been the explosive growth in the population of cryptographers. Before this time, perhaps tens of thousands of people around the world made up this community and were working directly for military and intelligence cryptographic programs; a very small number of academics and theorists published a few papers on the topic. As the 1980s arrived, this community of amateur and professional cryptographers just kept growing. Estimates are very difficult to make, but today this community must number in the millions of people, black hats and white hats included. Add to that the number of people involved in peer review of open source systems and software for operating systems, browsers, applications programs, *and* cryptography, and Kerckhoff's and Shannon's observations about the enemy knowing your system seem all the more prescient!

One other revolution must be recognized in terms of its effects on cryptographic algorithm design the personal computer revolution. Personal computing provided the market demand for millions of powerful graphics processing units (GPUs) as well as for far more powerful central processing units (CPUs). When a million consumers are willing to spend an extra hundred dollars or so on the price of a home computer, suddenly there's a market advantage in having machines that can smoothly draw screens for classic games like Flight Simulator. GPUs are designed to take massive streams of data, perform the same kinds of repetitive manipulations on them, and stream the results quickly and efficiently, which provides graphics rendering necessary to take compressed video and render it to the screen smoothly. These same capabilities are useful in cryptanalysis, whether done by the white hats when designing new algorithms and cryptosystems or by the black hats while trying to attack them. Breaking modern cryptographic systems—*when they are correctly and effectively used and maintained*—still seems to be the province of the well-funded adversary. Millions of CPU cycles (and GPU cycles) might be out there for the taking, but the storage needed to keep huge rainbow tables, precomputed salts, and such is expensive, no matter where you find it.

Perhaps the biggest surprise, also in the 1970s, was that bastions of secrecy like the NSA saw the need to encourage public review, discussion, analysis, and debate about cryptography, leading to public competitions for new algorithms and systems concepts. Public key exchange and asymmetric algorithms, for example, became the new fundamental building blocks of cryptography, primarily because they were published, debated, and analyzed, and they competed against other ideas, new and old.

So while the modern cryptographic *era* is one of publish or perish, peer review, and widespread, global competition of ideas and their implementation, it's the technical factors that mark the change from classical to modern cryptography. These factors led to the widespread adoption of hybrid approaches to cryptography, which are what make *public key encryption*, *public key infrastructures*, and our modern e-commerce world possible.

## Diffie-Hellman-Merkle Public Key Exchange

One of the most vexing questions in cryptography has been how to establish secure, encrypted communication between two parties who have no previous knowledge of each other. In effect, this is about proving identity (of both parties) as well as jointly authorizing each other to participate in the session that's about to take place. One important distinction must be recognized at the start: key exchange is not about exchanging secret information between the parties; rather, it is about *creating* a shared key to use for subsequent encrypted sharing of secrets. Furthermore, it's important to realize that the "public" part of public key exchange is that you can quite literally publish parts of that key exchange without compromising the security of the encryption it supports. Whitfield Diffie and Martin Hellman, in a 1976 article published in *IEEE Transactions on Information Theory*, first showed that public key exchange requires the use of what they called *trapdoor functions*—a class of mathematical problems that are easy to do in one direction (like falling through a trapdoor in the floor) but extremely difficult if not impossible to do in the other direction.

---

### Distribution, Exchange, or Infrastructure?

It's important to keep the distinction between *key distribution* and *key exchange* clearly in mind, and then add the "secret sauce" that scales an exchange or distribution process up into an *infrastructure*:

- Classical cryptographic systems depend upon key *distribution* systems to ensure that all known, authenticated, and trustworthy parties on the system have current encryption keys. Key distribution is the passing of secret information—the keys—from the key originator and controller to the parties who will use it.

- Key exchange systems start with the presumption that parties do not know each other, and have no a priori reason to trust each other. They achieve this trust, and therefore can share in a secure, encrypted conversation, by *generating* their session key together, and keeping that session key secret to themselves.

In both cases, the underlying key *infrastructure* is the collection of systems, communications pathways, protocols, algorithms, and processes (people-facing or built into software and hardware) that make key distribution *or* exchange work effectively and reliability.

---

Let's start with a simple illustration. Suppose Bob and Carol wish to establish their own encrypted Internet connection with each other. Here's what happens:

1. Bob and Carol choose a suitable trapdoor function; they choose the key parameters that they will use. What they agree on can be shared in open, unsecured email with each other.

2. Carol chooses her private key and keeps it secret; she uses the trapdoor function to calculate her public key, which she sends to Bob. (Anyone can see her public key. More on this in a moment.) Bob, too, chooses a private key and uses the same trapdoor function to calculate his public key and sends that to Carol.

3. Carol applies the trapdoor function to Bob's public key, using her own private key; call the result the session key. Carol keeps this secret; she doesn't have to send it to Bob, and she shouldn't!

4. Bob applies the same trapdoor function to Carol's public key, using his own private key. This produces the same session key by the magic of the mathematics of the chosen trapdoor function. (The proof is left to the mathematically inclined reader.)

5. Carol and Bob now share a new secret, the session key. This key can be used with an appropriate (and agreed to) symmetric encryption algorithm so that Bob and Carol can exchange information with each other and keep others from being able to read it.

What about Eve, sitting along the sidelines of this conversation? Suppose Eve is, well, eavesdropping on Bob and Carol's key exchange; she somehow is trapping packets going back and forth and recognizes that they've agreed to an algorithm and its control parameters; she recognizes the exchange of Bob's and Carol's public keys for what it is. As long as Eve does not have a secret key that participated in the computation of the session key, she does not have anything that lets her read the traffic that Bob and Carol encrypt with the session key. Eve is left to using brute force, side channel, or other attacks to attempt to break the session encryption.

Ted, on the other hand, is someone Bob and Carol want to include in a three-way secure conversation (still keeping Eve out in the cold, of course). The process shown in steps 1 through 5 can easily be expanded to include three or more parties who share the choices about algorithms and parameters, and who then compute their own public keys and share them; they then use everybody else's public keys to compute their own copy of the session key.

Obviously, this simplified description of the Diffie-Hellman key exchange process has some vulnerabilities. (We note that since 2002, Hellman asked this be known as Diffie-Hellman-Merkle, to recognize Ralph Merkle's foundational work in 1972 that paved the way for Diffie and Hellman's work four years later.) It doesn't actually authenticate that Bob is Bob, or Carol is Carol, thus tempting Ted to be the "man in the middle" who masquerades as the other party from the initial handshake and key generation through to the end of the session. The choice of trapdoor function, and the control values for it, can also present exploitable vulnerabilities. But in its simplest form, this is where the public key infrastructure (PKI) got its start.

Building a public key infrastructure starts with the algorithms used to generate the shared secret keys used to establish trustworthy communications. Those algorithms have to be implemented in some combination of software and hardware, and made available to users to incorporate into their systems or use as stand-alone messaging apps. These apps themselves, and the software and hardware distribution channels (wholesale, retail, original equipment manufacturer [OEM], or other) all have to be part of a network of trust relationships, if two end users are going to trust such apps to protect their communication with each other. So the problem of building a public key infrastructure must also embrace the problem of updating trusted software (and hardware) distribution.

Let's start by looking at the hybrid encryption systems components of such a public key exchange infrastructure; then we'll look at some of the protocols that are part of scaling such an infrastructure up to global levels of acceptance and use.

---

### Bob, Carol, and *Who*?

Many books, lectures, papers, and presentations on cryptography, cybersecurity, and information assurance revolve around four hypothetical actors, who take their names from the 1969 movie *Bob & Carol & Ted & Alice*. Typical of the era, this film focused on wife-swapping, and thus on lies, deceit, secrets shared, and secrets compromised. Much like the *Mad Magazine* characters in its near-trademark "Spy vs. Spy" cartoon strip (by Antonio Prohías, first in 1961, and still in print!) and their iconic white and black wardrobes, its character names and their roles became stereotypes for many things—including the good, the bad, and the bystanders in information security. We do not recommend any of these characters as role models, nor offer any speculation as to why they became the traditional placeholders in information security examples.

## RSA Encryption and Key Exchange

Immediately after Diffie and Hellman published their article in 1976, two MIT computer scientists, Ron Rivest and Adi Shamir, teamed with MIT mathematician Leonard Adleman and set out to create a suitable trapdoor or one-way function for use in a public key exchange process. These three focused on both an algorithm (based on modular exponentiation) as well as a process by which users could authenticate themselves, hence eliminating the risk of the man-in-the-middle attack. As is typical in the scientific and technical literature, they named the algorithm after themselves (Rivest-Shamir-Adleman or RSA). The three authors founded RSA Security, Inc., in 1982, and MIT was granted a U.S. patent in 1983 that used the RSA algorithm. Prior publication in 1973 by Clifford Cocks in the United Kingdom of very similar concepts precluded patenting RSA in other countries, and had that publication by Cocks been known, it would have invalidated even the U.S. patent (it was not disclosed by GCHQ until 1997). RSA later released the algorithm into the public domain in September 2000.

Like Diffie-Hellman, RSA uses the properties of modulo arithmetic applied to exponentiation of very large integers, where the modulus is also a very large prime number. Prior to the 1990s, the compute power needed to perform such operations (just to create the keys) was substantial, and the compute power necessary to break such algorithms was thought to be unaffordable by even the security services of major nation-states.

The founders of RSA did spend most of the 1980s and 1990s in what can only be called a pitched battle with the NSA and the White House. As this was during the heart of the Cold War and the Reagan-Bush defense buildup, it's not surprising that the government saw any widespread use of powerful encryption by *anybody* as a threat to national security. (It still sees that threat, particularly since anybody can be a terrorist, while in the same breath it knows that our modern digital economy cannot function without widespread public use of highly secure encryption.) This history in and of itself is worth your time and study, as an SSCP and as a citizen, but it is beyond the scope of this book and the SSCP exam.

## ElGamal Encryption

First described by Taher ElGamal in 1985, this asymmetric encryption algorithm is based on the mathematical theory of cyclic groups and the inherent difficulties in computing discrete logarithms in such groups. Borrowing from Diffie-Hellman-Merkle key exchange concepts, ElGamal provides for asymmetric encryption of keys previously used in symmetric encryption schemes. ElGamal also proposed a digital signature mechanism that allows third parties to confirm the authenticity of a message signed with it; this signature mechanism is not widely used today, but it did lead NSA to develop its Digital Signature Algorithm (DSA) as part of the Digital Signature Standard (DSS). DSS was adopted as FIPS 186 in 1996, and has undergone four revisions since then. (Don't confuse DSA with ElGamal signature schemes.)

Some hybrid encryption systems use ElGamal to encrypt the symmetric keys used to encrypt message content. It is vulnerable to the chosen-ciphertext attack, in which the attacker somehow tricks or spoofs a legitimate user (an *oracle*) into decrypting an arbitrary message block and then sharing those results with the attacker. (Variations on this kind of attack were first known as *lunchtime attacks*, since the user's machine was assumed to be available while they were at lunch.) ElGamal does provide padding and other means to limit this vulnerability.

ElGamal encryption is used in the GNU Privacy Guard system (GPG), which we'll look at in concert with PGP in a moment.

## Digital Signatures

Publication of RSA also led to widespread understanding, and later implementation, of digital signatures as an important application of cryptography. Suppose our friend Carol wishes to send a message to Bob, but in doing so, she needs to prove to Bob that the message is inarguably from her and not from some imposter:

1. Carol produces a strong hash of the message content.

2. Carol decrypts that hash value, using the trapdoor function and her private key. This new value is her digital signature.

3. Carol sends the message and her digital signature to Bob.

4. Bob encrypts Carol's digital signature, using the same trapdoor algorithm and Carol's public signature, to produce the signed hash value.

5. Bob uses the same hash function to produce a comparison hash of the message he received (not including the signature). If this matches the value he computed in step 4, he has proven that Carol (who is the only one who knows her private key) is the only one who could have sent that message.

In 1985, Taher Elgamal published a paper that argued for a public key infrastructure and signature scheme based on discrete logarithms. The ElGamal discrete logarithm cryptosystem and ElGamal signature scheme became important drivers for the National Institute of Standards and Technology's (NIST's) development of the Digital Signature Algorithm (DSA), which then became the centerpiece of NIST's Digital Signature Standard (DSS) in 2013. What took so long, you might ask?

## Digital Certificates and Certificate Authorities

The decade of the 1990s created the conditions in which the next major step forward in public key infrastructures became necessary. By January 1991, the world's first Web server was turned on, culminating the work by Tim Berners-Lee, with the strong support of Robert Cailliau and others, and it introduced the world to HTTP and HTML. Secure HTTP was developed in 1993 (originally named S-HTTP and later changed to HTTPS). By 1994, it was already becoming clear that millions of average, technically unsophisticated users around the world were ready to take personal interests and business online in a really big way. Many experts and governments could easily see the need for an infrastructure that supported all of the CIANA attributes, if *electronic commerce* (a new word in the 1990s) was to become a profitable, safe, and secure reality.

As Diffie-Hellman's own work suggested, growing a particular public key exchange *circle of trust* beyond just a few users needs a lot of work! Netscape is credited with inventing the Secure Sockets Layer (SSL) protocol, which defined the key elements of this new infrastructure, in 1994. It went through several iterations before its shortcomings led to the creation of TLS, described in more depth in the accompanying sidebar.

---

### SSL, TLS, or HTTPS?

Try to research why the name of this protocol family went from SSL to TLS, and you find an interesting array of opinions and assertions but little in the way of demonstrable fact. One argument, put forth by Tim Dierks in 2014, says that the Internet Engineering Task Force (IETF) "had to make some changes to SSL 3.0 so it wouldn't look [like] the IETF was just rubberstamping Netscape's protocol...and thus was born TLS 1.0. And now, of course, in retrospect, the whole thing looks silly."

Another point to keep in mind is that HTTPS actually says "use HTTP over secure sockets," which either meant "over SSL" or "over TLS," depending on whom you ask and when.

The bottom line is that one "S"—*secure* or *security*—is what matters. So if you know how HTTPS works, you know how TLS plays its role in that, and you know how SSL used to do the same.

SSL is still in use around the world, although it's been proven to have some serious vulnerabilities. As an SSCP, if you're confronted with users who still use it, get them to move to TLS!

---

## Hierarchies (or Webs) of Trust

We now have some of the major building blocks to provide for trustworthy distribution of the software (and hardware) elements of a public encryption system. Before we can start building an infrastructure with them, we first need to look more closely at what "trustworthy" means and how we establish this sense of trust, share it with others, and encourage strangers to trust each other—or at least, trust enough to communicate with them.

You first must recognize that a trust relationship between two parties is actually the sum of two one-way trust relationships: Bob *confers his trust* upon Carol, and Carol confers her trust upon Bob, which we observe by saying "Bob and Carol trust each other." (If you think that looks like a grant of privilege from Bob to Carol, you're right!) A *transitive trust relationship* occurs when Carol trusts Alice, and so therefore because Bob trusts Carol, he now also trusts Alice. And since Alice trusts Ted, Bob and Carol each trust Ted. Thus a transitive chain of trust is created. (If Ted trusts Alice, but chooses not to trust Bob, you can see that the Web or mesh of trust relationships can get. . .murky.) Strictly speaking, these are peer-to-peer trust relationships, as no one person in this group is the designated or accepted authority regarding trustworthiness.

Conversationally, we talk about chains of trust, webs of trust, and hierarchies of trust. Implicit in each of these ideas is the notion that those trust architectures have some "coin of the realm," some agreed-to set of ideas, messages, data, or other things that are both the token of that trust and what is being exchanged in a trustworthy fashion. Money, for example, is exchanged as a token (a representation) of both value and of trust.

In information and communications systems terms, the foremost token of trust is a *certificate* that asserts that the identity of the certificate holder and the public key associated with that certificate are linked or bound with each other. This gives rise to two different concepts of how trust conferred by one node upon another can be scaled up to larger numbers of nodes:

- A *hierarchy of trust* exists when a single node is recognized as the authority for asserting or conferring trust. This conferring of trust can be delegated downward (made transitive) by that trust authority conferring a special status to a set of intermediate nodes, each of which can act as a trust authority for other intermediary nodes or end user nodes (recipients of trust), which (in tree structure terms) are the leaf nodes. *The trust anchor* is the trust authority, as the root of this tree of trust, conferring trust downward through any number of intermediaries, to the leaf nodes. Hierarchies of trust resemble forests of trees (in data structure terms!), with one root branching out to start many sub-trees, which may further branch, until finally we reach the *leaf* nodes at the very tip of each twig.

- A *certificate authority (CA)* is the anchor node of a hierarchy of trust, issuing the certificates that bind individual identities with their corresponding public keys.

- A *web of trust* has no designated or accepted single authority for trust, and acts in peer-to-peer fashion to establish chains of trust.

**Trees Grow Down?**

In nature, of course, trees grow from their roots upward; information systems designers, out of habit, start drawing trees by putting the anchor node at the top of the page, and thus grow their digital trees downward.

In both hierarchies of trust and webs of trust, any given node can be a member of one or more trust relationships, and therefore be a member of one or more chains or webs of trust.

In hierarchies of trust, end users, seeking to validate the trustworthiness of a certificate, infer that a certificate from a trusted end (leaf) node is trustworthy if the intermediary who issued it is, on up to the anchor. Webs of trust, by contrast, involve peer-to-peer trust relationships that do not rely on central certificate authorities as the anchors. Hierarchies of trust are much more scalable (to billions of certificates in use) than webs of trust. Both systems have drawbacks and issues, particularly with respect to certificate revocation, expiration, or the failure of a node to maintain trustworthiness. (The details of those issues are beyond the scope of the SSCP exam, but you do need to be aware that these issues exist and are not straightforward.)

TLS, and secure HTTP (HTTPS), require the use of a certificate, granted by a certificate authority (CA). SSL and TLS established what was called the *chain of trust*, shown in Figure 7.4. The chain of trust starts with the CA itself generating a self-signed certificate, called a *root certificate*; this anchors the chain of trust. This root certificate can be used to generate and authenticate any number of intermediate certificates, which can also be used to authenticate (sign) other intermediate certificates. The end-entity, or end-user certificate, is the distant end of the chain of trust; it authenticates the end user's identity and is signed by an intermediate certificate issuer (or, hypothetically, it could be signed by the root authority). End-entity or *leaf* certificates (borrowing from tree structure terminology) are terminal—they cannot be used to sign other certificates of any kind.

**FIGURE 7.4**   Chains of trust

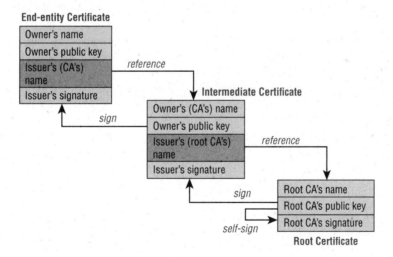

Certificates of this kind allow browsers or other client-side programs to use a certification path validation algorithm, which has to validate that (a) the subject of the certificate matches the host name being connected to, and (b) the certificate is signed by a trusted authority, has not been revoked, and has not expired. Figure 7.5 shows this in simplified form.

**FIGURE 7.5**   Certification path validation algorithm

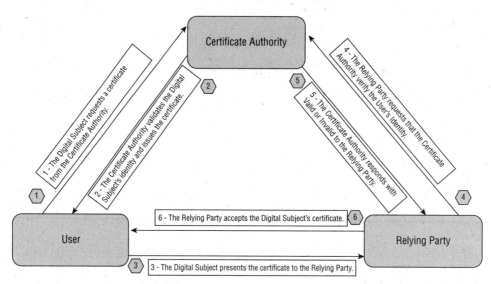

In 2008, the IETF published updated versions of the X.509 standard, which define these certificates and the protocols for their use.

As it turns out, *anyone* can become a self-authenticating certificate authority! This could be very helpful if your organization requires an isolated LAN in which certificate-based services are necessary but all use of those services stays within that LAN, for example. To become part of the world-spanning infrastructure, however, those wishing to become CAs have to have their certificate implementations adopted by the major Web browsers, which means getting their certificates bundled in with Edge, Firefox, Chrome, Safari, or Opera, for example. In fact, one of the key elements of these major vendor root certificate programs is that by becoming a root certificate member with them, your company adds significant value to their user community. CA applicants then have to go through rigorous technical demonstrations of their domains and their services. Each of those vendors has its own standards and processes to ensure that as a would-be CA, your company is not about to harm their reputation or the reputations or interests of their customers, partners, clients, and users worldwide.

What this all boils down to is that if you want to be an anchor of many trust chains, we, the rest of the Internet-using world, really do require that you prove your trustworthiness, your reliability, and your integrity to us. This may be why the four CAs with the largest market share between them are IdenTrust, Comodo, DigiCert, and GoDaddy, according to W3Techs surveys. In 2017, Google and Mozilla rejected Symantec's certificates from their browser bundles, citing numerous repeated violations of trust—including incorrect or unjustified issuance of over 30,000 HTTPS certificates. Some of this involved issuing free "domain validated" certificates, thought to be a great way to stimulate further small business development; in reality, it made it trivially easy for malicious sites to spring into action, typically with phishing attacks on unsuspecting targets. Prior to this, Symantec had been the market leader; that same year, DigiCert acquired Symantec.

The certificate validation process also demonstrates another important aspect of cybersecurity and cryptography that SSCPs must deal with every day: every system your organization uses is the result of an information technology supply chain, a chain that runs from designers and developers, through subsystems vendors and parts suppliers, to end-user sales and service, and then into your own organization's technology support staff. Every step of that process is a potential opportunity for threats to find vulnerabilities and exploit them. In fact, one definition of an advance persistent threat is that it is an organization or entity that looks at as much of the IT supply chain as it possibly can, seeking points of entry or influence.

## Pretty Good Privacy

In much the same timeframe in which Rivest, Shamir, and Adleman were battling with the U.S. government over making powerful encryption available to private citizens, businesses, and others, another battle started to rage over a software package called Pretty Good Privacy. PGP had been created by Phil Zimmerman, a long-time antinuclear activist, in 1991; he released it into the wild via friend who posted it in Usenet and on Peacenet, which was an ISP that focused on supporting various grass-roots political and social movements around the world. Almost immediately, the government realized that PGP's use of 128-bit (and larger) encryption keys violated the 40-bit limit established for *export of munitions* as defined in the Militarily Critical Technologies List; the government began a criminal investigation of Zimmerman, his associates, and PGP. Zimmerman then published the source code of PGP and its underlying symmetric encryption algorithm (the Bassomatic) in book form (via MIT Press), which was protected as free speech under the First Amendment of the U.S. Constitution. By 1996, the government backed down, and did not bring criminal charges against Zimmerman.

PGP uses a web of trust concept, but does embody a concept of key servers that can act as a decentralized mesh of repositories and clearinghouses. Its design provides not only for encryption of data in motion, but also for data at rest.

Initially, PGP as a software product allowed end users to encrypt any content, whether that was a file or the body of an email message. Various distributions used different encryption algorithms, such as ElGamal, DSA, and CAST-128. The designs and source code of PGP have moved through a variety of commercial products, including the z/OS encryption facility for the IBM Z mainframe computer family.

Described by some as being "the closest you're likely to get to military-grade encryption," as of this writing there do not seem to be known methods, computational or cryptographic, for breaking PGP encryption. Wikipedia and other sources cite a 2006 case in which U.S. Customs agents could not break PGP-encrypted content, suspected to be child pornography, on a laptop they had seized. A bug in certain implementations of PGP was discovered in May 2018, which under certain circumstances could lead to disclosing the plaintext associated with a given ciphertext of emails encrypted by these email variants.

Since its inception, PGP has evolved in several directions. It still is available in various free software and open source distributions; it's also available in a variety of commercial product forms.

## OpenPGP

A variety of efforts are underway to bring PGP and its use of different algorithms into an Internet set of standards. Some of these standards support the use of PGP by email clients; others look to specify the encryption suites used by PGP in different implementations. RFC 4880 is the main vehicle for change within the IETF for bringing PGP into the formally accepted Internet baseline. There is also work ongoing to develop a PGP-compliant open source library of JavaScript routines for use in Web applications that want to use PGP when supported by browsers running the app.

## GPG

GNU Privacy Guard (GPG) is part of the GNU project, which aims to provide users with what the project calls the *four essential freedoms* that software uses should have and enjoy. GPG provides a free and open source implementation of the OpenPGP standard, consistent with RFC 4800. It provides key management and access modules, support for S/MIME and SSH, and tools for easy integration into a variety of applications. It's also available as Gpg4win, which provides GPG capabilities for Microsoft Windows systems, including a plugin for Outlook email.

*Free*, in the context of free software, should be thought of in the same way as *free speech* rather than *free beer*, as explained on https://www.gnu.org/home.en.html. Free software advocates assert that the conflux of corporate and government interests are all too willing to sacrifice individual freedom of choice, including the freedom to speak or to keep something private. Without freely available source code for important infrastructure elements such as GPG and the GNU variant of Linux, they argue, individuals have no real way to know what software to trust or what information and communications they can rely upon. Whether you agree or disagree with their politics, GPG and other free software systems are increasingly becoming common elements in the IT architectures that SSCPs need to support and defend.

It is interesting to note that the German government initially donated 250,000 Deutschmarks (about $132,000) to the development and support of GPG.

## TLS

*Transport Layer Security* (TLS) provides for secure connections, but it's hard to say exactly where in the TCP/IP or OSI protocol stacks it actually sits. It runs on top of the transport layer, and yet it is treated by many applications as if it *is* the transport layer. But applications that use TLS must actively take steps to initiate and control its use. It's also further confusing, since the presentation layer is normally thought to provide encryption services for higher layers (such as the application layer in the OSI model). Perhaps it's best to think of it as providing services at the transport layer and above, as required, and leave it at that. It has largely replaced its predecessor, Secure Sockets Layer (SSL), which was found to be vulnerable to attacks on SSL's block cipher algorithms. (SSL also had this identity problem in terms of which layer of the protocol stack it did or didn't belong to.)

The TLS handshake dictates the process by which a secure session is established:

1. The handshake starts when the client requests a TLS connection to a server, typically on port 443, or uses a specific protocol like STARTTLS when using mail or news protocols.

2. Client and server negotiate what cipher suite (cryptographic algorithms and hash functions) will be used for the session.

3. The server authenticates its identity, usually by using a digital certificate (which identifies the server), the (CA that authenticates that certificate), and provides the client with the server's public encryption key.

4. The client confirms the certificate's validity.

5. Session keys are generated, either by the client encrypting a random number or by using Diffie-Hellman key exchange to securely generate and exchange this random number.

   If any of these steps fail, the secure connection is not created.

6. The session key is used to symmetrically encrypt and decrypt all subsequent data exchanges during this session, until the client or server signals the end of the session.

   The process is shown in Figure 7.6.

**FIGURE 7.6**   TLS handshake

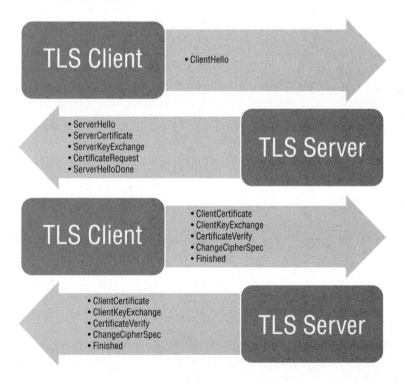

TLS has gone through two revisions since its first introduction, and in creating TLS 1.3, RFC 8446 in August 2018 added significant improvements to TLS. One key set of changes involved strengthening forward secrecy of TLS sessions. *Forward secrecy* (also known as *perfect forward secrecy*) provides for protection of past sessions in the event that the server's private key has been compromised. This protection is ensured by requiring a unique session key for every session a client initiates; in doing so, it offers protection against the Heartbleed exploit that affected SSL and OpenSSL, first reported in 2014. TLS 1.3 also removes support for other cryptographic and hash functions that have proven weak.

The *TLS cipher suite* is the set of cryptographic algorithms used within TLS across its four major operational phases of key exchange and agreement, authentication, block and stream encryption, and message authentication. This suite is updated as older algorithms are shown to be too vulnerable and as new algorithms become adopted by the Internet Engineering Task Force (IETF) and the Web community. As with all algorithms and protocols involving security, the two versions of the TLS cipher suite now in common use, V1 and V1.2, are coming to their end of life. On June 30, 2018, SSL, TLS 1.1, and TLS 1.2 were declared obsolete by the IETF. The major browsers, such as Firefox, Chrome, and Bing, have been phasing them out in favor of their replacements. Be sure to check to see if your organization is using them anywhere. Note that the Payment Card Industry Data Security Standard (PCI DSS) requires use of the new versions, so any credit, debit, or payment processing systems you support may need to be double-checked as well.

# HTTPS

*Hypertext Transfer Protocol Secure* (or HTTPS) is an application layer protocol in TCP/IP and the OSI model; it is simply HTTP (HyperText Transfer Protocol) using TLS (now that SSL is deprecated) to provide secure, encrypted interactions between clients and servers using hypertext. HTTPS is commonly used by Web browser applications. HTTPS provides important benefits to clients and servers alike:

- Authentication of identity, especially of the server's identity to the client
- Privacy and integrity of the data transferred during the session
- Protection against man-in-the-middle attacks that could attempt to hijack an HTTP session
- Simplicity

By building directly on TLS, HTTPS provides for strong encryption of the entire HTTPS session's data content or payload, using the CAs that were preinstalled in the browser by the browser application developer (Mozilla, Microsoft, DuckDuckGo, Apple, etc.). This leads to a hierarchy of trust in which the end user should trust the security of the session only if the following conditions hold true:

- The browser software correctly implements HTTPS.
- Certificates are correctly installed in the browser.
- The CA vouches only for legitimate websites.

- The certificate correctly identifies the website.
- The negotiated encryption sufficiently protects the user's data.

Users should be aware that HTTPS use alone cannot protect everything about the user's Web browsing activities. HTTPS still needs resolvable IP addresses at both ends of the session; even if the content of the session is kept safe, traffic analysis of captured packets may still reveal more than some users wish. Metadata about individual page viewings may also be available for others to sniff and inspect.

## Symmetric Key Algorithms and PKI

There's an elegance to the hybrid cryptographic systems model that should not go unappreciated by the SSCP. On the one hand, we are forced to use hybrid approaches because with any given technology base, we simply do not have enough computing power to affordably encrypt everything we need to protect using end-to-end asymmetric encryption, or get that encryption and decryption done in a reasonable amount of time. On the other hand, if such hardware capabilities did exist, they'd probably be sufficient to turn the computationally infeasible problems of breaking those asymmetric algorithms into easier, more affordable opportunities! Currently, TLS 1.0 through 1.2 support six different block or stream ciphers: RC4, Triple DES, AES, IDEA, DES, and Camellia. RC4 has been proven insecure and is left in TLS to support legacy systems; Camellia has been adopted as the International Data Encryption standard by the International Standards Organization and is similar in security and design to AES. With that in mind, let's take a closer look at DES and AES.

### DES

The Data Encryption Standard (DES) was, and still is, quite controversial. It was the first published and open competition by the U.S. government for a new symmetric key block encryption algorithm. It had elements (the "S-box" circuits) that some claimed NSA had inserted into the design to allow DES-encrypted traffic to be decrypted by NSA without needing the original encryption key; others, in turn, insisted these S-boxes were there to defeat still other back doors built into DES. (To date, no one has been able to convincingly confirm or deny these fears; the disclosure of many NSA secrets by Edward Snowden only reheated this simmering controversy. There were many arguments about the key length, which in IBM's original proposed used 64 bit keys, and which were downsized at NSA's insistence to 56 bits. (The key actually remains 64 bits in length, but since 8 bits are used for parity checking, the effective key length is still 56 bits.) DES was made a U.S. Federal Information Processing Standard in 1977, despite much outcry within the community that it was insecure right from the start.

DES used 16 rounds of processing, and its design reflects the capabilities of 1970s-era hardware. (This was the era of the first 8-bit microprocessors, and most minicomputer architectures had only a 16-bit address space.)

Although many people argued whether DES was in fact breakable, the Electronic Frontier Foundation (EFF) spent $250,000 to build a custom *DES Cracking Machine* to prove their point. It used brute force techniques (trying every possible key) and could break DES encryption in about two days' time.

Significant work was done to try to tighten up DES, including the Triple DES standard published in 1999. But it remained unsecure, and DES in all forms was finally withdrawn as a U.S. government standard in 2002 when superseded by AES.

DES remains important, not because it is secure, but because in the opinion of academics, industry, and government experts, it stimulated the explosive growth of the study of cryptography by those who had no connections at all to the military and intelligence communities and their cryptographers. Even today, it is still worth studying as you begin to understand cryptography, cryptanalysis, and common attack strategies.

## AES

The Advanced Encryption Standard (AES) was published by the U.S. government as FIPS Publication 197 in November 2001. It replaced DES, and although like DES it is a symmetric block encryption algorithm, it is significantly more secure. It remains in widespread use today, usually as part of hybrid encryption systems. NIST ran another open, public competition for a replacement to DES, and the Rijndael (pronounced "rhine-dahl") cipher by Vincent Rijmen and Joan Daeman was selected as the winner. It is the first and only publicly available cipher that is approved by NSA for use on government classified information up through Top Secret when used in an NSA-approved cryptographic module.

AES is a multiple-round algorithm that executes very fast in hardware or software implementations. The number of rounds is in part determined by the size of the key: 10 rounds for 128-bit keys, 12 rounds for 192-bit keys, and 14 rounds for 256-bit keys.

From a math perspective, AES looks pretty simple: nothing but a series of substitutions, permutations, and exclusive ORs, done on rows and columns of matrices in which plaintext and intermediate ciphertext are held. Surprisingly, it has withstood a number of attacks (in theory and in practice).

## PKI and Trust: A Recap

We've looked in some depth at the different piece-parts of the public key infrastructure; let's put them all into a (hopefully!) simple perspective:

- Key exchange processes, such as Diffie-Hellman-Merkle, provide both the architecture and the protocol framework for co-generation of session keys used by two parties to establish secure communications with each other.

- Session keys are then used with symmetric encryption algorithms, such as DES or AES, to provide fast, efficient, and secure communication during the session that they apply to.

- Asymmetric encryption algorithms using trapdoor functions, such as RSA or ElGamal, provide the foundation for generating public and private keys for parties to use in key exchange processes.

- Digital certificates provide digitally signed ways to assert that a given entity's identity and public key are in fact associated (bound) with each other. These certificates can be issued by any node on the Internet or within a system.

- Digital signatures provide highly secure, reliable ways to authenticate that software components (such as encryption suites) and certificates are authentic—that is, that they are in fact issued by the entity that they came from.

- Hierarchies of trust provide a certificate authority (CA) as the source of a top-level assertion of trustworthiness; the CA issues certificates regarding specific parties (and their identity and corresponding public keys) and can delegate certificate issuing authority downward to intermediate nodes. This provides a self-scaling architecture for conferring trust via certificates.

- Endpoint devices use encryption suites to participate in key exchange, enjoy secure communications, and authenticate software, data files, or other components via digital signatures from their originators or providers.

Figure 7.7 summarizes the families of cryptographic algorithms by types, mathematical algorithms, and use. It also gives a quick roundup of the various protocols used in the public key infrastructure and in key management in general. As an SSCP, you're going to need to be on a first-name basis with most if not all of the items shown on this "family tree"—if not for the SSCP exam itself, then certainly out on the job.

**FIGURE 7.7**  Crypto family tree

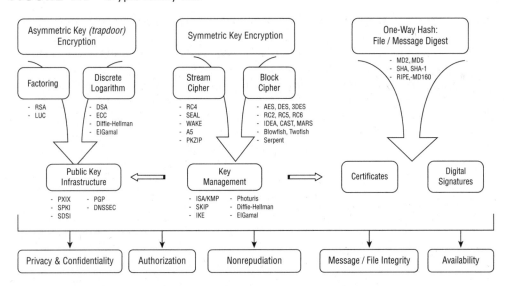

At this point, it's worth considering hierarchies of trust from the end *user's* perspective. Stop for a moment and think about what goes through your mind when you follow a URL to a website you've never visited before. How do you decide just how far you can trust that site's owners and operators? Don Norman and Jakob Nielsen, at NN/g, built on Maslow's Hierarchy of Needs to see this as a journey you go on as you pass from having no trust at all to a willingness to commit to an ongoing, valuable relationship (in whatever domain of activity you are pursuing with that website's owners and operators). At each step of the relationship-building process, they argue, there's the potential that the website's designers (and the business logic it embodies) assume that users are already at higher levels of trust than individual users may actually see themselves as being at. This misalignment of expectations about trust may in fact lead to lost opportunities!

Certainly, secure software and systems design, implemented with the right set of secure protocols, play a major part in building trust with end users; PKI, for example, *manages the trust relationship* across that user-to-systems interface.

What else can (and should) be considered to help manage and maintain that trust?

# Other Protocols: Applying Cryptography to Meet Different Needs

There are many places where cryptography is put to use in ways that go well beyond what we can cover in this book. That said, let's take a closer look at four main protocols and the applications or user needs that they support.

## IPSec

*Internet Protocol Security (IPSec)* reminds us that the first-generation Internet (or ARPANet) was built in a very different era than we're accustomed to now. Full racks of computing and communications equipment (standing 6' tall and perhaps 9' wide) were needed to implement what now lives on a small part of a chip in your smartphone; the CPUs in these computers might have had 64 KB worth of RAM, and their clocks ran at 1-microsecond cycle times! Simple protocols like network address translation (NAT) turned out to be quite demanding of the CPU and memory resources on these early minicomputers. Without more processing capability and speed, early Internet Protocol (even v4) could not deliver significant security services. As a result, the ARPANet, and then the early Internet, were designed on a best-efforts basis, one that trusted users to always do what was in the best interests of the network as a whole. (After all, they reasoned, would the U.S. Navy's computer centers want to disrupt the U.S. Air Force's?)

IPSec was developed during the late 1980s and early 1990s to provide Internet-layer (level 3) security functions, specifically the authentication and encryption of packets as they are transferred around the Internet. It needed to provide a variety of security benefits: peer authentication, sender (data origination) authentication, data integrity and confidentiality, and protection against replay attacks. IPSec can provide these services automatically, without needing application layer interaction or setup.

IPSec provides two methods of operation, known as transport mode and tunnel mode. *Transport mode* encrypts only the payload (data content) of the IP packets being sent, which leaves all of the routing information intact. However, when transport mode uses the

IPSec authentication header, services like NAT cannot operate because this will invalidate the hash value associated with the header and the routing information in it. *Tunnel mode*, by contrast, encrypts the entire IP packet, routing headers and all; it then encapsulates that encrypted payload into a new IP packet, with a new header. This can be used to build virtual private networks (VPNs) and can also be used for private host-to-host chat functions. Since the as-built packets from the sending system are encrypted and encapsulated for actual transmission through the network, any packet-centric services such as NAT can function correctly.

IPSec can be implemented in three different ways. It's normally built right into the operating system by including its functions within the *IP stack* (the set of operating systems service routines that implement the Internet Protocol in that environment). When such modification of the operating system is not desired, IPSec can be implemented as a separate set of functions that sit (in effect) between the device drivers and the operating system's IP stack, earning it the name *bump-in-the-stack*. If external cryptoprocessors are used (that is, not under the direct, integrated control of the operating system), it's also possible to do what's called a *bump-in-the-wire* implementation.

Originally developed for IPv4, work is in process to fully port IPSec over to IPv6.

## S/MIME

Secure Multipurpose Internet Mail Extensions (S/MIME) provides presentation layer authentication, message integrity, nonrepudiation, privacy, and data security benefits to users. Using PKI, it requires the user to obtain and install their own certificate, which is then used in forming a digital signature. It provides end-to-end encryption of the email payload and thus makes it difficult for organizations to implement outgoing and incoming email inspection for malware or other contraband without performing this inspection on each end-user workstation after receipt and decryption.

S/MIME has other issues, which may mean it is limited in the security it can offer to users of organizational email systems. Its signatures are *detached*—that is, they are not tied to the content of the message itself, so all that they authenticate is the sender's identity and not that the sender sent the message in question. In May 2018, the EFF announced that there were critical vulnerabilities in S/MIME, particularly when forms of OpenPGP are used. EFAIL, as this vulnerability is called, can allow attackers to hide unknown plaintext within the original message (using various HTML tags). EFAIL affects many email systems, and as such, it will require much coordination between vendors to fix.

## DKIM

Domain Keys Identified Mail (DKIM) provides an infrastructure for authenticating that an email came from the domain its address information claims it did and was thus (presumably) authorized by that domain operator or owner. It can prevent or limit the vulnerability of an organization's email system to phishing and email spam attacks. It works by attaching a digital signature to the email message, and the receiving email service validates that signature. This confirms that the email itself (and possibly some of the attachments to it) were not tampered with during transmission, providing a degree of data integrity protection. As an infrastructure service, DKIM is not normally visible to the end users (senders or recipients), which means it does not function as an end-to-end email authentication service.

Both the original RFC that proposed DKIM and work since then have identified a number of possible attack vectors and weaknesses. Some of these are related to the use of short (weak) encryption keys that can easily be brute force attacked; others relate to ways that clever spammers can spoof, misroute, forward, or otherwise misuse the email infrastructure in ways DKIM cannot help secure.

## Blockchain

Think about the message digest process; it produces a hash value of a message (or file) that demonstrates that the content of that message has not been changed since the message digest was computed. A *blockchain* is nothing more than a series of messages, each with its own message digest, that taken together represent a transaction history about an item of interest; the message digest for the first block is computed normally, and then this is used as an input into the message digest for the next block, and so on. Thus, any attempt to make a change to the content of a block will invalidate all subsequent block-level message digests.

A digital wallet uses this approach when it treats each new transaction against the wallet as a new block. The current balance in your wallet is represented by the message digest of the entire wallet, which is the sequential digest of each transaction from the first onward. When a new transaction is posted, that existing balance message digest is used as input to compute the message digest of everything associated with the transaction. (If the wallet is tracking a bank or currency account, then this might be information about the date, amount, other party, purpose, and the resulting balance in the wallet or account.)

By providing strong nonrepudiation and data integrity for the transactions contained in the individual blocks, blockchains can implement digital provenance systems:

- Chain of custody control, auditing, and record keeping for cyberforensics could use blockchains to irrefutably record who touched the evidence, when, how, and what they did to it.

- Provenance systems, such as for hardware or documents, could use blockchains to prove the authenticity of the underlying data to help prove that safety-critical components (physical hardware, computer or network hardware, software, or firmware) are in fact what they claim to be.

- Representations of any kind of value can be made extremely difficult to counterfeit.

It is this last that explains the dramatic rise in the use of cryptocurrencies—the use of blockchains to represent money and to record and attest to the transactions done with that money:

- The cryptocurrency *miner* uses significant computing power to generate a new unique cryptocurrency identifier (similar to printing a new piece of paper currency with a unique combination of serial numbers, paper security markings, etc.). This "cryptodollar" is represented by a blockchain and is stored in the mining company's wallet.

- Bob buys that cryptodollar from the miner, and the underlying blockchain transfers to Bob's wallet; the new message digest reflects this transfer into Bob's wallet. The blockchain in the miner's wallet is updated to show this transaction.

- Later, Bob uses that cryptodollar to buy something from Ted's online store; the blockchain that is Bob's wallet is updated to reflect the sell, and the blockchain that is Ted's wallet is updated to reflect the buy.

This is shown in simplified form in Figure 7.8.

**FIGURE 7.8**    The blockchain concept

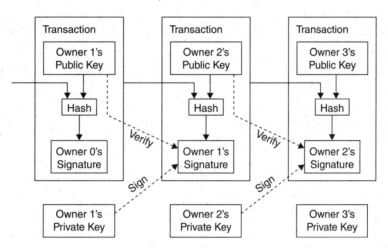

If all we do is use strong message digest functions in the blockchain, we provide some pretty powerful nonrepudiation and data integrity to our cryptocurrency users. We must combine this with a suitable exchange of public and private keys to be able to protect the confidentiality of the data and to ensure that only people or processes Bob authorizes (for example) can see into Bob's wallet, read the transaction history that is there, or initiate a new transaction.

Finally, cryptocurrency systems need to address the issue of authority: who is it, exactly, that we trust as a miner of a cryptodollar? Bitcoin, for example, solves this problem by being a completely decentralized system with no central bank or authority involved. The miners are actually the maintainers of copies of the total Bitcoin ledger, which records every Bitcoin owner's wallet information and its balance; voting algorithms provide for each distributed copy of the ledger to synchronize with the most correct copy. This maintenance function is computationally intensive, typically requiring many high-performance workstations running in parallel, and so the Bitcoin system rewards or incentivizes its miners by letting them earn a fraction of a Bitcoin as they maintain the system's ledger.

One irony of the rise in popularity and widespread adoption of blockchains and cryptocurrencies is the false perception that since money launderers, drug smugglers, and organized crime use these technologies, anyone using them must also be a criminal. Of course, nearly all criminals use money, but that does not mean that all users of money are criminals!

## Access Control Protocols

One of the most important uses of cryptographic systems is in implementing access control protocols, such as SSH, LDAP, Kerberos, or SSO. We looked at these in greater depth in Chapter 6, "Identity and Access Control," so refer to that chapter to see them in context.

---

 **Real World Scenario**

**Architecting Your Secure E-Registration and E-Voting System**

The work you've done on this project should now give you a pretty good understanding of the needs for information security. It's probably time to offer some strawman implementation thoughts.

How might some of the cryptographic systems we've explored be put to use in your system?

"Test-fit" some of those systems, and see what that reveals to you—either about the cryptosystems elements themselves, your project, or both.

---

# Measures of Merit for Cryptographic Solutions

From the standpoint of the owners, operators, and end users, what makes one cryptographic system a preferred solution over others? Key questions to consider when making such assessments might include the following:

- What are the costs to implement, maintain, manage, and operate the system?
- Does the system provide security commensurate with the value of the information and decisions being used?
- Are the throughput, flow rate, and other runtime performance impacts to our business processes within reason?
- Is the system simple for our users to use so that we minimize avoidance or corner-cutting by staff?
- How does the system add value, cost, or both to customer and prospective customer interactions with us?

- How does using the system enhance or maintain our reputation for trustworthiness?
- What new risks does investing in or using this system possibly expose us to?

It's fairly straightforward to trace most of these to technical performance measures, such as speed of processing, complexity of the tasks to initialize a new user, user training, and the known weaknesses in such systems. Integrating those parameters together into well-considered value propositions, however, is a necessary part of making such investment decisions—or making the decision that your current cryptosystems aren't fulfilling your needs in cost-effective ways.

# Attacks and Countermeasures

The good news is that there is one proven unbreakable cryptosystem—the ancient one-time pad! Claude Shannon's work at Bell Labs proved that the one-time pad is unbreakable, provided that the keying material is truly random, not reused, kept secret, and of equal or greater length than the message. Take a close look at that list of provisos, though, and you'll see that making practical one-time pad systems that are scalable to millions of users, simple to use, and yet secure day after day is just a bit of a challenge. All cryptosystems, from one-time pads through the most advanced of public key–based systems, still suffer from all of the problems that face other symmetric key systems—with distribution and key management being the hardest things to keep secure and scalable.

As you've seen, hybrid cryptographic systems are a form of a one-time pad, and like all one-time pad systems, they are still only as strong as the randomness the session key can provide.

Recall what we said earlier about what sort of attackers might be doing any or all of these kinds of attacks on a cryptosystem. The white hats might include:

- Law enforcement and national security organizations when taking captured devices or systems (or ones seized under a court order or other lawful process) and examining them for evidence
- Cryptosystems engineers, designers, and builders when attacking their own products or other systems provided to them under contract as part of systems vulnerability assessments
- Ethical hackers employed or under contract as part of penetration testing or system vulnerability assessment activities
- Students and teachers conducting ethical hacking and cryptanalysis as part of learning activities

The black hats list would include hostile national intelligence, security, and military services; business competitors (at home or abroad) willing to commit industrial espionage; private investigators, journalists, or others willing to break the law to seek incriminating, embarrassing, or other information they can use; and the whole gamut of criminal individuals and organizations.

With that in mind, let's look at a roundup of the most common assaults on cryptosystems. The details of how each attack works—and more importantly, how you can defend against them—are beyond the scope of this book and the SSCP exam. However, you will need to appreciate these typical attacks so that you can recognize when your organization may have taken actions that make such attacks likely or successful.

We'll look at countermeasures across the whole spectrum of "keeping the crypto safe" so as to avoid getting too far into the technical details.

## Brute Force and Dictionary Attacks

Lexically based ciphers first taught us that given enough cryptanalysts and enough dictionaries, we could probably break any such cipher system. In essence, the attacker makes assumptions about the cryptosystem being used and about its control parameters, and then uses randomly generated plaintext to see if its encrypted results match any substring in captured ciphertext. Such "brute force" (try every possibility—there's bound to be a winner in there somewhere!) approaches are also used as password-cracking schemes. Consider the typical four-digit personal identification number used on automated teller machine (ATM) and online banking systems. Only 10,000 guesses are the most required to break into your account! Of course, we rely on our banks to notice this and shut off the card after a much smaller number. Social engineering approaches can often find information that drastically reduces that search space.

Dictionary attacks often rely on precomputed tables of values, and of course, the larger the key space, the larger these tables have to become, requiring both more storage and faster storage access to be able to apply a brute force approach in a reasonable amount of time.

## Side Channel Attacks

Since every cryptosystem has to have *some* kind of hardware to run on—even it if is purely implemented in software—that hardware can be observed to see if it offers any kind of signatures that indicate something about the internals of the algorithms being used. Side channel attacks get their name because the channel the attacker is listening to is alongside the channel that the cryptosystem is *supposed* to be operating in and are limited only by the attacker's imagination. All start from the premise that computing systems show tiny variances in some kind of physical or operational signature based on the actual data being processed; if you can observe enough of these variations and correlate them to the data stream itself, perhaps you've found an exploitable weakness. Some possibilities include:

**Cache attack**   Monitoring the contents and use of processor or I/O board caches or software-managed caches in virtual machine and cloud systems.

**Timing attack**   Tightly monitoring the time each step takes.

**Power monitoring or power variation attack**   Monitoring power usage by specific hardware elements in the cryptosystem. Many RSA implementations are vulnerable to fluctuations in electrical power.

**Electromagnetic attack**   Measuring the tiny (sometimes not so tiny!) radio waves emitted by elements of the cryptosystem.

**Acoustic analysis**   Measuring mechanical vibrations in system elements.

**Differential fault analysis**   Introducing faults into your test copy of the system and seeing what that reveals.

**Data remanence**   Well-designed cryptosystems should not leave partial or intermediate results, pad counts, etc., lying around in their innards after processing has been completed; most, however, do leave something, somewhere, which is why system zeroization is important. These partial values can be swept up in a test environment and may be revealing.

**Software-initiated fault attacks**   By attacking other aspects of the system that hosts the cryptosystem, faults in the host environment or the cryptosystem may be triggered.

**Optical attacks**   Passive optical attacks that work by reading the disk activity lights or the lights on your routers and modems might seem old hat, but they can work. Attackers can also physically open the hardware of a cryptosystem under test, open the microchips, and use instruments to look for stray photons emitted as the system is operating. Active attacks involve using light, lasers, or even scanning electron microscopes to interact with the cryptosystem's circuits, similar to injecting noise or test signals, to observe the results.

**Branch predictor attacks**   Using software engineering analysis tools to predict when and how branches in the algorithm will be executed, and then using those predictions to reveal characteristics of the data being processed.

Although no one side channel attack will reveal everything, the combination of these and other possible investigative techniques could in fact lead to breaking the cryptosystem under test.

## Numeric (Algorithm or Key) Attacks

Almost every cryptosystem depends on logical assertions that lead to concluding that "system X is unbreakable provide that conditions A, B, and C hold true." Consider all of the algorithms that depend on very, very large prime numbers. If your system for *finding* the next three very large prime numbers has a bug in it and occasionally picks a value that is *not* prime, this can lead to an unintentional backdoor in your trapdoor function and allow attackers to crack your encryption by defeating the algorithm. (This is a front channel attack, as opposed to the side channel attack described earlier.) Much like purely random numbers that turn out not to be very random at all, *any* logical or mathematical error in the way that the cryptosystem is *implemented* can lead to incorrect operation and a possible exploitable weakness.

Without going into the math, some of the names you may encounter as you look at such mathematically based attacks or the weaknesses they are based on include the following:

- Small values for exponents and other control parameters in algorithms

- Chinese Remainder attacks   This theorem (which dates from the third century CE) can be applied when some parts of the control parameters can be guessed, or when too many users share same plaintext and some of the same parameters (such as $e$, but not $p$, $q$, and therefore $n$).

- Coppersmith's attack    A form of Chinese Remainder attack, which also can work when attacker knows part of the secret key.

- Broadcast attacks    The attacker sends the same plaintext or the same ciphertext to multiple recipients, collects (or intercepts) responses, and analyzes the results.

- Related message attack    If two ciphertext messages differ in part in some known or understandable ways, other analysis may reveal more about the keys or control parameters in use.

- Short padding attacks    Most cryptosystems have to deal with padding out variable-length message content so that the encryption and decryption algorithms can work on expected block sizes. Incorrect or short padding can open an exploitable weakness.

- Algorithmic weaknesses    Some algorithms are just not as logically or mathematically strong as they claim to be (think about DES).

- Usage weaknesses    Patterns of use that reveal information about algorithms, keys, or content.

- Faulty prime numbers in key generation    Values that actually aren't prime, or two primes that aren't far enough apart (on the number line) to meet strong encryption needs.

- Pseudorandom number weaknesses    Too small, or not random enough (can predict their generator's output sequence).

- Anticipated or predicted plaintext can also be useful in such attacks, as well as using a related message attack, in which two ciphertexts thought to be very similar can be compared and analyzed to possibly reveal weaknesses in the cryptosystem.

- And many more.

## Traffic Analysis, "Op Intel," and Social Engineering Attacks

We'll group these three attack vectors into one group, not because they use similar analytical attack processes, but because they often exploit the human frailties in our organizations and the ways we put cryptographic systems to work. They are useful as part of an attacker's ongoing reconnaissance efforts, and as such they can quite often break the protection that cryptosystems were supposed to provide.

*Operational intelligence* is the gathering of information and insight by watching how your organization operates, at the fine-grained, step-by-step process or task level, and looking for patterns. Observing that a Coast Guard unit often places phone orders for dozens of pizzas or other meals to be delivered might, for example, be a tip-off that a cutter is about to launch to do an intercept of a suspect vessel at sea. *Traffic analysis* looks at how communications ebb and flow across the organization, even if the content is encrypted;

changes in these patterns can often be reliable predictors of changes in behavior. *Social engineering* encompasses almost any effort to learn about the people in the organization and find exploitable weaknesses via those people. Sadly, the greatest human strength we have—that we are "herd animals" and we live best by helping others in our "herd"—is the most exploitable social engineering weakness that we have. Think of the total of these intelligence and reconnaissance processes as reverse-engineering how your organization gets its work done, finding exploitable vulnerabilities along the way. If this all sounds like what *you* should have been doing during the vulnerability analysis phase yourself, you'd be right!

We'd like to think that we've come a long way since the days when journalists could construct an organizational map of the Central Intelligence Agency headquarters by starting with the phone number listed in the public phone records, and just *war dial* numbers around that, asking each person who answered who they were and what office they were in. The infamous "I'm from IT, could you let me log on as you?" trick is still used for one reason only: *because it works*. So-called *dumpster diving*, going through the trash thrown out by a target organization, is still quite revealing (if a bit messy). This is especially useful when planning algorithmic attacks that need fragments of ciphertext, expired keying material, user or maintenance documentation (about the cryptosystems or other systems and processes), customer and subscriber information, or even equipment declared surplus and sent to the salvage yard or the dumpster.

In nearly all cases, these traditional espionage techniques still work because people and organizations tend to take shortcuts, make mistakes, or make incorrect assumptions. We cannot overemphasize this point! Product and systems implementations get rushed, because the deadlines are important; design assumptions can be inadequately tested or validated; and risk assessments can and are often curtailed or done only in a summary fashion.

## Massively Parallel Systems Attacks

In many, if not all, cryptographic systems, we assume that attackers will find it computationally infeasible to successfully apply brute force, pattern matching, or many other numerical or number theory–based attack approaches. This assumption about what is feasible—whether it is affordable or even doable—is part of that race against time we talked about earlier. Consider the the arguments over key length when DES was being created and competed, and how AES has had to push to even longer keys, as just one indicator. National security and intelligence services have long been one of the biggest drivers on the supercomputer and massively parallel computing market (and the ones with the deepest pockets to pay for such systems, typically), so we already have many examples of using such systems to break encryption schemes. (This is nothing new; if you think about it, the Bombe that Alan Turing and his team built for the British during World War II was far more expensive, physically larger, and demanded a larger team of talented brainpower than the cryptosystem they were trying to defeat. Compared to Enigma, the Bombe was a supercomputer of its day.)

Massively parallel architectures are also readily available to the rest of us, especially if we have a bit of money to invest. As the Stone Soupercomputer project at Oak Ridge National Laboratories demonstrated, clever engineering can take most any set of computers and mesh them together to solve complex numerical problems on the cheap. Academics (even high schools) learned from this example, as did the hacking community. And of course, we've seen that massive zombie botnets can easily be organized and used to conduct distributed denial of services attacks. If it hasn't happened already, the time when a massive zombie botnet figures prominently in an attack on a cryptographic system, its algorithms, or its keys is not very far away.

## Supply Chain Vulnerabilities

As you saw when we looked at hierarchies of trust, virtually every element of our IT systems comes from some supplier, who got it from some manufacturer, who built it out of parts and subsystems built by other companies, and so on. Every element of that value chain is a potential point of vulnerability, a place where otherwise trustworthy designs can have backdoors inserted or key parameters tweaked to create a weakness. Intelligence services have long been adept at surreptitiously modifying equipment, and later software, while it was en route to a target that they wished to gain insider access to or manipulate in some fashion.

The dangers of an inadequately protected supply chain are not just limited to surreptitious manipulation (legal or otherwise) by outsiders. Many of the attacks against cryptosystems exploit errors in design and use, and one such logical error is if too many devices in too many client or server systems are using the same prime numbers. As a systems administrator, you usually can replace the default administrator username and password, but on most commodity devices like modems, switches, routers, firewalls, VPN systems, or even printers, projectors, and VOIP systems, you'll have a hard time getting at the key parameters that dictate how those devices initiate and perform as elements in your cryptographically protected systems.

Does that sound farfetched? In 2013, four researchers documented just how prevalent this "common prime use" is in the IT industry, finding that the same common primes were integral to devices from over 30 manufacturers. Since then, one of this team, Nadia Heninger, has been quite outspoken about how national security services don't have to break everybody's codes to read everybody's information as a result of this supply chain weakness.

Supply chain weaknesses in IT security and cryptography are at risk of being exploited against us, whether by criminals, terrorists, foreign governments, or our own governments. A closer read of the reporting on the Edward Snowden information leaks, back in 2013, reveals that NSA had not only actively been soliciting the cooperation of information systems technology and services providers to build its Total Information Awareness system; it also shows how successful other governments had been at exploiting known supply side vulnerabilities.

## The "Sprinkle a Little Crypto Dust on It" Fallacy

The last vulnerability we'll mention is more of a mental failure than a systems or technology vulnerability. Far too many people—experts and neophytes alike—think that the obvious answer to our information security needs is just to *encrypt* everything in sight—and most things that are not in sight. We cannot blame people for thinking this way when we readily acknowledge the need for security for data in motion, in use, and at rest.

The bad news is that some software development management methodologies seem to promote sloppy software development and testing, particularly when the priority is placed on meeting user needs on time regardless of any possible errors in the implementation of that software. It is in such environments that we sometimes see simple encryption processes (perhaps overly simple!), downloaded from someplace on the Web, incorporated into systems with little end-to-end consideration of what the real security needs are and the steps necessary to achieve them.

The good news is that there are well-established, well-understood, and proven methodologies for developing software in ways that earn high assurance that the software does what it needs to, and nothing else, and that includes keeping data properly secure at all times. Good software design frameworks that encourage secure code development, such as the Open Web Application Security Project (OWASP), are a great place to start, but without the end-to-end commitment and support of the development *management* team, frameworks are not enough.

It takes dedication, forethought, time, and effort to apply sound systems engineering and software engineering methods up front; it's not free to "bake in" the safe and secure computing we need up front as we build our systems, applications, services, or even Internet of Things (IoT) products and gadgets. Much like any kind of product quality approach, too many businesses seem to believe that there's never enough money or time to do it right the first time, and the ones that usually decide this hope to have moved on to other pastures when someone else has to spend the time and money to do it over again, hopefully better.

# Countermeasures

Many of these countermeasures are steps you should be taking to support other risk mitigation problems, so perhaps they offer as a side benefit the ability to limit attacks on your cryptosystems. It is useful at this point to group them into physical, logical, and administrative sets of countermeasures. Remember that your organization's risk management profile should be dictating which sorts of threats you need to detect, which can merely be deterred, and which you have to prevent or constrain; let this drive how you choose to protect your protective systems themselves, such as your cryptographic systems.

## Physical Countermeasures

The physical security of your IT systems is the place to start. To the best degree possible, seek to restrict physical access to your Internet service provider's (ISP's) point of presence, your communications interfaces (such as modems and routers), and any other on-premises servers and systems. In doing so, your main concern is to prevent unauthorized modifications to hardware, firmware, and control settings; you also want to restrict as much as possible the ability of a stranger to attach a device anywhere on your system, such as a network sniffer or tap.

You may also want to inspect all electrical power connections to ensure that no power line–monitoring taps have been surreptitiously added. Uninterruptible power supplies and power conditioning equipment can protect your cryptographic systems from natural and man-made undervoltage, overvoltage, noise, or other power line–injected signals.

Systems configuration management information should also be physically protected. Keep such documentation, log analysis reports, and so forth in a locked container, and restrict access to this information to people with the right need to know.

The cryptographic elements of end-user systems, servers, and communications systems may need to be periodically zeroized or reset so that any potential leaks or data remanence can be reduced or eliminated. For most small office situations that do not have dedicated cryptologic systems, this can usually be accomplished by a thorough cold boot of systems— but be careful, as many systems have "fast boot" capabilities that actually restart the system from the way it was when it was last shut down. This can lead to data remaining in the system in a variety of ways. (Although you might think of clearing the memory as a logical operation, it usually does take a physical action to accomplish it—even if that's a manually invoked power-on reset.)

Disposal of systems components, documentation, log files, and all other information assets will ultimately lead to some physical item (such as a disk, a document, or a system) being thrown away. Your information classification guide, which you should have developed during your risk assessments, should guide you in determining which assets need destructive zeroization or clobbering and which can be safely disposed (possibly for salvage value).

## Logical Countermeasures

Assuming you've done a thorough vulnerabilities assessment and already addressed the most compelling of the common vulnerabilities your systems were exposing, dealing with the logical threats to your cryptographic systems mainly involves three sets of actions— key and parameter management, certificate management, and enforcement of user-level requirements:

- Management of cryptographic keys, seeds, control parameters, etc., should reflect the strongest level of protection that fits within any runtime performance constraints or targets your organization has established. Establish procedures that control how you decide to make changes, as well as how you control and audit that changes are made correctly.

- Your organization may provide its own local CA and issue end-user certificates to individuals or work units, or it may rely on the public key infrastructure completely and the CAs built into the browsers and other systems elements you're using. Either way, you'll need policies and procedures for handling certificate issuance and expiration, and quite possibly want to use software-enforced policies that control how end users can override any certificate validation issues they encounter.

- Your organization will no doubt write administrative policies that dictate acceptable use, control data exfiltration, and specify user privileges, auditing, and access control, just to name a few. Many of these require that users follow the policies' instructions and properly use protected systems, some of which involve use of cryptographically protected systems elements. You can use software-defined policies or other logical controls to help enforce these protections.

## Administrative Countermeasures

We cannot overemphasize that the number one, most important administrative countermeasure is configuration management and control. With a well-established, documented systems security baseline in your hands, you can quickly determine that a small office, home office (SOHO)-quality Wi-Fi router at the edge of your campus has had its firmware hacked by somebody; you can also verify that despite the lock on the wiring closet door being securely locked, someone has been in there playing around with your infrastructure!

The next most important administrative countermeasure is getting your people trained, motivated, and on side with your team. Initial and follow-on training, education, and motivation are imperative to transforming your people risk, yet doing so in ways that keep them customer-focused and engaged, and helpful to the degree their jobs and your team need. Having everyone on the staff know that modern IT systems use all sorts of cryptographic techniques to enforce access control, for example, can be a great way to build trust and confidence; most of your workforce, however, probably has no need to know how you manage certificates or keys.

## Timing Is Everything

One final set of countermeasures remains in your organization's hands: frequent change. You control when passwords must be updated, when caches must be flushed, and when keys must be reset or certificates revalidated or reissued. You control how often (or on what irregular basis) you attempt partial or complete vulnerability assessments, including penetration testing.

Classical encryption failed as often as it did because it could easily become *predictable*. Predicable patterns can drastically reduce the search space in which attackers have to hunt, poke, or attempt to break your encryption; patterns help traffic analysis find *more* data and *more* patterns.

Be surprise tolerant. Go beyond expecting the unexpected, and try to think ahead of your own business processes. Mix things up; change your rhythms; alter your operational signature.

# On the Near Horizon

As computing power, storage capabilities, and network throughput continue to increase dramatically, while the costs of using them keeps plummeting, no doubt more and more massively parallel computing attacks on cryptographic systems will find more vulnerabilities to exploit. Other changes in the technology of computing are here or on the near horizon; what might they hold for the future? We'll look at some of these issues through the lens of the cryptosystems user or designer right now, and save a peek at larger issues for Chapter 12, "Risks, Issues, and Opportunities, Starting Tomorrow," as we wrap up everything.

## Pervasive and Homomorphic Encryption

Securing data at rest, in motion, and in use provides an exceptional set of challenges to systems designers. Two distinctly different approaches to this problem address the in use aspect by asking whether the data actually must be decrypted—presented to users in plaintext form—in order to be put to use.

*Pervasive encryption*, as IBM calls it, is one approach that tries to keep sensitive information always encrypted, even when it is being used or displayed. This may dictate extensive changes to information systems architectures, from central systems to end-user devices, as well as changes to the ways we use our systems and information. Pervasive encryption may not be the right, or most cost-effective, answer for each need.

*Homomorphic encryption* demonstrates that with the right choice of encryption algorithms, complex data analytics can be performed on many individually encrypted data items to produce a meaningful, aggregate answer—without needing to decrypt any of the input data and without revealing its plaintext or exposing it to attack. (Homomorphic means that things have similar forms but different structures; set theory uses it to describe how the results of performing operations on elements of one set are mapped to the results of applying the corresponding operations to associated members, or images, in a second set. This does not necessarily mean that the reverse mapping can be done.) Individual patient medical data, for example, might be stored in individually encrypted records within many different clinics and care provider applications platforms; if all of these platforms were hosted in the cloud, a different application could access all of that data and draw inferences and conclusions about it without revealing PII or individual patient medical information. This could provide a near-real-time health alert system, detecting the possible outbreak of contagious diseases or spotting a possible toxic exposure event, much earlier than is currently possible. (ElGamal encryption is well suited to use in such homomorphic encryption applications.)

## Quantum Cryptography and Post–Quantum Cryptography

Over the last 10–15 years, quantum computing and quantum cryptography have continued to move out of the theoretical literature and into various technology demonstrator systems. It's quite likely that the next 10 years will see more and more demonstrators become market-worthy technologies. As an SSCP, you won't be expected to know the physics and the math that make them the unique, new approaches that they are, but you will no doubt need to become more and more familiar with them over time.

In the physical sciences, a *quantum* is the smallest unit of something that can exist. The ancient Greeks thought that this indivisible bit of matter was the atom, but over the last 200-plus years, we've continued to split the atom and its subatomic parts into finer and finer pieces. *Quantum mechanics*, the study of the behavior of the individual quanta of matter, has some very strange effects associated with it. One of these is that whenever you try to measure something about a quantum, the act of measuring interferes with it and changes the state of that quantum. The other is that when you prepare two (or more) quanta in a particular way, their states (their spin direction and orientation, for example) can become entangled, which means that if you physically separate them and force one to change, the other entangled quantum immediately changes state to match. This entanglement phenomenon has sometimes been called "spooky action at a distance."

---

### Schrödinger's Cat

Perhaps the most well-known example of a thought experiment in quantum physics was posed by Erwin Schrödinger in 1935. Suppose we have a system that consists of a cat in a box; in the box is a glass bottle of a toxic gas, a small sample of a radioactive isotope, and a mechanism that will cause a hammer to smash the bottle when a single atom of the isotope decays. The problem, he asked, is how do you describe the system at a particular time *t*? In classical physics, we'd say that at time *t*, the cat is either alive (the atom hasn't decayed) or it is dead, but since we can only estimate the probability of one atom decaying by that time, we really don't know until we open the box and look inside (preferably while wearing a gas mask).

Quantum mechanics, on the other hand, describes the system as the superposition of two states: one in which the atom has decayed and the cat has died, the other in which the atom has not decayed and the cat still lives. Until, of course, you open the lid and look; this causes the superposition to collapse, and the cat is either alive or dead but not both.

If that makes sense to you, there's a fortune to be made just waiting for you in quantum computing…

---

## Quantum Computers as Part of Cryptographic Systems

*Quantum key distribution (QKD)* systems can make use of the measurement effect to alert users that a third party has attempted to observe a key. This makes it ideal for one-time pad encryption systems, and in fact, it can work quite well with AES and other symmetric encryption systems as a result. QKD requires special protocols, two of which are the BB84 (developed by Charles Bennett and Gilles Brassard in 1984) and the E91 (developed by Artur Eckert in 1991). As of this writing, six different quantum key distribution networks were in operation, largely as test and demonstration systems. Photons (elemental particles of light) traveling in fiber-optic systems have been used to date, although the People's Republic of China has flown (in 2017) at least one spacecraft payload using laser links to connect ground stations in China and Austria in the first globe-spanning QKD network. Since the very act of attempting to sniff such a quantum key packet changes the value of the key, the potential here is profound.

### Quantum Computers as Part of Cryptanalysis Attacks

*Quantum computing* does not use binary digits (or bits) as we're familiar with, which store either a 0 or a 1. Every bit in a computer is in one of those two states, not both—and that bit cannot be in an undefined state, either! A *qubit*, or quantum bit, by contrast, exists in both the 0 and 1 states simultaneously until you observe it; then, it is said to *collapse* to a specific value. Without going into more detail, suffice to say that quantum computers can probably help us compute probabilistic problems far more efficiently than binary digital computers can. This could mean that a powerful quantum computer could be more effective at traditional attacks on known encryption algorithms. Mathematician Peter Shor published an algorithm in 1994 that could conceivably crack RSA's integer factorization problem once we can build a workable quantum computer (probably one measuring in mega-qubits or giga-qubits in capacity, and hundreds of millions or billions of qu-flops, or quantum floating-point math operations per second). While such machines are still far over the horizon, the argument rages on in the blogospheres. Watch those spaces!

## AI, Machine Learning, and Cryptography

*Artificial intelligence (AI)* is the name given to a broad set of approaches that try to make computer systems that can reason, think, solve problems, or interact with people and with each other in the same ways that healthy, rational humans do. The most familiar example of this might be natural language translation, such as that provided as a Web-based service by Google Translate. As a *machine learning* system, Google Translate uses a vast array of processing elements (software- and hardware-based), which form a web or mesh; that mesh looks at huge databases of phrases in the source language and, based on past experience, computes the probability that what you want is a particular phrase in the target language. If you agree with that translation, Google Translate increases the probably correct score for that pair of source and target phrases—but it still "knows" nothing about what those phrases mean to humans! (In Peter Watt's science fiction novel *Blindsight*, he shows this *Chinese Room* translation system and the misunderstandings it can lead to, to dramatic effect!) Machine learning is done by taking such a mesh of processing elements and training it with very large sets of data—in the case of machine language translation, some of those sets would be "correct translations," some might be "totally wrong," and others might be "technically correct but socially ill advised," at least *statistically*, that is. Each node in the mesh calculates coefficients as a result of both training and operational use. The problem with machine learning, as with many such analytics approaches, is that we humans can see that it works—it gets good answers—but we cannot explain why!

Cryptanalysts might make good use of machine learning approaches, especially if they have very large datasets of ciphertext to work with and some good starting points or *cribs* to work from. Machine learning is already being used in traffic analysis and pattern recognition as a way to infer meaning from encrypted traffic, even traffic routed through VPNs.

# Summary

We've taken as non-mathematical a look at cryptography as we can in order to gain a better understanding of what it can do (and what it cannot do!) to help us keep our organization's information and information systems safe and secure. The last three-plus decades have been nothing short of revolutionary, for they've seen cryptographic systems become commonplace—even your smart watch or fitness tracker uses cryptography to keep it paired with *your* devices, rather than someone else's.

At the heart of this revolution is the widespread adoption and use of public key encryption, which gave rise to digital certificates, digital signatures, and a host of other cryptosystems and uses. These have gone a long way to addressing many of the shortfalls in meeting CIANA's needs that previous generations of cryptography, networking, and systems could not fully address. We've seen how hierarchies of trust have been developed that enable and empower the vast majority of online users to conduct personal matters, business transactions, and financial transactions with reasonable assurance of safety. Nonrepudiation in the Internet world has become much more commonplace, largely as a result of this public key infrastructure. That said, PKI, certificates, and even the webs of trust we see in alternatives like PGP and GPG are not perfect solutions to all of our needs.

Since its first uses over 3,500 years ago, cryptography has protected one set of secrets with another—we protect the information we must keep safe and secure by means of algorithms, systems designs, and ultimately with cryptographic keys. The algorithms and the designs have been made public, and the millions of peer review pairs of eyes that subject them to constant scrutiny are part of the networks of trust we all depend on largely without thinking about them.

Although usually not cryptographers, cryptanalysts, or cryptographic engineers by training or inclination, most SSCPs do need to have a strong working knowledge of how to use cryptography, as well as have a healthy skepticism about being overly reliant on it. Cryptography is a vital element of almost every aspect of identity management, access control, and secure communications. As the market seeks to expand information protection to pervasively assure data in motion, data at rest, and data at use, more and more opportunities for smartly applied cryptography will no doubt arise; therein will the SSCP find even further professional opportunity.

# Exam Essentials

**Explain the fundamental concepts of cryptography and how they are used.**   Cryptography is the process of obscuring or hiding the meaning of information so that unauthorized persons or processes cannot read it or make a useful copy of it. The original information is called plaintext (no matter what form of data it is), which is encrypted to produce ciphertext, which can be transmitted to a recipient or stored for later retrieval. Upon receipt or retrieval, the ciphertext is decrypted to recover the original meaning and the original form of the plaintext. The encryption and decryption processes (or algorithms) require keys; without the keys, no encryption or decryption can occur. Symmetric encryption uses the same key (or a simple transform of it) for encryption and decryption, whereas asymmetric encryption uses different keys that are nearly impossible to derive from each other.

**Differentiate between hashing and encryption.**    Hashing is a one-way encryption process: plaintext goes in, a hash value comes out, but you cannot reverse this to "un-hash" a hash value to get back to the original plaintext. Hashing takes a plaintext message and uses an encrypting hash algorithm to transform the plaintext into a smaller, shorter value (called the hash or hash value), which must be unique to the input plaintext. The hash algorithm should make it impossible to decrypt the hash value back into the plaintext, without any way to determine the meaning of a particular hash value. By contrast, the purpose of non-hashing encryption is to safely store or communicate plaintext with its meaning hidden for storage and transmission so that the meaning can later be derived by means of the right decryption algorithm and key. Encryption for storage and communication is thus part of a two-way process.

**Explain the basic hashing algorithms and the role of salting in hashing.**    Hashing algorithms treat all input plaintext as if it is a series of numbers and use techniques such as modulo arithmetic to transform potentially large, variable-length inputs into fixed-length hash values. When the function is chosen correctly, the change of a single bit in the input will produce a significantly different hash value. This provides a fast way to demonstrate that two sets of input (two files, for example) are either bit-for-bit identical or they are not. It should not be possible to take a hash value and reverse-calculate what the input plaintext was that produced it. To improve the strength of a hash function, a large random number is added to the input plaintext as additional bytes of input. This makes it much harder for brute force attacks to attempt to break a hash value back to its original plaintext.

**Know how to use cryptography to provide nonrepudiation.**    Digitally signing documents, files, or emails makes it exceptionally difficult for a sender to claim that the file the recipient has is not the file that they sent or to deny sending it at all. Using digital signatures to prove receipt and use of files by the addressee or recipient, however, requires some form of digitally signed receipt process, which most email systems cannot support. However, add-on systems for email do provide this, and EU standards have been supporting their adoption and use as part of secure e-commerce. Some national postal systems and a growing number of Internet service providers now make such capabilities available to users.

**Explain how cryptography is used to support digital signatures and what benefits you gain from using digital signatures.**    Asymmetric keys provide a way to digitally sign a file, an email, or a document. Typically this involves calculating a cryptographic hash of the input file, and combining it with the originator's private key via a decryption process; the result is called the sender's digital signature of that file or document. Recipients use the matching encryption process on that digital signature, using the sender's public signature, to produce a received hash value, while also locally computing a hash of the received file. If these match, then the sender's identity has been validated. Digitally signing files assures recipients that software updates, transaction files, or important documents have not been altered in storage or transmission. This provides enhanced data integrity and nonrepudiation and can do so across space (sender to recipient) and across time (validating that files placed in storage have not been corrupted between the time they were created and the time they are retrieved for use, be that milliseconds or months).

**Explain what key management is, what different approaches can be used, and the issues with key management.** Key management is the process of creating encryption and decryption keys and then issuing, distributing, or sending them to users of the cryptographic system in question. The cryptographic keys are the fundamental secret that must be protected—all else, from systems design and usage through its fundamental algorithms, is known or will be easily known by one's adversaries. Keys must be distributed in ways that prevent loss or disclosure, and they need to be destroyed or zeroized if users leave the network, if keys are partially compromised, or as a routine security measure. Keys can be distributed as physical documents or in electronic message format; both are subject to compromise, corruption, and loss, and typically such key systems (if based on symmetric algorithms) cannot self-authenticate a sender or recipient. Public key infrastructures do not actually distribute keys; rather, they provide for sender and recipient to co-generate a unique, private session key, which is used only for that session's communication; these require asymmetric (public and private) keys have been generated for each user, typically authenticated by certificates.

**Explain how public key infrastructures (PKIs) are used.** Public key infrastructures provide two important benefits. First, by providing a secure means to generate, distribute, authenticate, and use public and private encryption keys, PKI has made widespread use of cryptographic protection a fundamental part of business, personal, and government use of the Web and the Internet. Second, by providing a scalable, decentralized capability to digitally sign documents, files, email, or other content, PKI provides not only enhanced confidentiality and integrity of information, but also nonrepudiation protection. It also strengthens authentication mechanisms. The total is that it makes secure, reliable information more available when it is needed, where it is needed.

**Explain the important differences between symmetric and asymmetric encryption algorithms.** Symmetric encryption uses the same key (or a simple transform of it) for encryption and decryption. The underlying mathematical operations are ones that can run in reverse so that the ciphertext can be decrypted back to the form and content of the original plaintext. Once compromised, this key can be used to decrypt all previously encrypted ciphertext—there is no forward privacy or secrecy. Asymmetric encryption uses a very different mathematical construct to encrypt than it does for decrypting; it is required that there be no computationally feasible or doable way to take ciphertext and solve for the original plaintext without having both the corresponding decryption algorithm and the decryption key. There should also be no way to mathematically derive the decryption key from the encryption key. Asymmetric encryption, when implemented with computationally difficult algorithms using very large numbers as factors and keys, provides inherently better security than symmetric encryption can, given the same size keys. It can also provide forward secrecy (protect previously encrypted ciphertext from being decrypted) when keys are changed or compromised. Asymmetric encryption and decryption are compute-intensive, using a lot of processing time, whereas symmetric encryption can be built to run very fast in hardware, software, or both. Thus most public key infrastructures use asymmetric encryption while establishing a session key and then use symmetric encryption, using that session key for the bulk of the session's communication.

**Understand the reasons for using cryptography as part of a secure information system.** Unique identification of users, processes, files, or other information assets is a fundamental cornerstone of building any secure information system. Cryptographic techniques, from hashes through digital signatures and to encryption and decryption of data at rest, in motion, and in use, can provide a wide range of confidentiality, integrity, authentication, nonrepudiation, and availability benefits to systems designers. Modern cryptographic systems provide a wide range of choices, which allows systems builders to achieve the protection they need for costs (in money, time, effort, runtime resources, and operational complexity) commensurate with the risk.

**Explain why cryptography does not answer all information security needs.** Most information systems security incidents occur because of flaws in business process design, implementation, and use; this includes the training, education, and proficiency of the human users and other workers within the organization as much as it includes the IT systems and components. Cryptography can strengthen access control, enhance the integrity and confidentiality of information, and add nonrepudiation as well—but it cannot prevent the unanticipated. Cryptography helps implement hierarchies of trust, but these are reliable only insofar as the human or supply chain aspects of those hierarchies are as trustworthy as is required.

**Know the regulatory and legal considerations for using cryptography in private business.** Private businesses, in almost all jurisdictions, are subject to a variety of legal, government, and financial and insurance regulations regarding their safekeeping of information; these requirements are best summarized as CIANA, or confidentiality, integrity, availability, nonrepudiation, and authentication. Taken together, these should establish high-level, strategic needs for information security processes and systems, including cryptographic systems where applicable, for that business. Failing to do so puts customers, employees, owners, and the business at risk.

**Explain the major vulnerabilities in various cryptographic systems and processes.** The encryption and decryption keys are the most critical elements of any cryptographic system, be it symmetric, asymmetric, or hybrid, paper or electronic. If the keys cannot be protected, then all is lost. Keys can be stolen. Algorithmic weaknesses can be discovered and exploited to enable partial or complete attacks on ciphertext. Physical characteristics, such as mechanical or electrical noise, timing, stray emanations, or data remaining after part or all of an encryption operation, can be accessed, analyzed, and used to identify exploitable weaknesses.

**Explain the difference between hierarchies of trust and webs of trust.** Both concepts strive to establish associations or logical networks of entities. The topmost node of such a network, its trust anchor, confers trust upon intermediaries, which can then assert their trust to end (leaf) nodes. In hierarchies of trust, certificate authorities are the trusted anchors, which can issue certificates to intermediaries, which can issue certificates to the leaf nodes. End users, seeking to validate the trustworthiness of a certificate, infer that a certificate from a trusted end (leaf) node is trustworthy if the intermediary that issued it is, on up to the anchor. Webs of trust, by contrast, involve peer-to-peer trust relationships that do not rely on central certificate authorities as the anchors. Hierarchies of trust are much more scalable (to billions of certificates in use) than webs of trust. Both systems have drawbacks and issues, particularly with respect to certificate revocation, expiration, or the failure of a node to maintain trustworthiness.

**Explain the difference between character, block, and stream ciphers.**   Character ciphers encrypt and decrypt each single character or symbol in the input plaintext, such as is done by a simple alphabetic substitution cipher; the encryption key is used to encrypt (and decrypt) each character. Block ciphers encrypt and decrypt fixed-length groups (blocks) of symbols or bytes from the input plaintext, typically in fixed-length blocks, which are then encrypted via transposition, substitution, or both; block ciphers may also transpose blocks, and multistage block encryption can do that at any stage in the process. The keys for block ciphers are applied to each block for encryption and decryption. Stream ciphers treat the input plaintext and the key as if they were continuous streams of symbols, and they use one element of the key to encrypt one element of the plaintext. Stream ciphers must use a key whose length is longer than the input plaintext and is random across that length to prevent attacks against the ciphertext.

**Understand how encryption strength depends on the size of keys and other parameters.**   The simplest way to break an encryption system is to capture some ciphertext outputs from it, and using its known or assumed decryption algorithm, try every possible key and see if a presumed cleartext output is a meaningful message. Since even pure binary cleartext files (executable programs, for example) contain a lot of error checking and parity information, if a presumed cleartext output is error free, it probably is meaningful and might even be what the attacker is looking for. Key length determines how many possible keys must be tried— keys of 8-bit length require trying only 256 possible keys, for example. The larger the key, the larger the search space of possible keys. Using large, random salt or seed values as part of the encryption and decryption effectively enlarges that search space again. If the encryption and decryption algorithms depend on numbers, such as integer factors or exponents, the larger these values, again, the larger the search space.

# Review Questions

1. Cryptography protects the meaning or content of files and messages by means of all of the following except which?

    **A.** Obscuring meaning by misdirection, concealment, or deception

    **B.** Obscuring meaning by making it difficult or impossible for unauthorized users to access, view, copy, or change it

    **C.** Transforming the meaning and content of something into a unique value

    **D.** Digitally signing files and messages to authenticate senders

2. Which of the following best describes symmetric encryption?

    **A.** Uses one key to encrypt blocks of text to be ciphered and another key to decrypt it back

    **B.** Uses the same key or a simple transform of it to encrypt plaintext into ciphertext, and to then decrypt the ciphertext back into plaintext

    **C.** Was used extensively in classical encryption but has since been superseded by much stronger asymmetric encryption

    **D.** Is best suited to plaintext that has a very high degree of regularity to its structure and content

3. Which statement about hashing is most correct?

    **A.** Hashing performs lossy compression on the input cleartext data file by representing the digest of its meaning in a much smaller number of bits.

    **B.** Hashing is almost exclusively used to produce indexes and pointers for database and file systems.

    **C.** Hashing is one-way cryptography in that you transform a meaningful plaintext into a meaningless but unique hash value but you cannot go from hash value back to the original meaning or plaintext.

    **D.** Hashing the contents of a file or a message is the first step in producing a private key.

4. How would you use cryptographic techniques to protect the integrity of data in a file if you do not require its content to remain confidential? (Choose all that apply.)

    **A.** Use pervasive encryption techniques to secure the file contents at rest, in motion, and in use.

    **B.** Encrypt the file using the private key of the creator, and make sure all legitimate users can find the corresponding public key.

    **C.** Digitally sign the file, as is done with software patch files, device driver executables, and so forth.

    **D.** Use an encrypting hash to produce a message digest; even a single bit change in the file will cause a subsequent message digest to be different, indicating a loss of integrity.

5. Properly used, cryptographic techniques improve all aspects of CIANA except which of the following?

    **A.** Confidentiality

    **B.** Authentication

    **C.** Nonrepudiation

    **D.** All aspects of CIANA can be enhanced via proper cryptographic techniques.

**6.** Nonrepudiation relies on cryptography to validate which of the following?

   **A.** The sender or author of a document or file is who the recipient thinks it is.

   **B.** The file or message has not been tampered with during transit or storage.

   **C.** The file or message has not been viewed by others or copied without the sender's and named recipient's knowledge.

   **D.** The certificate, public key, or both associated with the sender or author match what is associated with the file or message.

**7.** How can cryptography provide confidentiality and integrity across both time and space? (Choose all that apply.)

   **A.** By protecting data in transit (via Internet or other means), it protects data when en route between two or more physically separated points (in space).

   **B.** Since much of the Internet is carried on long-haul backbone circuits that go via satellite, encryption is used to protect data while being transmitted via radio through space to and from the satellite and ground stations. Without encryption, anybody could receive these signals and break out the data being exchanged.

   **C.** Despite traveling at the speed of light, Internet traffic takes time to go from one user's system to another (i.e. from a client to a server); thus, encryption protects the data in motion during this time.

   **D.** Encrypting a file for storage ensures that it cannot be read or tampered with by unauthorized users or processes (which do not have the key); later, authorized users with the key can read the file.

**8.** Which statement best describes how digital signatures work?

   **A.** The sender hashes the message or file to produce a message digest and applies the chosen encryption algorithm and their private key to it. This is the signature. The recipient uses the sender's public key and applies the corresponding decryption algorithm to the signature, which will produce a matching message digest only if the message or file is authentically from the sender.

   **B.** The sender hashes the message or file to produce a message digest and applies the chosen decryption algorithm and their public key to it. This is the signature. The recipient uses the sender's private key and applies the corresponding encryption algorithm to the signature, which will produce a matching message digest only if the message or file is authentically from the sender.

   **C.** The sender hashes the message or file to produce a message digest and applies the chosen decryption algorithm and their private key to it. This is the signature. The recipient uses the sender's public key and applies the corresponding encryption algorithm to the signature, which will produce a matching message digest only if the message or file is authentically from the sender.

   **D.** The sender encrypts the message or file with their private key and hashes the encrypted file to produce the signed message digest. This is the signature. The recipient uses the sender's public key and applies the corresponding decryption algorithm to the signature, which will produce a matching message digest only if the message or file is authentically from the sender.

9.  What is the role of a hierarchy of trust in using digital signatures? Select the best answer.

    **A.**  Digital signature processes work at the transport layer of TCP/IP, which is below where browser-supported hierarchies of trust function.

    **B.**  The client's operating system, browsers, and applications either embed certificate authorities as trust anchors or use peer-to-peer trust anchors; the client's user must then trust these systems vendors and the installation of their products, and the client's user own use of them, to completely trust that received digitally signed files or messages are legitimate.

    **C.**  The client's operating system, browsers, and applications either embed certificate authorities as trust anchors or use peer-to-peer trust anchors; the recipient of digitally signed files or messages from that client trusts that the client is properly configured and uses valid certificates, and thus can trust the received content.

    **D.**  Certificate authorities, working with government agencies, establish trust anchors on which digital signatures are based; this assures recipients that digitally signed content they receive is from authenticated senders.

10.  Which statements correctly describe the information security risks to most routine uses of email systems? (Choose all that apply.)

    **A.**  Almost all emails are sent unencrypted, with content, file attachment content, and address and routing information open to anyone who chooses to intercept it. This also means that content can be altered en route, and senders and recipients have no reasonable way to detect this.

    **B.**  No existing email systems have strong nonrepudiation capabilities, allowing senders to claim they never received emails or received ones with different content than what was sent.

    **C.**  Since most email server connections use HTTPS, only the routing information is exposed to potential disclosure via traffic analysis.

    **D.**  Most email systems provide ways of using encryption for message content, including attachments, or users can use peer-to-peer solutions like PGP, which will minimize the risk if used properly.

11.  What is required to make a one-time pad encryption system truly unbreakable?

    **A.**  Use an obscure, published book, with a secret way of choosing the key from words, lines, or phrases in that book; this secret must be known only to sender and recipient. This simplifies the key distribution and management process.

    **B.**  Generate the one-time pad key using a cryptographically strong pseudorandom number generator, with a very large random number as seed. Ensure that no portion of it is ever reused, and ensure that only one sender and one recipient have copies of it. Destroy sections of the pad as they are used. Protect the one-time pads at both sender and recipient from loss, theft, or compromise. Provide secure, immediate means to signal both parties of any loss or compromise or change in identity of sender or recipient.

    **C.**  Generate the one-time pad key in a truly random fashion, ensure that no portion of it is ever reused, and ensure that only one sender and one recipient have copies of it. Destroy sections of the pad as they are used. Protect the one-time pads at both sender and recipient from loss, theft, or compromise. Provide secure, immediate means to signal both parties of any loss or compromise or change in identity of sender or recipient.

    **D.**  Combine it with asymmetric encryption systems to create a hybrid architecture, using peer-to-peer certificate authority mechanisms that mask the real identity of the CA, sender, and recipient. This keeps the public keys very private (rather than published) for improved reliability.

**12.** How do webs of trust and hierarchies of trust differ? (Choose all that apply.)

  **A.** Webs of trust are based on peer-to-peer architectures and as such are not very scalable to large numbers of users. Hierarchies of trust rely on certificate authorities as publishers of intermediate certificates, which supports much larger numbers of users.

  **B.** Webs of trust work best when the peer trust anchors are incorporated into the IT logistics supply chain; hierarchies of trust do not need to have information embedded in vendor-provided product systems such as operating systems or browsers.

  **C.** Webs of trust, as peer-to-peer architectures, are not part of the IT logistics supply chain; hierarchies of trust work best when CAs become part of the architecture of hardware, operating systems, browsers, and other applications.

  **D.** They are actually common terms for the same set of architectures and implementations.

**13.** What are information risks that cryptography cannot address? (Choose all that apply.)

  **A.** Display of data to humans, or output of data as device commands in control systems, needs to be in an unencrypted form to be usable.

  **B.** Even cryptographic support for nonrepudiation cannot prove that a recipient (authorized or not) actually read and understood or made use of the contents of a protected file or message; it can only prove that they accessed it.

  **C.** Cryptography cannot be used to reduce risks to information availability.

  **D.** Users with legitimate access to a variety of information at one level of classification, when decrypted for use, may be able to infer the existence or value of information at higher levels of classification.

**14.** Which statement about the use of cryptography by private businesses is true?

  **A.** In most countries, public law and government policy severely restrict the use of cryptography by anyone but the government.

  **B.** Government policies and actions mean that most cryptographic systems available to business are easily broken when government needs to, for law enforcement or national security needs.

  **C.** In many jurisdictions, law and regulation place significant responsibilities for information protection and due diligence on businesses; these can only be met in practical ways by using cryptographic systems.

  **D.** Governments implement cryptographic module verifications programs, which assure businesses that systems they use that contain such modules will meet regulatory and legal constraints for privacy, data protection, and product safety.

**15.** How would you compare the relative security of character, block, or stream ciphers against cryptanalytic attacks?

  **A.** They all depend on the security of the cryptographic key being used.

  **B.** Character ciphers are the least secure, and stream ciphers the most secure.

  **C.** Block ciphers support the best levels of security but with performance penalties that make stream ciphers suitable for some applications.

  **D.** They all have comparable levels of security and depend on algorithms, control parameters, keys, implementation, and use to deliver the required security.

**16.** Why does cryptographic security tend to increase as the key size gets larger?

 **A.** No matter what kind of cryptanalytic attack, the larger the key, the larger the possible space of key values that an attacker must test; each additional binary bit doubles this search or testing time. Ultimately, this requires more computing power and storage than even the most well-funded governments can afford.

 **B.** This is a commonly held belief, but it's not actually true in most cases. Properly chosen algorithms and properly managed cryptosystems are proven to be unbreakable at current key sizes, and making the keys larger will only cause additional throughput delays.

 **C.** This is only a concern for block ciphers, since if the key size is too small, these ciphers are easily broken with rainbow table or dictionary attacks.

 **D.** Larger keys require more complex algorithms to execute without unacceptable runtime impacts, and this combines to provide even greater security.

**17.** What are the most common attacks that business or commercial use of cryptography might be exposed to?

 **A.** Invalid, expired, or fraudulent certificates accepted for use

 **B.** Optical, acoustic, or power line technical monitoring and analysis

 **C.** Social engineering

 **D.** Operational errors in use, such as incorrectly choosing control parameters or mismanaging keys or certificates

**18.** What is the most common source of exploitable vulnerabilities that business or commercial use of cryptography might present to attackers?

 **A.** Invalid, expired, or fraudulent certificates accepted for use

 **B.** Optical, acoustic, or power line technical monitoring and analysis

 **C.** IT supply chain compromises that allow corrupted cryptographic modules to be inserted into systems

 **D.** Operational errors in use, such as incorrectly choosing control parameters or mismanaging keys or certificates

**19.** Should a hash function be reversible?

 **A.** No, because this would allow the plaintext to be decrypted from the hash, rendering message digests and digital signatures unworkable.

 **B.** Yes, because this would allow the hash to contribute to error detection and correction operations.

 **C.** In a limited way, they are reversible, because the hash acts as a pointer or key into database and file management systems where the plaintext comes from.

 **D.** No, because a hash is a many-to-one function and thus must have a collision detection and avoidance mechanism as part of its implementation; being reversible would negate this.

**20.** What conditions might cause you to stop using a key? (Choose all that apply.)

 **A.** Notification that a key has been lost or compromised

 **B.** Suspicion that a user of that key is not who or what they claim to be

 **C.** Indications that your public key has been hijacked by someone masquerading as you

 **D.** You've used it more than 2048 times.

# Chapter

# 8

# Hardware and Systems Security

---

## THE SSCP EXAM OBJECTIVES COVERED IN THIS CHAPTER INCLUDE:

**Domain 7: Systems and Application Security**

✓ 7.1: Identify and Analyze Malicious Code and Activity

✓ 7.2: Implement and Operate Endpoint Device Security

✓ 7.3: Operate and Configure Cloud Security

✓ 7.4: Operate and Secure Virtual Environments

Underneath all of our administrative and logical controls, we find the physical. Without the underlying hardware and without the mix of firmware and operating systems software that makes that hardware actually do something, our applications and data and our business logic and our risk management plans would have nowhere to run and no ability to make work happen. But how do we build trust and confidence that this foundation layer of our trust pyramid is still trustworthy? From the individual chip level up to huge datacenters, hardware and systems vendors build in the features that SSCPs need to utilize to keep the business logic and the business data safe, secure, and resilient. Operating systems developers then layer on both the device-specific OS and the network operating system (NOS).

In this chapter, you will learn how to ensure that the logistics elements of your information risk management plans deliver a trustworthy base of computing, communications, and information storage power. We are taking the *infrastructure* view of our systems security practice. The economics of the cloud have changed our thinking about when or whether to own our own servers or rent them by the millisecond. Regardless, there are a lot of devices between the servers (whoever owns them) and our users, so device security is still a paramount concern and probably always will be. As a result, this chapter will deal with operating and securing the systems your organization "owns" rather than rents time on; Chapter 9, "Applications, Data, and Cloud Security," will extend that thinking into the cloud. We'll also focus here on systems, while leaving Chapter 9 to look at applications (homegrown or vendor-supplied platforms) and data security.

# Infrastructure Security Is Baseline Management

We take the viewpoint in this chapter that to keep your organization's information systems secure, as infrastructures and as they are in use, you have to manage them as a baseline. You have to *control* that baseline, and know how to be able to validate or confirm that what's in the real, live, deployed, and in-use baseline *right now* is what's supposed to be there, no more and no less. This infrastructure-as-managed-baseline view starts with the lowest level of physical devices you use; layer by layer, you increase your span of what you *should* control as you add on capabilities, connections, and utility.

Recall our definition of an infrastructure as a set of systems that work together to provide a common set of capabilities to a wide variety of users. Your organization's accounting department, for example, needs the same set of communications, data storage and retrieval, and computing capabilities (the same common infrastructure) as the product design group uses. On top of that infrastructure, the accountants add their "Big Four" software to handle accounts payable, accounts receivable, payroll, and finance, while product development groups add in CAD/CAM packages, simulation systems, or bill of material planning tools. Users then go many steps further as they embed business logic into data, metadata, macros, formulas, and programs that they write, which at some point become so widely used that they're almost a part of the infrastructure. Then there are user-provided or user-owned hardware, software, systems, and data, which all seem to *need* to become part of your systems. Add to this the ever-growing wilderness of the Internet of Things (IoT), and it's no wonder you're facing baseline management concerns!

Management and leadership must set boundaries and priorities, and establish and direct them via policies and other administrative measures. As an SSCP, you may be asked to advise them on these; you most likely will have to help implement them, enforce them, and report on compliance issues.

## It's About Access Control...

...which of course means it's also about identity authentication and management. It's important to realize that as the SSCP on watch, so to speak, identity and access mean more than just software implementations in Active Directory, LDAP, or identity as a service (IDaaS) cloud-hosted IT-centric solutions! We'll discuss the details of people control in Chapter 11, "Business Continuity via Information Security and People Power," and we've discussed the software mechanics of identity management and access control in Chapter 6, "Identity and Access Control." But it's vitally important to realize that without controlling how people can get physical access to the actual hardware, cabling, spare parts and supplies, and the power and communications gear that make your IT infrastructure function, you're taking an incredible gamble. This access control need for safety and security should extend to everyone—staff, owners, senior stakeholders, and board of directors members, as well as clients, potential customers, and friends and family members of employees coming for a personal visit. Many larger organizations have recognized that, much like the military and intelligence communities, they have their "no lone zones," areas physical and logical into which no employee should be authorized to enter without someone else being with them—being aware of their entry and exit from the zone, monitoring their actions, or having a nonrepudiable audit trail of those actions. This "no lone zone" perspective protects the organization *and* the individual worker; it should start with the root of the hierarchies of trust your business depends on by starting at the physical reality of your offices and work spaces and the IT hardware you put into those spaces *or* allow to be brought into them.

**Safety First!**

Human safety always comes first. Law, custom, and natural expectation dictate this. Regrettably, we see any number of industries and even societies where this just doesn't seem to be the case.

We have to remember that in Western industrialized societies, putting worker and people safety first is a twentieth century innovation. It may have come about due to humanitarian thinking or because enlightened management realized that injured workers cost more and produce less. But there are still places around the globe that hold life cheap.

As SSCPs, we have to practice to the highest standards, and safety of life comes first for us. That drives how we design and operate our information systems, how we keep them safe, and how we prioritize our decisions when responding to an incident.

## It's Also About Supply Chain Security

Every element of your organization's IT systems runs on or with hardware, firmware, software, and data made by someone else, modified by someone else, and maintained or supported by someone else. Its parts and subsystems elements, layer by layer, come into being through long and complex value chains of organizations that buy and sell parts and subsystems from each other; they buy rights to chip-level or board-level design information. These supply chains wrap around the entire world—the most commonly licensed patents for cell phone technology originate in Finland and end up in chips designed in dozens of countries that are manufactured in a dozen more, before they end up in your company's products, systems, or end-user devices, or the IoT elements of your systems.

Many larger organizations form strategic partnerships with their top-tier suppliers and services providers to form a trusted supply chain. The trusted supply chain is an ancient concept—it may have originated in early agrarian societies that first used futures contracts to ensure sufficient grain production to meet bakers' needs. Each trusted supply chain has a set of values it seeks to protect, whether that is socially acceptable practices, environmentally friendly production, sustainability, or quality, safety, and reliability. Companies large and small need to rely on supply chains they can trust; trust needs to support your organization's risk management strategy and plan, and harmonize with rather than further threaten the findings of your vulnerability assessments. Ultimately, trusting your supply chain means a healthy dose of knowing the people and the players in it; being transparent about production, sources of supply, and design and production techniques; sharing insights from verification and validation testing; and letting your suppliers know and trust *you* as a customer.

It may seem at first glance that as an SSCP, you'd have a very small role at the edge of the "trusted supply chain problem set," if we could group all of these issues under one label. As we look deeper into what it takes to keep just the IT hardware, its firmware, operating systems, and the network systems they use safe, secure, and reliable, keep thinking about the supply chains *you* and the IT team need to rely on. As you see those supply chains in action—or as and if they fail to act in reliable ways—you may be called on or need to step up to make them more secure and more trustworthy.

## Do Clouds Have Boundaries?

Cloud services can be part of your organization's IT systems as private, public, or hybrid environments:

- *Private clouds* are those cloud systems that one organization has sole and dedicated use of. In one type of private cloud deployment, the organization owns (or rents) the host hardware, licenses the systems and hypervisor software for, and is responsible for all maintenance and provisioning of that cloud. Configuration management, from hardware on up, is the organization's responsibility. When renting service bureau or data-center capabilities, this can sometimes be called a *bare iron* cloud, since the supplier doesn't do much more than provide equipment, power, air conditioning, and physical premises security. Any requirement for geographically dispersed backup capabilities, load sharing, and so forth is the responsibility of the organization. The other type of private cloud deployment uses cloud services providers (such as Microsoft and Amazon) to provide fully secure, private services to the customer organization, guaranteeing the total privacy and integrity of these services via contract and service level agreements. The cloud services provider operates and maintains all equipment and facilities; software configuration management and licensing then are based on what sort of service model the client organization chooses to use.

- *GovCloud* is becoming the next major initiative in cloud-hosting arrangements. It provides cloud services tailored to meet the needs of the U.S. federal government, whether for a single agency or for an interagency federation of activities. Major cloud-hosting providers, such as Amazon and Microsoft, structure their GovCloud offerings in various ways to meet the needs of government, their contractors, and others that they work with to collaborate on sensitive information and processing needs. GovCloud provides ways for such participants to ensure that their work meets the U.S. International Traffic in Arms Regulations (ITAR) requirements when developing systems for sale or deployment internationally.

- *Public clouds* are cloud systems in which multiple, unrelated customers are hosted on the cloud provider's systems, sharing that set of hardware, systems, and software resources; the cloud services provider is responsible for the hardware, hypervisor, communications, and systems software, along with power, air conditioning, security, and maintenance. These customers may be competitors, partners in other business ventures, or totally unrelated to each other. Typically, service level agreements (SLAs) will define privacy requirements that keep the identity, usage patterns, and contract terms of one customer private from other customers. Public clouds may be hosted by very large companies (such as Microsoft Azure, Amazon Web Services, and Google Cloud Platform) or hundreds of much smaller cloud providers. The larger systems provide very large datacenters around the world, with varying capabilities for dynamic synchronization, load balancing, and backup of data across these centers.

▪ *Hybrid clouds* are cloud systems that have (as you'd expect) a mix of both public and private characteristics. A particular organization may have a need to host some business processes on a local, private cloud system that is fully under its control, while using public cloud services for other business processes.

From a security management perspective, think of this in *contractual* terms: if your organization signs a contract with a service bureau or cloud systems provider for any kinds of "as-a-service" arrangements, then that contract (or SLA) documents where your IT team's responsibilities for security end and the cloud systems provider's take over. In many respects, a private cloud is not that much different than a private datacenter that operates without a hypervisor and virtual machine capabilities; in both cases, your organization "owns" its success or failure, whether it purchased the equipment outright or is leasing it.

With that in mind, let's first look at the private cloud or the non-cloud private datacenter as the critical infrastructure you need to protect.

# Infrastructures 101 and Threat Modeling

Compare and contrast a typical small office/home office (SOHO) local area network (LAN), which might support a dozen users via a network attached storage, a router, and a Wi-Fi access point, to a typical datacenter design. The datacenter needs to provide redundant Internet connections; multiple connection paths from endpoints within the company premises; mobile device access management; remote access management; multiple compute servers capable of meeting the data processing needs of the organization; and much larger storage capacity, including backup capabilities. Adaptive, load-balancing switches are necessary to bring those capabilities together internally in a mesh architecture that can provide a degree of hot-swap repair and replacement as processor boards, RAM, or disk drives fail. Figure 8.1 shows a typical datacenter design, illustrating these concepts; datacenters along these lines started to appear in the 1990s and are still in use today.

What this notional diagram does not show are the additional infrastructure elements that provide endpoint access to the datacenter. This would probably involve another set of (redundant) domain controller servers, communications or network management servers, and adaptive, load-balancing switching, to bring authorized local and remote user login and access capability into the mesh of the core and aggregation layer routers.

**FIGURE 8.1**    Notional datacenter design

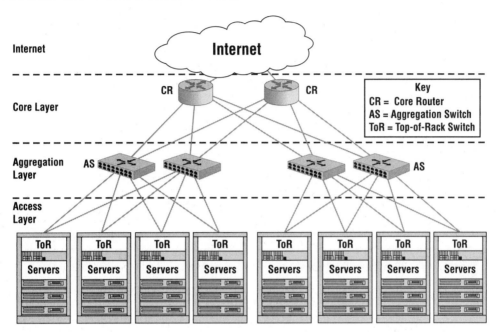

What's inside each of those blocks on that diagram (and the blocks on the diagrams not shown) are more layers of our IT infrastructure. At the lowest level is board-level computing hardware, along with its internal memory for firmware and software; these form the "bare metal" of most servers, processors, and even routers, switches, and gateways. Next, add on the input/output controllers, storage servers, and their associated disk drives. Electrical power and air conditioning come next, and of course, the interconnect cabling or fiber that knits it all together. On top of all that hardware, we need to cope with layers of programming, from closest to the hardware to closest to the user. This becomes clear if we look at the sequence of control as the hardware first starts its power-up sequence:

1.  Hard-wired logic starts the reset / restart sequence , and quickly turns control over to very low-level firmware in read-only memory at the chip level.

2.  Firmware in read-only memory chips or boards then starts to prepare for device-level initialization and control.

3.  More firmware comes next, which can be what initializes the system at cold boot or warm reset. In PC architectures, these functions were originally performed by the basic input-output subroutines (BIOS), which has largely been replaced by the Unified Extensible Firmware Interface [UEFI] bootstrap system.

4.  Then, control is turned over to the bootstrap loader software, either on hard disk, over the network, or other network attached storage.

5.  The bootstrap loader software loads, and turns control over to, the operating system loader and start-up routines.

**6.** Finally the OS system loader and start-up routines control the loading and initialization of the rest of the operating system, including user access controls, network logon and initialization, and other startup-time software.

At each step along the way, any number of configuration and control parameters are also read out of storage (firmware read-only memory, or files in the file system). These values are as critical to proper initialization and startup of the device as the instructions in the firmware or software. Many of these parameters can be edited by means of setup utilities, which users can access during the hardware boot process, once the operating system has finished loading, or both.

Whether the device in question is a router, a switch, a server, or an endpoint workstation, we see this same hierarchy of code. From the SSCP's perspective, the message should be clear: *everywhere you look, the hardware has embedded firmware, software, or other control parameters that must be protected from corruption or attack*. With that in mind, let's look closer at a few vulnerabilities along the way, from the lowest-level chip up to the datacenter and beyond.

### The Zero Day Exploit

It's clear that many people worldwide are actively seeking new vulnerabilities within the hardware and software systems we use every day. When *white hat*, or ethical, hackers discover a new vulnerability, they work with the system manufacturer or vendor to confirm that the vulnerability is real. The vendor can then work on a containment or prevention patch, while trying to resolve the underlying design or manufacturing flaw that led to the vulnerability.

To the black hat hackers, discovering a new, heretofore undocumented vulnerability or a new exploit against an existing, documented vulnerability represents a win in the race against time. There is a window of opportunity here for the black hat: until someone else discovers the same vulnerability and reports it to the manufacturer, the vendor, or the cybersecurity community at large, this new vulnerability may be open to undetected exploitation. This window of opportunity can exist for hours, days, or even months. Exploits done during that window are considered *zero day exploits*, not because they are exploited immediately (within 24 hours) of being found, but because the exploit happens before legitimate users, the manufacturer, or the cybersecurity community as a whole knows of the existence of the vulnerability.

The Stuxnet attack on the Iranian nuclear fuels processing systems is a case in point. Allegedly, Western intelligence and cyberwarfare experts discovered that previously unknown vulnerabilities existed in these fuels processing systems. These vulnerabilities could be exploited to command high-speed centrifuges to operate in ways that damaged or destroyed them, while simultaneously lying to systems operators by reporting falsified operating conditions. It apparently took months to infiltrate Stuxnet into these facilities, yet Stuxnet is considered a zero day exploit.

The key question to ask? How would you detect that somebody was running a zero day exploit against the systems you are defending?

# Hardware Vulnerabilities

This is a good time to remember that physical asset protection needs to consider theft, inadvertent or deliberate damage to, or tampering with equipment and systems as significant risks; risks that could lead to disruption to our business information systems. In Chapter 4, "Operationalizing Risk Mitigation," you considered these risks as part of the installed baseline of systems when doing the vulnerabilities assessment. This physical asset protection needs to extend across the lifecycle of that hardware, from identifying suppliers and vendors, purchasing, shipping it to your locations and receiving it; through installation and use; spare parts and maintenance activities; and finally, after it is decommissioned and disposed of. At each step in that physical asset lifecycle, those threats of accidental or deliberate damage or other loss are part of the risks you need to address.

Electrical power and other operating environment characteristics can also represent possible threat vectors to the hardware installed within your locations. Depending on your particular installation and its needs, there may also be safety needs to address, such as how power and data cabling are protected from becoming trip hazards to personnel, or kept from being exposed to pinch, crush, or other damage by others in the workplace.

## Protecting the Hardware

Physical access control is important. This can be as simple as antitheft cable locks for PCs, laptops, or other small and highly portable devices, or installing equipment (such as modems, routers, and servers in a SOHO environment) in locking cabinets. The point of presence (where your Internet service provider's physical cable or fiber enters your workplace) also needs to be physically protected; even in most SOHO facilities, most employees do not need routine, unrestricted physical access to the modem, router, signal, and power cabling.

Although it's perhaps obvious that an organization with its own on-premises datacenter needs to have that datacenter physically secured—restricting access to authorized IT department personnel, for example—even in smaller SOHO environments, physical security must be a consideration. Guests, visitors, or employees can easily reset unsecured equipment, which at a minimum causes a temporary disruption in service. It can also provide the opportunity for someone to reprogram the device (once it's been reset to its factory default settings, including its administrative login information).

Your organization may need to prevent or tightly control the use of removable media, such as USB, Firewire, or other devices. This may require blank panels that cover the USB ports on laptops or servers, for example. Don't forget the USB ports on the routers or modems—many network devices provide these as part of their feature set, and if your organization needs them blocked, do so.

## Trusted Platform Modules

*Trusted platform modules (or TPMs)* are specialized hardware devices, incorporated into the motherboard of the computer, phone, or tablet, that provide enhanced cryptographic-based device and process security services. A TPM is provided in a sealed, tamper-resistant hardware package that combines cryptographic services, host computer state descriptor information, and other data. TPMs are embedded into the computer's motherboard (so as to be non-removable), and in combination with device drivers and other software, achieve greater levels of security for that system. The Trusted Computing Group (TCG), a consortium of over 120 manufacturers, software houses, and cybersecurity companies from around the world, develops and publishes standards that describe what TPMs should do, and what they should not. The TCG defines trust in simple terms: a trusted device behaves in a particular, specified manner for a specified purpose. By storing key parameters about the host computer itself (chip-level serial numbers, for example), a TPM provides an extra measure of assurance that the computer system it is a part of is still behaving in the ways that its manufacturer intended. TPMs typically contain their own special-purpose, reduced instruction set computer; read-only memory for the control program; key, hash, and random number generators; and storage locations for configuration information, platform identity keys, and other data. TPMs are being incorporated into laptops, phones, and tablet systems, providing a world-class solution that is not strongly tied to or dominated by one manufacturer's chip set, operating system, or hierarchy of trust implementation.

TPMs protect the hardware itself by making it less attractive to steal, or less useful (easier to lock) when the host computer or phone is lost or mislaid. Although the TPM does not control any software tasks (system or application) running on the host, it can add to the security of processes designed to make use of it. It's probably fair to consider a TPM an additional hardware countermeasure to help make software and communications more secure.

## Firmware Vulnerabilities

Firmware is just software that has been put into nonvolatile, read-only memory; this memory can be onboard an integrated circuit chip, in programmable read-only memory (PROM) chips that can only be written (or "programmed") once; in erasable or alterable PROM; or in other special-purpose storage technologies associated with a device. We can think of firmware as either permanently embedded in the device, or subject to update or alteration (authorized or unauthorized).

- *Firmware has its own unique vulnerabilities, which you need to take into consideration as you develop plans to harden your systems:* In late 2017 and early 2018, multiple researchers reported finding errors in the design of several widely used CPU and GPU chips. Known by names such as Spectre, Meltdown, and most recently TL-Bleed, these errors in chip design and very low-level firmware (on board the CPU or GPU chip itself) could lead to significant compromises of data and process security. Since the chips themselves are used in computers from many vendors, almost all major operating systems were at risk. OS vendors quickly responded with patches (most of which turned off high-performance features that could expose these vulnerabilities to exploitation) and then worked to redesign, test, and distribute new versions of kernel portions of their OS. As of September 2018, no exploits of these vulnerabilities had been found in the wild—that is, outside of white hat cybersecurity research and test labs.

- *Network and communications firmware as targets:* From SOHO routers and switches on up, all of the hardware that makes our networks work has firmware in it, and that firmware has been provided with update mechanisms that can be compromised. (It doesn't help that all of these devices are shipped with well-known full administrative user IDs such as "admin" and default passwords of "password…"). Consider

Figure 8.2, an email received by the author recently. At first glance, it looks like a legitimate email notification from Netgear, announcing the availability of a new security update for its Nighthawk router family's onboard firmware. Great news! But... upon closer inspection, the email comes from a nonstandard email address for Netgear, and the embedded links are to definitely suspicious places on the Web (or maybe the Dark Web). Like many systems vendors, Netgear makes a lot of technical information available about its products, and encourages third-party and end-user customization; multiple hacks (presumably white hat hacks) of their device firmware are out there in the wild. Think about this, the next time you're staying in a bed-and-breakfast property or hotel and enjoying its free Wi-Fi connectivity.

**FIGURE 8.2**    Is this firmware update good news?

## Protecting Your Firmware

For critical devices, firmware that can be updated should be treated as part of the configuration-controlled baseline and be subject to change controls and audits. Change management tools that allow you to poll devices to report their current firmware versions can make this task easier, but beware: if you can do this over your internal networks, this may mean that external threat actors can do this as well. Some consumer-friendly network products (or IoT products) do not provide easy ways to verify the version and date of their firmware, and depending on your risk profiles, this may be acceptable or not. It would be prudent to replace these with other products that are more configuration-management friendly! Like all software updates, you should have policies and procedures in place that only those legitimate firmware updates, received from the device manufacturer or other trusted source, are applied to devices when and how you need them to be updated. Keep a backup of the device's firmware and settings before the update, if possible; keep change control records as you apply updates.

### Never Deploy the Factory Default Settings!

This *should* go without saying. Those defaults are downright necessary to initially configure the device, and to reset it when you've lost configuration control of it or lost your own sysadmin user ID and password! But that's no excuse for leaving these doorways into your systems wide open.

Critical systems elements, including routers, switches, and firewalls, should also have a test and validation plan, which you can use to verify that a firmware update has not caused a mission-critical feature to fail to operate correctly, or introduced other issues that you'll need to work around. Such test and validation plans and procedures can be run periodically, even without updates being installed, as part of validating that the system element and the overall system are still functioning properly.

## Operating Systems Vulnerabilities

Operating systems provide a lucrative and attractive target to hackers. As of September 2018, Windows 10, for example, showed at least 650 entries in Common Vulnerabilities and Exposures (CVE) databases that are published online. Many of these CVE entries refer to configuration settings, such as Group Policy Objects, which individual Windows systems administrators must choose to enable and tailor to achieve their required security levels. Apple's operating systems, and the many variants of Linux, have their own fair share of reported vulnerabilities. Mobile device operating systems, such as Android, IOS, and Windows in its phone variants also have many reported vulnerabilities.

Most widely used operating systems come with automatic update features built in. Enterprise IT environments can manage these updates (as "push" updates to groups of systems) as they need to, which provides an opportunity to first verify that the latest OS patch is still compatible with business-critical applications, platforms, and systems. SOHO systems users tend to just take the OS updates as and when they come.

## Malware and Your OSs

*Malware,* or software that is malicious in intent and effect, is the general name for any type of software that comes into your system without your full knowledge and consent, performs some functions you would not knowingly authorize it to, and in doing so diverts compute resources from your organization. Malware has its origins in what we now call *white hat hacking* attempts by various programmers and computer scientists to experiment with software and its interactions with hardware, operating systems, and other computing technologies. As malware continues to evolve quite rapidly, the lines between the classical Trojan horse, virus, worm, or other types of malware blur very quickly.

In general, malware consists of a vehicle or package that gets introduced into the target system; it may then release or install a payload that functions separately from the vehicle. Viruses, worms, scareware, and other types of malware typically bring payloads with them, in addition to performing other unauthorized and possibly harmful functions themselves. These payloads scan provide hidden, unauthorized entry points into the system (such as a Trojan horse), facilitate the exfiltration of sensitive data, modify data (such as system event logs) to hide the malware's presence and activities, destroy or corrupt user data, or even encrypt it to hold it for ransom. Malware payloads also form a part of target reconnaissance and characterization activities carried out by some advanced persistent threats, such as by installing keystroke loggers, spyware of various types, or scareware.

*Trojan horse* malware (classically named) disguises its nefarious payload within a wrapper or delivery "gift" that seems attractive, such as a useful program, a video, or music file, or a purported update to another program. Other types of malware, such as viruses and worms, got their names from their similarities with the way such disease vectors can transmit sickness in animal or plant populations. *Viruses,* for example, infect one target machine and then launch out to attack others; worms look to find many instances within the target to infect, making their eradication from the host problematic. Malware payloads can also transform your system into a launch platform from which attacks on other systems can be originated. Payloads can also just steal CPU cycles by performing parts of a distributed computation by means of your system's CPUs and GPUs; other than slowing down your own work, such cycle-stealing usually does not harm the host system. Codebreaking and cryptocurrency mining are but two of the common uses of such cycle-stealing.

*Rootkits* are a special class of malware that use a variety of privilege elevation techniques to insert themselves into the lowest-level (or kernel) functions in the operating system, which upon bootup get loaded and enabled before most anti-malware or antivirus systems are loaded and enabled. Rootkits, in essence, can give complete and almost undetectable control of your system to attackers and are a favorite of advanced persistent threats.

## Protecting Your OSs

First, make sure that each instance of an operating system (installed and operating on each computer, router, switch, or server) is included in your information systems baseline and in your configuration management and change control processes. Make sure that you can easily verify what version and patch or update level each such device is operating with. This is particularly important if your system does not support the ability to push updates to all such devices at the same time. Know which devices have not yet been updated, and, depending on the nature of the update, have plans in place for appropriate levels of extra monitoring to ensure that vulnerabilities are not exploited while waiting for the patches to be applied.

Almost all operating systems vendors provide their code in digitally signed release packages, which you can use to validate that the software distribution kit is authentic and has not been tampered with. Additionally, many operating systems have built-in tools that allow users to validate that OS libraries (directory trees) contain only authorized, signed, current files, matching a manifest list that came with the patch or update distribution. Your organization's systems administrators should be using these capabilities as part of the update installation and verification process.

It is vitally important to note that many of the published CVE items have been addressed by one or more patches or updates from the respective software vendor. Despite this, any number of headline-making data breaches are made possible (or made easier) because of patches and updates that have not yet been applied. It is common sense and good computing hygiene to routinely compare your organization's information systems security baseline against published CVE data.

As with all software changes, your organization should have a validation test process that confirms that updates have been successfully and completely installed, that they work correctly, and that all critical systems functions and services are still in working order.

---

### You've Been Orphaned—Now What?

More often than the industry might want to admit, users are faced with perfectly working hardware and applications that are no longer supported by their manufacturer or software vendor. This can happen to operating systems, device drivers for peripherals, applications that manage those peripherals, or general purpose applications. These become orphans when their vendor or manufacturer will no longer provide updates for them, particularly to port or migrate their software to a new version of the target operating systems. When Microsoft declared that Windows XP, for example, was (for many good reasons) beyond its support life, many printers, photo and document scanners, and even medical laboratory instrument manufacturers had to follow suit and orphan their products. The National Health Service in the U.K. faced a significant financial impact and an information security dilemma, as it had to either continue to run clinics all across the country on Windows XP, or purchase a substantial amount of new hardware and applications.

Sometimes, your business can protect itself from being stuck with an orphaned technology by means of negotiating a software escrow agreement. This places all of the source code, design, and maintenance documentation, and test drivers and test data into a third party's secure storage; if the vendor goes out of business, the escrow is opened and the code and related information are given to the escrow purchaser. While this may reduce the risk of being left high and dry if the manufacturer or vendor goes out of business, it can be very expensive—and it still leaves your business tied to an obsolete set of software that you now have to migrate to a new OS environment.

Software or source code escrow can also help insure that the source code developed by a third party specifically for your business is not at risk if the third party goes out of business. It can be a useful option, but it's not inexpensive.

# Virtual Machines and Vulnerabilities

More and more organizations are using virtual machine technologies to extend their computing capabilities, even before they move into a cloud environment. On a bare metal computer or server, as we saw earlier, the bootstrap process loads several layers of functionality before the operating system itself is loaded and takes control of the computer. Up until this happens, any operating system (that can execute on that CPU's instruction set) can be loaded. That OS will use physical RAM and virtual memory to load and manage the execution of applications programs. This copy of the operating system is in essence a virtual machine, running on top of the lowest level of kernel functions that deal directly with the hardware. Application programs "see" the OS and its set of services; they are insulated from the bare metal below it. As early as 1972, IBM created the first *hypervisor*—a program specifically designed to sit between the bare metal computer and multiple instances of operating systems and applications, each with its own virtual memory address space. This type of hypervisor architecture is perhaps the most prevalent in the industry today. Type two (or *hosted*) hypervisors load as applications under the control of a fully loaded operating system, and then load, execute, and supervise virtual machines to meet user needs. Most systems today require hardware support for virtualization to run efficiently. Regardless of which type of hypervisor your systems are using, one virtue of virtual machines is that the host environment (hypervisor on bare metal or hosted hypervisor) encapsulates the virtual machine's operating system, applications, and data storage; each VM has its own separate file system, and applications running on one VM cannot bleed into or access memory on another VM.

Creating a new instance of a virtual machine is a simple matter of a few mouse clicks. Instead of leasing new hardware, getting it shipped to your datacenter, installing it, testing it, and making it available for use, businesses can multiply the number of computers available to meet their processing needs within a few moments, and then give back the excess capability when they don't need it anymore. VMs in public or hybrid clouds rent by the second of CPU time. Private clouds still need the bare metal (and RAM, and disk space) to execute in, but a thoughtful VM strategy can get far more utility per month out of that hardware than a simpler strategy that preassigns users and tasks to specific machines.

This sounds ideal, doesn't it? Up until the VM needs to communicate to the outside world, and share resources on a network with other machines (virtual or not), it is. Software testing environments using VMs as containers provide robust sandboxes in which to test new versions of systems by means of this separation.

Once your VMs start to share resources—once they connect via software-defined networks to form a virtual cluster of processing and storage capabilities—problems on one VM do have the opportunity to bleed over onto other VMs. The most frequently reported problem in Amazon Web Services in 2017, for example, was poorly configured cloud data storage *blobs*, rather than "virtual disks"; user errors in setting up these blobs is the proximate cause cited by Amazon.

---

**Blobs: Binary Large Objects**

Cloud data storage services need to allow users to define how much storage they need without being tied down by the storage capacity of a disk drive. This gave rise to the blob, or binary large object, as the unit of cloud storage. Blobs (and that word is *not* an acronym) can range from the "tiny blob" of 64 KB, up through the blob, mediumblob, and longblob. This allows the cloud services provider the freedom to spread blobs across disk drives of many types and sizes, support encryption at the blob level, or provide other storage management capabilities independently of the specific storage technologies being used.

---

That very capability for near-instant growth in your VM fleet is also an opportunity for complexity in your security architecture. Unless each VM you create is just another copy of a proven, tested, well-controlled baseline system, your security management workload goes up with each VM you instantiate.

### Protecting Your VMs (and Protecting Your Other Systems from Them!)

The nature of your organization, its IT system needs, and its risk profile may very well dictate limits or constraints on which users can create what sort of virtual machines, for what purposes, and in what sort of environments. Software development and test, for example, should have procedures that control creation, use, and disposal of VM containers used as part of such development and test activities. Typically, most users would not need to do this; instead, they'd be interacting with some kind of platform or infrastructure set of services, and as they demand more from those services, this would lead to VMs being *spun up* (created or instanced) to meet their needs.

Once such policy considerations have been made, and administrative actions taken to publish and promulgate them, the IT experts can work to implement the right set of controls so that those users who need to create and use VMs can do so. Policy should also dictate suitable logging and monitoring, as required.

## Network Operating Systems

It used to be that individual computer systems (be they desktops or minicomputers) had operating systems that did not have networking capabilities built into them; add-on products like NetWare or Banyan VINES needed to be used to make networking with other devices or the Internet possible. As the market drove toward a monoculture solution—almost the entire world uses TCP/IP—these support stacks of software functions got integrated with the operating systems. Today, all supported variants of Windows, macOS, and Linux are network operating systems as much as they are computer operating systems. The line between being a computer and being a network device has largely disappeared.

What this means is that the network operating system has morphed into a distributed set of subsystems. The datacenter shown in Figure 8.1 suggests that the operational command, control, and synchronization services, the resource allocation, assignment, and task or process control functions now are shared responsibilities. The routers (at all levels), each rack full of servers, and each server itself, all become elements in a shared resource pool, often called a *service fabric*. Individual subjects (human users or processes invoked at their behest) have their needs addressed by the datacenter, which is managed by this distributed set of operating system functions, which are collectively controlled by the service fabric manager functions.

Whether that network operates as an integrated, tightly coupled set of subsystems or a loosely coupled set of systems that cooperate on a best-effort basis depends on choices made by its designers, builders, and managers. From the SSCP's perspective, the question is whether its security functions work together in an integrated, cohesive way or not. Do all of the security features and functions, in all of the hardware and software on the network, provide integrated command, control, and communications regarding security functions, alarms, and conditions? Or does the SSCP have to become the commander and orchestrate, dispatch, run, review, and monitor all of the security functions, and *then* collate all of the outputs, log files, and alarms from all of those security "troops" into a common security operational picture?

## Protecting the Networks

As you saw in Chapter 5, "Communications and Network Security," there's a wealth of technology and procedural countermeasures and protective measures regarding network systems security that ought to be part of your overall systems security approach and strategy. Let your risk mitigation planning drive your needs here—use that to identify timelines for prompt detection and response.

## Intrusion Detection and Prevention

Intrusion detection systems (IDSs) monitor attempts to access system resources to determine if such attempts are legitimate or are potential hostile intrusions. Host-based intrusion detection systems (HIDSs) are software applications that run on a host computer, such as a server, workstation, laptop, or smartphone or other mobile devices. They are installed so that they become part of the operating system boot sequence, much like antivirus systems are, and they typically work by focusing on attempts to violate access control policies and mechanisms. Network-based intrusion detection systems (NIDSs) are separate hardware and software platforms that sit between the protected, managed portions of your network and less secure zones (such as the Internet). Unlike HIDSs, NIDSs monitor network traffic and alert when packets attempt to access ports, services, or addresses, or attempt other actions that the NIDS is configured to detect.

Both kinds of intrusion detection systems can use either an anomaly-based detection or a signature-based detection approach. Anomaly detection requires that the IDS be able to "learn" from normal system or network usage, typically using machine learning approaches. For example, if normal traffic sees very small upload data volumes compared to download, a sudden spike in outbound data might be an anomaly worth noting, perhaps a data exfiltration attempt underway. Signature-based detection requires analytical efforts to take a known exploit, observe and identify key parameters that are associated with that exploit, and then scan traffic through the IDS looking for that signature. Detection of a possible intrusion, in any case, signals an alarm condition, which may result in a real-time notice to an administrator, log entries, or other alert actions. Some IDS systems of either type may also be able to act as intrusion prevention systems (IPSs). IPSs can be programmed to shut down or block a suspect connection, route it instead to a quarantine area or *honeypot*, or take other actions to contain the impacts of the potential intrusion.

 Given the millions of exploits being discovered each month, you can see that signature-based detection may soon become impractical.

## MDM, COPE, and BYOD

For many very sensible reasons, many businesses and organizations turn to mobile computing as a part of their IT infrastructure. As you saw in Chapter 5, this approach avoids many of the costs of a physical, wired infrastructure but brings with it the need for added attention to wireless security and mobile device management. Company-owned or provided mobile devices, such as laptops, phablets, phones, or even printers, can be a great way to leverage the IT budget quickly. *Mobile device management* (MDM) systems provide a variety of integrated tools that can help the organization maintain awareness of its mobile assets, track their usage, and provide management with insight and control of software, firmware, and data updates on these devices. When the organization controls these devices, it's reasonable to expect that the full gamut of acceptable use, configuration management and control, and other risk management policies apply to employees using such devices. These devices are of course subject to loss or theft, and as a result, the better MDM solutions provide ways to ensure that lost devices can be locked or zeroized to prevent data on the device being accessed, or the device being used to access the organization's networks and systems.

*Bring your own devices (BYOD)* is the term for when organizational IT infrastructures have to deal with computing and communications equipment, software, security tools, and data that do not belong to the organization and are not under its legal span of control. From its early days of floppy disks, thumb drives, and telecommuting to today, this has grown bewilderingly. Vendors, customers, prospective employees, and visitors of any kind to the business's locations, even family and friends of employees, all can bring in their own phones, laptops, tablets, and smart watches, and all have varying expectations about connecting to or making use of your organization's IT infrastructure. In many cases it's to the company's advantage to encourage employees to own and operate their own equipment, but it comes with up-front and downstream costs and risks.

*Company-owned personally enabled (COPE)*, as the name suggests, refers to strategies in which the organization owns and exerts some configuration management, application whitelisting, and security feature enforcements on the device that it issues to an individual employee. The employee can then (within policy limits) install applications and data for work-related or purely personal use. An example might be a university that provides laptops to its full-time faculty for the purpose of work-related teaching, courseware development, research, and organizational service tasks, knowing that the laptops can and will be used for purely personal (professional or other) activities.

**CYOD?**

Choose your own device (CYOD) is a common variation on the COPE theme, in which the organization owns or leases a smaller set of device types and issues them to employees to use with company systems and data. Employees can choose from this limited set, but are restricted from using personally owned devices with company data or systems. While this reduces the IT configuration management issues and makes the threat surface more manageable, it doesn't directly address visitor, customer, client, or guest use of mobile devices at the edges of the organization's systems.

Note that CYOD and COPE can refer to *company* or *corporate* ownership (or lease) and management of the devices.

Key issues that the SSCP can advise management about include but are not restricted to:

- Device access control, possibly using multifactor authentication
- Lost device locking or erasure of company content, software, encryption keys, and certificates
- Commingling of personal, non-work-related data and apps on the same device with company data
- Roaming security policies and practices that BYOD company users must abide by
- Device location tracking, usage tracking, and security analytics to support ongoing network and systems monitoring
- Policy restrictions on other non-employees using the BYOD device
- Restrictions on use of the BYOD device as a Wi-Fi hotspot or as part of other networks
- Auditing of the BYOD device content and usage
- Software and firmware update control and audit, both of software required for the business and software desired by the device-owning employee

At the moment, the MDM marketplace and community of practice is still struggling to find a common set of requirements that can be addressed by a common infrastructure solution. One major problem is deciding whether the BYOD security problem is anything different than what we face with endpoint security and data in motion regardless of who owns or exerts configuration management and control over the endpoint. This is a fundamental concern that has to be addressed in the context of the organization and its mission.

## BYOI? BYOC?

Many businesses and organizations have to deal with a greatly expanded version of the BYOD problem set, sometimes called *bring your own infrastructure* (BYOI). BYOI calls attention to the potential security issues that arise when smartphones, laptops or phablets, and even wearable computing devices bring hotspot connectivity, shared storage, and even shared or personally managed cryptographic resources to the workplace. In some situations, the nature of work itself, and the nature of the employee-employer relationship, morphs in innovative and disruptive ways. Taxi drivers, for example, are often using their personally owned devices to communicate with dispatchers, provide contact with customers for private bookings, conduct payment and billing operations, and even provide a W-Fi hotspot for passenger use. *Bring your own cloud (BYOC)* is an example of this, as it combines personal, consumer-facing cloud services (such as Dropbox) with enterprise-level cloud capabilities. While a SharePoint or other integrated platform as a service typically won't work well with personal cloud systems (or even other vendors' PaaS capabilities), the real security risk is that such mixtures of capabilities provide fertile ground for covert paths, aggregation of privileges, and aggregation of sensitive information across data classification boundaries.

 **Real World Scenario**

**It's the Endpoints, Isn't It?**

It's tempting to believe that thoroughly securing the endpoints would solve all of our information security problems. Let's look at a clinical situation and see if it is indeed the endpoints where the risks are most challenging.

A modern postoperative recovery room needs to provide highly responsive patient monitoring capabilities, which can be tailored in real time to meet the needs of each individual patient's immediate recovery from surgery. Medical instrumentation has become network-enabled, tied into the hospital's information infrastructures. Medical and nursing staff must be able to quickly set up a postoperative monitoring environment for a patient coming out of surgery, and in some instances tie that monitoring into real-time trending and analysis tools that can promptly alert nurses and doctors to changes in patient condition (be they good news or bad news). Privacy is as important as data segregation: cross-connecting Patient A's vital signs data into Patient B's real-time treatment monitoring and alerting processes could be fatal for both patients, and possibly business-terminal for the hospital as well!

In a mobile device–enabled clinical environment, each care team member might have their own personal digital assistant, phablet, or other device that they use as they interact with each patient and the devices monitoring that patient's condition. In other clinical environments, bedside "care terminals" might be used by the care staff instead.

As you think about the CIANA set of information security needs, what do you see as some of the most challenging information security needs to address in such situations? Are they really just the endpoints, or do they go deeper?

## Protecting Your Systems and Your Mobile Devices

Much as you saw when thinking about virtual machines, mobile device use with your systems brings with it a two-part question: how do you protect the mobile devices themselves from loss, compromise, or attack, and how *else* do you need to protect your core systems and infrastructure from mobile devices that might have gone rogue? Multiple technology and policy actions have to come together in a concerted fashion to provide the required set of information security needs when you include mobile devices in the mix. These include the following:

- Identity management and access control systems need to be robust enough to ensure that mobile devices of any kind have a very restricted set of entry points into your bastion systems. Unless there is a true mission-critical need, consider blocking off, disabling, or removing any dial-in telephone access, for example.

- Although network management systems can do MAC address filtering, and thus block all but authorized user devices from connecting, when your mobile user population gets large this can become unwieldy. Instead, you're forced to rely on validating the user, not the mobile device, in most cases. MDM systems may help here, but only if your organizational mission and business processes can be achieved with a reasonably static list of devices being connected. Retail establishments, schools, and many public-facing government organizations may need to allow almost any device to connect, instead relying on user-level authentication for access control.

- Network firewall systems provide additional protection by filtering on services, ports, and so on; this requires that the organization can identify what services to allow and which ones to block, to be practicable.

- Antimalware technologies and processes should also be part of the layered defense between mobile devices and the core system infrastructures.

- Emergency procedures need to be developed and in place that provide for timely locking, zeroizing, or *bricking* of mobile devices that are under company management, either as company-owned, COPE, or BYO devices covered by usage policies.

# Malware: Exploiting the Infrastructure's Vulnerabilities

Having looked at some of the most common exploitable vulnerabilities in the hardware, firmware, and software that make up our information infrastructures, let's turn and look at how those vulnerabilities get exploited. Simply put, it usually takes a combination of hacker activities, including specialized software tools, to be able to scan your system for vulnerabilities, identify and characterize them, and then interact with those vulnerabilities to achieve the desired outcomes. Those outcomes may be end goals in themselves, or steps in a larger plan of attack. One of the most common categories of exploit tools is called *malware.*

Malware is best classified not by type of malware, but by the discrete functions that an attacker wishes to accomplish. For example, attackers might use malware as one way of:

- Providing undetected or backdoor access into a system
- Creating new users, including privileged users, surreptitiously
- Gathering data about the target system, its installed hardware, firmware, and software, and peripherals
- Using the target system to perform reconnaissance, eavesdropping, or other activities against other computers on the same LAN or network segment with it
- Installing new services, device drivers, or other functions into operating systems, applications, or utility programs
- Elevating the privilege of a task or a user login beyond what normal system controls would allow
- Elevating a user or task to root or full, unrestricted systems administrative privilege levels
- Bypassing data integrity controls so as to provide undetected ability to modify files
- Altering or erasing data from log files associated with system events, resource access, security events, hardware status changes, or applications events
- Copying, moving, or deleting files without being detected, logged, or restricted
- Bypassing digital signatures, installing phony certificates, or otherwise nullifying cryptographic protections
- Changing hardware settings, either to change device behavior, or to cause it to damage or destroy itself (such as shutting off a CPU fan and associated over-temperature alarm events)
- Surreptitiously collecting user-entered data during login events or other activities
- Recording and later transmitting records of system, user, or application activities
- Allocating CPU, GPU, and other resources to support surreptitious execution of hacker-desired tasks
- Generating and sending network or system traffic to other devices, or to tasks on other systems
- Launching malware-based or other attacks against other systems
- Establishing webpage connections and transacting activity at websites of the hacker's choice
- Encrypting files (data or program code) as part of ransomware attacks
- Establishing hidden peer-to-peer or virtual private network connections with other systems, some of which may possibly be under the hacker's control

- Running tasks that disrupt, degrade, or otherwise impact normal work on that system

- Controlling multimedia devices, such as webcams, microphones, and so forth, to eavesdrop on users themselves or others in the immediate area of the target computer

- Monitoring a mobile device's location and tracking its movement as part of stalking or tracking the human user or the vehicle they are using

- Using a variety of multimedia or other systems functions to attempt to frighten, intimidate, coerce, or induce desired behavior in the humans using it or nearby it

*Procedural misuse* of built-in capabilities, whether by honest mistake or deliberate choice, has also exploited (and in some cases discovered) systems vulnerabilities. As early as the 1960s, many batch job computer systems were known to be vulnerable to denial-of-service attacks by simply submitting a *rabbit*, a job that made six copies of itself. Input queues would fill up and put the system into a wait state until the backlog of jobs could complete. Such misuse is not "malware" per se, but whether it's an attack, a penetration test, or a mistake depends upon intent.

### Beware Attackers Living Off the Land

In July 2017, Symantec's research showed an increasing number of ransom attacks—*not* ransomware!—in which the attackers used social engineering and other surreptitious, non-malware-based means to gain initial entry into target systems; they then used built-in systems functions to prepare target file systems for encryption at their command. In many cases, these attacks create few if any files at all on the target system, making it extremely difficult for most antimalware, software whitelisting, or intrusion detection and prevention technologies to recognize them for what they are. The attackers can also use the same systems functions to cover their tracks.

Symantec's bottom-line recommendation: multifactor user identification, combined with strong access control, is still the foundation of any well-managed IT security program.

It's interesting to note that many of the behaviors of common malware can resemble the behavior of otherwise legitimate software. This can lead to two kinds of errors. False positive errors are when the malware detection system marks a legitimate program as if it were malware, or quarantines or blocks attempts to connect to a webpage mistakenly "known" to be a malware source. False negative errors occur when actual malware is not detected as such and is allowed to pass unreported.

Malware can be introduced into a system by direct use of operating systems functions, such as mounting a removable disk drive; just as often, malware enters a system by users interacting with "applications" that are more than what they seem, and come with hidden side effects. Malware often needs to target operating systems functions in order to be part of a successful attack. Most of what you have to do as an SSCP to protect your infrastructure from malware intrusions must take place inside the infrastructure, even if the path into the system starts with or makes use of the application layer. (Some applications, such as office productivity suites, do have features that must be tightly controlled to prevent their being misused to introduce malware into a system; we'll explore these in Chapter 9.)

# Countering the Malware Threat

It would not be too much of an exaggeration to say that everything else in this book is part of what you need to do to block malware from entering into your protected infrastructures, detecting it when it does, and then eradicating it or limiting its impacts to your ongoing business operations. From user awareness, training, and education on down to adroit and effective configuration management and change control, keeping unwanted software and data *out* of your systems requires every tool in your SSCP bag of tricks brought to bear at the right time, the right place, and in the right ways.

Rather than repeat all of those countermeasures here, let's just focus on antivirus or antimalware systems. Software antimalware or antivirus systems perform a range of functions as they help protect your computer systems:

- Scanning your system to check for files that may be malware-infected or malware in disguise
- Inspecting the digital signatures of specific directories, such as boot sectors and operating system kernels, to check for possible surreptitious changes that might indicate malware
- Inspecting processes, services, and tasks in main memory (or in virtual page swap areas) to detect any infected executable code
- Inspecting macros, templates, or other such files for suspicious or malicious code or values
- Moving suspect files or objects to special quarantine areas, and preventing further movement or execution of them
- Inspecting operating systems control parameter sets, such as the Windows Registry hives, for signatures or elements suggestive of known malware
- Monitoring system behavior to detect possible anomalies, suggestive of malware in action
- Monitoring incoming email or Web traffic for possible malware
- Monitoring connection requests against lists of blacklisted sites

Similar to intrusion detection and prevention systems, malware detection and prevention systems can use a combination of anomaly detection and signature analysis to look for probable malware. Most consumer-grade antivirus systems (freeware and paid-subscription both) rely heavily on signature analysis, and thus frequent updates to the signature files are necessary to maintain your infrastructure's "immune system."

Malware defense can run in layers, and in larger enterprise systems, it is probably best to deploy it in multiple ways. Incoming email should be scanned by a malware-scanning server before email and its attachments are allowed to enter into the email server for later pickup by addressees; similar approaches can also scan outbound email and attachments, and in doing so can also be part of a data exfiltration protection system (more on this in Chapter 9). Individual user workstations, PCs, laptops, or smartphones should also have antimalware systems installed, as it's probably most effective (and runtime and throughput efficient) to scan for possible infected downloads, blacklisted websites, and so forth at the individual user system level rather than attempt this task centrally.

# Privacy and Secure Browsing

Because the use of Web browsers is such an integral part of the hierarchies of trust that we rely upon for secure e-commerce, e-business, and e-personal use of the Web and the Net, it's important to consider two sides of the same coin: how well do our browsers protect our privacy while they purportedly are keeping us secure? The majority of Web browser software is made freely available to users and systems builders alike; it comes preinstalled by the original equipment manufacturers (OEMs) on many computer products for consumer or enterprise use. The development and support costs of these browsers are paid for by advertising (ads placed within webpages displayed to users), by analytics derived from users' browsing history, or by other demographic data that browser providers, search engines, and websites can gather during their contact with users. Browsers support a variety of add-on functions, many of which can be used by websites to gather information about you and your system, leave session-specific or site-related information on your computer for later use, or otherwise gain more insight about what you're doing while you are browsing than you might think possible or desirable.

Browsers, like many modern software packages, also gather telemetry data—data that supports analysis of the behavior and functioning of the browser while the user is interacting with it—and makes that telemetry available to its vendor. (Many products say that users opt into this to "improve the user experience," whether the user feels such improvement or not.) Whether we recognize this or not, this paradigm has transformed the Web surfer from user-as-customer into user-as-product. In some circumstances, that can be of benefit to the user—it certainly provides the revenue stream that developers and infrastructure builders and maintainers need, at no additional direct cost to the user. But it can also be of potential harm to the user, be that user an individual or a business enterprise, if that aggregation of user-entered data, action history, and analytics violates the user's reasonable expectation of privacy, for example.

Let's start with a closer look at each side of that coin.

*Private browsing* is defined as using a Web browser in such a way that the user's identity, browsing history, and user-entered data when interacting with webpages is kept confidential. Browsers such as Mozilla Firefox or Microsoft Edge provide ways for users to open a new window (supported by a separate task and process stream) for private browsing, in which location tracking, identification, cookie handling, and various add-ons may change the way that they provide information back to websites or leave session-tracking information on the user's computer. For most mainline browsers, telemetry is still gathered and made available to the browser's authors. To put private browsing into perspective, consider one data point: the unique identification of the system you're browsing from. Fully nonrepudiable identification of your system would require every device on the Internet to have a unique key or ID assigned to it that was an amalgam of IP address, hardware identifiers, software identifiers, and even your user ID on that system. A suitable cryptographic hash of all of this data would produce such a unique ID, which could not be de-hashed (decrypted) to get back to your specific username, for example. But if the search engine or webpage keeps a history of activity tagged to that system identification, then every time you browse, your unique history continues to be updated. If that concerns you, can't you just avoid this by opening up a new *private* browser window, tab, or session? According to tests by the Electronic Frontier Foundation and others, no; so-called "private" browsing still generates an ID of your hardware, software, and session that is unique to one of a billion or more such addresses. And, of course, the browser telemetry is still going back home to its developers. In the meantime, private browsing usually does not prevent ads from being displayed or block pop-up windows from occurring; and some ad blockers and pop-up blockers are incompatible with private browsing modes.

*Secure browsing* is defined as using a Web browser in such a way that it actively helps keep the user's system secure, while more assertively or aggressively protecting the user's privacy, data about the user's system, and data about the user's browsing history. Competition between the mainstream browsers as products (that is, as platforms for revenue generation for advertisers or for search engine providers) has driven some of them to incorporate more of these features, and so the line between "highly secure and safe" and "private" browsing continues to blur. Some of the more well-respected secure browsers, such as Waterfox and Pale Moon, are offshoots (or forks) from earlier points in the development of Mozilla Firefox. By eliminating many of the data-intensive add-in capabilities, telemetry gathering, and other features, these secure browsers are also relatively lightweight as compared to native Firefox (that is, they run faster and use fewer system resources to do so).

If you truly need private and secure browsing, consider using add-ons such as HTTPS-Everywhere, which go a step further by using HTTPS for all of your browsing and then routing it through The Onion Router (TOR). TOR, incidentally, was designed by the U.S. Naval Research Laboratory as a way to provide anonymous communication and Web use for social advocates, journalists, and ordinary people living or working in repressive or totalitarian countries. TOR takes every packet exchange and routes it to different members of its peer-to-peer backbone infrastructure; by the time the connection leaves TOR and goes to the requested URL, the only thing the distant server can see is that last TOR node's IP address. This is very similar to using a VPN to hide your pathway, but with a serious twist: most VPNs bulk encrypt from your entry node to the landing node, providing anonymity and security, but try to minimize dynamic rerouting of your path for improved performance. TOR, on the other hand, dynamically reroutes to further mask your path and your identity, at the cost of sometimes significantly slower browsing.

One final approach to secure and private browsing is a sandbox system—a separate computer, outside of your organization's demilitarized zone (DMZ), that has no organizational or individual identifying data on it. The system is wiped (the disk is hard reformatted and re-imaged from a pristine image copy) after each session of use. Most businesses and many individuals do not have need of such a sandbox approach, but when the occasion warrants it, it works. Strict data hygiene practices must be in force when using such a sandbox; ensure that the bare minimum of information is put in by users as they interact with external systems, and either prevent or thoroughly scan, test, and validate any data or program brought in via the sandbox from outside before introducing it into any other system in your infrastructure. (This is an excellent opportunity to consider the *write-down* and *read-up* restrictions in some of the classical access control models, as they apply to systems integrity and data confidentiality protection.)

### The Downside of a VPN

VPNs can do a marvelous job of keeping not only your data but the fact of your connection to a specific webpage totally confidential; it's only on that last hop from the VPN's landing site in the country of your choice to the website of interest that actual IP addresses get used as packets flow to and from. Whether cookies make it back to your system, or whether browser telemetry makes it from your system to the browser's home, may require additional tweaking of the VPN and browser settings.

If your connection requires some rigorous security verification, however, you may need to turn off the VPN. This is particularly true if the server in question blacklists IP addresses originating in certain regions or countries. The author discovered this some time ago as he spent a 10-minute Skype conversation with PayPal security without using a VPN. PayPal security noted that the author's previous login and transaction attempts, moments before, seemed to move around between six different countries on four continents, including Iran and Chechnya, in as few as five minutes. This caused PayPal's security algorithms to block the transaction attempts. Turning off the VPN allowed a "static" IP address (dynamically assigned by the author's ISP) to be used for the next entire session, which was successful. We cannot blame PayPal for being overly protective of the author's bank information in that regard.

# "The Sin of Aggregation"

People within military and intelligence communities often encounter situations in which a series of facts at one level of security classification, when taken together and thoughtfully considered, directly or indirectly point to the existence of other facts that are classified at higher levels of security. A particular soldier, for example, may have access to unclassified information about individual military units, such as the quantities of supplies that they are purchasing from commercial vendors. Unclassified training schedules or leave calendars might show that over the next two months, significantly fewer soldiers are taking leave or being sent to training classes. This might reveal plans for an upcoming operational deployment, which no doubt would be information classified at Secret or higher levels. Aggregating information together to see what it reveals about otherwise well-kept secrets has long been a problem for military, government, and commercial organizations alike. This is also an example of a covert path, albeit in this case, the "path" is inside the mind of the human who is aggregating the information.

When we shift into a commercial setting and introduce mobile devices (BYOD, COPE, or a mix of both), we see the potential for covert paths that aggregate data across different lines of business as well as across the business-personal divide. An independent consultant, acting as a third-party adviser to a number of businesses, faces this problem repeatedly: she cannot allow what she learns in confidence from one client to color, influence, aid, or abet her advice and solutions for another client without violating her professional ethics and maybe her contracts' nondisclosure terms. Even if she studiously avoid this in her own mind, in her mobile device, the potential for aggregation across those "compartments" is real—especially if her mobile device is lost or stolen, and the value of that information is recognized.

To some degree, data exfiltration and access control methods can help limit this risk; other endpoint security measures can also limit inadvertent disclosure that could lead to aggregation of information. Ultimately, end-user awareness and training play a vital role in preventing such covert pathways in the mind or on the phablet from becoming real risks.

# Updating the Threat Model

We've surveyed the information infrastructure, putting its various types of vulnerabilities into perspective. Now is the opportunity to take the threat modeling that you and your information security team did during the vulnerabilities assessment phase and update it, reflecting further consideration of vulnerabilities and potential countermeasures. (We normally consider vulnerabilities first, weigh them against our risk management strategy, and *then* choose and apply countermeasures; it can be useful to have classes of countermeasures in mind as you look for vulnerabilities, if you don't treat the countermeasures as the hammer in your hand and make every problem into the nail you need to whack! Learn from the experience of the countermeasure providers and their user communities—but don't be a slave to their recommendations.)

Reexamine your threat model, and see if you've got the threat surfaces (the boundaries between one security zone and the next) in the right place. Verify that you've identified the frontier posts or gateways through which authorized functions must travel, and inspect the rest of what's inside the boundary to make sure no other paths exist that could allow a threat to jump over the boundary. (A maintenance backdoor access point, with a direct-dial modem attached, is an excellent example of what *not* to leave inside your protected bastions.) Update the documentation of your threat model as part of your updates to the information security baseline.

Your risk mitigation planning identified and prioritized the risks, and made choices about which risks to accept as-is; which to transfer; which to bound, contain, or limit the effects of; and which to correct or mitigate. It's these last two sets—the risks to contain and the risks to correct—that you'll need to apply countermeasures to as part of your efforts to reduce or eliminate your exposure to loss.

# Managing Your Systems' Security

In our earlier studies of risk management and risk mitigation, we looked at the use of security-related information management systems, and their dashboards and displays, as ways of addressing key stakeholder decision needs. Some of these systems focus on event-related information; others take a broader look at the entire security process. Typical dashboards provide at-a-glance insight into several aspects of a critical information infrastructure's security situation:

- Real-time and near-real-time incident information
- Real-time and near-real-time indicators and warnings (flags or conditions that *might* signal an incident of interest in the offing)
- Current status of ongoing risk mitigation projects and activities
- Systems health information, whether for critical nodes in the information architecture, or across the user base of systems
- Current status of "Top Ten" vulnerabilities and ongoing remediations

The point is not that every organization needs a security information management systems product and its color-glossy dashboards with which to manage its systems security. Nonetheless, all organizations, from the smallest of SOHO operations on up, need to treat security as a set of processes that are *managed* and *led*. Both of those key tasks require the right information, organized and presented in timely, accurate, and trustworthy ways. In other words, to achieve CIANA, you as the SSCP-in-charge need CIANA's support of the information *you* need to do your job!

# Summary

There's an absolutely daunting range of threats that attackers can use to find, fix, and exploit vulnerabilities in your systems in ways that disrupt your operations. That "kill chain" kind of focus—that first you locate a possible target; then you determine how to keep it in a known, fixed location (so you can find it again when you need to); and then you attack—is how the threat actors and the black hat hackers think about *your* IT infrastructure. You need to outthink them; you need to think ahead of their OODA (observe–orient–decide–act) loop if you're going to keep your infrastructure safe, secure, and resilient. And defending that infrastructure has to happen from the ground up, so to speak. Infrastructures run on hardware—on physical systems of some kind.

The same systems approach that organizations use in specifying, designing, and building those infrastructures supported us when we did the vulnerabilities assessments of the as-built information systems baseline. We've seen in previous chapters how risks apply to the information and the business processes that use it, and we've come through the networks layers that virtually all IT infrastructures rely on. By focusing here on the CPU and chip-level hardware, and then back up through the layers of firmware and systems software, we've identified vulnerabilities and possible countermeasures to reduce, contain, or eliminate risks associated with them. We also used the notional design of a typical on-premises datacenter as a way to focus our thinking about security (and vulnerability) at the device, subsystems, networks, and systems levels.

One thing we saw throughout is that in order to deliver trust and confidence to our users and our organization's stakeholders, we have to demand and expect trustworthy support from all aspects of our IT supply chain. The fastest-moving piece of that supply chain is the software update process for applications and operating systems, which seems to deliver updates almost every night. We, as SSCPs, need to support the IT department or team in managing those updates, as well as updates to device-level firmware. And as President Ronald Reagan said, when talking about the Strategic Arms Limitation Talks with the Soviet Union, we do need to trust our partners—but we equally need to *verify* that their actions live up to that trust.

From the systems baseline and the business impact analysis on to the fine-grained details in our configuration management and control systems, there's a *lot* of information *about* information systems and their security needs. That information is the foundation we stand on as we choose countermeasures to mitigate risks with. We will build upon this infrastructure of ideas about securing our information infrastructures as we move into cloud-hosted environments, applications security, and data security in Chapter 9.

# Exam Essentials

**Explain the relationship between the information systems baseline, the vulnerability assessment, and adequate hardware and systems security.** The information systems baseline documents all elements of the information system, including identification of versions, patch and update levels, critical subsystems or programs, and location. This forms part of the configuration-controlled and managed baseline of the information system. It should drive vulnerability assessment, including physical and logical inspection of systems elements and components. By including vulnerability assessment and risk mitigation planning, it becomes the information systems security baseline, documenting the as-is, in-use set of both the protected systems elements and known but still unresolved vulnerabilities.

**Describe the different types of malware or malicious code and possible effects related to its presence and execution.** Malware is any type of software designed and used for a variety of malicious purposes, which can include installing unwanted software, reading files, copying and exfiltrating files, damaging data, software, or hardware, or logging system usage information. Malware can also misguide users into taking actions through fear or misdirection that cause even further damage to the target system. Malware can cause degraded system performance, and can also turn your system into a platform from which it launches attacks upon other unsuspecting systems. Some of the key types have been classified as viruses, Trojan horses, worms, scareware, ransomware, keyloggers, sniffers, and botnets. Rootkits are a particularly pernicious type which overwrite part of the operating system's bootstrap loader functions, and thus can be difficult to find and remove. Note, though, that as attacker's purposes and tactics evolve, so too do their malware and the payloads they carry.

**Know how to detect the presence of malware, either when installed and dormant or while it is executing on your systems.**   Malware, when present on a system, can be detected during or after its installation, by active scanning (typically via antimalware software systems). It can also be detected by systems configuration audits that compare directory structures and files against known, validated baseline copies; this typically relies on file- or directory-level hashes as signatures. Malware installations can also be surmised by close inspection or analysis of system activity and event logs. Malware that is actively running on a system may be detected by inspection of installed and running services or programs, or by large-scale behavioral changes in the system—runtimes of known tasks may change; tasks may be slow to load; data files may be missing, visibly altered, or corrupted. Changes in network traffic, particularly file uploads, may suggest that malware is attempting to exfiltrate data. Sandboxes can also be used, as quarantine areas or copies of the system in which any new software or suspected data files are loaded and closely examined.

**Explain the role of the systems' end users in malware prevention, containment, and removal.**   The first is user awareness, training, and engagement with your information security plans and procedures. Alert users can quickly spot when something is not quite right and should be suspicious enough to ask for help from IT security without fear of embarrassment. Users must also believe in, support, and follow all policies, such as acceptable use, safe browsing, and email attachment use. Users are also the first line of defense against social engineering attacks or reconnaissance probes, and the end user's level of training, awareness, and proficiency in the daily normal of business logic and business processes is the best protection against phishing, spear phishing, and whaling attacks. Once a malware infestation is observed, end users should cooperate with IT security staff as they attempt to identify all possible vectors by which the malware may have entered the systems or spread within it, but they should not attempt to remove it themselves.

**Explain the various types of malware countermeasures and briefly describe their use.**
Trained, motivated, and aware users are the first line of defense. Malware scanners, antivirus, or similar systems can also use a variety of heuristic approaches to recognize a potential malware package before it enters the system's secure boundaries. Port scanning, blocking, and other tools can limit users or processes from connecting to potentially harmful IP addresses or websites (sites known or suspected to harbor malware, hackers, or other

threat actors), using either blacklisting (lists of banned or blocked sites, ports, services, or addresses) or whitelisting (listing those that are acceptable and thereby banning all others). Requiring that all software be digitally signed by its creators or publishers, and that signature be supported by a trustworthy, valid certificate, can help reduce the threat of malware being installed on the system. Keeping all software (systems and applications) up to date with all vendor-provided security updates and patches is also an important countermeasure.

**Identify the primary types of malicious activities that an organization's information systems may face, and some of the countermeasures that might apply.**   Hostile or malicious insider activity is the first and perhaps most difficult to deal with. Many different motivations may lead an employee to choose to attack the organization by means of attacking its information and information systems. The best IT security countermeasures involve control of elevation or aggregation of privileges, separation of duties, and auditing of systems access and usage. Theft of private, proprietary, or sensitive data, by insiders or external attackers, can expose the company to legal action, loss of customers, or loss of revenue, or in some cases lead to injury or death of employees or others. Access control is the first defense; control of removable media (entry onto the premises, use with an organization's systems) are also important countermeasures. Mobile device management, particularly in "bring your own" environments, makes data theft harder to prevent. There are some data exfiltration detection systems that may suit some organizations and their systems as well. For Web-facing businesses, or for businesses dependent on Internet connectivity to other sites, large-scale denial-of-service (DoS) attacks can impact network communications systems; distributed denial-of-service (DDoS) attacks are ones conducted using hundreds or thousands of geographically separated computers to launch the attack. Adaptive firewall protection that can smartly detect a possible DDoS in progress, block it, and prevent itself from being flooded is a key countermeasure for a DDoS.

**Explain what a zombie botnet is, how to prevent your systems from becoming part of one, and how to prevent being attacked by one.**   A zombie botnet is a collection of computers that have had malware payloads installed that allow each individual computer to function as part of a large, remotely controlled collective system. (The name suggests that the owner of the system, and the system's operating system and applications, don't know that the system is capable of being enslaved by its remote controller.) Zombie botnets typically do not harm the individual zombie systems themselves, which are then used either as part of a massively parallel cycle-stealing computation, as a DDoS attack, or as part of a distributed, large-scale target reconnaissance effort. Reasonable and prudent measures to protect your systems from unauthorized access, from unauthorized downloading and installation of software, and effective antimalware or antivirus systems are a part of keeping your systems from becoming part of a zombie botnet.

**Know what an endpoint device is, and explain the security challenges involved with endpoints.**   Endpoints are typically the devices at the end of networks or communications paths, at which the data from central systems is captured, created, displayed, or output to elements that are not part of the IT system itself. These can be people, computer-controlled manufacturing devices, robotic devices, or almost any IoT device. First, start with your information systems baseline, which should identify specific devices, their locations, users, and the systems and processes they are parts of. Endpoints can be people-facing terminals, personal computer workstations as thick clients or thin clients, phones, phablets, even smart watches and wearable computing devices; point-of-sale devices or other specialized information hardware may also be user-facing endpoints. The IoT can be serving computer-driven manufacturing, robotic warehouses, or other process control environments, in which every data-using, communications-capable device that translates data into the real world and back again is an endpoint. Smart products themselves—ones that can communicate usage and maintenance data into your systems—are also endpoints. Each of these devices involves data at rest (in the device), in use (interacting with humans or other machines or systems), and in motion (into and out of your overall systems). These devices can be stolen, their contents cloned, or their onboard software hacked. Many IoT devices have very little design provision for securing the onboard software and data. In most systems, endpoint devices can be easily and quickly connected to your networks via Wi-Fi, LiFi, or other remote access capabilities. Endpoint devices can be highly mobile, leading to a fast-moving, dynamic system of systems, which is difficult to monitor and control. Finally, one consideration is who owns, operates, and maintains the endpoints. Company-owned devices may be totally managed by the company, have shared management with the endpoint user employee, or be fully enabled for end-user management and control. BYOD and BYOI take these challenges further into how effectively software-enforced configuration management and control can help enforce acceptable use, identity authentication, access control, usage and location accountability, data commingling, and other risk mitigation policies.

**Explain what mobile device management (MDM) can do, and what some of its limitations are.**   Mobile device management (MDM) systems attempt to provide integrated sets of tools for identifying, tracking, and controlling the use of mobile devices as part of an organization's IT systems, as well as manage their software and data configuration. MDM systems primarily support organizational use of laptops, tablets, smartphones, and similar hybrid devices. As the line between the IoT and mobile personal computing continues to blur, MDM vendors are looking to support more kinds of devices. Some MDM systems can support mobile point-of-sale, inventory, process control, or other shop floor or clinical instrumentation as well. Most MDM systems claim to be able to facilitate a mix of company-owned and -managed, company-owned personally enabled (COPE), and bring-your-own device (BYOD). Organizations need to first realize that MDM systems cannot fill policy gaps. Each new device must be introduced to the MDM system, with supporting data as to user identification, authorized usage, or other policy-based security and control information. MDMs should be able to support device loss protections, either locking the device once it's declared missing or zeroizing or otherwise destroying (not just deleting) content stored on the device. MDM systems cannot by themselves deal with aggregation of privilege or aggregation of information by the device end users. Protections for data in the device (at rest, in motion, or in use) are also highly dependent on the device and its capabilities and may not be easily manageable by the chosen MDM system.

**Explain the role of intrusion detection systems and technologies in keeping hardware and systems secure.**   Intrusion detection systems (IDSs) use a variety of software technologies to detect attempted intrusions by an unauthorized user or process into a secure (bastion) portion of the organization's systems. A variety of patterns, heuristic rules, or signatures are used by the IDS to flag suspicious traffic to supervisors for further analysis. Some IDSs can also be configured to directly issue alarms and take containment actions, in which case they are known as intrusion prevention systems (IPSs). An IDS can be host-based (HIDS) or network-based (NIDS). Host-based systems are installed on one machine (the host), and they monitor for attempts to attack protected system resources or files. Protecting the operating system's boot image, bootstrap loader, kernel, and other files is a primary responsibility of most HIDSs. Vendor-supplied applications and their files, and even user- or organization-generated apps, as well as data files, can be part of an HIDS's span of monitoring and protection. NIDSs are hosted on a specific device placed at the perimeter of a protected subnet, and look at network traffic for possible intrusion attempts. NIDSs can be configured to look at some or all network traffic (connection-based and connectionless, control and data). Both HIDSs and NIDSs typically operate either by signature recognition (matching a pattern of events to predefined signature patterns of known attacks) or by anomaly detection (using machine learning approaches to observe the differences between normal and anomalous activities).

**Know what a trusted platform module (TPM) is and its role in protecting information systems.**   A trusted platform module (TPM) is a special hardware component, usually packaged in a single electronic chip, that uses on-chip hashing, encryption, and specialized software to store encryption keys, digital signatures, and other data. The TPM does not control how the host system it is a part of uses the TPM or the data kept within the TPM, but it does add an extra layer of tamper-resistant protection to these processes. TPMs are being included in many laptops, smartphones, and other devices. TPMs can be integrated into a wide variety of OS environments. The Trusted Computing Group (TCG) is the international de facto standards body that specifies TPM design and performance. With over 120 hardware and software companies as members, TCG is driving toward globally useful solutions for increased security. TPMs are well suited to scenarios that demand an exceptionally high degree of trust and confidence for user and service provider authentication, and for protection of data in use, in motion, and at rest.

**Explain the different kinds of firewalls and their use in protecting an organization's information infrastructure.**   Firewalls are systems that actively prevent some kinds of network traffic from crossing over a boundary. Firewalls typically work by signature recognition, anomaly detection, filtering rule sets, or any combination of these. Hardware-based firewalls (still with extensive firmware components) may be found in switches, routers, or standalone firewall systems products. They may also be part of modems or other Internet point of presence interface equipment. Software-based or host firewalls are programs that run on a specific computer, whether that be a server, a cluster management system, or an endpoint device. Hardware-based firewalls are placed on the perimeter of a protected subnet; ideally, there should be no entry points (perimeter crossings) into the protected subnet that are not protected by a hardware firewall of some kind. Many desktop, personal computing, and server operating systems now have firewall systems as a part of their distribution kits. In addition, many antimalware systems may provide firewall capabilities. Both kinds of firewalls can use either stateless or stateful detection techniques (that is, they look at traffic right in the moment, or at a history of traffic related to a port, a connection, and so forth).

**Compare and contrast firewalls with other malware countermeasures.**   Firewalls work to filter, block, or prevent network traffic that is unauthorized; this requires inspection of TCP/IP packets attempting to cross the boundary via the firewall, whether as a network-based or a host-based firewall. Other malware countermeasures are working in concert with the host computer's operating system to detect attempts to circumvent access controls, to use or attempt to change protected files, to thwart logon restrictions, or to elevate the privilege of a process.

**Explain what a DMZ is and its role in systems security.**   From a network security perspective, the demilitarized zone (DMZ) is that subset of organizational systems that are not within the protected or bastion systems perimeter. Systems or servers within the DMZ are thus exposed to larger, untrusted networks, typically the entire Internet. Public-facing Web servers, for example, are outside of the DMZ and do not require each Web user to have their identity authenticated in order to access their content. Data flows between systems in the DMZ, and those within the protected bastion must be carefully constructed and managed to prevent covert paths (connections into the secure systems that are not detected or prevented by access controls), or the exfiltration of data that should not go out into the DMZ and beyond.

**Explain the merits of using endpoint encryption as part of an information systems security approach.**   A variety of secure protocols should be considered and used to secure data in motion to and from the endpoint, in use within or at the endpoint, and at rest within the endpoint device. The organization's CIANA needs with respect to the endpoint and its use within the systems should dictate which protocols should be required or optional when the endpoint is a part of the organization's systems or processing, storing or displaying the organization's data. This may require encryption capabilities within browsers, email systems, or network services, at the endpoint device itself, to support secure browsing, digital signatures, secure virtual private network connections, or stronger identity authentication and access control. As most of these hierarchy of trust capabilities are now a part of consumer-grade endpoints, it is prudent to make their use a required part of the use of the endpoint with the system. For example, it's almost inexcusable to have endpoints using wireless connections in which packets are not protected via encryption.

**Compare and contrast a sandbox and a honeypot in terms of their roles in systems security.** A sandbox is an isolated, highly controlled software and hardware environment in which software and data can be tested, inspected, and evaluated. Sandboxes are frequently used as part of software systems development and testing so that new versions of production software can be evaluated, instrumented, and assessed without their execution (proper or improper) causing changes to production data, environments, and business activities.

Sandboxes are also useful as quarantine areas in which software or data suspected of carrying malware can be safely examined (with or without executing it). A honeypot is a sacrificial system placed on the outward-facing areas of the organization's network. It may use copies of production systems (such as webpages and Web-facing databases), new versions of such systems, or cut-down, limited-capability versions of production environments. The purpose of a honeypot is to allow an attacker limited, controlled access to the organization's systems so that more can be learned about systems vulnerabilities by watching the attacker attempt to exploit vulnerabilities in those systems.

**Explain what secure browsing is and how organizations should determine whether to use it as part of their systems.**   The most popular Web browsers are provided free to users (commercial or personal users); in doing so, their developers gain revenues by transforming their users into products—the browser delivers user browsing history to advertisers or other third parties who can derive value from analysis of browsing behavior and history. This exposes most users' systems (which host these browsers) to adware, spyware, and potential loss of user control over whom this information is shared with by the browser, by search engines the user accesses, and so forth. Although some adware and tracking apps are not malware, many malware packages can masquerade as *purportedly* safe adware and spyware. The major browsers attempt to address user concerns about security and privacy by providing private windows in which many advertising, tracking, login, and telemetry features are disabled or their use is restricted. If these do not meet your organization's needs, other, more secure browsers are available. Ultimately, a standalone sandbox system, typically positioned beyond the organization's DMZ and with no links back into secure (bastion) systems or data, may be used. Such a "throwaway" system can be used for browsing, uploading, and downloading, and then completely wiped (zeroized) and restored to a known, trusted state, if this is necessary to achieve the organization's security needs.

**Explain the importance of a trusted supply chain to IT security and how it can be achieved.**   Every system, subsystem, board-level part, or element of your organization's IT systems is designed and built by some other business, quite often one on the other side of the world. Most of those subsystem elements have board-level or device-level firmware in them; all of them depend on operating system software suites to integrate them, coordinate their actions, and turn those actions into services that end-user applications need. Every element of those systems is potentially a vulnerability you have brought inside your organization; by making those elements part of your information infrastructure, you rely on their continued safe, secure, and resilient operation to meet your objectives. Updates to software, firmware, and hardware add features, address known design or production errors, and may also introduce new vulnerabilities into your systems. As a customer of your suppliers, you cannot run their business for them—you cannot validate that all of their production processes are secure enough to meet your organization's CIANA needs. So you have to trust them to do their job right. This trust is supported by transparent and open sharing of information, by both sides, and often facilitated by creating strategic relationships or partnerships with key members of your supply chain.

# Review Questions

1.  When choosing your countermeasures and tactics to protect hardware and systems software, you should start with which of the following?

    A.  Published Current Vulnerabilities and Exposures (CVE) databases

    B.  The information systems baseline that documents the systems your organization uses

    C.  Your organization's business impact analysis

    D.  Your organization's IT vulnerabilities assessment

2.  Does the SSCP have a role in IT supply chain security issues? (Select the most correct statement.)

    A.  No, because this really is for the logistics, purchasing, or IT departments to focus on.

    B.  No, because if supply chain security is a concern to the company, it needs to be addressed by senior directors via a strategic partnership or relationship with key vendors or suppliers.

    C.  Yes, because the SSCP can and should advise on all potential security considerations affecting purchase, installation, use, maintenance, and disposal of IT equipment and systems.

    D.  Yes, because most of the supply chain risks to IT stem from purchasing or leasing systems at lowest cost, typically from discounters who offer little product support.

3.  What kind of malware attacks can corrupt or infect device-level firmware? (Choose all that apply.)

    A.  SNMP-based attacks that can trigger the device to download and install a firmware update remotely

    B.  Remote or onsite device management (or mismanagement) attacks that allow a hacker to initiate a firmware update using a hacked firmware file

    C.  Phishing or misdirection attacks that fool operators or users into initiating an upload of a hacked firmware file

    D.  None, because firmware updates require operator intervention to download trusted updates and patch files from the manufacturer's or vendor's websites, and then initiate and monitor the update and restart of the device

4.  What is a zero day exploit?

    A.  An exploit conducted against a vulnerability within the same day as it is reported

    B.  An exploit that impacts a system immediately, rather than having a delayed effect like ransomware or scareware

    C.  There are no real zero day exploits, but the mass media has exaggerated the dangers of unreported vulnerabilities

    D.  An exploit conducted against a newly discovered vulnerability before it becomes known to the cybersecurity community or the system's vendor or owners

5. The most important security vulnerability to your IT infrastructure's hardware elements would be which of the following?

   **A.** Being "orphaned" when the manufacturer no longer provides technical support, spare parts, or firmware updates

   **B.** Electrical power fluctuations, air conditioning issues, or other workplace environmental issues

   **C.** Unauthorized devices or software installed during maintenance by an off-site maintenance vendor or computer store

   **D.** Theft, or being misplaced or lost

6. Trusted platform modules provide which of the following benefits to an organization's IT infrastructure?

   **A.** By means of hardware implementations of encryption, hashing and key generation, they greatly simplify the use of certificate authorities and PKI.

   **B.** As a trust root, a TPM can make hierarchies of trust more reliable.

   **C.** The TPM replaces the host system's random number generators and hash routines with its hardware-accelerated, more secure versions. This enhances system security as well as runtime performance.

   **D.** As a signed part of operating systems kernels, TPMs make it possible to validate software updates more reliably.

7. Malware is best classified and understood by which of the following?

   **A.** The ways that it spreads from one system to another

   **B.** The capabilities it grants the exploiter, and the impacts it has on the target system

   **C.** Which of many strains of code, originally developed by national governments, it is descended from or modeled after

   **D.** Which operating systems, applications, or network systems it targets

8. How is malware detected when it has infected a target system? (Choose all that apply.)

   **A.** Users notice abnormal behavior of their systems, ranging from sluggish response, to strange crashes, to unusual warning messages or pop-ups.

   **B.** User files disappear, are corrupted, or become unusable, and then inexplicably they come back.

   **C.** It's very difficult to detect without examining the executable code of systems kernel files.

   **D.** Malware scanner programs look for signatures in program files that match known malware, or look for patterns of behavior that are suspicious.

**9.** Do firewalls play a role in countering or preventing a malware infestation from striking a system?

**A.** Yes, because firewalls can be programmed to allow only known and approved files to be received by the systems on their network, thus implementing software whitelisting as a form of protection.

**B.** Yes, because firewalls can use sandboxes or quarantine areas to analyze suspected files to see if they match known malware signatures or show anomalous behavior that indicates the presence of malware.

**C.** Yes, because firewalls can restrict or filter connections by outside devices to the network, and block connections to ports or the use of protocols or services that may be attempts to infiltrate your systems and possibly bring malware with them.

**D.** No, because firewalls look only at network traffic and network protocols, and do not inspect the contents of files that might contain malware.

**10.** Which statement about host-based firewalls is correct?

**A.** Host-based firewalls can be set to prevent applications programs from other systems from connecting to resources on the host computer, including preventing those applications from loading and executing on the host.

**B.** Host-based firewalls can filter, restrict, or block connection attempts by programs running on the host computer to external networks.

**C.** Host-based firewalls are very similar to antimalware systems in that they scan files or packets coming into and out of the host system for possible malware.

**D.** Network-based firewalls offer greater protection against malware intrusions than host-based firewalls can.

**11.** What information do you need to manage your IT infrastructure security activities? (Choose all that apply.)

**A.** Incident characterization and warning data, in real time

**B.** Status of planned systems upgrades and performance improvements

**C.** Traffic, systems utilization, and systems health and status information, updated in near real time

**D.** Status of open vulnerabilities, planned resolution efforts, and affected systems

**12.** Is secure browsing the same as private browsing? Why or why not? (Choose all that apply.)

**A.** They are different in that private browsing may not effectively mask your identity or the identity of your system but secure browsing can.

**B.** They started out being different but are rapidly converging to offer the same set of privacy and system protection features.

**C.** The only truly secure and private browsing is what you do on a sterile, sandbox system, with no PII or company data made available to the browser or sites you browse, and no files transferred from the sterile sandbox system into your protected systems.

**D.** No matter how secure your browser, it's your use of search engines that compromises your privacy.

13. Malware can be introduced into your protected systems by all of these methods except:

    A. Using removable media such as thumb drives

    B. Connecting to a webpage containing malware embedded in its pages

    C. Opening data files on a webpage via your Web browser

    D. Watching a streaming video or listening to streaming music or audio files

14. What are the limitations of mobile device management (MDM) when it comes to security needs? (Choose all that apply.)

    A. MDM systems can handle company-owned devices well, but most cannot support the wide range of user preferences that bring-your-own situations can involve.

    B. Most MDM systems can handle only market-leading mobile phones and laptops and cannot support wearable computing, smart watches, and so forth.

    C. MDM systems, by themselves, cannot make up for shortcomings in organizational policies or plans for risk management.

    D. MDM systems usually do not provide visibility or management control over mobile device software updates.

15. Can encryption solve all of your endpoint security problems?

    A. No; by itself, this does not offer protection if the device is lost or stolen.

    B. No; many endpoints may still allow users to create covert paths that move information across security boundaries or aggregate information in ways they should not.

    C. Yes, provided the endpoint device has a TPM in it to implement PKI in reliable ways.

    D. Yes, if encryption fully protects both endpoint communications and data storage and use.

16. How does bring your own infrastructure (BYOI) affect information security planning? (Choose all that apply.)

    A. Since it's just a special case of bringing your own devices, it adds very little in the way of new concerns or issues.

    B. By including mobile hotspots, cloud services, and other elements in the mobile device category, BYOI actually makes the security planner's job easier by transferring these concerns to the mobile system's users.

    C. BYOI potentially opens the organization's infrastructure up to previously unknown connections with other people, organizations, and so forth; the potential for new and surprising risks is very great.

    D. BYOI often uses consumer-grade services, particularly for cloud services, which are not compatible with typical enterprise systems.

**17.** What do you have to do differently to protect virtual machines, as compared to protecting your physical hardware systems?

    **A.** Nothing; you'll still need to do everything you do to protect the operating systems, applications, data, and networks that your real machines use, for your virtual machines.

    **B.** Since virtual machines are more easily sandboxed, you can run on them unprotected, and not have the performance penalties associated with malware scanning or firewalls.

    **C.** Because it's so easy to create (and destroy) VMs, you may need policy and procedural controls over who can do this and what protections need to be in place.

    **D.** Because it's so easy to create (and destroy) VMs, you don't really need to worry about them. The protections in place on the rest of your systems will keep them isolated.

**18.** Of the many things you could do to improve endpoint security, which would you recommend as most effective?

    **A.** Ensure that users promptly report missing, lost, or stolen endpoint hardware devices.

    **B.** Ensure that each endpoint has multiple, secure means to connect to your systems to enhance availability and productivity.

    **C.** Ensure that identity management and access control systems will not allow unauthorized users or processes access to system resources, regardless of what device they are from.

    **D.** Provide fully encrypted links for all data flows to and from endpoint devices.

**19.** Which of the following statements about malware are not true? (Choose all that apply.)

    **A.** Malware may corrupt your data and software, but it cannot damage your hardware.

    **B.** Most SOHO environments have very little to lose to a malware infection, so they are justified in not spending a lot of effort or money on defensive systems.

    **C.** If you operate your system within a hierarchy of trust, and you do not go beyond its boundaries, you do not need to do anything else to protect against malware.

    **D.** Doing all of your browsing in fully secure (HTTPS) sessions will prevent any malware from entering your system.

    **E.** None of these statements are true.

**20.** Which of the following statements about email and malware are correct? (Choose all that apply.)

    **A.** For most enterprise systems, a separate server that scans all incoming email and attachments, before email is sent to its addressees, should be used.

    **B.** As long as all of your email is digitally signed, such as with S/MIME, even the attachments will be free from malware.

    **C.** Limiting the total size of an incoming email and all of its attachments is a practical way to prevent malware coming into your systems.

    **D.** Email scanning for malware may be 100% effective at stopping malware from entering your systems directly, but it will not help with phishing, whaling, or other such attack vectors.

# Chapter

# 9

# Applications, Data, and Cloud Security

---

**THE SSCP EXAM OBJECTIVES COVERED IN THIS CHAPTER INCLUDE:**

Domain 7: Systems and Application Security

✓ 7.2: Implement and Operate Endpoint Device security

✓ 7.3: Operate and Configure Cloud Security

✓ 7.4: Operate and Secure Virtual Environments

Now that we've got a secure infrastructure under our user's work spaces, how do we keep their work from being its undoing? People need to use that infrastructure to accomplish the goals and objectives of the business or organization; they get that value-adding work done by taking data in, manipulating it, creating new data with it, and outputting it in ways that inform and enable action at a profit. People get all of that value-added work done by using *application programs*, or *apps*. This combination of software, data, and human interaction can keep the overall information systems secure, expose the business to substantial vulnerabilities (and liabilities!), or both in combination.

At one end of this problem are vendor-provided resources such as applications, data, and services; at the other are end user–created apps, formulas buried in spreadsheets, macros, webpages—the list of possible risk vectors is endless. Then there are the risks of what incorrect data, or correct data misused, can bring to bear.

Let's see how SSCPs can bring this final technical component of our information security architectures under control.

# It's a Data-Driven World...At the Endpoint

Let's face it—from the perspective of the information systems designer and builder, *all of the action happens at the endpoints*. These endpoints are where the real, tangible physical world of *things* and *people* is transformed by modeling, abstraction, and reduction into a handful of data values. It's where a similar handful of data values causes huge industrial equipment to *move*, to change its "end effectors" by swapping out one cutting tool for another, or hoisting *this* instead of *that*, and the result is physical, real *change* in the world we live in. There's a tangible, real, permeable barrier at the endpoint: on one side lives the world of the abstract information movers and shakers, and on the other side, "stuff happens." Money changes hands; merchandise is picked from shelves and prepped for shipment; 40-foot containers are loaded onto ships or taken off of them and stacked *just so* along the wharf. People laugh or cry, are fed or go hungry on the physical side of that boundary layer; data may model their needs, their wants, their hopes and aspirations on the other. *The model is not the reality. Forget this at your peril.*

You, the SSCP, have a role to play within the information systems "ivory tower," the abstract world in which data is manipulated, processed, calibrated, and combined to produce the other layers of the Data-Information-Knowledge-Wisdom pyramid. Inside the boundary, you translate business logic and security concerns into the software and data structures that implement identity management, access control, and a host of other security measures. Outside of that boundary, your work with physical and administrative controls, for example, is by nature part of the real, physical world; so are the sensor and control technologies used throughout your information security systems. The boundary itself represents the threat surface—that logical construct at which subjects attempt to cross into your virtualized data world. Data-driven logic helps you separate the legitimate attempts to enter your systems from those that are not. As the on-scene SSCP, you constantly move across the boundary as you shift your thinking across the data, control, and management planes of your organization's information architectures. (Yes, those planes—and the identity plane as well—should extend beyond just the world of the digital circuits and systems.)

But what about that boundary layer? What happens at that interface between the world you can *touch* and the world you can only *think about?* What about those two-way acts of abstraction and reification (making real) that happen across that boundary layer? And perhaps most germane to you, what is the role the SSCP plays in making that boundary *safe?*

That boundary layer is defined and implemented by the application programs, or apps, that users need and use to gather information, transform it, use it in making decisions, and then use it to control and monitor how well those decisions pan out. That boundary layer is many layers deep. Apps layer upon each other, using interface handlers and *middleware* to broker information between them and to interface with applications that are so large and feature-rich that we call them *platforms*—huge suites of applications programs, brought together via their underlying databases and data models, which provide broad and deep business logic capabilities to many different businesses. Salesforce, for example, provides broad, standardized capabilities in customer relationship management, business logic fulfillment, and decision support needed by businesses in almost any industry. Campus Solutions, by contrast, provides these same capabilities specifically tailored to meet the unique needs of the education and training industry; while Apollo is even more narrowly focused on the passenger air travel industry alone. These are all based on their data models; they are all data-driven embodiments of business logic. But whether an application is a huge, complex, feature-rich platform or a small, single-purpose, lightweight app on a handheld or smaller device, the action happens at the endpoints. *That's* where the organization makes its livelihood.

This is why this chapter separates apps and data from the *infrastructures* that support them. We've looked in depth at the security issues pertaining to those infrastructures in previous chapters. Many of those same issues, such as access control, pertain to the "apps and data and endpoints" view of the world as well. Yet one powerful truth remains unexplored. *Endpoint security can make or break everything else you have done to manage your organization's information and decision risk.*

You should feel that you're using some familiar guides and instruments to explore what might seem to be unfamiliar territory here in this chapter. In particular, we'll focus on the top layers of the OSI model, the ones that layer onto the basic four of the TCP/IP protocol stack. Know that as application builders and users, as gatherers and manipulators of data, we count on those lower layers to be cast-iron bulletproof, rock-solid secure. We have to rely on the implementations of those lower layers, and the systems and infrastructures they run on, to be doing their assigned portions of our overall information security needs for confidentiality, integrity, availability, nonrepudiation, and authorization. As users in our day-to-day operational tasks, we have to trust that others—other people and other systems—deliver their parts of the organization's total CIANA needs. (You'll recall that CIANA embodies the key information security attributes of confidentiality, integrity, availability, nonrepudiation, and authentication.) As app builders and users, we're not going to reinvent the secure transport layer here, nor are we going to work around any shortcomings in physical security. Those are rightly someone else's jobs to get done reliably (and it is management's due diligence responsibility to ensure that they are).

But...

A cost-effective allocation of risk management and risk mitigation might decide that a particular risk is best addressed at the Application layer, rather than the Physical layer, or how the Presentation layer simply cannot cope with another kind of threat and must rely on "what's above or below" to keep things safe and secure. And we'll revisit our earlier work on *integrating* all aspects of information security together in appropriate ways so that our awareness, our cognizance if you will, of an incipient or evolving threat incident can be met because we have effective command, control, and communications in place to deal with it.

In other words, it's at the endpoints that information turns into value-producing *work* and that work becomes information of value. This transformation is app-driven and app-enabled, and many times people-performed. The infrastructure may reduce our exposure to risks causing those app-driven transformations to go awry (or not); our people may be capable of keeping surprise from becoming dislocation in the face of mistakes, failures, or attacks (or not). The data we need, from inside our systems or from the outside world, does not turn into value without applications.

This is not just about *information* security, is it? It's about assuring the ongoing operation of business functions *at the endpoints*, by means of the software, data, and procedures that implement the business logic. As SSCPs, we'll need to know more about how applications software gets created, used, maintained, and then replaced; we'll also need to know a lot more about the lifecycle of the data and information as well. We'll then have to place both of these lifecycles firmly within an information systems and IT security context if we are to deliver the levels of business function and decision assurance that's needed.

We'll start our investigations of data-driven endpoint security with applications software, sometimes called *apps* or *appliances*. We'll see what it takes to build them secure, use them securely, and keep them secure. Data quality and data assurance, two sides of the same information security coin, will be our next port of call. Taking all of this into the clouds does add some complexities that SSCPs need to know how to cope with.

 **Real World Scenario**

### Ghosts Moving the Machines

Ian works as an instrumentation calibration and repair technician aboard one of the world's largest off-shore oil platforms, out in the frozen middle of a large body of water somewhere north of the Arctic Circle. A consortium of six different multinational corporations designed, equipped, and now staff and operate this biggest of the "big rigs." As Ian describes it, "all of a sudden, tons of industrial machinery *start moving,* as if it had a life of its own. Sometimes members of the crew know what's going on; sometimes they don't. It can get scary out here."

One of Ian's key concerns is that there is no agreed-to software or data configuration management. There are no rules, and no configuration management boards that enforce those rules. Stuff simply happens, and maybe the human crew on that rig know about the stuff before it's going to happen, and maybe they don't. These six multinational players don't "play nice," you might say; each is too busy chasing the profit margin to worry about whether the changes in software, control parameters, or operational procedures it implements in macros, control parameter settings, and scripts work safely and harmoniously with the other five's sets of data.

Yes, data. Scripts that embody procedural steps are nothing more than data that the script execution engine swallows whole, spitting out machinery-driving commands in step with what the script asks for. If the script designer overlooked a fail-safe parameter check, then the script will run without interrogating the sensor that should be the authoritative source for that fail-safe.

So long as things work as planned, it may be cheaper and more efficient (in the short term) to operate without the overhead and delays of a configuration management system, both for applications and systems software (and hardware). A formal data modeling and control process, one that would define every control or critical parameter *once* and ensure that all software used it correctly, is only felt necessary when things go wrong.

Is this something that the SSCPs working in those multinationals should have concerns about? How should they address this situation?

And how does their experience, or Ian's, relate to the systems and practices *your* world uses?

# Software as Appliances

Almost every computing device we use today is a *general-purpose computer*, one that can run programs to accomplish almost any function or task users ask it to by loading and executing programs written to achieve such functions. We often say that the only limits on what we can do with such general-purpose computers are the limits of our own imagination. Contrast this with your kitchen or home appliances; you don't ever think of your toaster as being able to wash and dry the dishes or prepare your shopping list for you, no matter how "smart" or network-enabled your kitchen is (do you?). We quickly accept that a special-purpose device, provided it does that purpose well, is often a better use of money, time, space, and energy than trying to make things too general in their capabilities. We might have a full set of pots and pans, and a stove or a cooktop, with which we can cook almost any kind of meal. But we let our smart coffee pot make our coffee when we need it, perhaps when our smart house senses we're about to get out of bed (or when we've told it we *need* the smell of fresh-brewed coffee as part of our wake-up call!), rather than try to over-gadget our stovetop.

This same approach of encapsulating a limited set of functions into the right combination of hardware, systems software, application software, and data brings another set of trade-offs with it that the SSCP needs to consider. Let's look at a few common examples to see just how prevalent this appliance model is today:

- Small office / home office (SOHO) routers and the modems provided by ISPs combine specialized hardware, OSs, and applications that present users with very powerful capabilities.

- Point-of-sale terminals have morphed from the smart cash register into highly portable devices used by restaurant wait staff, rental car agents, and many other businesses.

- Network attached storage (NAS) appliances package terabytes of inexpensive disk with network and server functions, bringing these capabilities into the reach of many home and small office users.

- Home entertainment, gaming, and smart home appliances bring a variety of related functions together and make them more pervasively available throughout our living spaces (yet none of them, thus far, help you in preparing your income taxes!).

Step away from the typical office environment and look at today's factory floor, and you see even more software-intensive appliances in action:

- Industrial automation and control uses a wide range of programmable control devices. Many major tasks in factory or process automation are easily broken down into well-understood steps, which are packaged or hosted into highly modularized elements.

- Medical and clinical settings combine specialized sensors to gather patient data, operate laboratory processes and instruments, and combine them with caregiver observations, orders, and interventions to provide better, safer patient care. This holistic approach to patient wellness via smarter, focused use of information is often referred to as *medical informatics*.

- Physical security systems combine sensors, input and display devices, and control systems to monitor the motion of people, packages, or vehicles; restrict, prevent, or authorize their further movement; and invoke other security and protection functions automatically or at the command of human security operators.

---

### Does "App" Mean "Application" or "Appliance?"

Good question!

From the first introduction of cell phones in the 1980s, portable communications users wanted more functionality. Motorola's DynaTac 8000x phone hit the market in 1983, with only a very rudimentary contacts list manager built into its onboard software. This brick-sized, 2.5 lb cell phone had no real way to expand its onboard functionality, which further whetted the market's appetite for more capabilities while on the go. The limited display, processor, and storage capabilities of the first- and second-generation phones dictated that smaller, lightweight, limited-function applications were needed, as users and industry observers quickly pointed out back then. As Steve Jobs pointed out (also in 1983), a totally different software distribution business model, similar to the then-popular record stores, was the opportunity waiting in the wings to address these problems. But it was not until sometime in the first decade of the twenty-first century that the market started calling these "apps," possibly because Apple and Microsoft, and later Google, started making them available to users via their Web-based "app stores."

Enter the era of the smart watch, and these apps-as-applications start to take on more of an appliance look and feel. Devices like the Fitbit line of fitness trackers combine limited health measurements (like pulse rate, motion, maybe even blood pressure and respiration) with location tracking, all built around the user paradigm of a wristwatch and its date-and-time functions. When linked to a desktop or mobile phone application, such fitness trackers enable users to have greater visibility of their activities, perhaps enabling them to change habits and choices as they correlate the tracker's data with other offboard information. The question remains: is such a fitness tracker, as a package, an "appliance"? And when the tracker's user downloads and installs a software package to enable integration of offboard data more seamlessly, is that software an "app as appliance" or "app as application"?

This distinction of appliance versus application is poorly expressed in the marketplace today. It may in fact be becoming more fluid, as it shifts from a designer's paradigm to an end-user or use-case paradigm. As a user, I might build a smarter, healthier lifestyle around my fitness tracker by gathering virtual appliances together that help me stay active and fit, but this depends on those appliances plugging and playing together in simple, safe, secure, and reliable ways. As a designer, I'm focused more on the details of the interfaces, whether they be applications calls, network-enabled and data-driven, or combinations of both. As the SSCP in my household, I have to look through both lenses to meet my needs for CIANA as applied to my fitness and lifestyle information systems—be they apps, applications, appliances, or data.

---

If there is a trend, it is to see more and more endpoint functionality being packaged, deployed, and used as appliances, rather than as "traditional" feature-rich applications. From the designer's perspective, maybe it's time for other nonmanufacturing businesses and organizations to borrow a few pages from the industrial process control playbook. Software-based or software-intensive appliances are beginning to be treated as commodities, which lets the market's need for standardized, modularized function within a particular envelope of price, performance, and reliability be met in reliable, repeatable ways.

Another trend that may be emerging is that the line between an Internet of Things (IoT) device and an appliance is blurring. As a whole domain of systems components, IoT devices have a reputation for being too simple, perhaps. Many do not support even the most rudimentary of security features and come with little or no way to update their onboard firmware or change security-related control parameters such as their default login and password. IoT device makers are feeling the pressure from the market and are starting to "smarten up" their products.

As an example, consider a modern orchard, using smart irrigation and nutrient delivery systems individualized to meet each tree's needs. Such orchards use a wide variety of Wi-Fi-enabled, GPS-savvy sensors and controls; each tree is known by its GPS coordinates; and a geographical information system (GIS) brings all of that data together. Are those sensors, the irrigation control systems, and even the uninhabited aerial vehicles (UAVs) that are flying survey and surveillance missions IoT devices, appliances, or something else? *Does that distinction matter?* To the orchard operators, no; their IT staff may need to differentiate the type of *endpoint* device based on how "dumb" or "smart" it is, and therefore whether it is a "classic IoT device" or a smarter, more capable appliance, or something else entirely.

The key takeaway for the SSCP on this is that these boundary lines between categories of devices are blurring. What remains as key differentiators might best be thought of (by the SSCP) in security-centric terms: how much that device contributes to information security solutions, compared to how much it causes or aggravates our information security problems.

# Applications Lifecycles and Security

Software is the set of instructions we give to the hardware to make it do the things we need done. Your car just sits in the driveway until you instruct it to take you to work, doesn't it? You issue instructions to the car by physically interacting with its controls—door handles, ignition switch, gearshift lever, the pedals, and so on. You design that total set of instructions based on the needs of your journey, and as you saw in Chapter 3, "Integrated Information Risk Management," you manage risks along that journey by preplanned vulnerability assessment combined with observation throughout the journey itself. This analogy is useful not only because it relates ideas to actions, but also because it reveals something about risk. Simply put, the instructions (for the journey or for a program) are easy to create—you just write them down. Making the hardware is, well, *harder* to do. Making hardware requires "bending metal" and other tangible actions on materials; we trust that we can always make up for shortcomings in hardware design by "fixing it later in the software" (or letting the end user cope with it procedurally). Yet experience shows that finding the logical design errors, the simple coding mistakes, or the misuse of programming language features in the code is a lot harder than finding errors in the hardware.

Don't panic—as an SSCP you do *not* need to become an expert programmer or a software development manager to be able to keep your company's applications software safe and secure. You do, however, need to gain a working knowledge of what it takes to develop most of the significant software applications that businesses and organizations use in order to help those developers and users keep the business running safely and securely. That boils down to knowing how and why to ask a few important questions of the software developers, maintainers, and managers you support:

- How do we identify and resolve vulnerabilities in the apps we write? In the apps we get from vendors or others?

- Do we have formalized processes for all apps across the full lifecycle, from needs identification to deployment to end users to retirement or disposal?

- How do we handle apps that end users develop?
- How do we do configuration management and control of all applications?
- Do we work to continually improve and mature those software lifecycle processes?

Any of those questions that have negative, incomplete, or unclear answers are highlighting potential risk management areas that need urgent attention.

# The Software Development Lifecycle (SDLC)

When we talk about the *lifecycle* of a system, we are trying to include every step from first concepts through postretirement—"from cradle to grave," as many manufacturers sometimes refer to it. As you saw in Chapter 1, "The Business Case for Decision Assurance and Information Security," no organization operates in that hypothetically perfect world of unlimited time, resources, and budget; every step of every task, every day, must make compromises with cost, schedule, and technical satisfaction of the most important performance requirements. Systems analysis, design, development, validation testing, operational use and support, and finally retirement are no exceptions to this "golden rule" (which we might paraphrase as "without the gold, you don't get much of a system designed, built, tested, or put into use"). For software, we use the term *software development lifecycle* (SDLC) model as the collective name of processes, procedures, and systems used to plan, organize, manage, and direct the people processes necessary to go from ideas to design and development to in-use validated software and beyond. There are many different SDLCs in use today, and most of them are based on the waterfall model, shown in Figure 9.1. The waterfall model consists of the following major stages:

**FIGURE 9.1**   Waterfall software development lifecycle model

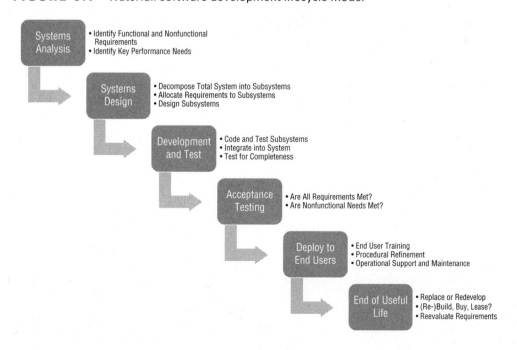

- *Systems analysis* is the process of capturing in human-readable form the needs for form, function, and purpose of a new information system, and grouping, structuring, and allocating those needs to broad, functional elements of software, hardware, networks and communications, people-facing processes, and other information-based processes. This phase is often called the *requirements phase*, as its main outcome is an agreed-to baseline set of statements about form, fit, and function that the system is required (in contractual terms) to meet. Its major output is usually a set of *performance requirements*, which are statements of what the system must do, and the measurement standards its functions will be assessed against, if the system (once it's built) is to meet the users' needs.

- *Systems design* translates the requirements for the system into a set of design elements; as such, system design makes choices about implementation approaches. The nature of the mission (the requirements) might, for example, dictate that this be a cloud-hosted, highly scalable architecture, or it might be that the mission requires most of the functionality to live in small IoT devices at the edge of the cloud or the network. System design also allocates requirements to elements of the design so that customers and users will know which features to use to accomplish business logic or mission needs.

- *Development and test* activities translate the system design into working software, which is verified to work correctly.

- *Validation or acceptance testing* provides a formal way for customers or users to see that each of the system's requirements have been correctly and completely built into the system and how they can be used to accomplish business or mission needs. Inspection and audit of the code, builds and control information, and configuration management records verify that no other functions were built into the product system—both to prevent excessive costs and to prevent backdoors or malware from sneaking in.

- *Operational deployment* moves the system from the developers to the users in two important ways: by installing it and having users start to "do business" with it, and by shifting the management of the systems baseline from developer-managed to user-managed. During development, the configuration management authority largely resides with the developer; once the system goes live, the business or organization's operational stakeholders now make the configuration management decisions.

- *Systems replacement and retirement* occurs when for whatever reason the organization chooses to stop using one set of systems and capabilities and replace that set with something else. New business needs might dictate this; increased risk exposure might also be a cause. Typically, the new systems are brought from concept to operational deployment, and then the old system is turned off, torn out, and disposed of.

Each of these critical steps in the life of a software application can present information security risks and the opportunities to manage and mitigate those risks. And it should go without saying that each of those steps involves compromises between functional requirements, safety and security needs, resources, time, budget, and risk tolerance. And if that's not enough, as you saw in Chapter 3, each time you compromise on some aspect of a system, you increase the likelihood of introducing a weakness in design that could be an exploitable vulnerability.

## SDLCs and IDEs

The waterfall model might seem to suggest that all software is developed in this highly structured manner, with well-defined turnover points between each step. Major systems that have safety-critical and mission-critical functions to perform, such as military command and control systems, medical information systems, and space flight and air traffic control systems, are often built this way. It allows for a clean decision point (often called a *milestone*) that controls the flow of activity and attention from one phase to the next. To successfully keep such a project on schedule and within cost is difficult; the more that the real world changes the mission requirements, the more that each subsequent step is put at risk.

Most business systems, however, do not have safety of life (or the survival of a nation) riding on the successful implementation of their performance or security requirements. In fact, many businesses and nonprofit organizations have to face new and different questions arising from their marketplaces, questions that require them to change the way their applications process and present information on an almost daily basis. This requires *agility* in those systems themselves—the ability to put a tool to a somewhat different use than was envisioned when it was made or purchased. It also requires these systems to be more resilient—more flexible and adaptable in the face of change—than a formal, tightly controlled requirements-driven software development lifecycle can usually manage.

Integrated development environments (IDEs) have come a long way in the last three decades. An IDE provides a complete, robust set of software tools that support one programmer, a team of programmers, or many teams at once, in all phases of development, test, deployment, and support of major or minor software systems. Many software and systems vendors provide one flagship IDE product, such as Microsoft's Visual Studio, which can support many different programming languages, and even support the integration of code from "foreign" libraries (those outside of the organization and its span of administration and control). Not all software is written in and managed by an IDE, however. Personal preferences for programming languages, libraries, tool sets, and integration strategies can make it hard sometimes to find the right mix of software development talent to get the new apps built and deployed, the old ones maintained, or both; this can add up to a less-than-integrated use of an IDE.

As an SSCP, you'll run into a number of different strategies for software development, with names like Agile, Scrum, Spiral, Rapid Prototyping, Code-First Design, Test-First, and others. *Don't lose sight of those key questions shown earlier.* Keep Kipling's six wise men handy; keep asking how things get done, what steps are taken to identify security needs, who decides what security needs to implement, where those implementations are done, and so forth.

# Why Is (Most) Software So Insecure?

It's almost an accepted part of our culture that the software we humans create is probably going to have mistakes in it. Although some of those mistakes may end up being minor inconveniences to its users, others might be exploitable vulnerabilities. Why?

First, the writing of software is a creative human process. We take ideas about functions we want to perform, translate those ideas into designs, and translate those designs into higher-level programming languages; and along the way, we create the user manuals, data structures, and everything else that should complete the bundle of new business capabilities. Since none of us are perfect, mistakes happen in each of these products.

Many of the mistakes made during design and development are preventable:

- *Poor design practices.* Applications are complex programs that designers build up from hundreds, perhaps thousands of much smaller, simpler units of code. This decomposition of higher-level, more abstract functions into simpler, well-bounded lower-level functions is the heart of any good design process. When designers consistently use proven and well-understood design rules, the designs are more robust and resilient—that is, their required functions work well together and handle problems or errors in well-planned ways.

- *Inconsistent use of design patterns.* A *design pattern* is a recommended method, procedure or definition of a way to accomplish a task. Experience and analysis have shown us that such design patterns can be built successfully and used safely to achieve correct results. Yet many programs are developed as if from scratch, as if they are the first-ever attempt to solve that problem or perform that task. Assembling hundreds or thousands of such "first-time" sets of designs can be fraught with peril—and getting them to work can be a never-ending struggle.

- *Poor coding practices.* Since the 1940s, we've known that about 20 classes of bad programming practice can lead to all-too-familiar runtime errors and exploitable vulnerabilities. The software industry teaches programmers these "thou shalt nots" of programming; still, they keep showing up in business applications and systems software.

- *Inconsistent use (or no use at all) of proven, tested design and code libraries.* Software reuse is the process of building new software from modules of code that have been previously inspected, tested, and verified for correct and safe execution. Such design and code libraries, when published by reputable development teams, are a boon to any software development effort—as long as the right library elements are chosen for the tasks at hand and then used correctly in the program being developed. High-quality libraries can bring a wealth of security-related features built into their designs and code; in many cases, the library developer provides ongoing technical support and participates in common vulnerability reporting with the information systems security community. Sadly, many software teams succumb to schedule and budget pressures and use the first bit of cheap (or free) code that they find on the Internet that seems to fit their needs. Sometimes, too, application programmers speed-read the high-level documentation of a library or a library routine and accept what they read as proof that they've found what they need. Then they just plug it into their application and pray that it works right, never taking the time to read the code itself or verify that it will correctly and safely do what they need it to do *and do nothing else* in the process.

This lack of discipline in using proper and proven design practices and patterns, as well as poor coding practices (or the lack of coding standards) can often produce *spaghetti code*, so called because trying to read it and follow its logic is as easy as following one strand of spaghetti when it's in a plateful on your dinner dish.

---

### Security "Baked In" to the Software, Right from the Start?

Strange as it may seem, most applications software is specified, designed, written, and tested by people who rather innocently assume that the world is not a dangerous place. So how do you, as a non-code-bending, non-software-trained SSCP, help your company or organization get more *defensive* in the ways that it builds and maintains its software? A blog post by the editorial team at Synopsys, in their Software Architecture and Design blog at www.synopsys.com/blogs/software-security /principles-secure-software-design/, highlights four key points to ponder:

1. Be paranoid. Know that somebodies, somewhere, are out to get you. Lots of them.

2. Pay attention to *abuse* cases, instead of just the "business normal" *use* cases, as sources of your functional and nonfunctional requirements. (They go on to mention three fallacies that lead to complacency about security needs among software developers.)

3. Understand that small vulnerabilities cascade together to become just as disruptive as a few large vulnerabilities can be.

4. Build things securely so that they *last*. Build for posterity.

One major problem has been that for decades, the software industry and academia have assumed that managers and senior designers are responsible for secure software design and development. It's no good teaching brand-new programmers about it, because they don't manage software projects, according to this view. As a result, an awful lot of *insecure* software gets written, as bad habits get engrained by use.

A great resource to learn with is the Open Web Application Security Project (OWASP), at www.owasp.org. OWASP is a nonprofit source of unbiased, vendor-neutral, and platform-agnostic information, and provides advice and ideas about the right ways to "bake in" security when designing Web apps.

As the SSCP, you are the security specialist who can help your organization's software developers better appreciate the threat, recognize the abuse cases, and advocate for penetration-style security testing *during* development—not just after deployment!

Baking the security in from the start of software development requires turning a classic programmer's paradigm inside-out. Programmers are *trusting* souls; they trust that others will do their jobs correctly. They trust that users will "do the right thing," that

*(continued)*

---

*(continued)*

network and systems security will validate the user, or that access control done by someone else will prevent any abuses. (Managers like this paradigm, too, because it shifts costs and efforts to other departments while making their jobs simpler and easier.) Instead, it's more than high time to borrow a page from the zero trust school of thought for networks:

> Trust no one, trust no input data, ever, and verify everything before you use it.

---

Next, we manage that process with other software—design tools, source code editors, compilers, integrated development environments, test systems, shells and data, configuration management tools, and analysis and inspection tools. This software, too, can have its own share of mistakes. It's also procedurally intensive work to plan, manage, build, test, integrate, and deliver major application packages.

Schedule concerns and budget limitations provide constraints on the development and test process. Usually, the new software has a hard and fast delivery date already set for it; the costs that delaying the delivery date are often too painful to tolerate. There's also a limit on how much money can be spent on testing, reprogramming to repair the errors, and retesting.

But that's not all. As we push on from design into coding, other common sources of *data errors* plague many software projects:

- *Weak enforcement of data typing and data modeling during software development.* A major business platform application, such as an enterprise resource planning (ERP) system, might have tens of thousands of identifiers—names for fields in records, for record types, for variables used in the software internally, and the like.

  - *Data modeling* is a formal process that translates the business logic into named data elements. It formalizes the constraints for initialization of each data item; how new values are input, calculated, produced, and checked against logical constraints; and how to handle errors in data elements. For example, one constraint on a credit card number field might specify the rules for validating it as part of a data set (including cardholder name, expiration date, and so forth); related constraints would dictate how to handle specific validation problems or issues.

  - *Data typing* involves the rules by which the programmer can write code that works on a data item. Adding dollars to dates, for example, makes no sense, yet preventing a programming error from doing this requires data typing rules that define how the computer stores calendar dates and monetary amounts, *and* the rules regarding allowable operations on both types taken together. Organizations that manage their information systems with robust data dictionaries and use rigorously enforced data typing in their software development *tend* to see fewer exploitable errors due to data format, type, or usage errors.

- *Inconsistent or no data quality efforts during operational use.* Think about what *should* happen when a clerk enters a customer's name into a data input screen but misspells it in the process; if it's an existing customer, the system ought to find a close match and query the clerk to identify the correct customer. The failure of this "pre-existing match test" logic then would prompt the clerk to ask, "Are you a new customer?" and only then create a new customer record in the system. This is an example of taking the business logic in the data dictionary (as a design standard for business processes) and enforcing it when the logic is used day to day. Customers change their address, even their name, sometimes a lot more often than mere programmers assume people will do; *data quality* focuses on keeping all of the related data together, logically consistent, correct, and up to date. (We'll look at some practical approaches to data quality later in this chapter.) Yet despite the proven payback of data quality efforts to almost any business, many organizations see it as a cost to be avoided; they simply trust that their operators, or sales clerks, or customers will find the errors and either tolerate them or fix them.

---

### Data Modeling Should Reflect Security Needs

Most data modeling is driven by use cases—who needs the data, what they use it for, and what happens to the data as they use it. Overwhelmingly, this use case analysis fails to recognize the abuse cases (as noted by Synoptics earlier); as a result, the data models assume trusted subjects doing trustworthy operations upon the data.

As the SSCP, perhaps you can bring your understanding of threat modeling to your organization's data modelers. Start small, perhaps over lunch or a coffee, and explore the possibilities for collaboration.

---

## Hard to Design It Right, Easy to Fix It?

This is perhaps the most pernicious thought that troubles every software development team, and every user of the software that they depend on in their jobs and in their private lives. *Hardware*, after all, is made of metal, plastic, glass, rubber, and dozens of other physical substances. *Changing the hardware is hard work*, we believe. A design error that says that our SOHO router overheats and burns out quickly, because we didn't provide enough ventilation, might require a larger plastic enclosure. That design change means new injection molds are needed to cast that enclosure's parts; new assembly line processes are needed, maybe requiring changes to the fixtures and tooling; and new shipping and packing materials for the empty enclosure and the finished product will be needed. That's a lot of work, and a lot of change to manage! But changing a few lines of code in something that exists only as a series of characters in a source code file seems *easy* by comparison.

This false logic leads many managers, users, and programmers to think that it's easy and simple to add in a missing feature, or change the way a function works to better suit the end user's needs or preferences. It's just a simple matter of programming, isn't it, if we need to fix a bug we discovered after we deployed the application to our end users?

Right?

In fact, we see that software development is a constant exercise in balancing trade-offs:

- Can we really build all of the requirements our users say they need?
- Can we really test and validate everything we built and show that it meets the requirements?
- Can we do that for a price that we quoted or contracted for and with the people and development resources we have?
- Can we get it all done *before* the marketplace or the real world forces us to change the build-to requirements?

As with any project, software development managers constantly trade off risks versus resources versus time. Some of the risks involve dissatisfied customers when the product is finally delivered; some risks involve undetected but exploitable vulnerabilities in that product system. And all projects face a degree of uncertainty that the people, money, time, and other resources needed for development and acceptance testing won't be as available as was assumed when the project was started—or that those resources will be there to support the maintenance phase once the project goes operational.

How much security is enough to keep what sort of applications secure? As with anything else in the IT world, the information security aspects of any app should be a requirements-driven process.

# CIANA and Applications Software Requirements

A maxim in the software industry is that any program large or small should do what its users asked the programmers to make it do; it should do those functions well, *and do nothing else at all*. This is the two-edged razor blade of software validation and test. First, you need to prove that requirements the customer paid for actually get done by the software you wrote. Second, you need to prove that no other surprises, special features, or hidden bells and whistles are built into your code, just waiting for the right series of operations and inputs to bring them to life.

(One good definition of *malware* is software that contains such unacknowledged or undisclosed features, after all.)

So how does the SSCP, who is probably not a programmer or systems analyst after all, assess their organization's applications software from this security requirements perspective?

Our old friend CIANA provides a great starting point to specify and definitize our information security needs as allocated to the applications that we use. Our systems analysis process should have allocated other functional requirements to specific applications (we don't normally expect bills to be paid to vendors or suppliers by the human resources management apps, for example). Then, as part of the design process, we decompose those functions into smaller sets of steps, and assign those sub-functional sets to elements of an application's design itself.

In a perfect world, systems analysts and designers would consult with the organization's information risk managers and get their current, detailed views on how confidentiality, integrity, authentication, nonrepudiation, and availability are related to each and every information asset that the system they're designing will come in contact with. As they flow high-level statements of need down into design-level subsystems and components, they would allocate the parts of CIANA that apply to that subsystem. Then they'd build it, and test it not only against the performance requirements, but also against security, operability, and all of the other "-ilities" that become part of the ways that systems stakeholders assess project success. (All too often, of course, compromises between this perfect set of needs and the imperfect but real world of schedules and budgets end up cutting corners, or more, off of many a well-intended design, build, and test process. This can often introduce vulnerabilities into the final as-delivered system, or fail to detect and remedy them.)

From the penetration tester's perspective, or the vulnerability assessor's point of view, we can work this in the reverse direction. Take any particular function in the as-deployed information system, and see how it is actually used in day-to-day business operations. Given that high-level CIANA statement, does the use of that function demonstrate what you think is adequate information security? Or is that particular function so trusting that "other functions" run by "somebody else" properly carried out the security needs? Take the simple task of an airline passenger service system accepting a boarding pass from a passenger and then signaling the gate agent that the passenger is cleared to board the flight. Air transport regulations, safety, and security all drive the due care and due diligence responsibilities that the airline and airport operators must meet as a part of loading the right passengers onto the right flight at the right time. CIANA might dictate a whole host of requirements, which might include:

- Confidentiality might require that the passenger's name, identification numbers, frequent flier numbers, etc., are not easily be seen by other passengers or bystanders in the gate area, and if further identification is required to verify that the right human being has the right boarding pass, that this can be done with due care to privacy needs.

- Authentication would require that the gate agents must sign on to the gate information system, and that their access privileges be authenticated as current and include their being assigned to process that particular flight at that particular gate; authentication is also the process that accepts that person X is the passenger that their boarding pass claims them to be, and thus, they are authorized to board.

- Integrity would require that any data entered or captured at the gate (such as boarding pass serial numbers) be error-checked and validated against the approved flight manifest, passenger list, and other information, right there at the endpoint (the gate and its terminal systems); then the data and its validation information are transferred to central systems for other uses as a signed, sealed bundle (to provide integrity protection while in motion).

- Nonrepudiation would demand that steps be taken to ensure that all manifested passengers who checked baggage onto the flight actually boarded it and are still on board when the order to close the cabin door is issued.

- Availability of passenger check-in *as a function* would dictate that there are backup (perhaps manual) processes for checking passengers onto the flight, verifying boarding passes and identification, etc., in the event that the IT system elements fail to operate during boarding.

---

### Security Requirements: Functional or Nonfunctional?

In systems analysis, a *functional requirement* is one that specifies a task that must be done; the requirement may also specify how users can verify that the task has completed successfully or if one of many error conditions have occurred. For example, the requirement might state that pressing the "start engine" button causes prerequisite safety conditions to be checked, then activates various subsystems, step by step, to start the engine; failure of any step aborts the start process, returns all subsystems to their safe pre-start condition, and sends alerts to the operator for resolution. By contrast, a *nonfunctional requirement* states a general characteristic that applies to the system or subsystem as a whole but is not obviously present in any particular feature or function. Security requirements are often considered nonfunctional. This can be confusing, as a few requirements examples can suggest:

- *Safety requirements* in a factory process control system might state that "the system will require two-factor authentication and two-step manual selection and authorization prior to allowing any function designated as safety-critical to be executed." As a broad statement, this is hard to test for; yet, when allocated down to specific subfunctions, either these specific verification steps are present in the module-level requirements, then built into the design, and observable under test, or they are not. Any as-built system element that *should* do such safety checks that does not is in violation of the requirements. So is such a safety requirement functional or nonfunctional?

- *Confidentiality requirements* in a knowledge bank system might state that "no unauthorized users can view, access, download, or use data in the system." This (and other) requirements might drive the specification, design, implementation, and use of the identity management and access control systems elements. But does the flow-down of this requirement stop there? Or do individual applications inherit a user authentication and authorization burden from this one high-level requirement?

- *Nonrepudiation requirements* for a clinical care system could dictate that there must be positive control for orders given by a physician, nurse practitioner, or other authorized caregiver, both as record of care decisions and as ways to prevent an order being unfilled or not carried out. The log of orders given is a functional requirement (somebody has to build the software that builds the log each time an order is entered). But is the nonrepudiation part functional or nonfunctional?

Many systems analysts will consider any requirement allocated to the human elements of the system as nonfunctional, since (they would argue) if the software or hardware isn't built to execute that function, that function isn't really a deliverable capability of the system. This also is the case, they'd argue, for functions "properly" allocated to the operating system or other IT infrastructure elements. Access control, for example, is rarely built into specific apps or platform systems, because it is far more efficient and effective to centralize the development and management of that function at the infrastructure level. Be careful—this train of thought leads to apps that have zero secure function built into them, even the most trivial of input data validation!

Performance requirements, those analysts would say, are by nature functional requirements in this sense. The "-ilities"—the capabilities, availabilities, and reliabilities, all of the characteristics of the system stated in words that end in *-ilities* or *-ility*—are (they say) nonfunctional requirements.

As an SSCP, you'll probably not be asked to adjudicate this functional-vs.-non argument. You may, however, have the opportunity to take statements from the users about what they need the system to do, *and* how they need to see it done, and see where CIANA-related concerns need to be assessed, analyzed, designed, built, tested, and then put to use. Monitored, too, of course; no sense building something if you do not keep an eye on how it's being used and how well it's working.

We live and work in a highly *imperfect* world, of course; it's almost a certainty that a number of CIANA-driven functional and nonfunctional requirements did not get captured in the high-level systems requirements documentation. Even if they did, chances are good that not all of them were properly implemented in the right subsystems, elements, or components of the overall application system. The two-view look as described earlier (from requirements downward, and from on-the-floor operational use upward) should help SSCPs make their working list of possible vulnerabilities.

*Possible* vulnerabilities, we caution. These are places to start a more in-depth investigation; these are things to ask others on the IT staff or information security team about. Maybe you'll be pleasantly surprised and find that many of them are already on the known vulnerabilities or issues watch lists, with resolution plans in the work.

But maybe not.

## Positive and Negative Models for Software Security

Ancient concepts of law, safety, and governance give us the idea that there are two ways to control the behavior of complex systems. *Positive control*, or *whitelisting*, lists by name those behaviors that are allowed, and thus everything else is prohibited. *Negative control*, or *blacklisting*, lists by name those behaviors that are prohibited, and thus everything else is allowed. (These are sometimes referred to as German and English common law, respectively.)

Antivirus or antimalware tools demonstrate both of these approaches to systems security. Software whitelisting, port forwarding rules, or parameters in machine learning behavioral monitoring systems all aim to let previously identified and authorized software be run or installed, connections be established, or other network or system behavior be considered as "normal" and hence authorized. Malware signature recognition and (again) machine learning behavioral monitoring systems look for things known to be harmful to the system or similar enough to known malware that additional human authorization steps must be taken to allow the activity to continue.

A quick look at some numbers suggest why each model has its place. It's been estimated that in 2018, over a million new pieces of malware were created *every month* "in the wild." As of this writing, AV-TEST GmbH notes on its website that it observes and categorizes over 350,000 new malicious or potentially unwanted programs (PUPs) or applications (PUAs) *every day*, with a current total exceeding 875 *million* species. Although many are simple variations on exploits already in use, that's a *lot* of new signatures to keep track of! By contrast, a typical medium to large-sized corporation might have to deal with authenticating from 1,000 to 10,000 new applications, or new versions of applications, that it considers authenticated to be used on its systems and endpoints.

Positive control models, if properly implemented, can also be a major component of managing system and applications updates. The details of this are beyond the scope of this book and won't be covered on the SSCP exam itself. That said, using a whitelisting system as part of how your organization manages all of its endpoints, all of its servers, and all of its devices in between can have several key advantages:

- As new versions of apps (or new apps) are authorized for use, a "push" of the approved whitelist to all devices can help ensure that old versions can no longer run without intervention or authorization.

- While new versions of apps are still being tested (for compatibility with existing systems or for operability considerations), the IT managers can prevent the inadvertent update of endpoints or servers.

- Individual users and departments may have legitimate business needs for unique software, not used by others in the company; whitelisting systems can keep this under control, down to the by-name individual who is requesting exceptions or overriding (or attempting to override) the whitelisting system.

- Whitelisting can be an active part of separation of duties and functions, preventing the execution of otherwise authorized apps by otherwise authorized users when not accessing the system from the proper set of endpoints.

- Whitelisting can be an active part in license and seat management if a particular app is licensed only to a fixed number of users.

## Is Blacklisting Dead? Or Dying?

SSCPs ought to ask this about every aspect of information systems security. Both blacklisting and whitelisting have their place in access control, identity management, network connectivity, and traffic routing and control, as well as with operating systems and application software installation, update, and use. Crowdsourcing for data (such as crowd-science approaches like Zooniverse) are impractical to operate if all users and data they provide must be subject to whitelisting, for example.

Let's narrow down the question for now to application software only. NIST and many other authorities and pundits argue that whitelisting is the best (if not the only sensible) approach when dealing with highly secure environments. These environments are characterized by the willingness to spend money, time, and effort in having strong, positive configuration management and control of all aspects of their systems. User-written code, for example, just isn't allowed in such environments, and attempts to introduce it can get its user-as-creator fired (or even prosecuted!). Whitelisting is *trust-centric*—in order for whitelisting to work, you have to trust your software logistics, support, and supply chain to provide you with software that meets or exceeds both your performance requirements *and* your information security needs across the lifecycle of that software's use in your organization. Making whitelisting for software control work requires administrative effort; the amount of effort is strongly related to the number of applications programs you need to allow, the frequency of their updates, and the numbers of systems (servers, endpoints, or both) that need to be under whitelist control.

Blacklisting is of course *threat-centric*. It's been the bedrock of antimalware and antivirus software and hybrid solutions for decades. It relies on being able to define or describe the behavior signatures or other aspects of potentially harmful software. If a behavior, a digital signature, a file's hash, or other parameters aren't on the blacklist, the potential threat wins access to your system. The administrative burden here is shifted to the threat monitoring and intelligence community that supports the blacklist system vendor (that is, we transfer part of this risk to the antimalware provider, rather than address it ourselves locally).

Whitelisting (or positive control) is sometimes described as requiring a strong authoritarian culture and mindset in the organization; it's argued that if users feel that they have an "inalienable right" to load and use any software that they want to, any time, then whitelisting stands in the way of them getting their job done. Yet blacklisting approaches work well (so far) when one central clearinghouse (such as an antimalware provider) can push signature updates out to thousands if not millions of systems, almost all of them running different mixes of operating systems, applications, vendor-supplied updates and security patches, and locally grown code.

Software development shops probably need isolated *workbench* or lab systems on which their ongoing development software can evolve without the administrative burdens of a whitelisting system. (Containerized virtual machines are probably safer and easier to administer and control for such purposes.) Academic or white-hat hacking environments may also need to operate in a whitelist, blacklist, or no-list manner, depending on the task at hand. Hopefully, other risk mitigation and control strategies can keep anything harmful in such labs from escaping (or being exfiltrated) out into the wild.

While the death certificate for negative control hasn't been signed yet, there does seem to be a strong trend in the marketplace. Until it is, and until all of the legacy systems that use blacklisting approaches are retired from the field, SSCPs will still need to understand how they work and be able to appreciate when they still might be the right choice for a specific set of information risk mitigation and control needs.

# Application Vulnerabilities

If we apply some old-fashioned wisdom to the art of writing software, there are some *right* ways to produce good, clean, secure, safe, and resilient apps—and then there are any number of just plain *wrong* ways to do that job. Those "right ways" can lead us to developing and maintaining software in reliable, repeatable ways; our programmer/analyst teams build on experience with each new app. At the same time, our IT security team gains experience with threat analysis and risk reduction throughout this regular, well-defined, controlled, repeatable, and *managed* development, deployment, and support lifecycle. Quality managers talk about such end-to-end sets of business processes as *capabilities*—the business or organization *can do* that set of tasks, end to end. Mature capabilities are those that are repeatable and that are continually monitored so that the business learns from mistakes and from successes; such mature capabilities will more likely produce higher-quality outputs (such as apps that they write) more often than less mature processes can do.

Note that there are no guarantees here! The "wrong ways" can be struck by blind luck and produce an application that works right and is reliable, robust, safe, and secure, perhaps just because some members of the team knew how to do things better. Similarly, very mature processes can still make mistakes.

Remember, software doesn't wear out; a set of instructions to ask the user for data, check it against constraints, and then send that data to the backend database server will not start to fade away, dropping out instructions or steps. The *hardware* it runs on might break down, but it's safe to say that all software vulnerabilities are human-induced.

Let's say that a different way: failures in the lifecycle process to specify, design, code, build, test, and use the software properly allow mistakes to go unnoticed—and some of those mistakes may result in exploitable vulnerabilities!

As you saw in Chapter 4, "Operationalizing Risk Mitigation," vulnerability assessment tells us that the larger and more complex the system, the greater the likelihood that it will contain more exploitable vulnerabilities. And as you saw in Chapter 8, "Hardware and Systems Security," unmanaged systems have a far greater likelihood that vulnerabilities will be found and exploited by attackers than do well-managed, well-controlled systems.

## Vulnerabilities Across the Lifecycle

As with systems software, applications are vulnerable across their lifecycle. For example, during development, several main threat vectors exist:

- The host operating system, network hardware and software, and other infrastructure elements may contain exploitable vulnerabilities that allow for exfiltration or infiltration of code and data, surreptitious monitoring of development activity, or other potentially harmful and unauthorized accesses to systems resources.

- The IDE software, other programming tools, test tools, library managers, and configuration management and control tools can have exploitable vulnerabilities in them, which can be used to "poison" or infect the ongoing development effort with malicious code fragments, as well as being used to exfiltrate sensitive design information about the project.

- All of the ideas, code, and documentation generated by the developers could be exploited by attackers to find vulnerabilities being built into the system (as if by accident). Requirements documents, design information, source code, test data and drivers, builds and controls scripts, development and test logs, and progress reports all contain valuable insight into both the team's processes and the product they are building.

- Development environments are also susceptible to attack. Insecure IDEs or the network or cloud-based library systems that they use are prime targets for *infiltration*, the insertion of hostile code and data fragments by attackers into the system being developed. (Such Trojan horse attacks during development have long been plot elements of cyber-*fiction* and espionage novels, which draw their inspiration from the demonstrated value of having insiders surreptitiously sneak in a few lines of hostile code *here*, substitute an entire module *there*,...)

During initial deployment, and later with redeployment of new versions, updates, or patches for the finished, tested, and trusted app, other potential weaknesses in process control and management could lead to any number of exploitable situations:

- Application software deployed as installation kits can be vulnerable to substitution of component files by a threat actor; whitelisting systems may not be able to check every component of a major application platform.

- During use, data input provided by users, over the Internet, or via databases or data files could drive the app to execute abnormally, which could expose system resources to further exploitation, malicious code being installed and executed, and so forth.

- Databases or data files used by the app, if not properly secured, can be hacked in ways that allow transactions to execute as if authorized and normal but in unauthorized and harmful ways. For example, hacking the payroll database to include a fictitious employee, complete with direct deposit information, can siphon off money from the company every pay period, and yet the payroll system itself may not be able to detect this "ghost employee."

- Data can be exfiltrated from the files or databases used by the app.

In general, it's hard for attackers to exploit these kinds of vulnerabilities in an app's source code, executable files, control parameters, or data files without some other failure of security:

- Failure of access control and identity authentication and authorization systems opening the door for the attacker

- Failure by the application logic itself to properly validate that user-supplied data is correct, consistent, and authorized

- Failure by the application logic itself to recognize out-of-limits conditions, or anomalous or unauthorized actions being requested, and safely abort those operations or shut down in graceful ways

In all of these cases, failure to notify information security and IT personnel of the potential violation of security just compounds the chain of violations. As does failure by the information security team to be monitoring, logging, and analyzing the results of all of that monitoring!

## Human Failures and Frailties

As with every information risk mitigation and control strategy, tactic, and operation, keeping applications programs free from deliberately or accidentally introduced vulnerabilities depends on the human elements in the organization's software development processes. Social engineering attacks may try to find a development team member, an administrator, or a file clerk who can be "turned" or subverted to the attacker's wishes. Whether through momentary bursts of incompetence or sustained and growing hostility toward the project, the company, or their teammates, the risks presented by the human element cannot be ignored.

Phishing attacks continue to proliferate and become more varied and sophisticated; as of December 2018, the latest variation on this theme, the "catfish" (or bottom-feeder) attack pattern, tries to develop a long-term relationship with staff members within the target organization. They may pose as a prospective vendor or customer, an educator, even a prospective employee! Over time, the attacker's e-credibility increases, and the target staff member's resistance crumbles. Such attacks can gather significant information about the software (applications and systems) being used at the target company, how tightly it is controlled, and how well it is maintained. Offering a sympathetic ear to complaints about the systems being used, attackers can spot potential vulnerabilities—either in those systems or with other humans in the organization to target with social engineering efforts.

Let's face it: people *need* to trust one another; we *need* to be able to bring the stranger in from beyond the pale and make them a member of our circles of acquaintances, friends, marketplaces, and tribes. This is why criminal law refers to the scam artist or the social engineer as a *confidence artist*, as one who plays on our needs for trust and confidence so as to deceive and exploit us. We defeat or deter such con men (and women, of course!) by bestowing our trust only when it is earned, rather than granting it blindly; this is nothing more than due care and due diligence require. Helping our organization achieve and maintain this kind of security posture takes training, teaching, and leading by example—all of which you can start delivering on your first day on the job.

# "Shadow IT:" The Dilemma of the User as Builder

Beware the end user! Armed with spreadsheet macros and formulas, end users can extract data from configuration-managed corporate databases, apply their own code and data magic, and produce decision-influencing answers that management and leadership depend on. Another user might build email-enabled and highly automated process flows, using some of the other features in the company's productivity suite. Still other users might be absolute wizards at organizing critical information, documents, spreadsheets, and information repositories in the company's shared storage resources. Using business intelligence analytical tools, another power user can build management and leadership just the decision support dashboards they want, when they want them. And all of these end users are doing this creative problem-solving work totally outside of the IT department's configuration management, builds and control, or quality management systems. Information security gurus in the company may not know any of these apps exist. Even the chief information officer (CIO) may appreciate the praise of other senior leaders for providing an IT infrastructure and tool set that lets people be so much more productive without even knowing that much of that productivity depends on "hobby shop" logic embedded in an uncontrolled, undocumented, and unmaintainable morass of files and file types.

*Shadow IT,* as you saw in Chapter 4, is the name for this "under the radar" set of people, products, and services that extract, create, gather, massage, and combine data to produce a whole set of answers to many different questions. *Shadow IT* is any process, business logic, or human procedure that is implemented in software, data, metadata, or other IT elements in ways that are outside of the normal processes the organization uses to manage the development, use, support, and security of its IT systems, infrastructures, data, and applications. Tom, for example, may be a wizard when it comes to setting up spreadsheet formulas; his department manager and others use his spreadsheets to extract data from the corporate database system on a regular basis. Nobody really understands how Tom's spreadsheets work, but they've used them for years, and they rely on them. Then Tom gets hit by a Powerball, winning a life-changing annuity from the state lottery, and retires. Now what happens? Who will maintain these spreadsheets?

Why does shadow IT exist in the first place? Simply put, far too many organizations, managers, and workers believe that the managed and controlled IT development process, with its multistep SDLC, takes too long and costs too much to get a quick and simple answer to a right-now need. They believe that the power and versatility of modern IT *applications* make these same-day solutions easy, safe, secure, and reliable. As a result, the balance between reliability and right-now gets upset.

Software vendors have worked hard to provide greater capabilities that enable the end user to create, manage, process, route, and control the way information is used within their office, their team, their company, or even with outside business associates. In the last few years, the reach and power of such "end-user-empowerment solutions" has grown almost tenfold.

---

### Why Is This Bad News?

It all comes down to whether the individual end users are skilled and experienced at designing, building, and maintaining IT systems that are safe to use, reliably produce correct answers, and protect the organization against misuse, bad data as input, or other hazards. It comes down to whether they have built and can maintain these self-created tools to meet or exceed the CIANA needs of the organization. If they can, great! Bring these people in from out in the cold of the shadows and recognize and reward them, for the survival of your business depends on them more than you might know.

If they cannot...in one IT manager's epithet, they are loose cannons looking for a ship to sink. They could *potentially* sink the business.

It is unfortunately true that throughout the history of computing, we have struggled with how to set this balance. SSCPs probably cannot influence how their organization sets this balance (and it may even be career limiting to try!). SSCPs can, however, work with others in the organization to gain a better understanding of the scope and severity of the information risks posed by shadow IT.

Shadow IT can take many forms:

- Application programs written in almost any programming language (even ones not supported by the organization's software development infrastructure)

- HTML, CSS, Java and JavaScript, or other web page elements

- Stored query procedures that users can create and then use with the company's formally supported database systems

- Batch files, shell scripts, or other procedures that users can create with a text editor and then run via the command line interpreter

- Visual Basic, self-recorded macros, or other procedural scripts generated by word processors, spreadsheets, presentation programs, email clients, etc.

- Process flows defined for email and attachments that interact with mainline company information systems

- Formula in spreadsheets (or in other documents) that check for conditions and then branch to process, present, or save data in particular ways

- Conditional logic for auto-repeating tasks, event schedules, and the emails that tie them together

Whitelisting is probably not going to help us here. In almost all cases, the shadow IT elements are loaded and executed by whitelisted programs (such as Microsoft Excel, PeopleSoft, or Quicken for Business). Those programs can be locked down to prevent all but a trusted set of macros, metadata, or other procedural information from being loaded and executed, but many organizations find this administratively difficult to manage. It's also very hard to get users and their managers to support "turning off all of the macros," for example. Except in the most security-conscious of organizations, too many users at too many levels in the chain of command have come to depend on their own quick and dirty shadow IT tools to solve today's problems today.

## Data and Metadata as Procedural Knowledge

In many organizations, data and metadata play both a formal and informal role. Strong data modeling and data quality processes may implement business logic that defines the right ways to gather new data, create new data, input it, change it, output it, and retire it. In other places—even in the same organization!—you could find significant amounts of data and metadata that is not managed and not subject to change control, auditing, or data quality measures.

First, let's look at data and metadata as procedural in nature, as information that tells the organization what to do and how to do it. Recall that we previously defined *procedures* as administrative, human-facing information products that provide the step-by-step instructions, constraints, and exception handling rules for portions of the organization's business logic. We also defined *data* as the values or fields that describe, model, or represent some aspect of a real entity, whereas *metadata* is data that describes, limits, or establishes constraints about data itself. For example, an accounts payable system might have data fields about a bank account, which would be the ACH routing number, SWIFT code, account number, account holder's name, bank name, and the like. Metadata might define that for banks located in certain countries (which don't use ACH routing), the account must have both SWIFT and IBAN bank routing codes, or the account cannot be used for payments or debits.

### Dealing with Domain-Specific Procedural Knowledge

Terms like SWIFT, ACH, IBAN, and others may dominate your thinking if you're involved with international funds transfers for personal or business reasons. They illustrate how just the acronyms as names themselves are the tip of a knowledge and insight pyramid, for people working in that field. These names are metadata specific to a particular business domain or activity; they embody the larger business or marketplace rules for such funds transfers, while associating that "how-to" knowledge and rule sets with specific data items or records in an individual transaction.

As an SSCP, you'll quickly find that the business or marketplaces your employer is in will dictate any number of such sets of metadata names. The better you know the language of your employer's business, the better you can help keep its information systems safe, secure, resilient, and reliable.

Data dictionaries provide centralized repositories for such business rules, and in well-managed applications development and support environments, the organization works hard to ensure that the rules in the metadata in the data dictionary are built into the logic of the application used by the business.

Without a data dictionary as a driving force in the IT infrastructure, the organization resorts to old-fashioned people-facing procedures to capture those business logic rules. That procedural knowledge might be part of initial onboarding and training of employees; it might only exist in the user manual for a particular application, or the desk-side "cheat sheet" used by an individual worker.

Think about that banking example again: *metadata* established a rule about when we needed more information about a bank in another country, but the list of specific countries was *data*, not metadata.

All organizations face a dilemma when it comes to procedural knowledge. The smarter your people at the *gemba* are, the more that they know *about* their job and the more they understand the meaning of the data that they retrieve, use, create, receive, and process, the greater their ability to protect your organization when something surprising or abnormal happens. But the more we depend on smart and savvy people, the more likely it is that *we do not understand all of our own business logic.*

What can happen when that procedural metadata is not kept sufficiently secure? Loss or corruption of this procedural and business logic knowledge could cause critical business processes to fail to work correctly. At best, this might mean missed business opportunities (similar to suffering a denial of services [DoS] attack); at worst, this could lead to death or injury to staff, customers, or bystanders, damage to property, and expenses and exposure to liability that could kill the business.

What can the SSCP do? In most cases, the SSCP is not, after all, a knowledge manager or a business process engineer by training and experience. In organizations where a lot of the business logic and procedural knowledge exists in personal notebooks, yellow stickies on physical desktops, or human experience and memory, the SSCP can help reduce information risk and decision risk by letting the business impact analysis (BIA) and the vulnerability assessment provide guidance and direction. Management and leadership need to set the priorities—which processes, outcomes, or assets need the most security attention and risk management, and which can wait for another day. And when the SSCP is assessing those high-priority processes and finds evidence that much of the business logic is in tacit form, inside the heads of the staff, or in soft, unmanageable, and unprotected paper notes and crib sheets, that ought to signal an area for process *and* security improvement.

But what about data as just *data*, information that models, describes, or represents people, employees, customers, inventory items, bills to pay, and the myriad other kinds of business objects organizations deal with every day? Bad data, as we saw earlier, can cause applications to malfunction, crash, or worse! How do we avoid those fates?

# Information Quality and Information Assurance

Think back to the relationship between information assurance and decision assurance, as we defined it in Chapter 3. Nobody gathers information just for the sake of gathering more information; whether today or years from now, they gather that information because they know it will help them make a better decision about something that matters to them! We also saw then that without taking steps to verify the quality of the data going into that decision, the rightness, the utility, and the *value* of that decision to us is suspect.

This is the "garbage in, garbage out" part of computing. Bad information in leads to waste, lost time and effort, and lost opportunity. Sometimes it leads to lost lives! (Think what happens if a hospital orders up two units of blood typed and cross-matched for the *wrong* patient, or an air traffic controller says "descend" when he really meant "climb" to avoid a possible midair collision.)

Thus, to make quality decisions—ones we can "bet our business on"—we need to ensure that we have sound business logic that uses quality information to come to those decisions.

### What Is "Information Quality?"

According to Larry English, author of *Information Quality Applied* and other books and articles on this subject, information quality for your organization is:

- Consistently meeting or exceeding *all* knowledge workers' and customers' expectations with information...

- So that knowledge workers can perform their work effectively and contribute to the enterprise mission...

- And so that customers are successful in conducting business with you, and are delighted with the products, services, and communications (or information) they receive from you.

English goes further, stating that the three key aspects of providing end-to-end or total information quality management must include:

- Specifying the data definition, valid business rules for use, formats, valid value sets or ranges, and the details it takes to implement such data with quality in database systems

- Information content quality

- Information presentation quality

How serious is the information quality problem? English, in 2009, cited sources showing that over 122 organizations suffered losses of over $1.2 trillion because of bad data. They lost customers; they wasted resources and labor; they redid work; in some cases, they went out of business. By 2016, IBM reported (in the *Harvard Business Review*) that this "garbage-in" impact had grown to $3.1 trillion. Nearly three times the growth in bad data losses in 7 years.

That's *not* loss and damage done by hackers. That's *not* losses due to data breach. That's self-inflicted wounds bleeding out.

## Information Quality Lifecycle

Like everything else, information has a lifecycle within an organization. This lifecycle starts with the business logic: why do we need the data, and what are we going to *do* with it? This logic should specify the kind of rules, constraints, or quality parameters that we need to ensure that good, useful, and complete information comes into our systems and bad information is rejected or routed to special procedures that may be able to clean, correct, or bridge over the faults in the original and make it useful to us again. We then store the information, use it in business processes, modify it, store it, display it, share it...

At some point in time, the information is no longer of value to the organization, and it needs to be disposed of. Again, our business logic ought to dictate whether such information can be sold or must be destroyed. Note, too, that legal and regulatory requirements may apply to how and when we must dispose of information and that failing to dispose of data that is past its legal limit can expose the company to legal liabilities.

Along the way, we keep backup copies of the information, typically in both snapshot sets that represent a moment in time and in full archival copies of our entire systems. These backups are a vital part of our business continuity and disaster recovery planning, which you'll learn more about in Chapter 11, "Business Continuity via Information Security and People Power."

## Preventing (or Limiting) the "Garbage In" Problem

As an SSCP, you might think you don't have much of a role to play in helping your organization limit the impact of "garbage in." Or do you? In many respects, there's a lot of similarity to how your role on the information security team can help the business grow and use higher-quality applications software. Get your best friends—Kipling's six wise men—and be prepared to ask a few questions to start your polite inquiries:

- Do we have a formal information quality program?

- Do we have and use a formal data dictionary or data model? How do we ensure that application programmers *and* business process owners and operators live and work by the business logic rules in that data dictionary or data model?

- Is our data dictionary or data model under formal configuration management and change control?

- Do we know how and when bad data impacts our business processes?

With those answers to start with, you're in a better position to talk with the knowledge workers who use those business processes as part of their jobs and ask them questions like these:

- How do you recognize bad input data, such as from customers, outside organizations, or other parts of our business, when you encounter it?

- How do you recognize bad output data when the system displays it to you?

- In either case, do you have formal, approved processes to handle these exceptions? Or do you have to just use your own best judgment?

### Be Careful Asking "Why"

As one of Kipling's six wise men, *why* is a powerful but two-edged sword.

Almost every answer to a "why" starts with "because," which can mean either "here's the cause" or "here's my judgment on that." You might want to save your *whys* for when you need to understand (and even challenge) motives and decisions, and use *hows* to look at cause and effect.

Much as we saw with the business process logic itself, with these answers in one hand, and the BIA and vulnerability assessment in the other, the SSCP can start to determine if there are data-driven exploitable vulnerabilities at the endpoints.

Remember, attackers can cause your business to go out of business by attacking the quality of the data your coworkers use to make decisions and carry out their assigned work. They don't even need to exfiltrate the data to do so.

That said, let's also consider how to protect the data (and metadata) from the effects of a vulnerability somewhere else in the systems being exploited against your organization.

# Protecting Data in Motion, in Use, and at Rest

This is the other critical part of keeping your information systems safe, secure, resilient; this is where you've got to know all of your CIANA requirements and have active, designed-in, and purposeful processes that deliver on those requirements. You then have to do the vulnerability assessment to see where your best-laid implementation plans got it wrong!

We might want to extend this three-part data security model a bit and add a few other steps in the data or information lifecycle into our thinking:

- Data modeling, definition, and metadata creation to assure information quality needs

- Input or acquisition of data from outside of the organization's quality span of control

- Data in motion to and from internal storage (or rest) facilities

- Data copied in backup sets, in archive sets, or to redundant and dispersed systems elements (for enhanced availability, or for business continuity and disaster recovery purposes)

- Data at rest in primary systems storage locations (datacenter, cloud storage, local hard drive, etc.), awaiting use

- Data at rest in primary systems storage locations, awaiting destruction

- Data in motion to and from endpoint devices, for use by users (or endpoint devices, such as robots and controls) via applications

- Data in RAM on servers, endpoints, or other devices

- Data retrieved from any system (primary or backup) to be delivered to attorneys, government officials, etc. as part of a digital discovery process

- Data on an endpoint or other device that has become lost, stolen, or misplaced, or that has been disposed of without properly being zeroized or randomized to destroy the data

- Data at rest on backup media, or in backup storage locations, that needs to be destroyed (expired, no longer fit for purpose, or to meet legal, contractual, or regulatory requirements)

- Data and information in tacit form, in the minds of employees, customers, vendors, or others

- Data that has been output from the systems (via some endpoint) and transformed into a printed or other format that can escape our security and control processes

- Data being displayed to an authorized user but observable by an unauthorized person or persons

---

### What about the Storage Devices the Data Is On?

We also have to shift our mental gears here and think not about the *data* but the *devices* that the data are stored on. Prior to the cloud, we stored all of *our* data on hard drives, tapes, floppy disks, disk cartridges, or even paper or punched cards; we controlled who could have access to those physical media, and (if we were practicing due diligence) we destroyed that media when it wore out or the data on it needed to be destroyed.

Moving our data into the cloud means that our data shares living space on the cloud provider's disk farm with data from many other users. If just *one* of those users is served with a subpoena, a national security letter (NSL), or a digital discovery order, or a search warrant seeks all of that user's data, your data that shares living space with that user's data get delivered to the requesting court or agency.

Your data can also "leak out" of the cloud if a malfunctioning disk drive is removed and thrown away without being zeroized or clobbered properly.

Most cloud providers deal with these risks with a combination of striping of files and directories across multiple physical devices and encrypting each customer's data separately before storing it. That said, as an SSCP, you need to check your service level agreement or terms of reference with your provider.

---

Every one of those steps in the life of a set of data needs to be thought of in CIANA risk terms. Are we at risk, for example, if data we *think* we ordered to be destroyed has actually not been destroyed yet? (Probably.)

By this point, SSCPs should recognize that almost every tool in their information security tool kit needs to be employed in a systematic, integrated way to achieve the CIANA needs of the *data and information* that is the lifeblood of the organization. This means the full range of physical, logical, and administrative controls are applied when, where, and how the risk assessment and vulnerabilities assessment indicate the greatest risks are. For example:

- Frequent and timely audit of identity management, access control, and applications logs should indicate that attempts to circumvent these controls have kept attackers out of the data itself, and the data hasn't been moved, copied, or otherwise exfiltrated.

- Physical and administrative controls, including audits and inspections, should verify that backup copies of information (and systems and application software) have been kept safe from attack or compromise.

- All of our people are educated on the job-killing risks of improper use of thumb drives, attachments to emails, personal cloud storage, or "bring-your-own-infrastructure" storage, and have been trained to properly use (or not use!) such capabilities as our policies and CIANA needs dictate.

This suggests that (like so many things in information security), our most powerful lines of defense can start with:

- Physical protection of the information systems, communications, and endpoints

- Identity management, identity provisioning, access control, and privilege management

- Integration of administrative (people-facing) policies and procedures with software and systems implementations of policies, controls, alarms, logs, and the systems, apps, and data themselves

- Ongoing and effective monitoring, inspection, and assessment

- Incident detection, characterization, and response

- Disaster recovery planning and business continuity measures, planned, in place, rehearsed, and evaluated

## Data Exfiltration I: The Traditional Threat

Most computer crime statutes define as *theft* the unauthorized removal or copying of data from someone's information system. Although that legally defines the crime, the IT security industry has been calling this *data exfiltration*. This threat has existed probably as long as people have been writing information down in any form.

Before an organization moves *any portion* of its business logic into the clouds, it is still faced with the significant risk of data exfiltration—data moving outside of the organization's span of control (and its threat surfaces), and "into the wild" for use by almost anyone for almost any purpose. This "traditional" exfiltration threat could involve the unauthorized movement of data via:

- Outbound (and draft) email content or attachments

- Downloads or file copies to poorly secured, insecure, or unauthorized devices (which could be thumb drives, laptops, smartphones, diskettes, or even paper print-outs)

- Tacit knowledge exfiltration, where the data or knowledge is read, heard, or seen by a person who then shares that data with other unauthorized parties or uses it themselves for unauthorized purposes

- Upload or transfer to unauthorized file sharing, storage, processing, or other services

- Downloading or transfer of data to secured or trusted devices, which are then removed from the workplace for data extraction to occur elsewhere

- Extraction of data from disposed hardware, particularly disk drives

Clearly, identity management (of people, processes, and devices) can control some of these classes of exploitation risk events. Access control also has a powerful role to play.

Applying our risk management model, we see that we face a strategic choice: *deter, detect, prevent,* and *avoid.* Deterrence and prevention go hand-in-hand with having a solid access control and identity management system in place; the visible presence of a monitoring and surveillance activity can also deter the would-be data thief. But what about detection?

In recent years, data exfiltration attacks have taken on a pattern that looks at five major stages to an attack:

Stage 1: Reconnaissance

Stage 2: Initial compromise and entry (typically involving phishing attacks)

Stage 3: Establish command and control

Stage 4: Identify, select, acquire, and aggregate data

Stage 5: Exfiltrate data

(Some attacks do demonstrate a sixth stage, in which the attacker erases all evidence of their presence, including their command and control hooks, and then departs the scene.)

We've examined how to detect events of interest in those first three stages in other chapters. Stage 5, the actual exfiltration (or criminal export) of the data, presents unique challenges, since most such attacks take steps to actively obscure or mask the data being exfiltrated. Breaking the data up into packets, encrypting the packets, combining packets from multiple sources within the target, and spoofing the file types to attempt to have the data masquerade as some other kind of data stream are just some of the techniques that the data thieves use to let the outbound flow of data look normal. Even a simple screenshot of classified data may easily sneak past any filters set up to detect and block the exfiltration of that data in its normal form. All of these techniques aim to remove or mask data classification labels or tell-tale patterns in the data, and even remove, suppress, or alter digital signatures. Scheduling the flow of data so that it hides within other routine outbound flows can also minimize the chances of detecting the ongoing exfiltration.

So we have to focus on Stage 4 of this data exfiltration model if we are to gain any traction in detecting such thefts before the data leaves our premises.

## Detecting Unauthorized Data Acquisition

Imagine for a moment that as an SSCP, you're working in an extremely security-conscious environment. Every bit of useful information is kept in a locked, guarded library; every access to that library requires proof of identity, need to know, and validation of your stated purpose. The librarians are selected and trained to trust no one. Everything you do with that data is monitored, as if "Big Brother" were shoulder-surfing with you every moment you are at work. Your task complete, you return what you checked out from the library, *and* you place into the library the new work products you created in part from that information; you also enter into that library all of your loose notes, even the sketches on the back of a paper napkin, that in any way relate to that highly classified information.

The history of espionage and counter-espionage tells us that such systems will work only until they fail; *somebody* will defeat them. In the meantime, the audit trail of who asked for what information, why, for what purpose, and what did they actually do with it, is a powerful set of *telemetry* data about the movement of data, information, and even knowledge within our organization. This telemetry also can provide a warning if someone is requesting information in ways that suggest they are trying to put too many pieces together, pieces that need to be kept secret and safe.

Move that highly protected, human-operated library out of the spy thrillers and into a typical corporate IT infrastructure, its apps, and its business logic. Identity management and access control systems can indeed generate that telemetry data. The more information that we need to watch over so closely, the more system resources (CPU time, network traffic, and storage) are required to generate and maintain the telemetry logs.

Here's the rub: as in the fictional settings of a John le Carré novel, the real world of major national intelligence agencies or in modern IT-enabled organizations, we may have all of that log data but we can't make sense of it. We don't have the analytical capabilities to read all of those logs, search for patterns, and correlate those patterns to see if they're telling us that the copying, gathering, and clumping up of data that's going on is in fact an ongoing exfiltration attempt. For example, monitoring outbound email or Web traffic may help a small organization detect a change in the pattern of sending and receiving addresses, which might be a signal of something suspicious. A company with tens of thousands of employees may not find this practical or achievable.

Security systems vendors offer a variety of security event information management and analysis capabilities, many of which host a variety of machine learning functions that promise to solve this "drowning in log data" problem. As with any alarm system, they will produce both false positives and false negatives. The false negatives mean that data exfiltration escaped detection (and prevention). False positives can overload your investigative staff and even erode the moral support from end users and their managers that *all* information security is so depending on to be successful.

## Preventing Data Loss

There are, as some vendors say, no silver bullet solutions for this problem. Depending on the kind of data you need to protect and the level of protection it needs, your organization may be able to implement some or all of the following approaches:

- Use digital rights management (DRM), which encapsulates the protected files with encryption-based locks on owner-specified privileges.

- Encrypt data at rest, either by classification level or across all data assets in the organization.

- Implement dynamic digital watermarking to mark all screenshots, file copies, and printed documents as a deterrent measure.

### Steganography as Watermarks

Many copying machines, printers, and scanners use steganography to watermark each document copy they print or make, thus embedding information such as the date, time, and machine used to produce or process that copy. Such watermark information can be used for a variety of internal purposes, from process control and quality improvement to loss prevention. Consistently implemented, watermarking tactics can also provide evidence to support a forensics investigation after an information security incident has occurred.

These would be in addition to implementing identity management, using access controls, controlling the use of removable storage, and other techniques already addressed.

# Into the Clouds: Endpoint App and Data Security Considerations

When a business or organization moves its information systems and business logic "into the clouds," this typically refers to its choices of a mix of deployment models. Think back to the notional datacenter model that we examined in Chapter 8. What separates a datacenter from a cloud can be found in several key characteristics, all summed up in one word: *virtual*.

- Compute power, represented by the number of processors and the amount of RAM available to them, is finite in any case. In a datacenter, the only way to significantly expand computing capabilities is to lease or buy more CPUs, GPUs, and RAM, along with whatever it takes to interconnect them into the datacenter. Even if the datacenter supports the use of virtual machines, the business cannot double the number of VMs that can get work done per hour, for example, without investing in more hardware. And that takes time—time measured in weeks if not in months! Cloud systems, by contrast, in near real time can effectively expand the amount of real processor and memory resources available to a customer's VMs for the duration of that customer's demand. Quite often, this involves the minute-by-minute rental of VM support resources on other cloud centers the provider owns or has contractual service relationships with. Cloud-hosted systems can also quickly release these extra assets from use, again in near real time, as business needs shrink throughout the day or the season.

- Storage systems in datacenters also face a practical limitation on the amount of data that can be stored compared to the amount of time the organization is willing to wait to make the data available for use. At some point, the organization must invest in more physical space to store disks, tapes, etc.; the systems themselves; and people to keep them managed effectively if their overall needs for storage must grow. Cloud systems providers can dynamically expand storage capabilities to meet both increasing and decreasing demand for data storage (and timely access) by a customer, again via minute-by-minute rental of storage resources "local" to the cloud provider or from other providers.

The first and most important issue to understand is that your organization, as a user, is still completely responsible for the security of information and processes it hosts via cloud system providers. The CIANA needs of your organization do not change as you migrate systems to the clouds; what does change is your choice of controls and methods to achieve those needs. Your needs for disaster recovery and business continuity services, in terms of responsiveness, alternate operating locations, and security, do not change, even though using a cloud provider may make them easier to achieve.

Regardless of deployment model and degree or types of services, your organization is going to have to depend on its technical staff in the IT department and on the information security team to understand the many different service capabilities your cloud hosting provider can offer. *Your people* will have to understand how to use these features to get the best performance and security for the money being spent on the cloud. To illustrate this, consider that early in 2018, research by Gartner and others showed that the number one cause of data breach or compromise for information stored by clients in the cloud was incorrect settings of security and access control parameters, on that storage, by the end users themselves. Thomas Fischer, reporting at IDG Connect (www.idgconnect.com/ idgconnect/opinion/1002869/common-causes-cloud-breaches), goes on to point out that by 2020, according to Gartner's research, "over 95% of cloud security incidents will be the customer's own fault."

Your organization, and you as an SSCP, must thoroughly understand the contract, service level agreement, or terms of reference document that sets the legally enforceable duties and obligations that you and your cloud host provider have with respect to that contract. This cannot be overemphasized! To most cloud-hosting providers, especially the market-leading ones, your organization is one of thousands if not millions of businesses moving into their clouds; they do not know your organization, and they do not understand your CIANA needs. For a (potentially) hefty consulting fee, they will work with your team, of course; even so, your team needs to know the legal as well as the technical ground on which you're going to operate. This is often called the *shared responsibility model* in which the cloud services provider and the customer organization document their agreement about different responsibilities.

Please note that much of the detailed mechanics of identifying and resolving information security risks for cloud-hosted business logic are beyond the scope of this book, as well as beyond the scope of the SSCP exam. Other certifications, such as (ISC)[2]'s Certified Cloud Security Professional (CCSP), may provide you the path you want to take if you need to become more of an expert at keeping cloud deployments safe, secure, and resilient. With that caveat, let's soar onward and upward!

# Cloud Deployment Models and Information Security

Currently, industry offers three basic models for deploying your business logic and business processes into the clouds: public, private, and a mix of the two commonly called *hybrid*.

All use the same basic virtualization technologies to provide processing, storage, network definition, webpage and Web service hosting, database capabilities, and a variety of other services. The key differentiator is not so much who owns the underlying hardware and software that is the cloud infrastructure itself, or who maintains it, but what other organizations or businesses share that infrastructure as cloud customers:

▪ Private clouds restrict user organizations to a specific, named set (such as a single business, its vendors, and its strategic partners).

▪ Public clouds provide access to any organization that wishes to contract with the cloud-hosting service provider.

▪ Hybrid clouds serve the needs of a single organization, or its designated partners, vendors, etc., by means of a mix of private cloud and public cloud systems.

A special case of the private cloud model is the government cloud. In this model, a specific government agency (local, state, regional, or national) contracts for cloud-hosting services for its business processes, which may be inward-facing (serving agency users only), public facing, or a combination of users to suit the agency mission. Whether the government cloud is hosted on hardware and systems exclusive to that agency (regardless of who owns and maintains them, or where on the planet they are physically located) or on shared, fully public clouds is largely a moot point.

From the SSCP's perspective, the difference in deployment models and the security capabilities they provide is largely one of degree. Private clouds may allow the organization full visibility into, control over, and responsibility for proper disposal of computing equipment that may have residual data still in it, for example. Public cloud providers have this responsibility, and their own business case dictates to them how they handle zeroizing or randomizing of storage media before it leaves their physical control in order to meet the confidentiality needs of all of their customers put together. Private clouds hosted on equipment the organization owns, leases, or manages, at locations it has complete control over, may allow a safe transition path from private datacenter to the clouds, while the organization is still learning about cloud system capabilities and security capabilities. As you might expect, the many different ways that hybrid deployments can be done provide a wide range of options to consider in terms of capabilities and information security approaches.

## Cloud Service Models and Information Security

On top of the decision to go private, public, or hybrid is another choice, driven as much by the organization's business logic as by its applications and data architecture and strategy. Recall from Chapter 4 that everything we do in the clouds is done by requesting and using *services*. The major service models you'll find today are:

▪ *Infrastructure as a service (IaaS)* provides CPU, storage, software-defined networking, and server capabilities on which users can host databases, compute-intensive applications, and other elements of their business logic. IaaS can be as simple as bare metal servers that require (and enable) the user to be in total control of defining, creating, dispatching, and using virtual machines, running on hypervisors selected by the user, or they can include a variety of system capabilities to make virtual machine creation, deployment, use, and retirement from use easier to manage.

- *Software as a service (SaaS)* provides a layer of application software on top of an IaaS foundation. End users who need cloud-hosted productivity suites, for example, or a rich set of software development environments, tools, and test facilities may find SaaS an effective service model.

- *Platform as a service (PaaS)* provides a large-scale, feature-rich applications platform, again on top of an IaaS foundation. Platforms usually integrate data modeling, data management, and data backup, restore, and failover capabilities focused on the application services the platform delivers to its users.

- *Identity as a service (IDaaS)* delivers integrated sets of identity management services. In some respects, this is a PaaS, focused on the infrastructure-level services of defining, managing, provisioning, and monitoring identities of end users, tasks, processes, and other information assets (such as hardware devices and databases).

Consider a small desktop publishing content firm as a simple example illustrating the differences between SaaS and PaaS implementations. Prior to considering a migration to the cloud, the firm may be using a variety of applications for word processing, page layout, webpage design and implementation, and other content development, provisioning, and management tasks. As a set of separate applications, they may not have an integrated document library management system or integrated backup and restore capabilities that provide versioning, fallback points, or other features that would empower the firm's growing needs for business continuity as its customer base grows. Moving to the cloud via SaaS merely moves those same apps, and their folder trees, into the cloud. PaaS models, by contrast, would look to use a larger, more feature-rich platform application that brings all of those features together, around an integrated data model. At some point, moving from applications to a platform may make a lot of sense for this business.

Think of these models as layering on capabilities, as they go from bare-metal infrastructure on up to platform services. Each new layer of functionality changes the way the cloud customer organization thinks about defining its business logic in that cloud, how it carries it out, and how it protects it to meet its overall information security needs:

- In a bare-metal IaaS environment (with or without the hypervisor provided by the host), the customer must select and build the operating system and other infrastructure services, such as identity management and access control, that they need both within their cloud space and at the threat surface where it faces the rest of the Internet (be that customers or crackers). As the customer adds on additional applications or app platforms, further attention to detail is necessary to ensure that these are implemented safely and securely. Disaster recovery and business continuity capabilities, even simple restore point recovery functions, must be added in by the customer.

- Moving up to SaaS environments usually means that the VMs that the customers deploy (as their workload demands more CPU power, for example) bring with them a built-in set of security policy capabilities. The apps themselves (that are the "software" in SaaS that the customer is renting time with) are probably preconfigured to provide a reasonably secure operating environment.

- Moving up to PaaS environments usually relies on the customer defining work roles (such as "order entry" or "HR hiring manager") to people on their staff and assigning built-in sets of privileges associated with those roles. The roles bring with them platform-defined and platform-enforced identity management and access control functions, which make use of the virtual host operating system's own such features.

## Clouds, Continuity, and Resiliency

We've seen how the combination of deployment models and service models give your business or organization a rich set of options when it comes to providing a new home for your business logic and information systems. The inherent flexibility and scalability of *any* cloud solution, as you apply it to the growing needs of your business, bring with it key aspects of availability: *continuity* and *resilience*.

Both of these related terms describe how well business processes and logic can operate correctly, safely, and securely despite the occurrence of errors, failures, or attacks by threat actors (natural or human). It's important to keep these two terms separate and distinct in your mind as you plan your cloud migration and keep it up and running:

- *Continuity* measures the degree to which a system can produce correct, timely results when input errors, missing data, failed or failing subsystems, or other problems are impacting its operations. Designed-in redundancy of critical paths or components can provide a degree of graceful degradation—as elements fail, or as system resources become exhausted, the system may provide lower throughput rates, produce more frequent but tolerable errors, or stop executing noncritical functions to conserve its capabilities to fulfill mission-essential tasks. Cloud-based systems might slow down dispatching new instances of VMs to support customer-facing tasks, for example, when there aren't enough resources to allow new VMs to run efficiently; this might slow the rate of dealing with new customer requests in favor of completing ongoing transactions.

- *Resiliency* measures the ability of the system to deal with unanticipated errors or conditions without crashing or causing unacceptable data loss or business process interruption. Auto-save and versioning capabilities on a word processor application, for example, provide resiliency to an author in two ways. Auto-save protects against an unplanned system shutdown (such as inadvertently unplugging its power cord); at most, the user/author loses what was typed in since the last automatic save. Versioning protects against the off chance that users make modifications, save the file, and then realize that they need to undo those modifications.

There's an interesting natural chain of consequences here, best illustrated by one key feature of loud solutions and the datacenters that support them alike: *load balancing*. Suppose our datacenter has 100 compute servers, each consisting of 16 CPU cores and 1 TB of onboard RAM; such a bare-metal server might be able to host 30 good-sized, highly functional virtual machines. As customer (or system) demand for more VMs increases, the load balancing and dispatching tools put each new VM on a different hardware server and on a different CPU core. The failure of one CPU or even one server therefore disrupts fewer customer work streams than if the dispatcher fully loaded the first core on the first server, then the second core, and so on.

Load balancing is an excellent example of a built-in capability to provide continuity in the face of rapidly changing demands for services. It also provides a degree of resiliency. Many systems, such as a national electrical power grid, have to deal with larger-than-anticipated swings in demand (or supply), often caused by natural disasters or other major events. As a designer, you can only plan for so much; after that, you trust that the inherent flexibility of what you've built will help it weather the storm.

## Clouds and Threat Modeling

Still, the real security question that the SSCP must grapple with is this: *where is the threat surface between what we keep "private" inside our cloud and what we expose or offer to the outside world?* Chapter 4 introduced us to threat modeling, which is a deliberate, purposeful task that seeks to define these boundaries between "inside, keep it safe" and "outside, let it be exposed to some risk." Concentric layers of threat surfaces are common in any IT system, after all; as design paradigms, these surfaces guide systems analysts and administrators in deploying the bare metal, the OS, then layer upon layer of functionality (such as identity management and access control management systems), finally adding layers of applications. On top of that apps-shielding threat surface is a space in which the typical end user has a limited set of privileges over some assets—he can create or delete his own files, in his own area of the file system, but not touch someone else's, for example.

It's also important to ask how the threat model (or threat surfaces) have changed, or will change, by migrating into the clouds. If the underlying business logic remains the same, the logical relationships between subjects (people or tasks) and information assets doesn't fundamentally change; roles, purposes, and trust criteria should not change just because of where assets or functions are hosted. (Should they?) What does change is the physical, logical, and administrative connection from subject to asset. At a minimum, this changes the nature of the crossing point on the threat surface; it may also introduce new threat surfaces interposed between subjects and assets, with their own crossing points or portals that need to be understood, controlled, and monitored.

It may be useful to compare a threat surface, or the idea of using threat surfaces, to maps and diagrams we use to plan and manage access to physical buildings, their surroundings, and their support systems. The paper map that shows the building, property entrance, alarm zones, and even the nearest fire hydrant is not the physical building, the plumbing, or pavements. It's just a model that helps us humans organize our thinking about normal workday traffic and activity, emergency responses, or how to increase security after business hours. We can drill down into that paper map by opening up other paper files, and learn where the fire alarm station is that seems to be ringing right now. When we put that map on an alarm annunciator panel or a dashboard, it still is showing us a model of the physical property—and as we make that display more interactive, and more integrated with the rest of our information systems, it becomes a geographic information system in miniature.

These threat surfaces do not need to be complicated. In fact, we can argue that if the SSCP starts out with simple threat surfaces, this can clarify everyone's thinking and drive toward identifying both potential vulnerabilities and appropriate control strategies for them. The key is to look at the overall system in terms of these perimeters and boundaries; information at rest is resting *within* a particular boundary, and it should not move across that boundary unless you and the system owners have decided to authorize that move. If it is authorized, you still need to worry about how (or if) to protect the data while it's on the move. (This, by the way, is the key to getting a grip on the data exfiltration problem.)

As we noted earlier, how your cloud host provider deals with data storage devices and protects your data while in motion, in use, and at rest in its cloud spaces should be part of your threat modeling considerations too.

---

 **Real World Scenario**

**Migrating the Threat Surfaces to the Clouds**

Amber is part of the information systems team at a small, private junior college, which has been using its own local network of computers to provide its own homegrown applications and platforms to handle student prospecting, student and class administration, faculty and staff human resources management, and other administrative functions. The school's website is hosted on a third-party Web hosting provider, and currently provides only email forms to request information or to contact the school. Right now, all of the administrative, IT, support, and classroom facilities are in the same building. There are about 40 faculty and staff and six classrooms; Wi-Fi access for faculty, staff, and students requires a valid network login (such as student or staff ID), and guest access is also supported.

As the school is growing, it needs to expand these systems to handle more classes, more students, and more buildings. It's considering cloud-hosted solutions, either as PaaS or SaaS models, or a combination of both.

Knowing you're an SSCP, Amber has asked you for some help with threat modeling. She thinks she needs to show her department head, and others, what the threat model looks like now, and what it might look like after the school moves into a PaaS-plus-SaaS environment.

Key risk areas that Amber knows must be addressed include:

- Student and staff personally identifiable information; other information protected by law (such as student records, payment records, employment files, etc.)

- Admissions, enrollment, class participation, and progress data (to prevent clever students from hacking a "straight-A" record for themselves or their friends)

- IT labs, currently hosted on hardware in the IT classroom, that are used for cybersecurity, white-hat hacking, and malware analysis student projects

How would you draw the threat surface (or surfaces), or model the threat environment, for the school as it is currently operating? Does this model represent a requirements baseline it should seek to achieve when it migrates into the cloud?

How would you see that threat model changing as the school migrates into the cloud?

## Cloud Security Methods

As with any information system, security depends on choosing the right set of cloud system features and capabilities to meet the CIANA needs of the organization.

Key to these are access control, authentication and audit, data integrity and data recovery capabilities, and protection of information at rest, in use, and in motion. The choice of cloud-hosting provider should consider both the deployment model (platform, software, or infrastructure as a service) and the inherent security capabilities provided by that host; security-related expectations and requirements need to be defined in a contractually binding terms of service (TOS) or service level agreement (SLA) between the organization and the cloud host.

It's also a question of scale. When securing your on-premises LAN, consisting of a few servers and a dozen or more workstations, you know all of the things you need to do to keep that LAN safe and secure. You'd limit or eliminate public-facing IP addresses, using proxy services to allow the public, potential customers, or real customers to access your systems. You'd segregate functions so that services and functions that had to face the Internet were isolated from those that needed greater protection. You'd use whitelisting strategies to lock down ports and services that you don't need to expose to the Internet, and control what apps can install and execute. You'd manage this set of systems as a baseline. You'd monitor it and assess its ongoing security effectiveness, possibly even with penetration testing.

In the cloud, your same business now may be seeing a dynamic, ever-changing number of virtual machines that are providing much that same set of functions, maybe even segregated out in similar ways. The only real difference is that the number of VMs that are running *copies* of those functions, in coordinated, load-balancing ways, changes moment by moment based on user demand for services.

This may actually be the silver lining in the cloud. Limit the number of *types* of VMs that you're going to use; make sure you thoroughly understand everything that each of them needs to do. Know which security capabilities the cloud-hosting provider offers that make it easy to define the VM template as fully secure as you need it. Then you just create and control the load-balancing rules that allow the cloud host to spawn more copies of each template when conditions demand it.

Finally, ensure that you and your networks team members thoroughly know how to exploit your cloud host's features for software-defined networks (SDNs). The same threat modeling and security techniques we looked at in Chapter 5, "Communications and Network Security," still apply (no matter where that virtual SDN is, it's still running TCP/IP, after all).

## SLAs, TORs, and Penetration Testing

We've looked at this in other sections of this book, but it bears repeating. When you decide to conduct penetration testing of *any* system, law and contracts require that you have the knowing consent of the target system's owners, operators, and responsible managers. If your well-intentioned penetration test takes down business processes, or causes other disruption or damage to the business, that signed, binding acknowledgment and acceptance by your own company's officials may be all that keeps you employed, or even out of jail! This situation gets even more complex as your business moves parts of its business logic and systems into a public or hybrid cloud, for it's conceivable that your pen tests against those systems could inadvertently disrupt other customers of that cloud-hosting provider or the cloud host's overall operations.

Before any serious planning of such cloud-based penetration testing begins, get with your managers and consult the contracts, the service level agreements (SLAs) or terms of reference (TORs), sometimes called terms of service, or TOS, that your organization has with its cloud-hosting provider. Understand any requirements to notify the cloud host; work with them to ensure that your test plan makes sense and contains the proper safeguards that they require.

## Data Exfiltration II: Hiding in the Clouds

Once in the clouds, the data exfiltration threat landscape facing your organization may see one important factor change in ways that can favor the attacker. Simply put, most organizations see everything about the IT side of their business expand dramatically as they move from on-premises computing into a cloud system. The numbers of attempted connections, numbers of authenticated users actually connecting, and number of services requested per day increases, perhaps by a factor of 10, 100, or more. Transaction volumes increase; the amount of data stored overall, on a per-function or per-user basis, increases to support the business logic that services the needs of all of these new prospects, customers, and transactions.

If data thieves want to steal your entire customer file, then of course their target of choice has gotten bigger. Huge file movements might be easier to detect (probably after they've happened). But if thieves want only a few customers' PII, credit card, or billing information, or have a way to take just one or two customers' worth of data out on any given attack, then those small transactions seem even smaller in contrast with the overall volume of activity.

# Legal and Regulatory Issues

Whether your business or organization has the IT systems that support its business process cloud-hosted, on local on-premises computers and LANs, or on paper files doesn't matter very much when it comes to the ever-growing complexity of legal and regulatory constraints and requirements organizations must live up to. In many nations, laws and regulations can exist at the local (municipality) level, at the state or province level, and at the national level. Treaties and international agreements entered into by their host nation also bind the corporate citizens of that nation to those international constraints and obligations as well. Industry groups may also impose standards, such as the Payment Card Industry Data Security Standard (PCI DSS), to ensure that transactions across their marketplaces are safe and secure.

Three major sets of issues arise when we consider doing information-based business in ways that touch upon multiple jurisdictions:

- Data in motion, as it crosses the borders between jurisdictions

- Data at rest, and the abilities of authorities to search it, copy it, seize it, censor it, or otherwise interfere with its use by the organization

- Data in use, which one jurisdiction may find objectionable while another does not

The continuing controversy of Google's attempts to deploy search engine capabilities that meet the needs of the marketplace but also meet the demands of the governments of countries such as the People's Republic of China, illustrate all three of these sets of issues. A number of nations in the Middle East also have attempted to control, restrict, or outright block the movement of data across their borders. Privacy concerns cover a wealth of information, such as identity, health, insurability, education, employment history, and credit data, and the processing, storage, and disposal requirements for each of these sets of information differ across different jurisdictions. Even data about prior arrests and convictions can be private and protected in one jurisdiction but public and published information in another.

Cultural standards also can cause a border-crossing information enterprise a variety of problems, often incurring legal problems. For example, the *anime* genre of illustrated novels and animated movies often depicts relationships and activities involving young people that are quite acceptable in Japan, where anime originated and much of it is produced. But in other cultures, it is sometimes considered to be child pornography or encouraging the sexual exploitation of children. Other images, art, or music that might be critical or satirical in one context can be blasphemous, heretical, or treasonous in another. (If you've been looking for another good reason to update your organization's acceptable use policies for your IT systems, this might be it!)

Legal and regulatory requirements also dictate how individuals can discover data that organizations hold that pertains to them, examine it, dispute its accuracy, and seek corrections and redress. Other requirements dictate both minimum and maximum periods that organizations must hold data of different types, and how and when they must dispose of it.

These requirements fall upon the organization that gathers, creates, stores, uses, moves, and destroys or disposes of the data. They also flow down onto third-party organizations, such as service providers working with that business or organization. Note that in most jurisdictions, your organization (as the prime contractor) is on the "hot seat" for whatever your subcontractors or third-party service providers do on your behalf. As with your employees, they are working under conditions you set, paid by you to perform tasks, and that includes staying within the laws and regulations that apply to them in their place (or country) of jurisdiction. So while these third parties are responsible and liable to the courts themselves, so are you! Even if you can show that they acted outside of the scope of your agreement, and without your prior knowledge and consent, your company is at risk—in the courts of public opinion and marketplace goodwill if nowhere else.

Consider one complication that could arise when moving to the cloud. *Where, physically, does your data reside?* What borders does it cross on its way to and from your company? Which sets of laws, customs, regulations, and expectations apply?

As you can imagine, a full understanding of many of these legal and regulatory issues is well beyond the scope of work that the typical SSCP will encounter. That said, you'll still need to know that such laws and regulations exist and that *someone* in the company's legal team needs to be the resident expert on what they mean to the company.

# Countermeasures: Keeping Your Apps and Data Safe and Secure

Whether the apps in question are large-scale, complex platforms or small, lightweight, appliance-sized bits of functionality, the same countermeasure strategies and approaches should be considered as part of an overall IT risk management and mitigation program. We've worked through the mechanics of each of these steps earlier in this or in previous chapters; let's see them taken together in a high-level summary fashion:

- Know and understand your organization's tolerance for information risk.

- Document and maintain the baselines that keep your organization alive and well: its information, information systems and processes, and IT infrastructure.

- Establish and use sufficient configuration management and change control over all information resources, including software development, test, deployment and support systems, tools, files, and other resources.

- Perform a thorough vulnerabilities assessment, making use of common vulnerability and exploit information, vendor-supplied security information, and the insight and experiences of your own people.

- Prioritize risk mitigation and control implementations in accordance with risk tolerance and guided by the vulnerabilities assessment.

- Implement, maintain, and monitor identity management and access control systems and procedures.

- Monitor application-generated and system-generated log files for suspicious activity.

- Work with applications end users throughout the organization to address training and education needs related to applications and data security, safety, and protection.

- Use design paradigms, patterns and templates, coding standards, and development processes that are reliable and repeatable and that support the development of secure, safe, and resilient applications.

- Use rigorous test processes (including analysis of test results) to ensure that high-risk functions are as free from vulnerabilities as possible *and* work correctly.

- Ensure that vendor-supplied updates, patches, and security fixes are assessed for applicability and compatibility with your systems, applications, and business processes, and implement them as soon as practicable.

- Work with developers and maintainers to ensure that initial and ongoing secure software development training needs are being met.

- Work with management and leadership to address human factors, such as insufficient separation of duties.

- Train and educate all staff members regarding the real, present danger of social engineering attacks. Strong application of the *need to know* principle would exclude almost all outsiders from the generalities *and* the details of our internal processes for building, maintaining, and solving problems with our applications and data.

- Perform ongoing security assessments of all aspects of applications and data development, deployment, use, retirement, and disposal.

- Ensure that disaster recovery and business continuity planning can be effective in providing failover and restore capabilities; fallback to earlier known, safe configurations; and archival copies of systems and data as required.

- Review all contracts, TORs, SLAs, or memoranda of understanding that transfer any element of risk, service performance, or service support to any outside party, to ensure that your information security needs as they pertain to those agreements are correctly and completely documented.

Yes, that looks like the complete set of task areas that information systems security teams need to address in many organizations. If we look at that list strictly from the point of view of our apps—if we apply this list *only* to the way we get apps built, tested, deployed, and then how we use those apps day to day in our business—we are seeing that entire "information security" job jar from the *endpoint* perspective.

# Summary

Keeping the endpoints of your organization's information systems safe, secure, reliable, and resilient has never been more important. In many respects, endpoint security is vitally dependent on the CIANA approaches you take to securing the information infrastructures that support those endpoints. Identity and access, monitoring and analysis, ongoing assessment, and *constant vigilance* apply at all levels of our information architectures. All of this, as you've seen, is or should be driven by the prioritized risks as identified by the BIA. Moving parts or all of your organization's business logic into the clouds adds many technical nuances to achieving information security

The endpoint perspective we've explored together in this chapter is very object-oriented in nature. By itself, this perspective says, data just sits there. It takes other objects, processes, or people, *subjects* as we called them in Chapter 6, to create, change, destroy, move, or copy data to another location. When we combine this idea with the basics of threat modeling and use a threat surface approach, we reveal those channels in which subjects can access our data objects; this focuses our attention on those channels we want to authorize, control, and monitor and on those we want to block (and monitor).

Applying a lifecycle model to the development and use of both applications and data has also helped reveal key opportunities to achieve better information security. Many of the common vulnerabilities in applications software, we've seen, stem from ineffective management of the software development process used to specify, create, deploy, and maintain that software. This is another example of the claim in earlier chapters that unmanaged systems are most vulnerable to exploitation. Data quality, or the "garbage in" side of the equation, also contributes to information insecurity; data quality, as we've seen, is separate and distinct from the CIANA benefits of strong and effective access control, for example.

Moving parts or all of your organization's business logic into the clouds adds many technical nuances to achieving your information security requirements; the good news is that it does not really add any new fundamental ideas or principles to consider. Just more details!

# Exam Essentials

**Explain the software development lifecycle (SDLC) in security terms.**    All applications software goes through a lifecycle of a number of phases as it evolves from initial ideas, to requirements analysis, system design, software development and test, deployment, operational use, support, and retirement. There are many SDLC models, but they all have these same basic elements. At each phase, the information used and produced, such as design notes or test strategies and plans, can reveal exploitable vulnerabilities in that software. Ideally, design validation and test should evaluate how real these vulnerabilities are as risks to the user's data or to the organization. In most cases, this software design and test information should be treated as proprietary information at least.

**Explain application whitelisting and its use.**    Whitelisting is a positive security control model—it explicitly names or lists approved activities, connections, files, users, or (in this case) applications that can be used. Organizations should only whitelist applications that come from trusted providers, that have been through the organization's security assessment process, and for which provider-supplied security patches and other updates are readily available. Whitelisting should be able to provide specific users or classes of users with the specific list of apps necessary for their job functions; all others would be blocked from being installed or executed by these users. Software development organizations usually cannot use whitelisting, as they are frequently compiling, building, and testing new versions of software repeatedly through the day. Whitelisting systems and the administrative policies that support their use may, at organizational discretion, allow for one-time exceptions or for users to submit requests for exceptions or additions to the whitelist. Obviously, the less control over the whitelist itself, the greater the risk of unauthorized apps being executed.

**Compare and contrast positive and negative models of applications and data security.** Positive models of security explicitly name and control allowed behaviors and thus automatically block anything not defined as allowed. Negative security models explicitly define prohibited behaviors and therefore authorize or allow anything that does not fit the definition of what is blocked. Antivirus systems are examples of negative security models, using either signature analysis or anomaly detection to flag suspicious or known malware and then block it from executing or spreading. Applications whitelisting is an example of a positive control model, as it defines a list of allowed executables to be used by a class of users or an individual user. Identity management and access control systems can be a combination of both positive and negative security models at work. It is estimated that perhaps a million pieces of new malware are created every day across the world, but any particular organization may only create a handful of new legitimate applications each day. Thus, whitelisting or positive security approaches are probably easier to implement and manage, and are more effective, than blacklisting or negative security models can be.

**Explain the role of IDEs in applications software security.** Integrated development environments (IDE) provide software developers and software project managers with a range of tools, frameworks, and processes that support many of the steps in the software development lifecycle process. Depending on organizational needs and culture, the right IDE can enforce the use of design patterns, data typing rules, test strategies, and problem analysis and error correction, all within an integrated configuration management and control framework. By providing visible management of the software lifecycle, the right IDE and configuration management (or builds and control) tools can reduce the risk that unmanaged software is deployed with known but unresolved exploitable vulnerabilities, which reduces the information security risk the organization faces.

**Identify possible security risks in various software development lifecycle models and frameworks.** Managing software development and deployment is a constant trade-off between how many required functions can be built, tested, and validated, in a given timeframe, using a given set of development resources; further, the deployed product may contain an undetected exploitable vulnerabilities. Some models and frameworks emphasize up-front requirements analysis, data validation, and other quality approaches, which may reduce the risk of producing software with such vulnerabilities. Other approaches, such as agile and rapid prototyping, quickly produce working software as a way of understanding the desired functionality. Test-driven or test-first methodologies may reduce these risks, with their emphasis on quickly writing code that tests what the requirements are trying to get accomplished (that is, testing what the business logic needs to do). Each is only as good at reducing the risk of producing insecure code as the manner in which it is managed.

**Explain the need for threat modeling when considering migration of business processes into cloud-hosted environments.** Threat modeling uses the concept of the threat surface, the logical, physical, and/or administrative boundary between the information assets inside the boundary, and all processes, users, or systems outside of the boundary that attempt to communicate with, confirm the existence of, learn about, access, or change those assets. Complex systems usually have multiple such threat surfaces. Migrating into any cloud-hosted environment demands that this threat surface be well understood and that all ways that such a threat surface can be crossed are known and under control.

**Describe the key issues in operating and configuring security for cloud-hosted systems.**   The first and most important issue to understand is that your organization, as a user, is still completely responsible for the security of information and processes it hosts via cloud systems providers. The CIANA needs of your organization do not change as you migrate systems to the clouds; what does change is your choice of controls and methods to achieve those needs. For example, moving to a public or hybrid cloud system means that your data, processes, and users are sharing CPU, network, and storage resources with other users—possibly even with your competitors. This may dictate more stringent means to ensure data is secure at rest (when stored in the cloud host's systems), in motion, and in use on your authorized users' endpoint devices and systems. You'll need to ensure that the host can meet or exceed your business continuity needs, such as maximum allowable outage. Finally, you should thoroughly understand the contract, SLA, or TOR document that sets the legally enforceable duties and obligations that you and your cloud host provider have with respect to that contract. For example, you may be liable for damages if malfunction of your processes cause other users of that same cloud host to suffer any performance degradation or data losses.

**Explain the key security issues pertaining to various cloud deployment models.**   Organizations can deploy information processes to the cloud(s) using systems that support their needs exclusively, that are fully shared with other unrelated user organizations, or that are a mix of both. These private, public, or hybrid cloud deployment models present different information security issues—but in and of themselves, a choice of deployment model does not change the CIANA needs of the organization. The key difference between private cloud deployments and public or any hybrid approach is that in the private model, the organization has total control (not just responsibility) to carry out all actions necessary to ensure its information security needs are met. Public or hybrid cloud deployments depend on the cloud hosting provider making the business decision about how much CIANA implementation to provide for each of its customers—and for all of its customers in aggregate. Such business case decisions by the provider should be reflected in how it implements customer data and process segregation and isolation; how it provides for data integrity, backup, and restore capabilities; and how it handles both data disposal and disposal of failed (or failing) hardware that may have data remaining within it. Additional insight as to how well (or poorly) the cloud provider implements data security for all of its customers may also be found by examining how it handles encryption, access control, identity management, and audit, and how it addresses data remanence in these systems and technologies, too.

**Differentiate the security issues of SaaS, PaaS, and IaaS cloud service models.**   All three cloud service models (or any mix thereof) require user organizations to thoroughly understand their own CIANA needs for information security and be technically and administratively capable of working with their cloud services provider to implement and manage core security functions, such as identity management, access control and accounting, and anomaly detection, incident characterization, and incident response and recovery. The key differences in these models from the SSCP's perspective is the degree to which the user's organization has to depend on the cloud services host to implement, manage, and deliver the security functionality the organization needs. Software as a service (SaaS) solutions, for example, often involve using productivity suites such as Microsoft Office 365 to provide software functionality to users. SaaS providers manage the security of the applications themselves (as well as the underlying systems infrastructure), but in doing so they are not providing any integrated data management capabilities. Individual users are still responsible for keeping hundreds if not thousands of data files—documents, spreadsheets, databases, etc.—correct, up to date, and cohesive as meeting the organization's business needs. PaaS models provide a "platform" as an integrated set of software capabilities and underlying databases, which might represent a single line of business or function (such as human resources management) or the entire business. As a result, ensuring sufficient, cost-effective CIANA depends on thoroughly understanding how to configure, manage, and use the platform's capabilities, including those for business continuity and restoration. IaaS offers the "bare metal plus" of the infrastructure by providing little more than the hardware, communications, storage, and execution management capabilities, along with the host operating systems to allocate such resources to user tasks while keeping those user tasks and data separate and secure from each other. The user organizations must each use these infrastructure capabilities (powerful though they may be) to implement their own data, applications, and communications security needs. Ultimately, the choice of model may depend on whether the organization has its own robust, secure platforms it is migrating or if its current systems are less than well integrated from an information security perspective as a whole.

**Explain how the use of virtualization and related hypervisors relates to applications and data security.**    Almost all cloud deployment models use virtual machine (VM) technologies to provide user application programs and data in a logically separate execution environment. Hypervisors are the systems software that manage the allocation of hardware resources (CPU, memory, communications, and storage) to user VMs. VMs can be created, put into operational use, achieve their allocated piece of the business logic or purpose, and then terminated and decommissioned in less than a second. Since most cloud deployments will require many such execution environments (or VMs) being used simultaneously to meet their customer and end-user needs, it is imperative that the creation, deployment, use, and decommissioning (or disposal) of these VMs upon task completion is all configured and managed correctly. Most hypervisors will provide the management and deployment infrastructures necessary to keep individual VMs and their data streams separated and secure from each other; however, most organizational information processes and business logic will end up integrating all of the data used by those VMs into one cohesive data environment, keeping it current and secure throughout the business day. The specifics of VM configuration, deployment, and management are beyond the scope of the SSCP exam; however, SSCPs should be aware that effective use of cloud services in any fashion requires the user organization to understand and appreciate the implications of such deployments to organizational information security needs.

**Describe the possible legal and regulatory issues that may arise when deploying to public cloud systems.** In most cases, moving to a public or hybrid cloud environment exposes the organization to the legal, regulatory, and cultural requirements of different nations (if the business is not in the same country as its cloud systems provider); each nation can exert its separate jurisdiction over what information the business has and how it uses it. Different legal frameworks may have conflicting standards about what information is (or is not) privacy related, and what protections are required. They may also impose different controls on trans-border movement of information, possibly even prohibiting certain information from entering or leaving their jurisdiction at all. Legal processes for search and seizure, for court-ordered discovery processes, and data retention requirements can differ. Different jurisdictions also may have very different laws pertaining to government surveillance of information systems and their users, and they may also have very different legal notions of what constitutes criminal offenses with information, such as slander, liable, negligence, profanity, heresy, blasphemy, "counter-revolutionary thought," or otherwise politically unfavorable speech, subversion, incitement, and even espionage.

**Explain the role of apps and cloud systems providers regarding the security of data in motion, at rest, and in use.** If data is the lifeblood of the organization, then apps are the muscles and sinew with which the organization's mind uses that data to achieve purpose and direction; cloud systems, be they public, private, or hybrid, are part of the veins and arteries, the bones, the heart, and other organs, that make that possible. Apps must ensure (through their design and implementation) that only properly authorized user subjects are executing valid actions with validated data. The infrastructure itself (including the cloud systems providers) supports this with identity management, access control, service provision, and protection of all communication paths that cross threat surfaces. Note that this is a functional statement—apps do *this*, the infrastructure does *that*—and not a design statement that specifies *how* those capabilities are achieved. There are many choices to make to ensure that the combination of user education and training; application design and implementation; data quality; and infrastructure services selection, configuration, and use results in cost-effective information risk management. This choice is the essence of information risk mitigation.

**Explain the typical third-party roles and responsibilities pertaining to information storage, retrieval, and use.** Typically, businesses contract with customers, employees, and suppliers for goods and services; the business is one party to these contracts, and individual customers, employees, or suppliers are the other party. (Contracts are typically between two individual organizations or people and refer to those contracting as "the parties.") A third party is one whom the business contracts with to help it fulfill a contracted service with one of its customers, employees, or suppliers. These third parties may provide a variety of information transmission, storage, access, processing, or retrieval services for the business. Third-party contracts should address the conditions under which such information is kept secure during use, during movement, and when at rest. Since each such service may have its own specified degree or level of satisfaction or success criteria associated with it, these are often called service level agreements (SLAs). An SLA might specify that a cloud services provider ensure that data is always available even if one of its physical datacenters is unavailable but that in no account should it host backup or archival copies of the customer's data in datacenters located in specific countries. SLAs also should specify under what circumstances the third party is to destroy data, the destruction method to be used, and the acceptable evidence of such destruction. Since no agreement can hold if it is not enforceable, and no enforcement can happen without there being auditable records of performance against the SLA, the business and this third party need to agree to what constitutes such an audit. The audit is the detail-by-detail inspection, analysis, and proof that both parties have lived up to the spirit and the letter of the SLA they both agreed to.

**Explain the role of archiving, backup, recovery, and restore capabilities in providing for data security.** As organizations execute their business logic moment by moment across each business day, their data—their information model of the real world of their business—moves forward in time with each transaction, operation, update, or use. Archiving provides a snapshot of a moment in time in the life of that data, and therefore of the organization and its activities. Archives support audits, analysis, trending, and regulatory or legal accountability functions, all of which support or achieve data integrity, nonrepudiation, confidentiality, and authentication needs. Because an archive represents a moment in time of the data, it can be used as a point in time to reset or restore back to, either to correct errors (by reversing the effects of a series of erroneous transactions) or to recover from hardware, software, or procedural failures. Although this may introduce the need to reprocess or re-accomplish transactions or other work, this ability to restore the data that represents a time in the life of the organization is critical to continuity of operations; it is what provides the continued availability after the restore point has been achieved.

**Explain the shared responsibility model and how it relates to achieving information security needs.** In almost all cases, organizations transfer risks to other organizations as a part of their risk management and risk mitigation strategies. This incurs a sharing of responsibilities in terms of due care and due diligence to ensure that the organization's information security needs are met to the desired degree. The simplest example of this is when a company wholly owns and operates its information systems infrastructure, applications, and data capabilities; even then, it is reliant on its IT supply chain, and (presumably) its Internet service provider or other communications providers for ongoing support. At the other extreme, organizations that do full deployments of their business logic and data to a public cloud provider (relying on thin client endpoint devices and communications capabilities) place far greater reliance on that cloud host provider to keep their business operating reliably. This requires a contractual basis, such as an SLA or a TOR that clearly identifies how each partner in that agreement delivers services and reassurances to the other at their agreed-to point of service delivery and interface. As with all contracts, this requires a meeting of the minds—the contracting parties have to achieve a common understanding of the legal, administrative, procedural, and technical aspects of what they are agreeing to do with and for each other. Without such a meeting of the minds, no such contract can be successful; indeed, in some jurisdictions, it may not even be enforceable.

**Explain the basic concepts of operating and securing virtual environments.** Unlike a single-user desktop computing environment, virtual environments, whether in the cloud or not, involve three distinct phases of activity: definition, deployment, and decommissioning. First, the user organization defines each type of virtual machine and environment it needs; this definition sets the parameters that define its resource needs, how it interacts with other systems (virtual or not), how its access to system resources and user data resources are to be controlled, and what programs can run on that VM. This definition or template also can set the rules by which the VM relinquishes system resources when done using them. It is during definition that information security services, such as identity management or access control, are selected, and their control parameters and policies are set and made part of the overall virtual environment of the VM. Next, the hypervisor will deploy as many copies of that VM as are needed to meet the workload demands of the business. As each VM comes into existence (or is *instantiated*), its definition invokes the interfaces to hypervisor-provided security infrastructures and features. Finally, as each VM completes its assigned tasks or is otherwise ready for termination, its allocated resources are returned to the system, and it ceases to exist as a valid process in the overall systems environment.

**Compare and contrast the information security aspects of software appliances and virtual appliances with more traditional computing approaches.**   Using the *appliance* approach to deploying, maintaining, and using software allows organizations to trade flexibility, security, maintainability, and cost in different ways. As you move from highly flexible and adaptable general-purpose and open computing models to more specialized, closed systems models, you reduce the threat surface. Traditionally, users or systems administrators would install an applications program on each general-purpose endpoint device, such as a laptop, desktop computer, or even a smartphone. A *computer appliance* or hardware appliance is a physical device on which the application software, operating system, and hardware are tailored to support a specific purpose and users are prevented from installing other applications. A *software appliance* is an installation kit or distribution image of an application and just enough of the operating systems functions necessary for it to run directly on the target hardware environments. These turn general-purpose computers into special-purpose (or limited-purpose) appliances, much like a smart washing machine cannot make toast (even if its onboard computer is capable of loading and running a toaster control program). *Virtual appliances* are software appliances created to run direct as virtual machine images under the control of a hypervisor. In the traditional model, the application's user is exposed to all of the vulnerabilities of the application, other applications installed on that system, the general-purpose operating system, and the hardware and communications environment that supports the system. Appliances, by contrast, may reduce the exposure to OS and other applications vulnerabilities, depending on the nature of the tailoring done to create the appliance. Maintaining appliance-based systems by replacing failed units may improve system availability and reduce time to repair.

**Explain the key information, access, and data security issues related to the Internet of Things.**   The Internet of Things (IoT) concept refers to devices with Internet addresses that may or may not provide adequate information systems security as part of their built-in capabilities. Whether these are "smart home" devices like thermostats, industrial process control devices, weather data or soil data sensors, or data-gathering devices on uninhabited aerial vehicles (UAVs), these "things" generate or gather data, send it to organizational information systems, and receive and execute commands (as service requests) from those information systems. This provides an access point that crosses the threat surface around those information systems; to the degree that those IoT devices are not secure, that access point is not secure. IoT devices typically have minimal security features built in; their data and command streams can be easily hacked, and quite often, IoT devices have no built-in capabilities for updating firmware, software, or control parameters. IoT devices that cannot provide strong identity authentication, participate in rigorous access control processes, or provide for secure data uplink and downlink are most vulnerable to attack, capture by a threat actor, and misuse against their owner or others. To the degree that a business depends on data generated by IoT devices or business logic implemented by IoT devices, that business is holding itself hostage to the security of those IoT devices. Businesses and organizations that allow IoT devices to upload, input, or otherwise inject commands of any kind (such as SQL queries) into their information systems have potentially put their continued existence in the hands of whomever it is that is actually operating that IoT device.

**Differentiate continuity and resilience with respect to applications and data.**   Both of these related terms describe how well business processes and logic can operate correctly, safely, and securely despite the occurrence of errors, failures, or attacks by threat actors (natural or human). *Continuity* measures the degree to which a system can produce correct, timely results when input errors, missing data, failed or failing subsystems, or other problems are impacting its operations. Designed-in redundancy of critical paths or components can provide a degree of graceful degradation—as elements fail or as system resources become exhausted, the system may provide lower throughput rates, produce more frequent but tolerable errors, or stop executing noncritical functions to conserve its capabilities to fulfill mission-essential tasks. Cloud-based systems might slow down dispatching new instances of VMs to support customer-facing tasks, for example, when there aren't enough resources to allow new VMs to run efficiently; this might slow the rate of dealing with new customer requests in favor of completing ongoing transactions. *Resiliency* measures the ability of the system to deal with unanticipated errors or conditions without crashing or causing unacceptable data loss or business process interruption. Auto-save and versioning capabilities on a word processor application, for example, provide resiliency to an author in two ways. Auto-save protects against an unplanned system shutdown (such as inadvertently unplugging its power cord); at most, the user/author loses what was typed in since the last automatic save. Versioning protects against the off chance that users make modifications, save the file, and then realize that they need to undo those modifications.

**Describe common vulnerabilities in applications and data, as well as common ways attackers can exploit them.**   Almost all applications are built to need and use three broad classes of input data: commands that select options and features, control parameters for features and options, and end-user data for processing by the application itself. Errors or deficiencies in program design will quite frequently result in exploitable vulnerabilities that allow attackers to select a series of operations, disrupt the application with badly formed data, or otherwise outthink the application's designer and subvert its execution to suit the needs of their attack. Such exploits can allow the attacker to obtain unauthorized resource and information access, elevate their privilege state, cause a disruption of service, or any combination of those. The most common vulnerabilities in applications software are those that relate to incomplete or inadequate validation of all data input to the program, whether from command line parameters, files, or user input via screens, fields, forms, or other means. *Out-of-limits attacks* attempt to discover and exploit the lack of rigorous, resilient *exception handling logic*—extra programming in which the designer anticipated out-of-bounds inputs by building in the logic to handle them in resilient ways. Without such resilience designed in, most applications programs will fail to execute properly, generate abnormal results, or cause other systems problems. This may lead to loss of data (in memory or in files stored on disk) or corruption of stored data, or in some cases cause the program to mistakenly execute the bad data as if it was a series of computer instructions. Input of numbers that lead to arithmetic faults, such as an attempt to divide by zero, may also cause an application to be terminated by the operating system, unless the application's programmer has built in logic to check for such conditions and handle them safely. *Buffer overflow attacks* attempt to input data that exceeds the designed-in maximum length or size for an input field or value, which can cause the program's runtime system to attempt to execute the overflowing data as if it were a series of legitimate instructions. *SQL injection*, for example, occurs when an attacker inputs a string of SQL commands rather than a set of text or other data, in ways that cause the application to pass that input to its underlying database engine to execute as if it were an otherwise legitimate, designed-in query. *Inadequate user authentication* vulnerabilities exist when the application program does not properly authenticate the user or subject that is asking for service from the application, and through that service, access to other information resources. For example, a typical word processing program should not (normally) be allowed to overwrite systems files that control the installation and operational use of other applications, or create new user accounts. Related to this are attempts by applications programmers to take programming shortcuts with secure storage of user or subject credentials (such as storing credit card numbers in clear text "temporarily" while using them). *Data dump attacks* attempt to cause the application to terminate abnormally might result in a diagnostic display of data (a "postmortem dump") from which the attacker can extract exploitable information. *Backdoor attacks* attempt to make use of built-in diagnostic, maintenance, or test features in the application, which may be misused to violate access privileges to in-memory or other data, or to modify the application to have it include otherwise unauthorized sets of instructions or control parameters.

Many modern applications depend on code injection to provide runtime tailoring of features, control parameters, and other user-related or system-related installation features; Windows systems use dynamic link library (DLL) files for this. One example of a *Trojan horse attack* exploits an application's failure to validate the correctness of a DLL or other code injection, thus allowing attackers to embed their own logic within the application. Related to these are *input data file Trojan horse attacks*, in which attackers first exploit other systems vulnerabilities to replace legitimate and expected input files or data streams with their own data. For example, adding false transactions to a backup data set, and then triggering an abnormal application termination, could cause the system to process those transactions without detecting or flagging an error condition—such as transferring money between two accounts, even if one of them isn't legitimate.

**Describe the common countermeasures to prevent or limit the damage from common attacks against data and applications.**   In a nutshell, *constant vigilance* is the best defense. First, protect the software base itself—the applications, their builds, and installations files and logs, control parameter files, and other key elements. Stay informed as to reported vulnerabilities in your applications, keep the software updated with the latest security fixes and patches, and develop procedural workarounds to protect against reported vulnerabilities that might impact your business but for which the vendor has not yet released a fix. This would include procedural steps to reduce (or prevent) out-of-limits data input—after all, most out-of-limits data that might cause the application to behave abnormally is probably not data that makes business sense in your business processes or logic! Next, protect the data—what you already have and use, and each new input that you gather. Institute data quality and data assurance processes, with which you define each data item, its limits, and the constraints on its use within your business logic. Implement data quality review, inspection, and audit processes to help detect and characterize bad data already in your systems. Ensure that identity management, access control, authorization, accounting, and audit systems are properly configured and in use. Monitor and review usage logs to detect possible anomalies in usage, access attempts, execution, or termination. Finally, and perhaps most important, train and educate your users so that they know what reasonable and expected systems and applications behavior is and thus recognize that anything else is abnormal and perhaps suspicious.

**Explain ways to address the security issues of shared storage.**   Shared storage systems typically provide information storage, access, retrieval, archive, backup, and restore services for many different customer organizations. Each customer must have confidence that other customers and the storage provider cannot read, modify, or extract its information without its knowledge and consent. To meet the combined confidentiality, integrity, and availability needs of all of its customers, the storage system provider must be able to prevent any customer information from being accessed or modified by any other customer or by processes invoked by another customer. These protections should also be extended to customer's access histories, transaction logs, deleted files, or other information regarding the customer's use of its own data. Storage providers frequently have to replace failed or failing storage media, such as disk drives, and this should not lead to compromise of customer data written on that (discarded) media. Storage providers can meet these obligations by encrypting files and file directories for each customer, by striping or segmenting storage of data and directories across multiple physical storage media, and by using virtual file systems (which migrate files or directory trees to faster or slower storage media to meet frequent usage demands). End-user customer organizations can also use directory-level and file-level encryption to add an extra layer of protection. In many cases, storage providers and end-user customer organizations can also use integrated resource, access, and identity management systems, such as Microsoft Active Directory, to define, deploy, and manage their information assets in more secure, auditable, and verifiable ways.

# Review Questions

1.  Which statements best explain why applications programs have exploitable vulnerabilities in them? (Choose all that are correct.)

    **A.**  Commercial software companies rush their products to market and pay little attention to designing or testing for security.

    **B.**  In-house developers often do not rigorously use design frameworks and coding standards that promote or enforce secure programming.

    **C.**  End users write most of the real applications that businesses use, but without configuration management, they're impossible to update and keep secure.

    **D.**  Most users do not keep their software updated, so they are missing out on security patches.

2.  Why is whitelisting a better approach to applications security than blacklisting? Choose the most correct statement.

    **A.**  Whitelisting depends on government-certified lists of trusted software providers, whereas blacklisting needs to recognize patterns of malicious code behavior, or malware signatures, to block the malware from being installed and executed.

    **B.**  For most organizations, the list of applications they have chosen to trust is far smaller and easier to administer than huge lists of malware signatures and behavioral models.

    **C.**  Administering a whitelisting system can require a lot of effort, but when an unknown program is trying to execute (or be installed), you know it is not yet trusted and can prevent harm.

    **D.**  With blacklisting only, new malware may not be recognized as such before it installs, executes, and begins to harm your systems and information.

3.  What is the role of threat modeling when an organization is planning to migrate its business processes into a cloud-hosted environment? Choose the most correct statement.

    **A.**  Private cloud deployments should see no change in threat modeling or threat surfaces.

    **B.**  Migrating to the cloud may not change the logical relationship between information assets and subjects requesting to use them, or the way privileges are set based on roles, needs, and trust, but the connection path to them may change; this probably changes the threat surface.

    **C.**  This really depends on the choice of IaaS, SaaS, or PaaS service models.

    **D.**  Shared responsibility models will transfer much of the organization's needs for information security services to the cloud-hosting provider, and they will apply their standard threat models to the chosen service and deployment models

4. "Maintaining or improving information security while migrating to the clouds is more of a contractual than technical problem to solve." Which statement best shows why this is either true or false?

A. It is false. The contractual side is similar to any other service provider relationship and is done once; the technical challenge of mastering a whole new set of features and capabilities is far larger and is always ongoing.

B. It is true. Cloud service models are constantly changing, and this means that the contracts, terms of service, or service level agreements are continually being updated. The underlying software technologies, however, don't change as much or as frequently.

C. It is false. The contractual agreements do change quite frequently as the underlying technologies, threats, and business case for both the cloud host and the customer change with time. These changes cause about equal amounts of work on both administrative and technical elements of the customer organization.

D. It is false. The contractual agreements do change quite frequently as the underlying technologies, threats, and business case for both the cloud host and the customer change with time. However, even these changes cause less work, less frequently, for the administrative elements and more for the technical elements of the typical customer organization.

5. Fred is on the IT team migrating his company's business systems into a public cloud provider, which will host the company's processes and data on its datacenters in three different countries to provide load balancing, failover/restart, and backup and restore capabilities. Which statement or statements best addresses key legal and regulatory concerns about this plan? (Choose all that apply.)

A. Because Fred's company does not have a business office or presence in the countries where the cloud host's datacenters are, those countries do not have legal or regulatory jurisdiction over company data.

B. The countries where the cloud host's datacenters are located, plus all of the countries in which Fred's company has a business presence, office, or other facility, have jurisdiction over company data.

C. In addition to staying compliant with all of those different countries' laws and regulations, Fred's company must also ensure that it does not violate cultural, religious, or political taboos in any of those countries.

D. These jurisdictional arguments only apply to data stored on servers or systems within a given country, or that is being used in that country; nations do not control the movement of data across their borders.

6.  Many issues are involved when planning for a third party to perform services involving data storage, backup and restore, and destruction or processing services for your company. Which of the following statements is not correct with regard to such planning or to your actual conduct of operations with that third party? (Choose all that apply.)

    **A.**  Your data protection responsibilities remain with you; you need to be able to actively verify that such third parties are doing what you've contracted with them to do. Otherwise, you are blindly trusting them.

    **B.**  Your contracts with these third parties should use a shared responsibility model to clearly delineate which party has which responsibilities; this will, in most cases, hold you harmless when the third party goes outside of the contract

    **C.**  Since third parties are by definition on a contract with you, as your subcontractor, you are not liable or responsible for mistakes they make in performing their duties.

    **D.**  What your third party providers, subcontractors, or employees (for that matter) do in your name and in your service, you are ultimately responsible for.

7.  Which statements about the role(s) of archiving, backup, and restore in meeting information security needs are most correct? (Choose all that apply.)

    **A.**  These each contribute to availability in similar ways.

    **B.**  These each contribute to availability and nonrepudiation.

    **C.**  As part of an incident response or disaster recovery plan, prompt restore to a known good data configuration may prevent other data from being compromised or breached, thus contributing to confidentiality.

    **D.**  These have no role to play in achieving authentication needs.

8.  How does securing a virtual machine differ from securing a physical computer system? (Choose all that apply.)

    **A.**  The basic tasks of defining the needs, configuring system capabilities in support of those needs, and then operationally deploying the VM are conceptually the same as when deploying the same OS and apps on a desktop or laptop. You use many of the same tools, OS features, and utilities.

    **B.**  VMs cannot run without some kind of software-defined network and a hypervisor, which bring many more complex security concerns that administrators need to deal with to achieve required information security performance.

    **C.**  VMs can access any resource on the bare metal machine that is hosting them through the hypervisor, which requires administrators to take many extra precautions to prevent security breaches.

    **D.**  The bare metal server, host OS (if used), and hypervisor provide none of the security features you'll need to configure to keep other system users, processes, and data, and those in each VM, safe, secure, and protected from each other.

**9.** Why is endpoint security so important to an organization?

   **A.** Users, who interact with organizational IT infrastructures and information at the endpoints, are notoriously difficult to control; if we can better control and secure the endpoints themselves, then we can prevent most end user–introduced security problems.

   **B.** Endpoints are where information turns into action, and that action produces value; on the way into the system, it is where action produces valuable information. This is where business actually gets done and work accomplished. Without the endpoints, the system is meaningless.

   **C.** Endpoints are what most users and customers see, and if endpoints are not secure, users and customers will not engage with our security programs and help us keep the system safe.

   **D.** While endpoints are where many users do information work, organizational managers and leaders draw their decision support at the systems level, and not from an endpoint device such as a smartphone. Data quality and software quality processes need to ensure that once data enters the system from an endpoint, it is then protected to meet CIANA needs throughout its life.

**10.** Jayne's company is considering the use of IoT devices as part of its buildings, grounds, and facilities maintenance tasks. Which statements give Jayne sound advice to consider for this project?

   **A.** Since IoT devices can easily be configured, updated, or patched, they are just as capable of being secure as are laptops, desktops, or smartphones.

   **B.** Functions that change frequently are well suited to IoT devices.

   **C.** Typical IoT devices are best suited to use where security or human safety are a primary concern.

   **D.** It may be better to consider industrial process control modules, rather than IoT devices, to interact with machinery, such as pumps and landscaping equipment.

**11.** Which statements about continuity and resilience are correct? (Choose all that apply.)

   **A.** Continuity measures a system's ability to deal with events the designers didn't anticipate.

   **B.** Continuity and resilience are basically the same idea, since they both deal with how systems handle errors, component or subsystem failures, or abnormal operational commands from users or other system elements.

   **C.** Resilience measures a system's ability to tolerate events or conditions not anticipated by the designers.

   **D.** Continuity measures a system's ability to deal with out-of-limits conditions, component or subsystems failures, or abnormal operating commands from users or other system elements, by means of designed-in redundancy, load shedding, or other strategies.

**12.** In which phase or phases of a typical data exfiltration attack would a hacker be making use of phishing? (Choose all that apply.)

   **A.** Reconnaissance and characterization

   **B.** Data gathering, clumping, masking, and aggregating

   **C.** Installing and using covert command and control capabilities

   **D.** Initial access

**13.** What are some effective, practical strategies to detect data exfiltration attacks? (Choose all that apply.)

   **A.** Analyze access control and resource usage log data to alert when abnormal patterns of behavior are noted.

   **B.** Alert when failed attempts to access a resource (whether it is protected by encryption or not) exceed a specified limit.

   **C.** Use digital rights management in addition to other identity management and access control capabilities.

   **D.** Set filters and rules on network traffic, inspecting suspicious packets, streams, or addresses to check for data being exfiltrated.

**14.** Which statement about privacy and data protection is most correct?

   **A.** International standards and agreements specify that personally identifiable information (PII) and information about an individual's healthcare, education, and work or credit history must be protected from unauthorized use or disclosure.

   **B.** Some countries, or regions like the EU, have laws and regulations that specify how personally identifiable information (PII) and information about an individual's healthcare, education, and work or credit history must be protected from unauthorized use or disclosure. Other countries do not. It's up to the organization that gathers, produces, uses, or disposes of such private data to determine what protection, if any, is needed.

   **C.** Storing backup or archive copies of privacy-related information in a datacenter in another country, without doing any processing there, does not subject you to that country's data protection laws.

   **D.** Sometimes, it seems cheaper to run the risk of fines or loss of business from a data breach involving privacy-related data than to implement proper data protection to prevent such a loss. Although this might make financial sense, it is not legal or ethical to do so.

**15.** The "garbage-in, garbage-out" (GIGO) problem means:

   **A.** Noise on power supplies or signal cables can corrupt data in motion, which if processed can result in abnormal or incorrect "garbage" results.

   **B.** Most information processes involve a set of related data items that represent or model a real person, activity, or part of the world. When that set of data is mutually inconsistent, or inconsistent with other data on hand about that real entity, each field may be within range but the overall meaning of the data set is corrupt. This "garbage," when processed (as input) by apps, produces equally meaningless but valid-looking outputs.

C. Organizations that just throw away damaged storage devices; printed copies of their data, application source code, design notes; and so forth are putting this "garbage" right where a "dumpster diver" hacker attack can collect it, examine it, and possibly find exploitable vulnerabilities.

D. Data input attacks can cause some applications to abort or execute abnormally, sometimes in ways that allow the garbage data that was input to be executed as if it is command strings or machine language instructions.

16. Which of the following might be serious example(s) of "shadow IT" contributing to an information security problem? (Choose all that apply.)

A. One user defines a format or style sheet for specific types of documents that other users will create and manage.

B. An end user writes special-purpose database queries and reports used to forecast sales and project production and inventory needs, which are reviewed and used at weekly division meetings.

C. Several users build scripts, flows, and other processing logic to implement a customer service help desk/trouble ticket system, using its own database on a shared use/collaboration platform that the company uses.

D. Users post documents, spreadsheets, and many other types of information on a company-provided shared storage system, making the information more freely available throughout the company.

17. Sandi has suggested to her boss that their small company should be using a cloud-based shared storage service, such as OneDrive, Dropbox, or Google Drive. Her boss believes these are inherently insecure. Which of the following statements would not help Sandi make her case?

A. Check the reputation and business model of the shared storage providers; check what national/legal jurisdiction they operate in, compared to the one her business operates in.

B. Examine their stated, posted privacy and security policies; ask for a sample contract, terms of reference, or service level agreement, and see if they claim to provide what her company needs.

C. Sandi can always encrypt her files before moving them into storage; that way, even if another user, a hacker, or the provider themselves try to read the file, they can't.

D. Sandi can take advantage of a free trial offer and see if her information security staff can hack into other users' storage or into system logs and account information on the provider. If her "white hats" can't break in and peek, the system is safe enough for her.

**18.** Your boss tells you that securing the endpoints should consider all of the measures you would use to secure the information infrastructures themselves. Is she correct? Which statement best confirms or refutes her statement?

**A.** False. Many of the things we do to secure operating systems and networks, for example, just don't apply to an endpoint device, the apps on it, and the user's interactions with it.

**B.** True. After all, each endpoint is (by definition) embedded in or part of one or more threat surfaces; from there, the same threat modeling and assessment processes will lead us through the same risk management and mitigation processes, with choices tailored as needed.

**C.** True. All of the same risk management, vulnerability assessment, risk mitigation, and operational risk management processes apply to each node of our system and to the system as a whole, tailored to the specific risks, vulnerabilities, technologies, and operational needs.

**D.** False. What happens at the endpoints is a special case of information security and needs special attention that is very different than how we assess risk to servers, networks, or applications platforms.

**19.** What steps can you take to limit or prevent attacks on your systems that attempt to spoof, corrupt, or tamper with data? (Choose all that apply.)

**A.** Ensure that firewalls, routers, and other network infrastructures filter for and block attempts to access network storage without authorization.

**B.** Develop and use an organizational data model and data dictionary that contain all data-focused business logic; use them to build and validate business processes and the apps that support them.

**C.** Implement data quality processes that ensure all data is fit for all purposes, in accordance with approved business logic.

**D.** Implement information classification, and use access control and identity management to enforce it.

**20.** Your coworkers don't agree with you when you say that data quality is a fundamental part of information security. Which of the following lines of argument are true in the context of your discussion with them? (Choose all that apply.)

**A.** If our business logic doesn't establish the data quality rules and constraints, we have no idea if an input or a whole set of inputs makes valid business sense or is a spoof attack trying to subvert our systems.

**B.** Since we don't have a data quality program now, if we get served with a digital discovery order, who knows whether the data we surrender to the authorities is correct and complete? The attorneys might care, but that really has no effect on us.

**C.** We have users who complain that when they try to test and evaluate backup data sets, the backup data makes no sense. If a real disruption or disaster strikes, and our backups don't make any business sense, we could be out of business pretty quickly.

**D.** We mitigate information risk to achieve the CIANA needs that the business impact analysis and the risk management plan called for; since those high-level plans didn't conclude that we need a data quality program, then we probably don't.

# People Power: What Makes or Breaks Information Security

Part 4 emphasizes the central role that *people* must fulfill in every aspect of information security. Senior leaders and managers set the organization's culture, decision-making style, and risk tolerance. People make the day-to-day decisions and take the moment-by-moment actions that create value, with which the company pays its bills. People decide how to design, implement, and operate the information systems that enable that value creation, and people are the ones who keep those information systems safe, secure, and reliable—or expose those systems to risk and loss.

In Chapter 10, you'll use the NIST Computer Security Incident Response framework as a guide to planning, preparing, and responding to incidents of interest. By now, you've probably realized that this is not a case of *if* an information security incident strikes your organization, but rather *when*. You'll see how to tailor this framework to meet the needs of your own business or organization, and you'll identify key planning factors you'll need management's decision and action on to be ready to detect, contain, recover, and help guide the organization in preparing for the *next* such incident.

Chapter 11 takes us further on from the immediate incident response time frame and shows how organizations plan for and achieve continuity of business operations in the face of a disaster or major dislocation. This is the time when all of your team's efforts at backup and recovery strategies and preparation get put to the test as you help your traumatized company get back into business.

Taken together, Chapters 10 and 11 help bring together every aspect of the administrative aspect of information risk management and mitigation. Chapter 12 finishes this process and offers a look ahead at what's right around the corner on your journey as an information systems security practitioner. In the end, it is SSCPs like you who bring all of the technical, physical, and administrative measures together to help organizations keep their information systems safe, secure, private, reliable—and available!

# Chapter

# 10

# Incident Response and Recovery

---

## THIS CHAPTER COVERS THE FOLLOWING SSCP OBJECTIVE DOMAINS:

**Domain 3: Risk Identification, Monitoring, and Analysis**

✓ 3.3: Operate and Maintain Monitoring Systems

✓ 3.4: Analyze Monitoring Results

**Domain 4: Incident Response and Recovery**

✓ 4.1: Support Incident Lifecycle

✓ 4.2: Understand and Support Forensic Investigations

✓ 4.3: Understand and Support Business Continuity Plan (BCP) and Disaster Recovery Plan (DRP) Activities

Anomalies happen. Tasks stop working right. Users can't connect reliably, or their connections don't stay up as they should. Servers get sluggish, as if they are handling an abnormally high demand for services. Hardware or software systems just stop working, either with "blue screens of death" or by using normal restart procedures but at unexpected times. Now, your organization's computer emergency response team springs into action to characterize the incident, contain it, and get your systems back to operating normally.

What? Your organization doesn't *have* such a team? Let's jump right in, do some focused preparation, and improve your operational information security posture so that you can detect, identify, contain, eradicate, and restore after the next anomaly.

# Defeating the Kill Chain One Skirmish at a Time

It's often been said that the attackers have to get lucky only once, whereas the defenders have to be lucky every moment of every day. When it comes to *advanced persistent threats (APTs)*, which pose potentially the most damaging attacks to our information systems, another, more operationally useful rule applies. APTs must of necessity use a robust kill chain to discover, reconnoiter, characterize, infiltrate, gain control, and further identify resources to attack within the system; make their "target kill"; and copy, exfiltrate, or destroy the data and systems of their choice, cover their tracks, and then leave. Things get worse: for most businesses, nongovernmental organizations (NGOs), and government departments and agencies, they are probably the object of interest of dozens of different, unrelated attackers, each following its own kill chain logic to achieve its own set of goals (which may or may not overlap with those of other attackers). Taken together, there may be thousands if not hundreds of thousands of APTs out there in the wild, each seeking its own dominance, power, and gain. The millions of information systems owned and operated by businesses and organizations worldwide are their hunting grounds.

The good news, however, is that as you've seen in previous chapters, SSCPs have some field-proven information risk management and mitigation strategies that they can help their companies or organizations adopt. These frameworks, and the specific risk mitigation controls, are tailored to the information security needs of your specific organization. With them, you can first deter, prevent, and avoid attacks. Then you can detect the ones that get past that first set of barriers, and characterize them in terms of real-time risks to your systems. You then take steps to contain the damage they're capable of causing, and help the organization recover from the attack and get back up on its feet.

You probably will not do battle with an APT directly; you and your team won't have the luxury (if we can call it that!) of trying to design to defeat a particular APT and thwart its attempts to seek its objectives at your expense. Instead, you'll wage your defensive campaign one skirmish at a time. You'll deflect or defeat one scouting party as you strengthen one perimeter; you'll detect and block a probe from gaining entry into your systems. You'll find where an illicit user ID has made itself part of your system, and you'll contain it, quarantine it, and ultimately block its attempts to expand its presence inside your operations. As you continually work with your systems' designers and maintainers, you'll help them find ways to tighten down a barrier *here* or mitigate a vulnerability *there*. Step by step, you strengthen your information security posture.

By now, you and your organization should be prepared to *respond* when those alarms start ringing. Right?

 **Real World Scenario**

### Identity Theft as an APT Tactical Weapon

Since 2011, energy production and distribution systems in North America and Western Europe have been under attack from what can only be described as a large, sophisticated, advanced persistent threat actor team. Known as *Dragonfly 2.0*, this attack depended heavily on fraudulent IDs and misuse of legitimate IDs created in systems owned and operated by utility companies, engineering and machinery support contractors, and the fuels industries that provide the feedstocks for the nuclear, petroleum, coal, and gas-fired generation of electricity. The Dragonfly 2.0 team wove a complex web of attacks against multiple private and public organizations as they gathered information, obtained access, and created fake IDs as precursor steps to gaining *more* access and control. For example, reports issued by the National Institute of Standards and Technologies (NIST), as well as by Symantec, make mention of "hostile email campaigns" that attempted to lure legitimate email subscribers in these organization to respond to fictitious holiday parties.

Blackouts and brownouts in various energy distribution systems, such as those suffered in Ukraine in 2015 and 2016, have been traced to cyberattacks linked to Dragonfly 2.0 and its teams of attackers. Data losses to various companies and organizations in the energy sector are still being assessed.

You can read Symantec's report at www.symantec.com/blogs/threat-intelligence/dragonfly-energy-sector-cyber-attacks.

Why should SSCPs put so much emphasis on APTs and their use of the kill chain? In virtually every major data breach in the past decade, the attack pattern was *low and slow*: sequences of small-scale efforts designed to not cause alarm, each of which gathered information or enabled the attacker to take control of a target system. More low and slow attacks launched from that first target against *other* target systems. More reconnaissance. Finally, with all command, control, and hacking capabilities in place, the attack began in earnest to exfiltrate sensitive, private, or otherwise valuable data out of the target's systems.

Note that if *any* of those low and slow attack steps had been thwarted, or if any of those early reconnaissance efforts, or attempts to install command and control tools, had been detected and stopped, then the attacker might have given up and moved on to another lucrative target.

*Preparation and planning are the keys to survival.* In previous chapters, you've learned how to translate risk mitigation into specific physical, technical, and administrative controls that you'd recommend to management to implement as part of the organization's information systems security posture. You've also learned how to build in the detection capabilities that should raise the alarms when things aren't looking right. More importantly, you've grasped the need to aggregate alarm data with systems status, state, and health information to generate indications and warnings of a possible information security incident in the making *and* the urgent and compelling need to promptly escalate such potential bad news to senior management and leadership.

## Kill Chains: Reviewing the Basics

In Chapter 1, "The Business Case for Decision Assurance and Information Security," we looked briefly at the *value chain*, which models how organizations create value in the products or services they provide to their customers. The value chain brings together the sequence of major activities, the infrastructures that support them, and the key resources that they need to transform each input into an output. The value chain focuses our attention on both the outputs and the outcomes that result from each activity. Critical to thinking about the value chain is that each major step provides the organization a chance to improve the end-to-end experience by reducing costs (by reducing waste, scrap, and rework) and improving the quality of each output and outcome along the way. We also saw that every step along the value chain is an opportunity for something to *go wrong*. A key input could be delayed or fail to meet the required specifications for quality or quantity. Skilled labor might not be available when we need it; critical information might be missing, incomplete, or inaccurate.

The name *kill chain* comes from military operational planning (which, after all, is the business of killing the opponent's forces and breaking their systems). *Kill chains* are outcomes-based planning concepts and are geared to achieving national strategic, operational, or tactical outcomes as part of larger battle plans. These kill chains tend to be planned from the desired outcome back toward the starting set of inputs: if you want to destroy the other side's naval fleet while at anchor at its home port, you have to figure out what kind of weapons you have or can get that can destroy such ships. Then you work out how to get those weapons to where they can damage the ships (by air drop, surface naval weapons fire, submarine, small boats, cargo trucks, or other stealthy means). And so on.

You then look at each way the other side can deter, defeat, or prevent you from attacking. By this point, you probably realize that you need to know more about their naval base, its defenses, its normal patterns of activity, its supply chains, and its communications systems. With all of *that* information, you start to winnow down the pile of options into a few reasonably sensible ways to defeat their navy while it's at home port, or you realize that's beyond your capabilities and you look for some other target that might be easier to attack that can help achieve the same *outcome* you want to achieve by defeating their navy.

With that as a starting point, we can see that an *information systems kill chain* is the total set of actions, plans, tasks, and resources used by an advanced persistent threat to

1. Identify potential target information systems that suit their objectives.

2. Gain access to those targets, and establish command and control over portions of those targets' systems.

3. Use that command and control to carry out further tasks in support of achieving their objectives.

How do APTs apply this kill chain in practice? In broad general terms, APT actors do the following:

- Survey the marketplaces for potential opportunities to achieve an outcome that supports their objectives

- Gather intelligence data about potential targets, building an initial profile on each target

- Use that intelligence to inform the way they conduct probes against selected targets, building up fingerprints of the target's systems and potentially exploitable vulnerabilities

- Conduct initial intrusions on selected targets and their systems, gathering more technical intelligence

- Establish some form of command and control presence on the target systems

- Elevate privilege so as to enable broader, deeper search for exploitable information assets in the target's systems and networks

- Conduct further reconnaissance to discover internetworked systems that may be worth reconnaissance or exploitation

- Begin the exploitation of the selected information assets: exfiltrate the data, disrupt or degrade the targeted information processes, and so on

- Complete the exploitation activities

- Obfuscate or destroy evidence of their activities in the target's system

- Disconnect from the target

The more complex, pernicious APTs will use multiple target systems as proxies in their kill chains, using one target's systems to become a platform from which they can run reconnaissance and exploitation against other targets.

---

**Avoid Stereotyping the APTs**

APTs can be almost any kind of organized effort to achieve some set of objectives by means of extracting value from your information systems. That value might come from information they can access, exfiltrate, and sell or trade to other threat actors, or it might come from disrupting your business processes or the work of key people on your team.

APTs have been seen as parts of campaigns waged by organized crime, terrorist organizations, national governments, and even private businesses. The APT threat actors, or the people whom they work with or for, have motives that range from purely mercenary to ideological, from seeking power to seeking revenge.

APT threat actors and the campaigns that they attempt to run may be of almost any size, scale, and complexity. And they're quite willing to use any system, no matter how small, personal or business, if it can be a stepping-stone to completing a step in their kill chain.

---

## Events vs. Incidents

Let's suppose for a moment that your company and its information systems have caught the attention of an APT actor. How might their attentions show up as observable activities from *your* side of the interface? Most probably, your systems will experience a variety of anomalies, of many different types, which may seem completely unrelated. At some point, one of those anomalies catches your interest, or you think you see a pattern beginning to emerge from a sequence of events.

Back in Chapter 2, "Information Security Fundamentals," we defined an *event of interest* as something that happens that might be an indicator of something that might impact your information's systems security. We looked at how an event of interest may or may not be a warning of a computer security incident in the making, or even the first stages of such an incident.

But what is a computer security incident? Several definitions by NIST, ITIL, and the IEFT* suggest that computer security incidents are events involving a target information system in ways that

- Are unplanned
- Are disruptive
- Are hostile, malicious, or harmful in intent
- Compromise the confidentiality, integrity, availability, authenticity, or other security characteristics of the affected information systems
- Willfully violate the system owners' policies for acceptable use, security, or access

Consider the unplanned shutdown of an email server within your systems. You'd need to do a quick investigation to rule out natural causes (such as a thunderstorm-induced power surge) and accidental causes (the maintenance technician who stumbled and pulled the

---

*NIST is the National Institute of Standards and Technologies; IETF is the Internet Engineering Task Force; and the Information Technology Information Library has been known simply as ITIL since 2013.

power cord loose on his way to the floor). Yes, your vulnerability assessment might have discovered these and made recommendations as to how to reduce their potential for disruption. But if neither weather nor a hardware-level accident caused the shutdown, you still have a dilemma: was it a software design problem that caused the crash, or a vulnerability that was exploited by a person or persons unknown?

Or consider the challenges of differentiating phishing attacks from innocent requests for information. An individual caller to your main business phone number, seeking contact information in your IT team, might be an honest and innocent inquiry (perhaps from an SSCP looking for a job!). However, if a number of such innocent inquiries across many days have attempted to map out your entire organization's structure, complete with individual names, phone numbers, and email addresses, you're being scouted against!

What this leads to is that your organization needs to clearly spell out a triage process by which the IT and information security teams can recognize an event, quickly characterize it, and decide the right process to apply to it. Figure 10.1 illustrates such a process.

**FIGURE 10.1**    Incident triage and response process

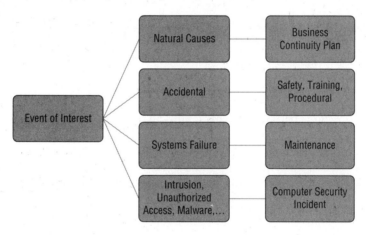

Note that our role as SSCPs requires us to view these incidents from the overall information risk management and mitigation perspective as well as from the information systems *security* perspective. It's quite likely that the computer security perspective is the more challenging one, demanding a greater degree of rapid-fire analysis and decision making, so we'll focus on it from here on out.

# Incident Response Framework

All organizations, regardless of size or mission, should have a framework or process they use to manage their information security incident response efforts with. It is a vital part of your organization's business logic. Due care and due diligence both require it. The sad truth is, however, many organizations don't get around to thinking through their incident response process needs until *after* the first really scary information security incident has taken place. As they sweep up the digital broken glass from the break-in, assess their losses due to stolen or compromised data, and start figuring out how to get back into operation, they say "Never again!" They promise themselves that they'll write down the lessons they've just painfully learned and be better prepared.

(ISC)² and others define the *incident response framework* as a formal plan or process for managing the organization's response to a suspected information security incident. It consists of a series of steps that start with detection and run through response, mitigation, reporting, recovery, and remediation, ending with a lessons learned and onward preparation phase. Figure 10.2 illustrates this process. Please note that this is a conceptual flow of the steps involved; reality tells us that incidents unfold in strange and complex ways, and your incident response team needs to be prepared to cycle around these steps in different ways based on what they learn and what results they get from the actions they take.

**FIGURE 10.2**    Incident response process

NIST, in its special publication 800-61r2, adds an initial preparation phase to this flow and further focuses attention on the detection process by emphasizing the role of prompt analysis to support incident identification and characterization. NIST also refines the mitigation efforts by breaking them down into containment and eradication steps and the lessons learned phase into information sharing and coordination activities. These are shown alongside the simplified response flow in Figure 10.3.

**FIGURE 10.3**    NIST 800-61 incident response flow

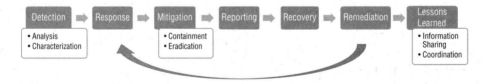

Other publications and authorities such as ITIL publish their own incident response frameworks, each slightly different in specifics. ISO/IEC 27035:2016 is another good source of information technology security techniques and approaches to incident management. As we saw with risk management frameworks in Chapters 3, "Integrated Information Risk Management," and 4, "Operationalizing Risk Mitigation," the key is to find what works for your organization. These same major tasks ought to show up in your company's incident response *management* processes, policies, and procedures. They may be called by different names, but the same set of functions should be readily apparent as you read through these documents. If you're missing a step—if a critical task in either of these flows seems to be overlooked—then it's time to investigate.

**Don't Even *Think* About a Counterattack!**

As part of your organization's information security team, you are strictly limited by law, regulations, and professional ethics in how you can deal with a suspected attacker. You can tempt them into a "honey net," where you can observe what they do *inside your isolated, quarantined network segment*. You can block their IP address and MAC addresses, or take other actions that prohibit traffic from them from coming into your networks and systems. But you simply cannot counterattack, or do counter-reconnaissance probes of your own, in any way, shape, or form. Period.

In most countries, the law looks negatively on self-appointed vigilantes, people or organizations who decide to take the enforcement of law into their own hands. You risk losing your job, possible criminal charges, and maybe even a prison sentence.

There is very little you could learn that would help you strengthen your own defenses by attempting counter-reconnaissance, probes, or scans of a suspected attacker's systems. It's not worth the risk.

Just don't do it.

## Incident Response Team: Roles and Structures

Unless you're in a *very* small organization, and as the SSCP you wear all of the hats of network and systems administration, security, and incident response, your organization will need to formally designate a team of people who have the "watch-standing" duty of a real-time incident response team. This team might be called a *computer emergency response team (CERT)*. CERTs can also be known as computer incident response teams, as a cyber incident response team (both using the CIRT acronym), or as computer security incident response teams (CSIRTs). For ease of reference, let's call ours a CSIRT for the remainder of this chapter. (Note that CERTs tend to have a broader charter, responding whether systems are put out of action by acts of nature, accidents, or hostile attackers. CERTs, too, tend to be more involved with broader disaster recovery efforts than a team focused primarily on security-related incidents.)

Your organization's risk appetite and its specific CIANA needs should determine whether this CSIRT provides around-the-clock, on-site support, or supports on a rapid-response, on-call basis after business hours. These needs will also help determine whether the incident response team is a separate and distinct group of people or is a part of preexisting groups in your IT, systems, or networks departments. In Chapter 5, "Communications and Network Security," for example, we looked at segregating the day-to-day network operations jobs of the network operations center (NOC) from the time-critical security and incident response tasks of a security operations center (SOC).

Whether your organization calls them a CSIRT or an SOC, or they're just a subset of the IT department's staff, there are a number of key functions that this incident response team should perform. We'll look at them in more detail in subsequent sections, but by way of introduction, they are as follows:

**Serve as a single point of contact for incident response.**   Having a single point of contact between the incident and the organization makes incident command, control, and communication much more effective. This should include the following:

- Focus reporting and rumor control with users and managers regarding suspicious events, systems anomalies, or other security concerns.

- Coordinate responses, and dispatch or call in additional resources as needed.

- Escalate computer security incident reports to senior managers and leadership.

- Coordinate with other security teams (such as physical security), and with local police, fire, and rescue departments as required.

**Take control of the incident and the scene.**   Taking control of the incident, as an event that's taking place in real time, is vital. Without somebody taking immediate control of the incident, and where it's taking place, you risk bad decisions placing people, property, information, or the business at greater risk of harm or loss than they already are. Taking control of the incident scene protects information about the incident, where it happened, and how it happened. This preserves physical and digital evidence that may be critical to determining how the incident began, how it progressed, and what happened as it spread. This information is vital to both problem analysis and recovery efforts and legal investigations of fault, liability, or unlawful activity.

- Response procedures should specify the chain of command relationships, and designate who (by position, title, or name) is the "on-scene commander," so to speak. Incident situations can be stressful, and often you're dealing with incomplete information. Even the simplest of decisions needs to be clearly made and communicated to those who need to carry it out; committees usually cannot do this very well in real time.

- The scene itself, and the systems, information, and even the rooms or buildings themselves, represent investments that the organization has made. Due care requires that the incident response team minimize further damage to the organization's property or the property of others that may be involved in the incident scene.

**Investigate, analyze, and assess the incident.**   This is where all of your skills as a trouble-shooter, an investigator, or just being good at making informed guesses start to pay off. Gather data; ask questions; dig for information.

**Escalate, report, and engage with leadership.**   Once they've determined that a security-related incident might in fact be happening, the team needs to promptly escalate this to senior leadership and management. This may involve a judgment call on the response team chief's part, as preplanned incident checklists and procedures cannot anticipate everything that might go wrong. Experience dictates that it's best to err on the side of caution, and report or escalate to higher management and leadership.

**Keep a running incident response log.**   The incident response team should keep accurate logs of what happened, what decisions got made (and by whom), and what actions were taken. Logging should also build a time-ordered catalog of event artifacts—files, other outputs, or physical changes to systems, for example. This time history of the event, as it unfolds, is also vital to understanding the event, and mitigating or taking remedial action to prevent its reoccurrence. Logs and the catalogs of artifacts that go with them are an important part of establishing the chain of custody of evidence (digital or other) in support of any subsequent forensics investigation.

**Coordinate with external parties.**   External parties can include systems vendors and maintainers, service bureaus or cloud-hosting service providers, outside organizations that have shared access to information systems (such as extranets or federated access privileges), and others whose own information and information systems may be put at risk by this incident as it unfolds. By acting as the organization's focal point for coordination with external parties, the team can keep those partners properly informed, reduce risk to their systems and information, and make better use of technical, security, and other support those parties may be able to provide.

**Before You Share Incident Information...Get Senior Leadership's Buy-In**

In almost all cases, you'll need senior leadership and management to make the real-time decisions regarding what information about an incident should be shared with outside organizations. Note, too, that your internal CSIRT or SOC should *not* be the liaison with the news media!

**Contain the incident.**   Prevent it from infecting, disrupting, or gaining access to any other elements of your systems or networks, as well as preventing it from using your systems as launchpads to attack other external systems.

**Eradicate the incident.**   Remove, quarantine, or otherwise eliminate all elements of the attack from your systems.

**Recover from the incident.**   Restore systems to their pre-attack state by resetting and reloading network systems, routers, servers, and so forth as required. Finally, inform management that the systems should be back up and ready for operational use by end users.

**Document what you've learned.**   Capture everything possible regarding systems deficiencies, vulnerabilities, or procedural errors that contributed to the incident taking place for subsequent mitigation or remediation. Review your incident response procedures for what worked and what didn't, and update accordingly.

## Incident Response Priorities

No matter how your organization breaks up the incident response management process into a series of steps, or how they are assigned to different individuals or teams within the organization, the incident response team must keep three basic priorities firmly in mind.

The first one is easy: *the safety of people comes first*. Nothing you are going to try to accomplish is more important than protecting people from injury or death. It does not matter whether those people are your coworkers on the incident response team, or other staff members at the site of the incident, or even people who might have been responsible for causing the incident, your first priority is preventing harm from coming to any of them—yourself included! Your organization should have standing policies and procedures that dictate how calls for assistance to local fire, police, or emergency medical services should be made; these should be part of your incident response procedures.

**Safety of Life and Limb First!**

Throughout every phase of an incident response, people safety is always priority one. *After* any issues involving the safety of people have been dealt with, you can deal with the often-conflicting needs to understand what happened versus getting things back up and running quickly.

The next two priority choices, when taken together, are actually one of the most difficult decisions facing an organization, especially when it's in the midst of a computer security incident: should it prioritize getting back into normal business operations or supporting a digital forensics investigation that may establish responsibility, guilt, or liability for the incident and resultant loss and damages. *This is not a decision that the on-scene response team leader makes!* Simply put, the longer it takes to secure the scene, and gather and protect evidence (such as memory dumps, systems images, disk images, log files, etc.), the longer it takes to restore systems to their normal business configurations and get users back to doing productive work. This is not a binary, either-or decision—it is something that the incident response team and senior leaders need to keep a constant watch over throughout all phases of incident response.

Increasingly, we see that government regulators, civic watchdog groups, shareholders, and the courts are becoming impatient with senior management teams that fail in their due diligence. This impatience is translating into legal and market action that can and will bring self-inflicted damage—negligence, in other words—home to roost where it belongs, and the reasonable fear of that should lead to tasking all members of the IT organization, including their information security specialists, with developing greater proficiency at being able to protect and preserve the digital evidence related to an incident, while getting the systems and business processes promptly restored to normal operations.

The details of how to preserve an incident scene for a possible digital forensics investigation, and how such investigations are conducted, is beyond the scope of the SSCP exam and this book. They are, however, great avenues for you to journey along as you continue to grow in your chosen profession as a white hat!

# Preparation

You may have noticed that this step isn't shown in either of the flows in Figures 10.2 or 10.3. That's not an oversight—this should have been done as soon as you started your information risk management planning process. There is nothing to gain by waiting—and potentially everything to lose. NIST SP800-61 Rev. 2 provides an excellent "shopping list" of key preparation and planning tasks to start with and the information they should make readily available to your response team. But where do you start?

Let's break this preparation task down into more manageable steps, using the Plan-Do-Check-Act (PDCA) model we used in earlier chapters, as part of risk management and mitigation. It may seem redundant to plan for a plan, but it's not—you have to start somewhere, after all. Note that the boundaries between planning, doing, checking, and acting are not hard and fast; you'll no doubt find that some steps can and should be taken almost immediately, while others need a more deliberative approach. Every step of the way, keep senior management and leadership engaged and involved. This is *their* emergency response capability you're planning and building, after all.

## Preparation Planning

This first set of tasks focuses on gathering what the organization already knows about its information systems and IT infrastructures, its business processes and its people, which become the foundation on which you can build the procedures, resources, and training that your incident responders will need. As you build those procedures and training plans, you'll also need to build out the support relationships you'll need when that first incident (or the *next* incident) happens.

**Build, maintain, and use a knowledge base of critical systems support information.**   You'll need this information to identify and properly scope the CSIRT's monitoring and detection job, as well as identify the internal systems support teams, critical users, and recovery and restoration processes that already exist. As a living library, the CSIRT should have these information products available to them as reference and guidance materials. These include but are not limited to

- Information architecture documentation, plans, and support information
- IT systems documentation, such as servers, endpoints, special-purpose systems, etc.
- IT security systems documentation, including connectivity, current settings, alarm indications, and system documentation
- Clean, trusted backup images of systems and critical files, including digitally signed copies or cryptographic hashes, from which trusted restoration can take place

- Networks and other communications systems design, installation, and support, including data plane, control plane, and management plane views
- Platform and service systems documentation
- Physical layout drawings, showing equipment location, points of presence, alarm systems, entrances, and exits
- Power supply information, including commercial and backup sources, switching, power conditioning, etc.
- Current status of known vulnerabilities on all systems, connections, and endpoints
- Current status of systems, applications, platforms and database backups, age of last backup, and physical location of backup images
- Contact information or directory of key staff members, managers, and support personnel, both in-house and for any service providers, systems vendors, or federated access partners

Whether you put this information into a separate knowledge base for your incident responders, or it is part of your overall software, systems, and IT knowledge base, is perhaps a question of scale and of survivability. During an incident itself, you need this knowledge base reliably available to your responders, without having to worry if it's been tainted by this incident or a prior but undetected one.

Use that list to identify the set of business process, systems architecture, and technology-focused critical knowledge that each CSIRT team member must be proficient in, and add this to your team training and requalification planning set.

**Assemble critical data collection, collation, and analysis tools.**   Characterizing an event in real time, and quickly determining its nature and the urgency of the response it demands, requires that your incident response team be able to analyze and assess what all of the information from your systems is trying to tell them. You do not help the team get this done by letting the team find the tools they need right when they're trying to deal with an ongoing incident. Instead, identify a broad set of systems and event information analysis tools, and bring them together in what we might call a *responder's workbench*. This workbench can provide your response team with a set of known, clean systems to use as they capture data, analyze it, and draw conclusions about the event in question. Some of the current generation of security information and event management systems may provide good starting points for growing your own workbench. Other tools may need to be developed in house, tailored to the nature of critical business processes or information flows, for example.

**Establish minimum standards for event logging.**   Virtually all of your devices, be they servers, endpoints, or connectivity systems, have the capability to capture event information at the hardware, systems software, and applications levels. These logs can quickly narrow down your hunt for the broken or infected system, or the unauthorized subject(s) and the objects they've accessed. You'll also need to establish a comprehensive and uniform policy about log file retention if you're hoping to correlate logs from different systems and devices with each other in any meaningful way. Higher-priority, mission-critical systems should have higher levels of logging, capturing more events and at greater time granularity, to better empower your response capability regarding these systems.

**Identify forensics requirements, capabilities, and relationships.**   Although many information-security incidents may come and go without generating legal repercussions, you need to take steps now to prepare for those incidents that will. You'll need to put in place the minimum required capabilities to establish and maintain a chain of custody for evidence. This may surface the need for additional training for CSIRT team members and managers. Use this as the opportunity to understand the support relationships your team will need when (not if) such an incident occurs, and start thinking through how you'd select the certified forensics examiners you'd need when it does.

By the end of this preparation planning phase, you should have some concrete ideas about what you'll need for the CSIRT:

- *SOC, or NOC?* Does your organization need a security operations center, with its crew of watch-standers? Or can the CSIRT be an on-call team of responders drawn from the IT department's networks, systems, and applications support specialists? In either case, how many people will be needed for ongoing alert and monitoring during normal business hours, for round-the-clock watch-standing, and for emergency response?

- *Physical work space, responder's workbenches, and communication needs* must also be identified at this point. These will no doubt need to be budgeted for, and their acquisition, installation, and ongoing support needs to fit into your overall incident response budget and schedule.

- *Reporting, escalation, and incident management chain of command procedures* should be put together in draft form at this point; coordinate with management and leadership to gain their endorsement and commitment to these.

## Put the Preparation Plan in Motion

This is where the *doing* of our PDCA gets going in earnest. Some of the actions you'll take are strictly internal and technical; some relate to improvements in administrative controls:

**Synchronize all system clocks.**   Many service handshakes can allow up to 5 minutes or more misalignment of clocks across all elements participating in the service, but this can play havoc with attempts to correlate event logs.

**Frequently profile your systems.**   System profiles help you understand the "normal" types, patterns, and amounts of traffic and load on the systems, as well as capturing key security and performance settings. Whether you use automated change-detection tools or manual inspection, comparing a current profile to a previous one may surface an indicator of an event of interest in progress or shed light on your search to find it, fix it, and remove it.

**Establish channels for outside parties to report information security incidents to you.**   Whether these are other organizations you do routine business with or complete strangers, you make it much easier on your shared community of information security profession-als when you set up an email form or phone number for anyone to report such problems to you. And it should go without saying that somebody in your response team needs to be *paying attention* to that email inbox, or the phone messages, or the forms-generated trou-ble tickets that flow from such a "contact us" page!

**Establish external incident response support relationships.**    Many of the organizations you work with routinely—your cloud-hosting providers, other third-party services, your systems and software vendors and maintainers, even and especially your ISP—can be valuable team-mates when you're in the midst of an incident response. Gather them up into a community of practice *before* the lightning strikes. Get to know each other, and understand the normal lim-its of what you can call upon each other for in the way of support. Clearly identify what you have to warn them about as you're working through a real-time incident response yourself.

**Develop and document CSIRT response procedures.**    These will, of course, be living docu-ments; as your team learns with each incident they respond to, they'll need to update these procedures as they discover what they were well-prepared and equipped to deal with effec-tively, and what caught them by surprise.  Checklist-oriented procedures can be very pow-erful, especially if they're suitable for deployment to CSIRT team members' smartphones or phablets. Don't forget the value of a paper backup copy, along with emergency lighting and flashlights with fresh batteries, for when the lights go out!

**Initiate CSIRT personnel training and certification as required.**    Take the minimum pro-ficiency sets of knowledge, skills, and abilities (often called KSAs in human resources man-agement terms), review the personnel assigned to the CSIRT and your recall rosters, and identify the gaps. Focus training, whether informal on-the-job or formal coursework, that each person needs, and get that training organized, planned, scheduled, and accomplished. Keep CSIRT proficiency qualification files for each team member, note the completion of training activities, and be able to inform management regarding this aspect of your readi-ness for incident response.  (Your organization's HR team may be able to help you with these tasks, and with organizing the training recordkeeping.)

## Are You Prepared?

Maybe your preparation achieves a "ready to respond" state incrementally; maybe you're just not ready for an incident at all, until you've achieved a certain minimum set of veri-fied, in-place knowledge, tools, people, and procedures. Your organization's mission, goals, objectives, and risk posture will shape whether you can get incrementally ready or have to achieve an identifiable readiness posture. Regardless, there are several things you and the CSIRT should do to determine whether they are ready or not:

**Understand your "business normal" as seen by your IT *systems*.**    Establish a routine pat-tern or rhythm for your incident response team members to steep themselves in the day-to-day normal of the business and how people in the business use the IT infrastructure to create value in that normal way. Stay current with internal and external events that you'd reasonably expect would change that normal—the weather-related shutdown of a branch office, or a temporary addition of new federation partners into your extranets. The more each team member knows about how "normal" is reflected in fine-grained system activity, the greater the chance that those team members will sniff out trouble *before* it starts to cause problems. They'll also be better informed and thus more capable of restoring systems to a useful normal state as a result.

While you're at it, don't forget to translate that business normal into fine-tuning of your automated and semiautomated security tools, such as your security incident event management systems (SIEMs), intrusion detection systems (IDS), intrusion prevention systems (IPS), or other tools that drive your alerting and monitoring channels. Business normal may also be reflected in the control and filter settings for access control and identity management systems, as well as for firewall settings and their access control lists. This is especially important if your organization's business activities have seasonal variations.

**Routinely demonstrate and test backup and restore capabilities.** You do not want to be in the middle of an incident response only to find out that you've been taking backup images or files all wrong and that none of them can be reloaded or work right when they are loaded.

**Exercise your alert/recall, notification, escalation, and reporting processes.** At the cost of a few extra phone calls and a bit of time from key leaders and managers, you gain confidence in two critical aspects of your incident response management process. For starters, you demonstrate that the phone tree or the recall and alert processes *work*; this builds confidence that they'll work when you really need them to. A second, add-on bonus is that you get to "table-top" or exercise the protocols you'd want to use had this been an actual information systems security incident.

**Document your incident response procedures, and use these documents as part of training and readiness.** Do not trust human memory or the memory of a well-intended and otherwise effective committee or team! Take the time to write up each major procedure in your incident response management process. Make it an active, living part of the knowledge base your responders will need. Exercise these procedures. Train with them, both as initial training for IT and incident response team members, line, and senior managers, and your general user base as applicable.

 **Real World Scenario**

**Checklist-Targeted Readiness**

Let's borrow another page from the NIST playbook, and consider preparation as a checklist-driven activity. NIST's Incident Handling Checklist is shown in Figure 10.4. Your preparation activities should *build toward* having your incident response teams equipped with such a checklist, tailored to your organization's needs, its systems and infrastructure, and business logic; not only that, your preparations should ensure that you've put the resources, tools, and information in place for the team to use when incidents occur. Then, your last preparation task is to *train* the team members on your newly developed internal, organization-specific procedures.

*(continued)*

(*continued*)

**FIGURE 10.4**     Incident Handling Checklist

| | Action | Completed |
|---|---|---|
| | **Detection and Analysis** | |
| 1. | Determine whether an incident has occurred | |
| 1.1 | Analyze the precursors and indicators | |
| 1.2 | Look for correlating information | |
| 1.3 | Perform research (e.g., search engines, knowledge base) | |
| 1.4 | As soon as the handler believes an incident has occurred, begin documenting the investigation and gathering evidence | |
| 2. | Prioritize handling the incident based on the relevant factors (functional impact, information impact, recoverability effort, etc.) | |
| 3. | Report the incident to the appropriate internal personnel and external organizations | |
| | **Containment, Eradication, and Recovery** | |
| 4. | Acquire, preserve, secure, and document evidence | |
| 5. | Contain the incident | |
| 6. | Eradicate the incident | |
| 6.1 | Identify and mitigate all vulnerabilities that were exploited | |
| 6.2 | Remove malware, inappropriate materials, and other components | |
| 6.3 | If more affected hosts are discovered (e.g., new malware infections), repeat the Detection and Analysis steps (1.1, 1.2) to identify all other affected hosts, then contain (5) and eradicate (6) the incident for them | |
| 7. | Recover from the incident | |
| 7.1 | Return affected systems to an operationally ready state | |
| 7.2 | Confirm that the affected systems are functioning normally | |
| 7.3 | If necessary, implement additional monitoring to look for future related activity | |
| | **Post-Incident Activity** | |
| 8. | Create a follow-up report | |
| 9. | Hold a lessons learned meeting (mandatory for major incidents, optional otherwise) | |

Source: NIST SP800-61 Rev. 2.

Let's apply this checklist to your current organization's incident response capabilities and posture; do this first as a *thought experiment*, by reviewing what you already know or can easily observe about your organization, its IT infrastructure, and how its user support or help desk respond to problems. Let this drive out questions you need to ask, or identify places where you've got strong doubts as to the real readiness posture. Speculate for a moment—do some *hypothesis generation*, as it's formally called—to think up ways to test each of those readiness items you've got doubts about.

Does this lead you to conclude that your organization is ready to respond to an information security incident? Or do you fear it is skating on thin ice?

Taken all at once, that looks like a *lot* of preparation! Yet much of what's needed by your incident response team, if they're going to be well prepared, comes right from the architectural assessments, your vulnerability assessments, and your risk mitigation implementation activities. Other key information comes from your overall approach to managing and maintaining configuration control over your information systems and your IT infrastructure. And you should already be carrying out good "IT hygiene" and safety and security measures, such as clock synchronization, event logging, testing, and so forth. The new effort is in creating the team, defining its tasks, writing them up in procedural form, and then using those procedures as an active part of your ongoing training, readiness, and operational evaluation of your overall information security posture.

# Detection and Analysis

On a typical day, a typical medium-sized organization might see millions of IP packets knocking on its point of presence, most of them in response to legitimate traffic generated inside the organization, solicited by its Web presence, or generated by its external partners, customers, prospective customers, and vendors. Internally, the traffic volume on the company's internetworks and the event loads on servers that support end users at their endpoints could be of comparable volume. Detecting that something is not quite right, and that that something might be part of an attack, is as much art as it is science. Three different factors combine to make this art-and-science difficult and challenging:

- *Multiple, different means of detection*: Many different technologies are in use to flag circumstances that *might* be a security-related incident in the making. Quite often, different technologies measure, assess, characterize, and report their observations at different levels of granularity and accuracy. Sometimes, technologies cannot detect a potential incident, and a human end user or administrator is the first to suspect something's not quite right. Often, however, the first signs of an incident in progress go undetected.

- *Incredibly high volumes of events that might be incidents*: Inline intrusion detection systems might detect and report a million or more events per day as possible intrusion-related events. Filtering approaches, even with machine learning capabilities, can reduce this, while introducing both false positive and false negative alarms into the response team's workload.

- *Deep, specialist knowledge, along with considerable experience is required* for a response team member to be able to make sense of the noise and find the signal (the real events worth investigating) in all of it.

So how does our response team sort through all of that noise and find the few important, urgent, and compelling signals to pay attention to?

## Warning Signs

First, let's define some important terms related to incident detection. Earlier we talked about events of interest—that is, some kind of occurrence or activity that takes place that just might be worth paying closer attention to. Without getting too philosophical about it, events make *something* in our systems change state. The user, with hand on mouse, does not cause an event to take place until they *do* something with the mouse, and it signals the system it's attached to. That movement, click, or thumbwheel roll causes a series of changes in the system. Those changes are *events*. Whether they are *interesting* ones, or not, from a security perspective, is the question!

A *precursor* is a sign, signal, or observable characteristic of the occurrence of an event that in and of itself is not an attack but that might indicate that an attack could happen in the future. Let's look at a few common examples to illustrate this concept:

- Server or other logs that indicate a vulnerability scanner has been being used against a system
- An announcement of a newly found vulnerability by a systems or applications vendor, information security service, or reputable vulnerabilities and exploits reporting service that might relate to your systems or platforms
- Media coverage of events that put your organization's reputation at risk (deservedly or not)
- Email, phone calls, or postal mail threatening attack on your organization, your systems, your staff, or those doing business with you
- Increasingly hostile or angry content in social media postings regarding customer service failures by your company
- Anonymous complaints in employee-facing suggestion boxes, ombudsman communications channels, or even graffiti in the restrooms or lounge areas

Genuine precursors—ones that give you actionable intelligence—are quite rare. They are often akin to the "travel security advisory codes" used by many national governments. They rarely provide enough insight that something specific is about to take place. The best you can do when you see such potential precursors is to pay closer attention to your indicators and warnings systems, perhaps by opening up the filters a bit more. You might also consider altering your security posture in ways that might increase protection for critical systems, perhaps at the cost of reduced throughput due to additional access control processing.

An *indicator* is a sign, signal, or observable characteristic of the occurrence of an event indicating that an information security incident may have occurred or may be occurring right now. Again, a few very common examples will illustrate:

- Network intrusion detectors generate an alert when input buffer overflows might indicate attempts to inject SQL or other script commands into a webpage or database server.
- Antivirus software detects that a device, such as an endpoint or removable media, has a suspected infection on it.
- Systems administrators, or automated search tools, notice filenames containing unusual or unprintable characters.
- Access control systems notice a device attempting to connect, which does not have required software or malware definition updates applied to it.
- A host or an endpoint device does an unplanned restart.

- A new or unmanaged host or endpoint attempts to join the network.

- A host or an endpoint device notices a change to a configuration-controlled element in its baseline configuration.

- An applications platform logs multiple failed login attempts, seemingly from an unfamiliar system or IP address.

- Email systems and administrators notice an increase in the number of bounced, refused, or quarantined emails with suspicious content or ones with unknown addressees.

- Unusual deviations in network traffic flows or systems loading are observed.

One type of indicator worth special attention is called an *indicator of compromise (IOC)*, which is an observable artifact that with high confidence signals that an information system has been compromised or is in the process of being compromised. Such artifacts might include recognizable malware signatures, attempts to access IP addresses or URLs known or suspected to be of hostile or compromising intent, or domain names associated with known or suspected botnet control servers. The information security community is working to standardize the format and structure of IOC information to aid in rapid dissemination and automated use by security systems.

In one respect, the fact that detection is a war of numbers is both a blessing and a curse; in many cases, even the first few low and slow steps in an attack may create dozens or hundreds of indicators, each of which *may*, if you're lucky, contain information that correlates them all into a suspicious pattern. Of course, you're probably dealing with millions of events to correlate, assess, screen, filter, and dig through to find those few needles in that field of haystacks.

## Initial Detection

Initial incident detection is the iterative process by which human members of the incident response team assemble, collate, and analyze any number of indicators (and precursors, if available and applicable), usually with a SIEM tool or data aggregator of some sort, and then come to the conclusion that there is most likely an information security event in progress or one that has recently occurred. This is a human-centric, analytical, thoughtful process; it requires team members to make educated guesses (that is, *generate hypotheses*), test those hypotheses against the indicators and other systems event information, and then reasonably conclude that the alarm ought to be sounded.

That alarm might be best phrased to say that a "probable information security incident" has been detected, along with reporting when it is believed to have first started to occur and whether it is still ongoing.

Ongoing analysis will gather more data, from more systems; run tests, possibly including internal profiling of systems suspected to have been affected or accessed by the attack (if attack it was); and continue to refine its characterization or classification of the incident. At some point, the response team should consult predefined priority lists that help them allocate people and systems resources to continuing this analysis.

Note the dilemma here: paying *too much* attention, too soon, to too many alarms may distract attention, divert resources, and even build in a "Chicken Little" kind of reaction within management and leadership circles. When a security incident actually does occur, everyone may be just too desensitized to care about it. And of course, if you've got your thresholds set too high, you ignore the alarms that your investments in intrusion detection and security systems are trying to bring to your attention. Many of the headline-grabbing data breach incidents in the past 10 years, such as the attack that struck Target stores in 2013, suffered from having this balance between the costs of dealing with too many false rejections (or Type 1 errors) and the risk of missing a few more dangerous false acceptances (or Type 2 errors) set wrong.

## Timeline Analysis

This may seem obvious, but one of the most powerful analytical tools is often overlooked. Timeline analysis reconstructs the sequence of events in order to focus analysis, raise questions, generate insight, and aid in organizing information discovered during the response to the incident. Responders should start building their own reconstructed event timeline or sequence of events, starting from well before the last known good system state, through any precursor or indicator events, and up to and including each new event that occurs. The timeline is different than the response team's log—the log chronicles actions and decisions taken by the response team, directions they've received from management, and key coordination the team has had with external parties.

Some IDS, IPS, or SIEM product systems may contain timeline analysis tools that your teams can use. Digital forensic workbenches usually have excellent timeline analysis capabilities. Even a simple spreadsheet file can be used to record the sequence of events as it reveals itself to the responders, and as they deduce or infer other events that *might* have happened.

This last is a powerful component of timeline analysis. Timeline analysis should focus you on asking, "How did event A cause event B?" Just asking the question may lead you to infer some other event that event A actually caused, with this heretofore undiscovered event being the actual or proximate cause of event B. Making these educated guesses, *and making note of them in your timeline analysis*, is a critical part of trying to figure out what happened.

And without figuring out what happened, your search for all of the elements that might have caused the incident to occur in the first place will be limited to lucky guesswork.

## Notification

Now that the incident response team has determined that an incident probably already occurred or is ongoing, the team must notify managers and leaders in the organization. Each organization should specify how this notification is to be done and who the team contacts to deliver the bad news. In some organizations, this may direct that some types of incidents need immediate notification to all users on the affected systems; other circumstances may dictate that only key departmental or functional managers be advised. In any event, these notification procedures should specify how and when to inform senior leadership and management. (It's a sign of inadequate planning and preparation if the incident responders have to ask, "Who should we call?" in the heat of battle.)

Notification also includes getting local authorities, such as fire or rescue services, or law enforcement agencies, involved in the real-time response to the incident. This should always be coordinated with senior leadership and management, even if the team phones them immediately after following the company's process for calling the fire department.

Senior leadership and management may also have notification and reporting responsibilities of their own, which may include very short time frames in which notification must be given to regulatory authorities, or even the public. The incident response team should not have to do this kind of reporting, but it does owe its own leadership and management the information *they* will need to meet these obligations.

---

### Management Being Seen and Heard—A High-Payoff Incident Response Strategy

Experience with a variety of incidents demonstrates that when the incident has passed from suspected to *real*, and its direct impacts and the disruptions to normal operations are being felt around the organization, it's more than time for management and leadership to be *seen* and *heard* by everyone affected. This is not just a high-touch kind of communications *style* issue. Depending on the scale of the incident and its disruptions, employees can feel much greater levels of stress if they perceive their own jobs have been somehow put at risk. At first, it doesn't matter too much whether management and leadership know what happened or what it will take to recover from the incident. The message at Minute One after the attack should be, "Stay calm. We're still here. We've got work to do to sort this out, but we're going to come through this just fine."

When leadership and management are honest with these reassurances—when they stress "We're still investigating," for example—their calm, confident, and *visible* presence can go a long way to getting the organization, its systems, its processes, *and its people* back on their feet. This applies equally to external partners, customers, prospective customers, and key suppliers, too.

---

As incident containment, eradication, and recovery continue, the CSIRT will have continuing notification responsibilities. Management may ask for their assistance or direct them to reach out directly via webpage updates, updated voice prompt menus on the IT Help Desk contact line, emails, or phone calls to various internal and external stakeholders. Separate voice contact lines may also need to be used to help coordinate activities and keep everyone informed.

## Prioritization

There are several ways to prioritize the team's efforts in responding to an incident. These consider the potential for impact to the organization and its business objectives; whether confidentiality, integrity, or availability of information resources will be impacted; and just how possible it will be to recover from the incident should it continue. Let's take a closer look at these:

- *Functional impact* looks to the nature of the business processes, objectives, or outcomes that are put at risk by the incident. At one end of this spectrum are the mission-critical systems, the failure of which puts the very survival of the organization at risk. At the other end might be routine but necessary business processes, for which there are readily available alternatives or where the impact is otherwise tolerable. A hospital, for example, might consider systems that directly engage with real-time patient care—instrumentation control, laboratory and pharmacy, and surgical robots—as mission-critical (since losing a patient, terminally, because of an IT systems failure can severely jeopardize the hospital's ongoing existence!). On the other hand, the same hospital could consider post-release patient follow-up care management to be less urgent (no one will die *today* if this system fails to work today).

- *Information impact* considers whether the incident risks unauthorized disclosure, exfiltration, corruption, deletion, or other unauthorized changes to information assets, and the relative strategic, tactical, or operational value or sensitivity of that information asset to the organization. The annual holiday party plans, if compromised or deleted, probably have a very low impact to the organization; exfiltration of business proposals being developed with a strategic partner, on the other hand, could have significant impact to both organizations.

- *Recoverability* involves whether the impact of the incident is eliminated or significantly reduced if the incident is promptly and thoroughly contained. A data exfiltration attack that is detected and contained *before* copies of sensitive data have left the facility is a recoverable incident; after the copies of PII, customer credit card, or other sensitive data has left, it is not.

Taken together, these factors help the incident response team advise senior leadership and management on how to deal with the incident. It's worth stressing, again, that senior leadership and management need to make this prioritization decision; the SSCPs on the incident response team must *advise* their leaders by means of the best, most complete, and most current assessment of the incident and its impacts that they can develop. That advice also should address options for containment and eradication of the incident and its effects on the organization.

# Containment and Eradication

These two goals are the next major task areas that the CSIRT needs to take on and accomplish. As you can imagine, the nature of the specific incident or attack in question all but defines the containment and eradication tactics, techniques, and procedures you'll need to bring to bear to keep the mess from spreading and to clean up the mess itself.

More formally, *containment* is the process of identifying the affected or infected systems elements, whether hardware, software, communications systems, or data, and isolating them from the rest of your systems to prevent the disruption-causing agent and the disruption it is causing from affecting the rest of your systems or other systems external to your own. Pay careful attention to the need to not only isolate the *causal agent*, be that malware or an unauthorized user ID with superuser privileges, but also keep the damage from spreading to other systems. As an example, consider a denial of service (DoS) attack that's started on your systems at one local branch office and its subnets and is using malware payloads to spread itself throughout your systems. You may be able to filter any outbound traffic from that system to keep the malware itself from spreading, but until you've thoroughly cleansed all hosts within that local set of subnets, each of *them* could be suborned into launching DoS attacks on other hosts inside your system or out on the Internet.

Some typical containment tactics might include:

- Logically or physically disconnecting systems from the network or network segments from the rest of the infrastructure
- Disconnecting key servers (logically or physically), such as domain name system (DNS), dynamic host configuration protocol (DHCP), or access control systems
- Disconnecting your internal networks from your ISP at *all* points of presence
- Disabling Wi-Fi or other wireless and remote login and access
- Disabling outgoing and incoming connections to known services, applications, platforms, sites, or services
- Disabling outgoing and incoming connections to *all* external services, services, applications, platforms, sites, or services
- Disconnecting from any extranets or VPNs
- Disconnecting some or all external partners and user domains from any federated access to your systems
- Disabling internal users, processes, or applications, either in functional or logical groups or by physical or network locations

A familiar term should come to mind as you read this list: *quarantine*. In general, that's what containment is all about. Suspect elements of your system are *quarantined* off from the rest of the system, which certainly can prevent damage from spreading. It also can isolate a suspected causal agent, allowing you a somewhat safer environment in which to examine it, perhaps even identify it, and track down all of its pieces and parts. As a result, containment and eradication often blur into each other as interrelated tasks rather than remain as distinctly different phases of activity.

This gives us another term worthy of a definition: a *causal agent* is a software process, data object, hardware element, human-performed procedure, or any combination of those that perform the actions on the targeted systems that constitute the incident, attack, or disruption. Malware payloads, their control and parameter files, and their carriers are examples of causal agents. Bogus user IDs, hardware sniffer devices, or systems on your network that have already been suborned by an attacker are examples of causal agents. As you might suspect, the more sophisticated APT kill chains may use multiple methods to get into your systems and in doing so leave multiple bits of stuff behind to help them achieve their objectives each time they come on in.

*Eradication* is the process of identifying every instance of the causal agent and its associated files, executables, etc. from all elements of your system. For example, a malware infection would require you to thoroughly scrub every CPU's memory, as well as all file storage systems (local and in the clouds), to ensure you'd found and removed all copies of the malware and any associated files, data, or code fragments. You'd also have to do this for all backup media for all of those systems in order to ensure you'd looked everywhere, removed the malware and its components, and clobbered or zeroized the space they were occupying in whatever storage media you found them on. Depending on the nature of the causal agent, the incident, and the storage technologies involved, you may need to do a full low-level reformat of the media and completely initialize its directory structures to ensure that eradication has been successfully completed.

Eradication should result in a formal declaration that the system, a segment or subsystem, or a particular host, server, or communications device has been inspected and verified to be free from any remnants of the causal agent. This declaration is the signal that recovery of that element or subsystem can begin.

It's beyond the scope of the SSCP exam to get into the many different techniques your incident response team may need to use as part of containment and eradication—quite frankly, there are just far too many potential causal agents out there in the wild, and more are being created daily. It's important to have a working sense of how detection and identification provided you the starting point for your containment, and then your eradication, of the threat.

## Evidence Gathering, Preservation, and Use

During all stages of an incident, responders need to be gathering information about the status, state, and health of all systems, particularly those affected by the attack. They need to be correlating event log files from many different elements of their IT infrastructure, while at the same time constructing their own timeline of the event. Incident response teams are expected to figure out what happened, take steps to keep the damage from spreading, remove the cause(s) of the incident, and restore systems to normal use as quickly as they can.

There's a real danger that the incident response team can spread itself too thin if the same group of people are containing and eradicating the threat, while at the same time trying to gather evidence, preserve it, and examine it for possible clues. Management and leadership need to be aware of this conflict. They are the ones who can allocate more resources, either during preparation and planning, incident response, or both, to provide a digital forensics capability.

As in all things, a balance needs to be struck, and response team leaders need to be sensitive to these different needs as they develop and maintain their team's *battle rhythm* in working through the incident.

## Constant Monitoring

From the first moment that the responders believe that an incident has occurred or is ongoing, the team needs to sharpen their gaze at the various monitoring tools that are already in place, watching over the organization's IT infrastructure. The incident itself may be starting to cause disruptions to the normal state of the infrastructure and systems; containment and eradication responses will no doubt further disrupt operations. All of that aside, a new monitoring priority and question now needs to occupy center stage for the response team's attention: are their chosen containment, eradication, and (later on) restoration efforts working properly?

On the one hand, the team should be actively predicting the most likely outcomes of each step they are about to take *before* they take it. This look-ahead should also be suggesting additional alarm conditions or signs of trouble that might indicate that the chosen step is *not* working correctly or in fact is adding to the impact the incident is causing. Training and experience with each tool and tactic is vital, as this gives the team the depth of specialist knowledge to draw on as they assess the situation, choose among possible actions to take, and then perform that action as part of their overall response.

The incident response team is, first and foremost, supposed to be *managing* their responses to the incident. Without well-informed predictions of the results of a selected action, the team is not managing the incident; they're not even *experimenting*, which is how we test such predictions as part of confirming our logic and reasoning. Without informed guesswork and thoughtful consideration of alternatives, the team is being out-thought by its adversaries; the attackers are still managing and directing the incident, and defense is trapped into reacting as they call the shots.

# Recovery: Getting Back to Business

*Recovery* is the process by which the organization's IT infrastructure, applications, data, and workflows are reestablished and declared operational. In an ideal world, recovery starts when the eradication phase is complete, and the hardware, networks, and other systems elements are declared safe to restore to their required normal state. The ideal recovery process brings all elements of the system back to the moment in time just before the incident started to inflict damage or disruption to your systems. When recovery is complete, end users should be able to log back in and start working again, just as if they'd last logged off at the end of a normal set of work-related tasks.

It's important to stress that every step of a recovery process must be *validated* as correctly performed and complete. This may need nothing more than using some simple tools to check status, state, and health information, or using preselected test suites of software and procedures to determine whether the system or element in question is behaving as it should be. It's also worth noting that the more complex a system is, the more it may need to have a specific order in which subsystems, elements, and servers are reinitialized as part of an overall recovery and restart process.

With that in mind, let's look at this step by step, in general terms:

**Eradication complete.**   Ideally, this is a formal declaration by the CSIRT that the systems elements in question have been verified to be free of any instances of the causal agent (malware, illicit user IDs, corrupted or falsified data, etc.).

**Restore from bare metal to working OS.**   Servers, hosts, endpoints, and many network devices should be reset to a known good set of initial software, firmware, and control parameters. In many cases, the IT department has made standard image sets that they use to do a full initial load of new hardware of the same type. This should include setting up systems or device administrator identities, passwords, or other access control parameters. At the end of this task, the device meets your organization's security and operational policy requirements and can now have applications, data, and end users restored to it.

**Ensure all OS updates and patches are installed correctly...**   ...if any have been released for the versions of software installed by your distribution kits or pristine system image copies.

**Restore applications as well as links to applications platforms and servers on your network.** Many endpoint devices in your systems will need locally installed applications, such as email clients, productivity tools, or even multifactor access control tools, as part of normal operations. These will need to be reinstalled from pristine distribution kits if they were not in the standard image used to reload the OS. This set of steps also includes reloading the connections to servers, services, and applications platforms on your organization's networks (including extranets). This step should also verify that all updates and patches to applications have been installed correctly.

**Restore access to resources via federated access controls and resources beyond your security perimeter out on the Internet.**   This step may require coordination with these external resource operators, particularly if your containment activities had to temporarily disable such access.

At this point, the systems and infrastructure are ready for normal operations. Aren't they?

# Data Recovery

Remember that the IT systems and the information architecture exist because the organization's business logic needs to gather, create, make use of, and produce information to support decisions and action. Restoring the data plane of the total IT architecture is the next step that must be taken before declaring the system ready for business again.

---

**Backups: They Exist Only Because We Plan for Business Continuity**

When you're in the midst of responding to an information security incident, you do *not* want to discover that you have no backups of the business-critical software systems, databases, or other information resources. Yes, the CSIRT is the *primary customer* of these backups, but somebody else had to have planned and specified how to generate them, how often to make updated backups, and how they should be stored, kept safe, and yet available when urgently needed.

*Business continuity planning* is the broad functional area that should address these needs, and we'll cover it more in Chapter 11. As for the CSIRT, please note that your own *preparation* phase should have either found where the backups are kept and how to know which ones to use...or discovered that nobody's actually making any backups in the first place!

In most cases, incident recovery will include restoring databases and storage systems *content* to the last known good configuration. This requires, of course, that the organization has a routine process in place for making backups of all of its operational data. Those backups might be

- Complete copies of every data item in every record in every database and file.
- Incremental or partial copies, which copy a subset of records or files on a regular basis
- Differential, update, or change copies, which consist of records, fields, or files changed since a particular time
- Transaction logs, which are chronologically ordered sets of input data

Restoring all databases and file systems to their "ready for business as usual" state may take the combined efforts of the incident response team, database administrators, application support programmers, and others in the IT department. Key end users may also need to be part of this process, particularly as they are probably best suited to verifying that the systems *and* the data are all back to normal.

For example, a small wholesale distributor might use a backup strategy that makes a full copy of its databases once per week, and then a differential backup at the end of every business day. Individual transactions (reflecting customer orders, payments to vendors, inventory changes, etc.) would be reflected in the transaction logs kept for specific applications or by end users. In the event that the firm's database has been corrupted by an attacker (or a serious systems malfunction), it would need to restore the last complete backup copy, then apply the daily differential backups for each day since that backup copy had been made. Finally, the firm would have to step through each transaction again, either using built-in applications functions that recover transactions from saved log files or by hand.

*Now*, that distributor is ready to start working on *new* transactions, reflecting *new* business. Its CSIRT's response to the incident is over, and it moves on to the post-incident activities we'll look at in just a moment.

## Post-Recovery: Notification and Monitoring

One of the last tasks that the incident response team has is to ensure that end users, functional managers, and senior leaders and managers in the organization know that the recovery operations are now complete. This notice serves several important purposes:

- *Back in business.* This notice gives the green light to the organization to get back into normal business operations. Each department or functional division of the organization may have a different approach to this, based on its business logic and processes. This is particularly true as to how each department addresses any work lost during the overall downtime.

- *Proceed with caution.* Users and their managers should be extra vigilant as they start to use the systems, applications, and data once again. They may wish to start with load-balancing constraints in place so that processes can be closely monitored as they start up slowly and then throttle up to the normal pace of business.

- *Get the word out.* Senior leaders and managers should help make sure that key external stakeholders, partners, and others are properly informed about the successful recovery operation. They may also need to meet legal and regulatory obligations, and keep government officials, shareholders or investors, customers, and the general public properly informed. This is also a great opportunity for leadership and management, from the top down to the first-rung supervisors, to help ensure that every member of the team can be confident in the post-recovery state of the organization.

At this point, the incident response team's real-time sense of urgency can relax; they've met the challenges of this latest information security incident to confront their organization. Now it's time to take a deep breath, relax, and *capture their lessons learned*.

# Post-Incident Activities

Before you as team chief send your responder crews home for some rest, you need to get them to look at their notes and the team log, and make some quick memory-jogging notes about anything that happened that's not immediately obvious in those logs. Then (perhaps the next morning), the team should walk through a formal debrief process, using their logs and their event timeline as a framework. This debrief needs to capture, as completely as possible, the immediate memory of the experiences the team has just shared.

The process of *appreciative inquiry* can be a great help in such a team debrief. Appreciative inquiry starts from the assumption that what happened was good and useful, even if it didn't quite fit what was needed; this can lead the team to a blame-free examination of why or how the chosen procedures didn't suit the situation as best as they could have. Appreciative inquiry sets the stage for learning from experience by valuing that experience and, in doing so, reassuring those on the team that they played valued roles in the incident recovery process.

Good questions can and should be used to drive this debriefing process:

- Exactly what happened, and when?
- How well did we observe each event and capture information about it?
- Did we have documented procedures for such an event? If so, were they used? Did they help?
- What information did we need sooner than we actually discovered or received it?
- What did we do that actually hindered our recovery efforts? What mistakes did we make? How could we have done such steps more effectively?
- What can leadership, management, and staff do differently, both *before* the next incident and *during* the next incident, to make containment and recovery work more effectively?
- How could our information sharing with other organizations be improved?
- What precursors and indicators did we miss, or do we still not have insight about, that might have made a key difference to our recovery process?
- What other tools, resources, or talent and experience do we need to help us better detect, analyze, and respond to such incidents in the future?

This debriefing process may take several iterations as the team discovers that they need to learn more from the data collected from the systems during the incident and their response actions. They may also need to consult with others, such as system developers, key end users, or other partners, to more fully appreciate just what *did* happen and how well the team and the organization responded to it.

## Learning the Lessons

The debriefing process will no doubt surface a number of actions, suggestions, and areas for further exploration and analysis. All of these need to be captured in a manageable form, which the team leader, IT director, chief information security officer, or others in leadership and management can use to manage and direct the learning process that's been started by the debrief. In general, you'll see several broad types or categories of action items flowing out from the start of this "lessons learned" process:

- Immediate updates to administrative, technical, and physical controls, including the response team's procedures
- Prompt updates to procedures and content for internal and external communication and coordination during and after an incident response
- Prompt development, installation, and use of new or modified controls and their corresponding procedures
- Updated training and education of response team members, IT and other support staff, managers, leaders, and the overall workforce
- Longer-term, additional investment in information security risk mitigation and management approaches

The question is often asked: did we really *learn* lessons from such an experience, or did we just write them down and put them in the files for later? That set of action item categories bears a striking resemblance to how software, systems, or product developers manage successive builds or versions of their own products. They *plan* what should be in each of the next several releases or versions; they task members of their teams to develop those incremental changes, write them, test, and validate them, and then the team integrates them together into the next release.

Make those observations you and your team wrote down be more than just observations—prioritize them, plan and schedule their resolution, and assign resources and people to update systems, controls, procedures, and training as required to get the *learning* from those lessons reflected in your new and improved ways of doing incident response.

## Support Ongoing Forensics Investigations

The incident responders may be done at this point, but other investigations may still be ongoing. Criminal or civil proceedings may mean that digital discovery motions have been served on the organization, or it's anticipated that they'll be served very soon. Ongoing internal investigations may be examining suspicious or careless behavior on the part of one or more employees, which could lead to disciplinary actions or even dismissal for cause. Most employers will not take such actions unless they are reasonably certain that they've got the evidence to back up such accusations, should the employee seek redress via a labor relations tribunal or the courts. In addition, the nature of the incident may bring with it still more regulatory or legal burdens that require the organization to thoroughly document exactly what happened; what information was compromised, disclosed, or corrupted; and whether any business decisions and actions were taken unadvisedly based on such loss or impact to decision support data.

---

### Preserve the Chain of Custody!

We've got to beat the drum loudly about this: *any* post-incident investigation, for any purpose, will *fail* if the investigators cannot show a solid chain of custody for each piece of evidence they build their case with!

From pre-incident preparation and planning through the heat of battle of incident response itself, your incident response team has to do its utmost to preserve the incident scene, keep good records and logs, catalog evidence, protect that evidence, and document every instance of someone doing something with or to that evidence.

Ideally, your organization will have dedicated, trained personnel who can ensure that the chain of custody is properly established and maintained. As the on-scene SSCP, you must work with them to protect the value of any subsequent investigation.

If you're interested, you might also consider seeking additional training and earning certifications as a computer examiner or digital forensics technician.

---

# Information and Evidence Retention

In almost any jurisdiction, there are many different and sometimes conflicting rules, regulations, laws, and expectations regarding how long information pertaining to such an incident must be retained. There are even laws and regulations that set maximum retention periods, and companies and individuals can cause themselves *more* legal troubles if they don't dispose of information when required to do so. When any aspect of an incident becomes a matter for the courts to consider, these retention timelines can change yet again.

As an SSCP, your role in the midst of all of this may be as simple as ensuring that somebody in the organization produces a records and information retention schedule and that this schedule states how long data collected during an information security incident and response activity must be retained.

You'll also need to be aware that storage and retention of evidence requires more stringent controls than the storage and retention of other forms of business records, including data gathered or produced during an incident response. Any of that information that has been deemed evidence to a legal proceeding of any kind will probably require a separate storage and accountability process. Most digital evidence is a *copy* of the original—the contents of a system's RAM when it was executing malware has to be read out and written onto some kind of systems image media, and that disk image is what must be kept free from harm and under positive accountability. The *chain of custody* is the sequence of each step taken to originally gather the evidence, record or copy it, put it into storage, and then control and keep account of persons or processes who accessed that evidence; it further has to account for anything that was done to the evidence. Gaps in this chain of custody suggest that someone had the opportunity to tamper with the evidence, at which point the evidence is worthless.

You probably won't encounter questions on the SSCP exam as to the details of records retention, evidence protection and its chain of custody, and the many different laws, regulations, and standards that apply to all of this. You may very well encounter these topics on the job, and the more you know about the nature of these requirements, the better you'll be able to serve your organization's overall information security needs.

# Information Sharing with the Larger IT Security Community

It's good practice to be an established, respected, and trusted member of your local area information security communities of practice, as well as of larger communities. Once you're into the post-event phase, it's a good time to share information about the incident, your responses to it, and the residual damage or actions, if any, that you're facing. (Such sharing must of course be tempered by your organization's information security classification guidelines!) Those communities—much like your fellow (ISC)² members—are there to help each other learn from experiences such as you and your team have just been through. Share the wealth, as well as the pain, of that learning with them.

# Summary

From preparation through response and to post-response wrap-up, organizations need to invest in, create, and maintain their capabilities to respond to information systems security incidents. It's a vital part of getting back into business and may be the difference between *being* in business after the incident or allowing the incident to put you *out* of business completely. Prompt detection, identification, and characterization of an incident are the first major steps; these inform the incident response team, who (after notifying their senior leadership and management) begin the tasks of containment and eradication of the damage-causing agent, malware, or illicit identities. Once those are thoroughly eradicated, the team begins the process of restoring systems and data, finally notifying managers and users that all's well, and the systems are back online and ready for business as usual.

But it's not just *our* systems and *our* end users and business needs anymore, is it? Increasingly, our businesses and organizations become parts of larger digital communities via extranets, federated access, and other collaboration arrangements. Thus, our response to information security incidents takes on both greater urgency and a greater burden of coordination and cooperation. We may have done everything right in our own systems, and yet still, our systems were struck down, perhaps by a zero day exploit, and corrupted; that's our loss. If we then fail to promptly notify our federated partners, or organizations who share *their* information resources with us via their own extranets, we can be liable for damages *they* suffer as well.

Being part of an incident response team is perhaps the closest we in the IT world can come to being part of a hospital emergency room's urgent care team. The alarms start going off; systems start behaving abnormally or crash completely. Normal work starts to slow down or halt completely, either directly because of the incident or because of the containment, eradication, and recovery efforts your team is taking. Senior leaders and managers need to know, *now*, what's going on, and what your best prognosis is as to the possible damage, the extent of the downtime, and what else it might take to get things back to normal. It's demanding and challenging, and it can be quite stressful; it also demands broad and deep specialist knowledge and experience from the SSCPs and others who work on that team.

# Exam Essentials

**Describe the information security incident lifecycle.**   There are many published lifecycle models and frameworks, which differ in some of their details. Conceptually, however, they all agree on the following major phases of activity. Preparation comes first, because this is where the business or organization first starts to plan to respond to such incidents. Key needs for equipment, information, communications, and skills are identified, and manageable plans are put in motion to attain them and build up the team. The actual response cycle starts with detecting the indicators or precursors of such an incident, whether it happened earlier or is just now occurring. Analysis and characterization are necessary to determine the nature and extent of the incident and to guide the next set of activities. Containment, which attempts to restrict or quarantine the damage and its cause to a subset of the overall systems, comes next, followed by eradication or removal of the causal agent, malware, illicit identity, or other elements that are the cause of the incident and its related damage. Once eradication is complete, recovery can begin. Recovery operations restore systems to their pre-incident, known good state, usually by zeroizing or clobbering the systems and reloading them from known good backup images. Data restoration comes next, including connectivity to off-board or third-party data systems and applications platforms. Finally, the restored systems are turned back over to operational users and managers, and the incident response team begins post-incident analysis, documenting lessons learned in the experience and finishing any longer-term data analysis tasks.

**Explain how the incident response team and process support digital forensics investigations.** Digital forensics investigations are conducted to gather and assess digital evidence in support of answering legal, regulatory, or contractual questions of guilt, fault, liability, or innocence. Most such questions require that evidence gathered and used to answer such questions be subject to chain of custody standards, which dictate how access to the evidence is controlled and accounted for. In an information security incident, much of the same digital information that the incident response team needs to analyze and understand so that they can appropriately identify, contain, and eradicate whatever caused the incident may also end up being needed as evidence by forensics examiners. The procedures used by the incident responders should try to respect the needs of potential follow-on forensics investigations, wherever possible, so that problem-solving information still meets chain of custody and other evidentiary standards for use in courts of law. This balance can be difficult to maintain in the immediacy of responding to an incident. Proper preparation can reduce the chance that key information will become unusable as evidence.

**Understand the relationship between incident response, business continuity, and disaster recovery planning.** A disaster is an incident that causes major damage to property, business information, and quite possibly injures or kills people. A disaster may be one very extensive incident or a whole series of smaller events, which, taken together, constitute an existence-threatening stress to the organization. The extensiveness of this damage can be such that the organization cannot recover quickly, if at all, or that such recovery will take significant reinvestment into systems, facilities, relationships with other organizations, and people. Disaster recovery plans are ways of preparing to cope with such significant levels of disruption. Business continuity, by contrast, is the general term for plans that address how to continue to operate in as normal a fashion as possible despite the occurrence of one or more disruptions. Such plans can address alternative processing capabilities and locations, partnering arrangements, and financial arrangements necessary to keep the payroll flowing while operational income is disrupted. Business continuity can be interrupted by one incident or a series of them. Incident response narrows the focus down to a single incident and provides detailed and systematic instruction as to how to detect, characterize, and respond to an incident to contain or minimize damage; such response plans then outline how to restore systems and processes to let business operations operate again as normal.

**Describe some of the key elements of incident response preparation.**   Preparation usually starts with those possible incidents identified by the risk management process, and documented in the business impact analysis (BIA) as being of highest priority or concern to senior leadership and management. These are used to identify a key set of information resources, tools, systems, skills, and talent needed to respond effectively. The incident response team's structure, roles, and responsibilities should be defined, and the team established, whether as an on-call resource, an ongoing security operations watch team, or some other structure best suited to the organization's business logic and security needs. The team should then ensure that system profiles and other information be routinely gathered and updated so that the team understands the normal behavior of the IT systems and infrastructure when servicing routine business loads and demands. Testing and validation of backup and restore capabilities, and team exercises, should also be part of becoming and staying well prepared for information security incidents when (not if) they occur.

**Explain the challenges of precursors and indicators in incident detection.**   An incident is a series of one or more events, the cumulative effect of which is a potential or real violation of the information security needs of the organization. As an event occurs, it makes something change—it changes the contents of a storage system or location, triggers another event or blocks a preplanned trigger, etc. These outcomes of an event may be either precursors or indicators. Precursors are signals that a security event may happen some indeterminate time later but that such an event is not happening right now. Indicators signal that a security event is taking place now. The problem is one of sheer volume; even a small SOHO system might see hundreds of thousands of events each working day, some of which might be legitimate precursors or indicators. Intrusion detection systems, firewalls, and access control systems generate many more signals, but by themselves, these systems cannot usually determine whether the event in question was legitimate and authorized or might be part of a security incident. Filters and logical controls can limit these false positive alarms, but if set too high, alarms that should demand additional investigation are never reported to security analysts. This sense of false negative (the absence of alarms) may not reflect reality. Conversely, set the filters too low, and your analysts can spend far too much time on fruitless investigation of the false positives.

**Explain why containment and eradication often overlap as activities.**   As part of incident response, containment needs to keep the damage-causing agent, activity, process, or data from spreading to other elements of the system and causing further damage. Containment should also prevent this agent (malware, for example) from leaving your systems and getting back out onto the Internet where it could be part of an attack on another organization's systems. Many containment techniques, such as antimalware quarantine operations, logically or physically move the suspected malware to separate storage areas that are not accessible by normal user processes. This simultaneously removes them from the infected system and prevents their spread to other systems.

**Describe the legal and ethical obligations organizations must address when responding to information security incidents.**   The first set of such obligations come under due diligence and due care responsibilities to shareholders, stakeholders, employees, and the larger society. The organization must protect assets placed in its care for its business use. It must also take reasonable and prudent steps to prevent damage to its own assets or systems from spreading to other systems and causing damages to them in the process. Legally and ethically, organizations must keep stakeholders, investors, employees, and society informed when such information security incidents occur; failure to meet such notification burdens can result in fines, criminal prosecution, loss of contracts, or damage to the organization's reputation for reliability and trustworthiness. Such incidents may also raise questions of guilt, culpability, responsibility, and liability, and these may lead to digital forensic investigations. Such investigations usually need information that meets stringent rules of evidence, including a chain of custody that precludes someone from tampering with the evidence.

**Describe the key steps in the recovery phase of responding to an information security incident.**   Once the incident response team is confident that the damage-causing agents have been eradicated from the systems, servers, hosts, and communications and network elements, those systems need to be restored to their normal hardware, software, data, and connectivity states needed for routine business operations. This can involve complete reloads or rebuilds of their operating systems, reinstallation of applications, and restoring of access control and identity management information so that each device's normal subjects (users or processes) can function. The team then can ensure that databases, file systems, and other storage elements have their content fully restored. Data recovery may also need to include re-execution of transactions lost between the time of the last data system backup (complete, incremental, differential, or special) and the impact of the incident itself. At that point, end users can be notified that the system is back up and available for normal use.

**Describe the key steps in the post-incident phase of incident response.**   After the systems have been restored to normal operations, the incident response team in effect stands down from "emergency response" mode, but it's not through with this incident yet. As soon as possible after the incident is over, the team should debrief thoroughly to capture observations and insights that team members made during the incident or as a result of their response to it. An appreciative inquiry process is recommended, as this will encourage more open dialogue and avoid perceptions of finger-pointing. This should generate a list of actions to take that update procedures and risk mitigation controls, and may lead to additional or changed training and education for the team, users, or managers and leaders. Other actions may take considerable investment in resources or time in order to realize improvements in the incident prevention, detection, response, and recovery processes.

**Explain the benefits of doing exercises, drills, and testing of incident response plans and procedures.**   Exercises, drills, and testing of incident response plans and procedures can help the organization in several ways. First, they can verify the technical completeness and correctness of the plans and procedure *before* attempting to use them in response to an actual incident. Second, they give all those involved in incident response the chance to strengthen their skills and knowledge via practice and evaluation; this supports in-classroom or self-paced training. Third, it can enhance team morale as it focuses on creating unity of effort. By instilling a sense of confident competence, the practice effect of such exercises, drills, and testing can prepare the team and the organization to better cope with the stress of real incidents.

**Describe the role of monitoring systems during incident response.** Monitoring of IT infrastructures is performed by a combination of automated data-generating tools (such as event loggers), data gathering and correlation systems (such as security information and event monitoring systems, or dashboards of any kind), and the attentive engagement of IT operations and incident response team members to what these systems are attempting to alert them to. Each step of the incident response cycle depends heavily on monitoring, by systems and by people, to notice out-of-tolerance conditions, abnormalities, or anomalies; to understand what more detailed data about such events is suggesting; and to validate that their efforts at containment, eradication, and recovery have been successfully completed. Continued monitoring well after the incident response is over will contribute to the assurance that the incident is safely in the past.

**Explain the use of the kill chain concept in information security incident response.** Attacks on information systems by advanced persistent threat (APT) actors almost invariably involve sequences of steps to support the many phases of such attacks, such as reconnaissance, entry, establishing command and control, and achieving the outcomes desired by the threat actor. This chain of events, called a kill chain, can be quite complex and take months, or even a year or more, to run through to completion. Many of its steps are *low and slow*, small-scale intrusions or attacks that are designed to not attract too much attention or set off too many alarms. Systems defenders who can detect and defend against any step in the kill chain may deter or delay other steps in the chain to the point where the attacker gives up and chooses a less well-defended target instead. Thus, the white hat defenders don't need to be successful against major attacks every day but against the low and slow small steps that may be part of such attacks.

**Describe the use of logs in responding to information security incidents.** Almost every element of modern IT infrastructures, systems, and applications can generate event log files that can record the time-tagged occurrence of events that incident responders may need to learn about. Changes in access control settings, changes in the status or content of an information resource, the loading and execution of tasks or process threads, or the creation of a user ID and elevation of its privileges are but a few of thousands of such log file events responders need to know about. Correlating log files from different systems elements can help produce or enrich an incident timeline, which is built by the incident response team as an analysis tool and as a description of what happened step by step as the incident unfolded. To correlate log files, they must use a common time of reference; it's therefore important to synchronize all system clocks, preferably to a network time standard. Different logs quite frequently record different kinds of events, to different levels of granularity and accuracy; thus, the team can find it challenging to find all of the observable events, across multiple logs, which are actually signaling a specific event in the incident itself. This is an important way to identify cause and effect relationships between events that take place during the incident.

**Explain why and how the incident response team communicates and engages with organizational management and leadership.** The incident response team acts as a single point of contact or focus regarding the response to an ongoing information security incident. It is important that the team not be overwhelmed by calls from every end user, or need to communicate with each of them individually. The team may also need senior organizational leadership and management's authority to call in additional personnel or emergency responders, or to activate other contingency plans. Management and leadership also have the burden to notify regulators, partners, legal authorities, customers, and the public. During the preparation phase, decisions should be made and procedures developed that dictate how the team reaches out to which specific leaders and managers in the organization, to share what kind of information. These procedures should also provide ways for the team to ask leadership for key decisions, as well as seek guidance from them in dealing with the incident if they need to prioritize some efforts over others. This communication can be face to face or by phone, email, or any means available, as specified in procedures.

# Review Questions

1. You're part of the CSIRT for your organization; during an incident, you take a call from a rather upset production manager who demands you put their systems back online right away. You explain that the team hasn't finished containment activities yet. He insists that their systems were working fine until you pulled the connections to everything and that production activities could continue while you're doing that. Which statement or statements would best support you in your reply? (Choose all that apply.)

    A. We could assume that your systems were not contaminated by the attack, and let you run on them. We'd take them down and inspect them later, when you're not using them.

    B. We cannot run the risk that whatever caused the attack isn't dormant in your systems and that it wouldn't spread to our other systems or back out onto the Internet if we did that.

    C. We have to comply with our policies that tell us how to handle incidents like this, and so, we can't do that.

    D. Yours are not the only systems affected by this attack; we've had to shut down most of our IT operations to make sure that our critical data and systems are protected.

2. You're the only IT person at a small tool and die machine shop, which uses a LAN and cloud-hosted platforms to run the business on. Your boss is not worried about the business being the target of a cyberattack and doesn't want you to spend time preparing the company to respond to such an incident. What would you advise your boss to consider? (Choose all that apply.)

    A. Since we don't handle consumer-level payment cards, and we don't have any proprietary information, we probably don't have to worry about being a target.

    B. We do share an extranet connection with key customers and suppliers, and an attack on our systems could lead to an attack on theirs; whether we'd be liable for the damages or not, it could cost us our relationships with those companies.

    C. Our cloud systems hosting company provides most of our security, and as long as we keep our systems on the factory floor and the workstations our staff use properly updated, we should be okay.

    D. Since we've not really done even a basic vulnerabilities assessment, we don't know what risks we could be facing. Let's do that much at least, and let that tell us what the next step should be. Soon.

3. As an SSCP, you're a CERT team member at your company. At a team meeting, some of the team members seem confused as to whether they have a role in disaster recovery or business continuity. How would you answer their question? (Choose all that apply.)

    A. Since even a disaster starts with an incident, and we're the first responders, we quickly have to figure out how disruptive the incident could be; the more disruptive, the greater the impact on our ability to keep doing business. We don't execute those other plans, but we do have to call our bosses and let them know what we think. They decide whether to activate those other plans.

**B.** Since all incidents have the potential for disrupting business operations, the BCP should cover everything and provide us the framework and scope to respond within. It also covers the DRP.

**C.** Those other plans focus primarily on people issues, facilities, and cash flow kinds of problems, and those don't concern the CERT.

**D.** Those other plans mostly handle legal, regulatory, and shareholder notification requirements, so we're not involved with those.

4. What role, if any, does an incident response team play in supporting any subsequent forensics investigation? (Choose all that apply.)

**A.** None. The investigators have their own procedures to follow, and it's best if the incident response team just cooperate but stay out of their way.

**B.** Since any information security incident might lead to a follow-on forensics investigation, the team needs to make sure that any of the data they collect, or systems they restore or rebuild, are first preserved and cataloged to meet chain-of-custody requirements as evidence. Thus, the responders also need to be trained and certified as investigators.

**C.** As the first responders, the team should take steps to control the scene of the incident, and keep good logs or records of the state of systems and information throughout their response activities. These records need to be retained in case there is a later investigation.

**D.** Management needs to make sure that the procedures used by the response team will preserve the incident scene and information gathered during the incident response in ways that will meet rules of evidence; if that cannot be done without interfering with prompt incident response and recovery, management has to take responsibility for that risk.

5. Which of the following sets of information would not be useful to a CSIRT during an incident response? (Choose all that apply.)

**A.** Contracts with service providers, systems vendors, or suppliers

**B.** Information systems baseline information

**C.** Information technology baseline information

**D.** IT hardware maintenance manuals

6. Which of the following information about networks and infrastructures should be readily available for information systems security incident responders to consult during an incident response? (Choose all that apply.)

**A.** Networks and systems designs showing data, control, and management planes

**B.** OSI reference model design descriptions of networks, systems, and platforms

**C.** Organization charts and staff directories, including contact information

**D.** Systems requirements documentation

**7.**  The CSIRT team members are discussing incident detection. They seem convinced that it's almost impossible to detect an information security incident until it's already started to disrupt business operations. They're trying to find actions they can take now to help deal with this. They ask your opinion. Which of the following statements would you not use as you reply? (Choose all that apply.)

**A.**  Most incident precursors are so general that they provide broad warning, but nothing specific you can act on.

**B.**  We miss the most important incident precursors because we've set our IDS alarm thresholds too low.

**C.**  Many indicators of a possible attack can also be indicators of routine and legitimate business activities or network traffic; since we cannot investigate them all, we just have to hope that the first damage an attack causes is small enough not to hurt badly, but visible enough that we'll see it in time to react.

**D.**  Actually, this is because we've designed our networks wrong. We can fix this, but it will take time, money, and effort.

**8.**  Which statement about precursors and indicators is most correct?

**A.**  Precursors are events that prepare the way for an attack, such as an intrusion, to take place.

**B.**  Precursors are the observable signals from an event, which may suggest that an information systems security event may happen later.

**C.**  Indicators are the observable signals from an event, which may suggest that an information systems security event may happen later.

**D.**  Indicators are events that are part of an information security incident kill chain; warnings are the observable effects that we can detect, that tell us of the occurrence of the indicator.

**9.**  Why is escalation part of the detection and analysis phase of an incident response?

**A.**  It will require additional resources, such as IT staff, to begin carrying out the next phases of the response plan, and this would require management approval and action.

**B.**  Management and leadership need to know that an information security incident may have occurred and that investigation continues. Depending on the nature of the incident as understood thus far, management may need to take additional action.

**C.**  Most organizations are unwilling to delegate authority to an incident response team leader and thus need to control every action in order to exercise due diligence.

**D.**  This is required by NIST SP800-61 Rev. 2 and in regulations that apply to the particular business or organization.

**10.**  What are some of the key tasks to consider as part of containment of an information security incident? (Choose all that apply.)

**A.**  Suspending processes related to applications platforms

**B.**  Disabling network traffic at the points of presence with ISPs

**C.**  Disabling connections to servers or hosts suspected of having been attacked

**D.**  Notifying external users of extranet or other shared resources and requesting that they suspend activities

11. Which statements about containment and eradication are most correct?

   **A.** Containment and eradication are separate and distinct tasks; once containment is complete, the incident response team moves on to eradication of the causal agent(s).

   **B.** Containment and eradication usually involve the same tools and procedures, and so they often are performed simultaneously.

   **C.** Malware quarantine operations are an example of containment and eradication achieved with the same task.

   **D.** Containment primarily addresses shutting down connectivity between networks, subnets, systems, and servers. Eradication addresses locating the causal agents (malware, bogus user IDs, etc.) and removing them from each system.

12. Which of the following are not legal or regulatory issues that a CSIRT would have to be concerned with?

   **A.** Incidents caused by employee negligence or accident

   **B.** Incidents caused by misuse of systems by an employee

   **C.** Incidents that may involve competitors attempting to access company proprietary information

   **D.** Incidents that disrupt normal business operations

13. What are some of the key steps or processes in the recovery phase of responding to an information security incident? (Choose all that apply.)

   **A.** Documenting lessons learned

   **B.** Restoring, rebuilding, or reloading servers and hosts with clean backup images or distribution kits

   **C.** Restoring databases and network storage systems to backup copies made prior to the incident

   **D.** Setting filters and rules on network traffic, and inspecting suspicious packets, streams, or addresses to check that containment and eradication have been successful

14. Which set of plans and procedures should define how the organization makes backups of systems, applications, device settings, databases, and other data, for use during the recovery phase of an information systems security incident response?

   **A.** Information security incident response plans and procedures

   **B.** Disaster recovery plans and procedures

   **C.** Business continuity plans and procedures

   **D.** Information technology configuration management plans and procedures

**15.** You're the only SSCP in your small company's four-person IT team, and you've just been part of an emergency response team that's spent six nonstop days of overtime dealing with a major malware incident. The chief operating officer (COO) wants to skip the post-recovery phase, both to save costs and to get you and the other team members back onto your regularly assigned job tasks. Which statements would you base a reply to the COO on? Choose the statements that best support your reply.

A. Although it's recommended that we produce a lessons-learned file from this and every incident, we can do that as a part-time, background task, over the next several weeks or months, so we won't miss anything important.

B. Right now, the data we gathered as we investigated the incident is just in working files, notes, and such, and if we need to retain any of it, for any reasons, we've got some housekeeping to do before we're done.

C. The labor days we'd spend doing proper post-recovery procedures review, update, and process improvement will have us much better prepared for the next time something like this happens.

D. Since we don't really know how the malware came into our systems in the first place, we might want to continue that investigation now, while it's still fresh in our minds.

**16.** You've suggested to the IT team that all systems and servers, and all network devices, have their clocks synchronized and that synchronization checked frequently. One of their team members says this is not necessary. Which of these statements would be best to support your reply?

A. When we see a device whose clock is not in sync, it's probably because of a spoofed Wi-Fi access point, but if we don't have the clocks synchronized by policy, we can't see this.

B. This should be easy to do; just have every device initialization script make network time service calls.

C. Clocks that aren't synchronized properly might indicate anomalies on that system or device, which could be a precursor of an information security incident.

D. In the event we're investigating an anomaly or an incident, having all systems event logs using the same time standard will make them a lot easier to correlate and analyze.

**17.** Several months ago, your company suffered from a serious information systems security incident, which crippled its production operations for days. As a result, the CSIRT and other managers have seen the need to make a number of changes to a number of information security procedures, including those for incident response and continuity of operations. As CSIRT team chief, they've asked you what else they should consider, and why. Which of the following might you recommend? (Choose all that apply.)

A. Exercise the new procedures to verify that they work and deliver the improvements we need.

B. Increase our penetration testing activities to see if our new procedures help us detect and respond better.

C. Train the key team members, managers, and leadership on the new procedures.

D. Keep the news about the new procedures very low-key; most of our employees don't have a need to know about them, and letting them become widely known may inadvertently disclose other vulnerabilities.

**18.** Which of the following kinds of events might not be part of an advanced persistent threat attack?

**A.** Inquiries or requests for employee or staff contact information

**B.** Anomalies in applications behavior

**C.** Recurrent problems with data corruption in database entries

**D.** Routine ping or other ICMP packets coming to your systems

**19.** You've suggested that your CSIRT should create its own timeline of an incident, as part of their efforts to understand and assess it. Other team members say that this is what correlating event logs should take care of. Which statements would you base your reply on? (Choose all that apply.)

**A.** Our timeline is how we capture our assessment of the cause and effect relationships between events; the systems logs show us only events that happened.

**B.** Event logs need to be annotated to show relationships between events, and if we had the right set of security information and event management tools, that would be all we need.

**C.** Event logs only show when the hardware, operating systems, or applications saw an event and logged it; they don't cover actions taken by us or by other staff members.

**D.** We have to explain to management, in simple terms, what happened and when; they don't want to see hundreds of events in a log, which are nothing more than the evidence that led us to conclusions about what happened.

**20.** Which statements about the role of end users in detecting information security incidents are correct?

**A.** Most end users may have significant experience with the routine operation of the business systems and applications that they use, but they really cannot produce useful precursor or indicator information regarding possible information security incidents.

**B.** Most end users and their first-level supervisors have the best, most current insight as to the normal business rhythm and flow, and therefore normal loads on the systems and their throughput. They will most likely see anything abnormal quickly as a result.

**C.** Users think that they know a lot about business normal, but we need to rely more heavily on well-instrumented intrusion detection systems, access control, and other monitoring capabilities.

**D.** Since most APT kill chains use low and slow attack methods to reconnoiter and gain access, by the time users see things behaving abnormally, it's too late.

# Chapter

# 11

# Business Continuity via Information Security and People Power

---

## THIS CHAPTER COVERS THE FOLLOWING SSCP OBJECTIVE DOMAINS:

**Domain 1: Access Controls**

✓ 1.3: Participate in the Identity Management Lifecycle

**Domain 2: Security Operations and Administration**

✓ 2.1: Comply with Codes of Ethics

✓ 2.2: Understand Security Concepts

✓ 2.3: Document, Implement, and Maintain Functional Security controls

✓ 2.4: Participate in Asset Management

✓ 2.5: Implement Security Controls and Assess Compliance

✓ 2.6: Participate in Change Management

✓ 2.7: Participate in Security Awareness and Training

✓ 2.8: Participate in Physical Security Operations (e.g., Data Center Assessment, Badging)

**Domain 3: Risk Identification, Monitoring, and Analysis**

✓ 3.1: Understand the Risk Management Process

Disasters can happen. Natural disasters might strike in seconds or mere minutes to disrupt your information systems and your ability to conduct business so totally that you go out of business. An advanced persistent threat's attacks on your systems might take months to achieve the same cumulative effect. Without a well-considered business continuity plan, and without management and leadership committing the resources that the plan needs to make it real, chances are that major disruptions will put your organization out of business. It takes a solid, well-prepared team of people to take a badly disrupted organization, one that's been hit by a disaster-sized major information systems security attack, and get it back on its feet again.

In doing so, we'll have to go beyond Layer 7 of the OSI model and get into the people-centric functions, features, and protocols that are where the business operates. It's at these rarified, nontechnical layers that SSCPs may face their organization's weakest links in their overall information security chain of defenses.

Let's take what we've explored thus far and put all of that administrative, logical, and physical CIANA thinking into the context of managing how people and systems get ready to survive to operate.

# A Spectrum of Disruption

Despite our best-laid plans, things don't always work right. Business logic failed to anticipate some special conditions, and as a result, well-meaning employees are forced to make educated guesses to attempt to satisfy a customer's needs. The assumptions that one employee made in handing a special situation may not be documented well enough for other employees, further along the information processing chain, to notice where errors were made that need to be corrected. Bad data, or not quite complete data, gets accepted as valid as a result. In product design, perhaps those poorly captured assumptions and educated guesses lead to features (in hardware or software) that *almost* get the right job done. But not quite. Every business or organization could probably write its own list of such "Murphy's Law" events, those things that can go wrong and therefore *do* go wrong. This *should* be part of the vulnerability assessment process as risk managers work to identify what kind of events can disrupt the company's business logic or prevent it from achieving its goals and objectives.

Chapter 10, "Incident Response and Recovery," focused our attention on information security incidents—those events the directly or indirectly threaten to disrupt, deny, degrade, or destroy some or all aspects of the confidentiality, integrity, authentication, nonrepudiation, and availability characteristics of our organization's information systems. Planning for, preventing, and responding to such incidents is the main responsibility of an SSCP. However, as you saw in Chapter 10 and earlier chapters, a broad spectrum of disruption can occur, whether it's caused by a black-hat hacker or attacker, by accident, or by Mother Nature. SSCPs can play a vital role in helping their organizations survive each of these types of incidents, at any scale of disruption. This will require a far greater administrative attention to concepts and details as you assist in orchestrating the people power inherent in your organization to achieve what it takes to *survive to operate*.

Let's review what Chapter 3, "Integrated Information Risk Management," showed us about this spectrum of disruptive events—or events of interest, as information security professionals sometimes refer to them. Figure 11.1 graphically reminds us that these things-that-go-wrong can, in some circumstances, put the organization completely out of existence and, along the way, inflict significant levels of pain and suffering on its employees, owners, stakeholders, and others in its business ecosystem.

**FIGURE 11.1**   The descent from anomaly to organizational death

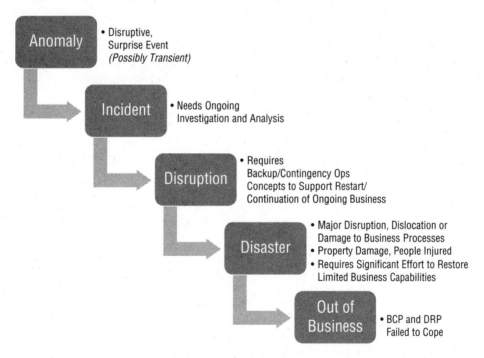

*Anomalies* are events that are unexpected or unanticipated. Computers, for example, do turn themselves off under software control—but they're not supposed to do it in the middle of my typing this paragraph. *That* would be an anomaly. Whether that anomaly is an *event of interest* to me as an information security issue or just a software and hardware fault will affect which path on my *problem analysis and error correction* checklist and flow I should take. Either way, it's disrupted my work and my train of thought.

Scale that situation up to when a company's intranet database servers decide to shut down or stop accepting connections from users or transactions from applications.

Depending on the nature of the organization, the business disruption this can cause may be significant, resulting in lost sales opportunities, delays in handling emergency services dispatch center calls, or even a safety-critical shutdown of an assembly line or processing pipeline if the server isn't there to provide support when needed. That's two of our five CIANA* factors, maybe more; we'd want to elevate the status of such an event, on a business-critical system, by calling it an *incident* and track it in our incident logging, reporting, and analysis systems. That's our first decision as information systems first responders. Note that we still don't know whether this is a security incident or not.

This brings us to the next major decision we have to face, and that concerns the urgency of our response to the incident. Key to this decision will be our assessment of the damage already inflicted on the organization, damage that is ongoing, and our anticipated very near-term future damage. This damage is both the immediate damage caused by the incident—the property or assets damaged by a fire, for example—and the downstream losses caused by the disruption to business operations. Continuity of business operations planning should help responders, managers, and organizational leadership decide in real time which of any preplanned or previously considered contingency operations plans or concepts ought to be put into action.

At some point, the damage already caused and the damage that most likely will continue to happen in the aftermath of this incident may be so severe that the organization simply cannot continue to operate as it normally does; it has to switch to a *disaster recovery* mode. This may require massively scaling back on the numbers and types of employees coming to work, customer orders going unfulfilled, and incoming materials and supplies being diverted or turned away due to lack of safe facilities in which to receive, store, and process them.

Of course, a single event can be a disaster all by itself—a major storm or earthquake, for example. In many other cases, it is a chain of events and a cascading sequence of anomalies, which lead to an almost total disruption of normal business operations. Sometimes organizational leadership cannot declare an incident as a disaster until after the smoke has died down, so to speak; other times, the nature of the incident is all too painfully obvious.

---

### Chapter 11 Bankruptcy

In most nations, when a business or organization can no longer meet its legal, contractual, or financial obligations to pay its bills, make its payroll, or deliver goods or services to customers, we say it has *gone bankrupt*. United States Code, Title 11, defines the ways that such bankrupt organizations are reorganized under the supervision of a court so that creditors, shareholders, and others with claims on the business have a reasonable degree of assurance that their claims will be heard and honored, perhaps partially. "Filing for Chapter 11" with the court offers a limited form of risk protection to those with claims—before Title 11 was enacted into law, it was those with the fastest lawyers who got to feed on the dying company's assets, often leaving the employees with no salary or pension benefits as a result.

Had this book been written in the United Kingdom, we'd still be here in our Chapter 11, but we'd be talking about the UK's Companies Act and its insolvency process and protections as defined by the UK's Insolvency Act instead.

---

*Confidentiality, integrity, availability, nonrepudiation, and authentication.

# Surviving to Operate: Plan for It!

Figure 11.2 puts these many different planning processes in a loosely arranged hierarchy; while many formal frameworks, such as those from NIST, ISO, and ITIL, offer sage advice, no one specific set of plans in any particular relationship is the most correct or most compliant with law and regulation. As a result, this figure shows no direct connecting lines or arrows from one plan to another; they all mesh together in the context of business planning and risk management planning. What this figure does illustrate, however, is that there are many interrelated and mutually supportive planning tasks or processes that organizations can and should use to be better prepared to adapt, survive, and overcome the anomalies. As an SSCP, you won't need to have deep knowledge of each of these plans or the planning processes that produce them. You *will*, however, serve your employers or clients best as you can to offer advice and assistance in helping them achieve their CIANA needs by protecting their information, information systems, IT infrastructures, and people from harm.

**FIGURE 11.2**    Continuity of operations planning and supporting planning processes

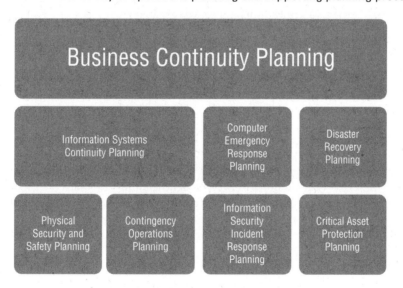

Each of these layers of planning is (or should be) driven by the business impact analysis (BIA), which took the results of the risk assessment process to produce a prioritized approach to which risks, leading to which impacts to the organization, were the most important, urgent, or compelling to protect against. Let's take a brief look in more detail at some of the planning processes that SSCPs will typically participate in, the plans those processes produce:

- *Business continuity planning* considers how to keep core business logic and processes operating safely and reliably in the face of disruptive incidents; it also looks at how to restore these core processes after they have been disrupted. The *business continuity plans (BCPs)* that are produced are at the "high tactical" level; they use the strategic plans of the organization as context to take the prioritized core business processes (as defined by the BIA), specifying the tasks needed to recover from such a disruption. This includes all phases of incident response, as you saw in Chapter 10. BCPs do not normally go into the step-by-step operational details necessary to achieve effective preparation, response, or recovery; they rely on other, subordinate plans and procedures to do so.

- *Disaster recovery planning* must concern itself with significant loss of life, injury to people, damage to organizational assets (or the property or assets of others), and significant disruption to normal business operations. As a result, *disaster recovery plans (DRPs)* look to ways to prevent a disruption from turning into panic or hysteria, while at the same time meeting the organization's due care and due diligence responsibilities to keep both stakeholders and the community informed. DRPs, for example, often must consider that organizational cash flow will probably suffer significantly as business operations are suspended, or greatly reduced, perhaps for months.

- *Contingency operations planning* takes business continuity considerations a few steps further by examining and selecting how to provide alternate means of getting business operations up and running again. This can embrace a variety of approaches, depending on the nature of the business logic in question:

  - Alternate work locations for employees to use

  - Alternate communications systems, internal and external, to keep employees, stakeholders, customers, or partners in touch, informed, and engaged

  - Information backup, archive, and restore capabilities, whether for physical backup of information and key documents or digital backups

  - Alternate processing capabilities

  - Alternate storage, support, and logistics processes

  - Temporary staffing, financial, and other key considerations

- *Critical asset protection planning* looks at the protection required for strategic, high-value or high-risk assets in order to prevent significant loss of value, utility, or availability of these assets to serve the organization's needs. As you saw in Chapter 3, these can be people, intellectual property, databases, assembly lines, or almost anything that is hard to replace and almost impossible to carry on business without.

- *Physical security and safety planning* focuses on preventing unauthorized physical access to the organization's premises, property, systems, and people; it focuses on fire, environmental, or other hazards that might cause human injury or death, property damage, or otherwise reduce the value of the organization and its ability to function. It works to identify safety hazards and reduce accidents. (Chapter 4, "Operationalizing Risk Mitigation," identified key approaches to physical risk mitigation controls with which SSCPs should be familiar.)

Finally, we as SSCPs come back to the *information security incident response planning* processes, as shown in Chapter 10. That planning process rightly focuses our attention on detecting IT and information systems events (or anomalies) that might be security incidents in the making, characterizing them, notifying appropriate organizational managers and leaders, and working through containment, eradication, and recovery tasks as we respond to such incidents.

The conclusion is inescapable: planning is what keeps us prepared, so that we can respond, but our planning has to be multifaceted and allow us to look at our organization, our operations, our information architectures, and our risks across the whole spectrum of business strategic, tactical, and operational concerns and details.

For example, consider how businesses in the Midwestern United States can combine forecasting and weather trending data to minimize the risk of loss from tornados and severe thunderstorms. As Yossi Sheffi points out in *The Resilient Enterprise* (2005, MIT Press), General Motors plant managers in Oklahoma City used data that shows how "tornado season" spans April, May, and June, with the peak *time of day* being from 3 p.m. to 9 p.m. local time. This insight empowered managers to focus attention on keeping the swing shift (afternoon and evening) workforce safer. The same data might suggest better, more cost-effective solutions to preserving and protecting IT infrastructures and key systems, especially if the commercial power, communications, and Internet systems can be prone to interruption or collapse during these peak periods of storm activity.

It's important to make a distinction here between *plans* and *planning*. *Plans* are sets of tasks, objectives, resources, constraints, schedules, and success criteria, brought together in a coherent way to show us what we need to do and how we do it to achieve a set of goals. *Planning* is a process—an activity that people do to gather all of that information, understand it, and put it to use. Planning is *iterative*; you do it over and over again, and each time through, you learn more about the objectives, the tasks, the constraints; you learn more about what "success" (or "failure") really means in the context of the planning you're doing. In the worst of all worlds, plans become documents that sit on shelves; they are taken down every year, dusted off, thumbed through, and put back on the shelf with minor updates perhaps. These plans are not living documents; they are *useless*. Plans that people use every day *become* living documents through use; they stay alive, current, and *real*, because the people served by those plans take each step of those plans and develop detailed procedures that they then use on the job to accomplish the intent of the plan.

In a very real sense, the planning you'll do to meet the CIANA needs of your organization or business does not and should not end until that organization or business does. Ongoing, continuous planning is in touch with what the knowledge workers and *knowledge-seeking* workers on your team are doing, every day, in every aspect of their jobs.

# Cloud-Based "Do-Over" Buttons for Continuity, Security, and Resilience

This is arguably the greatest boon to the organization that migrating its business logic *correctly* into the right cloud-hosting environment and service model can bring. In this chapter, as well as earlier chapters, we've examined some of the arguments for moving services into the clouds. Let's take a 50,000-foot view of this (as our aviator friends call it), and see just how these three attributes of secure, safe, and survivable computing show up in a typical organization by means of a common feature in almost every video game: the do-over button. This can show up in a number of everyday activities:

- *Transaction do-over*: Almost everything businesses and organizations need to achieve can be modeled as a series of transactions. Transactions are atomic by definition; that is, either you complete a transaction successfully, in its entirety, or you don't. (You don't partially make a deposit into your bank account, do you?) Undeleting a file is probably the most common IT example of this; this is straightforward when done on your local storage devices but requires multiple versions of files (or other approaches) to deal with shared, cloud-hosted, and synchronized storage supporting multiple users on multiple devices.

- *Session do-over*: As a writer, I might spend an hour or more editing a document, only to realize that I've made some horrible mistakes; I *really* want to just throw away this hour's work and start over from where I was first thing this morning. Document file versioning (or even frequent "save as" with a new name) is the simplest approach to this, since auto-save and cloud-synchronized backups often capture each change as an update to the file being edited as they occur. In fact, document versioning—saving a completely new instance of the file under a new name—is just about the *only* way to provide this kind of fallback at the user's work task level.

- *Complex service do-over*: Installing a new version of an OS or a major applications suite is complex, can take a lot of time, and may require a number of system reboots. Most systems and applications installation kits provide some kind of *fallback* capability, allowing the user to retry by reconfiguring the system to the way it was before the (aborted) installation or update was started.

You might say that a threat actor is the cause of every do-over capability that we need: the user made a mistake and needs to correct it; Mother Nature has intervened and shut the systems down in unclean ways; or an attacker, or just a software or data error, has caused the system to malfunction. The systems' managers and owners then detect that they're facing the Hob's choice of the computer era: abort what's already been done, retry the tasks by falling back to a known good point in the cumulative transaction history and redoing everything since, or ignore the compounding of errors and somehow move on. In the larger case of a total systems outage lasting days or weeks, the activation of disaster recovery and business continuity plans determines what to do about three categories of work (as reflected in the physical nature of the business and in its information systems).

What all of these do-overs have in common is that first, users and systems planners need to identify some baseline configurations of systems, software, and data that are worthy of extra efforts to keep available. These baselines need to be time and date stamped to be effective, of course! Whether we need to fall back to this morning's version of a file or completely re-create the system image onto new hardware after a disaster, users will need to know what backup set from what moment in time to reload. Once it's loaded, users can step through offline records of work steps taken and either redo them or deliberately choose to ignore them. Business logic should dictate this choice in advance or at least define the criteria to use in making this choice.

---

**Should All Updates Be Done Immediately?**

Updates to desktop operating systems, browsers, and applications suites are notorious for breaking some business processes while fixing others, aren't they? As individual end users in our SOHO environments, we tend to just grin and bear it, and figure out why what worked yesterday doesn't work quite the same way today. In the worst case, we have to restore the affected application or the OS to a previous checkpoint (a restore point) if the system made one for us before the updates were applied.

Larger organizations have to face this problem proactively to prevent overnight updates from disrupting business too much. Typically this involves:

- Using technical controls, such as policy settings, to block endpoints from automatically updating.

- Evaluating each new update in a test system configuration (possibly on virtual machines) to look for possible breakage to business logic, procedures, or other software. (This is a form of *regression testing*, done by the end users rather than by the developer.)

- Deploying those updates that passed evaluation to affected endpoints.

- Maintaining awareness and status on updates received, pending evaluation, and pending deployment to endpoints.

Clearly, this involves trading risks, which should be a priority-based call by management and leadership: how badly do we need the new security patches or feature updates, versus how little we wish to tolerate unknown disruption due to a "bad patch"?

---

Different cloud systems providers, their deployment models, and their services models provide different selections of features and capabilities that support a cloud-based do-over capability. Critical to making the right choice is to know your organization's real needs in each of these three areas, and the BIA should give you a solid foundation from which to start. Some key questions to consider include these:

- How many connections to the cloud-hosted business platforms, from how many of our end users, must meet what degree of reliability?

- Does our current physical communications architecture, including connections via our ISPs, provide us with that degree of reliability?

- If our fallback options include greater reliance on end-user mobile devices, what happens to our connectivity and business continuity when the local area mobile networks are overloaded or crash (as often happens during severe storms, earthquakes, and accidental or deliberate large-scale disruptions)?

We also must consider where our cloud-hosted data and applications platform systems actually, physically reside. Can the same natural or man-made hazard that disrupts our on-site business operations and people also disrupt our cloud host? If there's a possibility of this, we need to explore how the cloud host itself can provide backup, distributed, or alternate site storage, as well as processing and access control support. Again, our business needs for this should drive the CIANA components of our discussions and negotiations with alternative cloud services providers. (One comforting thought: the major cloud host providers, such as Amazon, Google, and Microsoft, have already worked out solutions to these problems for very large, multinational customer organizations using their clouds; this drove them to build in capabilities that smaller organizations, be they local, regional, or international, can benefit from.)

This is the point in the information security risk management process where the "magic numbers" of risk come back into play:

- Exposure factor (EF)—The fraction of the value of the asset, process, or outcome that will be lost from a single occurrence of the risk event.

- Single loss expectancy (SLE)—The total direct and indirect costs (or losses) from a single occurrence of a risk event.

- Annual rate of occurrence (ARO)—The anticipated number of times per year that such an event may occur.

- Annual loss expectancy (ALE)—The anticipated losses for the year, which is the ARO multiplied by the SLE:

  $$ALE = SLE \times ARO$$

- Safeguard value (SV)—The costs to install, activate, and use the risk mitigation controls that provide protection from the impact of this risk event.

- Maximum allowable outage (MAO)—The greatest time period that business operations can be allowed to be disrupted by this risk event.

- Recovery time objective (RTO)—The time by which the systems must be restored to normal operational function after the occurrence of this risk event.

- Recovery point objective (RPO)—The maximum allowable latency or lag between having all data current versus the state of the data as a result of the risk event. The shorter the RPO, the more frequently data needs to be backed up. Longer RPOs reflect a willingness to operate on restored systems, handling new data (new business transactions) while still working to restore ones lost by the event.

Remember, these magic numbers are needed for *each* risk in the organization's risk register. Complex organizations, with their resultant complex IT infrastructures supporting their rich sets of information systems and services, may have hundreds or more lower-level, more granular risks, each with its set of risk assessment numbers. They may have many ways of aggregating subsets of these risks up into a much smaller set of numbers. Note that the reverse process is also true: first, you face a large, almost terrifying single risk idea or event, and you break it down into smaller, more manageable elements of risk, each of which has *its* own set of numbers, including the leftover *residual risk* that you don't quite know what to do with yet.

SLE is a good example of a magic number that can be quite simple to derive, or quite complex. Think about what happens when an electrical power transient "bricks" your modem/router in a SOHO environment, leaving you with no LAN and no ISP connection at all. This may mean that your staff can work to only 75 percent of their normal (budgeted) productivity until Internet services are restored. There's also the possibility that for every 10-hour day that you're offline, you might lose a customer order. The components of this single loss event might break down as shown in the following table:

| Item | Nature of impact | Loss | Exposure factor | Itemized SLE |
|------|------------------|------|-----------------|--------------|
| Modem/ Router | Nonrepairable after surge | $150 | 1.0 | $150 |
| Staff | 4 people idle for each hour, $20/hr. each | $80/hr. | 0.25 (reduced productivity) | $20/hr. |
| Loss of Business | Loss of customer order | $500 average value | 0.1 (10% probability of losing an order) | $50 |

If we assume that it's going to take you all day to get the ISP to bring you a replacement modem/router, your total single loss expectancy is $400 ($150 for the replacement modem/router, 10 hours of lost productivity, and a 10 percent chance of a lost order averaging $500). Depending on the ARO for this event as a whole, it might (or might not) be worthwhile to invest in a spare modem/router.

 **Real World Scenario**

**Too Many Numbers to Be Decidable? Aggregate Them!**

Cynthia is the owner of a small company that provides customized educational programs and courses to meet the needs of mid-career and senior managers and leaders at companies and government agencies in her local area. These courses specialize in global and regional political and economic issues, and she holds classes in her offices, which she rents in a local marina's office park. In 4 years, she's added 12 staff members to her team, all of whom work in the office space with her—this has been key to unleashing an incredibly high degree of collaboration and creativity that has given her business its unique competitive advantage.

All of her IT infrastructure is in-house: LAN-based simple file sharing desktops and laptops, and a single ISP connection, are the extent of her systems. Her business does not

*(continued)*

*(continued)*

serve the IT sectors, and since none of her client base needs her company to address IT-related security and resiliency in courses she builds and teaches to them, she does not have any "geeks" on her team. Recently, a major storm destroyed a part of the office park; she's now rethinking her business survival needs.

If another such storm strikes, with the business organized and structured the way it is, Cynthia stands to lose everything—all customer business records, all file copies of course materials, her reference library, and of course her computers, office furnishings, and the like. Conservatively, she estimates this could put her out of operation for a year; her team members might be forced to find other jobs, and ultimately, it could put her completely out of business. That storm was *supposed* to be a 100-year storm, but the area has seen three such storms in the last 15 years.

Last year, growth fueled her annual revenues to $1.8 million; salaries and operating expenses, taxes, and insurance left her with her own salary plus about $100,000 excess profit as retained earnings. Her business insurance would cover injury or death benefits to employees or visitors, and as its coverage assumes depreciated value of physical assets and equipment, it would only pay for about 10 percent of her estimated $100,000 in office furnishings, equipment, computers, and the library.

For this major storm, Cynthia's SLE would be calculated as her annual revenue minus anticipated insurance payout, or $1.790 million. (This assumes she has no other costs to liquidate her holding in the office space or her business property in it before the storm hits.) Her ARO would be 0.2, and thus her ALE would be $358,000. Clearly, there must be a better way!

Cynthia next looks to IT professionals among her friends and associates, and she believes that she can decompose this single-event business-killing risk into a collection of smaller risks if she can plan to move her business into a reliable public cloud–hosting service. She'd still maintain the offices as excellent collaboration facilities and continue to teach classes there. She thinks she might also need to migrate her existing LAN-based courseware development and teaching support into the cloud, possibly to a *learning management system* (LMS) platform of some kind, while redesigning her business processes to take advantage of the more managed environment that public clouds can provide. This will involve some training of her team of academics, of course! Along the way, she sees the need to engage with her most important clients and customers to gain their support, insight, and patience as she transitions her business processes to the cloud.

What kind of risks might her new business process model face during this transition period and after the transition is complete? How might you assess each, and how would you need the systems analysis process she'll start using for this migration to help support this assessment?

Although it's difficult at this point (in the face of very little hard data) to make a quantitative assessment of these new risks, how might you make a qualitative assessment? Do you believe Cynthia will be better off facing *more* risks than she is facing right now?

Thus, the circle should close: business or organizational goals and objectives drive the creation and design of business processes, which dictate IT infrastructure capabilities to deliver enough CIANA to achieve those goals while managing risk in cost-effective ways. Each step further refines the strategies, tactics, and operational approaches to risk management and mitigation, producing *more* entries in the risk registry, each of which is smaller in impact. At some point, each risk can be affordably managed, controlled, and monitored. Each step in that circle of decision, design, implementation, and operation can benefit greatly from what the SSCP can bring to the table.

# CIANA at Layer 8 and Above

**Remember CIANA?**

Back in Chapter 5, "Communications and Network Security," you saw that network security needs to address more than just the CIA triad of information security.

As an acronym, CIA reminds us of the need to maintain the confidentiality, integrity, and availability of our information.

CIANA adds nonrepudiation and authentication to those same three attributes.

Nonrepudiation, as you recall, is strongly linked to the use of the public key infrastructure and its use of asymmetric encryption. Authentication, of course, is provided by identity management and access control.

"What? Layer 8? I thought you said that the OSI reference model was a 7-layer model!" Well, that's true, but almost since it was first being drafted, there were any number of authors (including Michael Gregg, in his 2006 classic *Hack the Stack*) who referred to the people-facing administrative, policy, training, and procedural stuff as Layer 8. (Pundits have also pointed out additional layers, such as Money, Political, and Dogmatic, but for simplicity of analysis, SSCPs can lump those all into the "people layer.") Layer 8 by that name probably won't appear on the SSCP certification exam, but vulnerabilities, exploitations, and countermeasures involving how people configure, control, manage, use, *misuse, mismanage, and misconfigure* their IT systems no doubt will. Figure 11.3 illustrates this concept, and much like Figure 11.2, it too shows many process-focused aspects of running a business or organization that intermesh with each other. Note that just as every layer within the OSI protocol stack defines and enables interactions with the outside world, so too does every protocol or business architectural element in Figure 11.3. The surrounding layers might be immediate customers, suppliers, and clients; next, the overall marketplace, maybe the society or dominant culture in the nation or region in which the organization does business. This layer-by-layer view of interaction can be a powerful way to look at both the power and value of information at, within, or across a layer, as well as a tool that SSCPs can use to think about threats and vulnerabilities within those higher layers of the *uber*-stack.

**FIGURE 11.3**   Beyond the seventh layer

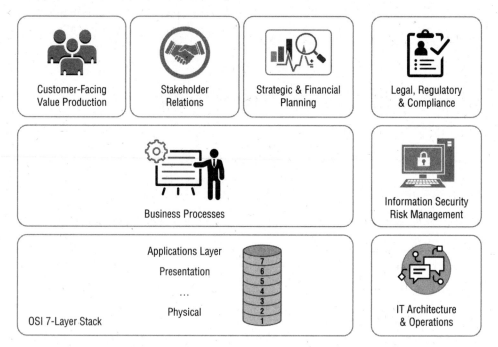

*Collaborative workspaces* are an excellent case in point of this. The design and manufacturing of the Boeing 767 aircraft family involves hundreds of design, manufacturing, and supply businesses, all working together with a dozen or more major airlines and air cargo operators, collaborating digitally to bring the ideas through design to reality and then into day-to-day sustained air transport operations. At Layer 7 of the OSI stack, there were multiple applications programs and platforms used to provide the IT infrastructure needed for this project. The information security rules that all players in the B767 design space had to abide by might see implementation using many physical and logical control technologies across Layers 1 through 7, yet with all of the administrative controls being implemented out in "people space" and the interorganizational contractual, business process, and cultural spaces.

To date, sadly, a number of IT security professionals have constrained their gaze to Layer 7 and below. The results? *Missed opportunities to better serve the information security needs of their organizations.* One irony of this is that almost by definition, *all* administrative controls are instantiated, implemented, used (and abused or ignored) *beyond* Layer 7.

Let's take a closer look at those next layers.

# It *Is* a Dangerous World Out There

If we were to redraw Figure 11.3, we might be able to see that the *people* element of an organization makes up a great deal of its outermost threat surface. Even the digital or physical connections our businesses make with others are, in one sense, surrounded by a layer of people-facing, people-powered processes that create them, operate them, maintain them, and sometimes abuse or misuse them. You can see this reflected in the dark humor of the security services of many nations: before the computer age, they'd joke that if your guards, secretaries, or janitors owned better cars, houses, or boats than you did, you might want to look into who *else* is paying them and why. By the 1980s, we'd added communications and cryptologic technical and administrative people to that list of "the usual suspects." A decade later, our sysadmins and database administrators joined this pool of people to really, *really* watch more closely. And like all apocryphal stories, these still missed seeing the real evolution of the threat actor's approaches to social engineering.

The goal of any *social engineering* process is to gain access to *insider information*—information that is normally not made public or disclosed to outsiders, for whatever reason. With such insider information, an outsider can potentially take actions that help them gain their own objectives at greatly reduced costs to themselves, while quite likely damaging the organization, its employees, customers, stakeholders, or its community. In Chapter 3 we looked at how one classical and useful approach to keeping insider information *inside* involves creating an information security classification process; the more damaging that disclosure, corruption, or loss of this information can cause to the company, the greater the need to protect it. This is a good start, but it's only a start. Social engineering attacks have proven quite effective at sweeping up many different pieces of unclassified information, even that which is publicly available, and analyzing it to deduce the possible existence of an exploitable vulnerability.

Social engineering works because people in general want to be well regarded by other people; we want to be helpful, courteous, and friendly, because we want other people to behave in those ways toward us. (We're wired that way inside.) But we also are wired to protect our group, be that our home and family, our clan, or any other social grouping we belong to. So, at the same time we're open and trusting, we are hesitant, wary, and maybe a bit untrusting or skeptical. Social engineering attacks try to establish one bit of common ground with a target, one element on which further conversation and engagement can take place; over time, the target begins to trust the attacker. The honest sales professional, the doctor, and the government inspector use such techniques to get the people they're working with to let down their guard and be more open and more sharing with information. Parents do this with their children and teachers with their students. *It's human* to do so. So, naturally, we as humans are very susceptible to being manipulated by the smooth-talking stranger with hostile intent.

Consider how *phishing* attacks have evolved in just the last 10 or 15 years:

- *Phishing attacks* tend to use email spam to "shotgun blast" attractive lures into the inboxes of perhaps thousands of email users at a time; the emails either would carry malware payloads themselves or would tempt recipients to follow a URL, which would then expose their systems to hostile reconnaissance, malware, or other attacks. The other major use of phishing attacks is identity theft or compromise; by offering to transfer an inheritance or a bank's excess profit to the addressee, the attacker tempts the target to reveal personally identifying information (PII), which the attacker can then sell or use as another step in an advanced persistent attack's kill chain. The attacker can also use this PII to defraud the addressee, banks, merchants, or others by masquerading as the addressee to access bank accounts and credit information, for example.

- *Spear phishing* attacks focus on individual email recipients, or very select, targeted groups of individuals, and in true social engineering style, they'd try to suggest that some degree of affinity, identification, or relationship already existed in order to wear down the target's natural hesitation to trusting an otherwise unknown person or organization. Spear phishing attacks are often aimed at lower-level personnel in large organizations—people who by themselves can't or don't do great things or wield great authority and power inside the company but who may know or have access to some *little* bit of information or power the attacker can make use of. The most typical spear phishing attack would be an email sent to a worker in the finance department, claiming to be from the company's chief executive. "I'm traveling in (someplace far away), and to make this deal happen, I need you to wire some large amount of money to this name, address, bank name, account, etc.," such phishing attacks would say. Amazingly, an embarrassingly large number of small, medium, and large companies have fallen (and continue to fall) for these attacks and lost their money in the process.

- *Whaling attacks*, by contrast, aim at key individuals in an organization. The chief financial officer (CFO) of a company might get an email claiming to be from their chief executive officer (CEO), which says much the same thing: "If we're going to make this special deal happen, I need you to send this payment now!" CFOs rarely write checks or make payments themselves—so they'd forward these whaling attack emails on to their financial payments clerks, who'd just do what the CFO told them to do. (One of the author's friends is the CEO of a small technology company, and he related the story of how such an attack was attempted against his company recently, and the low-level payments clerk in that kill chain was the only one who said "Wait a minute, this email doesn't look right...," which got the CEO involved in the nick of time.)

- *Catphishing* involves the creation of an entirely fictitious persona; this "person" then strikes up what seems to be a legitimate personal or professional relationship with people within its operator's target set. Catphishing originated within the online dating communities, but we've seen several notorious examples so far of its use in attack strategies that do not involve romance.

This list could go on and on; we've already had more than enough examples of advanced persistent threat operations that create phony companies or organizations, staffed with nonexistent people, as part of their reconnaissance and attack strategies.

Notice that by shifting from phishing to more sophisticated spear phishing, whaling, or even catphishing attacks, attackers have to do far more social engineering, in more subtle ways, to gather the intelligence data about their prospective target, its people, and its internal processes. Of course, the potential payoff to the attacker often justifies the greater up-front reconnaissance efforts.

This all should suggest that if we can provide for more *trustworthy* interpersonal interaction and communication, we could go a long ways toward establishing and maintaining a greater security posture at these additional layers of our organization's information architecture. Much of this will depend on your organization, its decision-making culture and managerial style, its risk tolerance, and its mission or strategic sense of purpose. Going back to Chapter 10's ideas, we're looking for ways to find precursors and indicators that some kind of reconnaissance probe or attack is in the works. For example, separation of duties can be used to identify "need to know" boundaries; queries by people not directly involved in those duties, whether insiders or not, should be considered as possible precursor signals. This can aid in key asset protection, security for critical business processes, or even by protecting information about the movement or availability of key personnel. Penetration testing or exercises that focus on social engineering attack vectors might also help discover previously unknown vulnerabilities or identify key ways that improved (or different) staff education and training can help "phishing-proof" your organization.

## People Power for Secure Communications

There's a lot of great advice out there in the marketplace and on the Internet as to why organizations need to teach their people how to help protect *their own jobs* by protecting critical information about the company. As an SSCP, you can help the organization select or create the right education, training, and evaluation processes and tools for this. A survival tip: use the separation of duties principle to identify groups or teams of people whose job responsibilities suggest the need for specific, focused information protection skills at the people-to-people level.

That's an important thought; this is not about multifactor identification or physical control of the movement of people throughout the business's office spaces or work areas. This is also *not* trying to convert your open, honest, trusting, and helpful team members into suspicious, surly, standoffish "moat dragons" either! All you need to do is get each of them to add one key concept to their mental map of the workplace: *trust, but verify*. Our network engineers need to build our *systems* in as much of a zero trust architectural way as the business needs and can afford, but the most flexible, responsive, surprise-tolerant *and* abnormality-detecting link in our security chain needs to stay trusting if it's going to deliver the agility that resilient organizations require. They just need to have routine, simple, safe, reliable, and efficient ways to *verify* that what somebody seemingly is asking them to do, share, or divulge is a legitimate request from a trustworthy person or organization.

Without needing to dive too deeply into organizational psychology and culture, as SSCPs we ought to be able to help our organizations set such processes in place, and keep them simple, current, and useful. This won't stop every social engineering attack—but then again, no risk control will stop every threat that's targeted against it either. And as organizations find greater value and power in actually sharing more information about themselves with far larger sets of outsiders—even *publishing* it—the collection of information "crown jewels" that need to be protected may, over time, get smaller. That smaller set of valuable nuggets of information may be easier to protect from inadvertent disclosure but may also become much more of an attractive target.

## POTS and VoIP Security

One last frontier we need to look beyond is the use of other communications technologies and systems, both for communications inside our organization and with the myriad of outside organizations and people that we deal with. Plain old telephone service (POTS) has traditionally been provided to businesses and organizations by using an on-premises switchboard systems to connect to a phone company's central office systems (at a point of presence, of course, within the organization's physical space). Endpoint devices such as desktop or wall-mounted phones, intercoms, or other devices provided both the voice connectivity and the routing and control of individual calls. But with the rare exception of encrypted telephone systems, the vast majority of these systems used unsecured analog encoding to transmit and receive digitized speech over the public switched telephone network (PSTN). In recent years, Voice over Internet Protocol (VoIP) has become a major communications alternative for many organizations and individuals. VoIP platforms, such as Skype, Viper, FaceTime, and Google Voice, have revolutionized the way we think about *talking* with others. We want to hear *and* see them; we want to be able to instantly add others to the call. We want to call *them*, not an endpoint device that happens to be where they were *yesterday* or might return to next week. Business and individual VoIP users have many legitimate reasons (and some illegitimate ones) to record such calls or incorporate other multimedia information into them.

Each of these major, and very appealing, features of VoIP systems brings with it the increased risks that well-intentioned users may disclose sensitive, proprietary, or other information to other parties on the VoIP session who may not have a valid need to know such information. Your organization must ensure that users understand your information security classification guidelines and that you have procedures in place that users can use to check what information can be shared in a VoIP session (especially with outsiders) and what information *must not be shared*. Without such a classification guide, and the awareness, education, and training to make use of it, your organization is putting a great deal at risk.

POTS systems tend to use a separate physical plant than the network systems in most locations. The same modem (at the same point of presence) may deliver POTS and Internet connectivity to your location if provided over the same "last mile" wiring or fiber distribution system used by the same communications company. Once we look past that modem, to date, the technologies involved in telephone call routing, control, and support of advanced calling and billing features have tended to be separate systems. POTS is call based, while the Internet is packet switching based.

We haven't looked at POTS technologies and security issues very much, since they tend to be beyond what SSCPs deal with. Nevertheless, the same need for awareness, education, and training of your staff in how to handle sensitive, proprietary, or other restricted information is paramount to *any* attempt to keep your information safe, secure, and reliable.

Clearly, VoIP touches the users at Layer 7 of the OSI model; all of the technical risk mitigation controls, such as encryption, access control, identity management, and authentication can be applied to meet the organization's needs for information security. We've addressed those for VoIP already to the degree that it's just another app that runs on our networks. However, the trivial ease with which a trusted team member of one organization can be VoIP calling from less-than-trustworthy surroundings does suggest that keeping VoIP safe and secure requires other specialized end-user knowledge, skills, and attitudes. This is another opportunity for you as an SSCP to identify ways to help your organization's VoIP users communicate in more information security–conscious ways.

# Summary

Business continuity is about staying in business, despite what risks may materialize. It's about achieving the organization's strategic, tactical, and operational goals and objectives despite the occurrence of accidents, deliberate attacks, or even natural disasters. In order to *survive to operate*, organizations must *plan* to make such survival possible, as well as plan for how to bring disrupted business processes back to something close to pre-incident normal. As we've seen in this chapter, SSCPs bring many different sets of knowledge, skills, and abilities to the table as they help their organizations prepare to survive, prepare to recover, and then carry out those plans successfully when incidents happen.

Much of this business continuity planning, including incident response activities, happens at the administrative level—in other words, it happens in nontechnical ways, as if at Layer 8 or beyond in our 7-layer OSI reference model. The organization's people are (once again) seen to be critically important to making these various layers of planning become reality under the stress of an anomaly becoming an incident and then an incident becoming a disaster. Awareness education and procedural training of our organization's workforce, focused on tasks, work units, or processes, and the critical assets or systems they need to perform their roles, can play a vital part not only in emergency response preparedness but also in day-to-day activities that enhance information security.

This is all part of how organizations become resilient, able to bend in the face of major disruptions without breaking under the strain. (That same resilience may also herald an unlooked-for opportunity for innovation and *positive* change, as you may recall from Chapter 3.) The ubiquitous nature of cloud-based or cloud-hosted systems, platforms, and services make many options available to support contingency operations plans, including backup and restore of systems and data. When combined with the people power the organization already depends on for success, the chances of surviving to operate can be better than ever. And that's what continuity of business operations planning is all about.

# Exam Essentials

**Understand the relationship between incident response, business continuity, and disaster recovery planning.**   A disaster is an incident that causes major damage to property, disrupts business activities, and quite possibly injures or even kills people. A disaster can also cause information critical to a business to be lost, corrupted, or exposed to the wrong people. A disaster may be one very extensive incident or a whole series of smaller events that, taken together, constitute an existence-threatening stress to the organization. The extensiveness of this damage can be such that the organization cannot recover quickly, if at all, or that such recovery will take significant reinvestment into systems, facilities, relationships with other organizations, and people. Disaster recovery plans are ways of preparing to cope with such significant levels of disruption. Business continuity, by contrast, is the general term for plans that address how to continue to operate in as normal a fashion as possible despite the occurrence of one or more disruptions. Such plans can address alternative processing capabilities and locations, partnering arrangements, and financial arrangements necessary to keep the payroll flowing while operational income is disrupted. Business continuity can be interrupted by one incident or a series of them. Incident response narrows the focus down to a single incident, and provides detailed and systematic instruction as to how to detect, characterize, and respond to an incident to contain or minimize damage; such response plans then outline how to restore systems and processes to let business operations can operate again as normally.

**Describe how business continuity and disaster recovery planning differ from incident response planning.**   These three sets of planning activities share a common core of detecting events that could disrupt critical business processes, inflict damage to vital business assets (including information systems), or lead to people being injured or killed. As risk management plans, these all look to identify appropriate responses, identify required resources and preparation tasks, and lay out manageable strategies to attain acceptable levels of preparedness. They differ on the scale of disruption considered and the scope of activities. Disaster recovery plans (DRPs) look at significant events that could potentially put the business out of business; as such, they focus on workforce health and safety, morale, and continuing key financial functions such as payroll and alternate and contingency operations at reduced levels or capacities. Business continuity plans (BCPs) look more at business processes, by criticality, and determine what the details of those alternate operations need to be. BCPs address more of the details of backup and restore capabilities for systems, information, and business processes, which can include alternate processing arrangements, cloud solutions, or hot, warm, and cold backup operating locations. Incident response plans focus on getting ready to continually detect a potentially disruptive incident, such as an attack by an advanced persistent threat, and how to characterize it, contain it, respond to it, and recover from it. Part of that process includes decision points (by senior leadership and management) as to whether to activate larger BCP recovery options or to declare a disaster is in progress and to activate the DRP.

**Describe the legal and ethical obligations organizations must address when developing disaster response, business continuity, and incident response plans.**   The first set of such obligations come under due diligence and due care responsibilities to shareholders, stakeholders, employees, and the larger society. The organization must protect assets placed in its care for its business use. It must also take reasonable and prudent steps to prevent damage to its own assets or systems from spreading to other systems and causing damages to them in the process. Legally and ethically, organizations must keep stakeholders, investors, employees, and society informed when such information security incidents occur; failure to meet such notification burdens can result in fines, criminal prosecution, loss of contracts, or damage to the organization's reputation for reliability and trustworthiness. Such incidents may also raise questions of guilt, culpability, responsibility, and liability, and they may lead to digital forensic investigations. Such investigations usually need information that meets stringent rules of evidence, including a chain of custody that precludes someone from tampering with the evidence.

**Describe the possible role of cloud technologies in business continuity planning and disaster recovery.**   Using cloud-based systems to host data storage, business applications platforms, or even complete systems can provide a number of valuable business continuity capabilities. First, it diversifies location by allowing data, apps, and systems to be physically residing on hardware systems not located directly in the business' premises. This reduces the potential that the same incident (such as a storm or even a terrorist attack) can disrupt, disable, or destroy both the business and its cloud services provider. Second, it provides for layers of secure, offsite data, apps and systems backup, and archive and restore capabilities, which can range from restoring a single transaction up to restoring entire sets of business logic, processes, capabilities, and the data they depend on. Third, hosting such systems in a third-party cloud services provider may make it much easier to transition to alternate or contingency business operations plans, especially if knowledge workers have to work from home, from temporary quarters, or even from another city or state.

**Explain the role of awareness, education, and training for employees and associates in achieving business operations continuity.**   All employees of an organization, or people associated with an organization, should have a basic awareness of its business continuity plans and strategy; this gives them confidence that this important aspect of their own personal security and continued employment has not been forgotten. Separation of duties, as a design-for-security concept, can play a role in developing focused, timely education and training based on teams or groups involved with specific, related subsets of the business logic. Education can build on that awareness to help selected teams of employees know more about how they are a valuable part of ensuring or achieving continuity of business operations for their specific duties and responsibilities; it gets employees engaged in making continuity planning and readiness more achievable. Training focuses on skills development and practice, which builds confidence for dealing with any emergency.

**Describe the different types of phishing attacks.**   Phishing attacks, like all social engineering attacks, attempt to gain the trust and confidence of the targeted person or group of people so that they will divulge information that provides something of value to the attacker. This can be information that makes it easier for the attacker to gain access to IT systems, money, or property. Phishing attacks originated as broadcast-style emails, sent to thousands of email addresses, and either carried a malware payload to the reader's system or offered links to tempt the user to browse to sites from which the attack could continue. Spear phishing attacks focused on selected individuals within organizations, often by claiming to be email from a senior company official, and would attempt to lure the recipient into taking action to initiate a transfer of funds to the attacker's account. These tended to be aimed at (addressed to) clerical and administrative personnel. Whaling attacks target high-worth or highly placed individuals, such as a chief financial officer (CFO), and use much the same story line to attempt to get the CFO to task a clerk to initiate a funds transfer. Cat phishing attacks involve the creation of a fictitious persona, who attempts to establish a personal, professional relationship with a targeted individual or small group of individuals. The attacker may be posing as a consultant, possible client, journalist, investor—in short, any-one business managers or leaders might reasonably be willing to take at face value. Once that trust and rapport is established, the manipulation begins.

**Explain how to defend against phishing attacks.**   Some automated tools can screen email from external addresses for potentially fraudulent senders and scan for other possible indications that they might be a phishing attack rather than a legitimate email. The most powerful defense is achieved by increasing every employee's awareness of the threat and providing focused education and training to improve skills in spotting possibly suspicious emails that might be phishing attacks. It's also advisable to apply separation of duties pro-cesses that establish multiple, alternative ways to validate the legitimacy of any such request to expose critical and valuable assets to risk.

**Explain the apparent conflict between designing zero trust networks but encouraging employees to "trust, but verify."**   Zero trust network design is sometimes described as "never trust, always verify." For example, it asks us to segment networks and systems into smaller and smaller zones of trust, and enforce verification of every access attempt and every attempt to cross from one zone or segment to another, because this seems to be required to deal with advanced persistent threats using low-and-slow attack methodologies. On the other hand, people are not terribly programmable, and this is both a weakness and a strength. Our businesses and organizations need our people to be helpful, engaging, and trusting—this is how we break down the internal barriers to communication and teamwork while strengthening our company's relationship with customers, suppliers, or others. We must educate and train our employees to *first verify* that the person asking for the conver-sation, help, or information is a trustworthy person with a legitimate business reason for their request, and *then* engage, be helpful, and establish rapport and trust. This way, we maintain the strength and flexibility of the human component of our organizations, while supporting them with processes, procedures, and training to keep the organization safe, secure, and resilient.

# Review Questions

1. Which of the following types of actions or responses would you not expect to see in an information security incident response plan? (Choose all that apply.)

   A. Relocation of business operations to alternate sites

   B. Temporary staffing

   C. Using off-site systems and data archives

   D. Engaging with senior organizational leadership

2. Your boss believes that your company must follow NIST guidelines for disaster recovery planning and wants you to develop the company's plans based on those guidelines. Which statement might you use to respond to your boss?

   A. As a government contractor, we actually have to follow ISO and ITIL, not NIST.

   B. Although we are not a government contractor, NIST frameworks and guidelines are mandatory for all US businesses, and so this is correct.

   C. NIST publications are mandatory only for government agencies or companies on government contracts, and since we are neither of those, we don't have to follow them. But they have some great ideas we should see about putting to use, tailored to our risk management plans.

   D. NIST publications are specifically for government agencies and their contractors, and most of what they say is just not applicable to the private sector.

3. Your boss has asked you to start planning for disaster recovery. Where would you start to understand what your organization needs to do to be prepared? (Choose all that apply.)

   A. Business impact analysis

   B. Business continuity plan

   C. Critical asset protection plan

   D. Physical security and safety plan

4. Which plan would you expect to be driven by assessments such as SLE, ARO, or ALE?

   A. Business continuity plan

   B. Contingency operations plan

   C. Information security incident response plan

   D. Risk management plan

5. Which statement best explains the relationship between incident response or disaster recovery, and configuration management of your IT architecture baseline? (Choose all that apply.)

   A. There is no relationship; managing the IT baseline is useful during normal operations, but it has no role during incident response or disaster recovery.

   B. As you're restoring operations, you may need to redo changes or updates done since the time the backup copies were made; your configuration management system should tell you this.

   C. Without a documented and managed baseline, you may not know sufficient detail to build, buy, or lease replacement systems, software, and platforms needed for the business

   D. There is no relationship, because the contingency operations procedures should provide for this.

6. Which statement about recovery times and outages is most correct?

   A. MAO should exceed RTO.

   B. RTO should exceed MAO.

   C. RTO should be less than or equal to MAO.

   D. RTO and MAO are always equal.

7. Which value reflects a quantitative assessment of the maximum allowable loss of data due to a risk event?

   A. RTO

   B. RPO

   C. MAO

   D. ARO

8. Which of the following statements about information security risks is most correct regarding the use of collaborative workspace tools and platforms?

   A. Because these tools encourage open, trusting sharing of information and collaboration on ideas, they cannot be used to securely work with proprietary or sensitive data.

   B. These tools require strong identity management and access control, as part of the infrastructure beneath them, to protect sensitive or proprietary information.

   C. Granting access to such collaboration environments should first be determined by legitimate business need to know and be based upon trustworthiness.

   D. First, the organizations collaborating with them should agree on how sensitive data used by or created by the team members must be restricted, protected, or kept safe and secure. Then, the people using the tool need to be fully aware of those restrictions. Without this, the technical risk controls, such as access control systems, can do very little to keep information safe and secure.

**9.** Which statement about phishing attacks is most correct?

**A.** Phishing attacks are rarely successful, and so they pose very low risk to organizations.

**B.** Spear phishing attacks are easy to detect with scanners or filters.

**C.** Attackers learn nothing of value from you, if you simply reply to an email you suspect is part of a spear phishing or whaling attack and say "please remove me from your list."

**D.** Phishing attacks of all kinds are still in use, because they can be effective social engineering tools when trying to do reconnaissance or gain illicit entry into an organization or its systems.

**10.** In general, what differentiates phishing from whaling attacks?

**A.** Phishing attacks tend to be used to gain access to systems via malware payloads or by getting recipients to disclose information, whereas whaling attacks try to get responsible managers to authorize payments to the attacker's accounts.

**B.** Phishing attacks are focused on businesses; whaling attacks are focused on high-worth individuals.

**C.** Whaling attacks tend to offer something that ought to sound "too good to be true," whereas phishing attacks masquerade as routine business activities such as package delivery confirmations.

**D.** There's really no difference.

**11.** Which statement best describes how does the separation of duties relate to education and training of end users, managers, and leaders in an organization?

**A.** Separation of duties would dictate that general education and awareness training be done by different people than those who provide detailed skills-based training for the proper handling of sensitive information.

**B.** Separation of duties should identify groups or teams that have little need for information security awareness, training, and education so that effort can be better focused on ones with greater needs.

**C.** Separation of duties should segment the organization into teams focused on their job responsibilities, with clear interfaces to other teams. Effective awareness training and education can help each team, and each team member, see how successfully fulfilling their duties depends on keeping information safe, secure, and reliable.

**D.** Separation of duties would dictate that workers outside of one team's span of control or duties have no business need to know what that team works with; education and training would reinforce this.

**12.** What should be your highest priority as you consider improving the information security of your organization's telephone and voice communications systems?

    **A.** Having in-depth, current technical knowledge on the systems and technologies being used

    **B.** Understanding the contractual or terms of service conditions, with each provider, as they pertain to information security

    **C.** Ensuring that users, managers, and leaders understand the risks of sharing sensitive information with the wrong parties and that effective administrative controls support everyone in protecting information accordingly

    **D.** Ensuring that all sensitive information, of any kind, is covered by nondisclosure agreements (NDAs)

**13.** Social engineering attacks still present a threat to organizations and individuals for all of the following reasons except:

    **A.** Most targeted individuals don't see the harm in responding or in answering simple questions posed by the attacker.

    **B.** Most people believe they are too smart to fall for such obvious ploys, but they do anyway.

    **C.** Most targeted individuals and organizations have effective tools and procedures to filter out phishing and related scams, so they are now better protected from such attacks.

    **D.** Most people want to be trusting and helpful.

**14.** You're the lone SSCP in the IT group of a small start-up business, which has perhaps 25 or so full-time employees performing various duties. Much of the work the company does depends on dynamic collaboration with many outside agencies, companies, and academic organizations, as well as with potential customers. The managing director wants to talk with you about ways to help protect the rapidly evolving intellectual property, market development ideas, and other information that she believes give the company its competitive advantage. She's especially worried that with the high rate of open conversation in the collaborations, this advantage is at risk. Which of the following would you recommend be the first that the company invest in and make use of?

    **A.** More rigorous access control systems, using multifactor authentication

    **B.** More secure, compartmented collaboration software suites, tools, and procedures

    **C.** Better, more focused education and open dialogue with company staff about the risks of too much open collaboration

    **D.** Better work on our information risk management efforts, to include an information security classification process that our teammates can use effectively

**15.** You've recently determined that some recent systems glitches might be being caused by the software or hardware that a few employees have installed and are using with their company-provided endpoints; in some cases, employee-owned devices are being used instead of company-provided ones. What are some of the steps you should take right away to address this? (Choose all that apply.)

- **A.** Check to see if your company's acceptable use policy addresses this.
- **B.** Review your IT team's approach to configuration management and control.
- **C.** Conduct remote configuration inspections and audits on the devices in question.
- **D.** Get your manager to escalate this issue before things get worse.

**16.** You've just started a new job as an information security analyst at a medium-sized company, one with about 500 employees across its seven locations. In a conversation with your team chief, you learn that the company's approach to risk management and information security includes an annual review and update of its risk register. Which of the following might be worth asking your team chief about? (Choose all that apply.)

- **A.** What do we do when an incident response makes us aware of previously unknown vulnerabilities?
- **B.** How does that relate to our ongoing monitoring of our IT infrastructure and key applications platforms and systems?
- **C.** Does that result in any tangible cost savings for us?
- **D.** Why do that every year, as opposed to doing it on some other periodic basis?

**17.** The company you work for does medical insurance billing, payments processing, and reconciliation, using both Web-based transaction systems as well as batch file processing of hundreds of transactions in one file. As the SSCP on the IT team, you've been asked to consider changes to their backup and restore strategies to help reduce costs. Which quantitative risk assessment parameter might this affect most?

- **A.** Recovery time objective
- **B.** Recovery point objective
- **C.** None; this operational change would not impact information security risks.
- **D.** Maximum allowable outage

**18.** Which statement about business continuity planning and information security is most correct?

- **A.** Plans are more important than the planning process itself.
- **B.** Planning is more important than the plans it produces.
- **C.** Plans represent significant investments and decisions, and thus should be updated only when significant changes to objectives or circumstances dictate.
- **D.** Planning should continuously bring plans and procedures in tune with ongoing operational reality.

19. One of your co-workers stated that he thought business continuity planning was a heartless, bottom line–driven exercise that cared only about the money and not about anything else. You disagree. Which of the following points would you not raise in discussing this with your colleague? (Choose all that apply.)

    A. Insurance coverage should provide for meeting the needs of workers or others who are disrupted by the incident and our responses to it.

    B. Due care places on all of us the burden to protect the safety and security of the business, its people, and stakeholders in it, as well as the society we're part of.

    C. As a professional, we're expected to take steps to ensure that the systems we're responsible for do not harm people or the property of others.

    D. The workers and managers are part of what makes the company productive and profitable in normal times, and even more so during the recovery from a significant disruption.

20. How can ideas from the identity management lifecycle be applied to helping an organization's workforce, at all levels, defend against sophisticated social engineering attack attempts? (Choose all that apply.)

    A. Most end users may have significant experience with the routine operation of the business systems and applications that they use; this can be applied, much like identity proofing, to determine whether a suspected social engineering attempt is taking place.

    B. Most end users and their first-level supervisors have the best, most current insight as to the normal business rhythm, flow, inputs, and outcomes. This experience should be part of authenticating an unusual access request (via email, phone, in person, or by any means).

    C. Users think that they know a lot about "business normal," but they tend to know only the narrow scope of their jobs and responsibilities; this does not equip them to contribute to detecting social engineering attacks.

    D. Contact requests by email, by phone, in person, or by other means are akin to access attempts, and they can and should be accounted for.

# Chapter 12

# Risks, Issues, and Opportunities, Starting Tomorrow

As an SSCP, you've chosen to be part of one of the most cutting-edge endeavors we know. The previous 11 chapters have explored the technical and social aspects of what it takes to deliver information security; they've given you the chance to build your skills with the physical, logical, and administrative controls as you help your organization or business cope with information risk mitigation and management.

Let's take several giant steps back from the details and look at a few current issues that are attracting attention and analysis in the cybersecurity field and see what they suggest about the future. We'll use that as our springboard to look at how that may suggest options for your personal and professional growth, as well as perhaps revealing business opportunities you might want to consider pursuing.

All of that will help us put the final task of preparing to take the SSCP exam itself in perspective; we'll also look at all of the places you might go, once you've crossed that Rubicon.

# On Our Way to the Future

Let's face it—most of what we do as SSCPs is still very brand new. Yes, there are fundamental concepts and theoretical models that are the core of what we do, that information security professionals have been making use of since the 1960s. Yet it was in 1965 that Gordon Moore, who would later found Fairchild Semiconductor and become CEO of Intel, coined what's become known as "Moore's Law." Every two years, Moore said, the number of devices we can put on a chip will double; that's *exponential growth* in complexity, interconnectedness, and the power of the devices we compute with. Since then, the number of people on the globe has more than doubled as well, while the number of devices using the Internet has increased from a paltry handful to billions and billions. We've had to invent new numbers to cope with the sheer amount of data created every minute, growing from kilobytes to terabytes and now zetabytes. And we're seeing over a million new pieces of malware cropping up in the wild *every day*, according to some cybersecurity threat intelligence sources.

Along that arrow of growth headed toward the future, we've also seen an equally explosive growth in the challenges that we as SSCPs face when we try to keep our organizations' information and information systems safe, secure, and reliable. We've seen *computer crime* go from a laughable idea that prosecutors, courts, and legislators would not think about, to the central, unifying concept behind national and personal security. The war on organized crime and terrorism, for example, is fundamentally a war of analytics, information security, and perception management.

With this explosive growth in capability and demand has come a mind-boggling growth in opportunity. Old ideas suddenly find ways to take wing and fly; new ideas spark in the minds of the young, the old, and children, who organize crowdfunding campaigns to launch new digitally empowered, cloud-hosted businesses. Things we used to think were nice ideas but simply had no business case can suddenly become profitable, successful, and worthwhile products. Think of how 3D printers enable the profitable creation of custom-engineered prosthetics for children as well as adults, for example, or stethoscope apps for your smartphone. What's next?

Each chapter has identified some ongoing issues, or problems not yet solved, in its subject domain; along the way, we've seen indicators that some of these might be worth keeping an eye on as we move into our future. Many of these are opportunities for the threat actor to find new ways to create mischief for us; then, too, these selfsame issues are opportunities for us, as SSCPs, to create new and more effective ways of combating the threat actors all around us.

Where there's a problem, there's an opportunity. Let's take a look.

## Access Control and Zero Trust

Access control and identity management have taken a center-stage role in our continuing struggle to secure information systems, as you saw in Chapter 6, "Identity and Access Control," in some depth. Recently, we've heard this entire topic area referred to as making *information access gates* for our datacenters. This gatekeeper function will no doubt continue to grow in importance in the coming decade. Of all of the access control paradigms, role-based access control (RBAC) looks to be the leading set of concepts and technologies to help implement the fine-grained, nonstop authentication and authorization capabilities we increasingly need.

This ties in directly with the notion of zero trust architectures. But I would raise a caution flag here by asking you a question: what should drive the detailed design, implementation, and operation of your business's zero trust networks, platforms, systems, and federated access arrangements? Should we start with an information risk assessment and work it top-down and, along the way, be developing an information security classification guide and process? Or should we start with the business logic as the known, as-built expression of how the organization achieves its objectives, and look at that logic from an information security, separation of duties, and constant verification perspective?

There are very tempting solutions in the marketplace today, ones that can do more and more for us as we strive to integrate identity management for every kind of subject (be it person, device, or process) and object with our access control needs. Applying Moore's Law and thinking about the network effect (when we connect things in a network, the power of the network grows as the square of the number of nodes does) leads us to think that large, complex organizations and their information systems are going to have tremendously large, complex RBAC databases, perhaps with some *very* complicated Boolean logic in them.

# AI, ML, BI, and Trustworthiness

Several trend lines are merging together, it seems, as we think about how our information and our information security tools are getting *smarter*. One trend we see is how applied artificial intelligence (AI) is creating many different paradigms for software to interact with other software and, in the process, make the physical hardware that hosts that software take action in ways that perhaps are not quite what we anticipated when we built it. We already have software tools that can "decide" to look for more information, to interact with other tools, and to share data, metadata, rules, and the results of using those rules to form conclusions. In 2018, The Verge reported on a 2016 video made by Google researcher Nick Foster called "The Selfish Ledger." Playing on ideas from selfish genes (and selfish memes), the video suggests that we're nearly at the point where the collection of data about an individual subject—a person, a company, or a set of abstract ideas—could decide by itself how and when to influence the software and hardware that hosts it to take actions so that the data object can learn, grow, acquire other data, and maybe even learn to protect itself. As a selfish ledger, it could and would do this without regard for any value this might have for the *subject* of that information. Imagine such selfish ledgers in the hands of the black hats; how could you defend against them?

Another trend is in *machine learning* (ML), which is a subset of applied AI. ML, as it's called, tends to use meshes of processing elements (which can each be in software, hardware, or both) that look for statistical relationships between input conditions and desired outputs from that mesh; this *training* takes thousands of sets of inputs and lets the mesh compute its own parameters by which each processing element manipulates its inputs and its memory of previous results to produce and share an output with others in the mesh. The problem is, these meshes cannot explain to us, their builders and users, why or how they computed the answer that they got and the action they then took (or caused to happen) as a result.

*Analytics*, the science of applying statistical and associative techniques to derive meaning from data, is already one of the hottest topics in computing, and both of its major forms are becoming even hotter as organizations seek ways to apply them to information security. *Business intelligence* (BI) takes this into the domain of making business or other decisions, based on what can be inferred about the data. Many of us see this when online merchants or media channels suggest that other users, like us, have also looked at *these* products or videos, for example. BI and machine learning drive the transformation of news from broadcasting to *narrowcasting*, in which the same major news channels show you a different set of headlines, based on what that ML "thinks" you're most likely to favor or respond to. BI looks to what has happened and strives to find connections between events. *Predictive intelligence (PI)* strives to make analytics-based predictions about possible outcomes of decisions that others might make. Both BI and PI are being applied to end-user (or subject) *behavior analysis* to determine whether a subject's behavior is "not quite business normal" or is a precursor or indicator of a possible change in behavior in ways that put information security at risk. Applied AI and machine learning techniques figure prominently in BI and PI, particularly when applied to information security problems.

One major worry about the dramatic growth in the capabilities and processing power of AI and ML systems is that our concepts of *computationally infeasible attacks* on cryptographic systems will be proven to be just an overly optimistic assertion. It was, after all, the birth of the supercomputer that allowed for massively parallel attacks by NSA on Soviet and other cryptosystems that drove even more growth in supercomputing, massively parallel software architectures, and network systems performance. Constructing a parallel processing system of hundreds of nodes is nearly child's play these days (high schools have been known to construct them from "obsolete" PC/XTs, following Oak Ridge National Laboratories' recipe for the Stone Soupercomputer Project). We're seeing the same approaches used to cobble together huge systems for cryptocurrency mining as well. It's hard not to feel that it's only a matter of time before our public key infrastructure and asymmetric encryption algorithms fall to the cracker's attacks.

By the way, one of these ML/AI tool sets, called Sophia, is incorporated or hosted in a partial human shape (just her face and upper body at present); she has demonstrated a continued growth in her conversational skills. While an earlier AI was voted onto the board of directors of a major Hong Kong venture capital firm, Sophia has gone one step further: as of October 25, 2017, she has been a *citizen* of Saudi Arabia. *This means that under international law, we now have a robot protected by the United Nations Charter and its declaration of human rights.* (Sadly, when Sophia travels, she travels in, not with, a set of matched hardened equipment cases, rather than sitting in business class; as of her 2019 visit to Montevideo, Uruguay, she did so on Customs clearance documents rather than her Saudi passport.) We're still a ways away from whether Sophia has a legitimate and defensible claim to having human rights or not; in the meantime, check out her story at Hanson Robotics' website, `www.hansonrobotics.com/Sophia`.

In one respect, this is an age-old problem in new clothes. We've never really known what was going on in someone else's head; we watched their behavior, we'd try to correlate that with what they *said* they'd do, and then we'd decide whether to continue trusting them or not. But at least with some people, we could *ask* them to explain why they did what they did, and that explanation might help us in our continual decision about how far to trust them. When our ML and AI and other tools cannot explain, how do we trust?

# Quantum Communications, Computing, and Cryptography

The algorithms have already been published for using the power of quantum computing architectures to break the integer factorization problem—the heart of the RSA encryption process and the heart of our public key infrastructure. All it would take, said mathematician Peter Shor, was a mega-qubit or giga-qubit processor. So far, the largest of quantum computer processors is claimed to have 2,000 qubits, while IBM's announcement in January 2019 of the System Q One uses 20-qubit processing elements.

The year 2018 saw a growing debate as to whether scalable, high-capacity, and *fast* quantum computing would threaten our current cryptologic architectures and key distribution processes. Some even went so far as to suggest that if they could, we might not even be able to recognize when such an attack took place or was successful. Elliptical curve algorithms for cryptography (ECC) may be a strong part of the "quantum-proofing" we'll have to implement.

## Paradigm Shifts in Information Security?

It's becoming clearer (say a number of commentators) that while the information security industry has paid a lot of attention to the *technical* aspects of keeping systems and information secure, we haven't made a lot of progress in strengthening the *human* element of these systems. It may be more than time for several ideas to start to gain traction:

- *Human security behaviors* need more of our attention, understanding, guidance, and management. At best, we've tended to focus on the attacker—their motives, goals, objectives, and methods of operations. This is especially important as we ask our insiders, the people purportedly on *our side* in the struggle for information security, to take on potentially more complex and demanding security-related awareness, understanding, and actions.

- *Transformational communication paradigms* are changing the ways in which our workforce, our customers, our prospective customers, our partners, suppliers, and stakeholders all come together to achieve *their* objectives. Social media technologies are not the issue here—it's the changes in the ways people think about finding, using, and sharing observations, insights, and data that are. Some businesses and organizations get this, and their market effectiveness and the loyalty of their customers and team members show this. Other organizations haven't gotten here yet. The classical systems geek approach to this offers mobile device management (MDM) approaches, and maybe natural language processing (are tweets *in* natural language, I wonder?), but this seems to be only scratching the surface of the possible.

- *Digital nomads* are becoming more the norm as virtual workspaces and virtual organizations proliferate. Whether this is because work in many industries is becoming focused on smaller parts of projects, or even atomized into discrete tasks, many talented people pack up their laptop and smartphone and tour the world while working for (or with) multiple businesses and organizations. Hotel and coffee shop Wi-Fi is becoming passé, as Airbnb-like entrepreneurial cafes offer hourly, daily, or weekly options for high-quality connections, comfortable work surroundings—and no bosses! This is as much a BYOI approach to infrastructure as it is becoming a case of OPI—other people's infrastructure.

- *The semantics of data* is becoming more integral to systems and business operations. In the last decade, we've seen significant growth in the use of metadata, tags, and other techniques to let packages of data incorporate their own meanings with them; smarter systems act on the meanings, interpret them, and then apply them as part of how that data is put to use. Security information event monitoring, analysis, and modeling systems are only beginning to look at ways to apply these concepts. Semantic analysis of data, and of its metadata, may be a high-payoff approach to dealing with far too many log entries and far too little human analytical power to spot the precursors or indicators.

- *Greater emphasis on safety and privacy* are changing the ways in which we think about managing projects. The traditional trio of cost, schedule, and performance still apply, of course, but in many ways we're starting to see a greater emphasis on product and system safety, as well as on protecting privacy-related information that will be part of the resulting system.

These and other similar mini-trends have a few things in common. First, they focus on the ways that the revolutionary changes in the nature of apps, platforms, tools, and systems have worked hand in hand with the revolutions in interpersonal and interorganizational work and communications patterns. Second, they are part of the pressure to further decentralize, fragment, or uncouple our organizations and our systems, whether we think about that electronically, contractually, or personally. Taken altogether, they strongly suggest that the core competencies of the SSCP and others in the information systems security ecology may have to change as well.

## Perception Management and Information Security

The art and science of perception management deals with a plain and simple fact: when it comes to human behavior, what humans perceive, think, and believe about a situation *is* the reality of the situation. Reality, to us humans, is not the tangible, physical objects, or the actions of others around us; it is the nonstop narrative we tell ourselves—the video we watch inside our heads, which is our *interpretation* of what our senses were telling us—and results in our *modeling* of what *might* have been happening around us.

Applying this to information systems security, we might see that

- Customers, prospective clients, and the public have their beliefs as to whether or not our company does a great job of protecting their information.

- Management and leadership want to believe that their employees understand the need for information security, have taken to heart the training provided, and are working hard to keep the company, their jobs, and shareholder value safe and secure by protecting critical information.

- Employees often perceive information security programs as saying "management doesn't trust you."

- Regulators believe that few private organizations report truthfully about every information security incident.

- Information security team members perceive that management isn't interested in taking information security seriously.

- Departmental managers might believe the company is spending too much on information security and not enough on *their* department's value-chain-impacting needs.

Think back to what we looked at in Chapter 10, "Incident Response and Recovery," using this perception management lens, and we might see that the people on the incident response team or the crew in the security operations center are *interpreting* what the systems are telling them *through their own internalized filters* that are based on their beliefs.

They *believe* they did a diligent job of setting alarm limits and programmed the right access control list settings into the firewalls, and thus what their dashboards and network security systems are telling them *must* be correct.

Right?

Part of the successful STUXNET attack on the Iranian nuclear fuels processing facility was that it managed the perceptions of the facility's engineering and operations crews by keeping them willing to believe what their instruments and dashboards were telling them about the plant's operating conditions.

Perception management might find gainful employment on several information security fronts:

▪ Presenting security needs, procedures, and techniques to employees, their managers, and leaders as part of gaining improved *usefulness* from our logical, physical, and administrative controls

▪ More effective communication with managers and leaders when escalating issues pertaining to an incident and incident response

▪ Better design of incident response procedures, particularly ones involved in the high-stress environment of disaster recovery

▪ Better engagement and support from customers, prospective customers, and others, with the controls built into webpages, apps, and even voice-to-voice interactions with the organization and its systems

## Widespread Lack of Useful Understanding of Core Technologies

In Chapter 7, "Cryptography," we saw that an unfortunate number of people look at cryptography as if it were a silver-bullet solution to our problems in meeting their CIANA needs for confidentiality, integrity, availability, nonrepudiation, and authentication; if only we could "sprinkle a little more crypto dust" on things, they all would work so much better. The same underinformed beliefs about migrating to "the cloud" (as if there is only *one* cloud) often lead to ill-considered decisions about migrating to the right set of cloud-hosted services and platforms. Some people think that the Internet needs a "kill switch," and they believe they know whose finger ought to hover over it. And so on… There could almost be a special section in the local computer bookstore, something like "key IT technologies for lawyers, accountants, and managers," just like all of the other self-help books focused on business management and leadership. There already are a *lot* of titles published as if they're aimed at that corner of the bookstore.

It's not that we as systems security specialists need *everyone* to be full-fledged geeks, steeped in the technologies and proficient in their use. On the contrary: *we need to communicate better* about these core technologies as they apply to our company's information security needs, the problems a client is having, or to the doubts and fears (or unbridled optimism) of those we work with.

This is where your knowledge, skills, and experience have much to offer.

## IT Supply Chain Vulnerabilities

In the late 1990s, it was just barely possible for U.S. government systems builders to spend the money, time, and effort to assure that mission-critical IT systems were built and dependent on a trustworthy IT supply chain. Inspection, auditing, test, and validation costs for these efforts were significant. Most major businesses could not afford that kind of risk management in the 1990s; small and medium-sized enterprises can afford it even less today. The hierarchies of trust that we all depend on have one element in them that we haven't made much mention of thus far, and that is our trust in the laws of large numbers. The vast majority of Internet users sleep easily after each day's surfing or e-banking because they *believe* that they are one of millions of "small fry," too insignificant to tempt hackers to attack, and reasonably law-abiding enough to not attract the attention of government agencies who might leave trapdoors behind for later exploitation. We blithely ignore how advanced persistent threat actors routinely use zombie botnet systems as elements in their attacks on more lucrative targets; after all, we have nothing at risk, we think.

Market demand for more and more computing power *now*, more and cheaper storage, faster and cheaper connectivity, are all colliding to amplify pressures on the IT supply chain that have always existed. Cycles of market fragmentation and consolidation combine with shorter and shorter design lifetimes (time to design and market viability of that design) to encourage shortcuts and compromises.

Our trust in "hiding in plain sight" as one of the "small fry" may be a blind trust, after all.

## Government Overreactions

National governments have the responsibility to protect and secure the property, interests, and lives of their citizens—rich and poor, weak and powerful alike. Whether that government is a totalitarian dictatorship or a parliamentary democracy operating with the consent of their governed, all governments see secret communications by others as a threat to their power. Governments tell us that they cannot keep us protected from organized crime, terrorists, or communists if they cannot read any message, email, file, or document that they think they have a "national security" need to read. Many noteworthy cases have hit the headlines recently in which governments could not crack the codes on a suspect's iPhone or other device, and the manufacturer both refused to help and claimed no technical capabilities to help decrypt such information. It's ironic that the companies trusted the least by many in the general public—Apple, Microsoft, Google, Amazon, etc.—are the ones that have fought against government efforts to force them to build trapdoors into the encryption systems they build into their products.

There are many civil liberties and social safety concerns tangled up in this issue; rather than address them here, let's look instead at the practicalities. Without something like PKI and the cryptosystems that make it robust, resilient, and secure, much of our e-commerce economy could not function. We know this.

We also know that the hierarchies of trust that make those infrastructures work are almost totally owned and operated by private businesses and not by governments. This may be the only thing that keeps those systems secure, rather than allowing them to become politicized.

# CIA, CIANA, or CIANAPS?

As you saw in Chapter 5, "Communications and Network Security," there's a powerful advantage we accrue as SSCPs when we add nonrepudiation and authentication to the CIA security triad of confidentiality, integrity, and availability. But it's not clear that there's any end to adding on requirements to CIANA's list of worthy attributes.

*Safety* considerations, as a fundamental systems engineering thought process, are becoming more and more important and more influential, as the work of Dr. Nancy Leveson and others at MIT are proving to be. Her initial work on the Systems Theoretic Accident Model and Process (STAMP) has seen significant application in software systems reliability, resilience, and accident prevention and reduction; it's also being applied to cybersecurity in many powerful and exciting ways.

Privacy concerns will no doubt continue to escalate. We've already seen that in the United States, NIST is strengthening its call for more thoughtful application of privacy protection methods to information systems security design and operation. It's possible that as the pressures on national governments and regional governance processes increase, we may see schisms developing between the ways that different governments and their national industries want to deal with data protection, data sharing, and privacy. The small differences we saw as the General Data Protection Regulation (GDPR) became effective in 2018 may only be the tip of many icebergs.

This is reminiscent of what has happened with the military's acronym for command and control. First, they added *communications* to it; then *intelligence*; *computers* was added to grow C3I into C4I (no one in the military types that "4" as an exponent, which they did with $C^2$, $C^3$, even $C^3I$, which they'd dutifully pronounce as "cee-cubed-eye"). As with C4ISR (adding *surveillance* and *reconnaissance* to the mix), the key is that the concepts layer on, one after the other, as the users of the terms look both broader and deeper at the why and how of using information to make decisions, carry them out, and monitor what happens as a result.

CIANAPS is much the same idea. Who knows? Perhaps we'll have to consider adding other measures of effectiveness in design and operation, such as resilience, or *understandability* (if we fear that without it, we'll never know what our machine learning *is* learning or doing), in the coming years.

# Enduring Lessons

Having gazed into the near-term future and seen some of the tantalizing opportunities that might be awaiting us there, let's return to the present. Our profession has over 60 years of experience to its credit; it's no surprise that some enduring lessons emerge. We've looked in depth at some of them across many of the preceding chapters, but they're worthy of a last few parting words and some thoughtful reflection at this point.

## You Cannot Legislate Security

Well, you *can* actually legislate better information security for your organization or company. It just doesn't get you very far. You can write all of the administrative controls that you want to; you can get the CEO to sign off on them, and you can push copies of them out to everyone involved. All of that by itself does not change attitudes or habits; none of that changes perceptions or behaviors. (And none of it changes the technical implementation of security policies within our networks, servers, endpoints, platforms, and apps, either.)

If the history of workplace safety is any guide, it will take significant financial incentives, driven into place by insurers, reinsurers, and the investment community, to make serious information security ideas become routine practices.

## It's About Managing Our Security and Our Systems

Experience has shown us, rather painfully, that unmanaged systems only stay secure through what can only be called *dumb luck*. Attackers may not have found them, hiding in plain sight among the billions of systems on the Internet, or if they did, a few quick looks around didn't tempt them to try to take control or extract valuable data from them. Managing our systems security processes requires us to manage those systems as collections of assets, as designs, as processes, as places people work, and as capabilities they need to get their work done. We must be part of the management and governance of these systems, and the data that makes them valuable and value-producing. We must manage every aspect of the work we and others do to deliver the CIANA, the privacy, the resilience, the safety, and the continuity of operations that our business needs. If it's an important aspect of achieving the business's goals or the organization's objectives, *we must actively manage what it takes* to delivery that capability and that aspect of *decision assurance*.

We have to become more adept at managing information risk. We need to become past masters at translating risk, via vulnerability assessment, into risk mitigation plans and procedures; we then must manage how we monitor those risk mitigation systems in action, and manage our interpretation of the alarm bells they ring at 5 minutes before quitting time on a Friday afternoon.

Our organizations' leaders are looking to us—their information security professionals—to also help manage the process that keeps what we monitor, what we do, and how we act to secure those systems aligned with the goals and objectives of the organization. We're the ones they'll look to, to fit the security processes into the organizational culture; that, too, is a management challenge.

## People Put It Together

No matter how much automation we put into our systems; no matter how simple or complex they are; around and above all of the technical and physical elements of those systems we find the people who need them, use them, build them, operate them, abuse and misuse them, don't believe them, or aren't critical enough in assessing what the systems are trying to tell them about. The people inside our organization, as well as those outsiders we deal with, are both the greatest source of strength, insight, agility, and awareness as well as potentially being the greatest source of anomalies, misuse (accidental or deliberate), frustration, or obstructivism. We have to worry about insiders who might turn into attackers, outsiders trying to intrude into our systems, and insiders who simply don't follow the information security and systems use rules and policies we've put in place for everyone's benefit.

What kind of people do our organizations need working for us if we are to really prepare for and achieve operational continuity despite accident, attack, or bad weather? Michael Workman, Daniel Phelps, and John Gathegi, in *Information Security for Managers* (2013), cited six basic aptitudes and attitudes we need from our people if they are going to help us get work done right, keep that work and the work systems safe and secure, and in doing so, protect the organization's existence and their own jobs. This kind of people power needs people who

- Know what their roles, duties, and responsibilities are

- Know the boundaries of those roles, and understand and appreciate the consequences (to themselves and to others) of going beyond those boundaries

- Understand the policies that apply to their jobs and roles, particularly the ones pertaining to information security

- Have been trained to do the jobs and tasks we ask them to do, and have demonstrated their proficiency in those tasks as a result

- Know how *and why* to monitor for signs of trouble, anomalies, or possible security incidents, as well as know what to do and who to contact if they think they've spotted such events

- Know how to respond when emergencies or security incidents occur; and then respond as required

As an SSCP working on information security and protecting the organization's IT infrastructure, you have a slice of each of those six "people power preparedness" tasks. Start by thinking about what *you* would want somebody else in the organization to know, as it pertains to information security, in each of those areas. Jot that down. You're starting to build an awareness, education, and training program! You can be—and *should* be—one of the security evangelists within your organization. Help set the climate and culture to help encourage better *information security hygiene* across the organization. Take that evangelism outside as well; work with key customers, partners, stakeholders, and others in your organization's marketplace or context. Keeping that community safer and more secure is in everyone's best interest.

If at this point you're concerned that your own interpersonal skills may not be up to the task, don't worry; go do something about that. Join Toastmasters, which can help even the most poised and confident among us improve our abilities to speak with a group of people. Check with your organization's human resources management group to see what kind of professional development opportunities you can participate in.

## Maintain Flexibility of Vision

Whether you're in the early days of a security assessment or down in the details of implementing a particular mitigation control, you'll find that you frequently need to shift not just *where* your focus and attention is directed but whether you're zoomed in closely on the details or zoomed far out to see the bigger picture and the surrounding context. This is sometimes referred to as having your own *strategic telescope* and knowing how and when to use it. Part of this is knowing when to zoom out, or zoom in, by walking around, talking with and listening to people in the various nooks and crannies of the organization. Hear what the end users are telling you, but also try to read between the lines of what they say. Catch the subtext. Think about it.

Most of what an organization knows about how it does what it does is not explicitly known (that is, written down in some tangible form); often, the people who possess this knowledge inside their own heads don't consciously realize what they know either.

As a point of comparison, consider different strategies in neighborhood security and policing. The world over, police departments know that "beat cops," the uniformed police officers out walking a beat in the neighborhoods, become known elements of the community. They become part of the *normal*; people become more trusting of them, over time, and look to them as sources of help and security, rather than as the power of authority. As one of your organization's information security team, that same opportunity may present itself to you. As Yogi Berra said, it's amazing what you can see if you only look!

## Accountability—It's Personal. Make It So.

High-integrity systems only happen when they are designed, built, used, and maintained by people of high integrity. High-integrity systems—the kinds of systems that we are willing to entrust with our lives, our fortunes, and our sacred honor—are all around us; we don't recognize how many of them are part of what makes our day-to-day electronic world keep on working. Key to every step in that journey of a high-integrity system, from initial requirements to ongoing operations, is the *accountability* of each person involved with that system and its processes.

When we step back from the sharp, demanding edge of the high-integrity systems, though, we should not be willing to stop demanding personal and professional accountability from those we work those systems with. What we can do, though, is model the very accountability we know we need to see in everyone around us.

Avoid waffle-speak; say "I made a mistake" instead of "Mistakes were made." Help others recover from the mistakes they've made, and work to find ways that prevent others from doing the same mistake as well. Do your homework; dig for the facts; verify them, six different ways from Sunday as they used to say, if the situation demands it. By showing the people around you that you are prepared to take your professional obligations seriously and that you deliver on those obligations in that way, every day, you'll find that you actually can lead by example in ways that count.

## Stay Sharp

Keep staying sharp—technically, about systems, about threats, and about the overall geo-political-economic landscape you're a part of. Read well beyond the immediate needs of what you're doing at work and well beyond the kind of subjects and sources you've usually, habitually used for information (or infotainment!). By studying to become an SSCP, you've already built a solid foundation of knowledge and skills; continue that learning process as you build onto that foundation.

You've a wealth of opportunities to feed that growing information security learning habit of yours! Podcasts; e-news subscriptions, and blogs that focus on IT issues, information security, compliance, and risk management; books; courses—no matter how you take in new ideas best, there's a channel and a format out there in the marketplace ready to bring you the insights and information you need. Work toward other certifications by studying and gaining experience that builds on your new SSCP and empowers you to dive deeper into topics and technologies that suit you.

That said, don't be afraid to wander away from that foundation now and then! Get playful—think outside the box and stretch your mind. Many of the great newspapers of the world (now in their online forms, of course) are deservedly respected for the reach, breadth, and quality of their explorations into all aspects of science and technology, the arts, cultures around the world, business, and industry, and of course for their in-depth analysis of current events in politics and economics. Take risks with ideas; let something *new* excite you and chase after it for a while, researching and thinking about it.

Play. Play logic games; go orienteering; read whodunits and other mysteries, occasionally challenging yourself to see if you can solve the mystery before the author reveals all in the last chapter. Playfulness engages the fun side of your brain; let that happen at work, too.

Teach. Become an advocate for your profession; participate in local school-age programs that help the next generation keep *their* world safe and secure too.

Speak; write. Attend information security conferences, meet with others, and network with them. Share ideas, and in doing so, become more of an active member of your community of practitioners.

Beware of two very common fallacies, and work to avoid becoming trapped in their webs. The first of these asserts that there is nothing left to discover: we have all of the answers on Topic X or Subject Y that we'll ever need. It's been done before; it's always been done this way; these are variants of this "nothing new under the sun" fallacy. The other is the drive to oversimplify; it demands almost trivially simple answers to what may *seem* to be simple questions or situations, but in reality are anything *but* simple.

We talked about this in an earlier chapter, too, but it's worth remembering Kipling's Six Wise Men. Hire these guys! Put them on your mental payroll. Who. What. Why. When. Where. How. Then, *put them to work by asking good questions, every day.* Open-ended questions such as "Why do you think that happened that way?" invite others to think along with you. Engage their curiosity by using your own.

# Your Next Steps

It's time to get ready for the next steps toward your SSCP. You've gone through this book, and you've made good use of the review questions in each chapter; you've done thought experiments as you've exercised applying the concepts in each section, drawn from each of the SSCP domains, to real situations you're involved with at work or familiar with from experience.

You've done the practice exams. You've reviewed all of the study materials. You're ready to take the exam.

What's next? Schedule, take, and succeed at the SSCP exam.

You take the SSCP exam in person, typically at a PearsonVue test center convenient to you. www.isc2.org will have the latest information about the test process and where to go to schedule your test appointment. Pay close attention to the policies about rescheduling your exam—and if you're a no-show for your scheduled appointment, for any reason, you will lose your entire testing fee!

Be sure to read and heed the test center's policies about food, drink, personal items, and such. You'll have to leave your phone, watch, car keys, and everything else in your pockets in a locker at the test site; you will be monitored during the testing process, and the test is timed of course.

If you have any conditions that might require special accommodation in testing, contact the testing company *well in advance.* Speak with them about the accommodation you are requesting, and be prepared to provide them authoritative documentation to support your request. Contact (ISC)² if you have any questions or need their assistance in this regard.

Schedule your exam for a day that allows you time to relax and unwind for a day or so beforehand; if possible, take the preceding day and the test day itself off from work or other studies and obligations.

If you can, schedule the exam for a time of day that is your best to do hard, thoughtful, detailed, concentrated work. The exam is quite demanding, so it's to your benefit to work to remove sources of worry and uncertainty about the test and the test process. Find the test center—drive to it to get a good idea of the time it will take you on the test day itself to arrive and still have plenty of time to relax for a bit before starting your test.

The night before, get a good night's sleep. Do the things you know work best for you to help you relax and enjoy a carefree, restful slumber. Set your alarm, and set a backup alarm if you need it, and plan to get to the test center early. Go on in, register, and succeed!

When you complete testing, the test center will give you a preliminary statement of the results you achieved. Smile, thank them for their help, and leave; whether you earned a "preliminary pass" or not, is not something you need to share with others in the testing center or their staff.

It may take a few days for (ISC)$^2$ to determine whether your preliminary pass is affirmed. If so, congratulations! They'll work with you on converting you from applicant to associate to full membership status, based on your experience and education to date that is applicable to systems security. Welcome to the team!

# At the Close

I want to take this final opportunity to thank you for coming on this journey with me. You're here because you value a world where information can enable and empower people to make their dreams become reality; you value truth, accuracy, and integrity. And you're willing to work hard to protect that world from accidents, bad design, failures in the face of Mother Nature, and enemy action large or small. Integrity matters to you. That's a tough row to hoe. It needs our best.

Let's get to it.

# Appendix

# Answers to Review Questions

# Self-Assessment

1.  D. Planning should be an ongoing, continuous, and iterative process; plans are thus continually tested against reality so that changes to plans and procedures stay harmonized. Thus, Option D is most correct. Option C, unfortunately, is a commonly held view and can lead to work being done to obsolete ideas or to assumptions long since proven to be incorrect by reality. Option B is good but not as correct and complete as D. Option A is incorrect; effective plans define and prioritize objectives, lay out major tasks and processes, assign resources to achieve those, and define success criteria for each; plans should be manageable and measurable.

2.  C. Options A, B, and D all demonstrate the hallmarks of social engineering attacks—they work (and have worked for thousands of years) because people are generally trusting, open, and willing to engage with strangers. Option C, the correct choice, is unfortunately not true; tools may help filter out some email-based social engineering attacks, but few organizations have truly been able to operate with a "loose lips sink ships" approach and deal openly with customers, clients, and many other outside stakeholders.

3.  A. Option A is correct; phishing tends to seek information, and whaling (and spear phishing) seeks action, typically the release of funds to the attacker. Option B is incorrect; whaling is primarily aimed at senior business leaders, whereas phishing can be aimed at anybody, anywhere, if the attacker perceives there is something worthwhile to learn in doing so. Option C has these reversed; whaling attacks depend on credibility of the business transaction they request. Option D is incorrect, since it reverses key characteristics of whaling and phishing.

4.  D. While Option A may be true, it is naïve and incorrect; the air conditioning company that serviced Target stores didn't handle retail (credit card) sales either, yet attackers found it to be an ideal entry into Target's payment processing systems. Option C is also incorrect; your cloud hosts will protect their systems, and their platforms, from malware attacks from your connections, but attackers who spoof bogus, privileged accounts into your systems can still destroy your business's presence in those cloud systems. Option B is incorrect; without doing a detailed vulnerability assessment of that architecture, you are at risk making this assumption. Option D offers the boss a sensible first step.

5.  A. Option A by itself won't do what is needed; at a minimum, Option D and its implementation of rigorous access control and identity management is necessary to protect network storage resources from being corrupted, tampered with, and so forth. The others are all valuable parts of a data governance and data security/data protection plan.

6.  A, B. The key determiner of whether user-defined and user-maintained "stuff" is shadow IT is the amount of business logic that it embeds or implements; the more such business logic is built into uncontrolled or unmanaged apps or tools, the greater the risk of something going wrong in undetected ways. Thus Option A is not a probable risk; Option B seems to have a lot of frequent, intensive reviews of the results of these queries, which would need to correlate or compare with what the production information systems would show. Option C implements customer relationship management and systems/product maintenance business logic; Option D seems to circumvent information classification, segregation of duties, and other access control principles. Both C and D bear close watching.

**7.** D. Option A is false; no such agreements apply worldwide. At best, regulations like the General Data Protection Regulation (GDPR) apply to EU member states. Option B is true as far as it goes, but with a catch: if the organization guesses wrong, it could end up in serious legal trouble in multiple jurisdictions. Option C is false; storage of data in a center in another country must involve movement of data from your jurisdiction into the one the datacenter is in, and movement in the reverse direction when you need to use the backup. In almost all cases, data protection laws and regulations apply to data in use, at rest, and in motion. Option D correctly illustrates the need to ensure that professional ethics have a voice in making risk management decisions.

**8.** B, C. Phishing and many other social engineering tactics have played a major role in over 60 percent of major data breaches in the past few years. Such tactics have high payoff to the attacker during their search for a possible target, gathering information about its systems and security, and then their initial entry into the target's systems. Thus Options A and D are likely phases for phishing attacks, and incorrect answers to this question (note the "not make use"). Option B and C are almost exclusively done surreptitiously, exploiting information that social engineering may have revealed to the attacker; few if any signs of phishing in these activities have been noted.

**9.** D. Starting with Option A is a common-sense approach to quickly implementing some reasonable and prudent protection, but it lacks any judgment as to which vulnerabilities are important to your organization's risk management strategy and which are not. Option B is the systems inventory, and you will need it because it describes the as-built systems. Option C is what drives D. Therefore, start shopping for countermeasures with D in hand.

**10.** B, C. Option A is false; Simple Network Management Protocol (SNMP) by itself cannot trigger a device to download and install a firmware patch file. Option D is false, because that operator action can be misdirected to use the wrong file as the update. Option B may be true in some cases, if the device is set to allow remote management from other than a connected endpoint system such as a laptop or smartphone. Attacks like those in Option C happen a lot!

**11.** D. While some zero day exploits have been discovered and exploited within the same day, typically after the release of a new software product to the market, attackers need to spend considerable time on most newly discovered vulnerabilities to understand them well enough to design an exploit against them, and then find a suitable target. So Option A is not correct. Option B incorrectly refers to exploits that leave behind payloads or features that will take action later. Option C incorrectly associates the media reporting of cybersecurity, in general, with the time from discovery to exploitation of a vulnerability.

**12.** B. Since TPMs are special, sealed hardware modules added to the motherboards of computers or phones by their manufacturers, Option D is incorrect, even though TPM device driver software must be incorporated into most OSs to enable their use. Option A is incorrect; the TPM doesn't simplify this but allows for a more trustworthy hardware storage and management of certificates, digital signatures, and so forth. Option C is not correct; these functions in the OS and host hardware remain, while all the TPM provides is its own implementations with which it secures keys, manages certificates, and hashes (preserves) machine identification information.

**13.** A.  Options B, C, and D all are parts of what cryptography entails and taken together sum it up. Option A is more suggestive of camouflage, honeypots, or other efforts to draw attackers away from what you wish to defend and divert their energies elsewhere, which do not directly involve the use of encryption, hashing, and so forth.

**14.** B.  Option A is an incomplete description of asymmetric encryption; Option C is false, since hybrid systems are in widespread use; and Option D is unrelated to symmetric or asymmetric encryption.

**15.** D.  Options A, B, and C are correct. Option D seems to confuse aspects of access control systems, which do have to keep track of—that is, account for—access attempts and allowed accesses.

**16.** D.  While Option A is tempting, cryptographic processes cannot confirm that the certificate and key are correctly associated with a specific human or organization. The Certificate Authority (CA) does that through other (noncryptographic) means, and as an anchor in the chain of trust, attests that this person and this certificate go together. Thus Option D is correct. Option B refers to integrity and Option C to confidentiality, which are not directly part of nonrepudiation.

**17.** C.  The incorrect answers show misapplication of the steps of the process. Option A has reversed who encrypts and who decrypts. Option B confuses the use of the sender's public and private key, and if the recipient knows the sender's private key it must no longer be private. Option D won't work, because decrypting the unencrypted hash won't produce anything that is useful.

**18.** A.  Subjects, by definition, want to *do something* that involves an *object*. Thus, Option A has these roles reversed. Subjects can be any kind of entity that can take action. Objects contain information but also can provide requested services—that is, take action upon request—so Options B and C are correct.

**19.** A.  The reference monitor is the functionality that checks every access attempt to see if it should be authorized or denied. As a result, Option D is false (accounting is a recordkeeping function, necessary to access control but done after the access request is granted or denied). Option C is false, since the reference monitor is in fact implemented in operating systems (typically in their security kernel) or as part of a trusted computing base (TCB) module on a motherboard. Option B is the reverse of what's required; we need to be able to inspect, analyze, and verify that the logic and code of the reference monitor does its job completely and correctly and that it does nothing else if we are to consider it highly trustworthy.

**20.** B, D.  Mandatory access control policies do not allow subjects or objects to modify the security-related aspects of the system, its subjects and objects; thus, granting the privileges in Option A or C cannot be allowed. Options B and D reflect reasonable and prudent access control checks that all systems should perform before granting access but that are not part of mandatory access control policies.

21. B. Item 1, proofing, is part of provisioning, and thus Options A and C are incorrect. Item 5, deletion, happens after revocation, but it is a cleanup of files, assets, and records, and is more properly part of a records retention and housekeeping process. It is not part of identity management per se. Thus Option D is incorrect. Option B correctly reflects that we start by provisioning an identity, we continually review the privileges assigned to it versus the needs of the job and the organization, and then we revoke it.

22. D. Option D is highly risky and therefore correct: plugging a device into an empty network connection should start a connection handshake that is an opportunity to block an unknown or unauthorized device from joining the network. Options A and C are parts of how Option B performs such an authentication, and therefore B is the most secure approach of the three.

23. B. A positive result of an authentication test means that the claimant is who (or what) they claim to be. Thus a false positive is allowing an incorrect identity to access the system, which probably is a threat actor. A negative result denies an identity's claim to be who (or what) they claim to be. Thus a false negative denies a legitimate identity from system access. Thus, Options A and D incorrectly use the concept of negative and positive authentication results (correct and false). While Option C is true, Option B indicates the situation of greatest risk—a threat actor has been legitimized and granted access.

24. B. Option A is false; each additional factor checked increases the challenge an attacker has to overcome to spoof an identity claim. Option C is false; hardware is only needed for factors involving what the subject has, such as a keyfob code generator or biometric factors. Option D is tempting, and high-risk functions might be best protected with additional security measures, but compared to Option B, it is not as compellingly correct.

25. D. Option D accurately reflects the use of both of these as conceptual models and protocol stacks—by builders, attackers, and defenders alike. Option A reflects an incorrect bias of many network engineers who somewhat dismissively ignore things above the Transport layer. Option B is incorrect, because both models drive the design and use of hardware, software, control, and systems management information. Option C is incorrect, since all three sets of concepts drive the design and operation of real hardware, software, and systems.

26. A. Option B is incorrect, because the changes in address field sizes, and therefore packet header structures, have nothing to do with security (although IPv6 does provide enhancements to security). Option C is incorrect; such a conversion could be done by a gateway, but that is not part of IPv6, although IPv6 supports it. Option D is incorrect, although the transport protocols (like TCP and UDP) have not changed, but this is not where the incompatibility comes from.

27. B. Options A and C both incorrectly leave out subnetting in IPv6 and misstate what classless inter-domain routing (CIDR) is about, even though the two options say different incorrect things about CIDR. Option D is partly correct in that IPv6 does have a 16-bit subnet field, and as Option B says, the overall address field size makes subnetting much easier to do, but there is no subnet field in IPv4.

**28.**  A, D. Ports are a fundamental part of the way apps request services from processes running on other nodes on the Internet. Standardized port numbers make applications designs easier to manage; thus, port 80 and HTTP are associated with each other. Therefore, Options A and D show a misunderstanding of what ports are and why they are necessary.

**29.**  B. From the Physical layer on up, the injection of unauthorized traffic into a network can cause almost any protocol to fall for a "mistaken identity" that leads to an MITM attack. Session stealing (Layers 5 and 7) is a prime example, making Option A false. Option C is incorrect, since IP (Layer 2) is inherently connectionless and prone to MITM attacks. Option D is also false, as session stealing (and others) demonstrates.

**30.**  B. Option A misstates the role of ongoing monitoring and conflicts with Option B. Option C suggests a redundant set of capabilities, which may be mission critical for a select few organizations but is not common. Option D may be a useful capability, but it is not the reason for ongoing monitoring.

**31.**  B. If Option A or C was plausible, then you wouldn't actually have a gap. Option D correctly defines the gap but fails to look to how to mitigate the risk posed by the gap.

**32.**  A. Fixing or applying patches to eliminate a vulnerability is the definition of remediating, mitigating, fixing, or repairing a vulnerability.

**33.**  A, B, C. Option D is typically an example of remediating, sometimes called fixing or mitigating the risk.

**34.**  C. Option B does correctly state the risk that attackers may know more about your systems than you do, if you haven't thoroughly checked CVE data as part of your vulnerabilities assessment. But it incorrectly goes on to suggest that you fix these first—they may not relate to your organization's highest-priority impacts as spelled out by the BIA. Option A is therefore false. Option D is also false, since even the most Linux-based of organizations will probably have non-Linux systems elements (such as network components) that CVE could have information about.

**35.**  D. Improving product quality is a laudable goal, but in and of itself it is not related to information systems security; thus Option A is incorrect. Option B refers to activities after an incident; mitigation activities happen before an incident occurs or result from lessons learned because of the incident. Option C is most likely being done to implement new or revised security policies. Option D is part of information risk management and should precede information risk mitigation.

**36.**  C. Option D incorrectly has the BIA first when it has to come after the organization's leadership has agreed to risk tolerance and set priorities. Option B is incorrect, partly because the basic "common-sense" posture is not part of a formal risk management process but a bare minimum immediate set of actions to take if needed. Option A has establishing a posture (which is policy and decisions that drive implementation and operation steps) and implementation in the wrong order.

**37.** B. Option B is the simplest and most effective definition of information risk. Options A and C do not include probability of occurrence (risks are not certain to happen), and describe how risks become events rather than what the risk actually is. Option D is one example, but it does not define information risk.

**38.** D. Proactive means (thinking ahead and planning for contingencies), rather than reactive (waiting until things break). Option A is both wrong and probably illegal in most circumstances. Option B might be true, but it is a general statement about "being proactive" rather than specifically about information security. Option C describes an integrated information security management approach.

**39.** A, B. Option C is the safeguard value, which we cannot compute until we have completed risk assessment and vulnerability assessment, and then designed, specified, or selected such controls or countermeasures. Option D is typically not the loss incurred by damage of an asset; of greater interest regarding impact to an asset would be the cost to repair it (if repairable), replace it, or design and implement new processes to do without it.

**40.** C. Options A and D reflect biases toward or against qualitative assessments (presumably for being "soft" or potentially based on emotions or intuition) or quantitative ones (the data is too hard to get or validate). Using published common vulnerability and exposure (CVE) information can be quite illuminating, but as in Option D, be careful to not just assume that other people's experiences and systems are a good match for your own, or to bow to authoritative statements without carefully considering whether they fit your situation.

**41.** C. Option B has the annual rate of occurrence (ARO) use incorrect; if the ARO was less than 1, the single loss expectancy is in effect spread over multiple years (as if it were amortized). Option A involves restore time and point objectives, which are not involved in the annualized loss expectancy (ALE) calculation. Option D misunderstands ALE = ARO * SLE (single loss expectancy) as the basic math involved.

**42.** A. Option A is a misstatement of RTO and RPO.

**43.** B. Item 3, perspective, should reflect priorities, risk appetite or tolerance, and decision-making culture, and this has to lead all risk management activities. Next comes Item 4, which feeds into the BIA. Item 2 should be a product of the business impact analysis (BIA) process, because it combines costs or magnitude of impacts with acceptable damage limitation strategies. Finally, we choose what to fix, transfer (pay someone else to worry about), accept, or avoid, and any residual risk is recast or re-expressed to reflect these decisions.

**44.** A, B, C. Option D is incorrect; almost everything that holds our IT world together is done via directly building protocols into hardware and software. Options A, B, and C are correct and show the human social communications need for signaling each other about the communication we're trying to achieve.

**45.** D. Options A and C are confusing information, and our systems or processes for using it, with the technologies with which we create, store, and use that information. Option B is a partial answer (it does not address anything other than confidentiality) and might be true, but this is a decision that company leadership and management should make (on advice from the SSCP). Option D is most complete and correct.

**46.** B. Option A incorrectly ignores that failures in security design or practice can lead to data input or systems usage that might be safe and reliable tomorrow, for example, but not today. Option C, true as far as it goes, does not address security at all. Option D incorrectly ignores that the vulnerability assessments that should drive security measures are all based on consequences if the risk becomes real.

**47.** C. Options A and B are both examples of due care; due diligence is the verification that all is being done well and nothing is not done properly. Option D can be an important part of due diligence, but it is missing the potential for follow-up action.

**48.** B. Disclosure of intellectual property in unauthorized ways can end up giving away any competitive advantage that IP might have had for the business.

**49.** D. If the equipment cannot run because there is no power, then no data stored in it can be displayed, printed, or shared with users—data is not available. Some transactions may have to be recovered and rerun once the power comes back up and everything is turned on again, but only if transactions were lost completely would there be a data integrity concern.

**50.** A. Keeping information secret means agreeing to limit or control how (or if) that information can be passed on to others. Privacy is the freedom from intrusion into your own affairs, person, property, or ideas. The other options either confuse confidentiality with privacy or do not use the concepts correctly.

# Chapter 2: Information Security Fundamentals

**1.** B. This is the scientific method in action: make observations, ask questions, make informed guesses, get more data, and see if it fits what you think you've learned thus far. Repeat until you are highly confident.

**2.** B. People make decisions based on what they know, what they remember, and what they observe; that data, information, and knowledge are independent of the paper, books, computers, or radio waves that brought those observations to them in the first place. Options C and D confuse the role of the technologies with the information itself; option A is a true statement that does not address the actual question.

**3.** B. The fact that systems monitoring and event data is collected at all indicates that Paul or his staff determined it was a necessary part of keeping the organization's information systems secure—they took (due) care of those responsibilities. But by not reviewing the data to verify proper systems behavior and use, or to look for potential intrusions or compromises, Paul has not been diligent.

**4.** A. Keeping information secret means agreeing to limit or control how (or if) that information can be passed on to others. Privacy is the freedom from intrusion into your own affairs, person, property or ideas. The other options either confuse confidentiality with privacy or do not use the concepts correctly.

**5.** A. The correctness or wholeness of the data may have been violated, inflating some employees' ratings while deflating others. This violates the presumed integrity of the appraisal data. Presumably, HR staff have legitimate reasons to access the data, and even enter or change it, so it is not a confidentiality violation; since the systems are designed to store such data and make it available for authorized use, privacy has not been violated. Appraisals have not been removed, so there are no availability issues.

**6.** C. What we say and do in public places is, by definition, visible to anyone who wants to watch or listen. Publishing a letter or a book, or writing on a publicly visible social media page, is also considered public speech. We have no reasonable expectation of privacy in social media—we have no basis on which to assume that by posting something on our private pages, others whom we've invited to those pages will not forward that information on to someone else.

**7.** D. If the equipment cannot run because there is no power, then no data stored in it can be displayed, printed, or shared with users—data is not available. Some transactions may have to be recovered and rerun once the power comes back up and everything is turned on again, but only if transactions were lost completely would there be a data integrity concern.

**8.** D. The logic is the set of steps and decisions necessary to achieve the objective; some of those decisions may compare intermediate results with constraints and then branch to alternate steps in the logic to make corrections, for example. The rules and constraints by themselves are not the business logic. Processes (software or people procedures) are not the business logic, but they should accurately and effectively implement that logic.

**9.** A. The sequence of steps in a process (such as a recipe for baking a cake) reflects the logic and knowledge of what needs to be done, in what order, and within what limits, as well as the constraints to achieve the desired conditions or results. That's what business logic is. Most businesses know how to do something that they do better, faster, or cheaper than their competitors, and thus their business logic gives them an advantage in the marketplace.

**10.** B. Although it is clear that the necessary parameter files are not available, this seems to have been caused because somebody could violate the integrity requirements of those files— deleting them does not seem to have been an authorized change.

**11.** B. Disclosure of intellectual property in unauthorized ways can end up giving away any competitive advantage that IP might have had for the business.

**12.** A. All other groups have a valid personal or financial interest in the success and safe operation of the company; a major chemical spill or a fire producing toxic smoke, for example, could directly injure them or damage their property. Although tax authorities might also suffer a loss of revenues in such circumstances, they are not involved with the company or its operation in any way.

13. A, C. "Safety" for information systems can mean keeping the system from suffering damage, keeping the system from failing in ways that cause damage, or both. Thus, Options A and C are correct, though they are different aspects of safety. Option B is true, but it reverses cause and effect. Option D is incorrect because it tries to separate safety and security when they are in fact related to each other.

14. A. Option A correctly interprets the words themselves of the preamble. Option B is incorrect. The preamble does not set personal values (such as honesty); these are in the canons and tied to actions we should take. Option C misses the point of the purpose of the code.

15. C. Options A and B are both examples of due care; due diligence is the verification that all is being done well and that nothing is not done properly. Option D can be an important part of due diligence but is missing the potential for follow-up action.

16. A, B, C, D. Options A and C represent direct or indirect stakeholders in the business that employs the SSCP. Options B and D represent other members of society, and you owe them professional service as an SSCP as well. The service you owe others in the marketplace would not include divulging your employer's private data, of course!

17. B. Option A ignores that failures in security design or practice can lead to data input or systems usage that might be safe and reliable tomorrow, for example, but not today. Option C, true as far as it goes, does not address security at all. Option D ignores that the vulnerability assessments that should drive security measures are all based on consequences if the risk becomes real.

18. D. Options A and C are confusing information, and our systems or processes for using it, with the technologies with which we create, store, and use that information. Option B is a partial answer (it does not address anything other than confidentiality), and it might be true, but this is a decision that company leadership and management should make (with advice from the SSCP). Option D is the most complete and correct answer.

19. A, B, C. Option D is incorrect; almost everything that holds our IT world together is done via directly building protocols into hardware and software. Options A, B, and C are correct, and they show the human social communications need for signaling one another about the communication we're trying to achieve.

20. B, D. In many respects the debate about what to call what we're studying is somewhat meaningless. Option D shows that in different communities the different terms are held in greater or lesser favor. It is how people use terms that establishes their meaning and not what a "language authority" declares the terms to mean. Option B describes this common use of different terms as if they are different ideas—defense and intelligence communities, for example, prefer "cybersecurity," whereas financial and insurance risk managers prefer "information assurance." And yet defense will use "information assurance" to refer to what senior commanders need when making decisions, and everybody talks about "information security" as if all it involves is the hard, technical stuff—but didn't cybersecurity cover that? Options A and C are other incomplete expressions of these ideas.

# Chapter 3: Integrated Information Risk Management

1. C. Option D incorrectly has the BIA first, but the BIA has to come after the organization's leadership has agreed to risk tolerance and set priorities. Option B is incorrect partly because the basic "common sense" posture is not part of a formal risk management process but a bare-minimum immediate set of actions to take if needed. Option A has establishing a posture (which consists of policies and decisions that drive implementation and operation steps) and implementation in the wrong order.

2. B. Option B is the simplest and most effective definition of information risk. Options A and C do not include probability of occurrence (risks are not certain to happen), and describe how risks become events rather than what the risk actually is. Option D is one example, but it does not define information risk.

3. B. Option B correctly shows the use of information to make decisions, as well as the roles of processes and technologies in doing so. Option A mistakenly suggests that the IT risks are more important; IT risks may be how important information is lost or compromised, but it is that information loss or impact that puts businesses out of business and not the failure of their IT systems. Option C confuses risk management with information risk. Option D also mistakes the role of information and the roles of processes and technologies, both in achieving objectives and in risk management.

4. D. Options A, B, and C are correct statements about each perspective, but they each falsely proclaim that their approach is the only one needed.

5. C. Option C shows both the purpose of an integrated approach (timely incident characterization and management) and the use of communications capabilities in doing so. Options A and D demonstrate that vendor self-description of their products can sound good but does not really address key needs. Option B is true, and partially addresses how point solutions need to be mutually supportive, but does not go far enough.

6. D. Proactive involves thinking ahead and planning for contingencies, as opposed to being reactive, or waiting until things break. Option A is both wrong and probably illegal in most circumstances. Option B might be true, but it is a general statement about "being proactive" rather than specifically about information security. Option C describes an integrated information security management approach.

7. D. Options A and C highlight what seem to be Tom's failures to adequately plan for or implement offsite backup storage of system images and data, and his failures to institute effective verification of the security of that storage. Option B is incorrect—the lack of records does not relieve Tom of the burden to check that things are working correctly anyway.

**8.** A, B. Option C is the safeguard value, which we cannot compute until we have completed a risk assessment and a vulnerability assessment, and then designed, specified, or selected such controls or countermeasures. Option D is typically not the loss incurred by damage of an asset; of greater interest regarding impact to an asset would be the cost to repair it (if repairable), replace it, or design and implement new processes to do without the damaged or disrupted asset.

**9.** A. The business impact analysis (BIA) is an integrated view of the prioritized risks and the projected impacts they could have on the business. Option B is a misstatement of the confidentiality, integrity, and availability (CIA) needs for information security. Options C and D suggest realistic management needs for bringing together plans, costs, budgets, and timelines, but they are incomplete as stated and may not even exist.

**10.** C. Options A and D reflect biases toward or against qualitative assessments (presumably for being "soft" or potentially based on emotions or intuition) or quantitative ones (the data is too hard to get or validate). Using published common vulnerability and exposure (CVE) information can be quite illuminating, but as in Option D, be careful to not assume that other people's experiences and systems are a good match for your own, or to bow to authoritative statements without carefully considering whether they fit your situation.

**11.** B, C, D. These are the expression of confidentiality, integrity, and availability for these data sets. Note that in military terms, information that exposes significant vulnerabilities that could place the organization at risk of great harm is often classified as "Top Secret."

**12.** C. Option B has the annualized rate of occurrence (ARO) use incorrect; if the ARO was less than 1, the single loss expectancy is in effect spread over multiple years (as if it were amortized). Option A involves restore time and point objectives, which are not involved in the annualized loss expectancy (ALE) calculation. Option D misunderstands ALE = ARO * SLE (single loss expectancy) as the basic math involved.

**13.** B, C, D. Option A is a misstatement of RTO and RPO.

**14.** B. Whether the system is small and simple or large and complex, its owners, builders, and users have to treat it like a "black box" and know what can happen across every interface it has with the outside world. Thus Option B is correct. Option A has the steps in the wrong order; detailed threat modeling and assessment needs detailed system architectural information to be valid. Option C misstates how threat modeling is done. While Option D may address a useful set of tools, it does not explain what threat modeling and assessment are or how to do them.

**15.** B. Choice 3, perspective, should reflect priorities, risk appetite, or tolerance, and decision-making culture, and this has to lead all risk management activities. Next comes Choice 4, which feeds into the BIA. Choice 2 should be a product of the BIA process, because it combines costs or magnitude of impacts with acceptable damage limitation strategies. Finally, we choose what to fix, transfer (pay someone else to worry about), accept, or avoid, and any residual risk is recast or re-expressed to reflect these decisions.

**16.** B. Although Options B and C seem to say the same thing, C is more confrontational and perhaps would seem judgmental—probably not an effective way to sell the benefits of using an RMF. Options A and D are similar, but perhaps they advise too much caution. As an SSCP, Jill has pledged to offer her best advice to her employers. Start the dialogue, according to Option B.

**17.** A, B. Options C and D may or may not be true in fact, but it's not clear whether these have any bearing on how the company determines priorities and risk tolerance, or what its decision-making processes and styles are. Options A and B are key elements of organizational culture that can impede or facilitate implementation of a risk management approach.

**18.** A. All are correct as far as they go in comparing "ignore" and "accept." However, the key to due care and due diligence is the standard of reasonable and prudent effort. You would not be prudent if you spent millions of dollars to relocate your business from Atlanta, Georgia (1,050 feet above mean sea level [MSL]) to Boulder, Colorado (5,328 feet above MSL) simply to avoid the risk of a tsunami flooding out your facility, given how astronomically huge that tidal wave would have to be! Thus, Options C and D do not apply, and Option B merely restates the due care or due diligence argument.

**19.** D. Despite the name, the 24 hours of a day have nothing to do with the element of surprise associated with attacking a heretofore-unknown vulnerability. Option C is false, since the term is well understood in IT security communities. Option D correctly explains the period from discovery in the wild to first recognition by system owners, users, or the IT community, and how this element of surprise may give the attacker an advantage.

**20.** B, C. Option A is correct in that tolerance or appetite for risk should drive setting the maximum allowable outage time; the costs incurred during a maximum outage are part of computing single loss expectancy. Option B is incorrect, since the power outages seem to be happening monthly, so SLE alone overstates the potential losses. Option C annualizes the expected losses, but comparing it to the safeguard value assumes a one-year payback period is required. Option D reflects that management may be willing to spend significant money on a safeguard that requires more than one year to justify (pay back) its expense in anticipated savings.

# Chapter 4: Operationalizing Risk Mitigation

**1.** D. Improving product quality is a laudable goal but in and of itself it is not related to information systems security; thus Option A is incorrect. Option B refers to activities after an incident; mitigation activities happen before an incident occurs, or result from lessons learned because of the incident. Option C is most likely being done to implement new or revised security policies. Option D is part of information risk management and should precede information risk mitigation.

**2.** C, D. Options C and D focus on trying to discern the "as-built" current state of the systems; whether this goes down to the cable-by-cable verification of what's plugged in where could depend on how thorough the baseline needs to be. Options A and B refer to ongoing operation of the system after mitigation steps have been taken to see if incidents of interest are happening or if there is a need for additional risk mitigation.

**3.** B. Option D is an exaggeration. Options A and C have the cart driving the horse: the IT architecture should only exist in the first place because it supports achieving business objectives, and the information architecture is where humans work and make decisions. This is what Option B states.

**4.** C. Option A seems to blindly assume that a contractual transfer of responsibility was necessary, sufficient, and agreed to, and this is normally not the case. Option B is false; platforms and infrastructures still require substantial effort by users (and their IT security team) to establish policies, implement them in controls, and monitor their ongoing correct operation. Option D seems to ignore BIA-driven risk assessment and is inherently misleading.

**5.** B, C. Option B correctly describes what shadow IT systems are; thus Option A is false. Options B and C demonstrate that in many cases, it cannot be shown that shadow IT systems taken as a whole correctly perform business logic or that they attain the CIA levels commensurate with the impacts if they fail.

**6.** C. Option B does correctly state the risk that attackers may know more about your systems than you do if you haven't thoroughly checked CVE data as part of your vulnerabilities assessment. But it incorrectly goes on to suggest that you fix those first—they may not relate to your organization's highest-priority impacts as spelled out by the business impact analysis (BIA). Option A is therefore false. Option D is also false, since even the most Linux-based of organizations will probably have non-Linux systems elements (such as network components) that common vulnerabilities and exploits (CVE) could have information about.

**7.** B. Option A is overcomplicating the threat modeling process. Options C and D misstate the purpose of threat modeling.

**8.** C, D. Option A may be a commonplace statement, but it incorrectly suggests this is where the assessment should start. The BIA should establish the priorities (which processes to assess first and which ones can wait until later). Option B's concerns about culture and context are irrelevant to whether a process step contains a vulnerability and whether the BIA has characterized that as of high interest or concern.

**9.** B. Option A confuses accepting a risk with accepting the assessment of all risks as an actionable basis on which to proceed with mitigation efforts. Option C confuses accepting with transferring a risk. Option D confuses accepting with ignoring a risk. Acceptance requires knowing, informed consent; ignoring a risk is simply choosing not to investigate, assess, characterize, or even think about the risk.

**10.** A, B, C. Option D is typically an example of remediating, sometimes called fixing or mitigating the risk.

**11.** A, B. Option C makes it seem that businesses are helpless to choose their goals, objectives, and where or how they will operate; this statement exaggerates. Option D confuses psychological avoidance behavior with an informed choice to step out of the way of a risk; it confuses ignoring with avoiding.

**12.** A. Fixing or applying patches to eliminate a vulnerability is the definition of remediating, mitigating, fixing, or repairing a vulnerability.

**13.** B. Option A misunderstands that controls are chosen and then implemented, and proper mitigation planning seeks to have controls or countermeasures mutually reinforce each other. Option C misstates the mitigation planning task. Option D suggests that if "administrators" are network or systems administrators, then we hope they *do* understand something about IT security; if they are not, they are probably not the ones who have to work to ensure these controls are part of an interlocking system of information security.

**14.** B. If Option A or C was plausible, then you wouldn't actually have a gap. Option D correctly defines the gap but fails to look to how to mitigate the risk posed by the gap.

**15.** A, B, C. Option D may reflect a legitimate need for ongoing insight, but this is rather like testing to verify that your testing was done correctly. It's not clear such a step would be productive.

**16.** A, B, D. Option C is incorrect—you cannot test systems before they are built (i.e. during the systems analysis phase).

**17.** A, B, C. Option D is an important task to do on a routine basis, but it involves monitoring the outside threat world and not the behavior or performance of the systems we are protecting.

**18.** B. Option A misstates the role of ongoing monitoring, and conflicts with Option B. Option C suggests a redundant set of capabilities, which may be mission critical for a select few organizations but is not common. Option D may be a useful capability, but it is not the reason for ongoing monitoring.

**19.** D. Options A and C both underestimate the value of a good key performance indicator, whether for real-time incident detection and response or for trending and analysis. Option B is also mistaken in that it suggests that aggregate measures such as link loading, resource utilization, and so forth have no value in incident detection.

**20.** A. Option B is incorrect; incident response and management is a vital part of risk management. Options C and D do not recognize that risk management includes all processes necessary to identify, assess, characterize, control, respond to, and recover from risks.

# Chapter 5: Communications and Network Security

**1.** D. Option D accurately reflects the use of both of these as conceptual models and protocol stacks—by builders, attackers, and defenders alike. Option A reflects an incorrect bias that many network engineers have, who somewhat dismissively ignore things above the Transport layer. Option B is its logical opposite, also false. Option C is incorrect, as all three sets of concepts drive the design and operation of real hardware, software, and systems.

**2.**  A. Option B is incorrect, because the changes in address field sizes, and therefore packet header structures, have nothing to do with security (although IPv6 does provide enhancements to security). Option C is incorrect; such a conversion could be done by a gateway, but that is not part of IPv6 and is only supported by it. Option D is incorrect, although the transport protocols (like TCP and UDP) have not changed, but this is not where the incompatibility comes from.

**3.**  B. Option A is false, as there is no one central node that serves the entire net; further, millions of Internet nodes have connections between them. Option C is incorrect, as many nodes on the Internet can fail, but this does not prevent alternate routing of frames around the failure; the Internet is "self-annealing" in this way. Option D is false, as there is no one straight line connection from the first Internet node to the last. Option B correctly identifies the billions of nodes on the Internet as being part of a very large mesh.

**4.**  C. Option A is incorrect; VPNs provide connectivity but have no more role in service delivery than other Layer 1 or Layer 2 network elements do. Option B is incorrect, as neither peer controls the other in service sharing. Option D is incorrect; in such a case, either the server is a peer to the other server or the peer is actually a client. Option C correctly identifies that most services need one node to control the service delivery process, and the other node, requesting the service, follows the first node's control of the conversation.

**5.**  B. Options A and C both incorrectly leave out subnetting in IPv6 and misstate what Classless Inter-Domain Routing (CIDR) is about, even though the two options say this differently. Option D is partly correct in that IPv6 does have a 16-bit subnet field, and (as Option B says) the overall address field size makes subnetting much easier to do, but there is no subnet field in IPv4.

**6.**  C. Option A is the backbone of most LANs, because physical cables can be protected in a variety of ways, and unless a hacker can access your patch panels or other hardware, it is difficult to intrude at the Physical layer. Option B is also very secure; it is harder to physically tap into a fiber as well. Option D tends to see use in limited circumstances, but this may change in time. Option C is correct because Wi-Fi is, quite literally, everywhere; it is *expected* to be available; people and businesses demand it; and many Wi-Fi devices, such as SOHO routers, are trivially easy to set up and leave unsecured. Wi-Fi is subject to many kinds of eavesdropping, snooping, and spoofing attacks unless properly secured.

**7.**  A, D. Ports are a fundamental part of the way apps request services from processes running on other nodes on the Internet. Standardized port numbers make applications designs easier to manage; thus, port 80 and HTTP are associated with each other. Thus, Options A and D show a misunderstanding of what ports are and why they are necessary.

**8.**  B. From the Physical layer on up, the injection of unauthorized traffic into a network can cause almost any protocol to fall for a "mistaken identity" that leads to an Man-in-the-Middle (MITM) attack. Session stealing (Layers 5 and 7) is a prime example; thus Option A is false. Option C is incorrect, since IP (Layer 2) is inherently connectionless and is prone to MITM attacks. Option D is also false, as session stealing (and others) demonstrates.

**9.**  C. Option A is incorrect, since the local host file (cache) is quite easily corrupted as part of an attack. Option B shows a misunderstanding of DNS and the role of DNS servers. Option D sounds tempting, but without this being part of an extensive data-at-rest protection scheme it may not work and would probably impede network operations.

**10.**  A. Option A is correct; this is "unwrapping" as datagrams have their headers and footers removed on their way up the stack. Option B is incorrect—wrapping happens on the way down from Transport (or higher) to Physical (by way of Data Link). Options C and D describe what the Presentation layer does as it passes datagrams to applications, which is beyond the Transport layer and going up, not down, the stack.

**11.**  B. Option B is correct; it is an internetworking layer security process and protocol set added to IPv4. Option A is incorrect; IPSec works with packets, not frames (IP addresses, not MAC addresses). Option C is also incorrect, because IPSec is not a transport protocol. Option D is incorrect; IPSec is not a session layer protocol.

**12.**  C. This IP address is the link local address, which is assigned to your system by the operating system and its network protocol stack when a DHCP server does not respond. Check the configuration settings for any switches, routers, and modems between your system and your ISP so that you know where the DHCP service resides; then find that device. Thus, Options A and B are incorrect. Option D may be a good step *after* you determine which device is supposed to be your DHCP server. Option C is your best next step. Ping it or use tracert it to see if it responds.

**13.**  B. In almost all circumstances, the boundary between an organization's information infrastructure and the outside world of the Internet is the highest-risk threat surface. Any channel crossing this boundary should be rigorously assessed for vulnerabilities, and all access via it should be well controlled and well monitored. Thus Option B is probably the best recommendation. Internal systems links, such as Options A and C, might help in containment of intrusions, but there may be other ways to do this than with IDS/IPS remotes. Option D restricts the effectiveness of the IPS or IDS to just those network segments and resources it can directly see and control, which may be a very small subset of your network.

**14.**  A, B. Option C is false; the physical access point itself needs to be protected from somebody attacking it with an unauthorized firmware update, for example, or simply plugging into an unblocked network jack on it. Option D is one component of mobile device management, but it is not sufficient. Option B can reduce exposure to many threats related to mobile device access, whereas a mobile device management system can help track, force compliance, block, or lock down a device reported lost or stolen.

**15.**  D. Option C is false; even if your company didn't use these planes as part of its design and build-out of the networks, this viewpoint can still help you as you look at what the protocol analyzers, SIEMs, IDSs, and IPSs are reporting to you. Options A and B are therefore partly correct; Option D brings all of your tools to bear on the problem.

**16.** B, C, D. Options B, C, and D all describe ways that having better insight into how your systems and networks are being used, right now, can help you determine if they might be suffering some kind of problems. And if they are, that data can help you resolve whether this is a security event or not. Option A is false and also lacks the insight to apply these systems to your overall information systems security strategy.

**17.** A. Option B is false; these products ship with everything wide open for a number of practical reasons, including making it easier for administrators to initially configure them. Option C is tempting fate. Option D is a little bit less risky than Option C, since at least you've prevented an intruder from reconfiguring your device to suit their needs and not yours.

**18.** D. Option D brings AES encryption to Wi-Fi. Option A is incorrect; WEP was easily broken early on. Option B, WPA, is also incorrect, since this was a step in the right direction while IEEE 802.11i was being developed as a standard. Option C, also incorrect, was part of the interim WPA design, and WPA2 supersedes WPA in all respects.

**19.** C. Option A is true in part (the range) but ignores other aspects of Bluetooth vulnerabilities. Option B is incorrect—it seems to assume keyboards and mice are the only Bluetooth devices to worry about. Option C is very real and not very well understood by many organizations. Option D isn't real. Yet.

**20.** B, C. Option A shows a conceptual misunderstanding about network operations and security operations, regardless of who conducts them or is responsible for them. Option D is also incorrect; many smaller organizations can easily and affordably have their network operations team handle the key security operations functions. Option B may indeed be true in some organizations and in some marketplaces, but the organization should always let its business case for security drive the decision. Option C is correct; NOC focuses on design, deployment, operation, and maintenance of the network and changes to it, and the SOC focus is on keeping it secure, detecting events and characterizing them, and containing and responding to them if necessary.

# Chapter 6: Identity and Access Control

**1.** B. Option A is false; each additional factor checked increases the challenge an attacker has to overcome to spoof an identity claim. Option C is false; hardware is only needed for factors involving what the subject has, such as a keyfob code generator, or biometric factors. Option D is tempting, and high-risk functions might be best protected with additional security measures, but compared to Option B, it is not as compellingly correct.

**2.** C. Option A is incorrect; proofing establishes the truthfulness of documents or other information that attest to a person's claim to be that person and is used during the identity provisioning process. Option B can be used as single-factor or as part of a multifactor system, for example, by using a Microsoft account to sign on to a Web service. Option D is incorrect; while this is two different measurements, they both attest to what the subject is (the physical body), and multifactor would require us to look at what the subject has or knows as well.

**3.** B. A positive result of an authentication test means that the claimant is who (or what) they claim to be. Thus a false positive is allowing an incorrect identity to access the system, which probably is a threat actor. A negative result denies an identity's claim to be who (or what) they claim to be. Thus a false negative denies a legitimate identity from system access. Thus, Options A and D incorrectly use the concept of negative and positive authentication results (correct and false). While Option C is true, Option B indicates the situation of greatest risk—a threat actor has been legitimized and granted access.

**4.** B. Option B is correct, as it emphasizes the need to have a rigorous threat modeling or vulnerability assessment drive the way you design and use access control at a very fine-grain level. Option A is only partially correct, because it considers SSO as if it's a one-ingredient answer to a complex situation. Option C confuses single sign-OFF with single sign-ON; it's correct in what it says, but single sign-off is relatively minor issue of little security risk. Option D is incorrect, as it exaggerates basic OS and network capabilities into a "support" that isn't really there. It also misinterprets managements' concern about security risk and addresses implementation risk instead.

**5.** B. Option D is high risk, and therefore incorrect; plugging a device into an empty network connection should start a connection handshake that is an opportunity to block an unknown or unauthorized device from joining the network. Options A and C are parts of how Option B performs such an authentication, and therefore B is the most correct answer and the most secure approach of the three.

**6.** B. Option A is incorrect; SSO is a subset of both the capabilities and security (issues and security solutions) that federated access can support. Option C correctly raises the issue of the trust architecture, but going from there to a full federated access control system, and keeping that secure, can be challenging. Keeping it secure will always require monitoring, analysis, and testing. Option D is incorrect; federated access, like SSO, can use any means of identity authentication that meets the organization's CIANA needs.

**7.** D. Option A demonstrates misunderstanding of the concept of a trust architecture, which Option D clarifies. Option B also misstates the purpose and intent of trust architectures and their role in reducing the risk of an unconstrained (or totally trusted) extranet. Option C does not correctly state what an extranet is (it allows those external to the organization to share in using the sponsoring organization's internal systems and data); it also is mistaken in saying that the same systems, technologies, connections, etc., that are the internal trust architecture would therefore be appropriate to secure and protect the extranet.

**8.** C. Option A is false; zero trust architectures have been used since 2007, and many systems vendors are actively supporting them with additional protocols and capabilities. Option B is only the first step in the process; risk mitigation is where implementation of network designs, including zero trust features, takes place. Option D is false; as an architecture, first you plan how to segment, secure, and "never trust, always verify." Then you build that design, and existing IPv4 commodity products are more than adequate to support such architectures.

**9.** C. Option A is incorrect; single sign on (SSO) provides sign-on capabilities for an organization's domain of users, while trust relationships refers to interorganizational trust of each other's users as domains or sets. Option B is correct as far as it goes, but it does not relate this to access control; Option C does this correctly. Option D is incorrect; federated access control deals with this in almost all cases.

10. B. Step 1, Proofing, is part of provisioning, and thus Options A and C are incorrect. Step 5, Deletion, happens after revocation, but it is a cleanup of files, assets, and records, and it is more properly part of a records retention and housekeeping process. It is not part of identity management. Thus, Option D is incorrect. Option B correctly reflects that we start by provisioning an identity, we continually review the privileges assigned to it versus the needs of the job and the organization, and then we revoke it.

11. B, C. Access control is not involved with resource chargeback, that is, billing; thus Option A is not correct. Option D has confused the roles of authorization and authentication, which Option C states correctly. Option B is correct—this is the "triple A" of access control.

12. D. Each of the options (A, B, C) is allowing a subject to modify the security enforcements in the system, either for an object it has been granted access to or for some other part of the system. Mandatory access control does not permit this. Thus Option D is correct.

13. C, D. Discretionary access control policies allow the systems administrators to grant capabilities (permissions) to subjects to modify aspects of access control restraints, but these must be uniformly defined for all subjects. Thus, Option C is correct, as is Option D. Options A and B apply to mandatory or nondiscretionary access control policies.

14. A. Option B looks at specific aspects of the subject, which might include duties and tasks in their job description, but Option A is more correct in that role-based access control can apply to subjects and objects both. Option D can contain role-based criteria, but normally this looks at many more conditions and criteria. Option C focuses more on the nature of the object—which may be used by more than one role.

15. D. Option D, attribute-based, can use complex Boolean logic statements to conditionally evaluate almost any criteria, environmental or situational conditions, and so forth, to authorize an access request. Each of the others provides limited capabilities by comparison; zero trust typically requires the most rigorous access control possible.

16. A, C. Be careful of the negative in the question! Mandatory access control policies do not allow subjects or objects to modify the security-related aspects of the systems, its subjects, and its objects; thus, granting the privileges in Option A or C cannot be allowed. Options B and D reflect reasonable and prudent access control checks that all systems should perform before granting access.

17. A. The reference monitor is the functionality that checks every access attempt to see if it should be authorized or denied. As a result, Option D is false (accounting is a recordkeeping function, necessary to access control but done after the access request is granted or denied). Option C is false, as the reference monitor is in fact implemented in operating systems (typically in their security kernel), or as part of a trusted computing base (TCB) module on a motherboard. Option B is the reverse of what's required; we need to be able to inspect, analyze, and verify that the logic and code of the reference monitor does its job completely and correctly and that it does nothing else if we are to consider it highly trustworthy.

**18.** D. Option A unnecessarily removes the identity from your systems and those of other systems in your federated access system; this would not be called for until the fate of the employee is known to warrant a permanent removal of access privileges. Options B and C still allow devices that the employee had been known to use to access your systems; if the employee, these devices, or both are in hostile hands, this places your systems at risk. Option D is the most secure response.

**19.** B, C, D. Option A confuses the roles of third-party service providers with those of organizations and individuals that collaborate with you via federated access and is not correct. The others are legitimate examples of third-party roles; note that Option D is still a relatively immature market, and if you're tempted to use IDaaS, choose your vendor with care!

**20.** A. Subjects, by definition, want to *do something* that involves an *object*. Thus, Option A has these roles reversed. Subjects can be any kind of entity that can take action. Objects contain information, but also can provide requested services (that is, take action upon request), so Options B and C are correct.

**21.** A. Option A correctly describes malware quarantine, and remediation by quarantine networks for systems not meeting requirements. Option B is incorrect, since antimalware systems do not quarantine systems but only files they encounter during scanning. Option C correctly describes captive portal quarantine by network access control systems, which differs from antimalware file-based quarantine. Option D misstates the capabilities of antimalware systems (unless they fully incorporate access control and identity management functions, of course).

**22.** A. Option B is partly correct, but Diameter never caught on in the market for a variety of reasons and is probably out of date by now. Option C is also incorrect—first came TACACS, which gave rise to both XTACACS, a proprietary product, and TACAC+, not the other way around. Option D is incorrect, since systems may be de facto "standards" (because a lot of companies use them), but they are not published standards by appropriate standards agencies.

**23.** C. Option A is false; not only does IPv6 contain and support IPSec, it also makes it mandatory. Option B is false; app-level encryption does not protect lower-layer traffic from being snooped or spoofed. Thus Option C is correct. Option D is false; IPv6 doesn't do this encryption, but it builds the features into the protocol stack so that user organizations can choose to implement it. IPv6 and IPv4 are not compatible, so a gateway of some kind will be required anyway, and the issue of security through the gateway will still need to be addressed.

# Chapter 7: Cryptography

**1.** A. Options B, C, and D all are parts of what cryptography entails, and taken together sum it up. Option A is more suggestive of camouflage, honeypots, or other efforts to draw attackers away from what you wish to defend and divert their energies elsewhere.

**2.** B. Option A is an incomplete description of asymmetric encryption; Option C is false, since hybrid systems are in widespread use; and Option D is unrelated to symmetric or asymmetric encryption.

**3.** C. Option A is false; this option confuses the message digest with the hash itself; a hash value contains no meaning. Option B is one use of hashing, but there are so many more, particularly in cryptographic systems like PKI and digital signatures. Option D contains a misunderstanding of the digital signature process.

**4.** C, D. Options A and B both suggest encrypting the file in some way, which hides its meaning; Option B is a concept being explored by IBM and is not readily available anyway. Options C and D would both accomplish this; Windows, Office, and many software systems use both techniques in their distribution and update processes.

**5.** D. Using proper cryptographic techniques, all aspects of CIANA (confidentiality, integrity, availability, nonrepudiation, authentication) can be enhanced, even availability and integrity.

**6.** D. Although Option A is tempting, cryptographic processes cannot confirm that the certificate and key are correctly associated with a specific human or organization. The CA does that through other (noncryptographic) means and, as an anchor in the chain of trust, attests that this person and this certificate go together. Thus Option D is correct. Option B refers to integrity and Option C to confidentiality, which are not directly part of nonrepudiation.

**7.** A, D. Option B confuses where the signals go (through space) with the movement of the information from one user as an endpoint to another. Similarly, Option C misses the point about protecting data at rest, which is from when it is written to storage to some time later, in the future, when it is read back.

**8.** C. The incorrect answers show misapplication of the steps of the process. Option A has reversed who encrypts and who decrypts. Option B confuses the use of the sender's public and private key, and if the recipient knows the sender's private key it must no longer be private! Option D won't work, because decrypting the unencrypted hash won't produce anything that is useful.

**9.** B. Option A shows incomplete understanding of the digital signature process. Option C confuses whether the sender or recipient needs to trust signed content and signatures. Option D is incorrect, as it is missing the receiving client's need for installed, trustworthy operating systems, browsers, or other signature-handling applications; it also misstates the role of government in the CA process.

**10.** A, B. Option C starts with an incorrect assumption, since many email systems use POP, IMAP, or other nonsecure connections. Option D may be correct as far as it goes, but this represents a tiny fraction of the routine uses of email.

**11.** C. Option A is one classical approach to using a one-time pad, but the key itself is the process for choosing key values out of the book, and that algorithm can easily be compromised, typically with lexical analysis. Option B is incorrect, as Shannon's work shows one-time pad is unbreakable only if truly random numbers are used as a key. Option D may be partially correct, but it does not address how the one-time pad itself is generated.

**12.** A, C. Option B is incorrect, reversing which concept (webs or hierarchies) have their trust anchors as part of the supply chain. Option D is incorrect, as the differences shown in Options A and C would indicate.

**13.** A, B, D. Option C is incorrect; by making significant contributions to access control, information integrity, and confidentiality, cryptography can reduce or eliminate many vulnerabilities that could lead to information or systems being unavailable when and where needed.

**14.** C. Options A and B are high on the "wish lists" of many governments but are just not obtainable, nor would they make widespread e-commerce possible, as there would be no basis of trust for it. Option D overstates the role of cryptographic module verification programs, since they validate only that the module does what it claims to and not whether it is suitable for any specific information security need.

**15.** C. Arguably, Option D as a blanket statement might be true, but in practice it's not true. Stream ciphers depend on the stream being shorter than the key (no repeat use of the key), which leads to implementations that are susceptible to algorithm attacks. Option B is also false for this reason. Option A is true but incomplete for the same reason.

**16.** A. Option B demonstrates complacency that's been disproven time and again; continued cryptanalysis suggests that even the largest keys in use today on RSA are not as secure as we think. Option C is true but for character and stream ciphers as well. Option D makes a mistaken assumption about requiring more complex algorithms.

**17.** C. Although all are real threats, Option B is probably of lowest likelihood for most small and medium-sized businesses. Options A and D are not technically attacks but vulnerabilities that user organizations inflict upon themselves.

**18.** D. Although all are real vulnerabilities, Option B typically arises only when disposing of equipment (or if physical security of equipment is lacking). Option C can be an issue, especially for software-based cryptographic systems, if access control and configuration management allow unauthorized or uncontrolled software update and installation. Option A is a subset of Option D.

**19.** A. Option B is incorrect; hash comparisons for purportedly the same text will reveal even a single bit difference in the inputs, which some error correcting and detecting codes cannot provide; reversible hashes do not improve on this. Option C incorrectly states what "reversibility" means for an algorithm. Option D is incorrect, because hash functions must be one-to-one; any attempt at collision avoidance (many-to-one) would negate reversibility and uniqueness, which are the essence of what we need secure hash functions for.

**20.** A, B. Option C misunderstands the use of a public key, which can only be used to authenticate your identity by decrypting something you've digitally signed with your corresponding private key. Option D seems to confuse key length with usage: although having key change intervals is something that policy and systems choices should dictate, it's probably not a fixed (suspiciously binary) number like this.

# Chapter 8: Hardware and Systems Security

1. D. Starting with Option A is a commonsense approach to quickly implementing some reasonable and prudent protection, but it lacks any judgment as to which vulnerabilities are important to your organization's risk management strategy and which are not. Option B is the systems inventory, and you will need it, as it describes the as-built systems. Option C is what drives Option D. Therefore, start shopping for countermeasures with Option D in hand.

2. C. Although Options A and B correctly indicate roles that others in the company fulfill in securing the IT supply chain, the SSCP does have the responsibility and opportunity to advise and assist. Option D may be a factor, but it is not the sole factor in IT supply chain risk management.

3. B, C. Option A is false—SNMP by itself cannot trigger a device to download and install a firmware patch file. Option D is false—that operator action can be misdirected to use the wrong file as the update. Option B may be true in some cases, if the device is set to allow remote management from other than a connected endpoint system such as a laptop or smartphone. Option C happens a lot!

4. D. While some zero day exploits have been discovered and exploited within the same day, typically after the release of a new software product to the market, most take the attackers understand a newly discovered vulnerability, design an exploit against it, and then find a suitable target. So Option A is not correct. Option B incorrectly refers to exploits that leave behind payloads or features that will take action later. Option C incorrectly associates the media reporting of cybersecurity, in general, with the time from discovery to exploitation of a vulnerability.

5. D. All of these are legitimate risks to worry about; some big box stores' computer repair services are known to do full scans and voluntarily report what they find to law enforcement, or possibly others, for example. Option A happens frequently, but it's more of an impact to ongoing availability than it is an exploitable vulnerability. Option B can cause equipment to fail or behave erratically. Option D is far and away the most prevalent hardware-related cause of data loss, systems breach, or information security failures, of the items on this list.

6. B. Since trusted platform modules (TPMs) are special, sealed hardware modules added to the motherboards of computers or phones by their manufacturers, Option D is incorrect, even though TPM device driver software must be incorporated into most OSs to enable their use. Option A is incorrect; the TPM doesn't simplify this but allows for a more trustworthy hardware storage and management of certificates, digital signatures, and so forth. Option C is not correct; these functions in the OS and host hardware remain, while all the TPM provides is its own implementations with which it secures keys, manages certificates, and hashes (preserves) machine identification information.

**7.** B. Option A was originally used, differentiating between Trojan horses (or "giftware"), worms, and viruses, for example; this has proved to be inadequate. Option C has merit for signature analysis, either as patterns of behavior or patterns in the executable code and other files that are part of the malware. Option D is of use when looking to specific systems and their vulnerabilities. Option B combines purpose, intent, design, and effect and is arguably the more important characterization to use.

**8.** A, D. Option B would be unusual for malware—but it might signify anything from loose connections to storage devices through congestion on networks slowing down directory updates. Option C is not correct; many behavioral effects are noticeable by the non-geeky user. Option D is how malware detection systems actually work.

**9.** C. Options A and B misstate the role of application whitelisting or an antivirus program; firewalls do not do these functions. Option C is what a network firewall does. Option D describes what a network firewall does but misstates the firewall's role in malware defense.

**10.** B. Option A misses the "destination" end of the connection attempt to the host: a program running on it. Option C is incorrect; firewalls do not do this. Option D is incorrect; although network-based firewalls may protect a lot of systems, they cannot control attempts by software on a host from exceeding prescribed limits of behavior.

**11.** A, C, D. Option B does not typically shed light on security-specific features, fixes, vendor-supplied updates, or patches. The other options go from real-time indications and warnings, to health and status monitoring in real or near-real time, to mitigation plans and status.

**12.** A, C. Option B overstates how the line between private and secure browsing is blurring; the "browser wars" continue to hold security and privacy hostage to revenue generation based on users and their history being products. Option D is only partly true, as it misses browser telemetry, your own interaction with webpages, and other ways that browsers leak information about you and your system.

**13.** D. In almost all cases, using a media player built into your browser will not allow malware to be stored on your computer. All of the rest are known vectors (paths) for malware infection.

**14.** B, C. Option A may be confusing a "blacklisting" approach (thou shalt nots) for bring your own devices (BYOD) and mobile device management systems (MDMs), rather than a whitelisting (permitted activities); nonetheless, this is a major problem with mobile devices regardless of ownership. Option D is one of the major problems MDMs are designed to help manage or solve, so this is false.

**15.** B. Option A requires other capabilities, such as mobile device management, to provide this protection. Option C overlooks many complexities of using encryption on an endpoint device. Option D seems tempting, but current practice does not provide seamless encryption-based protection of data in use, especially on most mobile / smartphone endpoints.

**16.** C, D. Option A is false; BYOI brings the potential for dynamic subnets of people and organizations becoming part of your infrastructure, and for loosely coupled cloud storage and processing to impact your business logic's use of enterprise systems. Option B is tempting but misleading, as most of your employees using BYOI capabilities do not have the capacity to solve the risks those capabilities can introduce.

**17.** C. Option A is safe, but may overstate the need. Option B may apply for VMs executing in a sandboxed or partially isolated way, but does not address VMs used for production systems. Option D does not recognize that VM software—the OS and applications—can still become infected with malware, or that software-defined networks that support the VMs can still suffer intrusions if not adequately protected.

**18.** C. Option A fails in practice, as lost or stolen devices may not be noticed as "missing" right away. Option B seems to subvert system security planning. Option D does not address identity or access control.

**19.** E. Option A ignores the many instances where malware has shut off safety features in computers or destroyed hard disk drives. Option B ignores the losses a small business can suffer if even one employee's or customer's PII is compromised, or if critical data is lost. Options C and D are strongly related to each other, but both ignore the many other pathways that malware can enter a system that don't involve a browser.

**20.** A, D. Option B confuses what signing an email does (it merely authenticates the sender's identity); it does nothing to ensure that the contents or attachments are safe. Option C mistakenly assumes that malware must be large executable files, when a few hundred bytes may be all that is needed.

# Chapter 9: Applications, Data, and Cloud Security

**1.** B. While many people feel that Option A is true, it's an overgeneralization; most commercial apps go through rigorous design and testing, and include information security requirements. Option C exaggerates how much shadow IT exists, while ignoring the widespread use of platforms and services, productivity suites, etc. Option D addresses why apps already installed still have known vulnerabilities in them, but it does not address how those vulnerabilities got there in the first place. Option B is the number one reason we see the same kinds of errors, decade after decade, baked into new programs as they are written.

**2.** C. Option C is correct in terms of the major benefit of whitelisting; Option D, its logical opposite, addresses the zero day risks of blacklisting approaches without saying why any other approach (such as whitelisting) is better. Option A is false on its face; no such program (thankfully!) exists to "trust-mark" applications. However, digitally signed installation kits do give some assurance that the software came from the vendor you thought provided it. Option B is true on its face but does not say why one approach provides better security than the other.

**3.** B. Option A is false; it effectively assumes that private clouds are as secure as private datacenters or LANs and desktops. Option C is correct as far as it goes, since PaaS (for example) may provide platform-based controls while introducing additional boundaries (or threat surfaces). Option D is false and misstates the shared responsibility concept. Option B focuses on where to start thinking about the proposed migration and the role of threat modeling in planning for information security in the chosen cloud.

**4.** D. Option A is incorrect by oversimplifying the ongoing need to understand changing conditions and how these affect the business relationship between host and customer. Option B is false; cloud systems technologies, whether Azure, Google Cloud, or Amazon Web Services, are updated virtually every week, with changes impacting customer-migrated systems utility and security. Option C overemphasizes the administrative/contractual burden of change. Option D better reflects the need to thoroughly understand both the contractual and the technical up front and how the effort spent on both will likely change over time.

**5.** B, C. Option A is false; the laws of the host nation apply to the cloud datacenter operator in that country, and that means they apply to all of the data and processing performed on that cloud datacenter. Option D is false, as nearly all countries claim the right to control the import and export of information, particularly (as in Option C) where that information violates, attacks, or ridicules a strong cultural, religious, or political value in that country. Options B and C are true.

**6.** B, C. Option D most correctly states the bottom line to most organizations in terms of how stakeholders, investors, legal and regulatory authorities, customers, and others will judge responsibility when things go wrong. Option A is a specific example; due care requires that you have the contractual, technical, and administrative ways to do such verifications, while due diligence requires that you actually *do* such verifications and hold the third party to task. Option B can only set day-to-day expectations; when a major data breach happens, Option D suggests that even if the service provider failed to fulfill their contract, your stakeholders will still hold you responsible. Option C is false.

**7.** A, B, C. Option D is incorrect. Authentication data, which defines user and process privileges, identity verification, and so forth, is as subject to being wiped out, corrupted, lost, or stolen as any other data on any information system.

**8.** A. Option B is partly correct but exaggerates the effort to set up an SDN or hypervisor. Option C is false, as it requires explicit actions by administrators to allow access to other system resources, devices, and so forth. Option D is also false, as the hardware, hypervisor, and host OS if used are where you start to define and configure VM images and the parameters that control their being dispatched to run and then retired.

**9.** B. Option A is true insofar as it describes a common malware vector, but it misses the key point. Option C may be true in a very limited sense (police call this the "broken window" theory of urban crime control), but it misunderstands the role of the endpoints in an IT system. Option D is false; all output that humans can use is done at an endpoint, be that a laptop, a phone, an annunciator, a process control status board, or even a printer. Option B correctly captures the value proposition of information work and the high-leverage role of action that happens at endpoints.

**10.** D. Currently, most Internet of Things (IoT) devices are limited to performing only a few related functions; it is also as difficult if not impossible to configure their access control or other security features (if they have any), or update or patch their onboard firmware. This means that Options A and B are probably not correct. Option C is also doubtful for this same reason—would Jayne's bosses want her to specify a human safety function be managed by an IoT device that anyone could hack into and subvert? Option D provides a sound alternative; the process control marketplace has many solutions available, all highly modularized.

**11.** C, D. Continuity is about planning for alternative modes of action—having a stack of "just in case" options already laid out in plans, procedures, software, or other IT elements. Thus, Option D is correct and Option A is false. Resilience is the ability to bend, adapt, tolerate, or even ignore unanticipated disruptions, without completely breaking down. Thus, Option B is incorrect, and Option C is correct.

**12.** A, D. Phishing and many other social engineering tactics have played a major role in over 60 percent of major data breaches in the past few years. Such tactics have high payoff to the attacker during their search for a possible target, gathering information about its systems and security, and then their initial entry into the target's systems. Thus Options A and D are correct. Options B and C are almost exclusively done surreptitiously, exploiting information that social engineering may have revealed to the attacker; few if any signs of phishing in these activities have been noted.

**13.** A, B. Option C makes it harder for an unauthorized user to use a resource, whether it's in its original form or it's been copied and exfiltrated; this does not help detect an ongoing attack beyond what proper access control should do. Option D is easily thwarted by attackers when they restructure, clump, aggregate, encrypt, or disguise the data; the rules and filters don't know what to look for as a result. Option A can reveal an attack in the early stages, but it is analysis intensive. Option B might usefully warn of attacks against data that is encrypted at rest but for which access control is not sensing a violation of privilege.

**14.** D. Option A is false; no such agreements apply worldwide. At best, regulations like the General Data Protection Regulation (GDPR) apply to EU member states. Option B is true as far as it goes, but with a catch: if the organization guesses wrong, it could end up in serious legal trouble in multiple jurisdictions. Option C is false; storage of data in a center in another country must involve movement of data from your jurisdiction into the one the datacenter is in and movement in the reverse direction when you need to use the backup. In almost all cases, data protection laws and regulations apply to data in use, at rest, and in motion.

**15.** B. Option A is a real risk but not what GIGO is about. Option C may involve throwing things in the "garbage" that should have been destroyed or zeroized first, but it's also incorrect. Option D is a very common attack attempt against many apps, but it usually does not lead to the application producing what looks like correctly formed outputs with distorted meanings. GIGO processing, as in Option B, can result in incorrect transactions being posted to an account, such as when a patient billing record has too many copies of the same lab procedure billed incorrectly to it.

**16.** C, D. The key determiner of whether user-defined and user-maintained "stuff" is shadow IT is the amount of business logic that it embeds or implements; the more such business logic is built into uncontrolled or unmanaged apps or tools, the greater the risk of something going wrong in undetected ways. Thus, Option A is not a probable risk; Option B seems to have a lot of frequent, intensive review of the results of these queries, which would need to correlate or compare with what the production information systems would show. Option C implements customer relationship management and systems/product maintenance business logic; Option D seems to circumvent information classification, segregation of duties, and other access control principles. Both Options C and D bear close watching.

**17.** D. Option D is probably illegal in most of the jurisdictions in question; even where it is not, it is certainly unethical to attempt to evaluate a storage provider's security by trying to hack into other customers' data without their express written consent and the consent of the provider. The rest are reasonable and prudent parts of due care and due diligence checks on a candidate third-party provider of this type.

**18.** B. Option A glosses over the growing "BYOx," where x can be infrastructure, device, or most any service; we might argue that Option A also ignores the blurring of the boundary between an endpoint and the information system itself. Option B reminds us to do integrated, coherent threat modeling and analysis across our total systems environment. Option C just echoes what the boss said, although it does add a minor bit about tailoring; overall, it doesn't contribute much to the conversation with the boss. Option D offers no support for this rather unusual viewpoint.

**19.** B, C, D. Option A by itself won't do what is needed; at a minimum, Option D and its implementation of rigorous access control and identity management is necessary to protect network storage resources from being corrupted, tampered with, and so on. The others are all valuable parts of a data governance and data security/data protection plan.

**20.** A, C. Option B is scary; it seems to assume that we can drown in data the government inspectors, auditors, or the attorneys who are suing us, and they'll never figure out it is meaningless. Very risky business! Option D suggests that perhaps senior leadership just did not realize the potential impacts that bad data (or a lack of data quality) can have on maintaining confidentiality, integrity, availability, nonrepudiation, and authentication of all information-based business processes. Options A and C are real risks that many organizations face each day.

# Chapter 10: Incident Response and Recovery

**1.** B, D. Option A is incorrect; this is a very high-risk strategy, as it allows the attacker to roam freely around some of your systems for an indeterminate period of time. Although Option C is probably true, it won't help defuse the production manager's frustration very much. Options B and D clearly explain the risk and put it in the context of impacts across the organization.

**2.** B, D. Although Option A may be true, it is naïve and incorrect; the air conditioning company that serviced Target stores didn't handle retail (credit card) sales either, yet attackers found it to be an ideal entry into Target's payment processing systems. Option C is also incorrect; your cloud hosts will protect their systems, and their platforms, from malware attacks from your connections, but attackers who spoof bogus, privileged accounts into your systems can still destroy your business's presence in those cloud systems. Option B points out a real business risks; Option D offers the boss a sensible first step.

**3.** A, B. Option D is false; the business continuity plan (BCP) and disaster recovery plan (DRP) should start with the broad strategic goals and flow them down into all activities necessary to keep the business operating, and to help it recover from a major disruption, respectively; this certainly includes the actions of the computer emergency response team (CERT) and the systems they support. Option C is true as far as it goes, but since all of those depend on continued use of business processes, which depend on the IT systems, the CERT plays a pivotal support role to those plans and the people who execute them. Options B and A are correct.

**4.** B, C, D. Option A is incorrect. Note that the question asks regarding a subsequent investigation; the team has to act in ways that don't make such an investigation pointless by destroying the evidence the forensics investigation may need. Thus, Options B, C, and D spell out what the responders should be mindful of and take due care to do, while management has the responsibility to strike the balance.

**5.** A, D. Option A is not normally useful; what the CSIRT does need at their fingertips is the emergency contact information for technical support, or information security incident coordination, with such organizations. Option D is also not normally useful, because the computer security incident response team (CSIRT) will more than likely work at the systems and networks level (data, control, and management planes), and if a hardware unit is not responding properly, they'll just isolate it, flag it for later maintenance, and move on. Option B captures business logic and translates it into major information flows or processes, akin to Layer 7 (Applications) in the OSI model. Option C is vital to problem analysis and correction.

**6.** A, B. Option D would not normally be useful during incident response, as the responders are dealing with abnormal behavior of as-built systems; the requirements that drove the design of these systems usually aren't helpful at that point. Option C is also not correct; what the team needs is more of a focused directory of key users and managers for different applications platforms or systems. Options A and B may prove valuable as the team tries to identify, characterize, and then deal with an attack or abnormal behavior. These both can guide choices about containment, eradication, and restoration tactics and priorities.

**7.** B, D. Option B has the alarm thresholds described backward: setting them low would let many more alarms through, setting them high filters more alarms out, passing fewer reports up to the security operations or response team. Option D may be correct—taking more of a zero trust approach and re-segmenting the network, for example, might be worth considering—but it won't help the response team today. Options A and C are correct statements regarding precursors (such as email threats claiming to be from activist groups) and indicators (such as changes to access control and accounting settings on a subject or object).

**8.** B. When it comes to incident detection, a precursor is an observable signal or result of an event, which may suggest to us that an event of interest (such as a security-related event) may happen in the near future. Precursors do not, in themselves, suggest that the incident is currently happening. Thus Option A is false. Option C mistakes indicators for precursors. Option D confuses events with the observable signals from them (such as the changes they make to target systems, which we can observe). "Warnings" in this context has no meaning—that is, our IDS or IPS technologies detect indicators and issue alarms. Thus, Option B is most correct.

**9.** B. Option A is incorrect; this may be a consequence of the way that the team's detection, response, and recovery responsibilities are defined and supported, but it's not generally the case. Option C is incorrect; though this might be true in some organizations, it is not related to due diligence and misstates that concept. Option D is incorrect; NIST publications provide guidance, while federal regulations can make them obligatory on federal and other government activities, they do not in general dictate what the private sector must do. Option B is correct; management and leadership may have legal, regulatory, or business reasons for knowing immediately that an incident might have occurred or might be occurring, but they cannot fulfill those obligations if no one on the response team tells them about it.

**10.** B, C. Containment looks to isolating systems that have been infected by a causal agent such as malware, or whose software and data may have been corrupted, so as to prevent either the causal agent or the damage from spreading. Thus, Option A wouldn't achieve containment, since an infected or corrupted application could have many service requests already sent to systems services, any of which could be a vector to spread the damage to other systems. Option D does not contain anything; the attack agent or damaged software and data can still flow from the affected systems to others. Shutting down that link, however, would contain the causal agent (by shutting down two-way traffic). Option B isolates the organization's LAN from the Internet, which is effective containment of the incident to the organization's systems. Option C addresses segmenting the organization's systems into infected (and thus contained or isolated) and not infected systems. Whether there's enough connectivity between the "believed healthy" systems to function as a network, or whether they are only capable of being islands of automation, will be determined by the network design and the incident's effects.

**11.** D. Option A is incorrect; containment may occur system by system or host by host as the networks are segmented and isolated, and thus the eradication specialists can start cleaning systems as they are isolated (or the causal agents on them are contained). Option B is incorrect, since different tools are needed to disable network connections than you'd use to scan systems for malware, as an example. Option C is incorrect; malware quarantine is more an example of eradication combined with recovery. Option D correctly explains isolating systems and then cleaning them.

**12.** A. Option A usually does not have a legal or regulatory obligation that the CSIRT must respond to (although there may be requirements for the organization to report statistics on such incidents to regulators or other authorities). Option B could lead to disciplinary actions or firing the employee involved, which could result in litigation. Option C may be criminal trespass or violation of other criminal laws. Option D may, depending on the nature of the business and its activities, require safety, security, or investor and consumer protection reporting and notification actions by the organization, regardless of cause.

**13.** B, C. Option A, documenting lessons learned, is a critical part of post-recovery activities and thus is incorrect. Option D is incorrect; verification of complete containment and eradication should be done as part of containment and eradication, prior to starting recovery tasks. Option B, restoring or rebuilding systems, and Option C, restoring databases and storage systems, are correct.

**14.** C. Option A is false; the response team should only need to know how to find and use such backups and should not be responsible for their initial generation or routine update. Option B is false; the DRP would address options spelled out in the BCP as to alternative processing locations, contingency plans, and so forth, all of which need the backups that the BCP directs be made. Option D is false; configuration management is the decision process that allows or prevents changes to hardware, software, or key data items or structures, but it doesn't manage backups. Option C correctly links the purpose of backups—continuing to get business done in the face of accidents, systems failures, attacks, or natural disasters—with the need for a specific set of resources, such as backups.

**15.** B, C. Option A is incorrect; delaying a post-event debriefing allows human memory to fade, and important insights can get lost very quickly. Option D may be true in this circumstance, but this is not strictly a post-recovery phase activity. It may very well be a great task for your many-talented IT team to take on, but just not as a CSIRT task. Option B addresses due care and due diligence, since there are many reasons why data from such incidents needs to be retained and kept secure. Option C is also a sound investment strategy, which will need to be weighed against the lost opportunity costs of your team continuing to fall behind on routine work tasks.

**16.** D. Option A might conceivably be true, but it's doubtful this could be a good indicator of an incident. Option B is technically correct, but it doesn't offer a justification for making clock synchronization be required. Option C, like Option A, might theoretically be true, but it's not clear this can easily be an indicator or precursor of a security incident. Option D correctly states the simple justification; networks with hundreds of devices, each producing dozens of event logs, will quickly overwhelm any manual attempts to bias the clocks in each log file to get things to collate together usefully.

**17.** A, C. Option D is incorrect; even if most employees won't need to know the details of new procedures, the fact of learning the lessons from the most recent, painful event will restore confidence in the "IT wizards" and in management. Option B is incorrect, or at least not strongly advised; it does not provide a strong link between pen testing, failure to detect and respond, and the new procedures. Option A should be a part of any procedural change process (how do you know the change did what you were promised it would?). Option C is critical to preparing these key people to respond properly when the next incident occurs.

**18.** D. Option A could be social engineering or other attempts to gain entry into your systems. Option B could be caused by malware, corrupted data entered by a user in attempting to exploit a vulnerability in the application. Option C could be the result of bogus data being entered in via an exploited vulnerability in a process or application, or it could indicate a corrupted application task (malware infected or otherwise exploited). Option D could be from any number of sources, most of which are not attackers.

**19.** A, C, D. Option B is incorrect; not only does it miss the actual value-added purposes of having the team do its own timeline analysis, but it also confuses the role of detailed evidence with broader cause-and-effect relationships (as in Option A). Option C is correct, as is Option D, in justifying the use of timeline analysis in incident investigation and response.

20. B. Option A is incorrect; it's actually rather dismissive of the knowledge that most line workers have when it comes to how business actually gets done every day. Users may need better training as to what to do when they think they see a problem, but that's not addressed by this answer. Option C is incorrect, demonstrating a narrow vision that only sees the technological solutions as useful. Option D is incorrect, notably that it is never too late to sound an alarm. Option B correctly expresses the value of knowledge and experience. Harnessing this insight in real time as part of an intrusion or anomaly detection process, however, is another story.

# Chapter 11: Business Continuity via Information Security and People Power

1.  A, B. Option A is incorrect; relocation of business operations is typically part of disaster recovery plans. Option B is incorrect, as temporary staffing implies that existing staff are not available to work or cannot work for some reason, and this is more in the scope of disaster recovery. Option C, off-site systems and data archives, may well be used in the restoration phase of an information security incident response. Option D is part of all incident response, continuity, and recovery planning.

2.  C. Option A is incorrect; NIST is mandatory for US government agencies and their contractors. Option B is incorrect, because NIST publications are not mandatory for the private sector. Option C correctly expresses the relationship of NIST publications to the private sector for this and many other aspects of information systems risk management. Option D is incorrect; most private organizations can learn a great many valuable lessons from NIST's publications.

3.  A, B. Option A is correct; it is the focal point for linking organizational priorities, goals, and objectives to risks and vulnerabilities and thence to impacts. The BIA should drive all other response plans. Option B is also correct; this is (or should be!) driven by the BIA, is the result of looking at significant disruptions to business operations, and shows concepts, plans, and resources needed to recover from the disruptions and continue to operate or get back to normal operations. Option C is incorrect; this would typically not address how the organization recovers from loss or damage to such an asset. Option D is incorrect, as like Option C, it looks at prevention and deterrence rather than recovery.

4.  D. These assessments look at cost and likelihood of loss or impact from a risk; thus, Option D is the right place to find them being used as part of the risk management decision process. The other answers all are incorrect, since they are response plans; these should be built to meet the time-based (or data loss–based) assessments such as recovery time objective as best as they can; during the incident response, you're not particularly worried about a probability of a loss when it's actually happening.

**5.** B, C. Option A is incorrect; without a known baseline to restore to (or rebuild if the primary systems are destroyed), you have no place to start from. Option B is correct, since restoring from backups needs to check for changes made to the production systems after the date/time of the backup. Option C is correct; in the event of major damage to the production systems, hardware, or facilities, you need to know what to start putting together to get back into operations. Option D is incorrect; the contingency operations procedures may identify assets (computers, etc.) in place for alternate operations locations, or for reduced capabilities, but they won't document the in-use production system at the requirements, design, and implementation detail level that the configuration managed baselines should do.

**6.** C. Option A is nearly correct—recovery time objective less than maximum allowable outage allows for some slack or reserve time before hitting the MAO constraint; however, the true condition is that expressed in Option C, which allows for when RTO and MAO are equal. Option B has this relationship backward; we plan to achieve the objective (RTO) so as to not exceed the maximum allowed. Option D is false; they do not have to be equal.

**7.** B. Option A is incorrect; recovery time objective (RTO) is not related to data loss. Option C, maximum allowable outage time (MAO), is incorrect. Option D, annual rate of occurrence (ARO), or the number of such events expected on a yearly basis, is incorrect. Option B is correct; the recovery point objective (RPO) sets the maximum time lag or latency time for data in order to be considered useful for business operations.

**8.** D. Option A is false; appropriate administrative and technical controls can and should be used to reduce information security risks to acceptable levels. Option B is correct in part, but without the users of the tool being fully aware of the CIANA needs pertaining to the data, information, and knowledge that are being collaborated upon, the technical controls are meaningless. Option C is correct in part, but it does not address user awareness, education, or training. Option D covers the key elements of user awareness and education, and supports the CIANA requirements for this collaboration; thus, the technical controls can do their job more effectively.

**9.** D. Option A is false; even if thousands of phishing emails are sent as part of a low-and-slow attack, one response can generate exploitable information for the attacker. Option C is false; in doing so, you confirm that your email address connects to a real (and somewhat underinformed) person. Expect more. Option B is false; attackers work hard to mimic the style, format, expression, and construction of their phishing emails, and continually attempt to spoof email addresses, domain names, and so forth. Tools may filter a lot of such junk email for you, but they won't catch it all. Option D is most correct.

**10.** A. Option A is correct; phishing tends to seek information, and whaling (and spear phishing) seek action, typically the release of funds to the attacker. Option B is incorrect; whaling is primarily aimed at senior business leaders, whereas phishing can be aimed at anybody, anywhere, if the attacker perceives there is something worthwhile to learn in doing so. Option C has these reversed; whaling attacks depend on credibility of the business transaction they request. Option D is false on its face; there is a significant difference, as shown in Option A.

**11.** C. Option A is incorrect; in general, the same core information security team members should actively shape and guide all information security awareness, education, and training efforts across the organization. Option B is incorrect; it shows a misunderstanding of separation of duties, which typically breaks a task for one trustworthy person or group into two or more sets of tasks for two (or more) trustworthy people or groups so as to provide a check and balance arrangement. This would typically involve information at the same level of sensitivity or classification. Option C is correct, since it links the opportunities that separation of duties can suggest for focusing such education and training. Option D, like Option B, does not apply separation of duties correctly. It is not intended to produce "compartments" that others cannot know about, in and of itself; rather, it drives the design of access controls or administrative controls to prevent one person from taking incorrect action.

**12.** C. Option A is not correct; most of the risk is in what people say to each other over these systems, and technical controls can do little to mitigate this. Option B is incorrect; the service provider has no role in how you keep your people from saying the wrong things to the wrong parties. Option C correctly focuses on what people in your organization need to know: how and why to protect the organization, by controlling what they say to others. Option D is incorrect; a signed NDA may make the employee signing it aware of the restrictions, and provide authority for sanctions (such as litigation, termination, etc.), but it doesn't help operationally in achieving information security.

**13.** C. Options A, B, and D all demonstrate the hallmarks of social engineering attacks—they work (and have worked for thousands of years) because people are generally trusting, open, and willing to engage with strangers. Option C, the correct choice, is unfortunately not true; tools may help filter out some email-based social engineering attacks, but few organizations have truly been able to operate with a "loose lips sink ships" approach and deal openly with customers, clients, and many other outside stakeholders.

**14.** C. Options A and B are incorrect; tempting as they are to the geek in us, they are not the first place that effort needs to be spent. Option D is a necessary and vital task, but given the dynamics of this organization, it sounds like Option C is the most immediate need. Getting this small group of people totally focused on protecting their own future while collaborating with many others in building that future is going to be key to success; thus, more dialogue (Option C) can lead to a better, more informed and effective information risk management and classification approach (Option D).

**15.** A, B. Option D is inadvisable as a first step; you need to first check to see if the company has policies that effectively set boundaries or constraints for acceptable use, bring your own device or software, and configuration management and control. Option C is also inadvisable, without first checking (again) with company policy and perhaps with company legal advisers, especially if you wish to scan employee-owned devices. Options A and B, starting with reviewing current policy, are your best first starts.

**16.** A, B. Option D is inadvisable; it's a legitimate thing for you to think about, but you might want to avoid such a confrontational question that seems to challenge the company's logic and reasoning for this practice. Option C is also inadvisable; it might be part of the decision logic to set the review period, but it shouldn't be high on your list of things to know as a new team member. Option A is a good, task-focused question that could very well be something you'd expect to encounter during or after incident response efforts. Option B is a good question, looking to the overall risk information architecture itself (what does the company learn from its monitoring for precursors and indicators?).

17. B.  Option B is correct; changing backup and restore strategies may affect backup data latency—the time between the last backup of the data, and the need to have the data in the system current and up to date, accurately reflecting all transactions since that last backup. Option A is incorrect, as RTO would set the goal for getting the system capabilities restored and able to accept new data; data latency is often assumed to be something that can be dealt with in parallel to processing new transactions after the system has been restored. Option C is incorrect; clearly, the ability to get back to normal business depends on the data being correct, complete, and current (that is, meeting integrity and availability needs). Option D is not correct; this is most likely set by business and market conditions, and not by the "how do we achieve this" that choices about data backup may affect.

18. D.  Planning should be an ongoing, continuous, and iterative process; plans are thus continually tested against reality so that changes to plans and procedures stay harmonized. Thus, Option D is most correct. Option C, unfortunately, is a commonly held view and can lead to work being done to obsolete ideas or to assumptions long since proven to be incorrect by reality. Option B is good, but not as correct and complete as Option D. Option A is incorrect; plans are good, useful and necessary, but it is the planning process that brings the team together to better understand needs versus resources.

19. A, D.  Options B and C both flow directly from the (ISC)² code of professional ethics, and they express the responsibilities we have to take due care of the people our actions might affect. They are points worth bringing up in this discussion. Option A may be technically or legally correct, but it suggests that the bottom-line financial measure of disruption and restitution is all that is required; this seems and may be heartless. Option D seems to treat people in the company, at any level, as objects that are merely parts of the productive processes that the company uses.

20. A, B, D.  Option C is incorrect; it ignores the ability of human experience, combined with focused awareness and training, to detect out-of-tolerance conditions and raise an alarm. Option A is a valid comparison of proofing (verifying that the offered claims of identity are legitimate). Option B is a valid comparison of authenticating that the person or subject in question is recognized as one entitled to access. Option D is a valid application of accounting for access attempts.

# Index

* (star) integrity property (Bell-LaPadula model), 262
* (star) security property (Bell-LaPadula model), 261

## A

AAA (authentication, authorization, accounting), identity, 254–255
ABAC (attribute-based access control), 263–264
acceptance testing, 76, 128, 146, 148, 421, 422, 428
access control, 555. *See also* NAC (network access control)
  ABAC (attribute-based access control), 263–264
  Active Directory and, 272
  answers to review questions, 586–589
  baselines and, 373–374
  Bell-LaPadula model, 260–262
  Biba model, 260–262
  Brewer and Nash model, 262
  centralized access control, 271–272
  CIANA and, 250–251
  Clark-Wilson model, 262
  data classification, 258–260
  datacenter gatekeepers, 256
  decentralized access control, 272
  discretionary, 264–265, 272–273
  Gogun-Meseguer, 262
  Graham-Denning model, 262
  mandatory, 264–265, 272

  non-discretionary access control, 273
  object-based, 264
  objects, 255
  protocols, 348
  RBAC (role-based access control), 263
  subject-based, 264
  subjects, 255
accountability, 180, 565–566
  due care, 17
  due diligence, 17
  due process, 17
  ethical, 18
  financial accounting, 18
  legal accountability, 18–19
  stewardship, 19
accounting. *See* financial accounting
  identity and, 254
ACL (access control list), 254, 266–267, 283, 286, 289
Active Directory, 269
  centralized access control and, 272
  identity and access, 373
  identity management and, 469
  single sign-on architecture, 283
  TACACS+ and, 270
address resolution, 185
addressing, 187–188
  link local address, 218
  loopback addresses, 218
administrative controls, 132, 141
administrative elements, 75
AES (Advanced Encryption Standard), 342
agents, NAC (network access control), 267
aggregating number, 535–536

Agile, 423

AH (Authentication Header), 211

AI (artificial intelligence), 360, 556

ALE (annual loss expectancy), 87, 534

algorithms
    attacks, 351–352
    cryptographic, 302, 307–308
    encryption algorithm, 308
    hash algorithms, 311–312
    rounds, 308
    SHA (Secure Hashing Algorithms), 312

analytics, 556

anomalies, 527

answers to review questions
    access control, 586–589
    application security, 594–597
    business continuity, 601–604
    cloud security, 594–597
    communications, 583–586
    cryptography, 589–591
    data security, 594–597
    hardware, 592–594
    identity, 586–589
    incident recovery, 597–601
    incident response, 597–601
    information security fundamentals, 576–578
    integrated information risk management, 579–581
    network security, 583–586
    operationalizing risk mitigation, 581–583
    self-assessment, 570–576
    systems security, 592–594

API (application programming interface), 208

APIPA (Auto-IP Address), 218

appliances, 416
    software as, 417–420

Application Layer 7 (OSI), 208–209
    CIANA
        countermeasures, 233
        residual risk, 233
        vulnerabilities, 232–233

applications
    answers to review questions, 594–597
    lifecycles, 420–421
        SDLC (software development lifecycle), 421–423
    vulnerabilities, lifecycle, 434–436

apps, 418–419

APTs (advanced persistent threats), 480–481, 484

architecture
    asset management, 151–152
    configuration control, 151–152
    IT architecture
        clouds, 124
        external system providers, 124
        information security baseline, 122
        information technology baseline, 122
        networks, 123–124
        service bureaus, 124
        software-defined service provision, 124–126
    zero trust, 281–282

ARO (annual rate of occurrence), 87, 534

ARP (Address Resolution Protocol), 209
    gratuitous ARP, 209
    Proxy ARP, 209

ARPANet (Advanced Research Projects Agency), 177, 195

asset management, 151

asset-based risk, 65, 68

assets
    information assets, 68
    information technology, 68
    intangible, 68
    tangible, 68

assurance, 9

asymmetric encryption, trapdoor functions, 318

asymmetric key cryptography, 318

attack surface, 181

attacks
  computationally infeasible attacks, 557
  cryptanalysis, quantum computing, 360
  cryptosystems, 349
    algorithm, 351–352
    brute force, 350
    dictionary, 350
    key, 351–352
    massively parallel computing,
      353–354
    numeric, 351–352
    operational intelligence, 352–353
    side channel, 350–351
    social engineering, 353
    supply chain vulnerabilities, 354
    traffic analysis, 352–353
  living off the land, 393
  phishing, 539–540
  threat actors, 54
authentication, 179
  cryptography and, 323
  handshake, EAPOL, 267
  identity and, 254
  multifactor, 274–276
authorization, identity and
  assigning privileges, 254
  authorizing specific request, 254
availability, 14, 31
  cryptography and, 325–326
avoidance, 97–98

**B**

backplanes, bus topologies, 190
bankruptcy, 528
baselines, 372–373
  access control and, 373–374
  cloud services, 375–376
  controlled, auditing, 152
  supply chain security, 374–375
  uncontrolled, 151–152

bases, 66
basis of estimate, 66
BCP (business continuity plan), 529–530
behavior analysis, 556
Bell-LaPadula model, 260–262
  * (star) integrity property, 261
  * (star) security property, 261
  discretionary security property, 261
  simple integrity property, 261
  simple security (SS) property, 261
Berners-Lee, Tim, 188–189
best effort services, 193
BI (business intelligence), 556
BIA (business impact analysis), 92,
  180, 270
Biba model, 260–262
  * (star) integrity property, 261, 262
  * (star) security property, 261
  discretionary security property, 261
  simple integrity property, 261, 262
  simple security (SS) property, 261
biometrics, 275
Bitcoin, 347
BITE (built-in test equipment), 153
black hats, cryptanalysis, 319
blacklisting, 432–433
BLOB (binary large objects),
  385–386
block ciphers, 307
blockchain, 346–348
Bluetooth, 215–216
Boyd, John, 115
Brewer and Nash model, 262
broadcast messages, 219
broadcast news, 37
browsing, 395–397
brute force attacks, 350
budgets, 22–23
bump-in-the-stack, 344–345
bump-in-the-wire, 344–345
bus topologies, 190

business
   boards of directors, 20
   C-Suite, 20
   competitors, 12
   corporations, 11
   customers, 12
   employees, 12
   executive directors, 20
   investors, 11, 19–20
   managing directors, 20
   owners, 19–20
   partnerships, 11
   sole proprietorships, 11
   stakeholders, 12
business continuity, 88
   answers to review questions,
      601–604
   planning, 529–530
business logic, 7, 14–15, 67
   patents, 15
   trade secrets, 15
business plan, 12–13
business process engineering, 121
business processes, 60–61, 67
BYOC (bring your own cloud), 390
BYOD (bring your own device), 388
BYOI (bring your own infrastructure),
   389–391

# C

C3 (command, control, communications),
   64–65
CA (certificate authorities), 332–333, 334
CADAM (computer-aided design and
   manufacturing), 13
captive portals, 268
case studies, voter registration, 59–60,
   70–72
catphishing, 540
causal agents, 503

CCITT (International Telegraph and
   Telephone Consultative Committee), 195
CCTV (closed-circuit television), 33
celebrities, 35
centralized access control, 271–272
CEO (chief executive officer), 20
CERT (computer emergency response
   team), 487
certificates, 334
   leaf, 335
   revocation, 335
   root certificate, 335
CFO (chief financial officer), 20
chain of custody, evidence, 510
chain of trust, 335
character ciphers, 307
checksums, 310
CIA (confidentiality, integrity, availability),
   9, 562
   government and, 36
   individual's needs, 34–35
   military and, 36
   nuclear medicine and, 39–40
   private business, 35
   product development and, 13–14
   real estate, 32
   society's need for, 36–37
   training, 38
CIANA (confidentiality, integrity,
   availability, nonrepudiation,
   authentication), 179, 562
   access and, 250–251
   applications software and, 428–433
   cryptography and, 322–327
   e-voting and, 326
   identity and, 250–251
   Layer 1 - Physical
      countermeasures, 225–226
      residual risk, 226
      tools, 224–225
      vulnerabilities, 223–224

Layer 2 - Data Link
  countermeasures, 225–226, 227
  residual risk, 226, 228
  tools, 224–225
  vulnerabilities, 226–227
Layer 3 - Network
  countermeasures, 228
  residual risk, 229
  vulnerabilities, 228
Layer 4 - Transport
  countermeasures, 229–230
  residual risk, 230
  vulnerabilities, 229
Layer 5 - Session
  countermeasures, 230–231
  residual risk, 231
  vulnerabilities, 230
Layer 6 - Presentation
  countermeasures, 232
  residual risk, 232
  vulnerabilities, 231
Layer 7 - Application
  countermeasures, 233
  residual risk, 233
  vulnerabilities, 232–233
layer 8, 537–538
CIDR (Classless Inter-Domain Routing),
  220, 240
CIFS (Common Internet File System), 208
CIO (chief information officer), 20
ciphers, 300–305
  block ciphers, 307
  character ciphers, 307
  stream ciphers, 307
  symbol ciphers, 307
ciphertext, 301
CISO (chief information security officer), 20
civil law, 19
CKO (chief knowledge officer), 20
Clark-Wilson model, 262
cleartext, 301–302, 322, 365

clients, star network, 191
cloud, 124
  answers to review questions, 594–597
  continuity and, 452
  *versus* datacenter, 448
  deployment models, 449–450
  do-over buttons
    complex service do-over, 532
    session do-over, 532
    transaction do-over, 532
  GovCloud, 375
  hybrid, 376
  penetration testing, 456
  private, 375
  public, 375–376
  resiliency and, 452
  security methods, 455
  services
    baseline management and, 375–376
    IaaS (infrastructure as a service),
      450–451
    IDaaS (identity as a service), 451
    PaaS (platform as a service), 451
    SaaS (software as a service), 451
  SLAs (service-level agreements), 456
  threat modeling and, 453–455
  TORs (terms of reference), 456
  updates, 533
CMIP (Common Management Information
  Protocol), 210
CMIS (Common Management Information
  Service), 210
CMVP (Cryptographic Module Validation
  Program), 310
code, 300–305
  decoding, 300
  encoding, 300
  prisoner's code, 300–301
  software security and, 424
Code of Ethics, 38–39
Code-First Design, 423

collaborative workspaces, 538

collision detection, 198

collision domain, 199

collisions, 308

    encryption, 311

common law, privacy and, 26–27

common sense, risk management

    and, 63–65

communications, 176

    answers to review questions, 583–586

    connectionless, 205, 211, 228

    intent, 178

    media, 178

    message content, 178

    parties, 178

    privileged, 29–30

    protocols, 178

    purpose, 178

    quantum communications, 557–558

    recipients, 178

    risk treatment and, 143–144

    senders, 178

    strategy, 180

    subtext, 178

    threat modeling, 180–181

company confidential information, 27

competitive advantage, 15

competitors, 12

complex service do-over button, 532

computationally infeasible attacks, 557

computing hygiene, 64

confidentiality, 14

    cryptography and, 298, 322

    privacy, 29–30

    privileged communications, 29–30

    requirements, 430

configuration control, 151–152

configuration management, 151–152

connectionless communications, 205,

    211, 228

connections

    logical, 185

    NIC and transmission medium, 198

    physical, 185

containment, incident response, 502–503

contingency operations planning, 530

continuity, cloud and, 452

control plane, 211

controlled paths, 181

controls

    risk treatment

        administrative, 141

        logical, 141

        physical, 140

        selecting, 141

        technical, 141

    user engagement and, 147–148

convergence of communications, 176–179

COO (chief operations officer), 20

COPE (company-owned personally enabled),

    388–389

core technologies, understanding, 560–561

corporate officers, 35

corporations, 11

counterattacks, 487

countermeasures

    applications, 458–459

    controls

        administrative, 141

        logical, 141

        physical, 140

        selecting, 141

        technical, 141

    cryptosystems

        administrative, 357

        logical, 356–357

        physical, 355–356

        timing, 357

covert paths, 320, 390, 398, 405

criminal law, 19

critical asset protection planning, 530
critical path, 69
CRM (customer relationship management), 13, 68
cross MAC scheduling, 210
cryptanalysis, 305
    attacks, quantum computing, 360
    black hats, 319
    white hats, 319
CryptGenRandom function, 313
cryptocurrency, 346–347
cryptographic module, 310
cryptographic systems, 304
    QKD (quantum key distribution), 359
cryptography, 298–299. *See also* encryption; quantum cryptography
    access control protocols, 348
    AI (artificial intelligence), 360
    algorithms, 302, 307–308
    answers to review questions, 589–591
    asymmetric key, 318
    blockchain and, 346–348
    certificate authorities, 332–333
    CIANA and
        authentication, 323
        availability, 325–326
        confidentiality, 322
        integrity, 323
        nonrepudiation, 323
    ciphers, 300–305
    ciphertext, 301
    classical *versus* modern, 326–327
    cleartext, 301–302, 365
    codes, 300–305
    computationally infeasible attacks, 557
    confidentiality and, 298
    definition, 305
    digital certificates, 332–333

digital cryptographic systems, 306
    block ciphers, 307
    character ciphers, 307
    stream ciphers, 307
    symbol ciphers, 307
digital signatures, 332
DKIM and, 345–346
e-voting and, 306
email and, 324–325
engineers, 320
entropy and, 313
functions and, 304
hashing and, 310
hybrid cryptosystems, 318–319
identity and, 298
integrity and, 298
IPSec and, 344–345
Kerckhoff's principle, 314
keys, 308–309, 314–315
    distribution and management, 309
    keying management, 309
    keying material, 309
    management, 314–315
    protection, 315
    protocols, 309–310
    pseudorandom numbers, 309
    revocation, 315–317
    space, 309
    storage, 315
    strength, 309
    zeroization, 315–317
Kryptos, 298–299
legalities, 321
lexical analysis, 298
measuring merit, 348–349
nonrepudiation and, 298
pervasive cryptography, 320
PKI (public key infrastructure), 341
plaintext, 301–302, 309, 322
primitives, 320

privacy and, 298
protocols, 309–310
public key, 318
S/MIME and, 345
sets and, 304
Shannon's maxim, 314
strength, 321
symmetric key, 317–318, 341
uniqueness and, 298
utility and, 298
zero value, 313–314
cryptolinguistics, 305
cryptology, 305
cryptosystems
attacks, 349
algorithm, 351–352
brute force, 350
dictionary, 350
key, 351–352
massively parallel computing, 353–354
numeric, 351–352
operational intelligence, 352–353
side channel, 350–351
social engineering, 353
supply chain vulnerabilities, 354
traffic analysis, 352–353
countermeasures
administrative, 357
logical, 356–357
physical, 355–356
timing, 357
design, 319
hybrid, 318–319
CSIRT (computer security incident response teams), 487
CSO (chief security officer), 20
CTO (chief technology officer), 20
customers, 12
CVE (Common Vulnerabilities and Exposures), 129–130, 223

CVSS (Common Vulnerability Scoring System), 129
cyber as prefix, 10
cybernetics, 61
cybersecurity, 10
CYOD (choose your own device), 389

## D

data, 6
acquisition, unauthorized, 446–447
answers to review questions, 594–597
cleaning, 7
errors, 426
exfiltration, 445–446, 456
hypotheses, 6
information and, 6
insight, 6
knowledge, 6
knowledge pyramid and, 8
loss, preventing, 447–448
modeling, 426
as procedural knowledge, 438–440
processed, 6, 7
processing, 7
quality assurance, 126
raw, 6
recovery, 506–507
semantics, 558
smoothing, 7
typing, 426
validation, 7
verifiability, 7
wisdom, 6
data classification
access control and, 258–260
privacy-related information, 258
reading up, 259
secret, 258

suitable for public release, 258
top secret, 258
unclassified, 258
writing down, 259
data encapsulation, 319
data in motion, 443–444, 443–445
data in rest, 443–444
data in use, 443–444
Data Link Layer 2 (OSI), 199–201
    CIANA
        countermeasures, 225–226, 227
        residual risk, 226, 228
        tools, 224–225
        vulnerabilities, 226–227
data plane, 211
data remenance, 317, 351, 356, 462
Data-Information-Knowledge-Wisdom
    pyramid, 414–415
datacenter keepers, 256
datacenters *versus* clouds, 448
datagrams, 182–183, 205
DDC (Dewey Decimal Classification), 310
decentralized access control, 272
decision assurance, 60–63
    zero trust architecture, 281–282
decision flow, airline flight purchase, 61–62
decision making, PDCA (Plan, Do, Check,
    Act), 82–84
decision work, 60–61
decoding, 300, 302
decryption, 301, 302
    collisions, 308
    substitution, 303
    transposition, 303
defense, 72–74
    due care, 76–77
    due diligence, 76–77
    layers, 74–75
    priority setting, 77–78
defense in depth, 54

Delta Airlines breach, 58
DES (Data Encryption Standard), 341–342
deserializing, 207
design pattern, 424, 461
design, software security and, 424
detection, 96–97
deterministic numbers, hashing
    and, 312–313
deterrence, 96
DHCP (Dynamic Host Configuration
    Protocol), 209
Diameter, 269
dictionary attacks, 350
Dierks, Tim, 333
Diffie, Whitfield, 328–331
digital certificates, 332–333
digital cryptographic systems, 306
    block ciphers, 307
    character ciphers, 307
    stream ciphers, 307
    symbol ciphers, 307
digital fingerprints, 310
digital identification, 313
digital nomads, 558
digital signatures, 332
    integrity and, 323
directives, 22–23
disaster recovery, 528
discretionary access control, 264–265,
    272–273
discretionary security property
    (Bell-LaPadula model), 261
DKIM (Domain Keys Identified Mail),
    345–346
DMZ (demilitarized zone), 397, 405–406
DNS (Domain Name System), 188, 210
do-over buttons
    complex service do-over, 532
    session do-over, 532
    transaction do-over, 532

DoS (denial-of-service) attack, 503–504

Dragonfly 2.0, 481

DRM (digital rights management), 447

DRP (disaster recovery plan), 530

DSA (Digital Signature Algorithm), 332

DSS (Digital Signature Standard), 332

DTLS (Datagram Transport Layer
    Security), 213

due care, 64, 76–77

due diligence, 64, 76–77

due process, 17, 27


# E

e-voting, cryptography and, 306

EAPOL (Extensible Authentication
    Protocol), 267
    authentication handshake, 267

ECC (elliptical curve algorithms for
    cryptography), 558

ECC (error correction code), 323

EF (exposure factor), 534

electronic commerce, 333

ElGamal encryption, 331–332

email, cryptography and, 324–325

emergency zeroization, 316

employees, 12

encapsulation, 185–187, 205
    data encapsulation, 319
    key encapsulation, 319

encoding, 300, 302

encryption, 301, 302. *See also* cryptography
    AES (Advanced Encryption Standard),
        342
    algorithm, 308
    collisions, 308, 311
    decryption, 301
    DES (Data Encryption Standard), 341–342
    ElGamal, 331–332
    homomorphic, 358

HTTPS (Hypertext Transfer Protocol
    Secure), 340–341
    pervasive, 358
    PGP (Pretty Good Privacy), 337
        GPG (GNU Privacy Guard), 338
        OpenPGP, 338
    public key, 328
    RSA (Rivest-Shamir-Adleman), 331
    symmetric, forward secrecy, 315
    TLS (Transport Layer Security), 338–340

endpoints, 213, 414–416

entropy, cryptography and, 313

Equifax breach, 56–57

error correction, 527

ESP (Encapsulating Security Payloads), 211

estimates, 66

Ether Type field, 200

ethical accountability, 18

European Union, 28

events, 527
    *versus* incidents, 484–485

evidence, incident response and, 504

executing code, 258

exercises, CIA and nuclear medicine, 39–40

exfiltration, data, 445–446

existential risk, 84

existential threats, 90

expected cost, 84

explicit information, 7

explicit knowledge, 121


# F

fake news, 37

false acceptance rate, 275–276, 288

false negative access control error, 275–276,
    288, 393, 447, 514

false positive access control error, 275–276,
    288, 393, 447

false rejection rate, 275–276, 288

fault tree analysis, 16

FCS (Frame Check Sequence), 200

FDFI (fault detection and fault isolation), 153

federated IAM system, 279

FERPA (Family Educational Rights and Privacy Act), 93–94

financial accounting, 18

    GAAP (Generally Accepted Accounting Principles), 18

firewalls, 97–98

firmware, vulnerabilities, threat modeling, 380–382

fishbone diagram, 16, 66

flexibility of vision, 565

forward secrecy, 315

four faces of risk, 65–66

    asset-based, 65, 68

    outcomes-based, 65, 67

    process-based, 65, 67–68

    threat-based, 65, 69

frames, 199

frequency of occurrence, 58

FTP (File Transfer Protocol), handshakes, 184–185

functional impact, 502

functional requirements, 430


## G

GAAP (Generally Accepted Accounting Principles), 18

gap analysis, 133–134

GDPR (General Data Protection Regulation), 28, 562

gemba, 21

    inverted pyramid chart, 22

GIS (geographical information system), 420

glueware, 121, 174

Gogun-Meseguer, 262

GovCloud, 375

government

    CIA and, 36

    overreactions, 561–562

government officials, 35

GPG (GNU Privacy Guard), 338

graceful degradation, 124, 137, 452, 467

Graham-Denning model, 262


## H

handshakes, 184–185

    EAPOL, 267

hardware, 427–428

    answers to review questions, 592–594

    vulnerabilities, threat modeling, 379–380

hashing, 310

    checksums, 310

    DDC (Dewey Decimal Classification), 310

    deterministic numbers, 312–313

    digital fingerprints, 310

    functions, 311

    hash algorithms, 311–312

    integrity and, 323

    mappings, 311

    pseudorandom numbers, 312–313

    SHA (Secure Hash Algorithms), 312

Hellman, Martin, 328–331

HIDS (host-based intrusion detection system), 387, 404

hierarchies of trust, 333–337

homomorphic encryption, 358

honeypot, 388, 405–406

hot-swap topologies, 190

HTTP (Hypertext Transfer Protocol), 189

HTTPS (Hypertext Transfer Protocol Secure), 340–341

human security behaviors, 558

hybrid clouds, 376

hybrid cryptosystems, 318
  data (payload) encapsulation, 319
  ElGamal, 332
  key encapsulation, 319
hypervisor, 374–376, 385, 450, 463, 466
hypotheses, 6

# I

IaaS (infrastructure as a service), 125,
    450–451
IAM (identity management and access
    control), 270
  authentication, multifactor, 274–276
  built-in solutions, 273–274
  centralized access control, 271–272
  decentralized access control, 272
  discretionary access control, 272–273
  integrated systems, 277–278
    federated system, 279
    IDaaS (Identity as a Service), 279
    SSO (single sign-on), 278
    trust frameworks, 279–281
  mandatory access control, 272
  non-discretionary access control, 273
  policy objects, 273
  server-based, 276–277
IANA (Internet Assigned Numbers
    Authority), 187
ICANN (Internet Corporation for Assigned
    Names and Numbers), 189
ICMP (Internet Control Message
    Protocol), 201
IDaaS (Identity as a Service), 125, 451
  integrated IAM systems, 279
identity
  accounting and, 255
  Active Directory and, 373
  answers to review questions, 586–589
  authentication and, multifactor, 254

authorization
    assigning privileges, 254
    authorizing specific request, 254
  CIANA and, 250–251
  cryptography and, 298
identity management, 251
  Active Directory and, 469
  lifecycle, 252
  privilege creep, 252–253
  provisioning, 252
    identity proofing, 252
  review, 252–253
  revocation, 253
identity plane, 415
identity proofing, 252
identity provisioning, 252
  identity proofing, 252
identity theft, APTs and, 481
IDEs (integrated development environments),
    423, 461
IDS (intrusion detection systems), 387–388
  HIDS (host-based intrusion detection
      system), 387, 404
  NIDS (network-based intrusion detection
      system), 387, 404
IEEE 802.1X, 267–268
IETF (Internet Engineering Task Force), 333
IGRP (Interior Gateway Routing
    Protocol), 201
IKE (Internet Key Exchange), 211
impact assessment, 113
InARP (Inverse ARP), 209
incident response
  answers to review questions, 597–601
  appreciative inquiry, 508–509
  APTs (advanced persistent threats),
      480–481
  causal agent, 503
  CERT (computer emergency response
      team), 487
  checklist, 495–496

containment, 502–503
counterattacks and, 487
CSIRT (computer security incident
    response teams), 487
detection
    initial, 499–500
    notification, 500–501
    timeline, 500
    warning signs, 497–499
DoS attack, 503–504
eradication, 504
evidence, 504
flow, 486
framework, 485–486
functional impact, 502
information impact, 502
kill chain, 482–484
monitoring, 505
point of contact, 488
post-incident, 508–509
    evidence chain of custody, 510
    evidence retention, 511
    forensics, ongoing, 510
    information retention, 511
    information sharing, 511
    lessons learned, 509–510
preparation
    implementing plan, 493–494
    planning, 491–493
priorities, 490
process, 486
quarantine, 503
recoverability, 502
recovery, 505–506
    answers to review questions, 597–601
    data recovery, 506–507
    post-recovery, 508
teams
    roles, 487–489
    structures, 487–489
triage, 485

incidents, 159–160
    *versus* events, 484–485
indicator of compromise, 499
individuals, CIA and, 34–35
industrial automation, 418
infiltration of code, 434–435
information, 4–5, 26
    company confidential, 27
    data and, 6
    explicit, 7
    *versus* information technology, 8–10
    knowledge pyramid and, 8
    privileged, 30
    proprietary, 27
    tacit, 7
information access gates, 555
information architecture
    assessment, 120
        cultural context, 120
        organization culture, 120
    business processes, 120–121
    decision flow, 120–121
    IT architecture
        information security baseline, 122
        information technology
            baseline, 122
information assets, 68
information assurance, 10, 440–443
information classification system, qualitative
    risk, 90
information processing, 4, 7
information quality, 440–441
    garbage in, 442–443
    lifecycle, 441–442
information risk
    financial data, 86
    internal business processes, 86
    PII (personally identifying
        information), 86
    proximate cause analysis, 86
    root cause analysis, 86

information risk management, 52
  consensus building, 84–85
  integrated information risk
    management, 54
  risk appetite, 85
  risk tolerance, 85
information security, 10. *See also* security
  answers to review questions,
    576–578
  baseline, 122
  hygiene, 564–565
  incident response planning, 530
information systems
  kill chain, 483 (*See also* kill chain)
  protocols, 5
information technology, 8–10, 26
  assets, 68
  baseline, 122
infotainment, 37
infrastructure, 415
  baseline management, 372–373
    access control and, 373–374
    cloud services, 375–376
    supply chain security, 374–375
  BYOC (bring your own cloud), 390
  BYOD (bring your own device), 388
  BYOI (bring your own infrastructure),
    389–391
  COPE (company-owned personally
    enabled), 388–389
  CYOD (choose your own device), 389
  malware, 391–393
    countermeasures, 394–395
    procedural misuse of capabilities, 393
  MDM (mobile device management),
    388
  NOS (network operating systems),
    386–387
    IDS (intrusion detection systems),
      387–388
  public key, 328

  threat modeling and, 376–378
    firmware vulnerabilities, 380–382
    hardware vulnerabilities, 379–380
    operating systems vulnerabilities, 382–384
    virtual machines vulnerabilities, 385–386
insight, 6
insure, 9
intangible assets, 68
integrated defense, 52
integrated IAM systems, 277–278
  federated system, 279
  IDaaS (Identity as a Service), 279
  SSO (single sign-on), 278
  trust frameworks, 279–281
integrated information risk management, 54
  answers to review questions, 579–581
integrity, 14, 30–31
  cryptography and, 298, 323
Internet, traffic, 196
Internet backbone, 185
Internet point of presence, 185
Internet segments, 188
Internet systems, 181–182
  addressing, 187–188
  Berners-Lee, Tim, 188–189
  best effort systems, 193
  datagrams, 182–183
  encapsulation, 185–187
  handshakes, 184–185
  packets, 185–187
  PDUs (protocol data units), 183
  routing, 187–188
  segmentation, 188
  switching, 187–188
  topologies
    bus, 190
    mesh, 192
    peer-to-peer, 189–190
    point-to-point, 189–190
    ring, 190–191
    star, 191

investors, dividends, 11
IOC (indicator of compromise), 499
IoT (Internet of Things), 419
IP (Internet Protocol), 210–211
IP addresses
    dynamic, 217
    link local addresses, 218
    loopback addresses, 218
    static, 217
IP masquerading, 210
IPS (intrusion prevention system), 388,
    404, 495
IPSec (Internet Protocol Security), 211, 344
    bump-in-the-stack, 344–345
    bump-in-the-wire, 344–345
    IP stack, 344–345
    transport mode, 344–345
    tunnel mode, 344–345
IPv4
    address exhaustion, 210, 220
    addressing, classes, 217–219
    *versus* IPv6, 221–222
    packet format, 202
    subnetting, 219–220
IPv6
    *versus* IPv4, 221–222
    packages, 222
ISAKMP (Internet Security Association and
    Key Management Protocol), 211
Ishikawa diagram, 16, 66
ISO (International Organization for
    Standardization), 195
ISP (Internet service provider), 185
IT architecture
    clouds, 124
    external system providers, 124
    information security baseline, 122
    information technology baseline, 122
    networks, 123–124
    service bureaus, 124
    shadow IT, 122–123

software-defined service provision,
    124–126
standalone systems, 122–123
ITU (International Telecommunications
    Union), 195

**J**

journalists, 35

**K**

Kerckhoff's principle, 314
key attacks, 351–352
key encapsulation, 319
keys, cryptographic, 308–309
    distribution and management, 309
    exchange, 211, 215, 315
    keying material, 309
    protection, 315
    protocols, 309–310
    pseudorandom numbers, 309
    public key exchange protocols, 318
    revocation, 315–317
    space, 309
    storage, 315
    strength, 309
    zeroization, 315–317
kill chain, 117, 482–484
KINK (Kerberized Internet Negotiations of
    Keys), 211
knowledge, 6
knowledge management, 7
knowledge pyramid, 6
Kryptos, 298–299

**L**

LANs (local area networks), objects, 257
law of diminishing returns, 68

Layer 1 - Physical layer (OSI model and TCP/IP), 198–199
  countermeasures, 225–226
  residual risk, 226
  tools, 224–225
  vulnerabilities, 223–224
Layer 2 - Data Link layer (OSI model and TCP/IP), 199–201
  countermeasures, 225–226, 227
  residual risk, 226, 228
  tools, 224–225
  vulnerabilities, 226–227
Layer 3 - Network layer (OSI model and TCP/IP), 201–202
  countermeasures, 228
  residual risk, 229
  vulnerabilities, 228
Layer 4 - Transport layer (OSI model and TCP/IP), 202–206
  countermeasures, 229–230
  residual risk, 230
  vulnerabilities, 229
Layer 5 - Session layer (OSI model and TCP/IP), 206–207
  countermeasures, 230–231
  residual risk, 231
  vulnerabilities, 230
Layer 6 - Presentation layer (OSI model and TCP/IP), 207–208
  countermeasures, 232
  residual risk, 232
  vulnerabilities, 231
Layer 7 - Application layer (OSI model and TCP/IP), 208–209
  countermeasures, 233
  residual risk, 233
  vulnerabilities, 232–233
layers, calls, 196
layers of abstraction, 182
LDAP (Lightweight Directory Access Protocol), 269

leaf certificates, 335
legal accountability, 18–19
legal issues
  privacy, 26–28
  public law, 27–28
legislation, 563
lessons learned, 563–567
lexical analysis
  cryptography, 298
  cryptography and, 298
Li-Fi, 214
licensed professionals, 35
link local address, 218
links, 188
living off the land attacks, 393
LLC (Logical Link Control), sublayer, 199
LMS (learning management system), 536
locators, 188
logical connections, 185, 199
logical controls, 141
logical elements, 75
loopback addresses, 218
loss prevention, 447–448
lunchtime attacks, 332

# M

MAC (media access control) address, 187
  cross MAC scheduling, 210
  spoofing, 200
  sublayer, 199–200
malware, 216, 254, 262, 317, 391–393
  countermeasures, 394–395
  definition file, 284
  procedural misuse of capabilities, 393
  quarantine and, 268
management plane, 211
mandatory access control, 264–265, 272
MAO (maximum acceptable outage), 87, 534
mappings, hashing, 311

massively parallel computing attacks, 353–354

MDM (mobile device management), 388

media control, transmission media, 198

medical informatics, 418

Merkle, Ralph, 330

mesh topologies, 192

messages, broadcast messages, 219

metadata, as procedural knowledge, 438–440

middleware, 415

military, CIA and, 36

mitigation, 95

ML (machine learning), 556

monitoring
  alert team and, 153–157
  continuous, 152–153, 152–155
  end users and, 157
  IT support staff, 157
  leadership and, 157–158
  management and, 157–158

MPLS (Multiprotocol Label Switching), 213

MTO (maximum tolerable outage), 87

MTPOD (maximum tolerable period of disruption), 87

MTTR (mean time to repair), 87

multicasting, 219

multifactor authentication, 274–276

## N

NAC (network access control), 265–266
  agent, 267
  agentless, 267
  IEEE 802.1X, 267–268
  inline, 267
  out-of-band, 267
  postadmission, 267
  preadmission, 267
  RADIUS (Remote Authentication Dial-In Service), 268–269

remediation
  captive portals, 268
  quarantine networks, 268

name resolution, 185

narrowcasting, 37, 556

NAT (Network Address Translation), 210

NBT (NetBIOS over TCP/IP), 208

need to know, RBAC (role-based access control) and, 263

negative security control, 431–432

NetBIOS (Network Basic Input/Output System), 208

Network Layer 3 (OSI), 201–202
  CIANA
    countermeasures, 228
    residual risk, 229
    vulnerabilities, 228

network management, functions, 210

networks, 123–124
  answers to review questions, 583–586
  SDNs (software-defined networks), 212

newspapers of record, 37

NFC (near-field communication), 216

NGOs (nongovernmental organizations), 280

NIC (network interface card), 185

NIDS (network-based intrusion detection system), 387, 404

NOC (network operations center), 234
  tools, 235–236

non-discretionary access control, 273

non-zero day exploit, 56–57

nonfunctional requirements, 425, 430–431

nonrepudiation, 179
  cryptography and, 298, 323
  requirements, 430

NOS (network operating systems), 386–387
  IDS (intrusion detection systems), 387–388

numeric attacks, 351–352

## O

OAuth, 279
object-based access control, 264
objects, 180
   access control, 255
   LANs, 257
   policy objects, 273
one-time pads, cryptographic keys and,
   308–309
one-way cryptography, hashing as, 310–313
one-way trust relationship, 285, 333
OODA loop (observe, orient, decide, act),
   115–117
Open Systems Interconnection Reference
   Model, 195
OpenID, 279
OpenPGP, 338
operating systems, threat modeling, 382–384
operational intelligence attacks, 352–353
operational risk mitigation planning, 95
operationalizing risk, 55
operationalizing risk mitigation, 118–119
   answers to review questions, 581–583
   control implementation, 141–145
   control selection, 135–141
   information architecture and, 119–126
   senior leaders and, 146
   threat assessment, 126–134
   treatment selection, 135–141
   vulnerability assessment, 126–134
organization chart as pyramid, 21
   inverted, 22
organization culture, 120
organizational death, 527
orphans, 384
OSI (Open Systems Interconnection)
   network
   Layer 1 - Physical layer, 198–199
   Layer 2 - Data Link layer, 199–201
   Layer 3 - Network layer, 201–202
   Layer 4 - Transport layer, 202–206
   Layer 5 - Session layer, 206–207
   Layer 6 - Presentation layer, 207–208
   Layer 7 - Application layer, 208–209
   mnemonics for remembering, 208
   TCP/IP comparison, 183–184, 197
OT&E (operational test and evaluation),
   148–150
OTV (Overlay Transport Virtualization), 209
outcomes-based risk, 65, 67

## P

PaaS (platform as a service), 125, 451
packages, IPv6, 222
packets, 185–187, 201
   IPv4, 202
partnerships, 11
PAT (Port Address Translation), 210
patent infringement, 15
patents, 15
PCCIP (President's Commission on Critical
   Infrastructure Protection), 145
PDCA (Plan, Do, Check, Act), 82–84
PDU (protocol data unit), 183
peer-to-peer topologies, 189–190
penetration testing, 456
perception management, 559–560
personnel reliability program, 131–132
pervasive cryptography, 320
pervasive encryption, 358
PGP (Pretty Good Privacy), 337
   GPG (GNU Privacy Guard), 338
   OpenPGP, 338
phishing attacks, 539–540
   catphishing, 540
   spear phishing, 540
   whaling attacks, 540
PHY scheduling, 210

physical connections, 185
physical controls, 140
Physical Layer 1 (OSI), 198–199
   CIANA
      countermeasures, 225–226
      residual risk, 225–226
      tools, 224–225
      vulnerabilities, 223–224
physical security and safety planning, 530
physical security systems, 418
physical systems elements, 75
PI (predictive intelligence), 556
PII (personally identifiable information), 6,
   30, 59–60, 86, 139, 313, 456
PKI (public key infrastructure), 328, 330, 341
   trust relationships, 342–344
plaintext, 301
planes
   control plane, 211
   data plane, 211
   management plane, 211
platforms, 415
point-to-point topologies, 189–190
policies, 22–23, 93
policy objects, 273
portals, captive portals, 268
Porter, Michael, 15
ports, 202
   TCP/IP, 203–205
postadmission, NAC (network access
   control), 267
POTS (plain old telephone systems), 187,
   542–543
preadmission, NAC (network access
   control), 267
Presentation Layer 6 (OSI), 207–208
   CIANA
      countermeasures, 232
      residual risk, 232
      vulnerabilities, 231

prevention, 97
priorities, 77–78
prisoner's code, 300–301
privacy
   common law and, 26–27
   confidentiality, 29–30
   cryptography and, 298
   European Union, 28
   private places, 28–29
   public law and, 27–28
   security and, 32–34
private browsing, 395–397
private business, CIA and, 35
private citizens, 35
private clouds, 375
private spaces, 27
privilege creep, 252–253
   RBAC and, 263
privileged communications, 29–30
privileged information, 30
proactive defense, 52
probability of occurrence, 58
problem analysis, 527
procedures, 93
process-based risk, 65, 67–68
processed data, 6
processing, 7
product development, CIA and, 13–14
proprietary information, 27
protocol stacks, 182, 194
protocols, 5
   cryptographic, 309–310
   public key exchange protocols, 318
   TCP/IP, 203–205
proximate causes, 126
Proxy ARP, 209
pseudorandom numbers, 309
   hashing and, 312–313
PSTN (public switched telephone
   network), 542

PUAs (potentially unwanted applications), 432
public clouds, 375–376
public key cryptography, 318
    public key exchange protocols, 318
public key encryption, 328
public key exchange protocols, 318, 327
    Diffie-Hellman-Merkle, 328–331
public law, privacy and, 27–28
public places, 28–29
PUPs (potentially unwanted programs), 432
pyramid chart (org chart), 21
    inverted, 22

## Q

QKD (quantum key distribution), 359
qualitative risk
    compartmentalization of information, 91
    existential threats, 90
    information classification system, 90
quality assurance
    data quality assurance, 126
    software quality assurance, 126–127
quantitative risk
    ALE (annual loss expectancy), 87
    ARO (annual rate of occurrence), 87
    calculating, 89–90
    MAO (maximum acceptable outage), 87
    MTO (maximum tolerable outage), 87
    MTPOD (maximum tolerable period of disruption), 87
    MTTR (mean time to repair), 87
    paint points, 88
    RPO (recovery point objective), 88
    RTO (recovery time objective), 88
    safeguard value, 87
    SLE (single loss expectancy), 87

quantum communications, 557–558
quantum cryptography, 358–359
    attacks, 360
    QKD (quantum key distribution), 359
quantum mechanics, 359
quarantine networks, 268

## R

RADIUS (Remote Authentication Dial-In Service), 268–269
    Diameter, 269
    roaming, 269
Rapid Prototyping, 423
RARP (Reverse ARP), 209
raw data, 6
RBAC (role-based access control), 263
real estate, CIA in, 32
remedial action, 137–138
remediation
    captive portals, 268
    quarantine networks, 268
reporting, 160
repudiation, 179
residual risk, 139, 534
resiliency, 452–453, 467
responder's workbench, 492–493
revocation, 243
    certificate revocation, 335
    key revocation, 315–316
RFID (radio frequency identification), 216
ring topologies, 190–191
risk, 55
    accepting, 98
    anticipating, 59
    ATM (automatic teller machine), 98–99
    expected cost, 84

four faces, 65–66
  asset-based, 65, 68
  outcomes-based, 65, 67
  process-based, 65, 67–68
  threat-based, 65, 69
ignoring, 98
operationalizing, 55
residual risk, 139
risk appetite, 85
risk assessment, 84
  impact assessment, 113
  information risk, consensus building,
      84–85
  qualitative risk
    compartmentalization of
        information, 91
    existential threats, 90
    information classification system, 90
  quantitative risk
    ALE (annual loss expectancy), 87
    ARO (annual rate of occurrence), 87
    MAO (maximum acceptable outage), 87
    MTO (maximum tolerable outage), 87
    MTPOD (maximum tolerable period
        of disruption), 87
    MTTR (mean time to repair), 87
    paint points, 88
    RPO (recovery point objective), 88
    RTO (recovery time objective), 88
    safeguard value, 87
    SLE (single loss expectancy), 87
  risk appetite, 85
  risk register, 91
  risk tolerance, 85
  vulnerabilities, 91
risk management, 81–82, 112
  common sense, 63–65
  concepts, 78–79
  frameworks, 78–79

risk mitigation, 112, 113
  asset management, 151–152
  configuration control, 151–152
  operationalizing, 118–119
    control implementation, 141–145
    control selection, 135–141
    information architecture and, 119–126
    senior leaders and, 146
    threat assessment, 126–134
    treatment selection, 135–141
    vulnerability assessment, 126–134
  planning, 114–116
  security assessments, 148
    assessment-driven training, 150
    OT&E, 149–150
risk register, 91
risk tolerance, 85
risk treatment
  command and control, 144–145
  communications, 143–144
  controls
    administrative, 141
    implementation, 141–145
    logical, 141
    physical, 140
    selecting, 141
    technical, 141
  countermeasures, 140–145
  self-insuring, 135
  strategies
    accept, 135–136
    avoidance, 138
    elimination, 138
    mitigation, 137–138
    recasting, 138–139
    remediation, 137–138
    residual, 139
    transfer, 136–137
risk-averse, 120

risk-tolerant, 120
RJ-11 connection, 182
RJ-45 connection, 198
RMF (Risk Management Framework), 52, 54, 78–79
    areas of concern, 79
    conceptual, 81
    phases, 80
robots, 221
roles, 35
root causes, 126
root certificate, 335
routers, 201
routing, 187–188
RPO (recovery point objective), 88, 534
RSA (Rivest-Shamir-Adleman) encryption, 331
RTO (recovery time objective), 88, 534
RTP (Real-Time Transport Protocol), 207

# S

S/MIME (Secure Multipurpose Internet Mail Extensions), 345
SaaS (software as a service), 125, 451
safeguard value, 87
safety requirements, 430
SAML (Security Assertion Markup Language), 279
sandboxes, 385, 397
SAs (security associations), 211
SCADA (Supervisory Control and Data Acquisition), 144
Scrum, 423
SDLC (software development lifecycle), 421
    development and test activities, 422
    IDEs (integrated development environments) and, 423
    operational deployment, 422
    performance requirements, 422
    systems analysis, 422

systems design, 422
systems replacement and retirement, 422
validation or acceptance testing, 422
waterfall software lifecycle model, 421
SDNs (software-defined networks), 212, 455
SDP (Session Description Protocol), 207
SDU (service data unit), 187
secure browsing, 395–397
security, 10. *See also* information security
    privacy and, 32–34
security evangelist, 564
security hygiene, 132
segmentation, 188, 199
self-assessment answers, 570–576
SEM (security event management), 65
semantics of data, 558
senior leadership, risk mitigation and, 146
separation of duties, RBAC (role-based access control) and, 263
serialization, 207
server-based IAM, 276–277
servers, star network, 191
service bureaus, 124
service fabric, 387
session do-over button, 532
Session Layer 5 (OSI), 206–207
    CIANA
        countermeasures, 230–231
        residual risk, 231
        vulnerabilities, 230
sets, cryptography and, 304
SFD (Start Frame Delimiter), 200
SHA (Secure Hash Algorithms), 312
shadow IT, 122–123, 436–438
    procedural knowledge
        data as, 438–440
        metadata as, 438–440
Shannon's maxim, 314
shared responsibility model, 449
shouldersurfing, 260

side channel attacks, 350–351

SIE (Search Improvement Engineering), 67

SIEM (security information and event management), 65

signal conditioning, ring networks, 190–191

signature recognition, 404, 432

SIM (security information management), 65

simple security (SS) property (Bell-LaPadula model), 261

SIP (Session Initiation Protocol), 207

SLAs (service-level agreements), 456

SLE (single loss expectancy), 87, 534, 535

SMB (Server Message Block), 208

SNMP (Simple Network Management Protocol), 210

SOC (security operations center), 234–235, 267

    tools, 235–236

social engineering attacks, 353

    insider information and, 539

sockets, 198, 205, 333

software

    as appliance, 417–420

    baked in security, 425

    blacklisting, 431–432

    CIANA and, 428–433

    confidentiality requirements, 430

    design

        data modeling, 426

        data quality, 427

        data typing, 426

    functional requirements, 430

    insecurity, 424–427

    negative control, 431–432

    nonrepudiation requirements, 430

    positive control, 431–432

    quality assurance, 126–127

    safety requirements, 430

    whitelisting, 431–432

software-defined service provision, 124–126

SOHO (small office/home office), 69

    migrating from, 270–271

    objects, 257

    subjects, 257–258

sole proprietorships, 11

spaghetti code, 425

span of control, 21–22

spear phishing, 540

Spiral, 423

SSL (secure sockets layer), 333, 335, 338–340

SSO (single sign-on), 270

    integrated IAM systems, 278

stakeholders, 12

STAMP (Systems Theoretic Accident Model and Process), 562

standalone systems, 122–123

star topologies, 191

stateful communications processes, 205

stateless communication processes, 205

steganography, 448

stewardship, 19

strategic plans, 180

strategic telescope, 565

stream ciphers, 307

subject-based access control, 264

subjects, 180

    access control, 255

subnets, 188, 199

    IPv4, 219–220

    IPv6, 240

substitution, cryptography, 303

supply chain vulnerabilities, 354, 374–375, 561

SV (safeguard value), 534

switching, 187–188

symbol ciphers, 307

symmetric encryption, forward secrecy, 315

symmetric key algorithms, 341

symmetric key cryptography, 318–319

syntax, 300–301

system security, 233–234

    answers to review questions, 592–594

    infrastructure, 372

    NOC (network operations center), 234

        tools, 235–236

    SOC (security operations center), 234–235

        tools, 235–236

    timeframes, 234

## T

TACACS (Terminal Access Controller Access Control System), 269–270

    Active Directory and, 270

    TACACS+, 270

    XTACACS (Extended TACACS), 270

tacit information, 7

tacit knowledge, 121

tactical choices, 95

tangible assets, 68

TCP/IP (Transmission Control Protocol over Internet Protocol), 194

    Application layer, 208–209

    ARPANet and, 195

    Data Link layer, 199–201

    IP (Internet Protocol), 210–211

    Network layer, 201–202

    OSI and

        cross-layer protocols, 209–210

        cross-layer services, 209–210

    OSI comparison, 183–184, 197

    Physical layer, 198–199

    ports, 203–205

    Presentation layer, 207–208

    protocols, 203–205

    Session layer, 206–207

    Transport layer, 202–206

technical controls, 141

technical elements, 75

telemetry data, 447

Test-First, 423

threat actors, 54, 69

threat modeling, 376–378

    administrative controls, 132

    administrative threat surface, 130–131

    clouds, 453–455

    communications systems, 180–181

    firmware vulnerabilities, 380–382

    hardware vulnerabilities, 379–380

    logical threat surface, 130

    operating systems vulnerabilities, 382–384

    physical threat surface, 130

    updating model, 398–399

    virtual machines vulnerabilities, 385–386

threat surface, 181

    migrating to cloud, 454–455

threat-based risk, 65, 69

threats, data exfiltration, 445–446

timeframes, 234

timeline analysis, 500

TLP (Traffic Light Protocol), 258

TLS (Transport Layer Security), 338–340

topologies

    bus, 190

    mesh, 192

    peer-to-peer, 189–190

    point-to-point, 189–190

    ring, 190–191

    star, 191

TORs (terms of reference), 456

tort law, 19

TPMs (trusted platform modules), 379–380

trade secrets, 15

traffic analysis attacks, 352–353

training, CIA and, 38

transaction do-over button, 532

transformational communication
  paradigms, 558
transitive trust relationships, 334
transmission media control, 198
Transport Layer 4 (OSI), 202–206
    CIANA
        countermeasures, 229–230
        residual risk, 230
        vulnerabilities, 229
transposition, cryptography, 303
trapdoor functions, 318
trust anchors, 334
trust frameworks, integrated IAM systems,
    279–281
trust relationships, 333–334
    chain of trust, 335
    PKI and, 342–344
    web of trust, 334
trusted installer, 273
trusted supply chain, 374–375
TTL (Time To Live), 201

# U

UAVs (uninhabited aerial vehicles), 420
UDP (User Datagram Protocol), 183
unauthorized disclosure, 57
unicasting, 219
uniqueness, cryptography and, 298
unwarranted actions, 27
updates, cloud, 533
URLs (Uniform Resource Locators), 189
US-CERT Traffic Light Protocol,
    258–259
user as builder, 436–437
    data/metadata as procedural knowledge,
        438–440
user identities, 258
utility, cryptography and, 298

# V

value chain, 15–16, 482
verifiability, 7, 76
vision, flexibility of, 565
VMs (virtual machines), 455
    vulnerabilities, threat modeling,
        385–386
VoIP (Voice over Internet Protocol), 207,
    542–543
voter registration case study, 59–60, 70–72,
    133–134
VPNs (virtual private networks),
    213–214
    downside, 397
vulnerabilities, 55–56, 69
    applications, lifecycle, 434–436
    supply chain, 354, 374–375, 561
vulnerability assessments, 126–127
    data quality assurance, 127
    proximate causes, 126
    as quality assurance, 127–128
    root causes, 126
    software quality assurance,
        127–128

# W

walking the gemba, 21–22
watermarks, 448
Web browsers, 189
Web crawlers, 189
web of trust, 334
WEP (Wired Equivalency Protocol),
    215
whaling attacks, 540
whistleblowers, 35
white hats, cryptanalysis and, 319
whitelisting, 431–432

wireless networks, 214
  data links
    access points, 212
    Bluetooth, 215–216
    NFC (near-field communication), 216
    Wi-Fi, 214–215
  security, 214–215
    Bluetooth, 215–216
    NFC (near-field communication), 216
    WEP (Wired Equivalency Protocol), 215
    WPA (Wi-Fi Protected Access), 215
    WPA2 (Wi-Fi Protected Access Version 2), 215
wisdom, 6
World Wide Web, 189

WPA (Wi-Fi Protected Access), 215
WPA2 (Wi-Fi Protected Access Version 2), 215

## X-Y-Z

XTACACS (Extended Terminal Access Controller Access Control System), 270

zero trust, 555
zero trust architectures, 281–282
zero value, 313–314
zero day exploits, 57–58
zeroization, 315–317
Zimmerman, Phil, 337